CW01673346

RadioTimes

COVER STORY

90 YEARS OF CLASSIC COVERS

IMMEDIATE MEDIA CO

First published in Great Britain in 2013 by Immediate Media Company London Limited,
Vineyard House, 44 Brook Green, London W6 7BT
ISBN 978-0-9567523-8-3 (Hardback)
ISBN 978-0-9567523-9-0 (Softback)
© 2013 Immediate Media Company London Limited
All rights reserved. No part of this publication may be reproduced or transmitted in any form or by any means, electronic or mechanical, including photocopying, recording or any information storage and retrieval system, without prior permission in writing from the publisher.
The book is sold subject to the condition that it shall not, by way of trade or otherwise, be lent, resold, hired out or otherwise circulated without the publisher's prior consent in any form of binding or cover other than that in which it is published and without a similar condition including this condition being imposed on the subsequent purchaser.

Editor and design Shem Law
Copy editor Ron Hewit
Forewords Ben Preston, Eddie Mair
Introduction Joe Moran
Words Jeremy Aspinall, Mark Braxton, Geraldine Brennan, Gill Crawford, Ellie Austin, William Gallagher, Ron Hewit, Jonathan Holmes, Laurence Joyce, Shem Law, Tom Le Bas, Patrick Mulkern, Paul Smith
Picture research Roger Dixon, Tristan Hopkins
Additional design Paul Smith, Stuart Manning
Photography Simon Vinall, Derek Hillier
Senior production co-ordinator Steve Calver
Image restoration and reprographic work Martin McCormack, Ian Crabb
Project manager Jessica Batten
Radio Times Head of Heritage Ralph Montagu

Printed and bound in the UK by Polestar Wheatons, Exeter

For Radio Times
Managing director, Radio Times Group Kathy Day
Associate publisher Zoë Helme
Editor Ben Preston
Associate Editor Tom Loxley

Very special thanks to Don Smith, *Radio Times* staff photographer from 1955 to 1997 – a great servant of the magazine to whom this book is dedicated

David Driver: Art editor & deputy editor: 1968–1978; features editor & deputy editor: 1979–1981
David Hodges, Steve Arnold, Darren Giddings, Roger Bickerton

***Radio Times* would like to thank past and present staff members and freelance contributors, writers, illustrators and photographers**

We have, where possible, credited illustrators and photographers where we have the information and records to do so. If you are a contributor, or relative of a contributor, who has not been credited, please contact us at **feedback@radiotimes.com**

To order more copies of this book and other *Radio Times* products visit **radiotimes.com/shop** or call **0844 848 9739**

Love *Radio Times*? You can get a subscription here: **radiotimes.com/magazinesubscription**

We welcome your feedback at *Radio Times* so please let us know what you thought of this book: **feedback@radiotimes.com**

www.radiotimes.com

Radio Times

COVER STORY

90 YEARS OF CLASSIC COVERS

CONTENTS

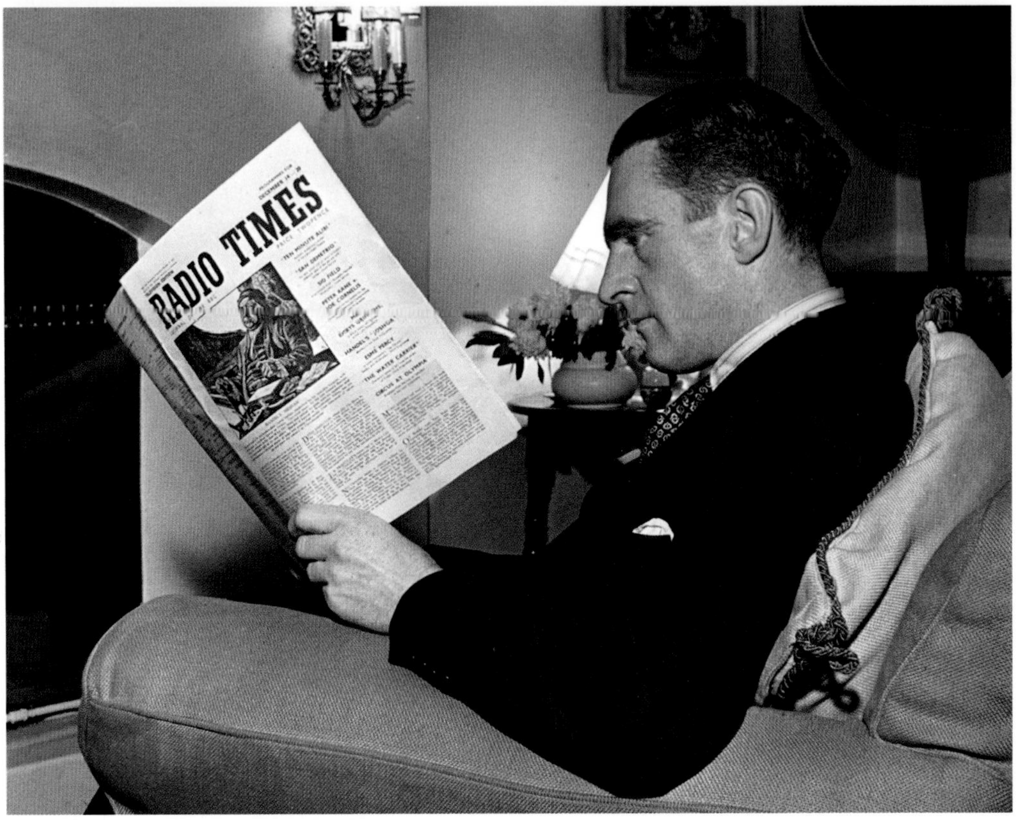

FOREWORD Just flick through the front covers of *Radio Times* over the past 90 years. What do you see? The story of Britain – and broadcasting – unfolding before your eyes.

Momentous events: the outbreak of war and peace, the Moon landings and even a World Cup victory. Royal weddings and funerals that mark out our age. Household names being created, stars being born. The hopeful new show that turns out to be the one that defines a decade. Names that burned brightly but are now remembered only by pub-quiz champions – for every *EastEnders*, there was an *Eldorado*. All grace the 4,600-plus covers – and counting – of *RT*.

Radio Times remains Britain's bestselling quality magazine, as it has been almost since its launch in 1923. It has surfed the waves created by radio and television, innovating and prospering through the Radio Age, the birth of colour TV and the 21st century's explosion of digital channels. It has kept pace with two media that in barely ten decades have altered for ever the way we see ourselves and what we talk about.

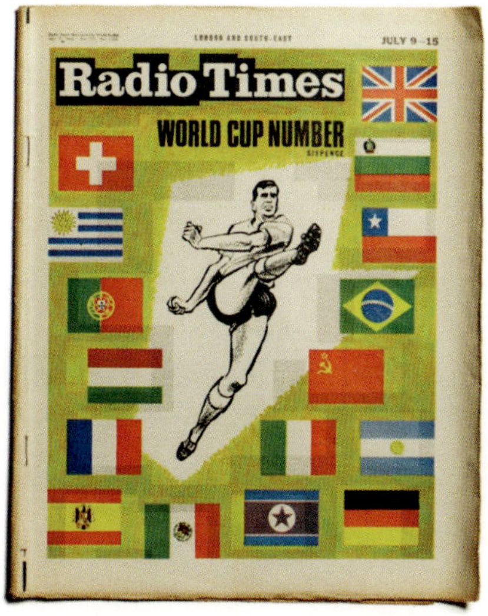

Broadcasting is, above all, the stuff people talk about and *Radio Times* has long been at the heart of that national conversation. Along the way, it has showcased the best writers, artists and photographers. Kingsley Amis, Tom Stoppard and Fay Weldon conjured with words, while Eric Fraser, Edward Ardizzone, Peter Blake and Nick Park all created remarkable cover images.

When John Peel, the broadcaster and *RT* columnist, tried to put his finger on the appeal of the magazine he grew up with, he was typically blunt. *RT* wasn't exciting in the way of magazines like *Eagle* or *Film Fun*, he said. But it was always there. In the living room. Dependable and necessary. "Radio changed, *Radio Times* changed and I changed. But hardly a day goes by without someone in the house shouting, 'Anyone seen *Radio Times*?' That hasn't changed."

Today, when that same cry for *Radio Times* goes up, the answer is easier. If the magazine isn't on the coffee table, then for millions of readers its currency of accurate information, incisive criticism and news-making interviews and articles is still close at hand, on a laptop, a tablet or, soon, on a mobile phone.

Proud of its past, confident of its future, *Radio Times* is thriving. Here's to another 90 years.

Ben Preston *editor, Radio Times*

EDDIE MAIR WRITES... At the age of 12, in December 1977, I walked into my local newsagent's in Dundee and asked for a copy of the Christmas and New Year *Radio Times*.

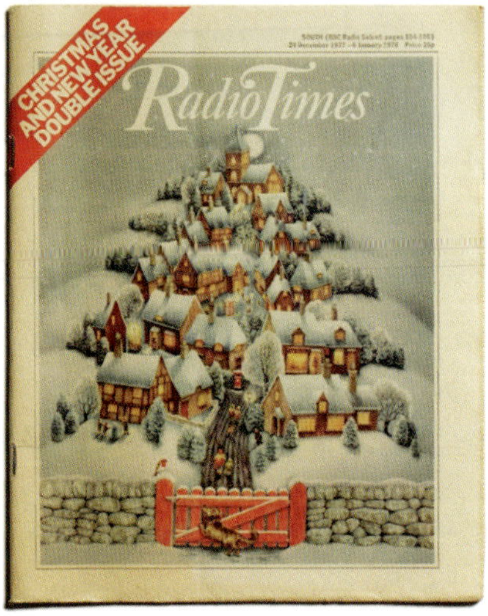

I remember being drawn to the clever cover that depicted a pretty village at Christmas time but that was at exactly the same time – and this was the clever part – a Christmas tree! I took the hefty issue home and spent about as long being mesmerised by the astonishing detail on the cover as all the sparkly programmes inside – and that's quite something when you consider that Brucie, Mike Yarwood and Morecambe and Wise were all on that Christmas night.

From that issue on, I bought *Radio Times* every week.

Yes, we can ask ourselves whether it was healthy for a growing lad to be spending his spare cash on a radio and TV listings magazine. We might also consider why he instinctively knew this was something he shouldn't discuss with his friends who might not consider it the coolest activity.

The mists of time do not afford clarity on the question of whether my interest in radio was piqued by that *Radio Times* cover, or vice versa, but the two have gone hand in hand ever since.

Why the people at *Radio Times* have waited until now to produce this book of covers is beyond me. I would buy an annual of covers every Christmas, though I accept I may be at the more overenthusiastic end of the cover-loving spectrum.

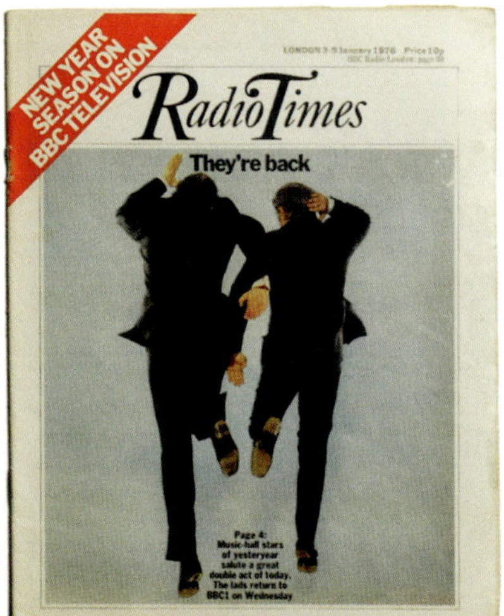

Can anyone fail to have personal memories triggered by this collection? I vividly recall standing in the aforementioned newsagent's being baffled by the 1976 Morecambe and Wise cover in which they are pictured doing their famous dancey-walk away from the camera, with the words "They're back" above their heads. When the word-play eventually dawned on me, I thought it was the cleverest thing since fractions.

I can't look at the *EastEnders* launch cover from 1985 depicting an astonishingly young Ian Beale and his family, without also instantly remembering the over-priced rented flat I was living in, and the experience of sitting down to watch this strange new drama for the first time. But this book transports beyond personal recollection. Take that first Christmas Number with its austere 1923 family captured by the fire apparently transfixed by something marvellously festive on the wireless. Or is Dad about to take them all out in a murder/suicide pact? I can't take my eyes off those wartime covers, either – depicting a BBC keeping the nation transfixed with its drama and diverted with its comedies. These covers tell the story of us.

Radio Times, after 90 years, is as buoyant as ever. It guides listeners and viewers cannily through broadcasting choices unimaginable in 1923, always fulfilling its primary function. In addition, its interviews make news every week. It features writers you want to read every week – and, no, I'm not talking about me.

But above all, it's the covers that set *Radio Times* apart. I once attended a photoshoot for a cover featuring Stephen Fry. Empires have risen and fallen in less time than the crew lavished on ensuring everything was perfect. I know for a fact household names and their agents jostle and get up to all sorts of shenanigans to try to get on the *Radio Times* cover. I know for a fact that the 2012 Christmas cover had its origins in a phone call made way back in the previous January.

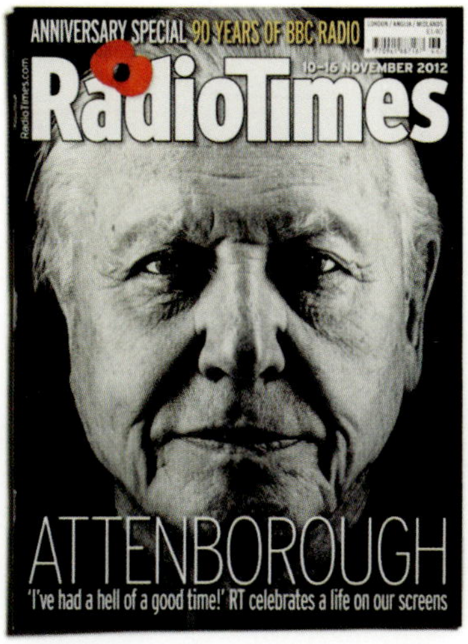

I still look forward to the covers every week and still spend a little too long looking at them. They are never worse than good and are sometimes breathtaking.

Changing fashions mean we don't see the beautiful illustrations and designs of yesteryear, and you might consider that a loss. Then you pick up a recent cover depicting Sir David Attenborough. Here is a face that's been part of our lives on screen for decades, suddenly revealed in close-up in black and white, staring back at us – and inviting us to stare at him... as indeed I did. And are there any other big-selling magazines that would be so bold while stripping the cover of the usual blurbs? It was a cover capable of standing alongside any of the greats.

And a magazine capable of this quality of work after all these years? Well, someone should do a book about it.

Eddie Mair is a regular columnist in *Radio Times* and presents *PM* on Radio 4

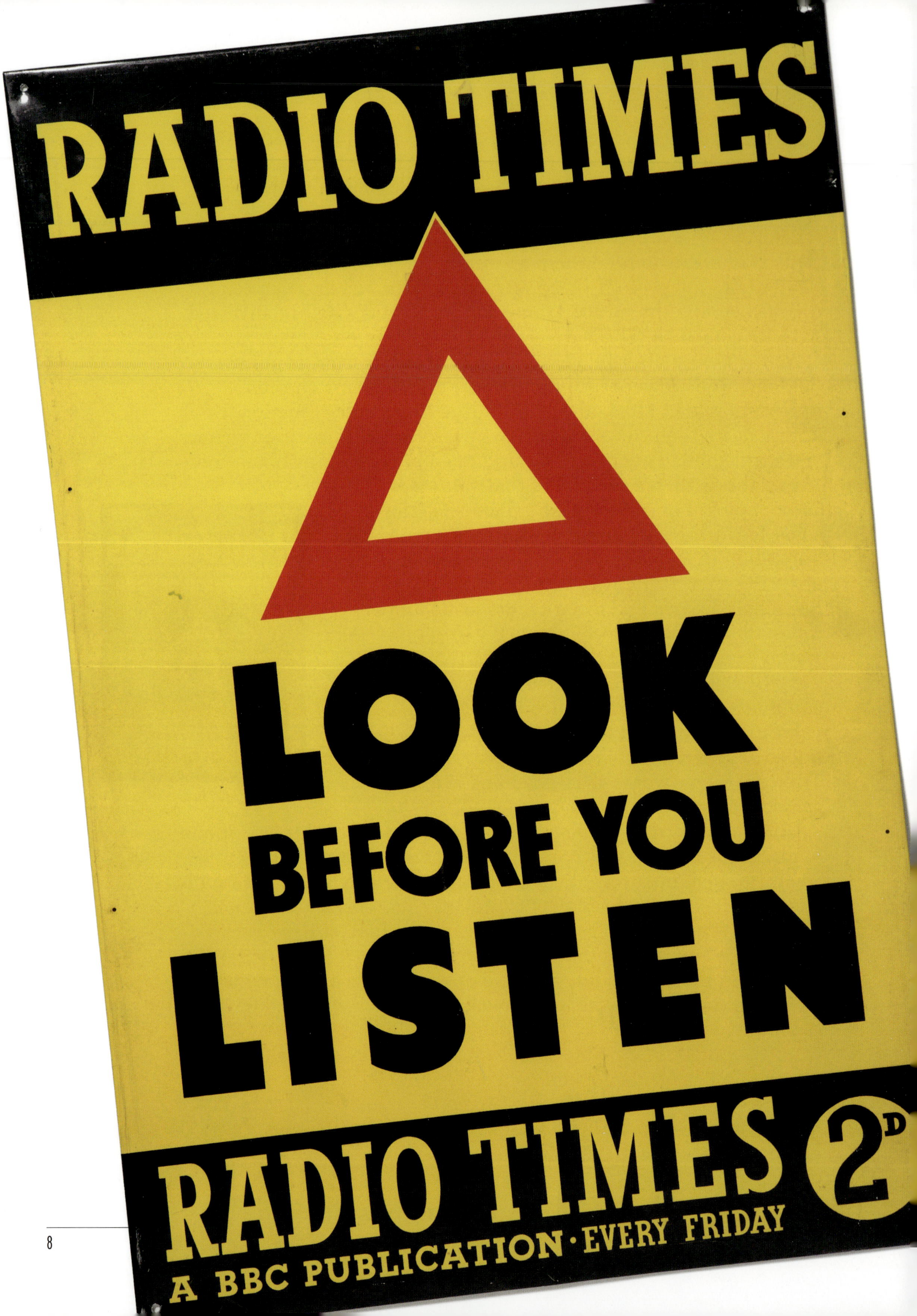
RADIO TIMES
LOOK
BEFORE YOU
LISTEN
RADIO TIMES 2D
A BBC PUBLICATION · EVERY FRIDAY

IT WAS LAUNCHED IN A FIT OF PIQUE.

In January 1923, the Newspaper Proprietors' Association announced that it would be charging the three-month-old British Broadcasting Company the standard advertising rates for publishing its radio listings in newspapers. Although the newspapers capitulated the following month, realising that not including the broadcasting schedules would affect their circulations, the BBC's general manager, John Reith, was irritated by their attitude and it gave him an idea. On 10 September he wrote in his diary: "Everything is now in shape for a BBC magazine, and from various alternatives I chose *Radio Times* for the title."

On the front cover of its first issue, Arthur R Burrows, the BBC's director of programmes, wrote in brisk, not very Reithian style: "HULLO EVERYONE! We will now give you the *Radio Times*. The good new times. The *Bradshaw* of Broadcasting. May you never be late for your wave-train. Speed 186,000 miles per second; five-hour non-stops. Family season ticket: First Class, 10s. per year." The new magazine, in which the word "listeners" was enclosed throughout in inverted commas, arrived in newsagents on Friday 28 September 1923. Its print run of 250,000 copies sold out almost immediately, and within a few weeks the circulation had risen to 600,000. *Radio Times* soon had an army of subscribers, the magazine being mailed out to them each week from its Addressing Department by Great War veterans with facial disfigurements – employed especially by John Reith, a scarred veteran himself. *Radio Times* quickly became the most widely read magazine in Britain and by May 1927 it had its own Braille edition.

A vintage tin panel advertising *Radio Times* in its early days

For the novelist Anthony Burgess, then a schoolboy called John Wilson living with his parents above a tobacconist's shop in a poor area of Moss Side, Manchester, *Radio Times* offered an entry point to another world. It was, he recalled, "a substantial publication like a weekly *Blast*, only better printed, and all for twopence. Its tone was intellectual, its artwork highly contemporary; it abounded with gratuitous erudition." Burgess had built his own crystal radio set to hear Adrian Boult's BBC Symphony Orchestra and he relied on the magazine to tell him when they were on.

Radio Times embodied Reith's notion that radio "must not be used for entertainment purposes alone" but that it should also be a purveyor of education and enlightenment. The inaugural issue had included a profile of Reith, which claimed that "his steadfast faith in the future… ensures that broadcasting will not become a commercialised form of entertainment consisting of cheap music and cheaper thrills". Reith had ruled that continual "tap" listening, ▷

◁ simply using the wireless as ambient noise, should not be encouraged, and so a few minutes' silence was often placed in between programmes to allow listeners to switch off. *Radio Times* duly urged listeners to prepare for a programme as if they were in a theatre or concert hall, advising them to turn the lights down and wait expectantly for it to start. The very idea of providing a week's listings in advance was designed to create the discriminating listener. "Plan your entertainment in advance," said the advertising slogans for the magazine. "Choose, don't chance your listening!'

Radio Times assumed the same sort of educative/ propagandistic role when the BBC's television service came along in 1936. It initiated the campaign for motorists to install suppressors on car ignitions, without which television would forever have been viewed through a snowstorm of static, and it tried to drum up business for the new medium by urging "viewers" to hold television parties for their non-viewing friends. "Only by a great expansion of the viewing habit can the present service develop – or perhaps go on at all," warned Ian Hunter in *Radio Times* in 1938. "When you arrange your television parties, take care to choose an evening when there is something good on – such as a short play, a cabaret, or an outstanding personality."

The magazine also tried to draw on the sense of *esprit de corps* among this tiny group of pioneers who had purchased a prewar television set. "A week or two ago I was introduced to a neighbour of mine," wrote the regular television columnist, "The Scanner", in February 1939. "We talked sweet nothings until I said as a brother-viewer I was glad to see his roof was graced with a television aerial. A reaction of delight was immediate; it was like the meeting of two anglers." *Radio Times* liked to identify celebrities with televisions, such as the cartoonist David Low, the dance-band leader Henry Hall and the comedian Will Hay. And it awarded the title of oldest viewer to 91-year-old Mr EC Rolls of Walton-on-Thames, who had dim memories of the Crimean War and who, after seeing Noël Coward's *Hay Fever* on Christmas night 1938, was hooked.

And yet, long after the Second World War, and in principled Reithian mode, *Radio Times* tried to discourage people from indiscriminately watching whatever was on. "Selective viewing is essential during this period," cautioned the magazine before the televising of the 1948 Olympics, "and to help viewers in making their plans, it has been arranged to announce at the end of each evening's programme details of the events which will be televised the next day." For several years *Radio Times* remained true to its name by printing the TV schedules, as an afterthought, at the back. Only in 1953 did it stop banishing them to a back-pages ghetto, and even then the radio schedules came first. The first television-dominated cover, featuring Victor Silvester and the final of *Come Dancing*, did not appear until December 1955, long after it was clear television was taking over from radio as the dominant mass medium. ▷

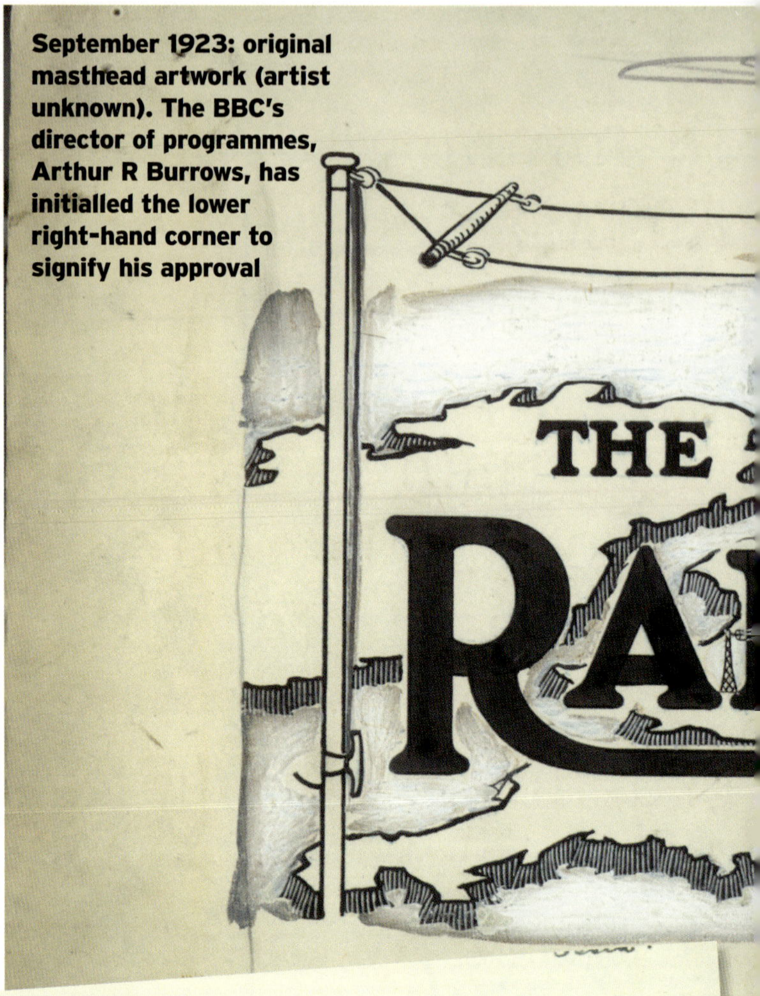

September 1923: original masthead artwork (artist unknown). The BBC's director of programmes, Arthur R Burrows, has initialled the lower right-hand corner to signify his approval

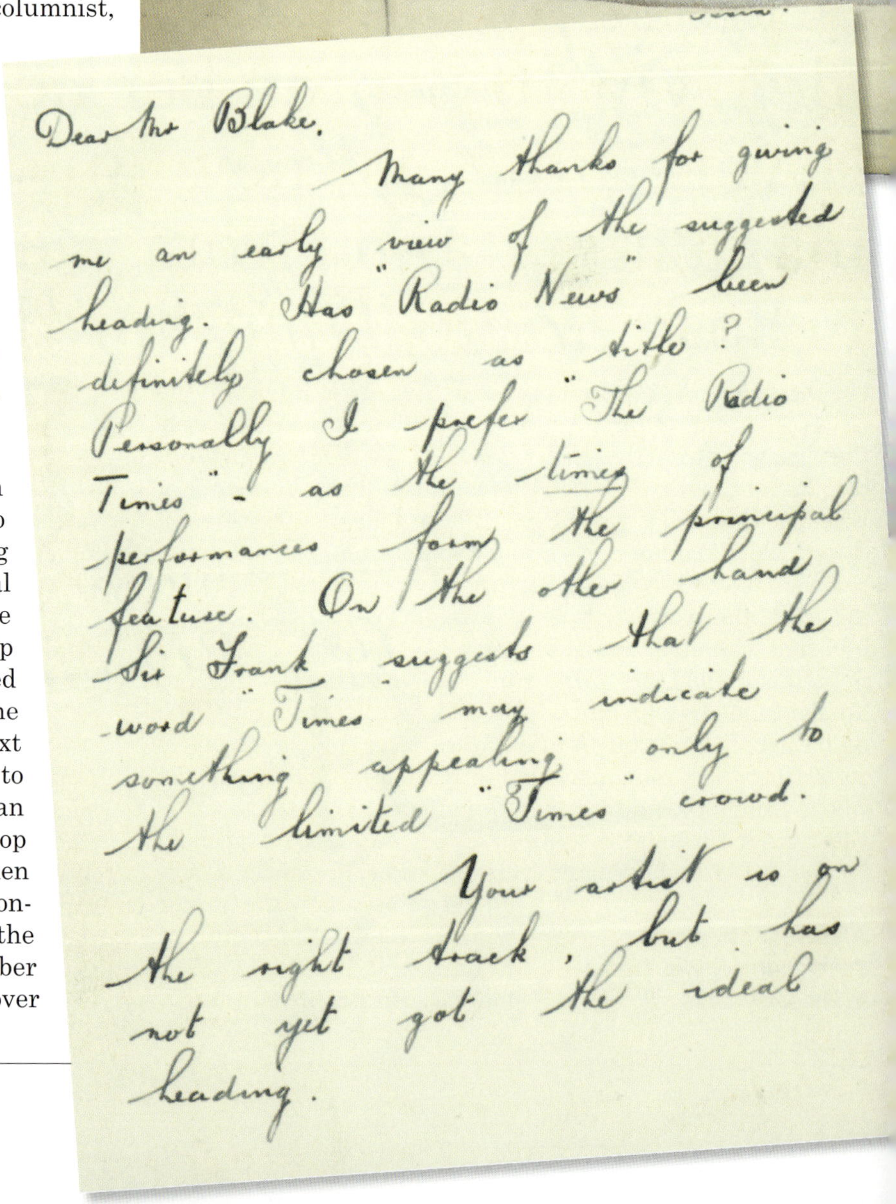

Dear Mr Blake,

Many thanks for giving me an early view of the suggested heading. Has "Radio News" been definitely chosen as title? Personally I prefer "The Radio Times" – as the times of performances form the principal feature. On the other hand Sir Frank suggests that the word "Times" may indicate something appealing only to the limited "Times" crowd.

Your artist is on the right track, but has not yet got the ideal heading.

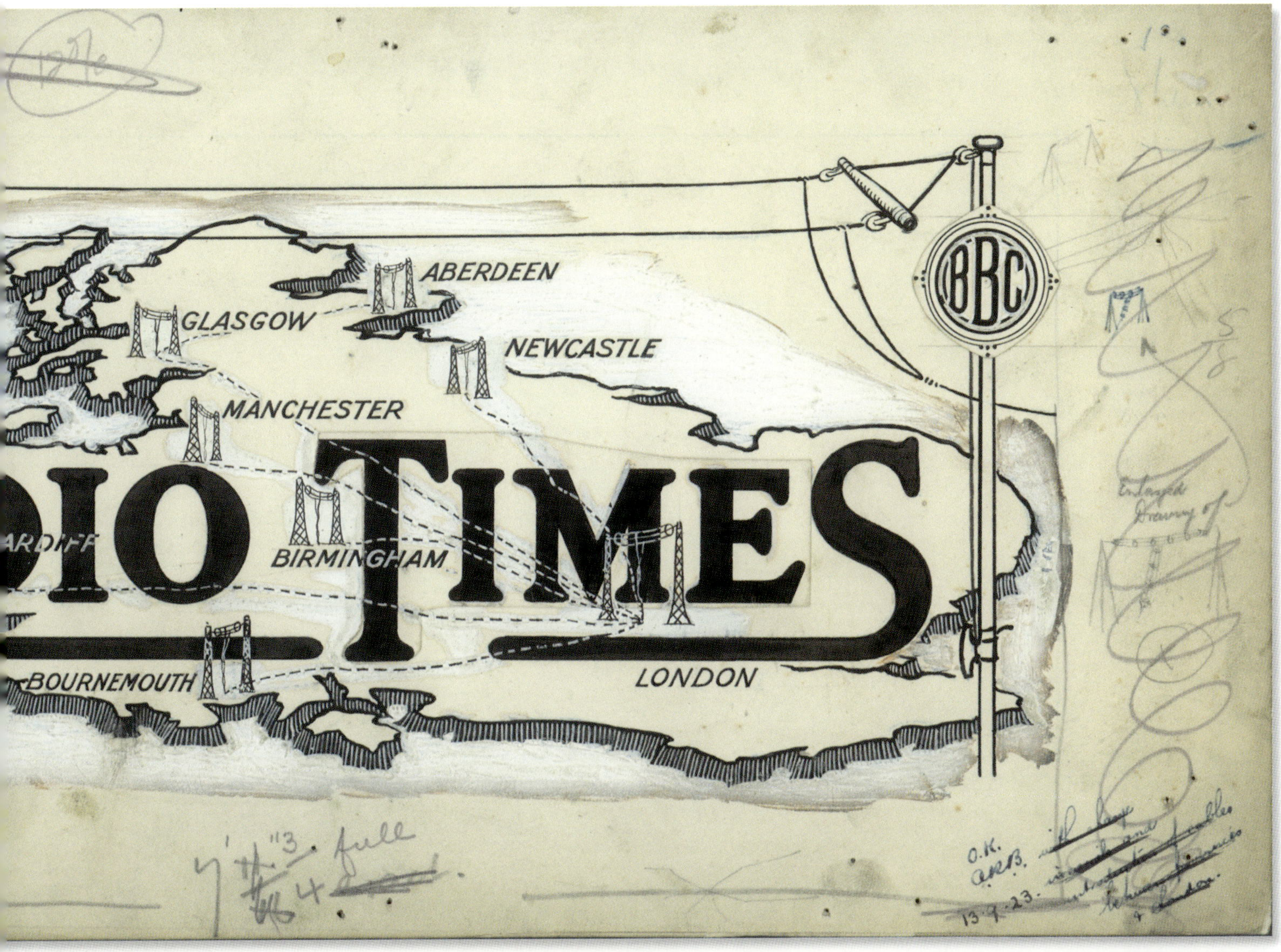

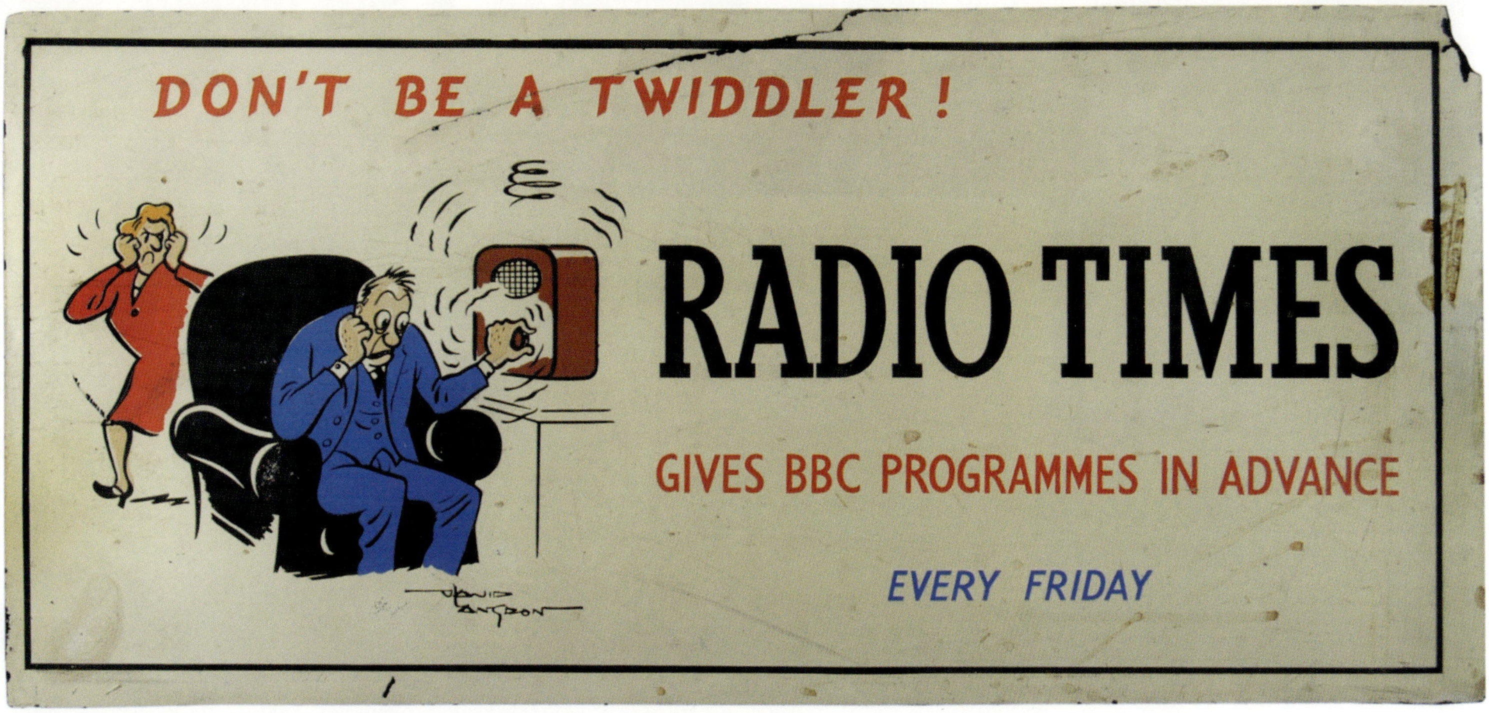

Above: A postwar advert for display on London Underground trains

Left: a letter from 1923, discussing the magazine's name and masthead, from the BBC's Arthur R Burrows to JH Blake, who worked for *Radio Times* publisher George Newnes

March 1939: a newsstand in Chelmsford, Essex, gets the *Radio Times* message across

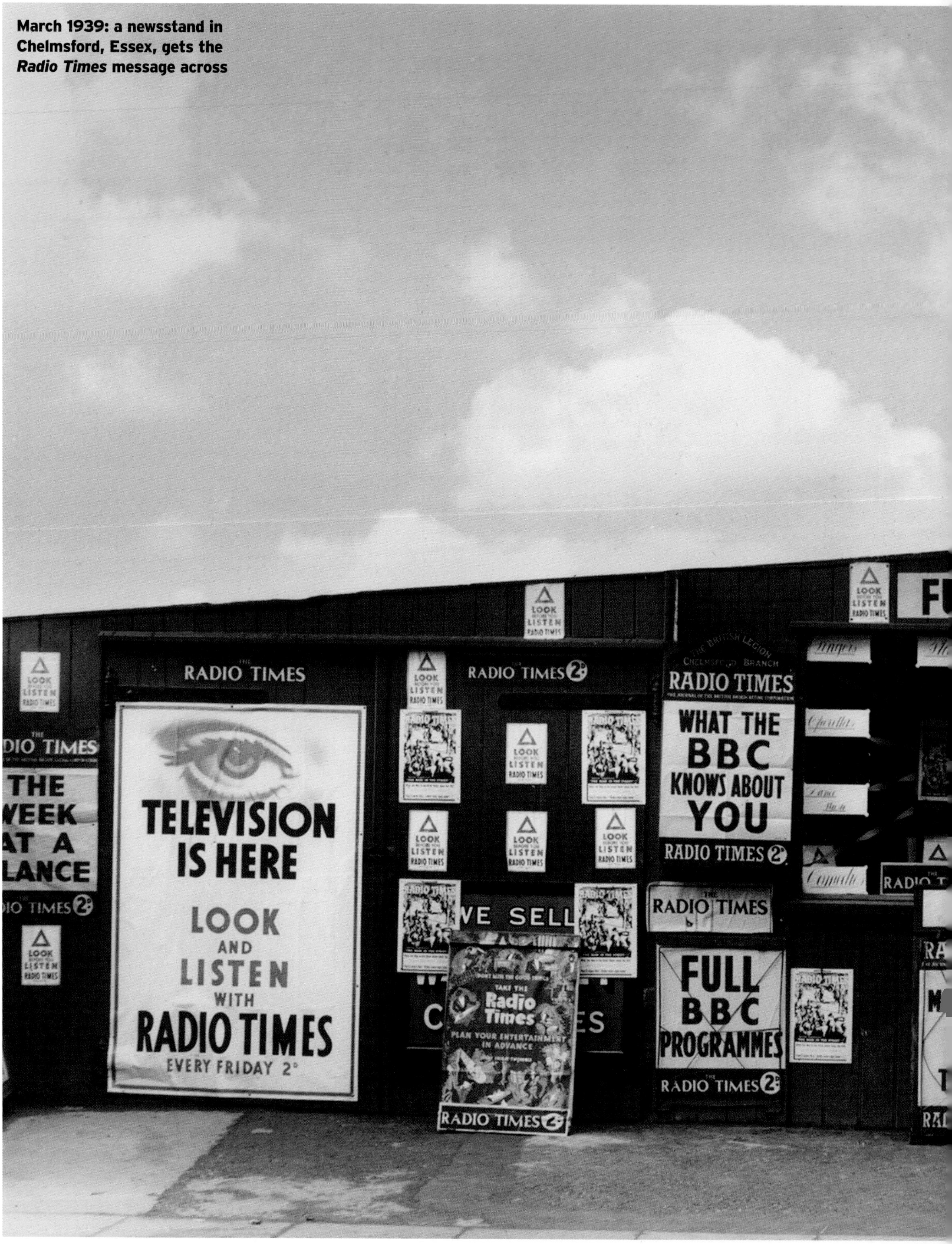

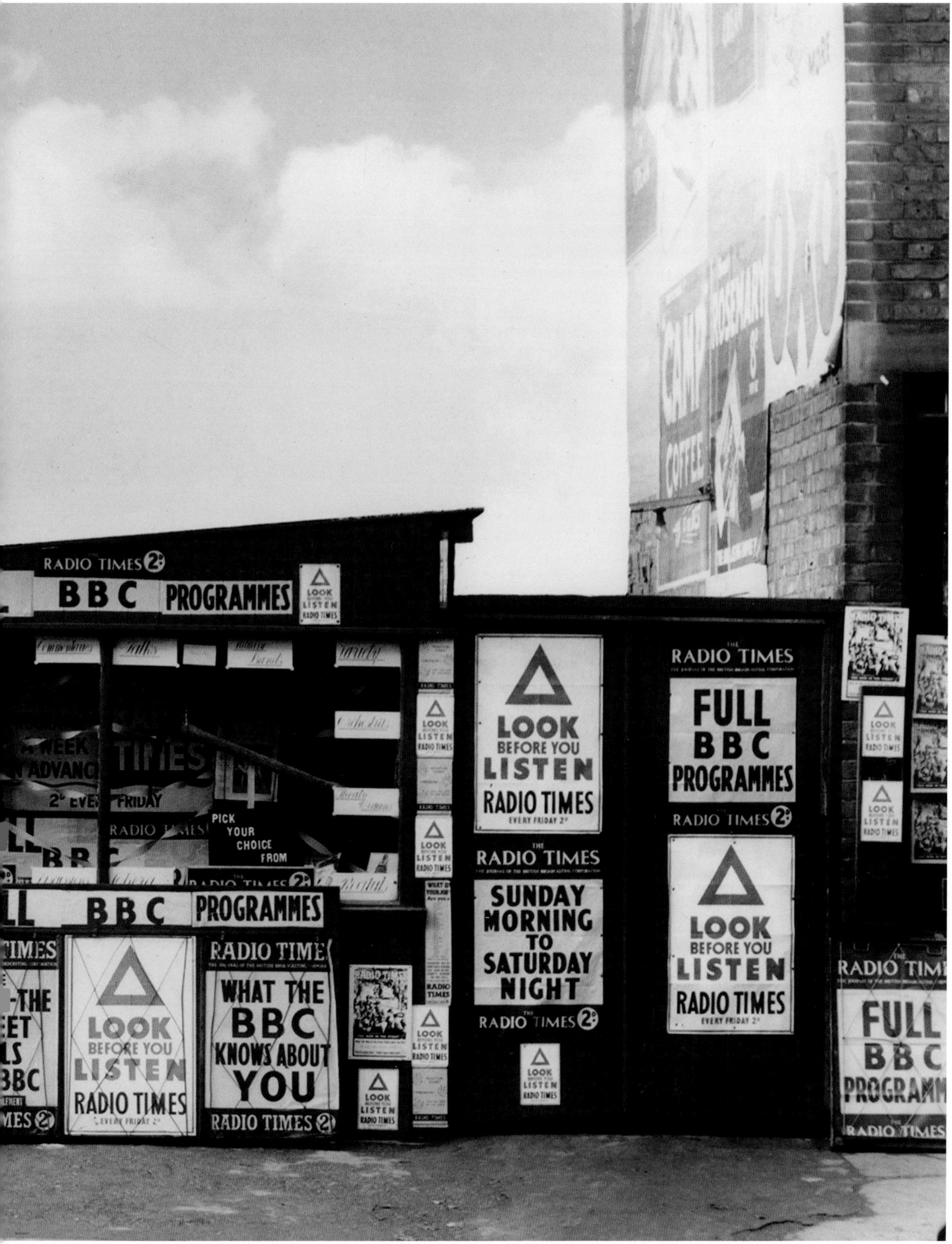
RADIO TIMES 2d
BBC
PROGRAMMES
LOOK BEFORE YOU LISTEN RADIO TIMES
CAMP COFFEE
ROSEMARY
OXO
PICK YOUR CHOICE FROM
BBC
PROGRAMMES
RADIO TIMES
WHAT THE BBC KNOWS ABOUT YOU
RADIO TIMES 2d
LOOK BEFORE YOU LISTEN
RADIO TIMES
EVERY FRIDAY 2d
LOOK BEFORE YOU LISTEN
RADIO TIMES
EVERY FRIDAY 2d
THE RADIO TIMES
SUNDAY MORNING TO SATURDAY NIGHT
THE RADIO TIMES 2d
THE RADIO TIMES
FULL BBC PROGRAMMES
THE RADIO TIMES 2d
LOOK BEFORE YOU LISTEN
RADIO TIMES
EVERY FRIDAY 2d
FULL BBC

◁ *Radio Times* was a significant sponsor of modern graphic art in these years. "Its cover could sometimes startle," remembered Anthony Burgess, "– a woodcut of Beethoven in terminal agony, the huge stark legend *Morning Heroes* to herald the first performance of Arthur Bliss's choral symphony of that name, a tortured Wagnerian fantasia for the 50th anniversary of the composer's death in 1933, the announcement *The End of the World* to signal an expressionist drama on that subject." Elegant little cartoons of flappers and dinner-suited bright young things listening to radiograms were the magazine's early marginalia. Maurice Gorham, assistant editor from 1926 and editor from 1933 to 1941, commissioned large numbers of artists; a single issue of his might contain 40-plus artworks. He got the best-known poster artists of the day to design covers, such as the Frenchman Cassandre and the American Edward McKnight Kauffer. Some of his regular artists, such as Victor Reinganum and Eric Fraser, represented the British public's main encounter with modernist abstraction and surrealism in these years, without ever being too intimidatingly avant-garde. Fraser, a former student of Walter Sickert's who first contributed to the magazine in 1926 and did his last illustration in 1982, a year before his death, was so omnipresent in the magazine that he virtually created its house style.

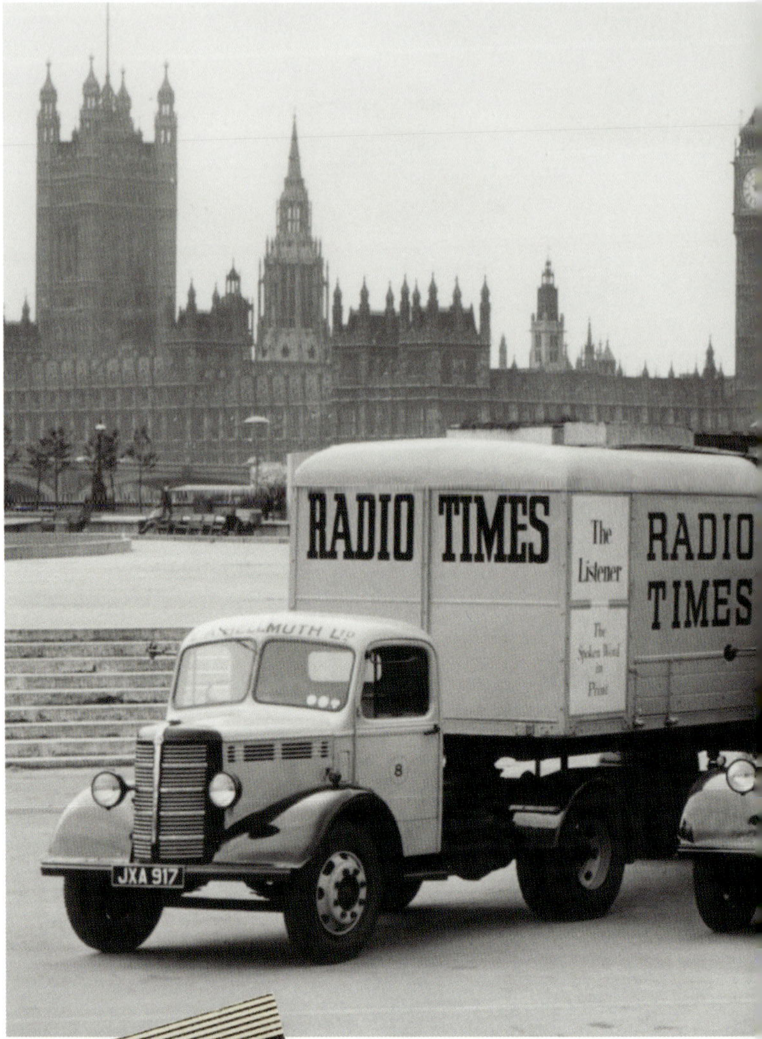

Radio Times preferred graphic art to photographs well into the 1950s (and even after that, artwork remained and remains an important part of the magazine). The effect was to claim this contemporary medium, broadcasting, as something reassuringly traditional and artisanal. During the late 1940s and early 1950s, as television spread across the land, the magazine put a series of the new TV transmitters on its covers, usually drawn by one of its favourite artists of the time, Cecil W Bacon: concentric circles of radio waves pulsing out from the top of the mast like ripples on water, and houses with aerials on top, waiting expectantly to receive the signal. Drawing in delicate pen or scraper-board in a way that resembled wood engraving, Bacon made these new structures seem both excitingly modern and familiarly British.

"The vulgarity of the *Radio Times* week by week makes me sorry I ever started it," complained 74-year-old Lord Reith in his diary for 7 September 1963. In fact, although its circulation was declining slowly from a peak of 8.5 million in the mid-1950s, *Radio Times* was flourishing. It now had more pages and a new prominence given to television – in 1960, it had made the momentous decision to list the TV schedules first – and BBC television was enjoying a new era of intelligent populism under its director-general, Hugh Carleton-Greene, having looked as though it might be obliterated by ITV in the late 1950s. The end of the decade saw the initiation of a much-loved ritual: the Christmas double issue of *Radio Times*, launched simultaneously with the first double issue of *TV Times* in December 1969. Their separate covers – *Radio Times* a tasteful montage of ribbons, wintry scenes and wassailers, and *TV Times* Des O'Connor in a Santa hat – said much about the cultural differences between the BBC and ITV and their idea of their viewers, and carried on doing so over the years. ▷

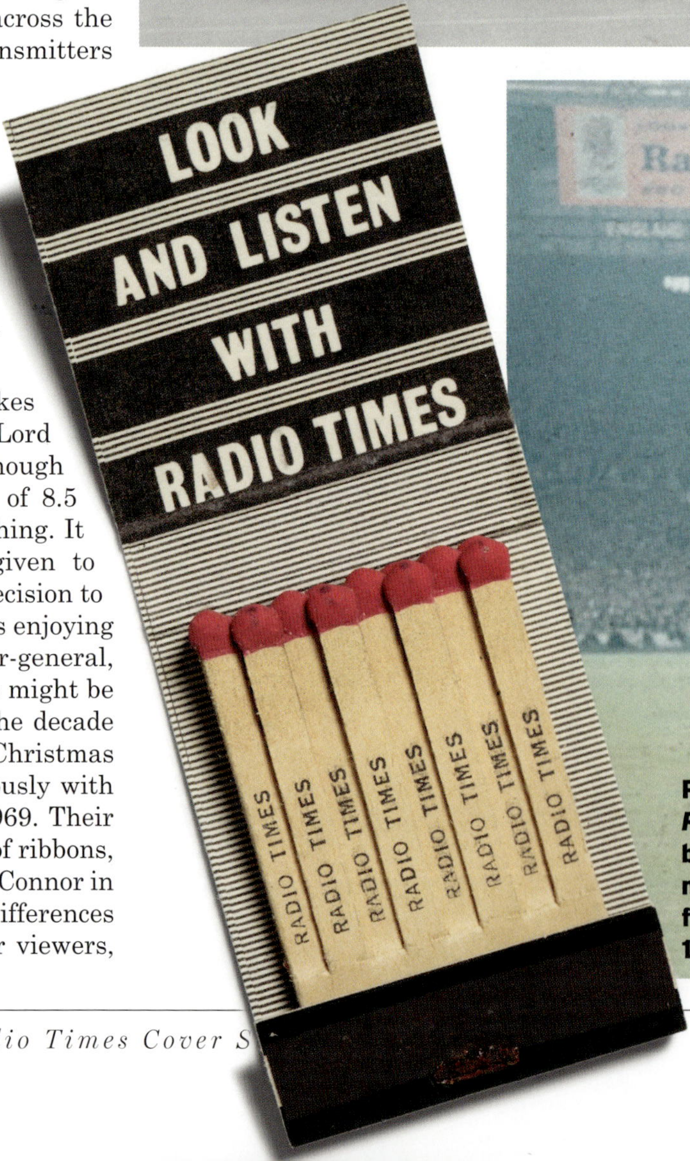

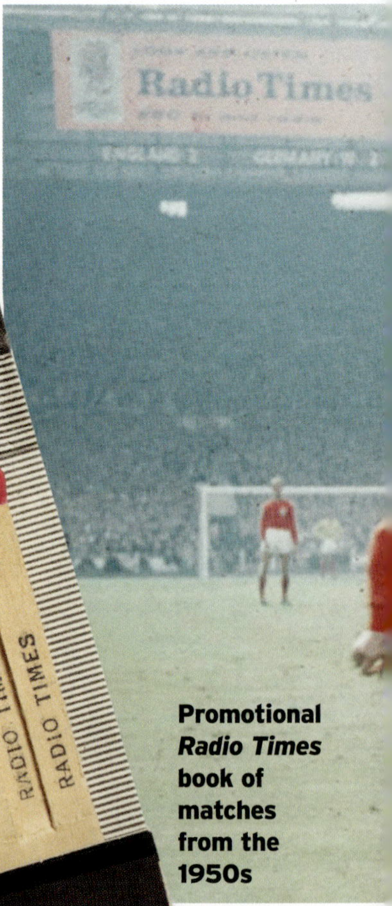

Promotional *Radio Times* book of matches from the 1950s

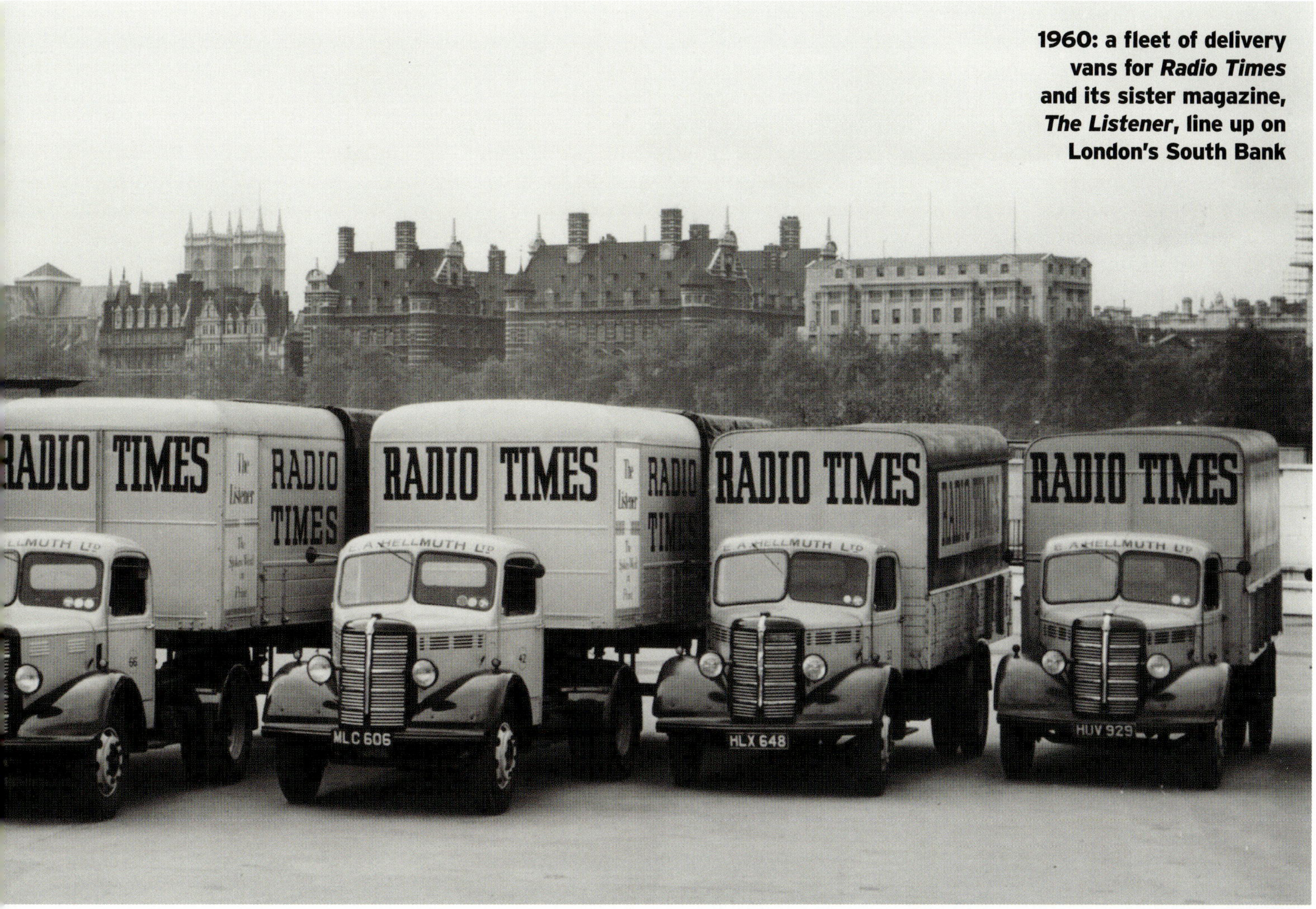

1960: a fleet of delivery vans for *Radio Times* and its sister magazine, *The Listener*, line up on London's South Bank

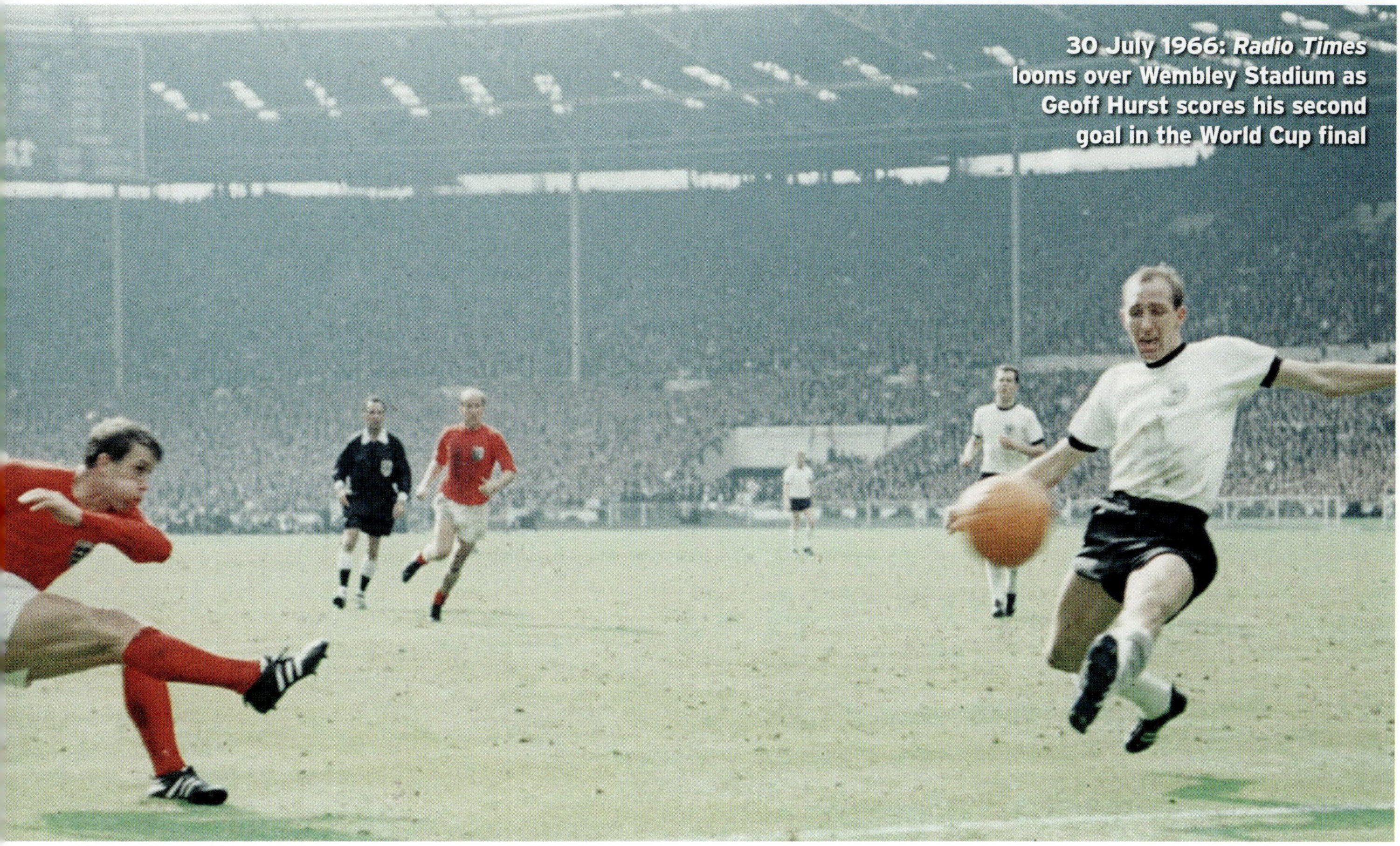
30 July 1966: *Radio Times* looms over Wembley Stadium as Geoff Hurst scores his second goal in the World Cup final

◁ Since it hung around homes for at least a fortnight, and would often sell 10–11 million copies, companies clambered over themselves for advertising space in the Christmas *Radio Times*. Quaintly, the magazine kept up its tradition of having small display ads for walk-in baths, rubber reducing corsets and garden sheds on its back pages. In the 1970s, now remembered as a golden era of three-channel colour television in which the most popular programmes regularly drew more than 20 million viewers, *Radio Times* employed heavyweight columnists like Kingsley Amis, Jonathan Raban and Margaret Drabble, who wrote happily about their love of *The Dick Emery Show* (Amis), *That's Life* (Raban) or *The Goodies* (Drabble). The philosopher AJ Ayer, a Tottenham Hotspur fan, declared his love for *Match of the Day* within its pages.

There was, of course, a reason for the magazine's dominance in these years. Not only did the BBC and ITV control the airwaves, they controlled our knowledge of what was on them, for both refused to allow newspapers to run listings except for the day of publication. (One might think of this as Lord Reith's revenge, served very cold, on the Newspaper Proprietors' Association.) *Radio Times* was so definitive in its listing of programmes that many a criminal would peruse a back issue at the local library in search of an alibi. Unfortunately for them, at the Television Duty Office at BBC Television Centre they kept a "Master", a copy of every *Radio Times* in which they noted any last-minute schedule changes and late runnings, of which there were many more then than today. Police and lawyers would thus regularly use the Duty Office to check the alibis of suspects who said they were at home watching TV when a crime took place. The BBC has recently completed a project to digitise programme listings from old copies of *Radio Times* – the so-called BBC Genome project – precisely because they are the only comprehensive record of every programme it has ever broadcast, and the best way for the corporation to identify shows missing from its archive.

"Nothing disturbs the ordered calm of my household more than an attempt to prevent me from watching *The Dick Emery Show*, and people who ring me up while it's on have been known to burst into tears"
KINGSLEY AMIS

Only once during this period of dominance did *Radio Times* properly acknowledge the existence of ITV: on its letters page, during the 11-week ITV strike in the summer of 1979. Here the magazine gave generous space to ITV viewers complaining about being "forced" to watch the BBC, suggesting that, more than 20 years after the arrival of commercial competition, some families still identified themselves as ITV or BBC households. "We have been without ITV for a few days now, and believe me, what a boring time it has been," wrote Mrs E Jackson from Formby. "You have two stations, I hope you never have any more." DJ Thompson from Blackpool said he had switched off the BBC and been "thoroughly entertained by reading what might have been in *TV Times*".

In November 1982 the arrival of Channel 4, which as a new channel made its listings freely available because it needed viewers, made this arrangement feel like an anachronism. The publisher of *Time Out* magazine, Tony Elliott, now took advantage of his midweek copy deadline to replicate the listings from the latest issues of *Radio Times* and *TV Times*. The magazines won a court ruling against him, but Elliott began an eight-year campaign for de-restriction of the listings, which had the support of much of the press. As newspapers competed among themselves for a declining readership, they were clinging parasitically to the younger medium as a source of news and gossip and they wanted to include more television coverage. *The Sun* and *Daily Mirror* now had double-page TV sections, which were the most read part of the newspaper. Pre-publicity for programmes, from on-air trailers to newspaper previews, was also becoming more important. The arrival of the VHS tape having enabled bulk copying, one of the familiar features of the London landscape in the 1980s was the number of motorcycle couriers racing through the streets sending preview tapes to critics. In this new environment, the copyright on listings was the kind of classically cosy cartel that Margaret Thatcher – never a fan of the BBC and what she called its "compulsory levy", the licence fee – had in her sights. In 1988 Home Secretary Douglas Hurd denounced what he called the "dotty duopoly". The 1990 Broadcasting Act, one of Thatcher's last major acts as prime minister, ended the copyright on listings.

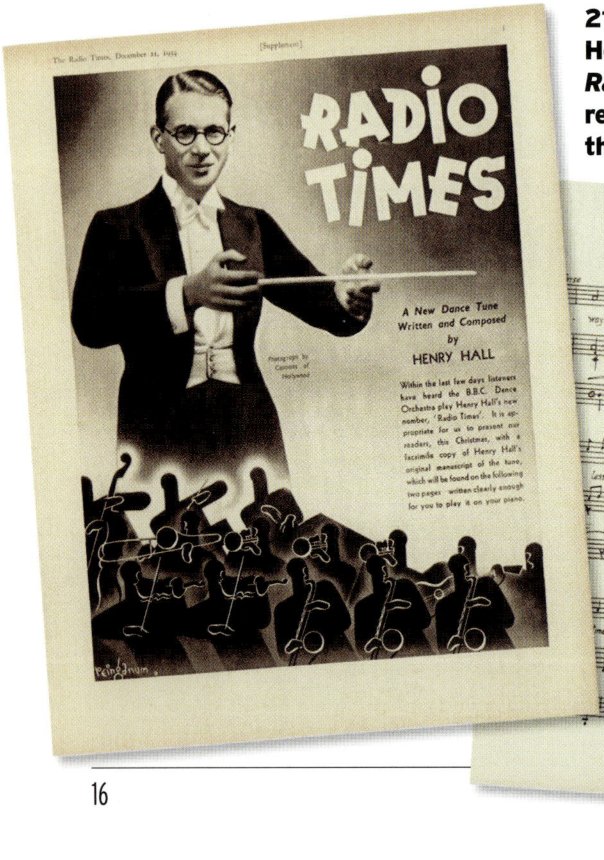

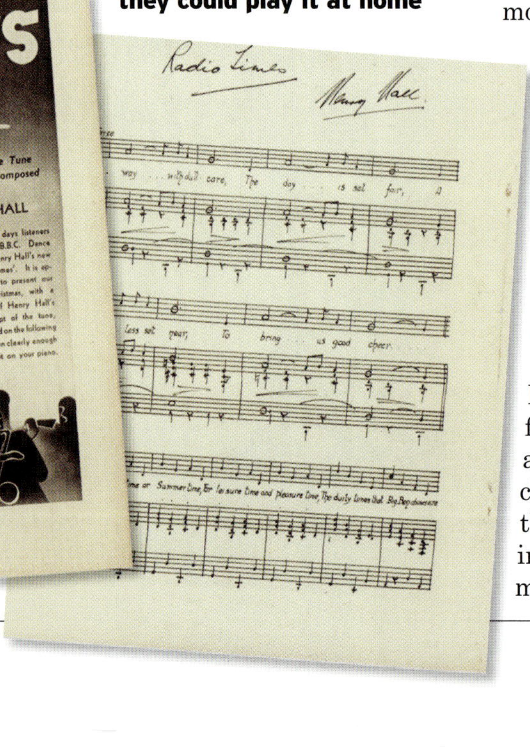

21 December 1934: Henry Hall composed the song *Radio Times* – given to readers in a supplement so they could play it at home

In March 1991, when the new rules came into force, the circulation of *Radio Times* fell instantly, and predictably, by almost half. After a legal challenge, the BBC was still allowed to advertise the magazine on its TV channels, as long as it included the disclaimer "other television listings magazines are available" – a phrase that entered

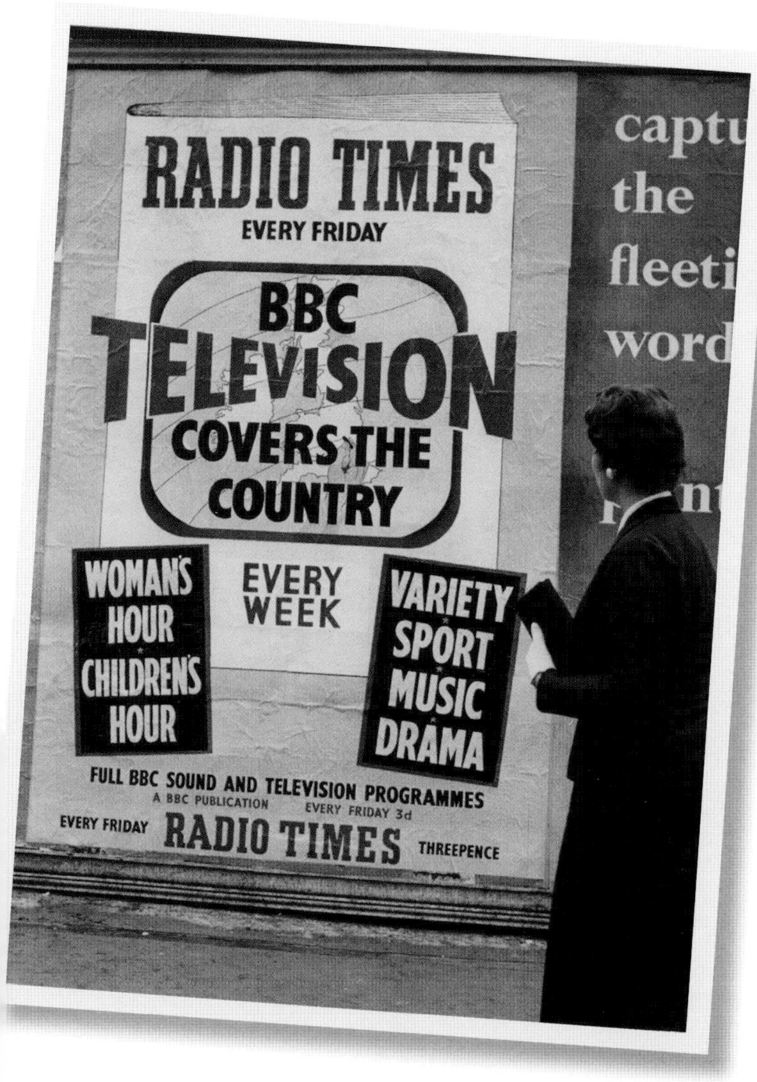

1950s: *Radio Times* provides full coverage as the BBC Television service expands across the UK

the common language. But while many of the cheap listings magazines that sprang up in the early 1990s are now extinct, *Radio Times* is still going strong. Even in the digital, multi-channel era, it has reliably made headlines, from *Ground Force's* Charlie Dimmock appearing naked on the cover in 1998, apart from some strategically placed foliage, to David Cameron declaring his youthful enthusiasms for *Tiswas*, *Neighbours* and the daytime quiz show *Going for Gold* to the magazine during the 2010 general election. The magazine still attracts big-name contributors, with Antony Beevor, Julian Barnes, William Boyd and Grayson Perry all writing for it recently, and artists David Hockney and Peter Blake creating covers.

Radio Times remains culturally significant for two reasons. First, although the BBC sold off the magazine in 2011, it is still strongly associated in the public mind with the corporation, which remains far more loved and respected than its commercial rivals, from Rupert Murdoch to the *Daily Mail*, would like to admit. Second, the habit of communal television watching has proved surprisingly resilient. The 1990 Broadcasting Act championed the idea that consumers, not the ITV/BBC duopoly, should decide what they watched, and that there should be more channels and more television for them to choose from. But despite the confident predictions at the start of the digital era about the end of "linear viewing", viewers still seemed to seek out that ephemeral, undemanding togetherness created by watching the same programmes. While governments recited the mantra of individual choice, television pointed to the residual longing for a collective national life. Just as the video recorder did in the 1980s, catch-up sites and digital recorders have encouraged an element of time-shifting but have not completely destroyed primetime or shared viewing. And precisely because there is so much television available and so many ways of watching it, programme-makers place a high worth on family-centred television that will be watched and talked about across the nation. Radio, the decline of which people have been confidently predicting since the 1950s, is also gaining listeners. All this means that the schedules still matter, and so *Radio Times*, which is partly a listings magazine and partly a celebration of the communal experience of broadcasting, also still matters.

This is what makes *Radio Times* such an important historical document: it offers textual evidence of our collective national life. This is particularly true of radio's boom years in the 1940s and 1950s, when millions listened to JB Priestley's and Winston Churchill's wartime broadcasts, *ITMA* and *The Goon Show*, or terrestrial TV's halcyon age from the 1960s to the 1980s. But it is broadly true of the whole 90 years *Radio Times* has been around: radio and TV have brought us together in a diasporic community, listening to or watching the same thing in 20 million living rooms.

Looking through decades of *Radio Times* covers is both a fascinating insight into changing fashions in graphic design and a primer in our recent social and cultural history, from the outbreak of war ("Broadcasting Carries On") to the launch of *Apollo 11* ("Target Moon"). It is rare that one comes across a face or event that is not instantly familiar, whether it be Fluck and Law's latex models of David Frost and Richard Nixon (created long before *Spitting Image*), Les Dawson's gurning features, Basil Fawlty's imperiously folded hands or Madonna in her peroxided pomp (although it seems unlikely she ever uttered the accompanying caption, "Wow! I'm on Wogan!"). Adorning the cover of *Radio Times* has long been the nearest British equivalent to being on the cover of *Time*, that definitive anointment of American celebrity.

Browsing inside old copies of *Radio Times* is, by contrast, a sweetly melancholy activity, an entry into a lost world of spent effort, used-up enjoyment and forgotten boredom. Most radio and television, to which talented, energetic people devoted months or years of their lives, has left momentary imprints on our retinas and eardrums and slightly less momentary imprints on our brains before vanishing into the uncaring ether. The programme listings have united us briefly, but they are swiftly forgotten, leaving little evidence behind – except for the back issues of *Radio Times*.

Joe Moran is Professor of English and Cultural History at Liverpool John Moores University. He's the author of Armchair Nation: an Intimate History of Britain in Front of the TV (published by Profile Books, 5 September 2013)

The making of a modern icon

Today, *Radio Times* covers are created with as much, if not more, care and attention as the covers of days gone by. In 2008, the Vote Dalek! cover (created by art editor Paul Smith three years earlier) was voted by the public the most iconic British cover of all time, and it's been shortlisted by the Professional Publishers Association for the Cover of the Century. While we feel that might be a little premature, it's a good example of the art and craft of a *Radio Times* cover.

The cover marked the return of the Daleks to TV after an absence of 17 years. It also happened to be the week of the 2005 general election, so *Radio Times* decided to bring the two events together by paying homage to a famous scene of Daleks crossing Westminster Bridge from the 1960s. Here's how it was done...

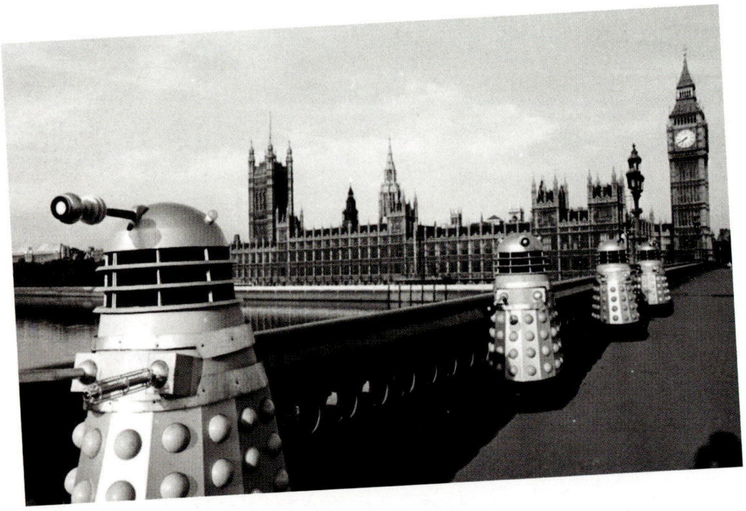

1 This image from the 1964 *Doctor Who* story, *The Dalek Invasion of Earth*, was the inspiration for our 2005 cover. It would be shot from a lower, more dramatic point of view, to let the Daleks loom menacingly, and photographed at dusk so that the Houses of Parliament were floodlit, with a dark moody sky behind.

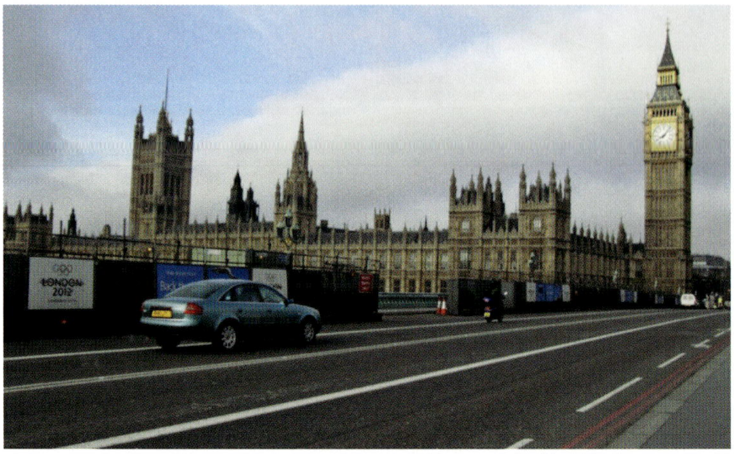

2 A recce for the shoot revealed that Westminster Bridge was undergoing renovation work – the pavement was cordoned off with barriers and portable buildings. The *Radio Times* team wasn't going to give up that easily and, with Westminster Council's help, the barriers were moved back and sufficient room was cleared for the shoot to go ahead. The barriers actually helped to shield the shoot from pedestrians and passing traffic at a notorious tourist hot spot, in the middle of the evening rush hour.

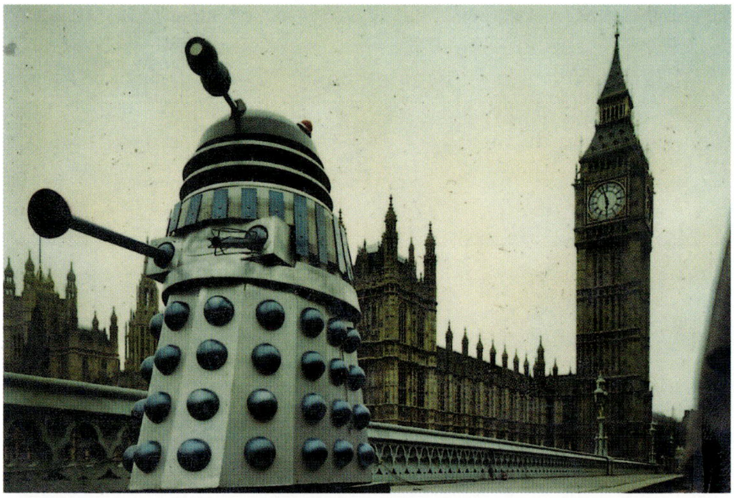

3 The next problem to overcome was that the Daleks' new look – chunkier, armoured and metallic bronze – was a closely guarded secret, so there was no way that any of the Daleks could be photographed on location. An old-style Dalek (above) stood in to work out the composition with exact positions and perspectives that could be re-created later when shooting the new-look Daleks in a studio. To prevent onlookers in passing buses or on the nearby London Eye seeing what was going on, the Dalek was hidden under a blanket, except for a brief moment when Polaroid tests were made for composition.

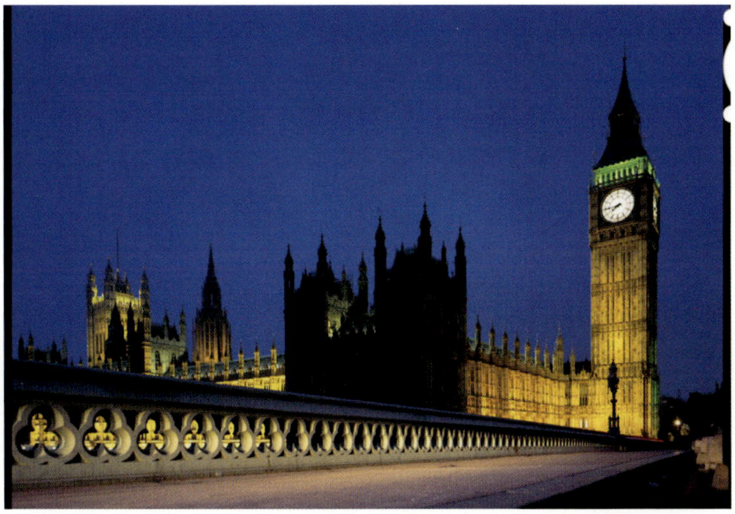

4 A fine afternoon soon became overcast and it started to rain. Mains electricity was available to light the foreground, but there was a risk of electrocution, so photographer Ian McKinnell's car headlights were used instead, and worked perfectly. The photo couldn't be taken until Parliament's floodlights were on and had warmed up sufficiently. With failing light, there was only a limited time window to get the shot. With a very long exposure, the rain didn't register, and the sky rendered as a deep blue, rather than dull grey.

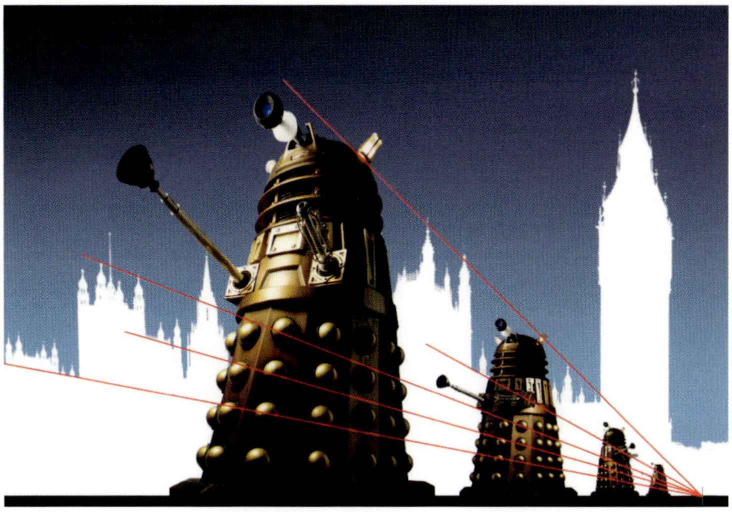

5 The new-look Daleks were photographed a week later at the *Doctor Who* studios in Wales – at exactly the correct distance and perspective, as if they'd been on the bridge. The image was then assembled in Photoshop. The Daleks were scaled to the correct perspective. Extensive retouching then followed to darken the foreground, add shadows and a more dramatic sky. The final cover with the cheeky coverline "Vote Dalek!" went on to be voted the Greatest British Cover of All Time in 2008 and has since been nominated for Cover of the Century.

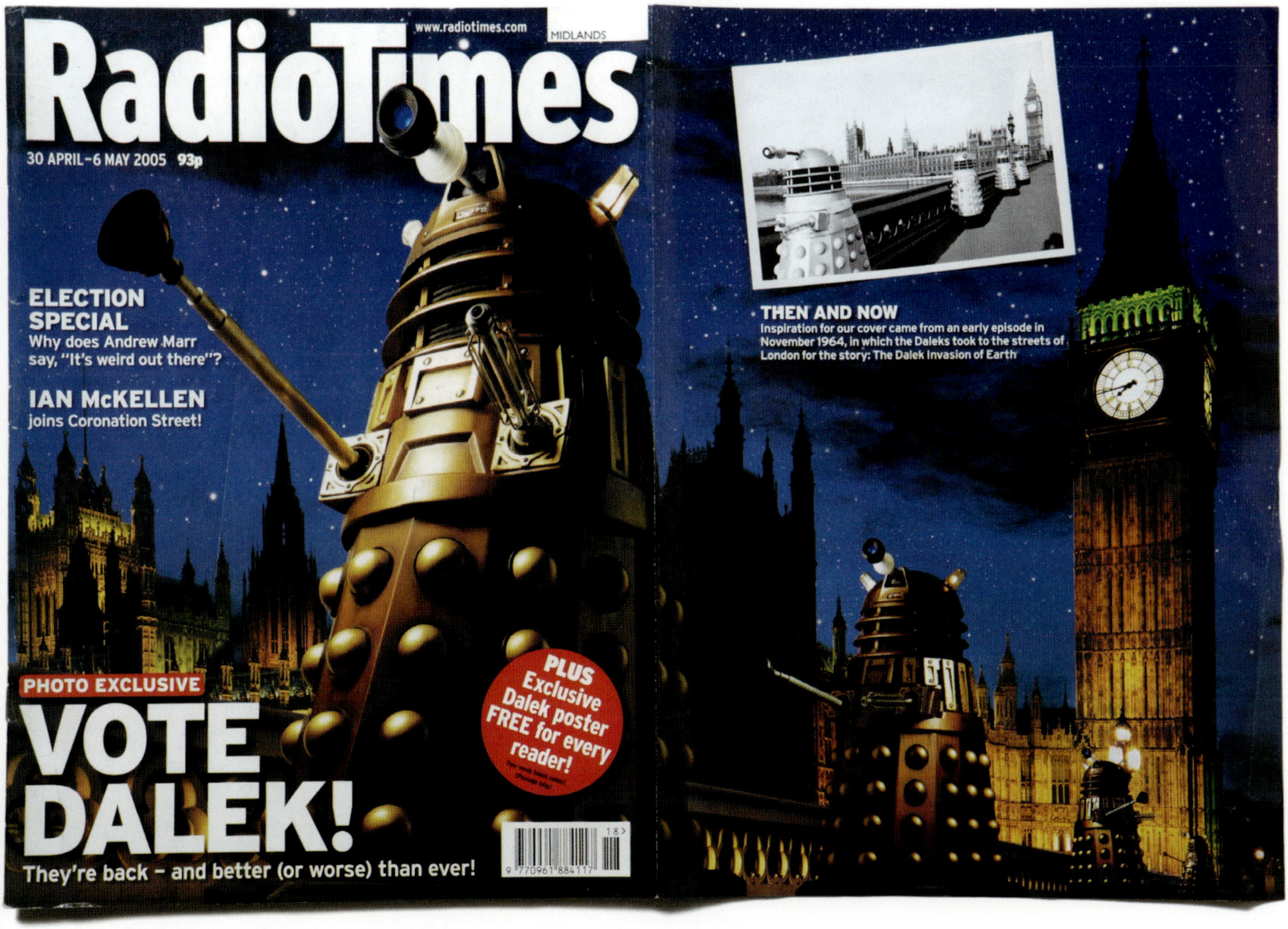

Doctor Who **The Daleks** *(photograph by Ian McKinnell)* *30 April–6 May 2005*

WIRELESS PROGRAMME—TUESDAY (Dec. 25th.)

The letters "S.B." printed in italics in these Programmes signify a Simultaneous Broadcast from the station mentioned.

LONDON.

6.30. **CHILDREN'S HOUR.**
S.B. to other Stations.

THE REV. J. A. MAYO will talk to the Children.

A Christmas Play adapted from "ON CHRISTMAS EVE" (Constance D'Arcy Mackay).

Cast :—

The Little Girl........ MONICA DISNEY
Wendy................ GILLY FLOWER
Alice................. BETTY THUMBLING
Goldilocks............. IRENE KEAMES
The Hush-a-Bye Lady AUNTIE PHYLLIS
Santa Claus........ UNCLE CARACTACUS

Scene : The bare living room of the Little Girl.

Christmas Night Programme.

7.30. *S.B. to other Stations.*
THE LONDON WIRELESS ORCHESTRA.
Conducted by L. STANTON JEFFERIES.
March, "Federation"............ *Klohr*
Overture, "Poet and Peasant".... *Suppe*

JOHN HENRY on "Christmas."

Orchestra.
Valse, "Chimes"............ *Windsor*
"A Musical Switch"........... *Alford*
"Baby's Sweetheart"........... *Corri*

A "MERRY CHRISTMAS" PARTY.
JOHN HENRY (the Host),
HELENA MILLAIS,
RONALD GOURLEY,
JAY KAYE.

Orchestra.
"Voice of the Bells"........... *Luigini*
Selection of the Popular Songs of Haydn Wood
Fox-trot, "Christmas"........... *Aston*
Old English Dance Music.
Polka.............. "Midnight Chimes"
Valse.......................... "Dorothy"
Barn Dance..................... "Lincke's"

9.30.—TIME SIGNAL, GENERAL NEWS BULLETIN. *S.B. to all Stations.* Local News and Weather Forecast.

9.45.—THE REV. G. W. KERR, B.A., LL.B., on "Wit and Humour." *S.B. to all Stations except Glasgow.*

10.0.—THE SAVOY ORPHEANS AND SAVOY HAVANA BANDS, relayed from the Savoy Hotel. *S.B. to all Stations (Glasgow 10.30).*

12.0.—Close down.

Announcer : R. F. Palmer.

BIRMINGHAM.

6.30. CHILDREN'S HOUR.
S.B. from London.

7.30. CHRISTMAS NIGHT PROGRAMME.
S.B. from London.

9.30.—NEWS. *S.B. from London.*

9.45.—THE REV. G. W. KERR. *S.B. from London.*

10.0.—THE SAVOY ORPHEANS AND SAVOY HAVANA BANDS. *S.B. from London.*

12.0.—Close down.

BOURNEMOUTH.

3.45. "AN AFTERNOON OF CAROLS."
GEORGE DALE (Solo Cornet).

4.45. WOMEN'S HOUR.

5.15. KIDDIES' HOUR.
DE VEKEY'S JUVENILE SERENADERS.
The Three Uncles.

7.10.—J. C. B. CARTER, B.A., on "Christmas Customs."

7.30. CHRISTMAS NIGHT PROGRAMME.
S.B. from London.

9.30.—NEWS. *S.B. from London.*

9.45.—THE REV. G. W. KERR. *S.B. from London.*

10.0.—THE SAVOY ORPHEANS AND SAVOY HAVANA BANDS. *S.B. from London.*

12.0.—Close down.

CARDIFF.

6.30. CHILDREN'S HOUR.
S.B. from London.

7.30. CHRISTMAS NIGHT PROGRAMME.
S.B. from London.

WAVE-LENGTHS AND CALL SIGNS.

LONDON (2LO)	-	350 Metres
ABERDEEN (2BD)	-	495 "
BIRMINGHAM (5IT)	-	475 "
BOURNEMOUTH (6BM)		385 "
CARDIFF (5WA)	-	435 "
GLASGOW (5SC)	-	420 "
MANCHESTER (2ZY)	-	400 "
NEWCASTLE (5NO)	-	370 "

9.30.—NEWS. *S.B. from London.*

9.45. THE REV. G. W. KERR. *S.B. from London.*

10.0.—THE SAVOY ORPHEANS AND SAVOY HAVANA BANDS. *S.B. from London.*

12.0.—Close down.

MANCHESTER.

4.0. "A CHRISTMAS CAROL."
(Chas. Dickens.)
Recited by
R. J. HEVER.
Incidental Music arranged and played by
ERIC FOGG.

5.15.—CHILDREN'S HOUR: Including a few words from everyone's Uncle, Father Xmas.

6.30. CHILDREN'S HOUR.
S.B. from London.

7.30. CHRISTMAS NIGHT PROGRAMME.
S.B. from London.

9.30.—NEWS. *S.B. from London.*

9.45.—THE REV. G. W. KERR. *S.B. from London.*

10.0.—THE SAVOY ORPHEANS AND SAVOY HAVANA BANDS. *S.B. from London.*

12.0.—Close down.

Announcer : Victor Smythe.

NEWCASTLE.

6.30. CHILDREN'S HOUR.
S.B. from London.

7.30. CHRISTMAS NIGHT PROGRAMME.
S.B. from London.

9.30.—NEWS. *S.B. from London.*

9.45.—THE REV. G. W. KERR. *S.B. from London.*

10.0.—THE SAVOY ORPHEANS AND SAVOY HAVANA BANDS. *S.B. from London.*

12.0.—Close down.

ALTERATIONS TO PROGRAMMES, Etc.

OWING to the enormous circulation of *THE RADIO TIMES*, it is necessary for the journal to go to press many days in advance of the date of publication. It sometimes happens, therefore, that the B.B.C. finds it necessary to make alterations or additions to programmes, etc., after *THE RADIO TIMES* has gone to press.

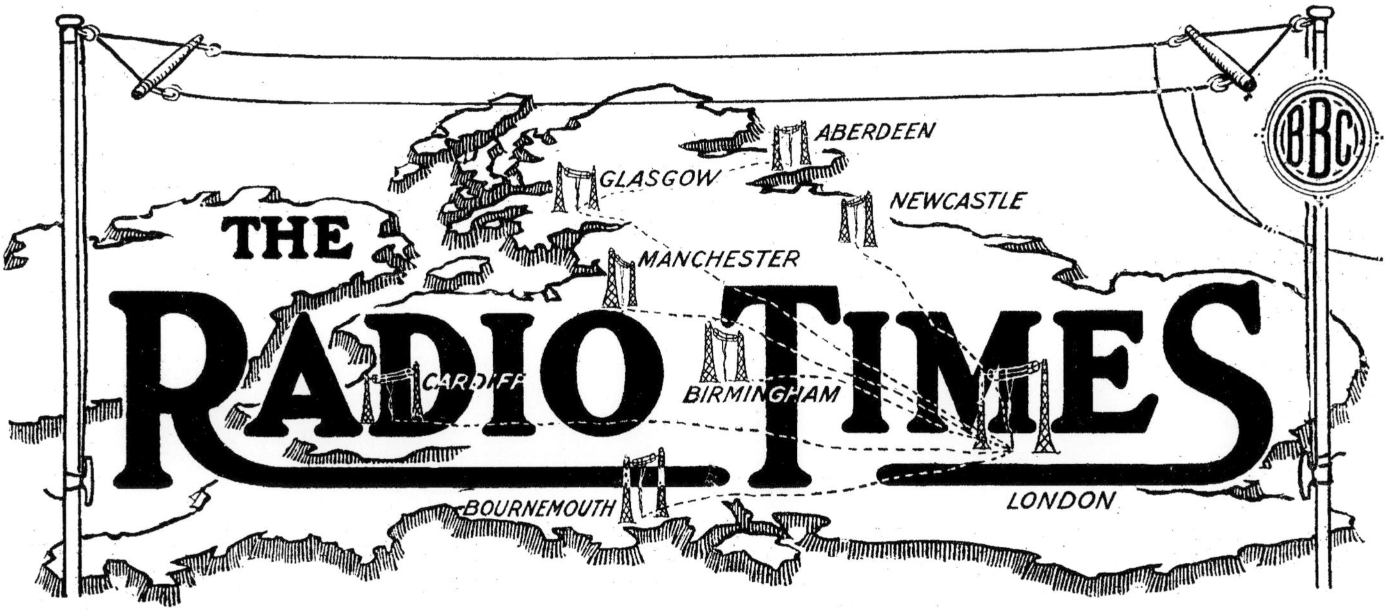

The Early Years 1923-1930

Vol. 1. No. 1.

28 September 1923

Necessity is the mother of success. Newspapers wanted to charge the BBC to run listings for its radio programmes, so the Corporation responded by launching a specialist magazine – *The Radio Times*. The first edition, published on 28 September 1923 and covering programmes for the week beginning 30 September, welcomed readers with a cheery "Hullo, everyone!" Ninety years later, *Radio Times* – the definite article was dropped from the title in January 1937 – is still going strong.

Every edition until 14 September 1928 (apart from Christmas issues) featured a version of this masthead, starting with eight transmitter sites and ending with 21. Radio was still so new that the technology was a focus of attention, and in the early years the magazine was loaded with technical puns. "May you never be late for your favourite wave-train," wrote Arthur R Burrows, BBC director of programmes.

But perhaps people are never happy: even this first issue included letters from listeners complaining about the BBC's announcers being too highbrow. *Radio Times* replied: "Even the greeting 'Hullo, Everybody' is considered undue familiarity amongst a class of listener. The tendency is towards introducing humour."

1923–1930

A publishing legend is born; the first Christmas special; Broadcasting House opens for business; and visions of the future

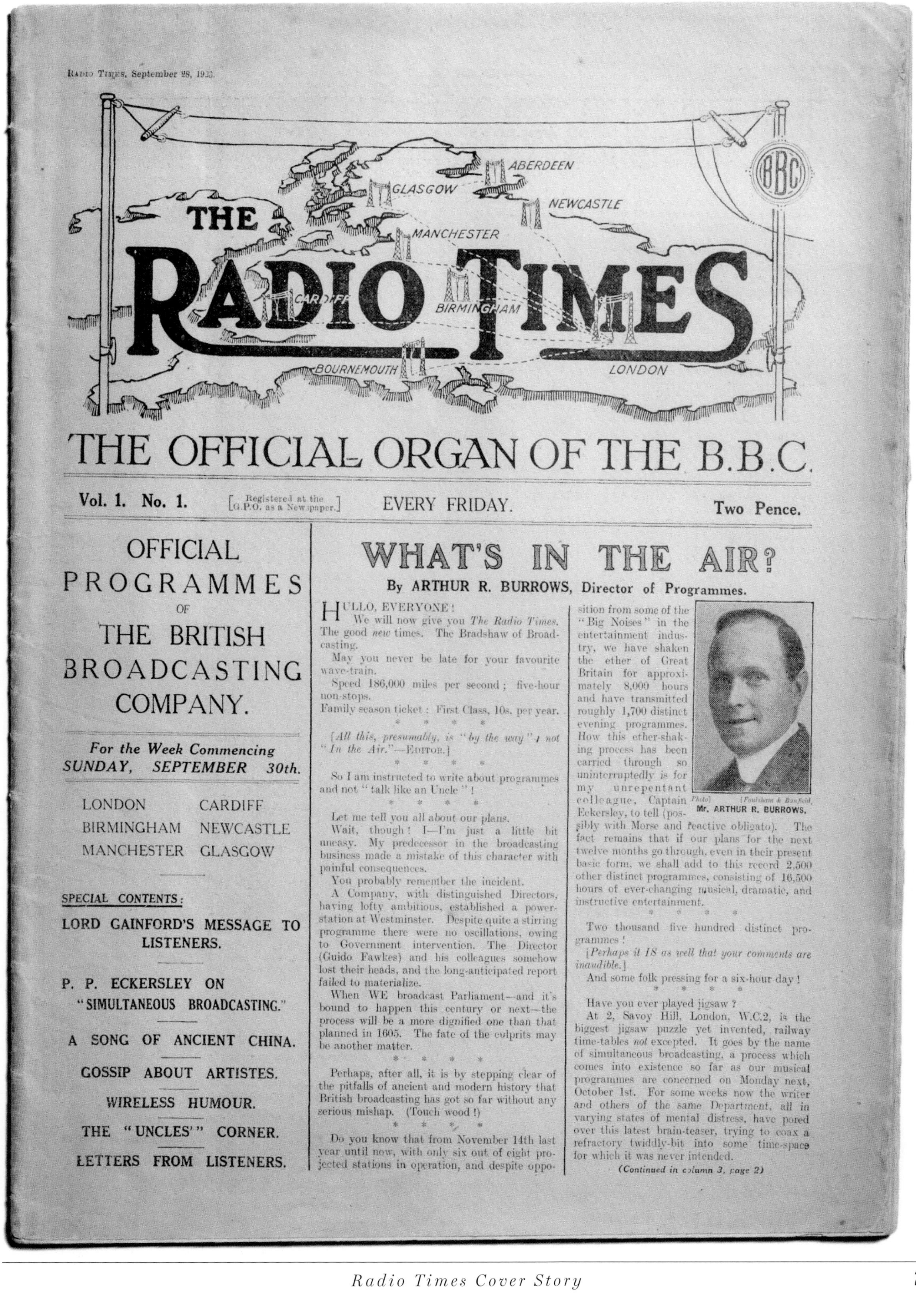

RADIO TIMES, September 28, 1923.

THE RADIO TIMES

THE OFFICIAL ORGAN OF THE B.B.C.

Vol. 1. No. 1. [Registered at the G.P.O. as a Newspaper.] EVERY FRIDAY. Two Pence.

OFFICIAL PROGRAMMES OF THE BRITISH BROADCASTING COMPANY.

For the Week Commencing SUNDAY, SEPTEMBER 30th.

LONDON — CARDIFF
BIRMINGHAM — NEWCASTLE
MANCHESTER — GLASGOW

SPECIAL CONTENTS:

LORD GAINFORD'S MESSAGE TO LISTENERS.

P. P. ECKERSLEY ON "SIMULTANEOUS BROADCASTING."

A SONG OF ANCIENT CHINA.

GOSSIP ABOUT ARTISTES.

WIRELESS HUMOUR.

THE "UNCLES'" CORNER.

LETTERS FROM LISTENERS.

WHAT'S IN THE AIR?

By ARTHUR R. BURROWS, Director of Programmes.

HULLO, EVERYONE!

We will now give you *The Radio Times.* The good *new* times. The Bradshaw of Broadcasting.

May you never be late for your favourite wave-train.

Speed 186,000 miles per second; five-hour non-stops.

Family season ticket: First Class, 10s. per year.

* * * *

[*All this, presumably, is "by the way" not "In the Air."*—EDITOR.]

* * * *

So I am instructed to write about programmes and not "talk like an Uncle"!

* * * *

Let me tell you all about our plans.

Wait, though! I—I'm just a little bit uneasy. My predecessor in the broadcasting business made a mistake of this character with painful consequences.

You probably remember the incident.

A Company, with distinguished Directors, having lofty ambitions, established a power-station at Westminster. Despite quite a stirring programme there were no oscillations, owing to Government intervention. The Director (Guido Fawkes) and his colleagues somehow lost their heads, and the long-anticipated report failed to materialize.

When WE broadcast Parliament—and it's bound to happen this century or next—the process will be a more dignified one than that planned in 1605. The fate of the culprits may be another matter.

* * * *

Perhaps, after all, it is by stepping clear of the pitfalls of ancient and modern history that British broadcasting has got so far without any serious mishap. (Touch wood!)

* * * *

Do you know that from November 14th last year until now, with only six out of eight projected stations in operation, and despite opposition from some of the "Big Noises" in the entertainment industry, we have shaken the ether of Great Britain for approximately 8,000 hours and have transmitted roughly 1,700 distinct evening programmes. How this ether-shaking process has been carried through so uninterruptedly is for my unrepentant colleague, Captain Eckersley, to tell (possibly with Morse and reactive obligato). The fact remains that if our plans for the next twelve months go through, even in their present basic form, we shall add to this record 2,500 other distinct programmes, consisting of 16,500 hours of ever-changing musical, dramatic, and instructive entertainment.

Photo] [Foulsham & Banfield.
Mr. ARTHUR R. BURROWS.

* * * *

Two thousand five hundred distinct programmes!

[*Perhaps it IS as well that your comments are inaudible.*]

And some folk pressing for a six-hour day!

* * * *

Have you ever played jigsaw?

At 2, Savoy Hill, London, W.C.2, is the biggest jigsaw puzzle yet invented, railway time-tables *not* excepted. It goes by the name of simultaneous broadcasting, a process which comes into existence so far as our musical programmes are concerned on Monday next, October 1st. For some weeks now the writer and others of the same Department, all in varying states of mental distress, have pored over this latest brain-teaser, trying to coax a refractory twiddly-bit into some time-space for which it was never intended.

(Continued in column 3, page 2)

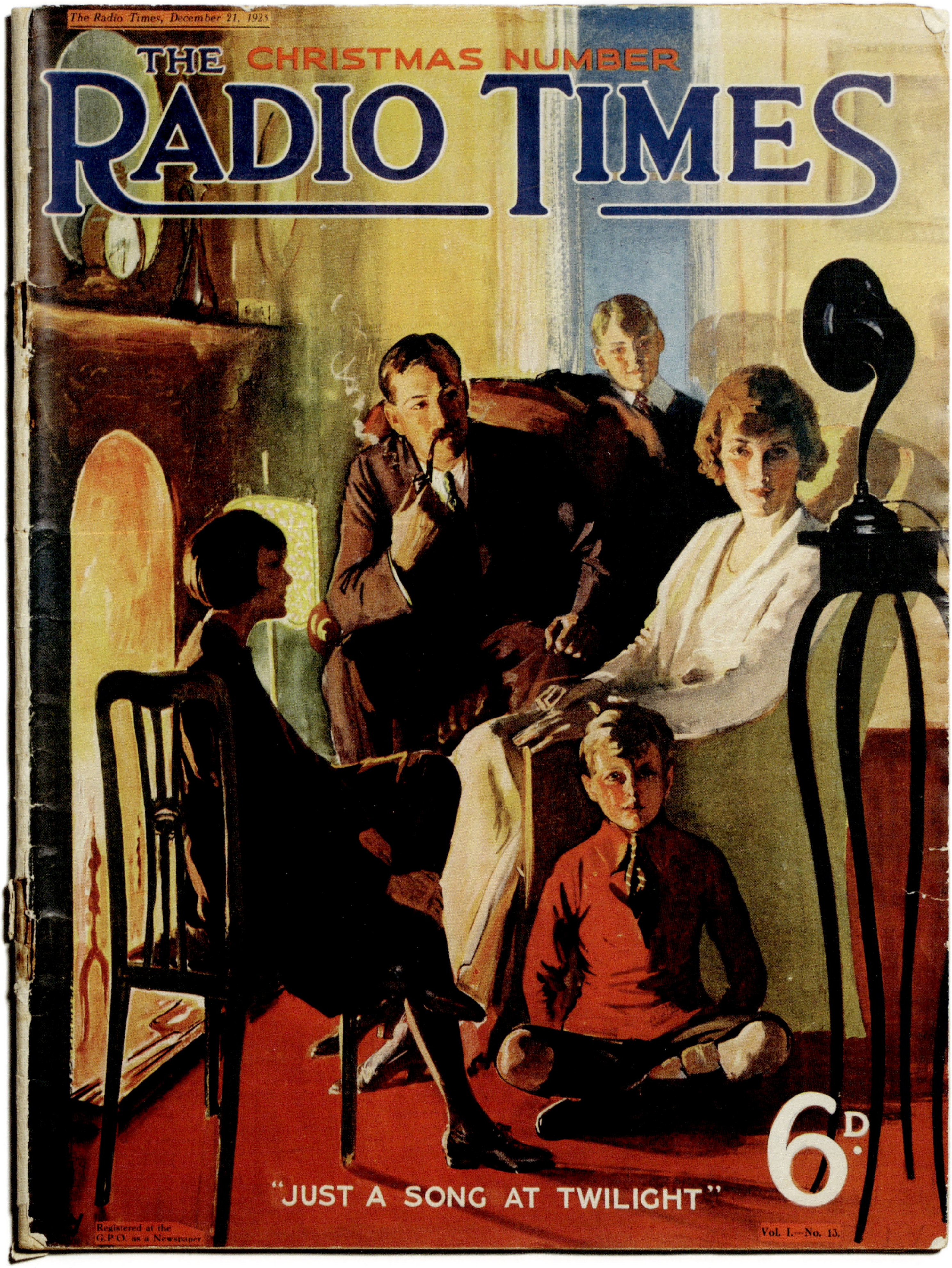
The Radio Times, December 21, 1923
THE CHRISTMAS NUMBER
RADIO TIMES
"JUST A SONG AT TWILIGHT"
6D.
Registered at the G.P.O. as a Newspaper
Vol. I.—No. 13.

Christmas 1923 *(left)*

Illustration by Kay

21 December 1923

Christmas has always been special in *Radio Times* and the very first festive edition made a big impact thanks to the colour illustration. John Reith, later Lord Reith, the BBC managing director who went on to become director-general, wrote in his letter that "this first wireless Christmas" meant the BBC could bring "some of the fellowship and good cheer of music and kindly message to those who cannot gather with others".

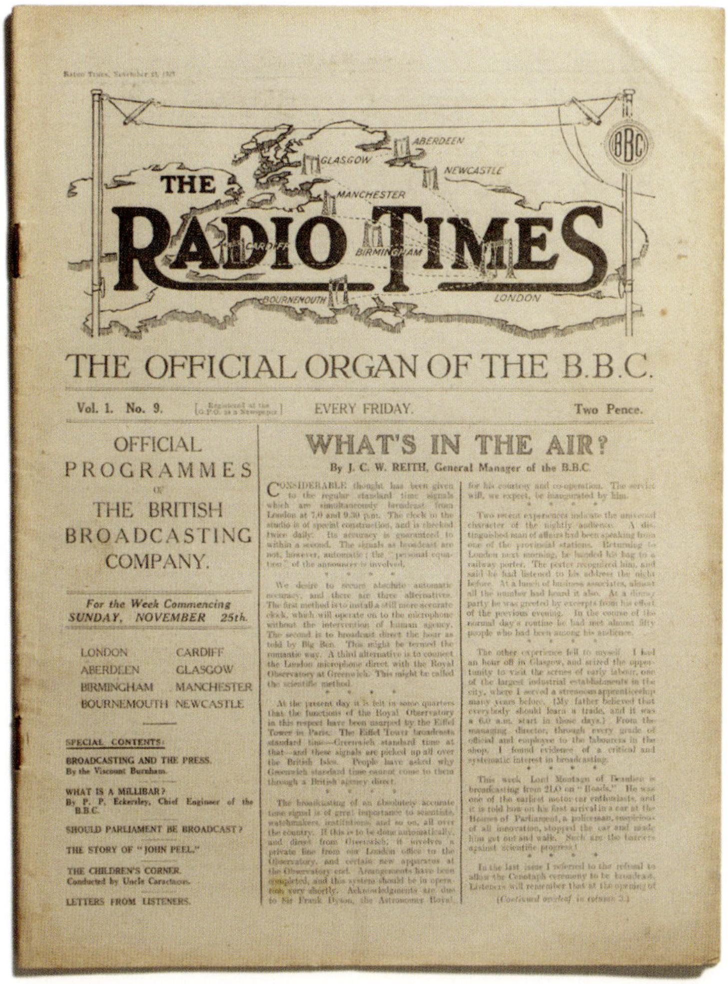

THE RADIO TIMES

THE OFFICIAL ORGAN OF THE B.B.C.

Vol. 1. No. 9. EVERY FRIDAY. Two Pence.

OFFICIAL PROGRAMMES OF THE BRITISH BROADCASTING COMPANY.

For the Week Commencing SUNDAY, NOVEMBER 25th.

LONDON, CARDIFF, ABERDEEN, GLASGOW, BIRMINGHAM, MANCHESTER, BOURNEMOUTH, NEWCASTLE

SPECIAL CONTENTS:

BROADCASTING AND THE PRESS. By the Viscount Burnham.

WHAT IS A MILLIBAR? By P. P. Eckersley, Chief Engineer of the B.B.C.

SHOULD PARLIAMENT BE BROADCAST?

THE STORY OF "JOHN PEEL."

THE CHILDREN'S CORNER. Conducted by Uncle Caractacus.

LETTERS FROM LISTENERS.

WHAT'S IN THE AIR?

By J. C. W. REITH, General Manager of the B.B.C.

What's in the air? *(right)*

23 November 1923

One of the first broadcasting controversies was whether to allow microphones in Parliament. The BBC's chief engineer, Peter Eckersley, was confident that broadcasting debates was possible, provided the microphone was held in a "gracefully designed carriage on rubber tyres" so it could be moved around. In the end, it was 1978 before the first live parliamentary debates were broadcast.

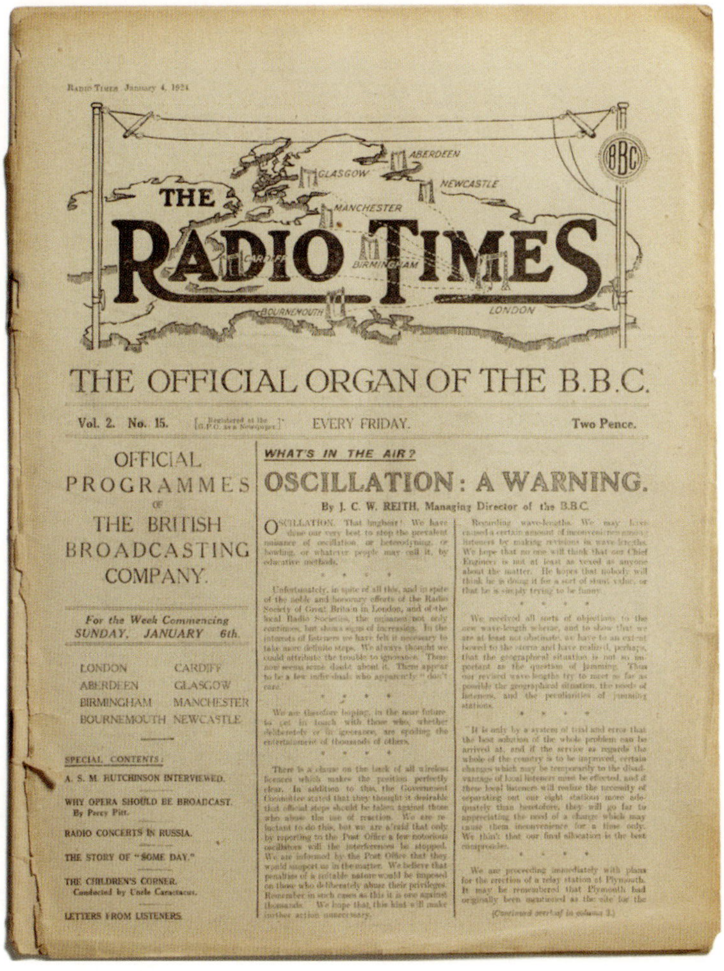

THE RADIO TIMES

THE OFFICIAL ORGAN OF THE B.B.C.

Vol. 2. No. 15. EVERY FRIDAY. Two Pence.

OFFICIAL PROGRAMMES OF THE BRITISH BROADCASTING COMPANY.

For the Week Commencing SUNDAY, JANUARY 6th.

LONDON, CARDIFF, ABERDEEN, GLASGOW, BIRMINGHAM, MANCHESTER, BOURNEMOUTH, NEWCASTLE

SPECIAL CONTENTS:

A. S. M. HUTCHINSON INTERVIEWED.

WHY OPERA SHOULD BE BROADCAST. By Percy Pitt.

RADIO CONCERTS IN RUSSIA.

THE STORY OF "SOME DAY."

THE CHILDREN'S CORNER. Conducted by Uncle Caractacus.

LETTERS FROM LISTENERS.

WHAT'S IN THE AIR?

OSCILLATION: A WARNING.

By J. C. W. REITH, Managing Director of the B.B.C.

Oscillation: a warning *(right)*

4 January 1924

Early wireless sets were sensitive instruments. Aerials often had to be hung from tall poles in the garden and the slightest miscalibration could result in poor reception or blown valves. Worse, a badly assembled set could trigger a howling noise on the equipment of everyone else for miles around, which was known as "oscillation" or "heterodyning". The pages of *Radio Times* were filled with jokes and cartoons about these "howlers" but John Reith didn't see the funny side. In his front-page letter he attacked the people "who, whether deliberately or in ignorance, are spoiling the entertainment of thousands of others".

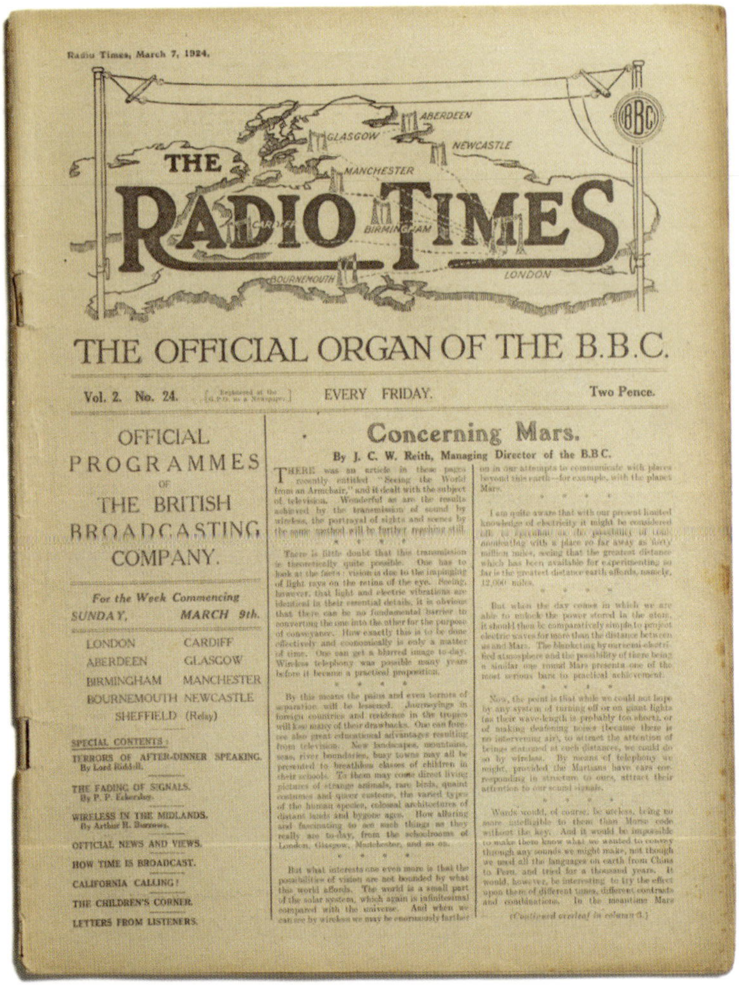

Radio Times, March 7, 1924.

THE RADIO TIMES

THE OFFICIAL ORGAN OF THE B.B.C.

Vol. 2. No. 24. EVERY FRIDAY. Two Pence.

OFFICIAL PROGRAMMES OF THE BRITISH BROADCASTING COMPANY.

For the Week Commencing SUNDAY, MARCH 9th.

LONDON, CARDIFF, ABERDEEN, GLASGOW, BIRMINGHAM, MANCHESTER, BOURNEMOUTH, NEWCASTLE, SHEFFIELD (Relay)

SPECIAL CONTENTS:
TERRORS OF AFTER-DINNER SPEAKING. By Lord Riddell.
THE FADING OF SIGNALS. By P. P. Eckersley.
WIRELESS IN THE MIDLANDS. By Arthur R. Burrows.
OFFICIAL NEWS AND VIEWS.
HOW TIME IS BROADCAST.
CALIFORNIA CALLING!
THE CHILDREN'S CORNER.
LETTERS FROM LISTENERS.

Concerning Mars.

By J. C. W. Reith, Managing Director of the B.B.C.

Concerning Mars *(left)*

7 March 1924

On 24 August 1924, Mars came within 35 million miles of Earth. It would not pass so close again until 2003. Public excitement in the months before this "perihelic opposition" became entangled with the technology of radio. Newspapers claimed mysterious "signals" had been received from the red planet, although *Radio Times* said such stories were "as unintelligible as the credulity of those who believe them".

Surprisingly, John Reith looked forward to a time when television would extend the BBC's audience to the stars. A famously severe man, he suggested we beam music and pictures of animals at Mars, along with their names in Esperanto. This would attract the attention of any aliens, "provided the Martians have ears corresponding in structure to ours".

Christmas 1924 *(right)*

Illustration by Edwin Austin Abbey

19 December 1924

This cover by American artist Edwin Austin Abbey is one of the most famous *Radio Times* images because it was used again – twice. The first time was for the Christmas cover in 1994 (below and page 255) when artist Bob Venables kept the air of innocence but reworked it to modernise the clothes and to erase the cigarettes. The second was an affectionate pastiche by *Doctor Who Magazine* in 2011.

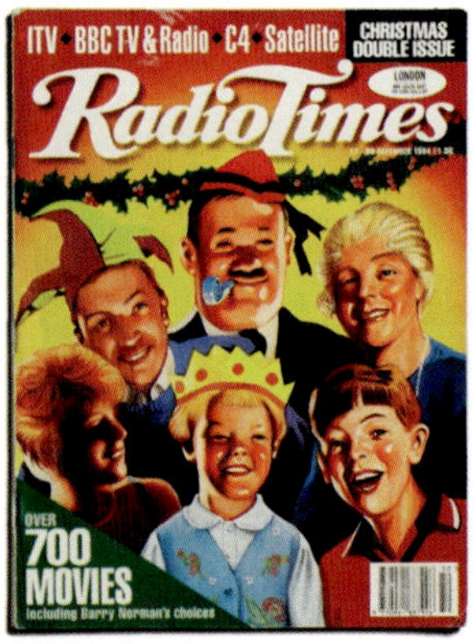

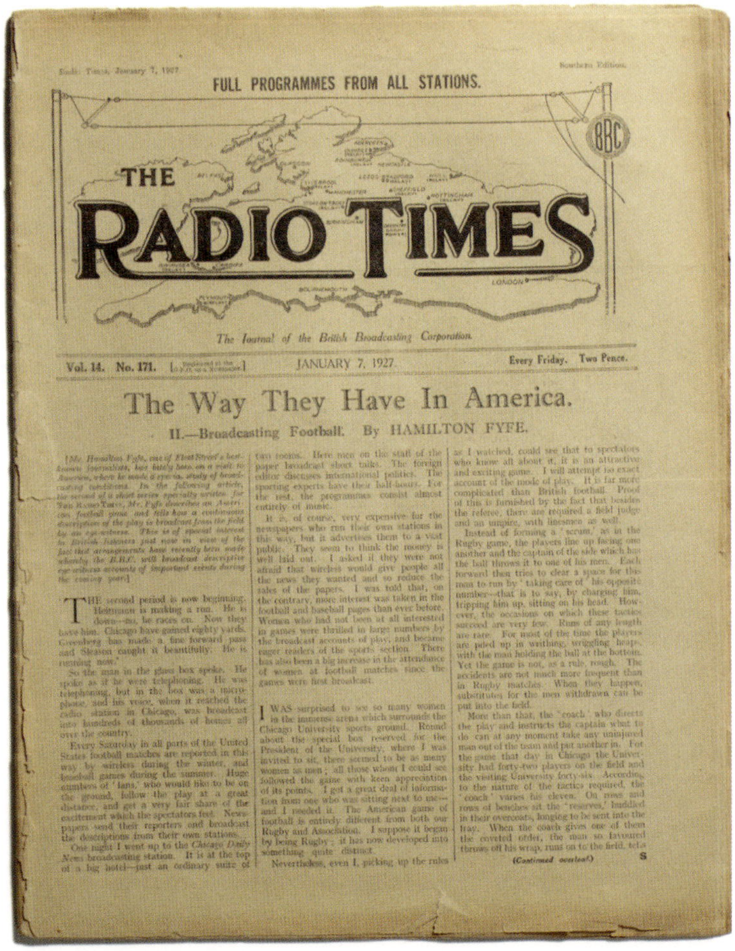

Radio Times, January 7, 1927.

FULL PROGRAMMES FROM ALL STATIONS.

THE RADIO TIMES

The Journal of the British Broadcasting Corporation.

Vol. 14. No. 171. JANUARY 7, 1927. Every Friday. Two Pence.

The Way They Have In America.

II.—Broadcasting Football. By HAMILTON FYFE.

The way they have in America *(left)*

7 January 1927

Broadcasting from outside the studio called for a new way of doing things. Hamilton Fyfe described a trip to an American football game in Chicago, where "a continuous description of the play is broadcast from the field by an eye-witness". Americans had heard sports commentary of this kind since 1921, but "the man in the glass box" appeared odd to British ears. However, the article announced the BBC's plans to "broadcast descriptive eye-witness accounts of important events during the coming year".

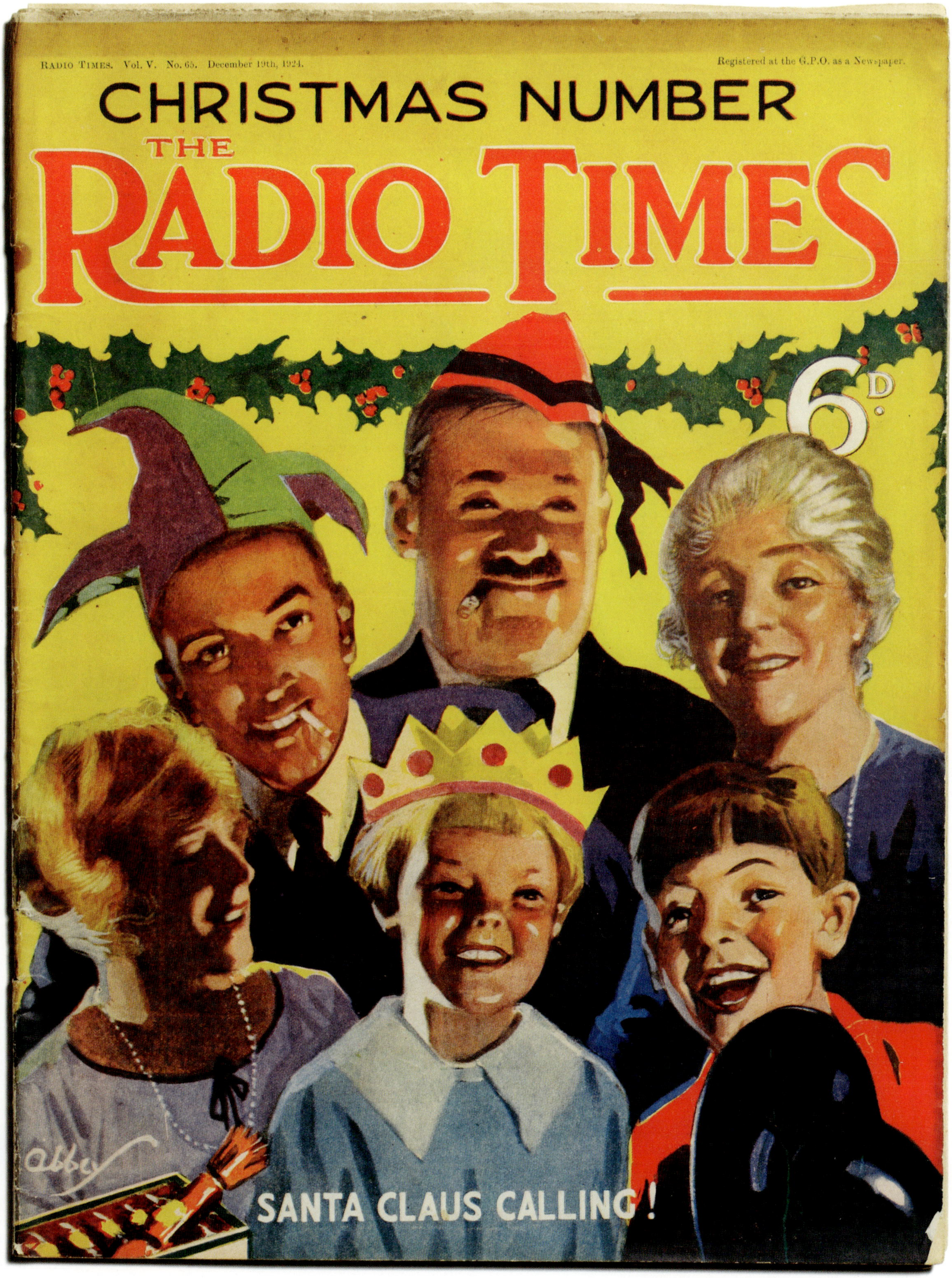
RADIO TIMES. Vol. V. No. 65. December 19th, 1924.
Registered at the G.P.O. as a Newspaper.
CHRISTMAS NUMBER
THE RADIO TIMES
6D.
abbey
SANTA CLAUS CALLING!

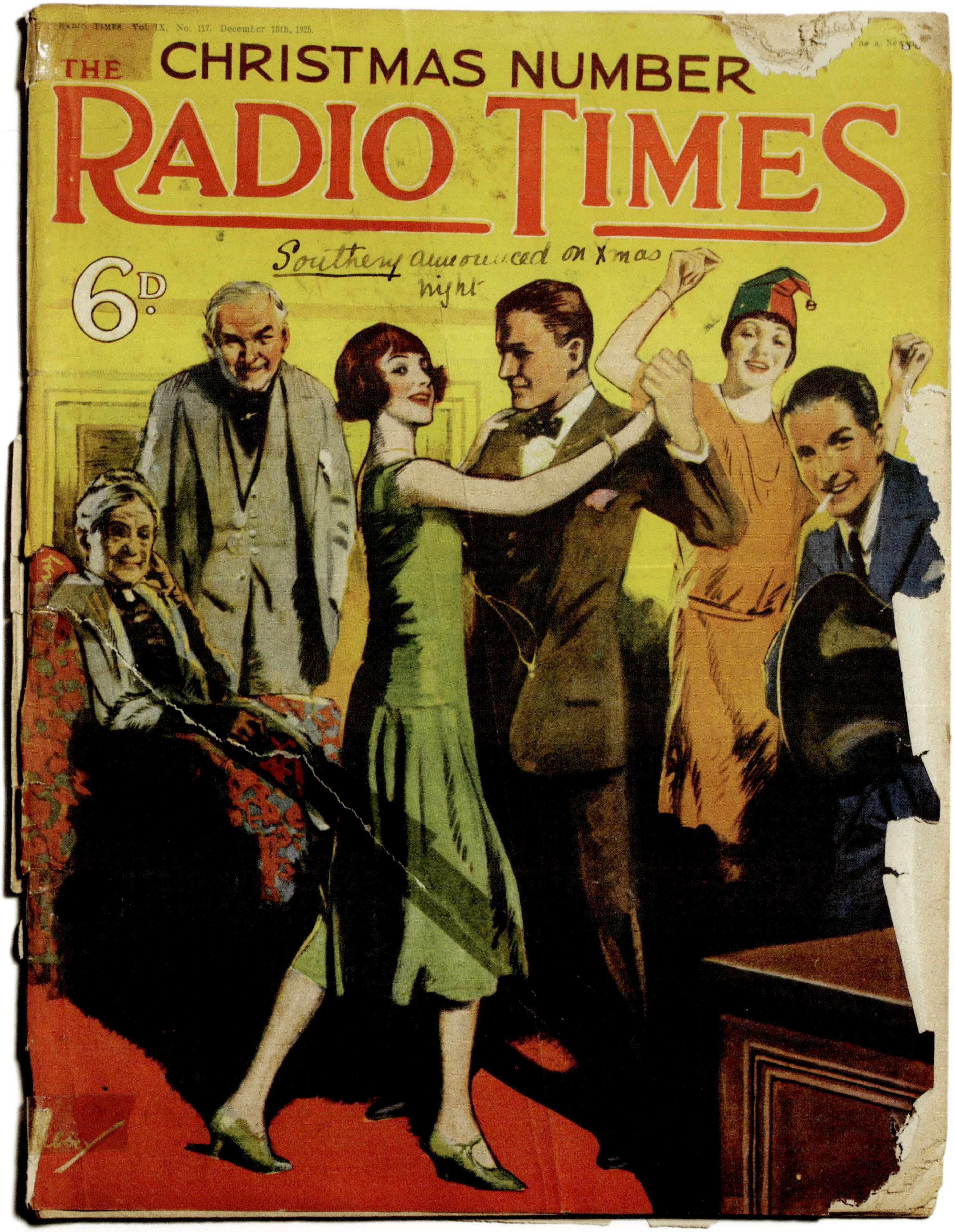

Christmas 1925 **Illustration by Edwin Austin Abbey** *18 December 1925*

Nothing changes. Where today we might have trouble getting a computer to work, in 1925 people had similar problems with their wireless. This issue featured a jocular story of an Aunt Lavinia battling with her valves... There was also a letter from a listener who was objecting to rumours that the government would take over broadcasting. RJF from Thornton Heath said if that were to happen, "I for one will dismantle my set."

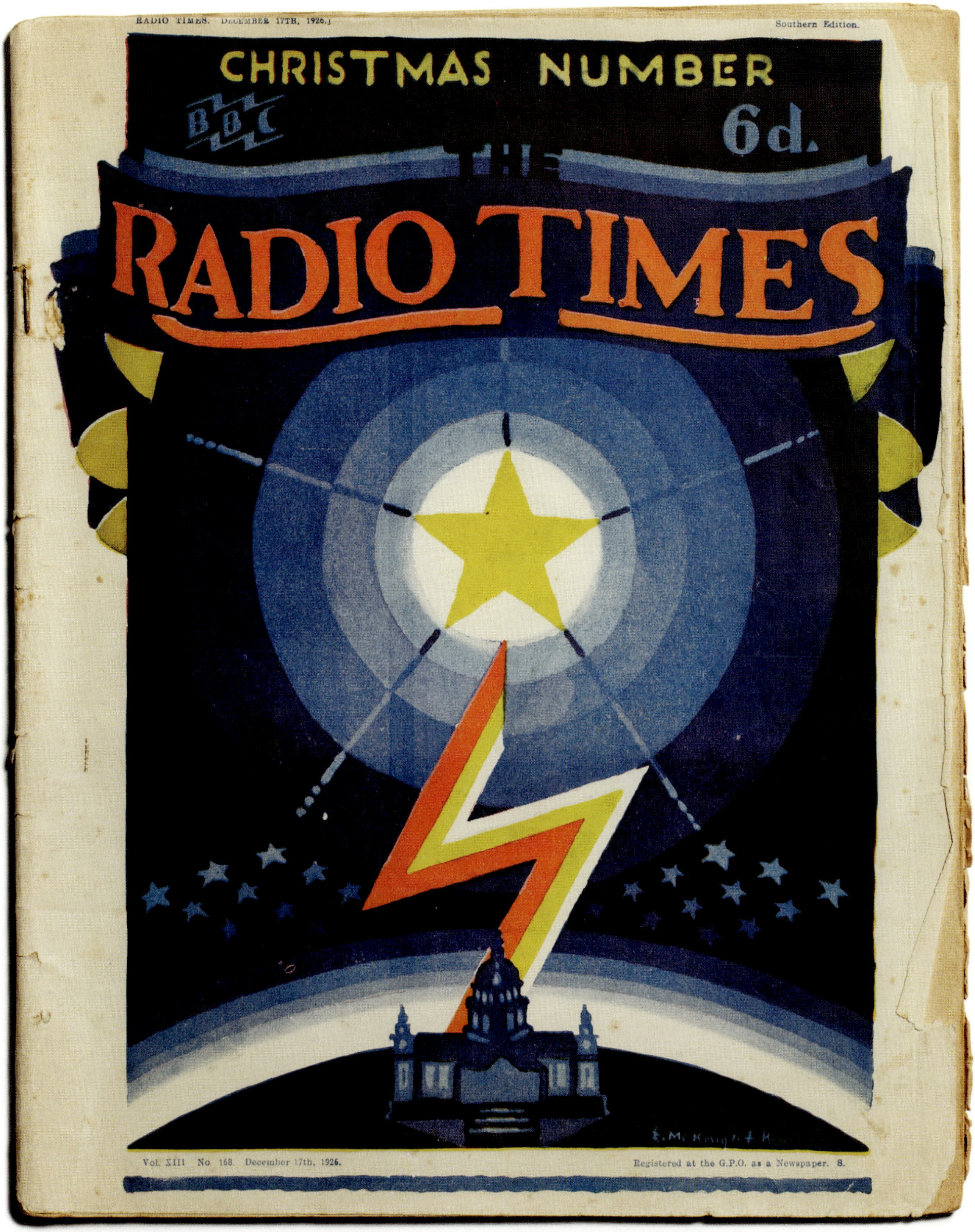

Christmas 1926 **Illustration by Edward McKnight Kauffer** *17 December 1926*

This cover was designed by American-born artist Edward McKnight Kauffer, who later designed posters for the London Underground. Inside was a story by Jerome K Jerome, who recalled the simple pleasures of a night out at the turn of the 20th century. Later, Denis Mackail prophesied that by 2026 the sky would be dark with aeroplanes queuing for runways, and homes would have so many bathrooms that families would live in them.

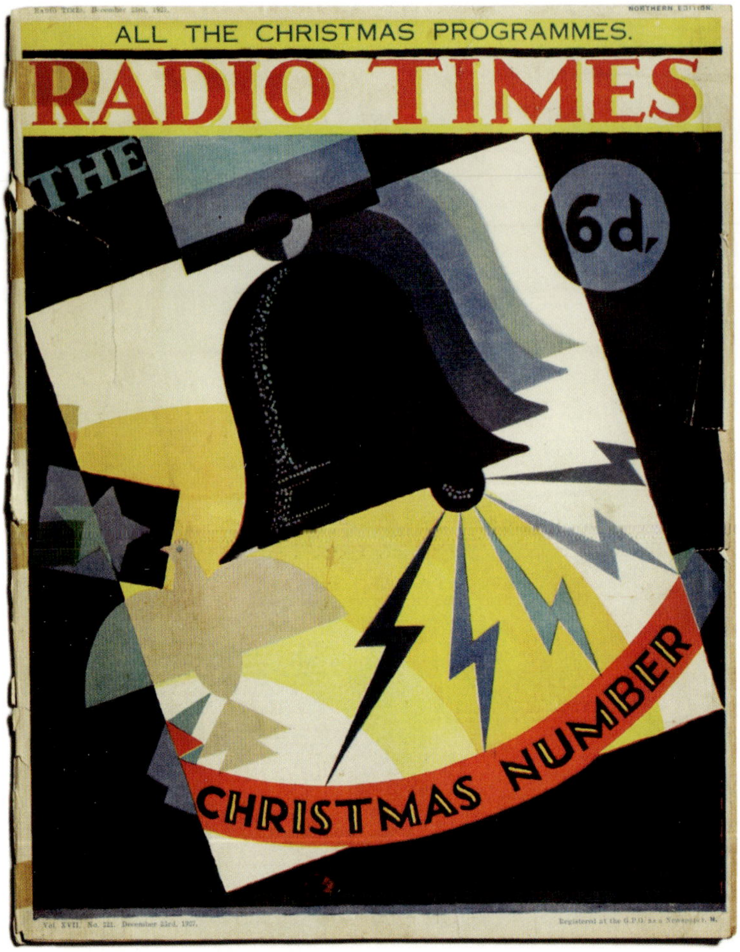

Christmas 1927 *(left)*
Illustration by Edward McKnight Kauffer
23 December 1927
In his letter John Reith reflected on the role of public service broadcasting: "Tolerance involves a recognition of the tastes of other listeners, and the endeavour to compile programmes to suit the taste of everybody is an obviously delicate and embarrassing business, requiring a resolute and steadfast policy of public service."

Whitsun number *(below left)*
Illustration by Steven Spurrier
25 May 1928
One of the first covers to feature an illustration that wasn't linked to Christmas. It took its cue from a story inside that imagined life in Britain in 2028.

Christmas 1928 *(below right)*
Illustration by Cassandre
21 December 1928
A Christmas cover by Cassandre – born Adolphe Mouron – a Ukrainian-French commercial artist famous for his classic posters advertising trains, cars and ocean liners.

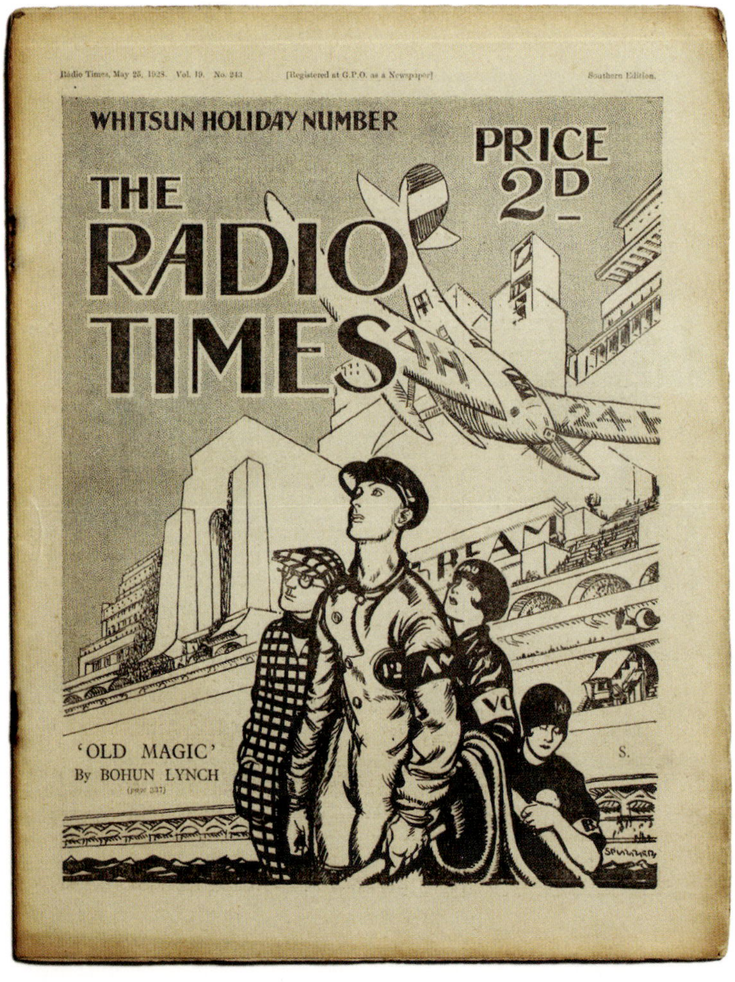

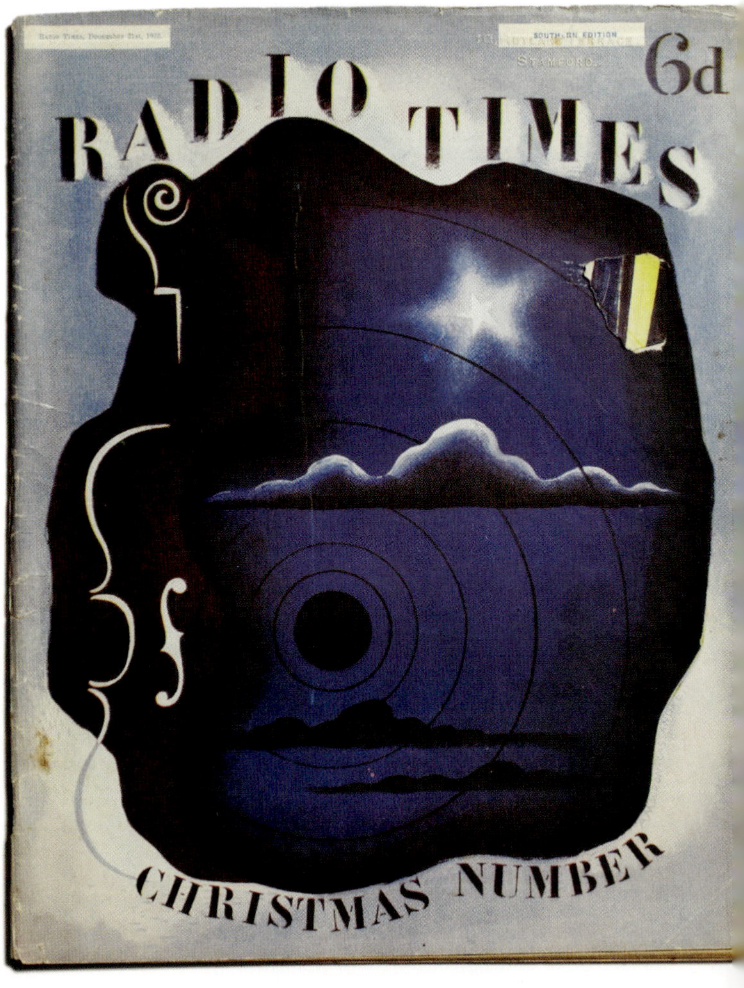

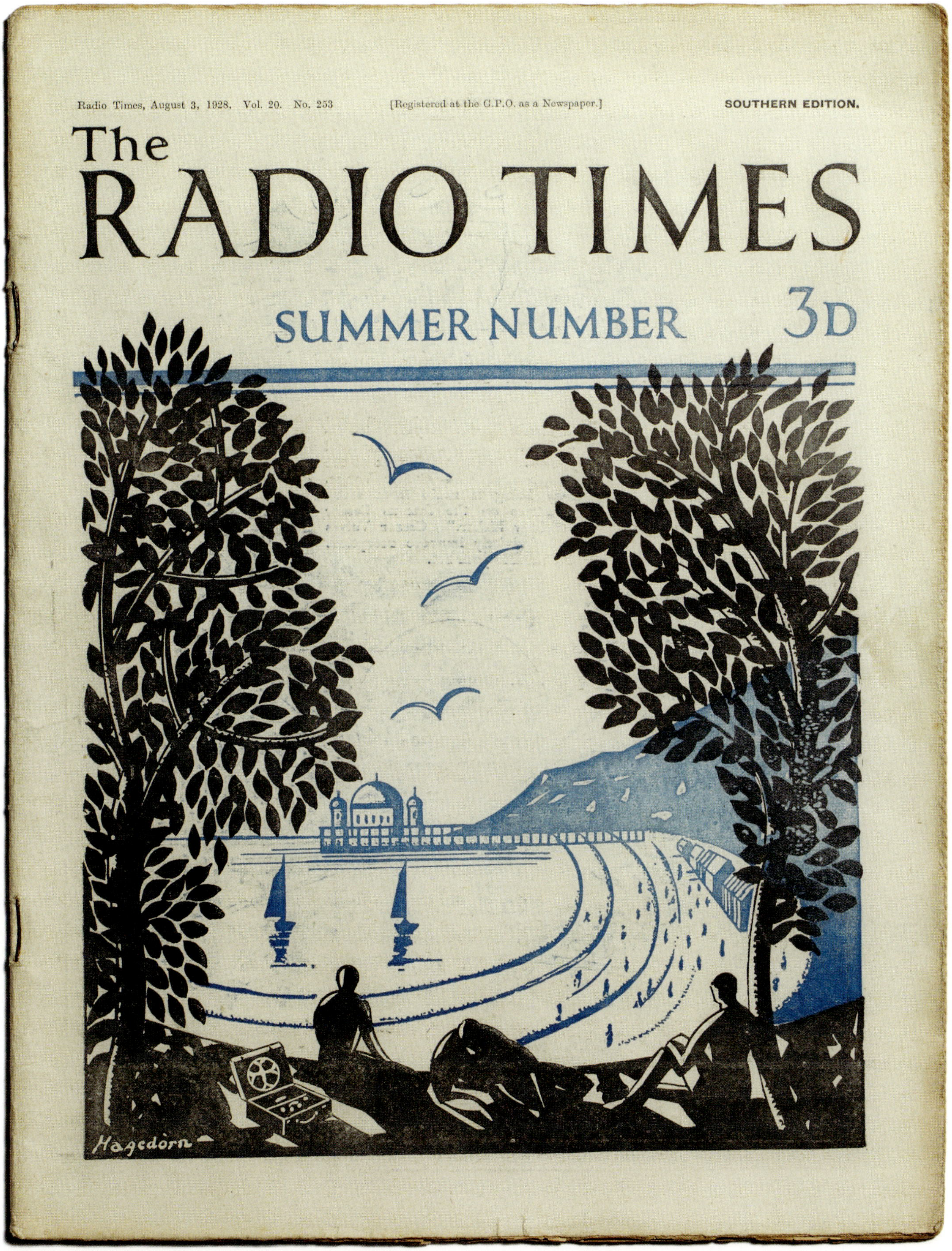

Summer number **Illustration by Hagedorn** *3 August 1928*

Many readers were asking when the BBC was going to branch out into television: the postmaster-general stated it was still an experimental, impractical technology, although it was hinted that "telephotography" (transmitting still photographs and diagrams) might be adopted "in the not very remote future".

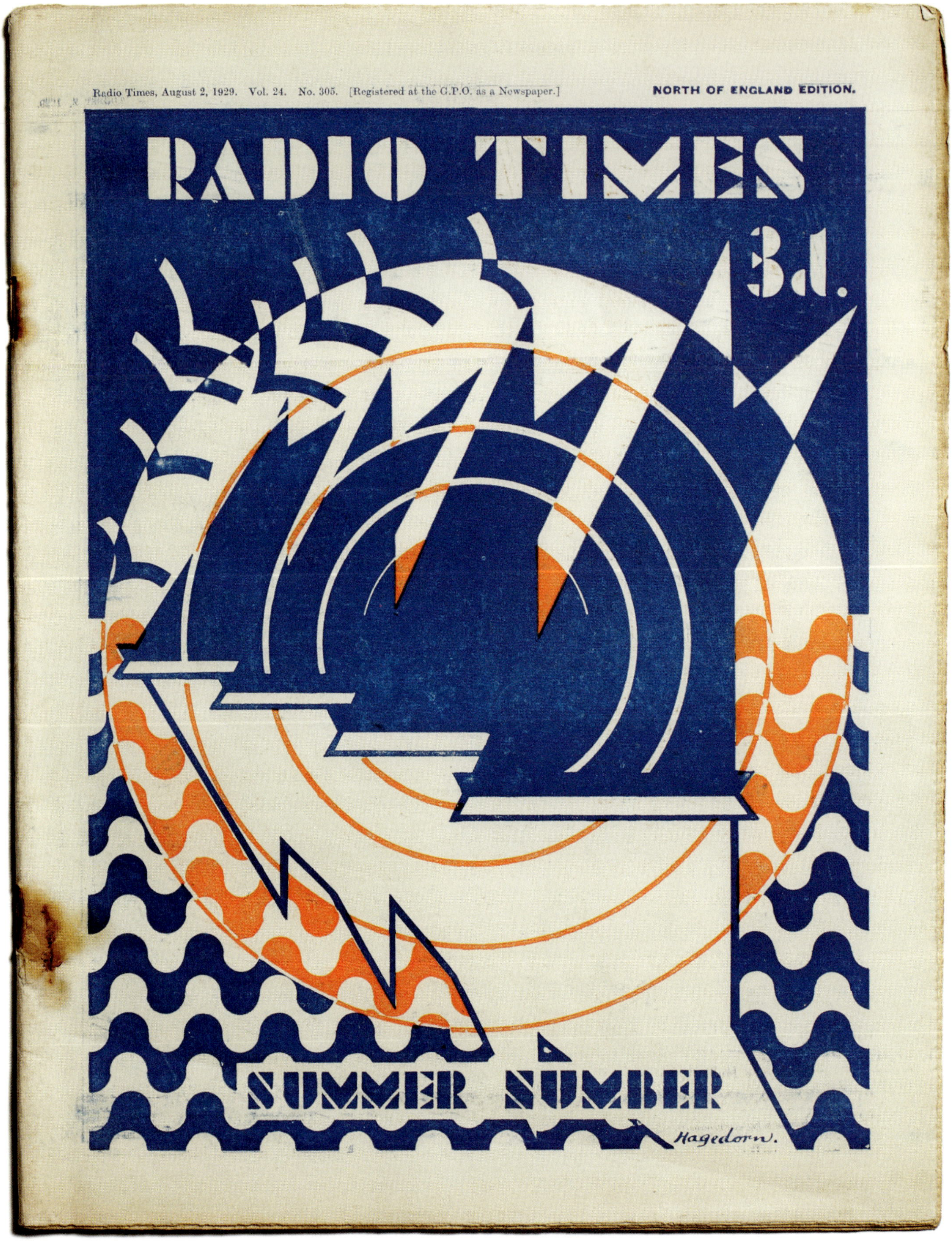

Summer number Illustration by Hagedorn *2 August 1929*

We still do this now: Compton Mackenzie – the writer of *Whisky Galore* – mocked the already common idea that summers in the past were always hotter. He put the record straight in this seasonal edition by describing how Cornwall had snow back in June 1888. For the record, the summer of 1929 was mainly dry and sunny.

His Majesty the King *(right)*

5 July 1929

The nation celebrated King George V's recovery from illness with a service at Westminster Abbey. *Radio Times* published the full order of service inside, and on the cover delivered the solemn message: "A Service of Thanksgiving to Almighty God for His good Providence whereby our Most Gracious Sovereign has been delivered from severe illness to the comfort of the whole Realm".

Broadcasting House *(below left)*

Illustration by Adrian Hill

21 November 1930

New Broadcasting House was opened by the Queen on 7 June 2013; this cover by artist Adrian Hill showed the original building under construction with its steel frame and facing of Portland stone. The first edition of *Radio Times* was placed under the foundation stone. The magazine's offices would move from Savoy Hill to Broadcasting House in 1932 and the first radio broadcast was made from the building on 15 March 1932.

Christmas 1930 *(below right)*

Illustration by Paul Nash

19 December 1930

The cover illustration by Paul Nash – a leading light of modern art in Britain – blurred the lines between transmitter, wireless receiver and a window on the world. Inside the issue were short stories, poems and an article about log-rolling.

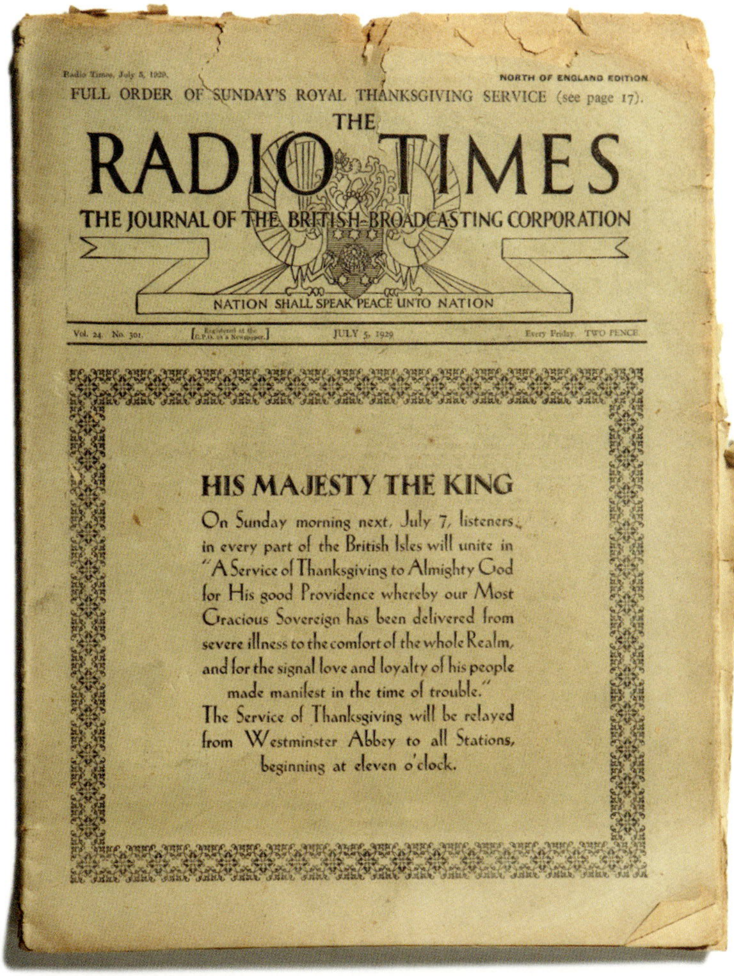

NORTH OF ENGLAND EDITION

FULL ORDER OF SUNDAY'S ROYAL THANKSGIVING SERVICE (see page 17).

THE RADIO TIMES

THE JOURNAL OF THE BRITISH BROADCASTING CORPORATION

NATION SHALL SPEAK PEACE UNTO NATION

JULY 5, 1929 Every Friday. TWO PENCE

HIS MAJESTY THE KING

On Sunday morning next, July 7, listeners, in every part of the British Isles will unite in "A Service of Thanksgiving to Almighty God for His good Providence whereby our Most Gracious Sovereign has been delivered from severe illness to the comfort of the whole Realm, and for the signal love and loyalty of his people made manifest in the time of trouble."

The Service of Thanksgiving will be relayed from Westminster Abbey to all Stations, beginning at eleven o'clock.

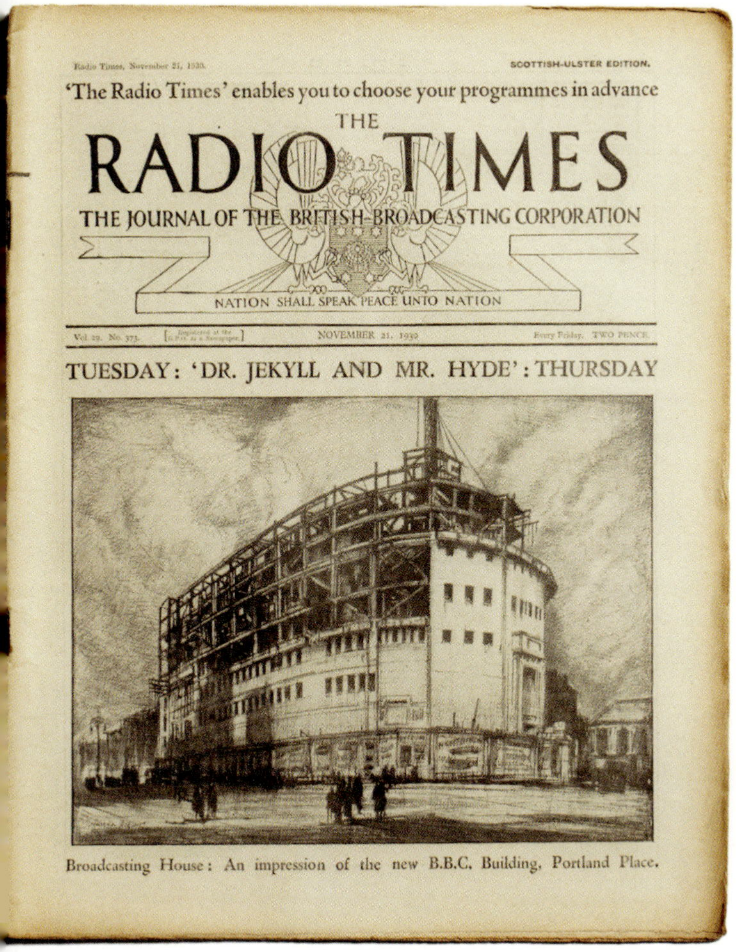

SCOTTISH-ULSTER EDITION.

'The Radio Times' enables you to choose your programmes in advance

THE RADIO TIMES

THE JOURNAL OF THE BRITISH BROADCASTING CORPORATION

NATION SHALL SPEAK PEACE UNTO NATION

NOVEMBER 21, 1930 Every Friday. TWO PENCE

TUESDAY: 'DR. JEKYLL AND MR. HYDE': THURSDAY

Broadcasting House: An impression of the new B.B.C. Building, Portland Place.

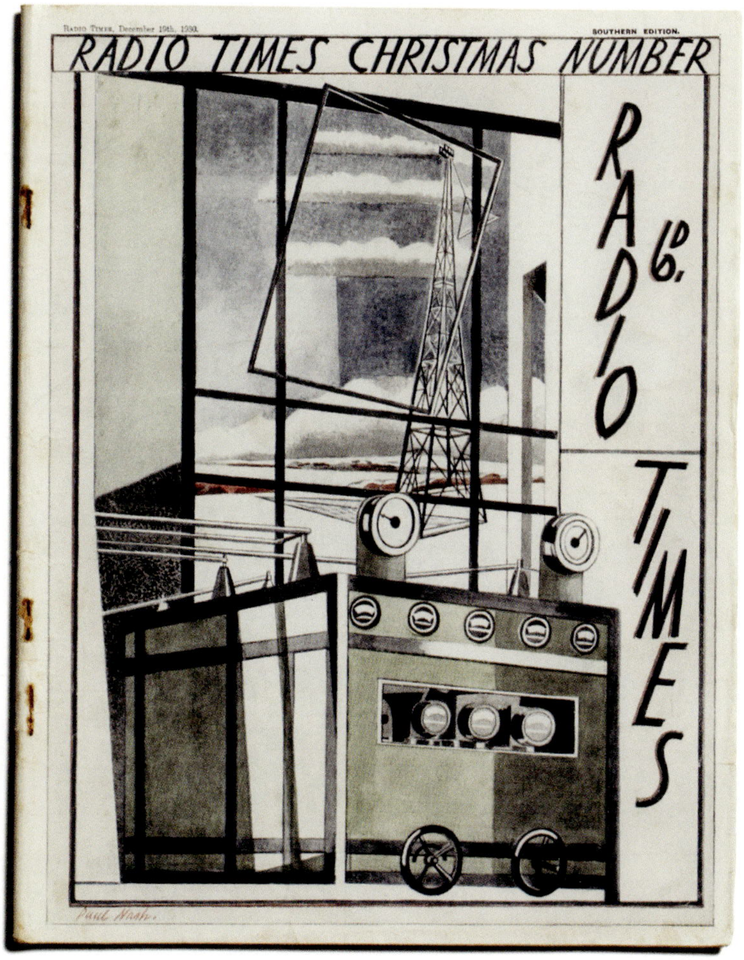

SOUTHERN EDITION.

RADIO TIMES CHRISTMAS NUMBER

RADIO TIMES

6D.

CHRISTMAS DAY

NATIONAL PROGRAMME | DROITWICH 200 kc's 1,500 m. | LONDON 1,149 kc's 261.1 m. | WEST 1,149 kc's 261.1 m. | NORTH 1,149 kc's 261.1 m.

(*Continued from previous page*)

3.5 Interval

3.15 THE HASTINGS MUNICIPAL ORCHESTRA

Conductor, JULIUS HARRISON

HENRY WENDON (tenor)

Relayed from the White Rock Pavilion, Hastings

ORCHESTRA

Here's a health unto His Majesty ... *arr. J. Harrison*
Christmas Overture ... *Coleridge-Taylor*
The Dancing Clock ... *Ewing, arr. Engleman*

HENRY WENDON

The Holy City ... *Stephen Adams*
On Wings of Song ... *Mendelssohn*

ORCHESTRA

Selection, The Gondoliers ... *Sullivan*
Folk Song, Fairy Tale ... *Komzak*
A Children's Overture ... *Quilter*
The Clock is playing ... *Blaauw*
The Toymaker's Dream ... *Golden*

HENRY WENDON

Sally in our Alley ... *Carey*
Come into the Garden, Maud ... *Balfe*

Carols by Audience and Orchestra, led by the Hastings Choral Union

The First Nowell, It came upon the Midnight clear, O come, all ye faithful ... *trad.*

4.45 THE JOHN MacARTHUR QUINTET

Directed by JOHN MacARTHUR

Selection, Harmony Lane ... *arr. Stone*
Waltz, Voices of Spring ... *Johann Strauss, arr. Winter*
A Dream of Christmas ... *Ketèlbey*
You are my lucky star ... *Egan, arr. Zalva*
Haymakers' Dance (Suite, Country Life) ... *King*

(*From Glasgow*)

5.15 THE BBC DANCE ORCHESTRA

Directed by HENRY HALL

6.0 *Time Signal, Greenwich*

Weather Forecast and Sports Bulletin

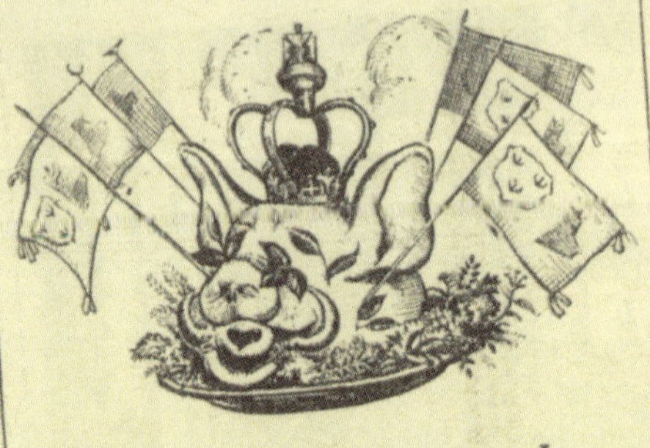

The Boar's Head in hand bear I,
Bedecked with bays and rosemary. . . .

6.10 'UNTO US'

A Pageant of Christmas

Literary Editor ... R. ELLIS ROBERTS
Musical Editor ... WALFORD DAVIES
Conductor ... TREVOR HARVEY

Devised and produced by ROBIN WHITWORTH

Composed from the Holy Bible, and from the works of Arnold, Blake, Chesterton, Gwent, Jonson, de la Mare, Milton, Myers, Shakespeare, Tennyson, and Wesley:

And from the works of Bach, Gibbons, Handel, Warlock, Parry, Sullivan, Vaughan Williams, Haydn, Hely-Hutchinson, and others

The cast:

Laidman Browne, Robert Farquharson, Frith Banbury, Barbara Palmer, Robert Speaight, and Ion Swinley

(*Ion Swinley by permission of Miss Lilian Baylis of the Old Vic, Robert Speaight by permission of Ashley Dukes*)

The BBC Chorus (Section B) with Orchestra and G. Thalben-Ball at the Organ

'Thou hast made us for Thyself, O God, and our hearts are restless until they rest in Thee'

(See the article by R. Ellis Roberts on page 14)

7.10 Interval

7.15 Boar's Head Ceremony

at The Queen's College, Oxford

Relayed from The College Hall

(By permission of the Provost and Fellows)

7.30 A Radio Christmas Party

Comedians—dance music—charades and musical games — Christmas Crackers — all kinds of happy-go-lucky entertainment —tune in at any time between 7.30 and 9.30 and take your chance

9.30 *Time Signal, Greenwich*

NEWS SUMMARY

Weather Forecast, Forecast for Shipping, and News

9.40 Wireless for the Blind

An Appeal on behalf of The British Wireless for the Blind Fund by the Rt. Hon. Viscount SANKEY, G.B.E., D.C.L., LL.D.

Contributions will be gratefully acknowledge[d] and should be addressed to the British 'Wi[re]less for the Blind' Fund, 226, Great Portla[nd] Street, London, W.1.

9.50 THE BBC MIDLAND ORCHESTRA

Leader, ALFRED CAVE

Conducted by LESLIE HEWARD

Overture, Das Christ-Elflein (The Christmas ... *Pfit*
Divertissement ... *K*
Summer Evening ... *Meye*
Torch Dance ... *L*
Ballade (From Olden Times) ...
Suite of Incidental Music to La Pisanella ... *Pi*

11.0-12.0 Ⓓ

Henry Hall's Hour

Ⓓ *Time Signal, Greenwich, at 11.30*

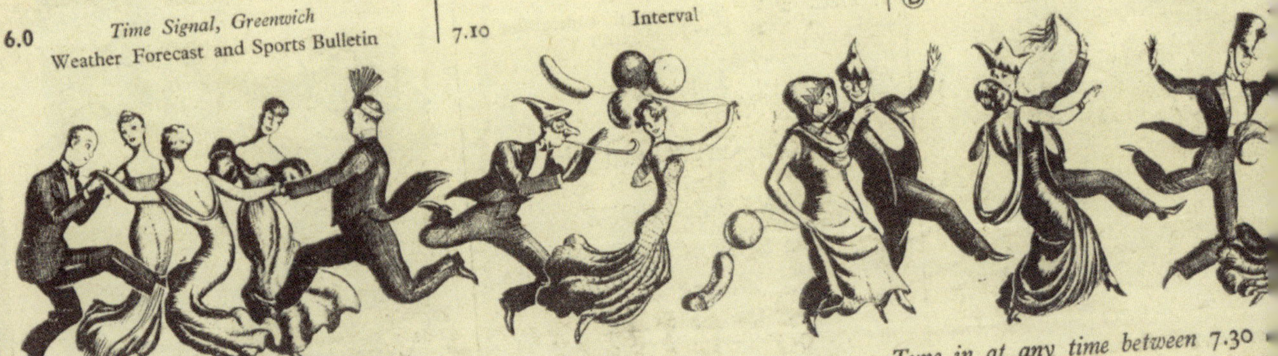

Tune in at any time between 7.30

All kinds of happy-go-lucky entertainment

THE RADIO TIMES

THE JOURNAL OF THE BRITISH BROADCASTING CORPORATION

NATION SHALL SPEAK PEACE UNTO NATION

Radio for the People

1931–1939

The FA Cup Final

Wembley Stadium *(photograph by Aerofilms)*

17 April 1931

It might have come from board games, it might have started with nursery rhymes, but one origin of the phrase "back to square one" is right in front of you. *Radio Times* printed diagrams of football pitches like the one on this cover and commentators used them to describe where the ball was so that listeners could follow the action more easily.

This issue, featuring the FA Cup final at Wembley Stadium between West Bromwich Albion and local rivals Birmingham City, included a bit of a rant against football clubs that were trying to get a ban on coverage of matches on radio: "Must listeners lose their football because the League blames the BBC for reduced gate-money?"

In fact, radio coverage of league football was banned two months later, although Cup finals continued to be broadcast.

1931–1939

The death of George V; the start of regular television broadcasts; and the final summer of peace before the Second World War

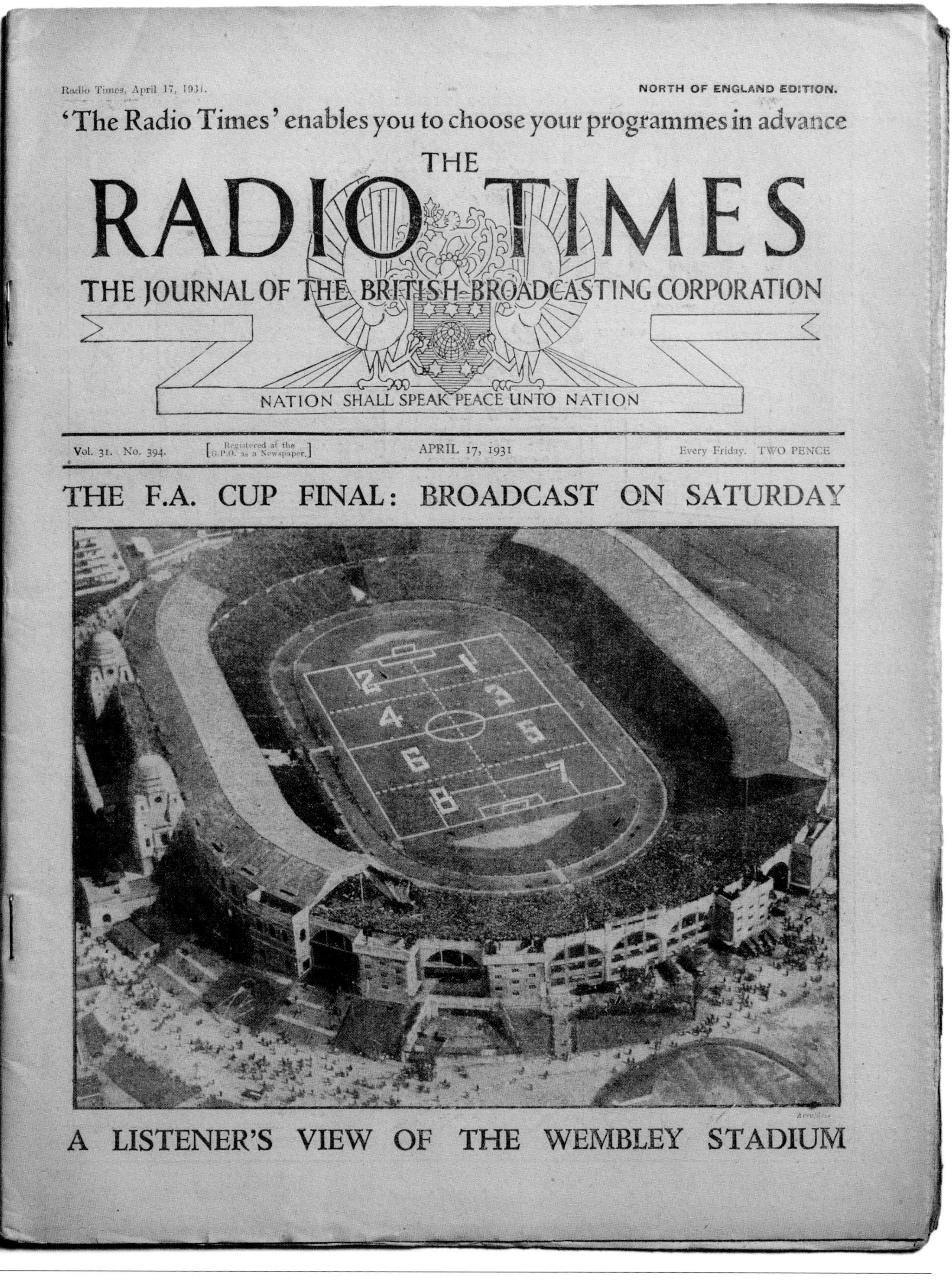

Radio Times, April 17, 1931. NORTH OF ENGLAND EDITION.

'The Radio Times' enables you to choose your programmes in advance

THE RADIO TIMES

THE JOURNAL OF THE BRITISH BROADCASTING CORPORATION

NATION SHALL SPEAK PEACE UNTO NATION

Vol. 31. No. 394. [Registered at the G.P.O. as a Newspaper.] APRIL 17, 1931 Every Friday. TWO PENCE

THE F.A. CUP FINAL: BROADCAST ON SATURDAY

Aerofilms

A LISTENER'S VIEW OF THE WEMBLEY STADIUM

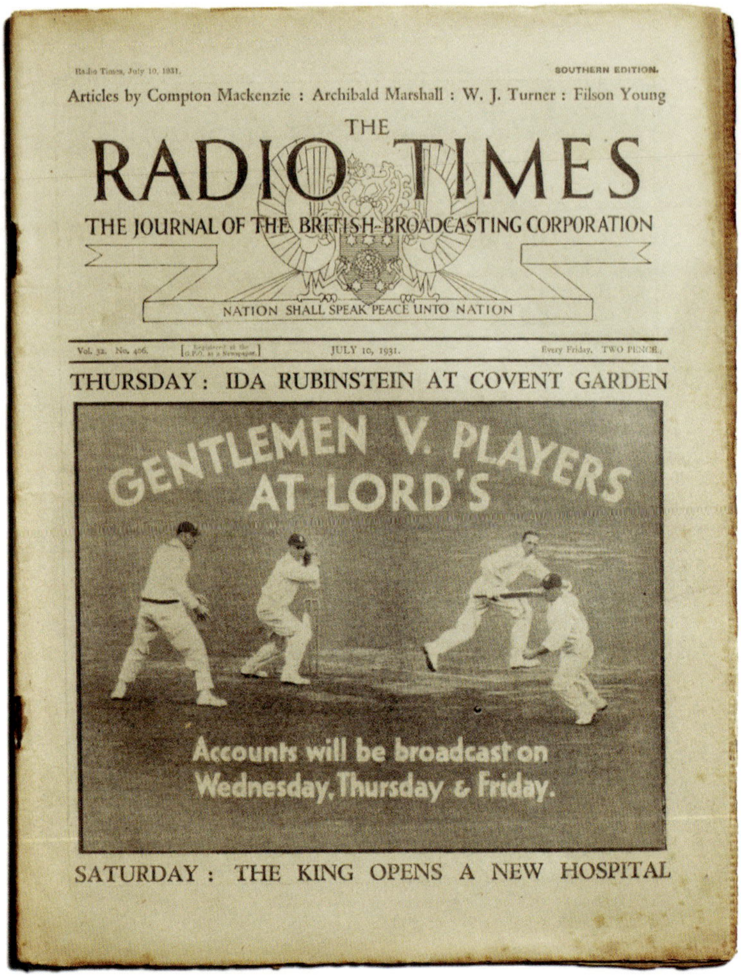

Gentlemen v Players *(left)*

10 July 1931

The 225th Gentlemen v Players fixture at Lord's graced the cover, even though coverage amounted to a short summary at the close of play. Meanwhile, the King George Hospital in Ilford, Essex, was opened by the man himself, with the broadcast of that event confined to just ten minutes.

The Schneider Trophy *(below left)*

4 September 1931

Coverage of the Schneider Trophy, an international race for seaplanes, was billed as the "year's most exciting broadcast". *Radio Times* helpfully published a map of the course off the north coast of the Isle of Wight and a scoring sheet to help engage listeners. It was won by the Supermarine S.6B flown by Flt Lt John Boothman. As France and Italy had both pulled out, he had to race against the two other British pilots in his team. The Supermarine S.6B was to become the basis for the iconic Supermarine Spitfire.

Strauss at the Queen's Hall *(below right)*

Paul Robeson *(photograph by Shaw Wildman)*

16 October 1931

His wasn't the first black face to appear on the cover of *Radio Times* – a documentary on the "Dark Continent" of Africa aired the year before – but actor Paul Robeson was the first black man to have the cover devoted to him, marking a performance of *God's Trombones*.

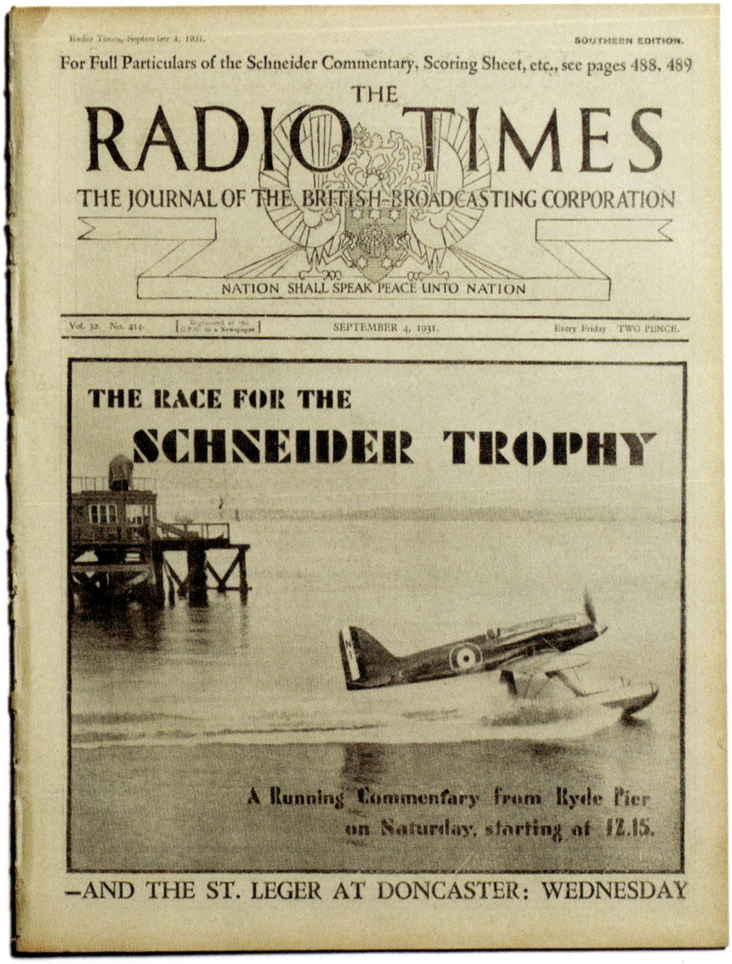

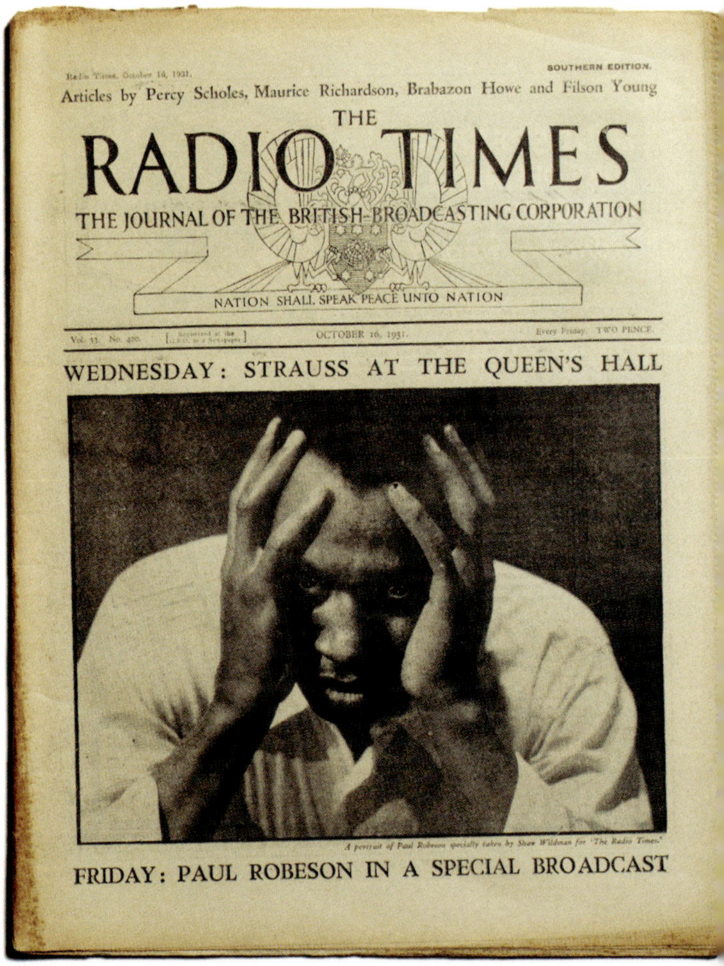

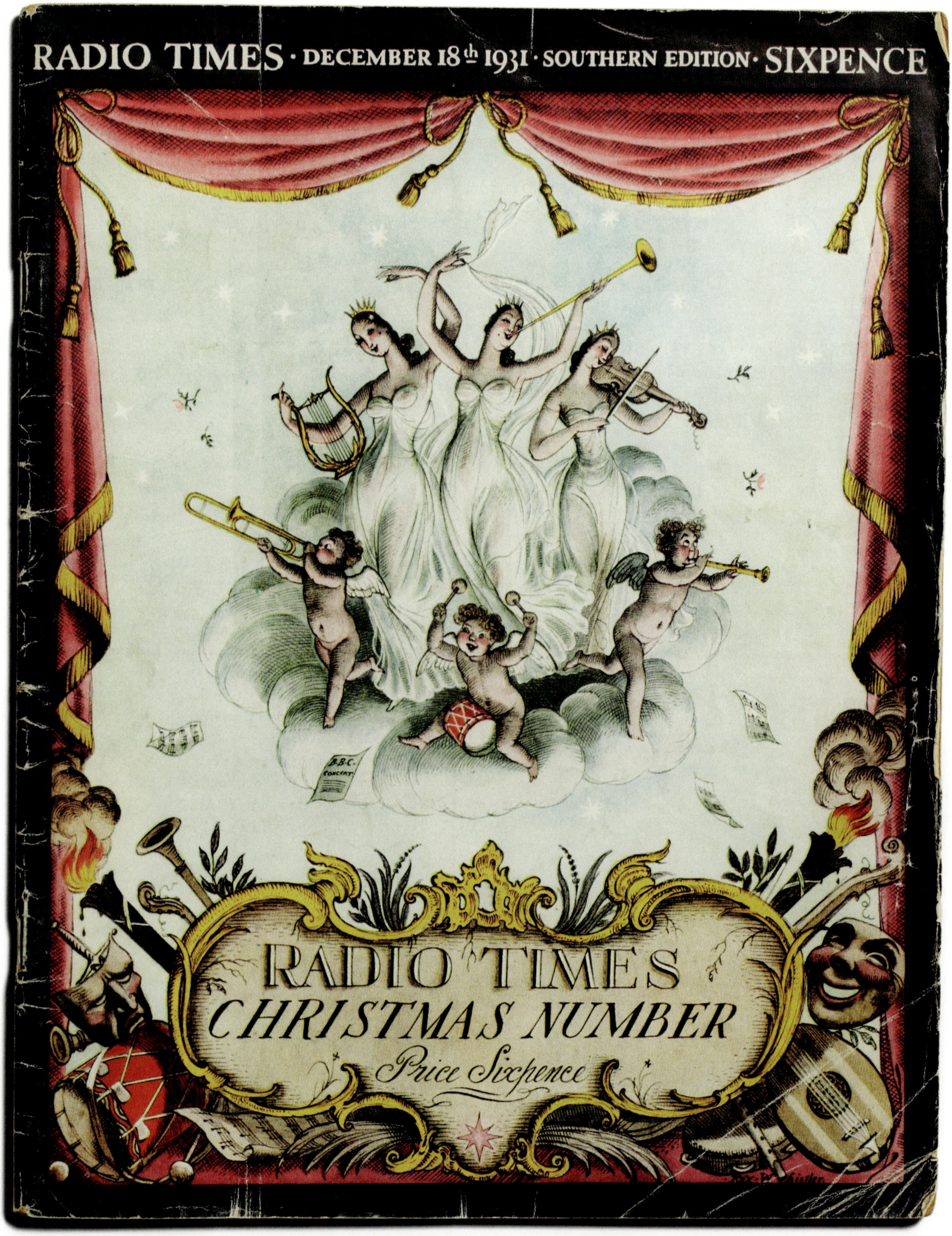

Christmas 1931 **Illustration by Rex Whistler** *18 December 1931*

Rex Whistler had studied art in London and Rome before he became famous for his murals, portraits and book illustrations. His best-known work is perhaps the mural at the Tate Gallery's refreshment room that he painted four years before he produced this cover. He was killed in action in Normandy in 1944.

White as snow *(right)*

Broadcasting House *(photograph by Aerofilms)*

18 September 1931

Broadcasting House was often described as a ship from the way its narrow entrance resembled a prow. Yet seen from above the building looks more like an island of white amid a startlingly filthy London.

Summer number *(middle right)*

Illustration by Eric Fraser

29 July 1932

Eric Fraser produced many colour covers for *Radio Times*. "To be given the opportunity of joining the band of capable illustrators in such a well-known publication was a great compliment," he said in 1981. But there was a caveat: "Every commission from *Radio Times* was an emergency."

Christmas 1932 *(far right)*

Illustration by Edward Ardizzone

23 December 1932

This series of sketches bounded by tinsel is typical of Ardizzone: "I think it really came from doodling," he said in a *Radio Times* interview shortly before his death in 1979. He also illustrated books such as Clive King's *Stig of the Dump* and was a war artist from 1940 to 1945.

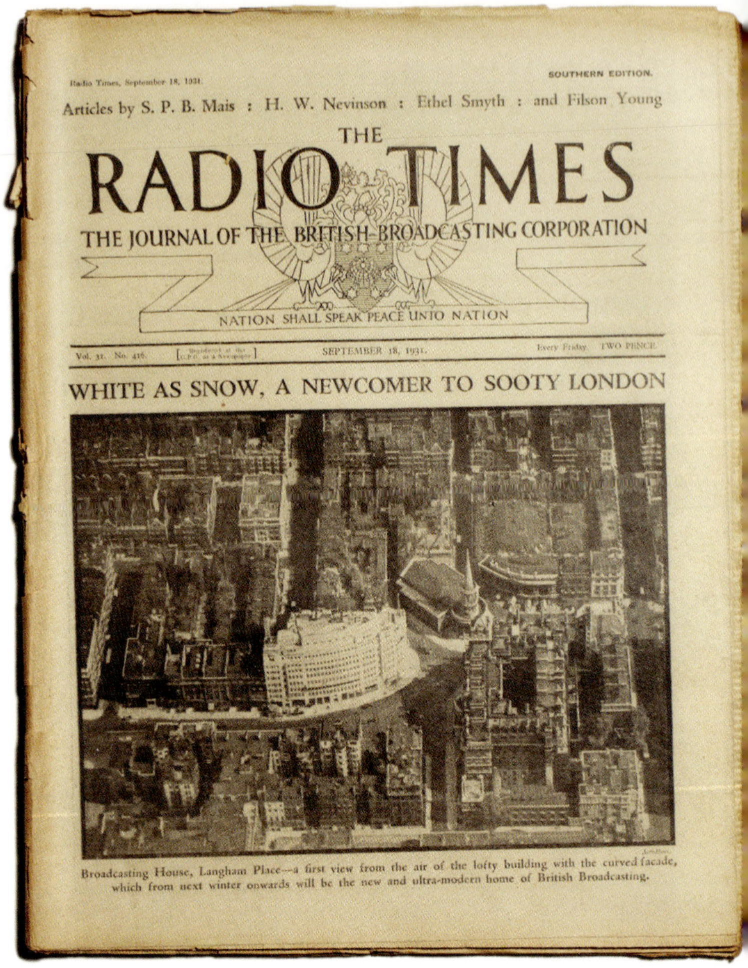

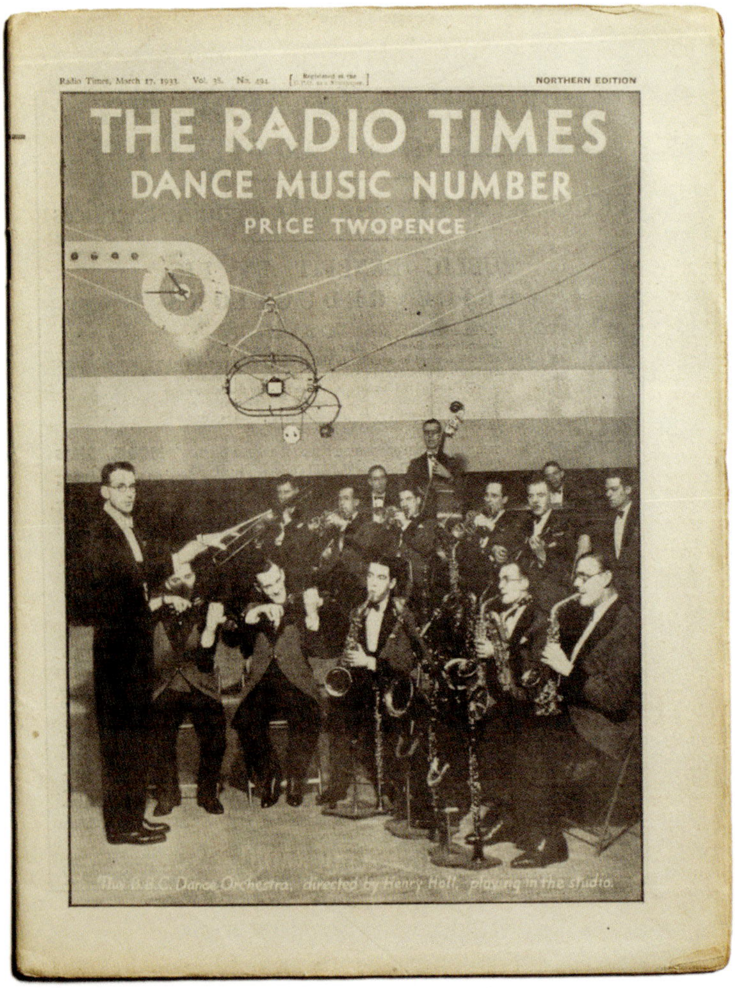

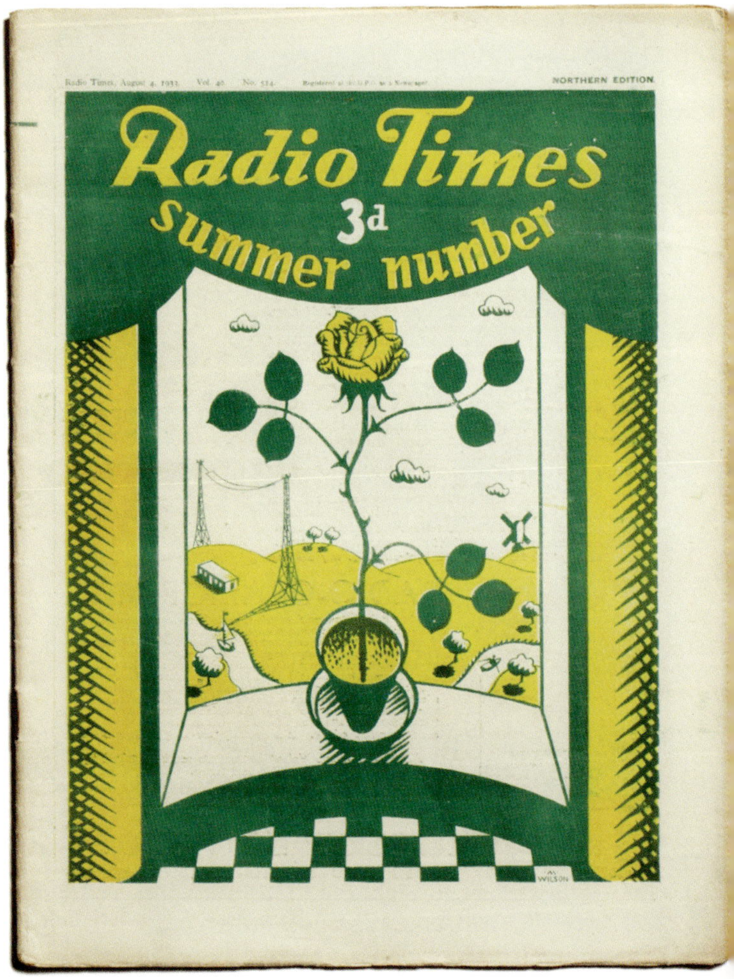

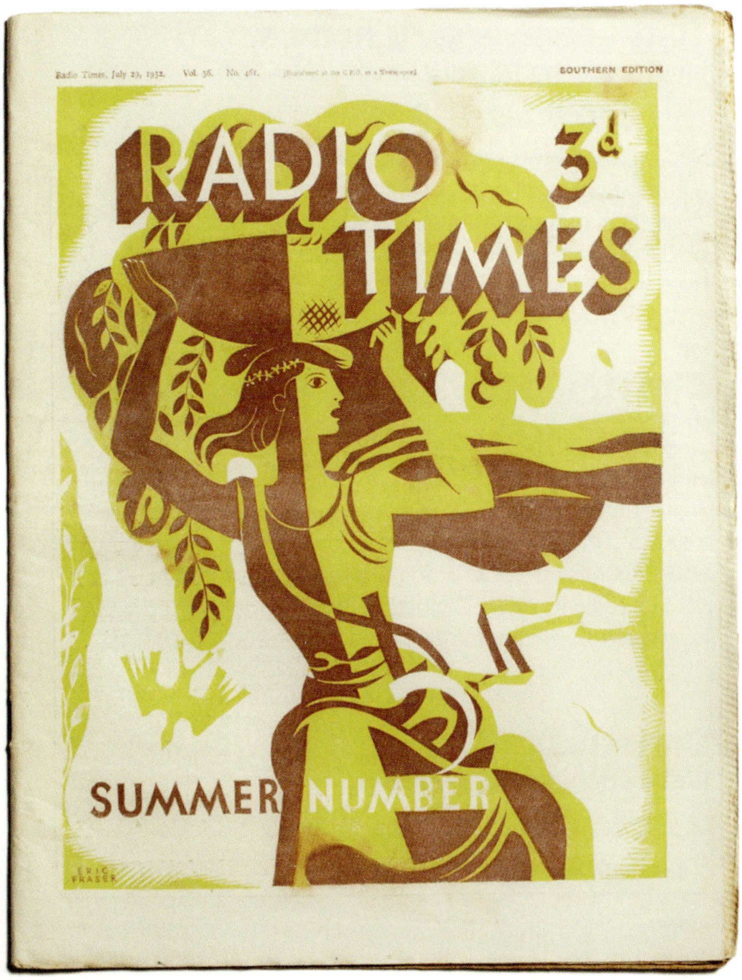

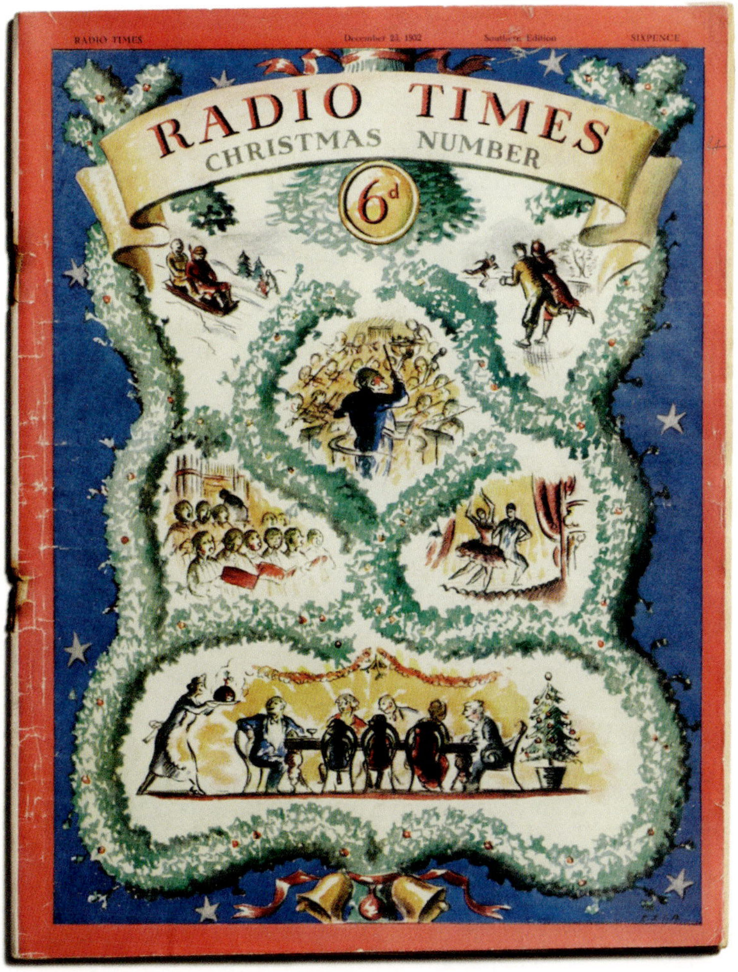

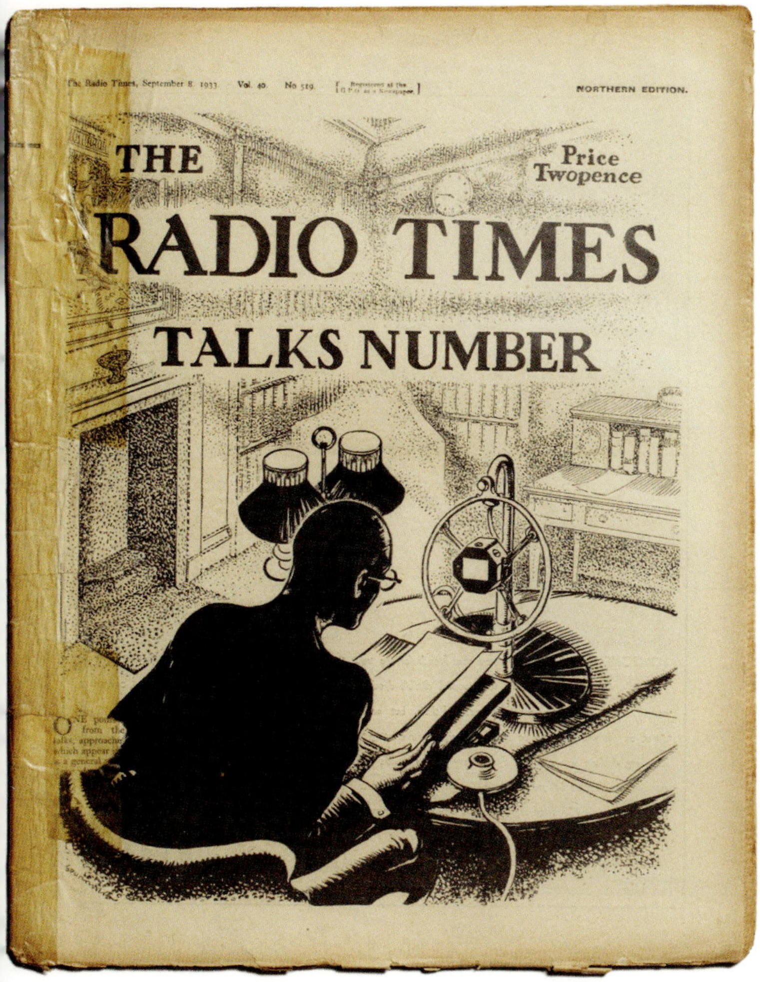

Dance music number *(far left)*

17 March 1933

"Conservative listeners may deplore such an innovation as this issue," said *Radio Times* for its first Dance Music number, which featured the BBC Dance Orchestra with its director Henry Hall on the cover. But there was no turning back: "Whatever may be our personal opinion of jazz, it is, incontrovertibly, the most popular music of the day."

Summer number *(middle left)*

Illustration by Mervyn Wilson

4 August 1933

In 1929, Mervyn Wilson was a serious artist who happened to show *Radio Times* staff a jokey drawing and became known for specialising in humorous illustrations. By his standards, then, this cover was comparatively serious.

Talks number *(left)*

Illustration by Steven Spurrier

8 September 1933

This evocative illustration was used to launch a season of programmes where speech, rather than music, would be to the fore, drawing listeners into unfamiliar subjects at home and abroad.

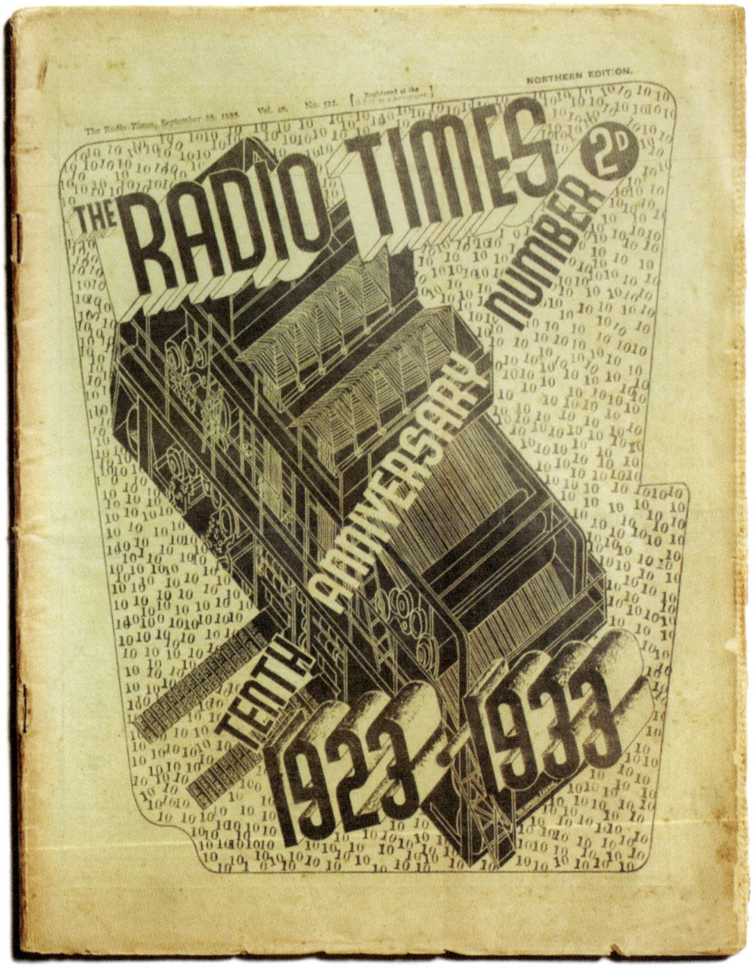

Tenth anniversary number *(left)*

Illustration by Richard Levin

29 September 1933

Radio Times celebrated its first decade by sharing a number of startling facts, including this one: "The total number of copies sold in ten years is over 600,000,000. If they were piled upon each other, they would form a skyscraper 62 miles high."

Christmas 1933 *(below left)*

Illustration by SC Johnson

22 December 1933

A startlingly colourful cover, and literary fireworks inside: a short story by Aldous Huxley, a poem by Walter de la Mare and GK Chesterton writing on the subject of laughter. And JB Morton, the *Daily Express's* Beachcomber, filled a page with odd but very straight-faced facts about Christmas.

Christmas 1934 *(below right)*

Illustration by Frank Brangwyn

23 December 1934

Radio Times was so pleased to get Frank Brangwyn, "one of the world's most famous artists", to create this cover that it devoted a feature to the man and his "two faithful friends": his dog Roger and Mrs Peacock, his housekeeper.

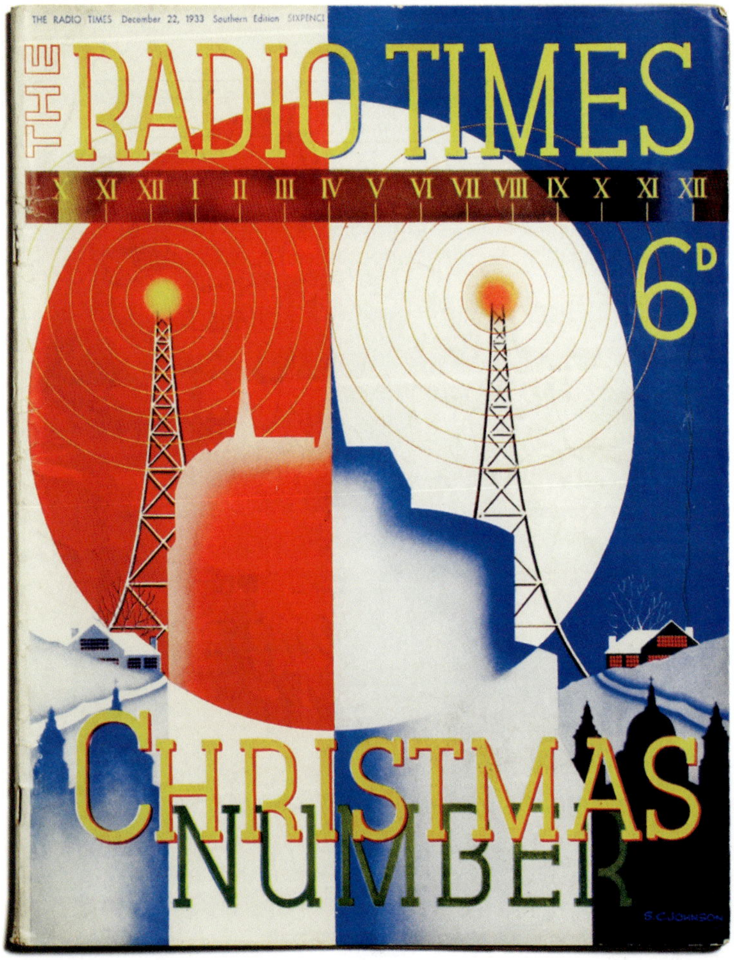

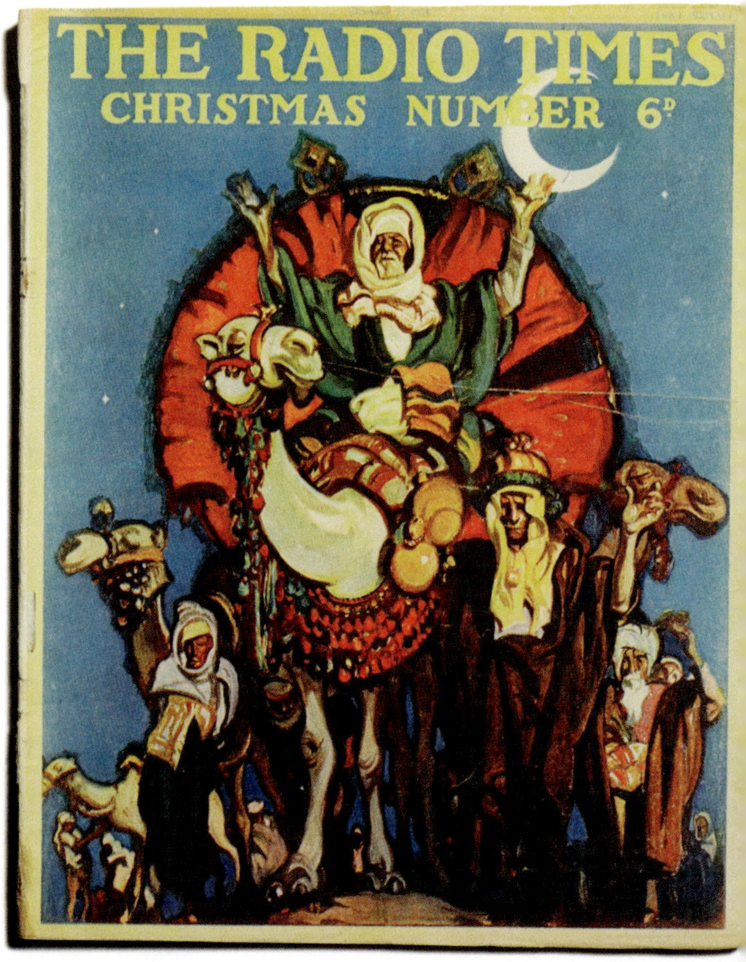

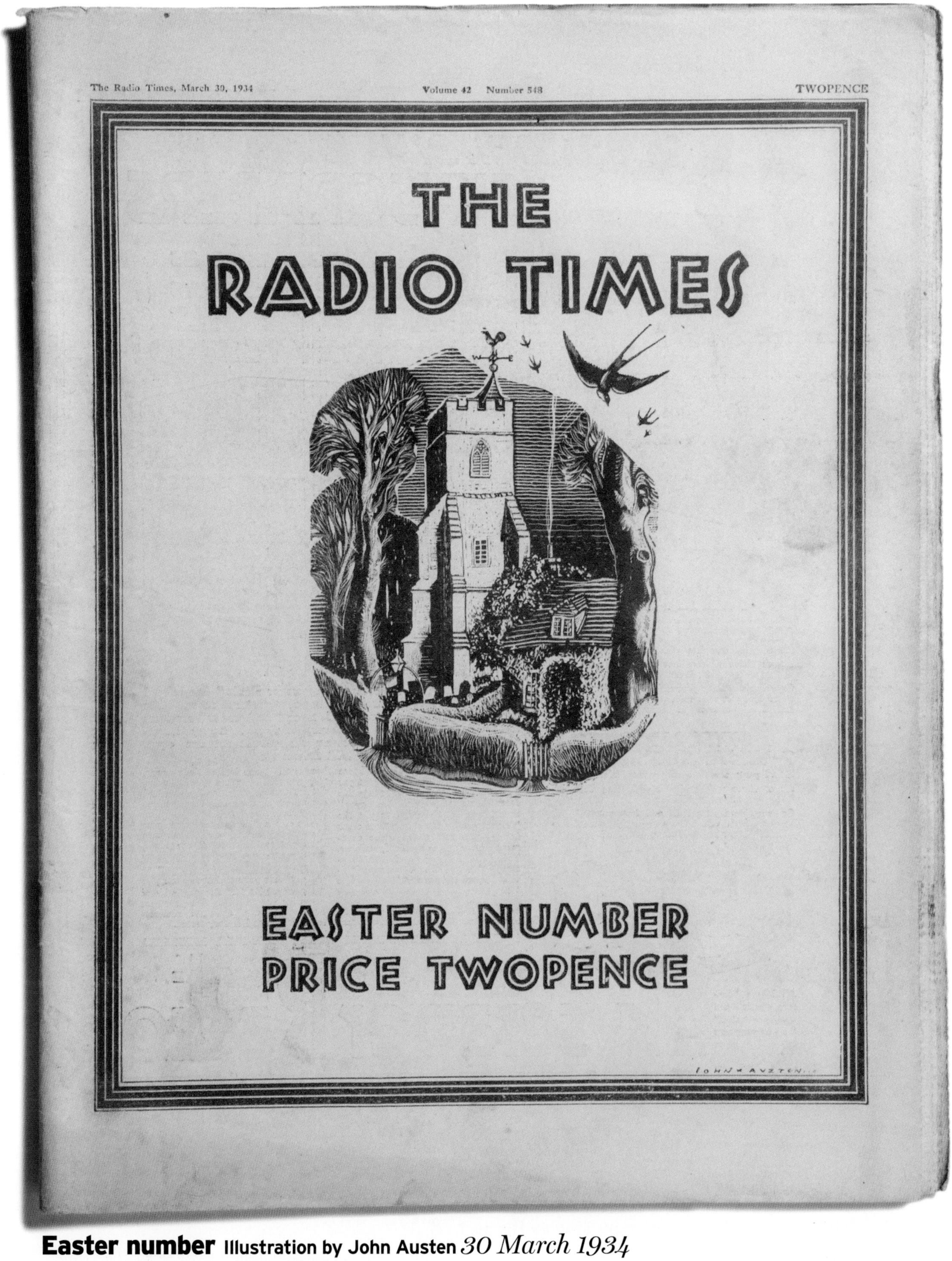

Easter number **Illustration by John Austen** *30 March 1934*

This beautifully simple cover was by a *Radio Times* favourite. John Austen "lives in an oast house in the wilds of Kent and comes up to London as seldom as he can". Inside, readers were treated to a guide to 50 regular outside broadcast venues, from the Beaufort Cinema in Washboard Heath near Birmingham to York Minster.

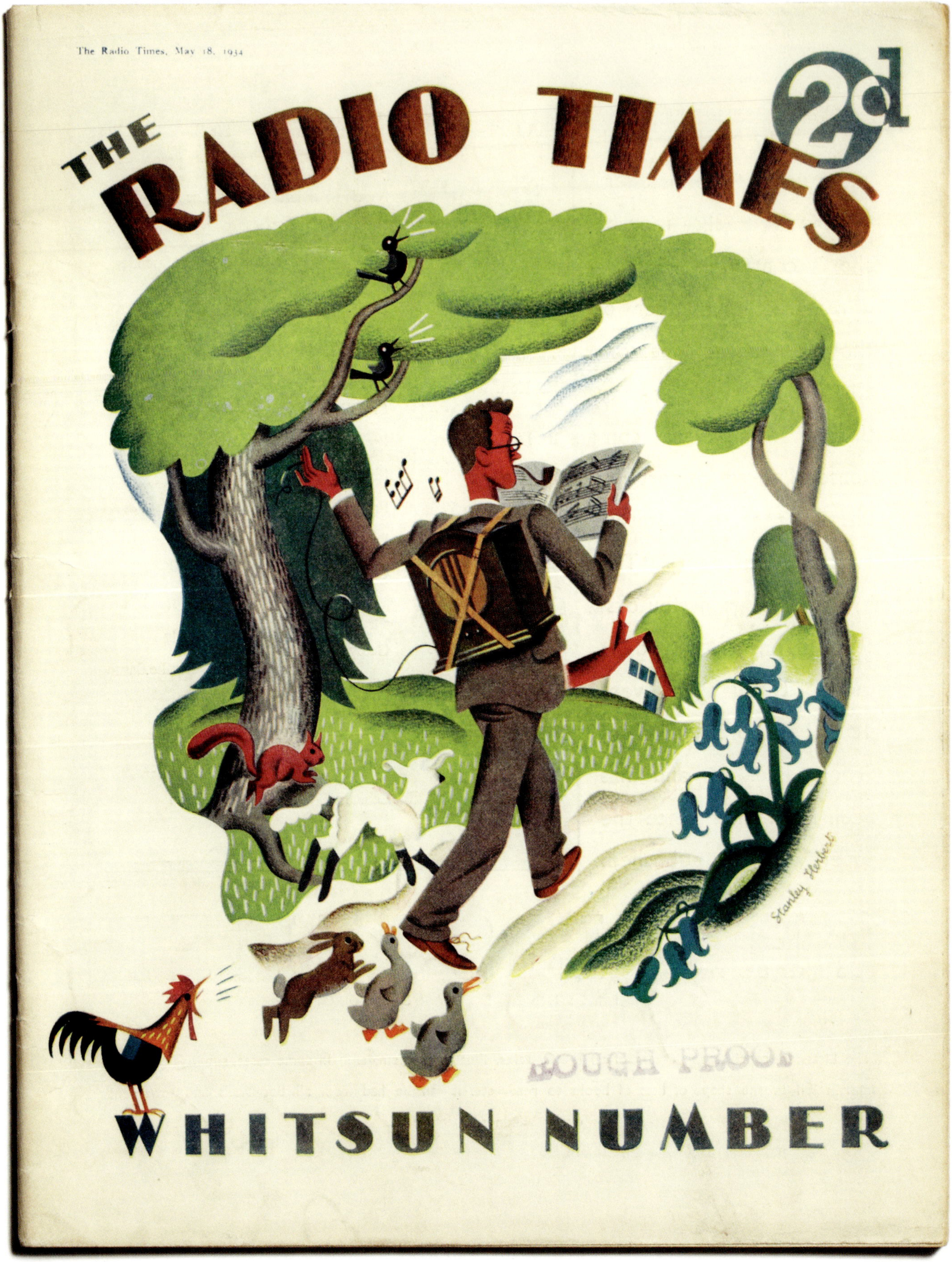

Whitsun number **Illustration by Stanley Herbert** *18 May 1934*

Stanley Herbert's jaunty cover shows a man enjoying a country ramble with a contemporaneous version of an iPod strapped to his back. Herbert famously produced posters for London Transport, but he also drew for comics including *Girl* and *Eagle*. Inside the issue, there was a fiery debate on the Americanisation of the English language and whether it was a good thing or something to be resisted.

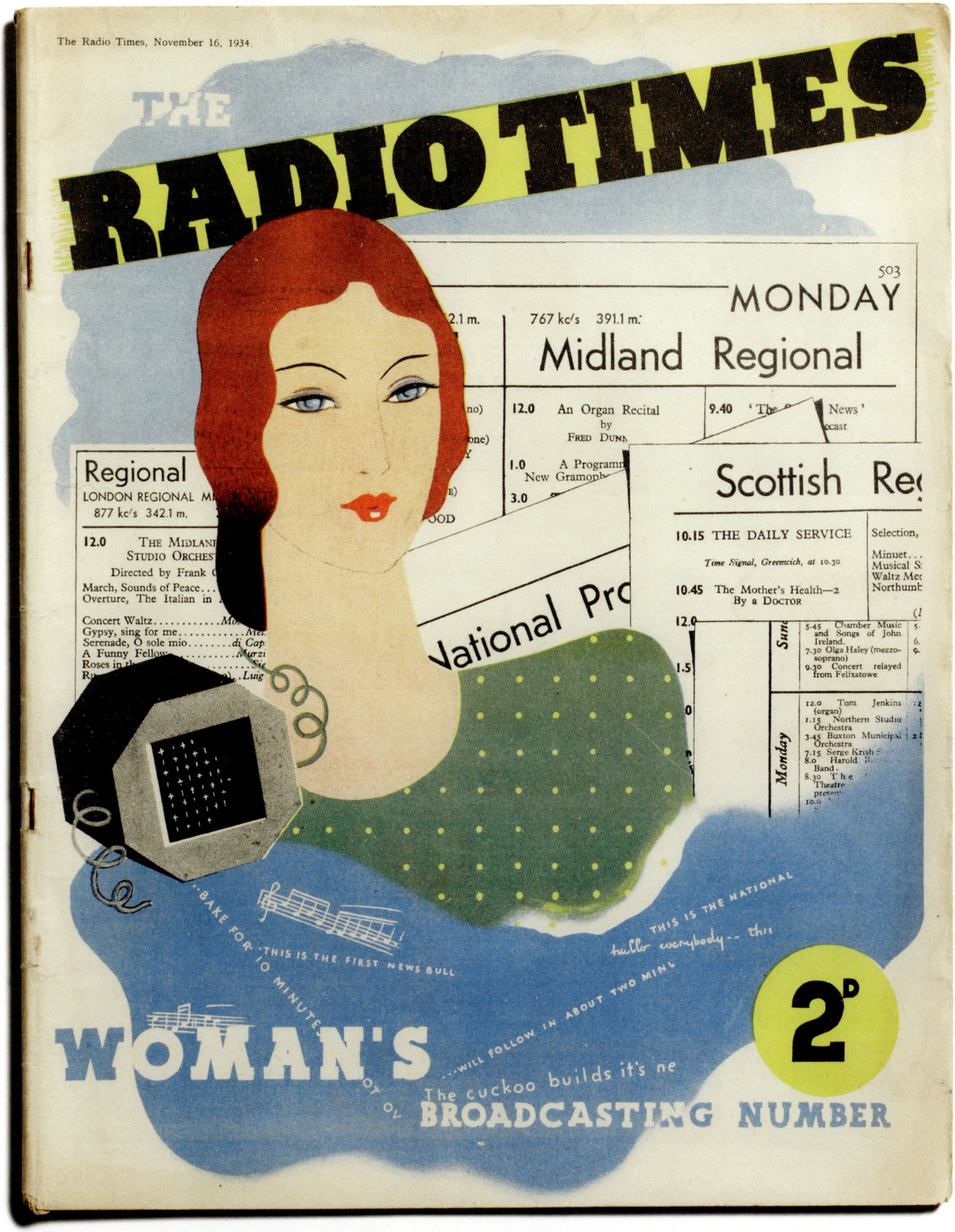

Woman's broadcasting number **Illustration by Ralph & Mott** *16 November 1934*

BBC governor Mary Agnes Hamilton declared, "In broadcasting, men and women work on a basis of equal and common concern – and equal pay!" Eighty years later, equal pay hasn't spread much further, but one thing has changed: "There are persons who do not like women's voices, either in the House of Commons or at the microphone, but they are getting over that." Ralph & Mott was an artists' agency that represented many different illustrators.

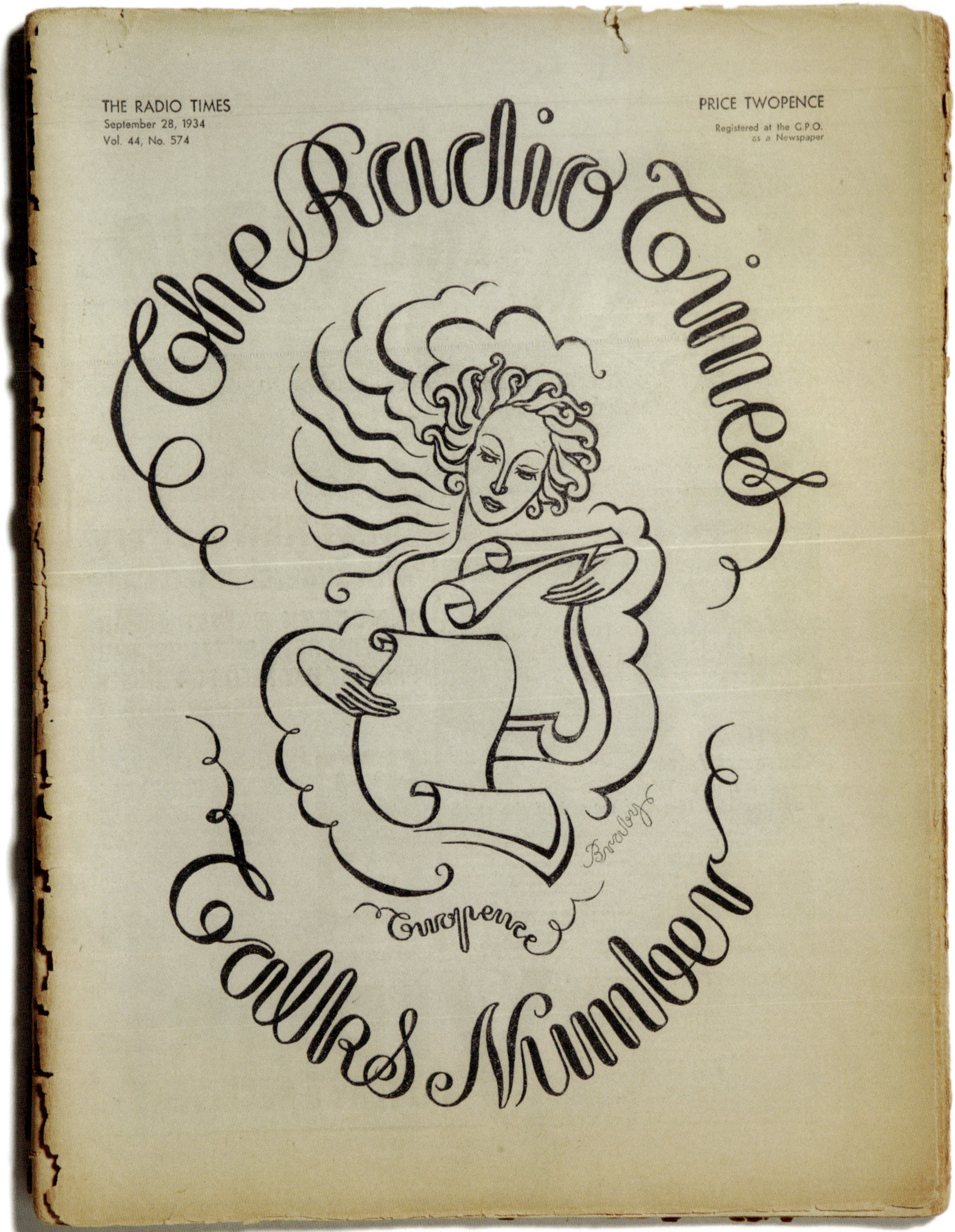

Talks number **Illustration by Dorothea Braby** *28 September 1934*

Cover illustrations by women were rare in this period, but painter and woodcut artist Dorothea Braby made this ethereal image for an issue describing changes in speech-based programmes that are still going strong today. From now on, said the BBC Director of Talks, programmes would include interviews and guest experts.

Jubilee number *(right)*
Illustration by Ralph Mott

3 May 1935

An unknown artist from the Ralph & Mott agency (sometimes, as here, just called Ralph Mott) showed the world in a 1930s microphone. *Radio Times* detailed the "modern miracle" of broadcasting that had so far allowed King George V to speak to his people 17 times.

Whitsun holiday number *(below left)*
Illustration by Robert Stewart Sherriffs

7 June 1935

While the cover partly extolled and partly mocked the British rush to travel on bank holidays, writer Filson Young decided to stay where he was and buy a better radio that could "pick up the programmes from every British station and at least 12 Continental stations".

Christmas 1935 *(below right)*
Illustration by Austin Cooper

20 December 1935

This fantastically original take on the subject of Christmas was by Austin Cooper, a Canadian commercial artist who moved to London after the First World War. By the mid-1930s he was a leading poster artist, best known for his work for the London Underground.

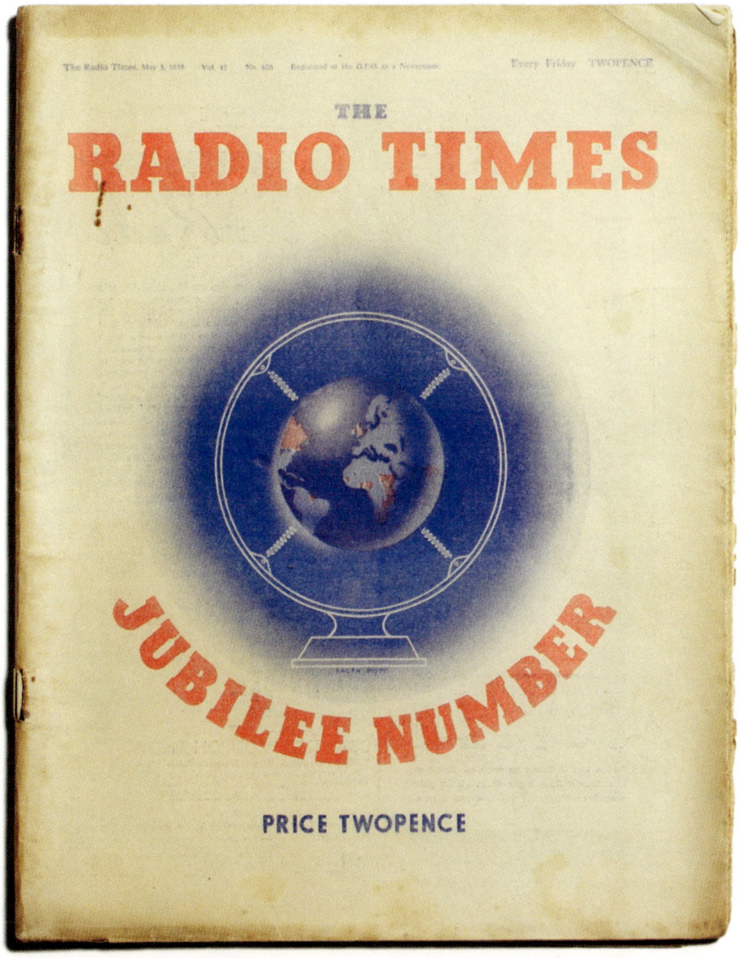

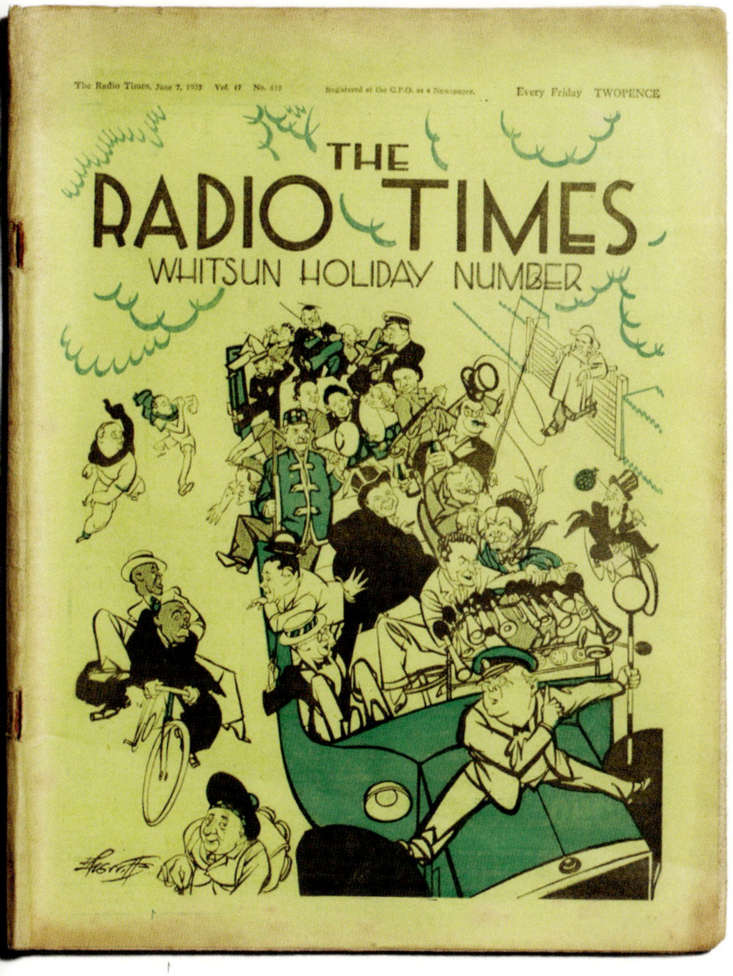

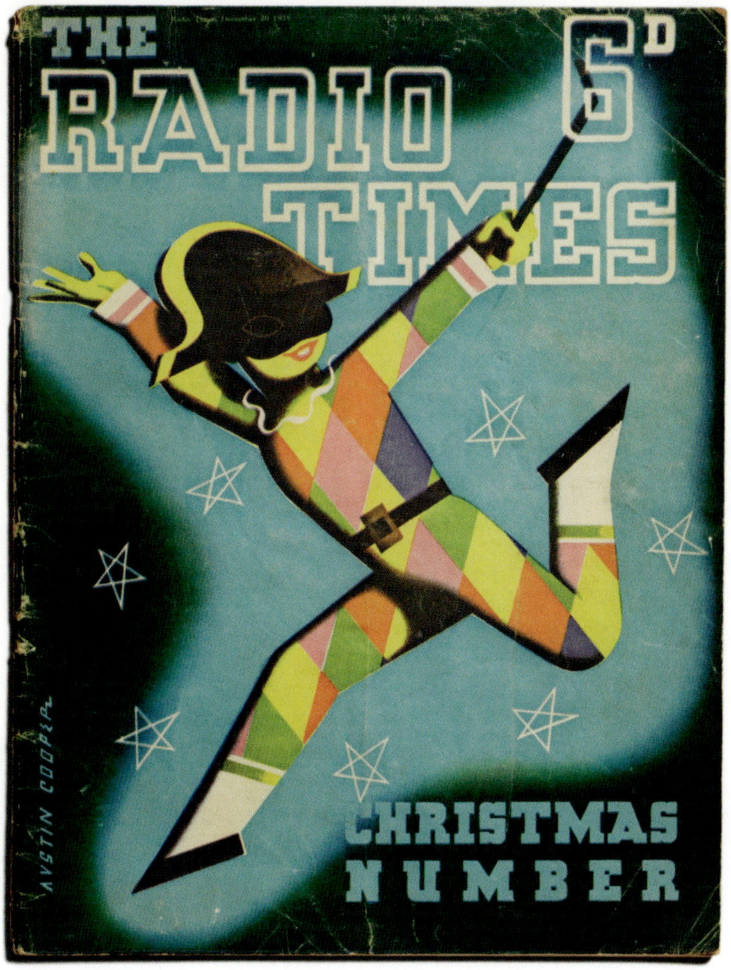

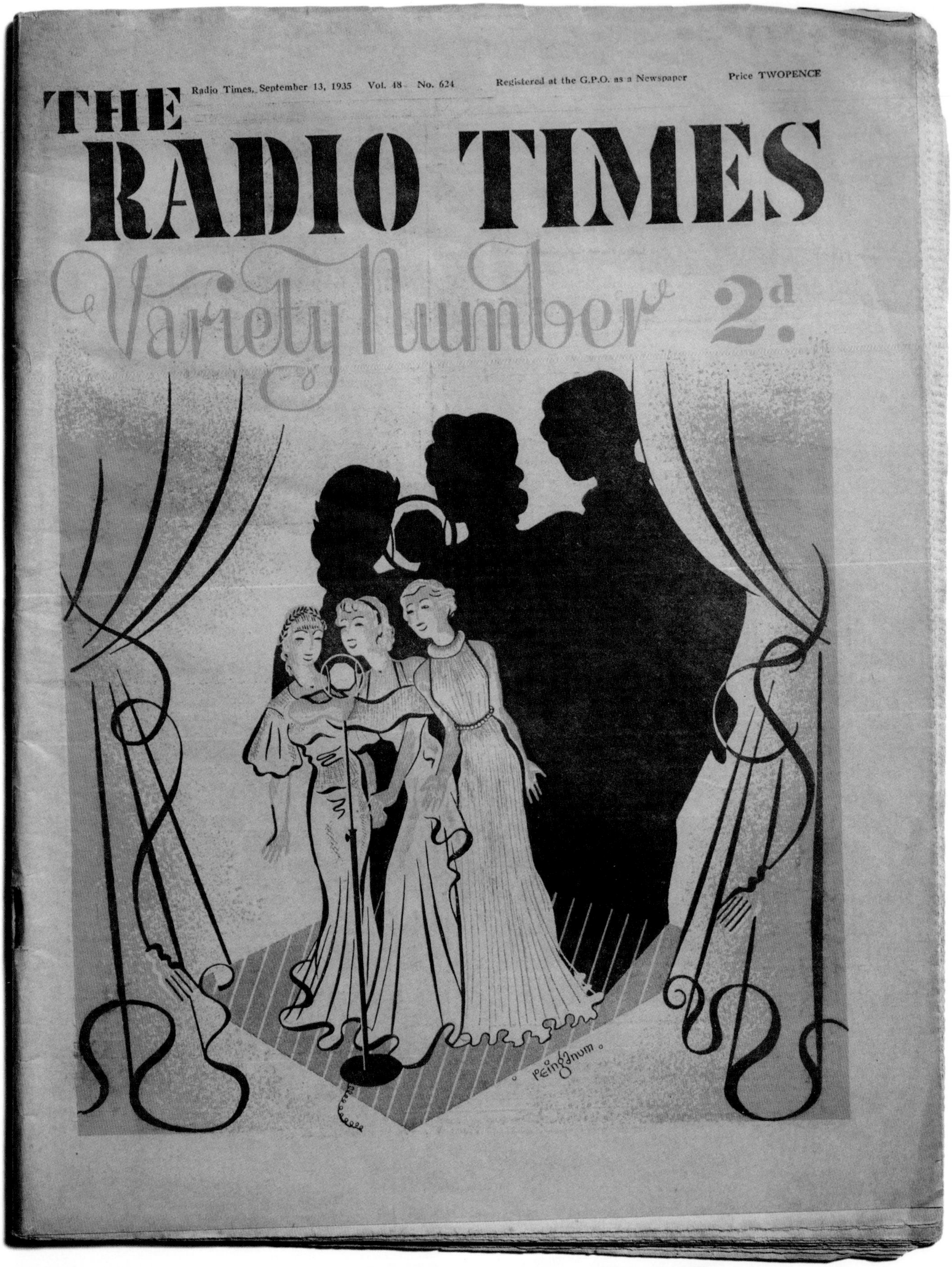

Variety number **Illustration by Victor Reinganum** *13 September 1935*

Victor Reinganum said that in 1926 he'd "tramped around London with a folio of rather poor drawings" and that, much to his surprise, *Radio Times* bought one. "It was a drawing in airbrush of a rather dashing dancing girl, slightly sexy" and it was used to illustrate a cabaret show. As well as his extensive range of work on *Radio Times*, he illustrated covers for many books, including Muriel Spark's *The Prime of Miss Jean Brodie*.

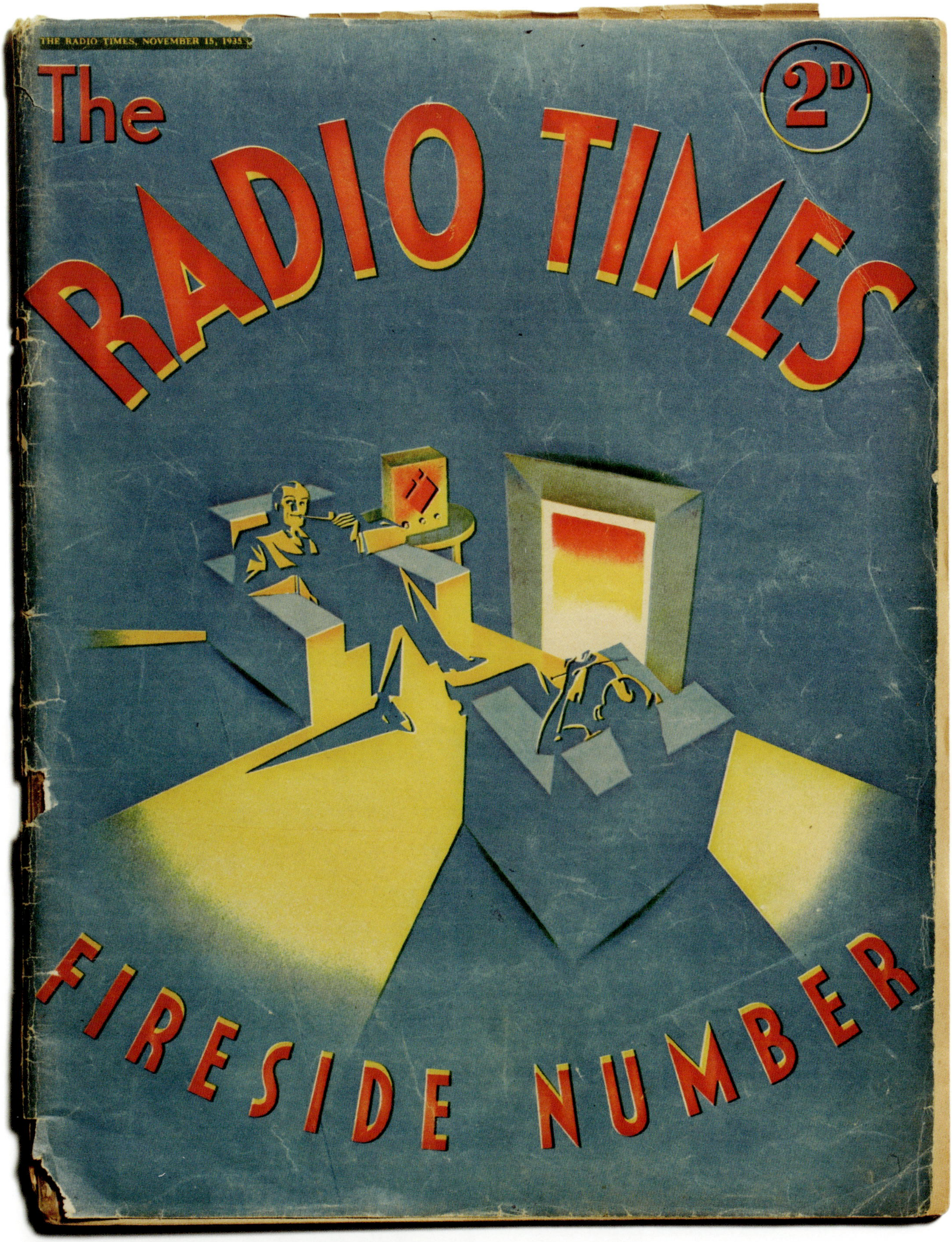

Fireside number **Illustration by Philip Zec** *15 November 1935*

Philip Zec's illustration provided a suitably warm, glowing feel for an issue extolling the many delights of spending long winter nights by a cosy fire listening to the wireless. Inside, the "Strolling Commentator" visited radio stars like Will Hay and Tommy Handley, who all lived in one fictitious town called Superhet Suburb – named after superhetrodyne receivers, which you'd know all about if this were still 1935.

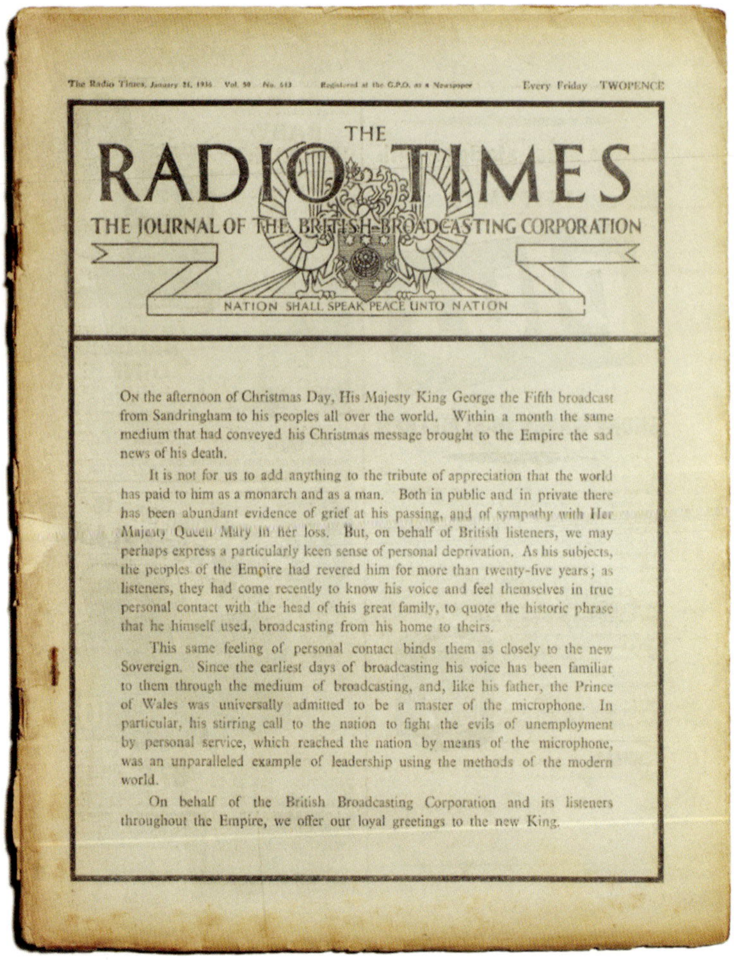

Every Friday TWOPENCE

THE
RADIO TIMES
THE JOURNAL OF THE BRITISH BROADCASTING CORPORATION
NATION SHALL SPEAK PEACE UNTO NATION

On the afternoon of Christmas Day, His Majesty King George the Fifth broadcast from Sandringham to his peoples all over the world. Within a month the same medium that had conveyed his Christmas message brought to the Empire the sad news of his death.

It is not for us to add anything to the tribute of appreciation that the world has paid to him as a monarch and as a man. Both in public and in private there has been abundant evidence of grief at his passing, and of sympathy with Her Majesty Queen Mary in her loss. But, on behalf of British listeners, we may perhaps express a particularly keen sense of personal deprivation. As his subjects, the peoples of the Empire had revered him for more than twenty-five years; as listeners, they had come recently to know his voice and feel themselves in true personal contact with the head of this great family, to quote the historic phrase that he himself used, broadcasting from his home to theirs.

This same feeling of personal contact binds them as closely to the new Sovereign. Since the earliest days of broadcasting his voice has been familiar to them through the medium of broadcasting, and, like his father, the Prince of Wales was universally admitted to be a master of the microphone. In particular, his stirring call to the nation to fight the evils of unemployment by personal service, which reached the nation by means of the microphone, was an unparalleled example of leadership using the methods of the modern world.

On behalf of the British Broadcasting Corporation and its listeners throughout the Empire, we offer our loyal greetings to the new King.

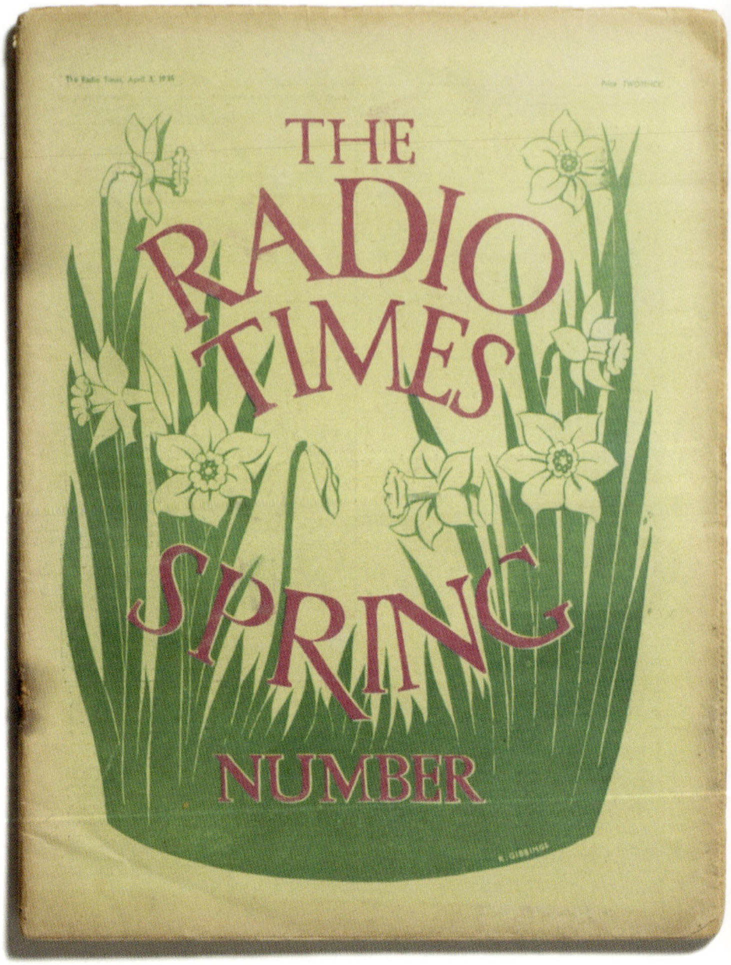

Autumn number *(right)*
Illustration by Rojan
11 September 1936

Artist Feodor Rojankovsky had a diverse career that ranged from children's books to erotic art. This issue focused on "big changes in programmes" such as "more news... brighter Sundays and so on".

Fireside number *(middle right)*
Illustration by Victor Reinganum
13 November 1936

An editorial spoke of mid-November with "the summer birds long fled... black leafless branches against a leaden sky" and "at home the firelight is glowing on the walls". Victor Reinganum produced a cover where the autumnal glow was very much on the outside – and perhaps slightly ominous.

Christmas 1936 *(far right)*
Illustration by Althea Willoughby
18 December 1936

Althea Willoughby's cover is like a catalogue of children's Christmas presents that no 21st-century child would ask for, or that no adult would give – such as the golliwog.

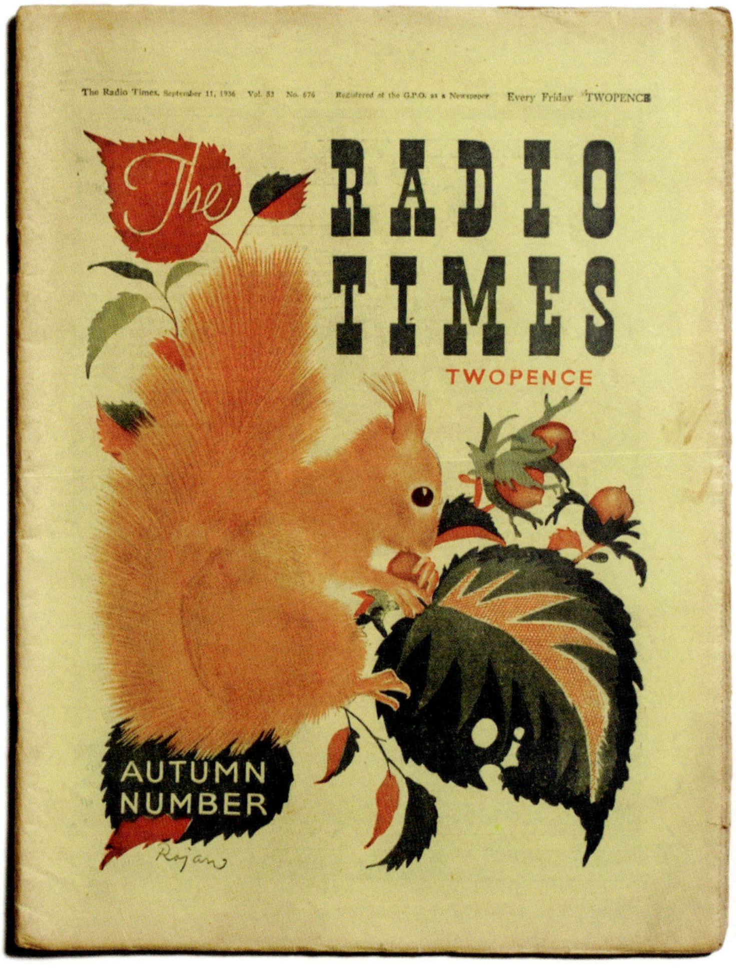

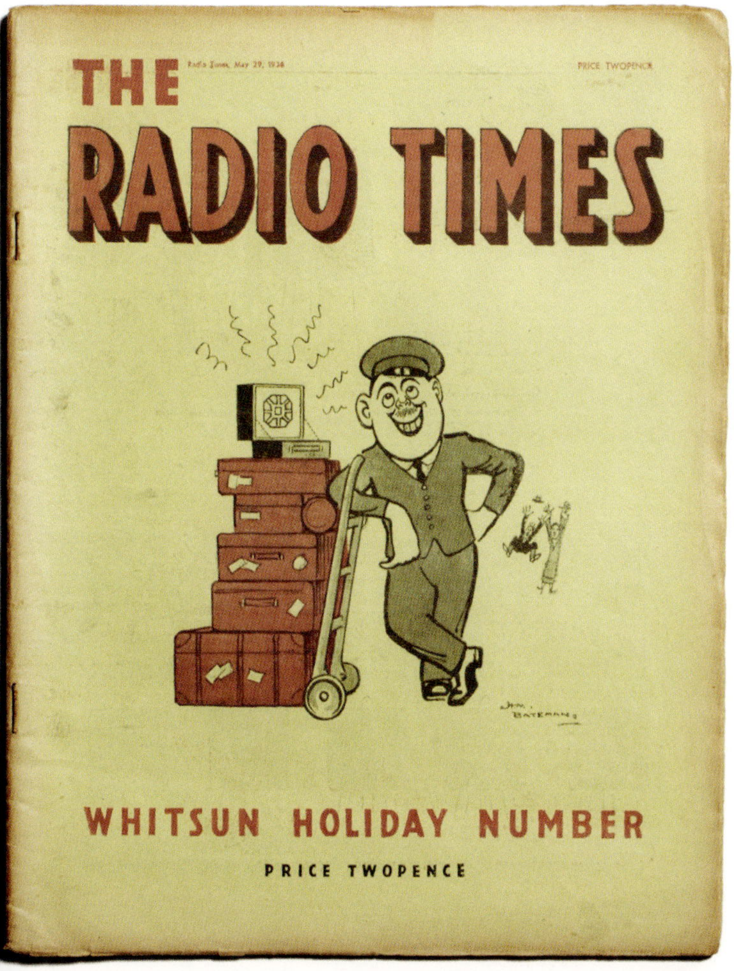

The death of King George V *(far left)*

24 January 1936

George V had given his Christmas message on radio a few weeks before and now *Radio Times* noted that "the same medium... brought to the Empire the sad news of his death". He was the first monarch whose subjects "had come recently to know his voice".

Spring number *(middle left)*

Illustration by R Gibbings

3 April 1936

Over the page from this cover by woodcut artist R Gibbings, poet Humbert Wolfe wrote a prose and verse sketch about a City financier who "looks importantly about him/while all the Spring goes on without him".

Whitsun holiday number *(left)*

Illustration by Henry Mayo Bateman

29 May 1936

Like many *Radio Times* artists, Bateman had a background in humour and cartoons. Unlike all the others, though, he later proposed a National Gallery of Humorous Art, which reportedly failed solely because no premises could be found.

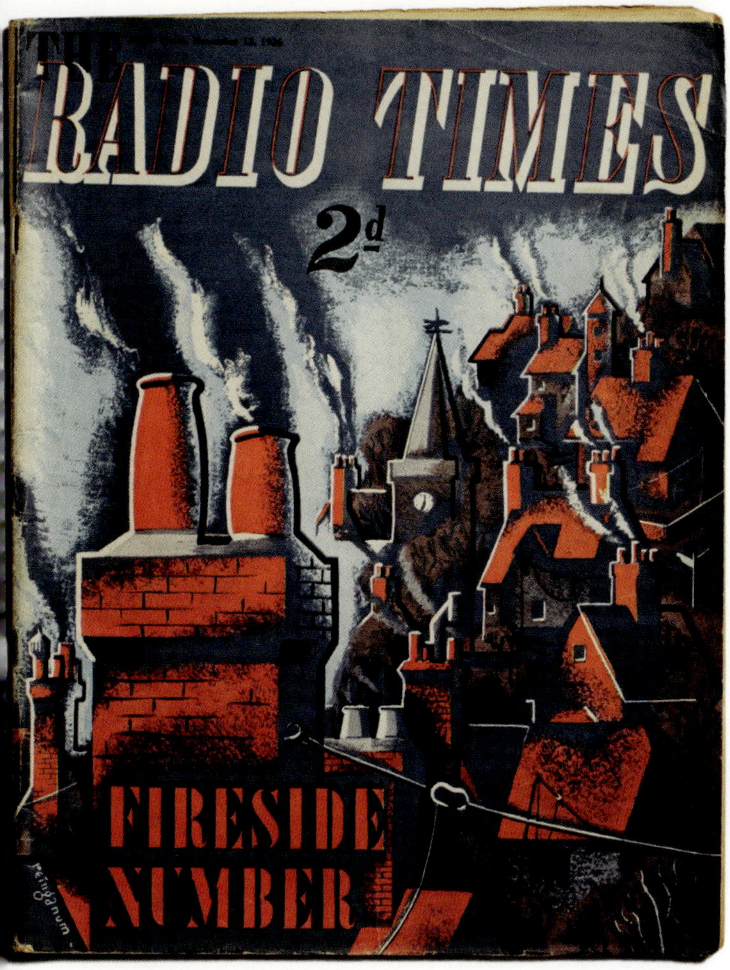

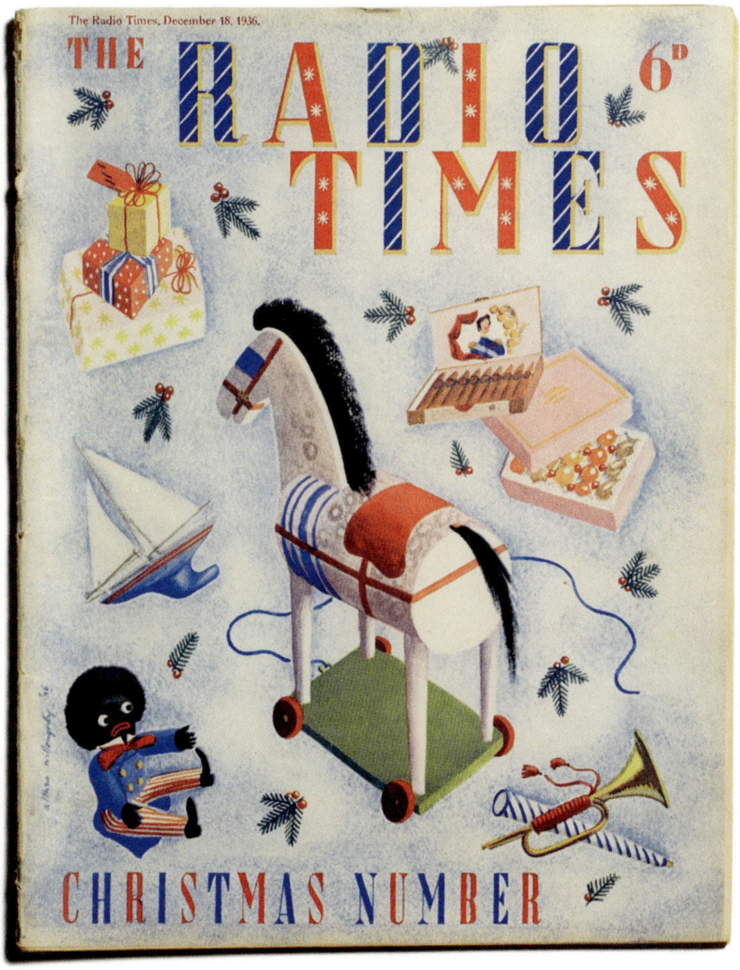

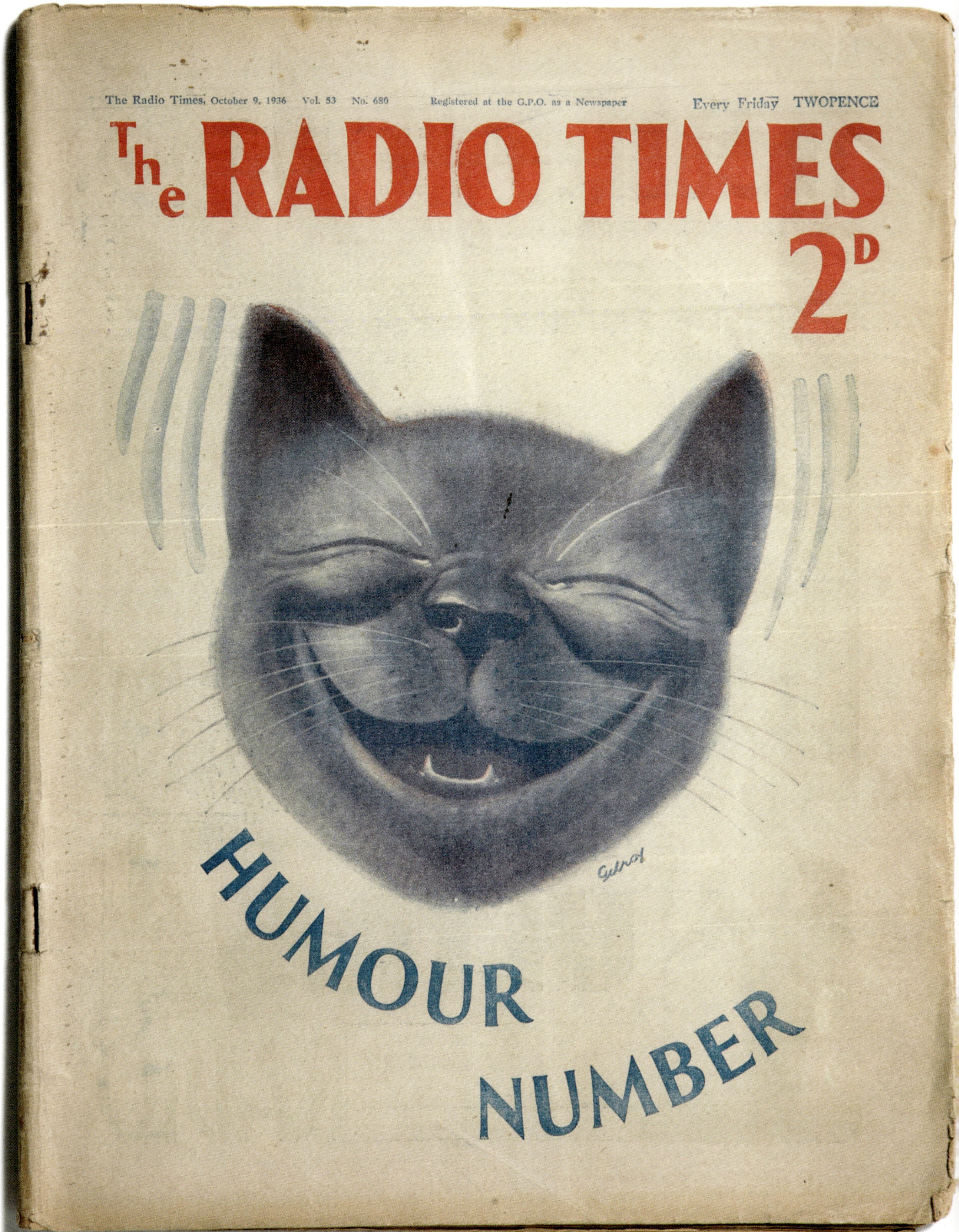
The Radio Times, October 9, 1936 Vol. 53 No. 680
Registered at the G.P.O. as a Newspaper
Every Friday TWOPENCE
The RADIO TIMES
2D
HUMOUR NUMBER

Television number *(right)*
Illustration by Eric Fraser
23 October 1936

This issue was devoted to television – yet there was no television in it: TV broadcasts started on 2 November but you had to live within 25 miles of Alexandra Palace in north London to receive them. However, the BBC declared: "The quality of pictures... is up to a standard at which we feel we may fairly offer it as being of real entertainment value." *Radio Times* wrote at length about television, including an aside about the soundproofing at "Ally Pally", which "of course" used asbestos.

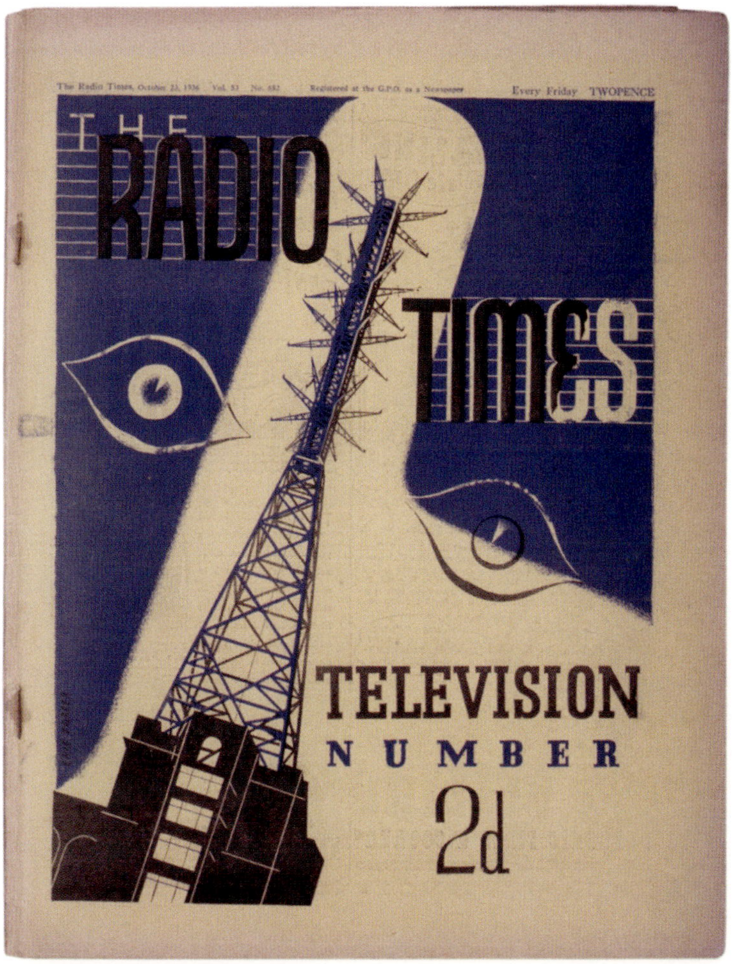

Humour number *(left)*
Illustration by John Gilroy
9 October 1936

John Gilroy became best known for his royal portrait paintings but he often produced covers for *Radio Times*, including this beaming cat for the Humour number. Inside, 24 radio comedians, including Tommy Handley and Stainless Stephen, were invited to write on any subject from health tips to how difficult it was to write for *Radio Times*.

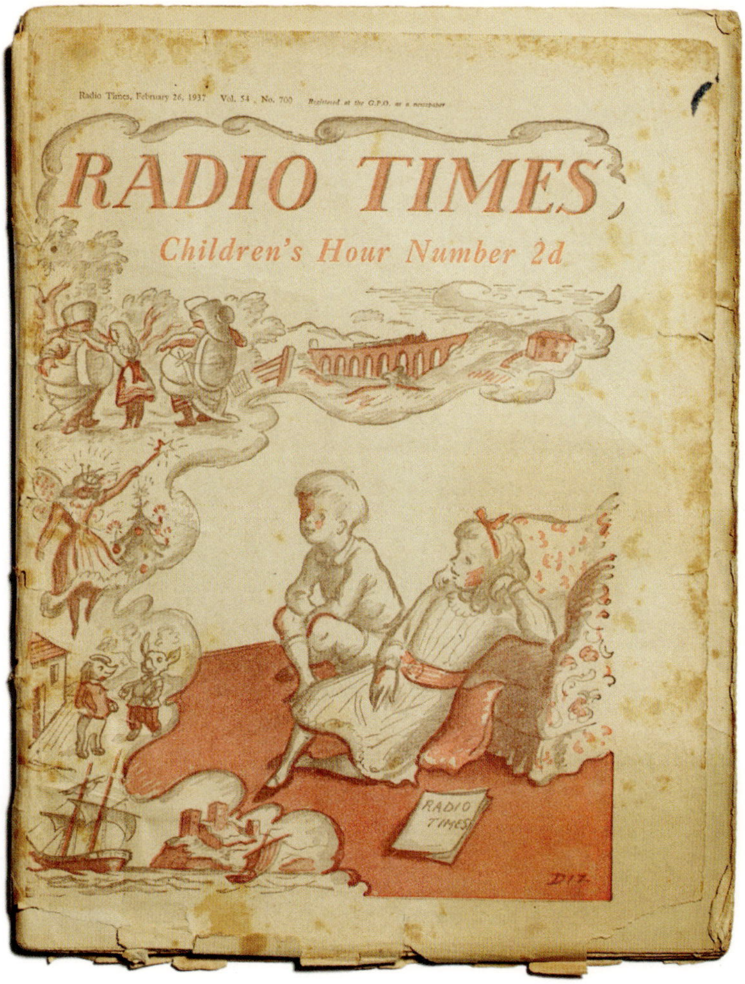

Children's Hour number *(right)*
Illustration by Edward Ardizzone
26 February 1937

Radio Times celebrated 14 years of *Children's Hour* – though noted that it had long been a 45-minute programme – and explained that the "haphazard" old days of BBC staff being Aunts and Uncles on air were over and programmes were planned as carefully as any for adults. "It is recognised that the children must be given nothing but the best."

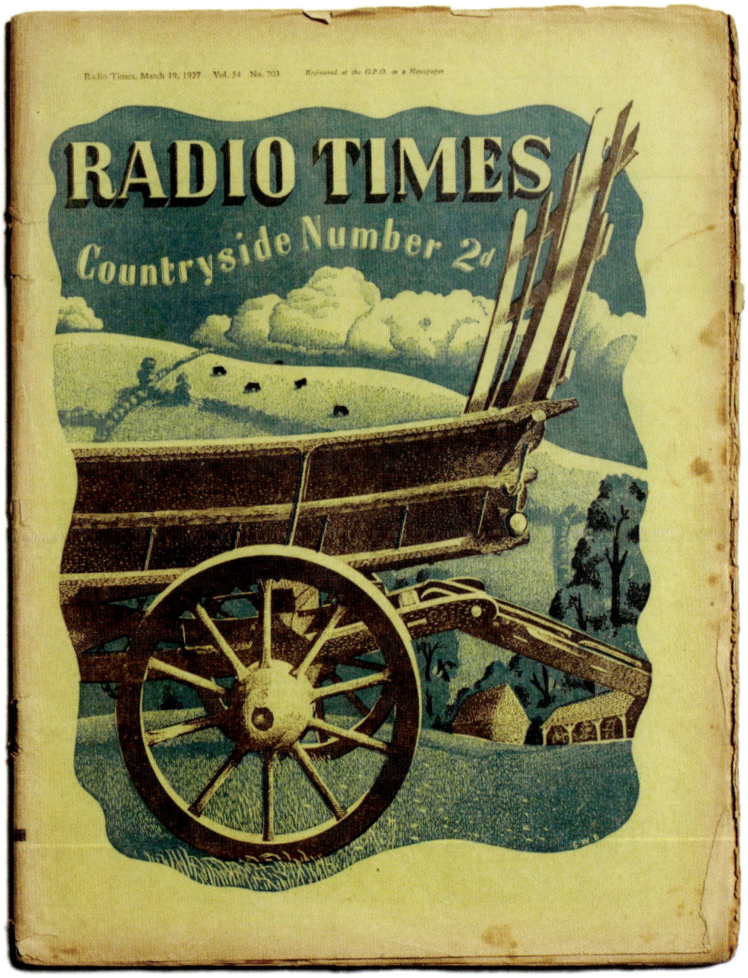

Countryside number *(left)*

Illustration by Cecil W Bacon

19 March 1937

Cecil W Bacon, whose *Radio Times* career ran for more than 30 years, provided this cover for an issue praising radio's ability to reach people in rural areas. Despite features on local farmers sharing their knowledge, *Radio Times* did betray some urban arrogance. The countryside is all very well, it suggested, but much of it "would be condemned as unfit for human habitation" if it were in a town.

The coronation *(right)*

Illustration by CRW Nevinson

7 May 1937

An issue devoted to "the most difficult broadcast ever attempted by the BBC" – the coronation of King George VI. In Westminster Abbey, a total of 28 microphones were employed to capture the event for the nation; in 2011, the BBC used 20 HD cameras in the Abbey for the wedding of Prince William and Kate Middleton. The full-size original painting of this cover by the landscape and portrait artist Christopher Nevinson would later be displayed from time to time in the *Radio Times* offices right up to the 2010s.

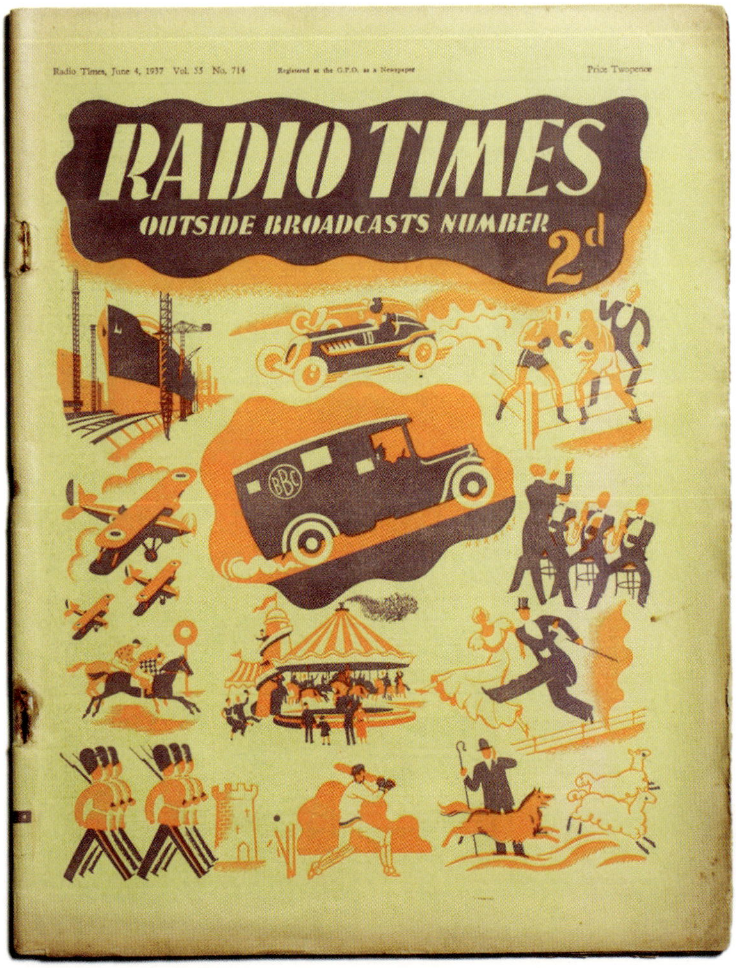

Outside broadcasts number *(left)*

Illustration by Stanley Herbert

4 June 1937

Most of this issue's focus was about how radio did outside broadcasts, and among the famous commentators featured was former motorcycle racer Graham Walker. His son, Graeme Murray Walker, would later follow his father into motorsport commentary. However, TV got a mention, too: until recently, cameras had been limited to no more than a thousand feet from Alexandra Palace – but now their range was increasing.

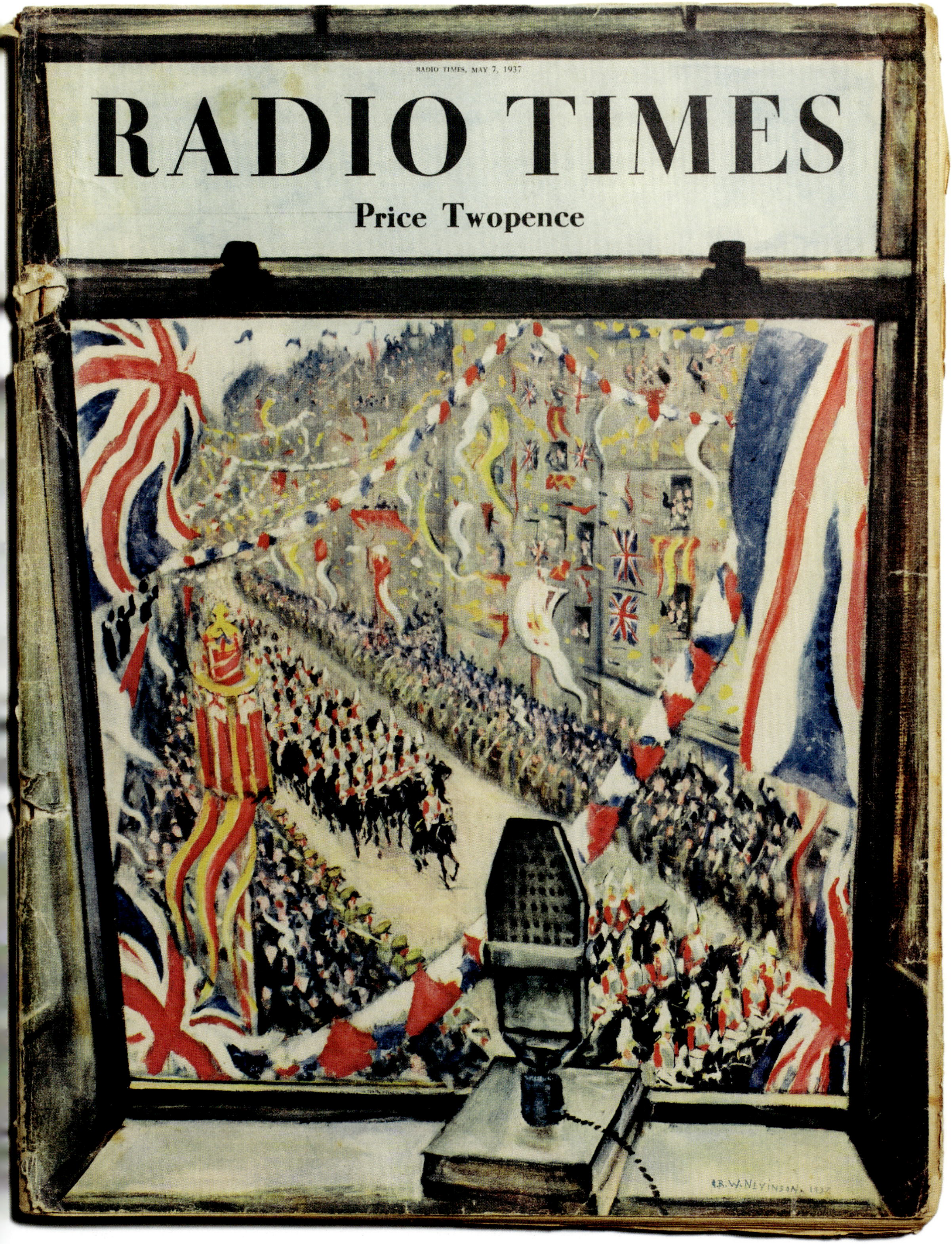
RADIO TIMES, MAY 7, 1937
RADIO TIMES
Price Twopence
C.R.W. NEVINSON. 1937

Memories number *(right)*

Illustration by JS Goodall

10 September 1937

The memories were chiefly of London broadcasting events, but Birmingham got a mention for the revelation that, in 1922, an announcer in Britain's second city had planned to read news bulletins twice – "first of all rapidly" and then slowly so listeners could take notes.

Autumn number *(middle right)*

Illustration by Stanley Herbert

8 October 1937

As *Radio Times* looked forward to autumn schedules full of "funny and simple" comedy, the BBC had asked for 1,000 listeners to join a panel reviewing programmes. It received 47,000 applications.

Woman's broadcasting number *(far right)*

12 November 1937

"Radio can open the door to a wider life for women," wrote the Rt Hon Margaret Bondfield, the first woman Cabinet minister. "But only if the women co-operate intelligently, using this new power with discrimination, and with self-control."

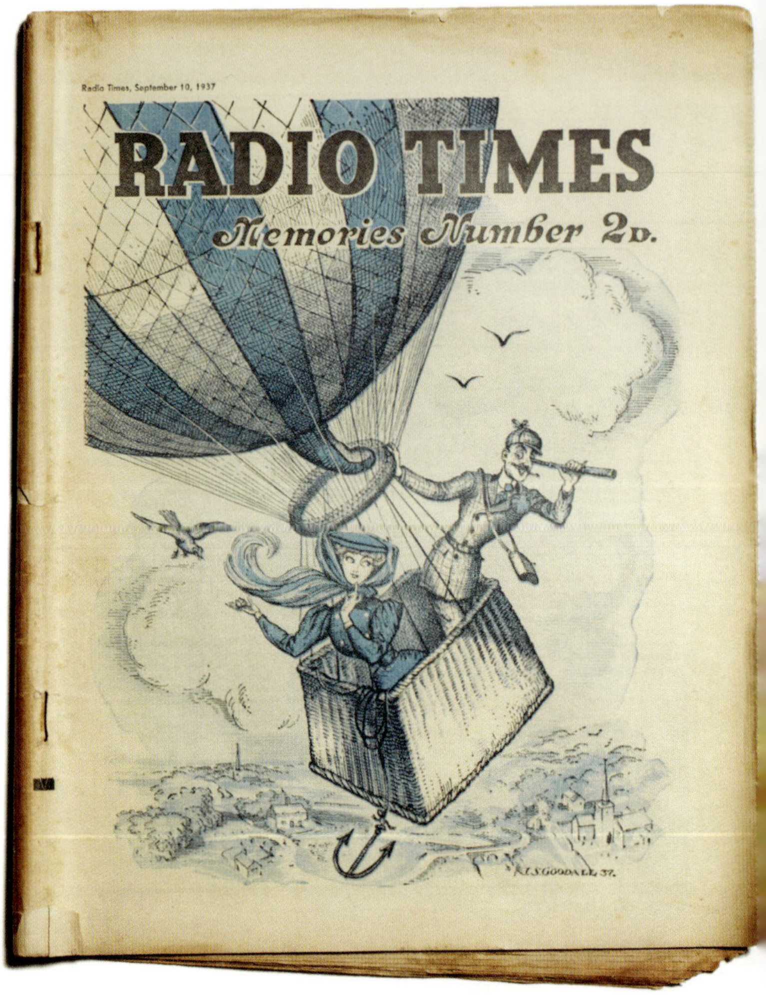

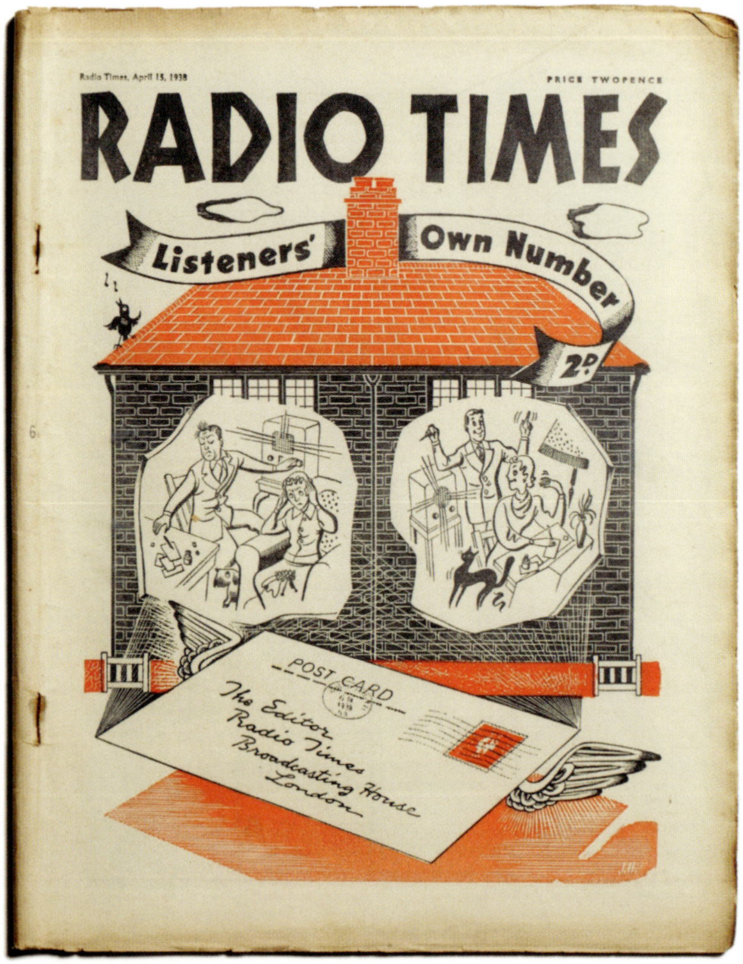

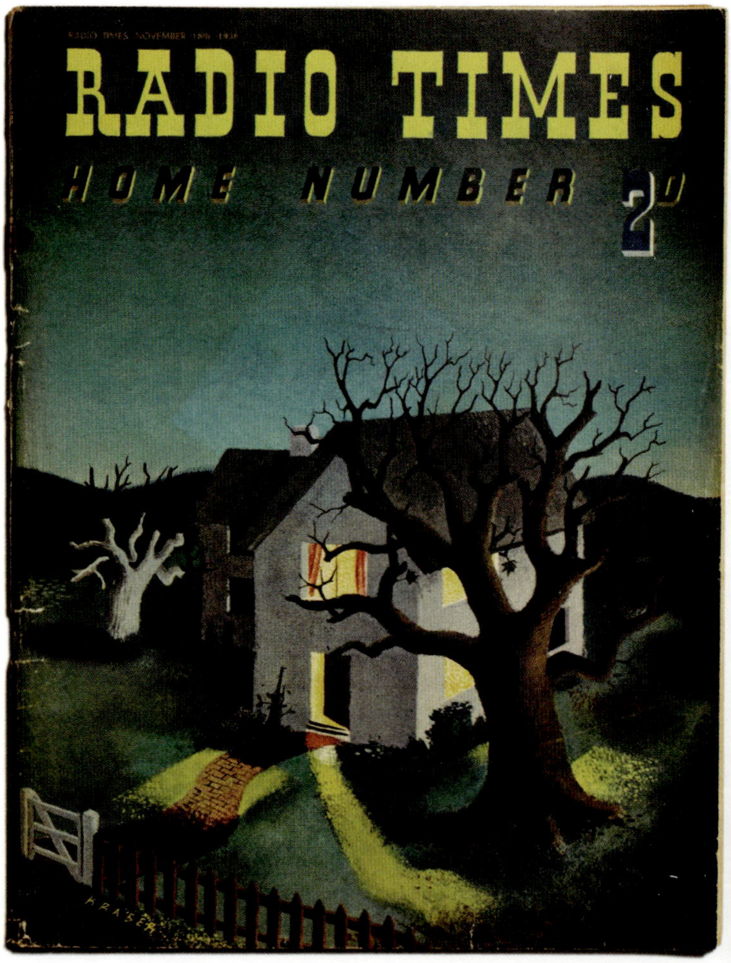

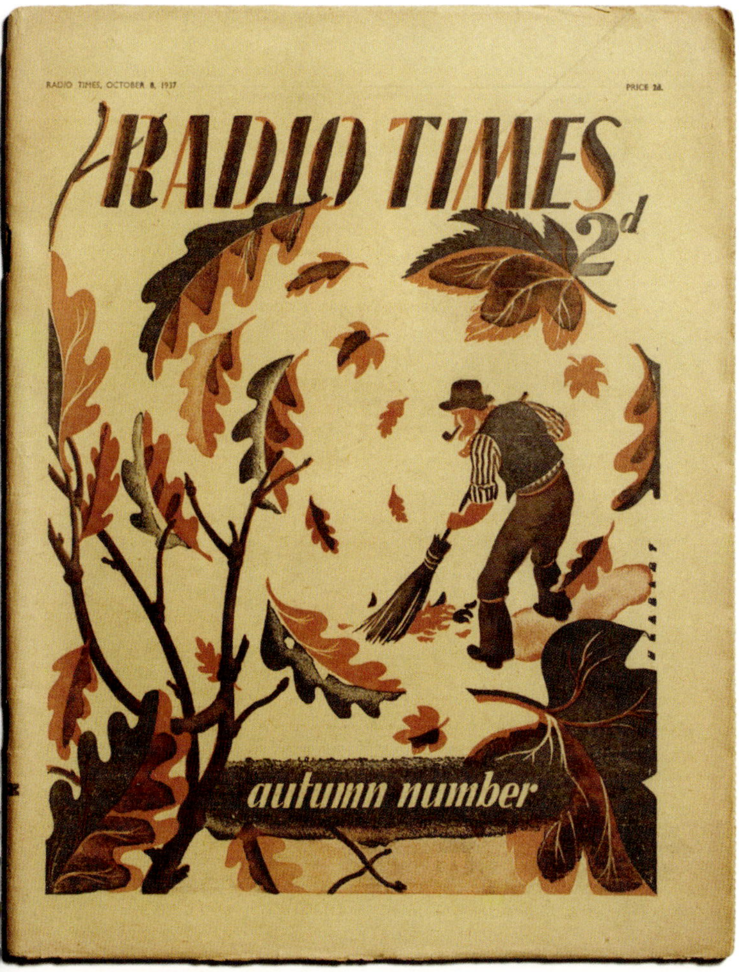

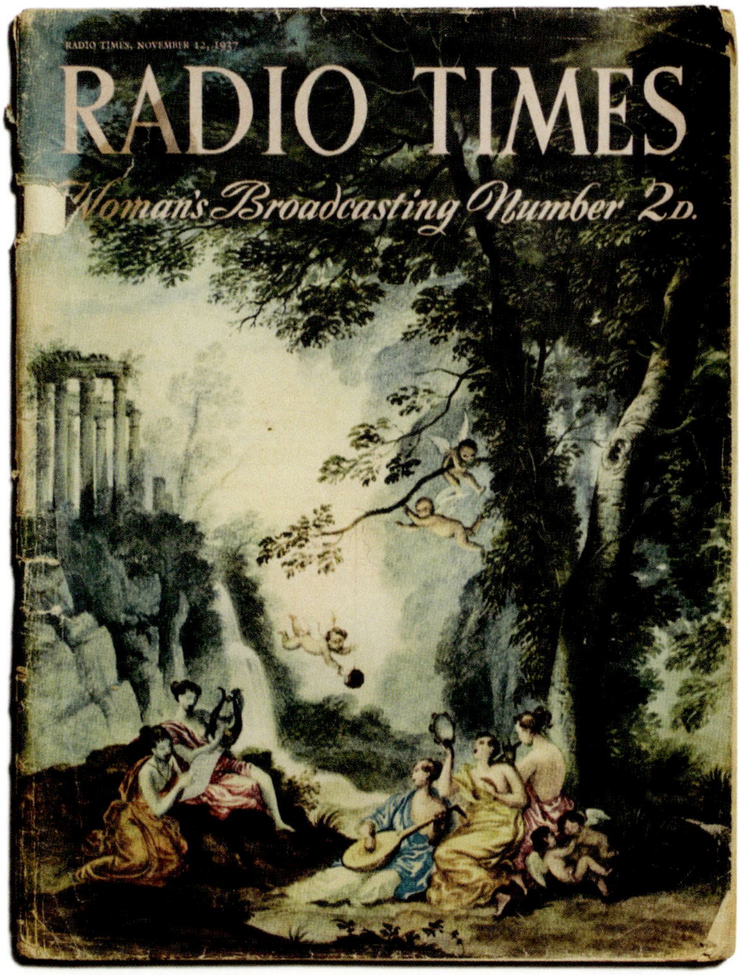

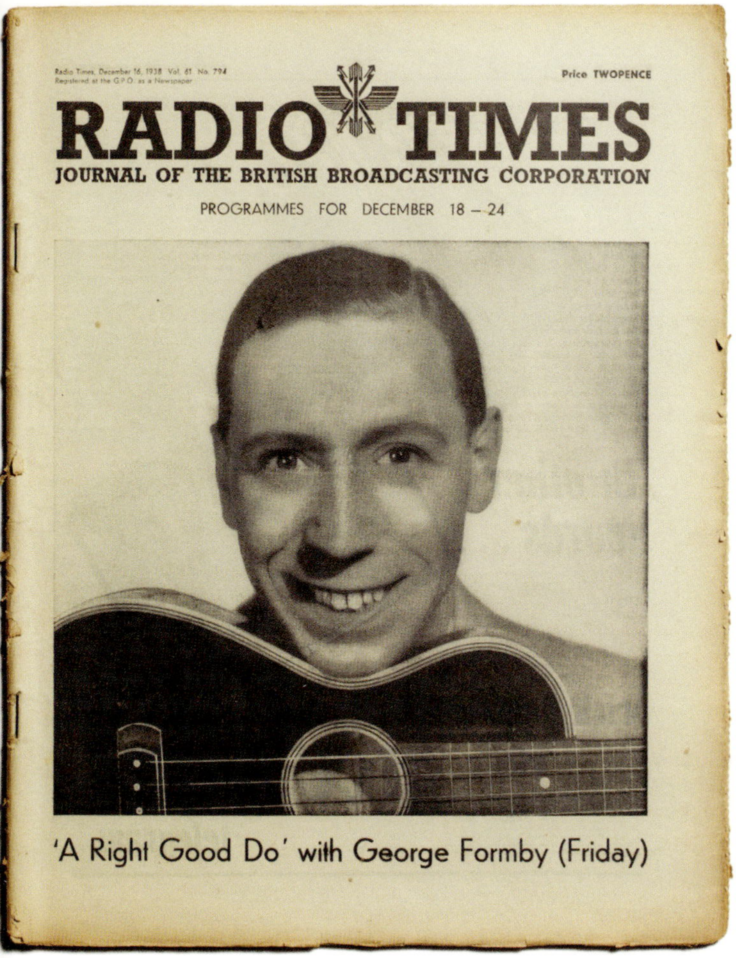

Listeners' own number *(far left)*

Illustration by JH

15 April 1938

"Can we have a pause for the comments of listeners after each really interesting item in the news?" asked John Philips of Cheshire. Perhaps he would be happier these days when many news programmes contain vox pop interviews.

Home number *(middle left)*

Illustration by Kraber

18 November 1938

Broadcasting stars were asked what home meant to them. "There's no place like home for me since I was a toddler on the cobbles of Lancashire," wrote Gracie Fields. "However long I live in London, I'll always be a Lancashire lass at heart." John Barker, who drew under the name Kraber, was a London Transport artist and began his career in 1934 as assistant to Austin Cooper, another *Radio Times* illustrator.

A Right Good Do *(left)*

George Formby *16 December 1938*

We might associate George Formby with songs, films and his toothy grin, but he was also a huge radio star. Here he presented "a Northern Christmas Party" with his guest, Beryl Reid.

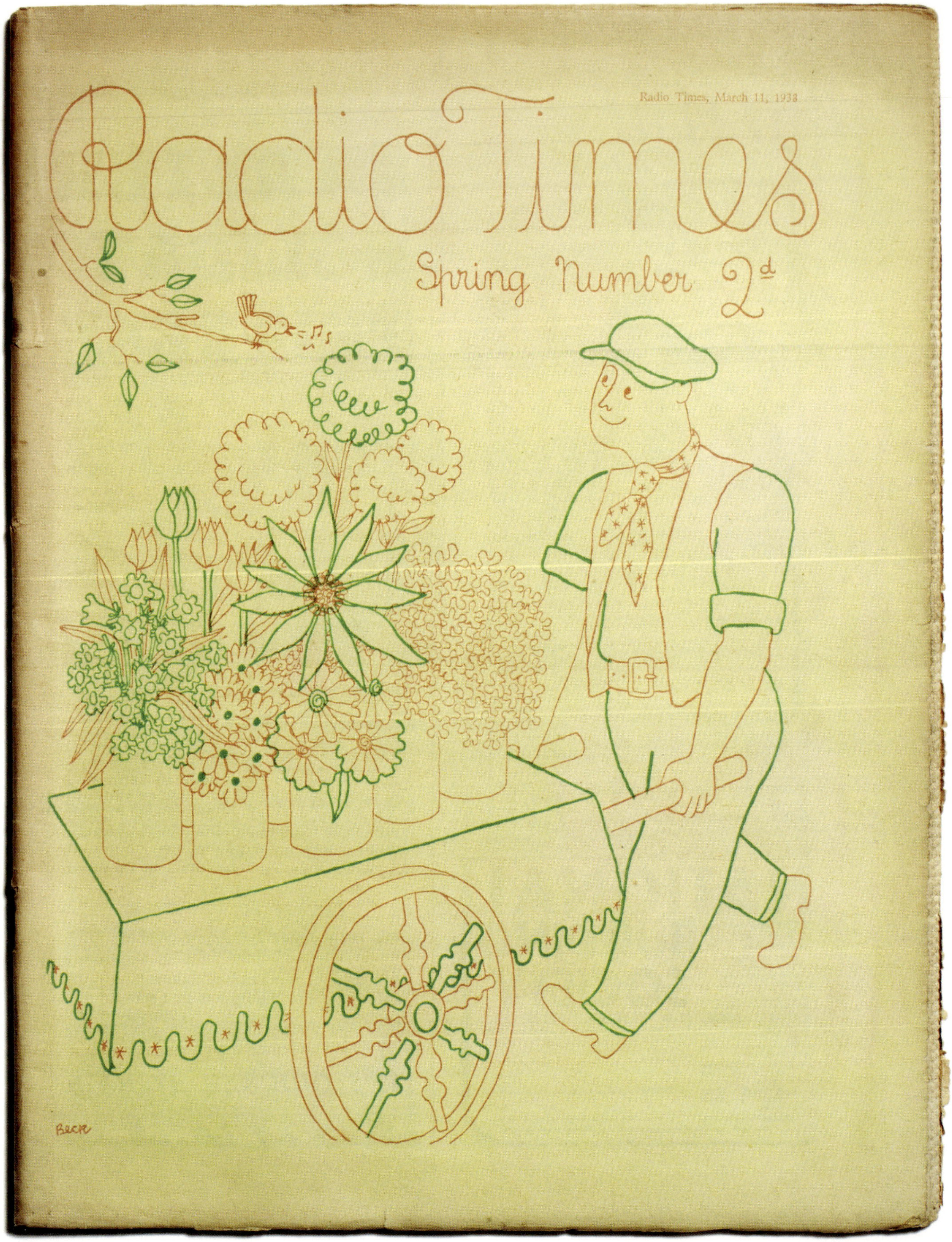

Spring number **Illustration by Beck** *11 March 1938*

Spring 1938 brought us a cheerily squiggly picture on the cover. Inside, four well-known broadcasters gave their thoughts and advice on spring hobbies: keeping bees, gardening, raising chickens for profit and, for the chaps, building a workshop. "Call it the workshop, not the shed," to avoid the tragedy of this sacred male environment becoming overcome with household clutter, was the advice.

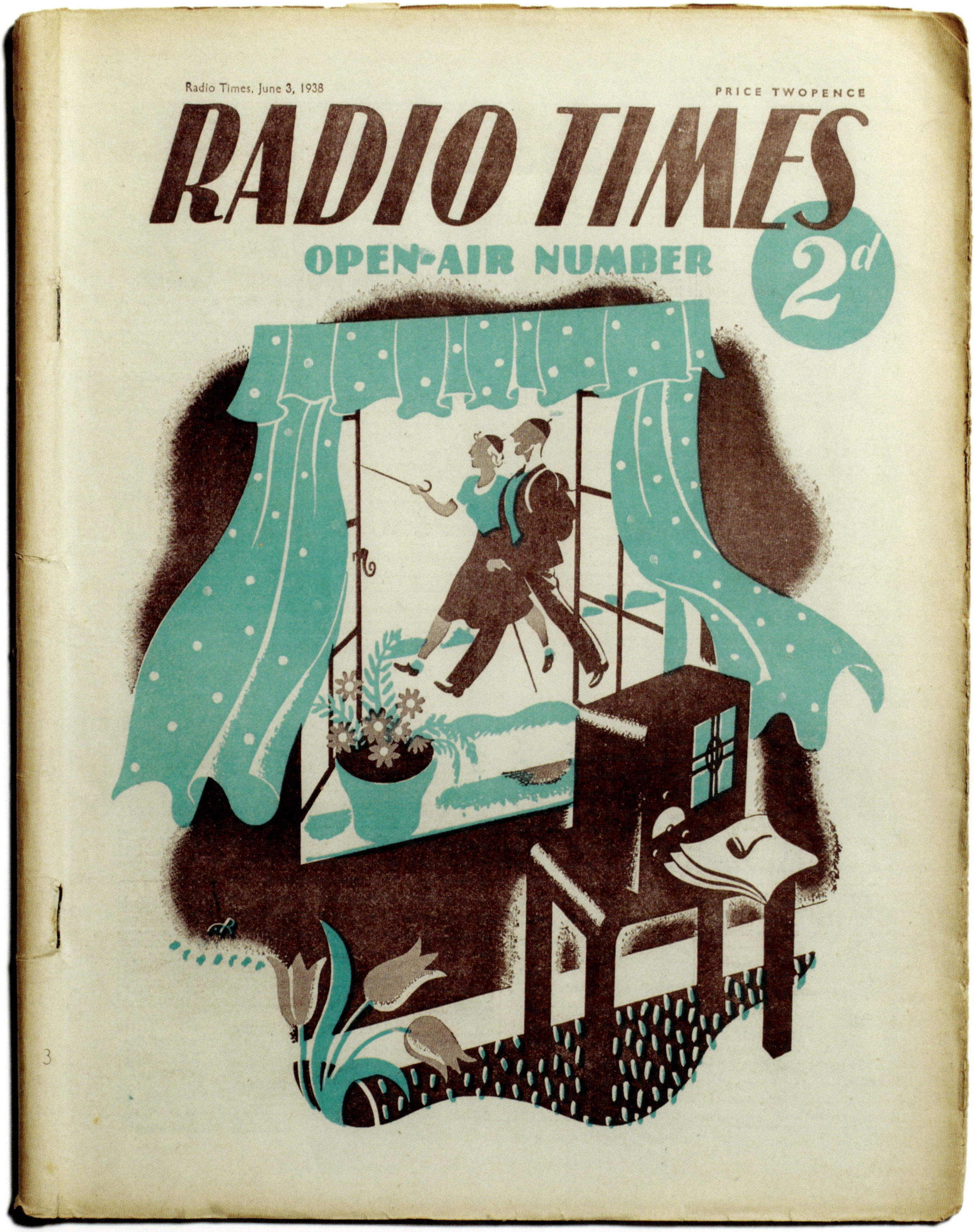

Open-air number **Illustration by Stanley Herbert** *3 June 1938*

This was as close to portable as you got back then: enjoy the great outdoors but first turn the radio round to the window so you can hear it. Ironically, *Radio Times* also complained that radio had dulled people's ears to the sounds of nature. Inside, five pages were devoted to some of the venues that would host outside broadcasts in the coming week, including, improbably, Cheltenham bus station – "the Charing Cross of the road".

Will Hay *(left)*

2 September 1938

Comedian Will Hay (centre) and co-stars Moore Marriott (left) and Graham Moffatt performed an extract from their forthcoming film *Old Bones of the River* for the opening of the Gaumont Cinema, Holloway, London.

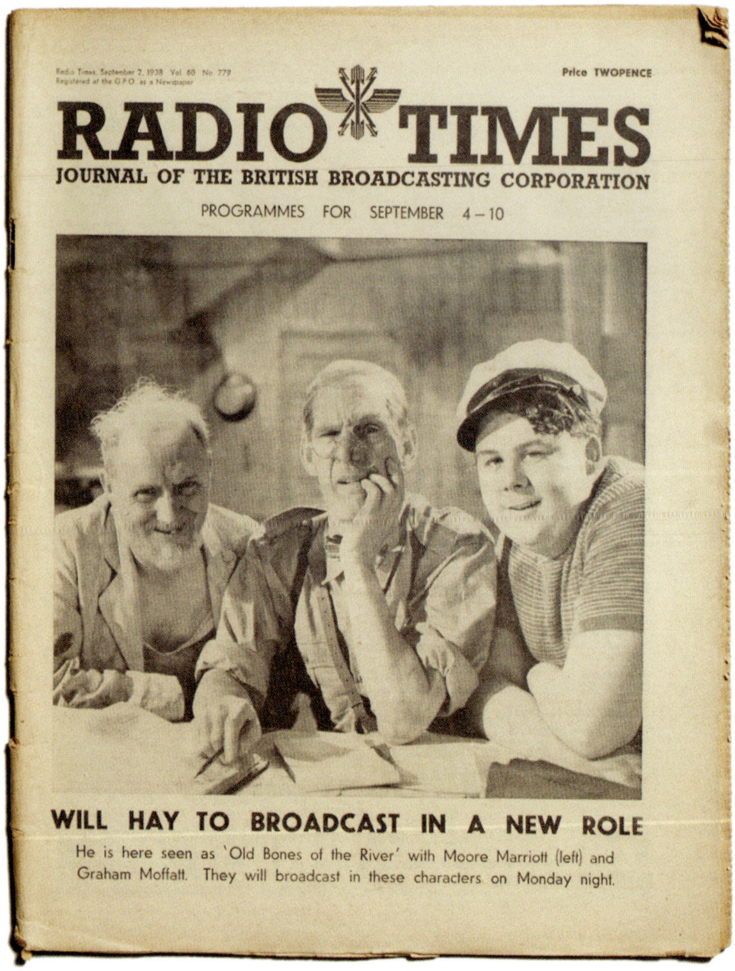

Gracie Fields *(below left)*

21 October 1938

Lancastrian superstar Gracie Fields was awarded her CBE this year and on Friday 28 October performed with military officers of the Kneller Hall Band at the Royal Albert Hall.

Behind the Broadcast News *(below right)*

Illustration by Eric Fraser

3 February 1939

A special supplement gave readers their first glimpse behind the scenes of "the men and the methods" of BBC News – then "only a small group of offices on the fifth floor" of Broadcasting House.

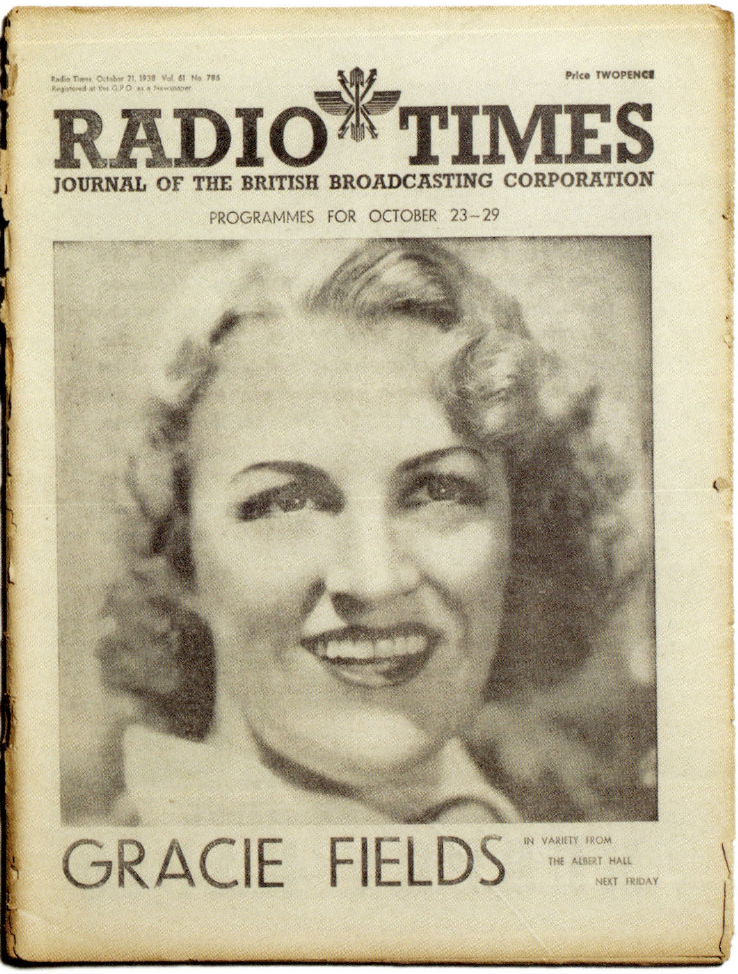

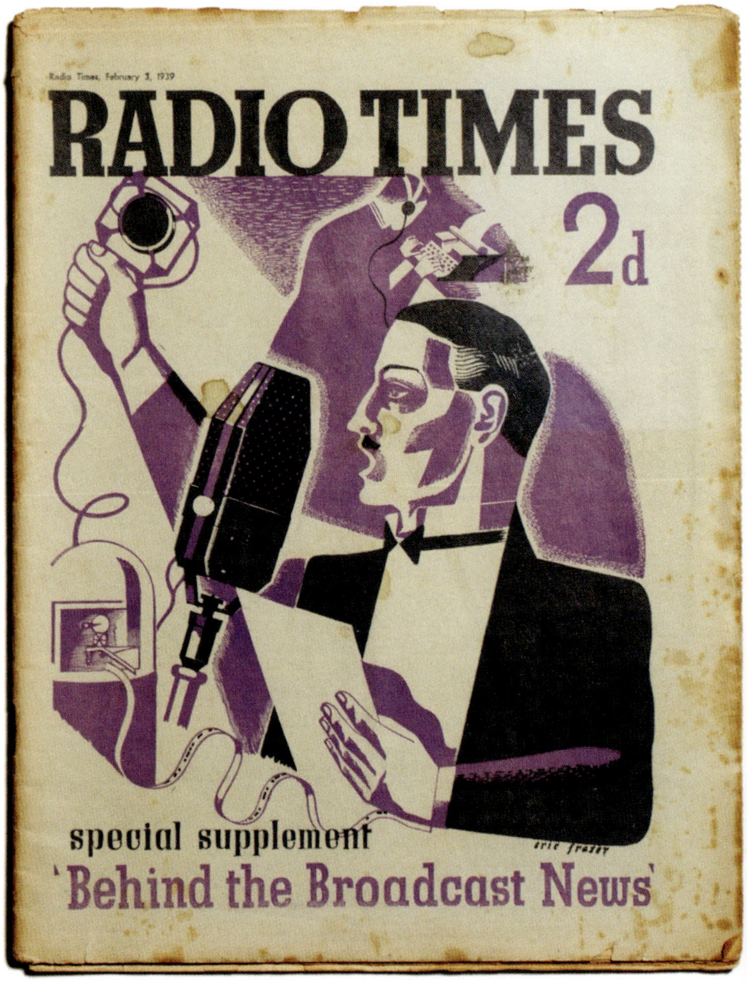

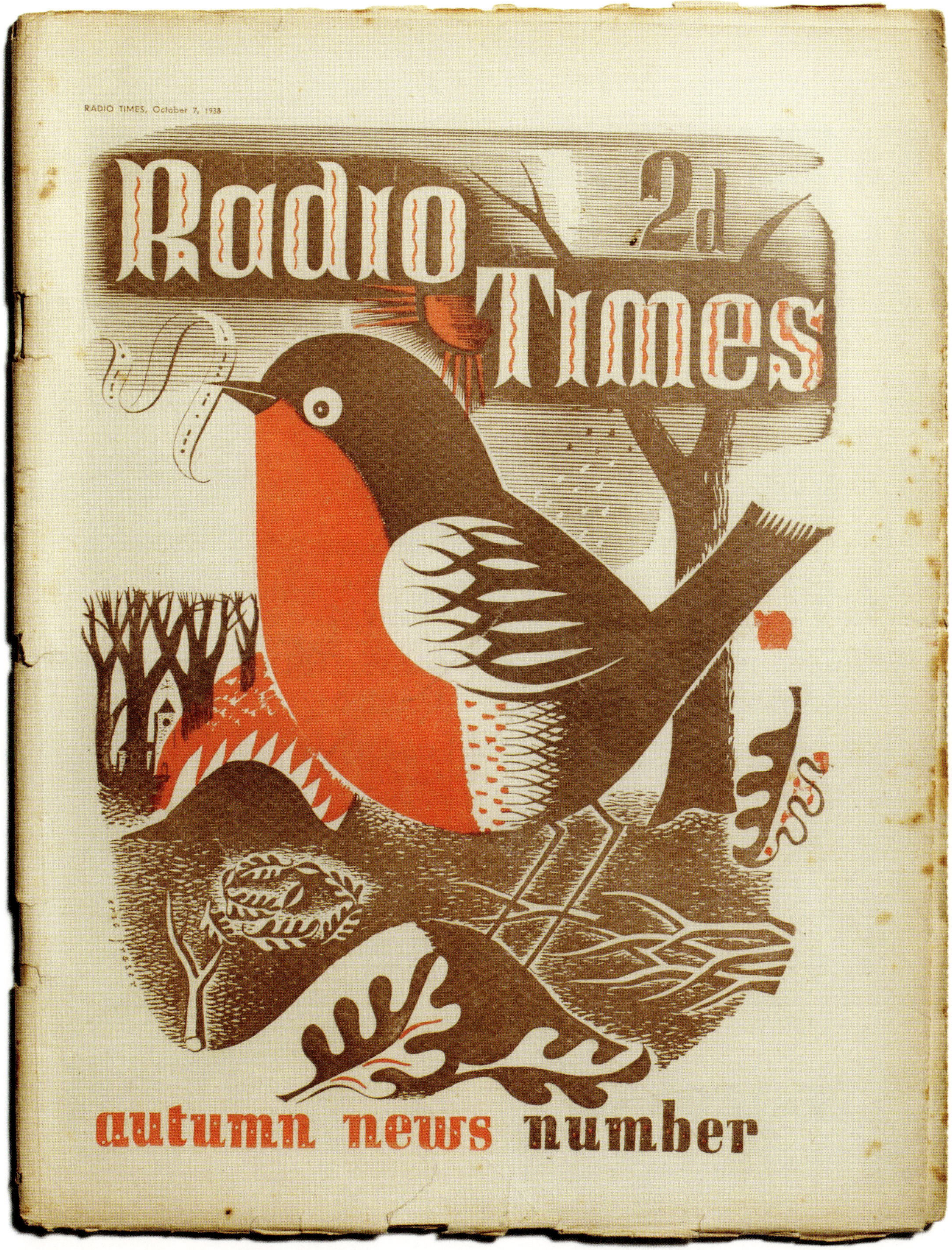

Autumn news number Illustration by Eric Fraser *7 October 1938*

The big news was that the BBC had taken delivery of a "recording car... a perfectly ordinary saloon, which can set off at a moment's notice to the scene of a news story". Also, after 11 years at the helm, Lord Reith, the BBC's first director-general, was replaced by Frederick Wolff Ogilvie (he lasted four years).

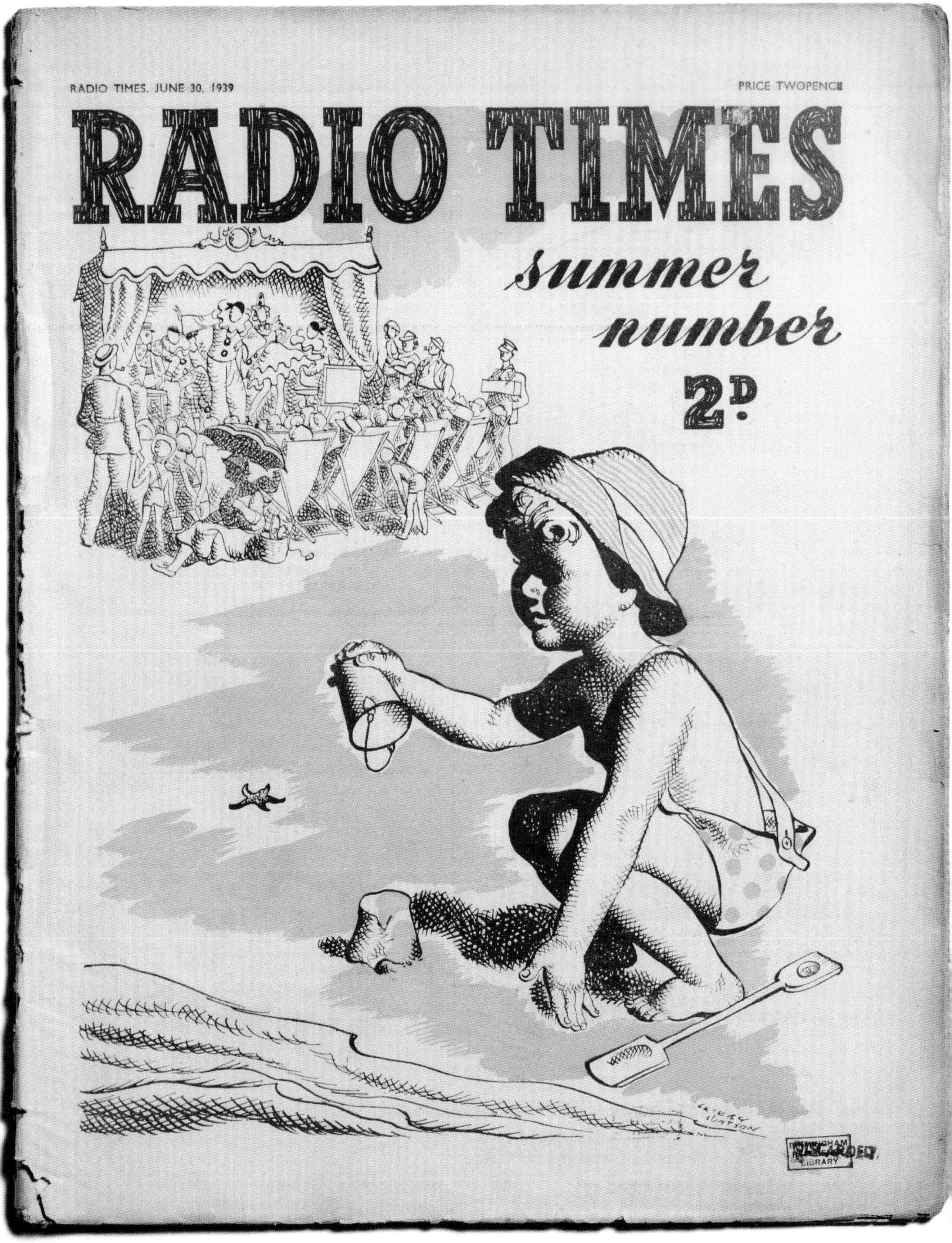
RADIO TIMES, JUNE 30, 1939
PRICE TWOPENCE
RADIO TIMES
summer
number
2D.

The man in the street *(right)*

Illustration by Relf

24 March 1939

Michael Standing from the programme *In Town Tonight* described the terrors of doing vox pop interviews live and how relieved he was when the first person he approached "didn't tell us to go to blazes". Standing was getting used to the job now: "Since then there have been over 20 of these broadcasts."

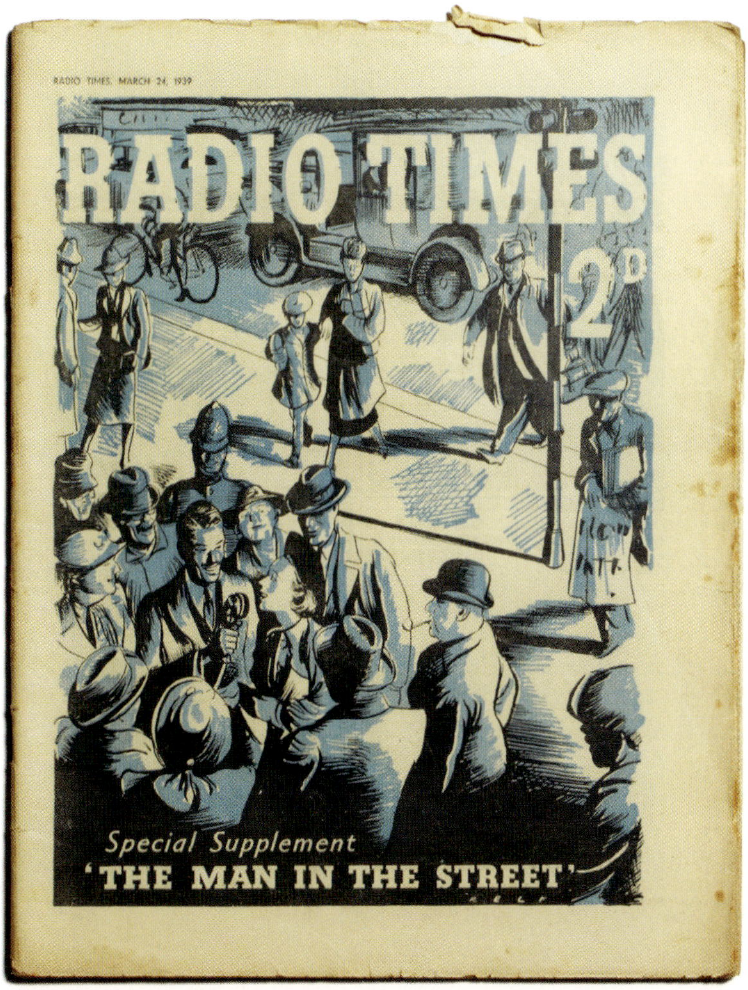

Summer number *(left)*

Illustration by Clixby Watson

30 June 1939

The summer of fun included a series of programmes from seaside towns around the country featuring the nation's favourite artists – a total of 56 concerts in all and a huge logistical problem for the production team. The cover illustration was by Clixby Watson, who began drawing at the age of five when he was confined to hospital with polio. He became an acclaimed painter and commercial artist.

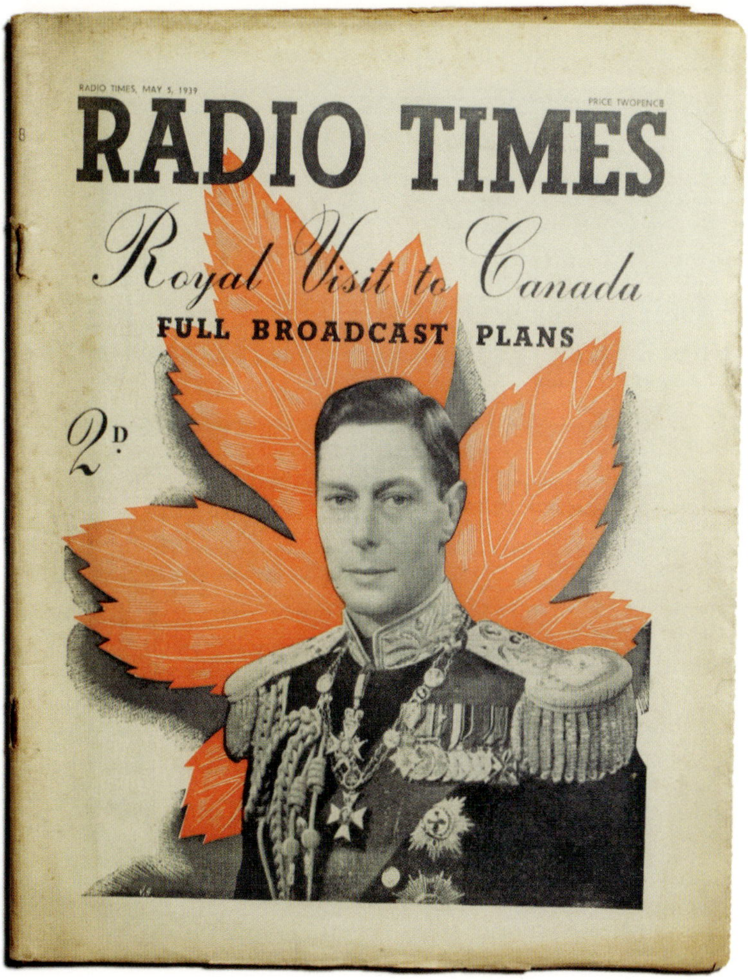

Royal visit to Canada *(right)*

Illustration of maple leaf by JH

5 May 1939

The King and Queen were heading off on a seven-week trip to Canada. It was big news – in a 14-page supplement detailing the coast-to-coast visit, *Radio Times* revealed that they would be met on the other side of the Atlantic by Richard Dimbleby: "one of the small 'flying squad' of BBC news observers".

CHRISTMAS DAY Home Service

203.5 m. 1474 kc/s
449.1 m. 668 kc/s
391.1 m. 767 kc/s
48.54 m. 6.18 Mc/s

DECEMBER 25

BLACK-OUT

	p.m.	a.m.
London	5.25 to	8.35
Plymouth	5.47 to	8.46
Cardiff	5.37 to	8.48
Leeds	5.18 to	8.54
Edinburgh	5.11 to	9.14
Aberdeen	4.58 to	9.18
Belfast	5.31 to	9.17

7.0 a.m. Time, Big Ben

'O come, all ye faithful'

NEWS

and summary of Forces programmes

7.15 This Week's Composer

RIMSKY-KORSAKOV

Gramophone records of excerpts from 'Scheherazade'

7.45 CHRISTMAS GREETINGS

from Uncle Mac, with verse and carols to start the day. Carols sung by Derek Barsham, the Boys' Brigade boy soprano (recording)

8.0 CAROLS

sung by the BBC Chorus: conductor, Leslie Woodgate

A Child this day is born *arr. Geoffrey Shaw*
God rest you merry, gentlemen ....*trad.*
I saw three ships........*arr. Geoffrey Shaw*
The Holly and the Ivy *arr. Rutland Boughton*
Good King Wenceslas...*arr. Geoffrey Shaw*

(BBC recording)

8.15 RICHARD CREAN ORCHESTRA

March of the Toys (Babes in Toyland) *Victor Herbert*
Waltz (The Sleeping Beauty)...*Tchaikovsky*
Selection: Snow White and the Seven Dwarfs..........................*Churchill*
Entry of the Little Fauns..............*Pierné*
All on a Christmas morning...*H. G. Amers*
Gingerbread Waltz (Hansel and Gretel) *Humperdinck*

(BBC recording)

8.40 'THE POSTMAN'S KNOCK'

In a London street—in a country village—town and country folk welcome the postman on his Christmas morning 'walk', accompanied in London by Michael Standing, and in Grantchester by Gilbert Harding

9.0 Time, Greenwich

'O come, all ye faithful'

NEWS

and Programme Parade

9.15 THE KITCHEN FRONT

9.20 CHRISTMAS BELLS

from the four corners of the British Isles. A message of greeting from the bells of Westminster Abbey; St. Cuthbert's, Edinburgh; Armagh Cathedral; St. John's, Cardiff; and St. Mary's, Lowdham, Nottinghamshire

9.30 FODEN'S MOTOR WORKS BAND

Conductor, Fred Mortimer

Idyll: All on a Christmas morning..*Amers*
Extracts from The Royal Water Music *Handel*
Trombone Solo: Down the Vale......*Moir* (Soloist, Ellis Westwood)
Selection: A Southern Maid.*Fraser-Simson*
Minuet and Galop (Orpheus in the Underworld)..............................*Offenbach*

10.0 'MESSIAH'

Selections from Handel's oratorio, on gramophone records

10.45 GUERNSEY CHILDREN SINGING

Choir of the States Intermediary School, of Guernsey, conducted by Winifred Roughton

Now once again our hearts we raise; Jean Grosjean; Le jour du lavage (Washing-Day)..............................*anon.*
Minuit chrétien (The Watch-Service Carol) *arr. Rodney Bennet*
Voici Noël.....................*arr. Weckerlin*
Lift your heads, rejoice...*arr. Martin Shaw*

(BBC recording)

11.0 Time, Big Ben

CHRISTMAS MORNING SERVICE

from St. Mary's, Lowdham, Nottinghamshire, conducted by Canon Anthony Otter

O come, all ye faithful (S.P. 78: C.H. 55)
Sentence
General Thanksgiving
The Lord's Prayer
Versicles and Responses
Venite
Psalm 8
Lesson: St. Luke 2, vv. 1-20
While shepherds watched their flocks (S.P. 82; C.H. 42)
Creed and Collects
Carols: Little Jesus, sweetly sleep (S.P. 383); Angels from the realms of glory (S.P. 71; C.H. 65)
Address
Behold, the great Creator (S.P. 72)
Prayers
Hark! the herald angels sing (S.P. 74; C.H. 46)
Blessing
Organist, Arthur Cowen

P.M.

12.0 WORKS WONDERS

Munition-workers entertain their colleagues in a Christmas Day concert at a factory in Scotland

12.30 'CHRISTMAS CHARIVARIA'

A 'hubbub' of recorded music and song, prose and poetry for today, contrasted and introduced by Raymond Raikes, with Bransby Williams, Joseph Macleod, and Geoffrey Wincott, and the recorded voices of Harry Hemsley, Peter Dawson, Ernest Lough, and Paul Robeson. Programme edited by Peter Eton

1.0 Time, Greenwich: NEWS

1.15 THE ARCHBISHOP OF CANTERBURY

gives a Christmas message

1.30 VIOLIN MUSIC

played by Eda Kersey (violin)

Sonata in D ....*Vivaldi—Respighi*
Sonatina in G, Op. 100..............*Dvořák*

2.0 'WE ARE ADVANCING' towards Victory, towards Understanding

A Christmas reunion of the peoples of the British Commonwealth and of the United Nations, linked by radio from all parts of the world to exchange greetings on the fifth wartime Christmas Day

Christmas in the British Isles: at home—with the workers—with British and Allied Forces
Christmas with the Imperial Forces Overseas: Italy—New Guinea—India
Christmas in Occupied Europe
Christmas in the United Nations: Russia—China—Brazil—U.S.A.
Christmas in the Holy Land

Narrator, Howard Marshall. Music by Victor Hely-Hutchinson, played and sung by the London Symphony Orchestra and Alexander Choir, conducted by Muir Mathieson. Written and produced by Laurence Gilliam and Leonard Cottrell

(Full details will be found in the article on page 3)

3.15 NATIONAL ANTHEMS OF THE ALLIES

3.30 BBC SCOTTISH ORCHESTRA

Conductor, Ian Whyte. Janette Sclanders (soprano)

Overture: Iolanthe.......................*Sullivan*
Four Scots Songs: O whistle and I'll come to ye, my lad; Flora MacDonald's Lament; Robin Adair; Comin' thro' the rye.......................................*trad.*
Berceuse; Praeludium..................*Järnefelt*
Waltz: The Skaters.................*Waldteufel*

4.0 'WHAT ELSE DO THEY DO?'

with C. H. Middleton, Mary Ferguson, 'The Radio Doctor', C. A. Lejeune, and Douglas Houghton (recording)

Five radio 'regulars' take a brief holiday from their regular subjects

4.20 'IS YOUR GENIE REALLY NECESSARY?'

A satirical pantomime for a war-time Christmas, written by Michael Barsley. Produced by John Glyn-Jones

Fairy Godmother........Mabel Constanduros
Cinderella....................Marjorie Westbury
Aladdin........................Stephen Manton
Ali Baba.............................Antony Holles
Man in off-black..................Roy Emerton
Taxi-men, thieves, Ministry officials played by members of the BBC Drama Repertory Company

5.0 Time, Greenwich

NEWYDDION (News in Welsh)

5.5 'CYFARCHION NADOLIG'

Oddi wrth fechgyn a merched Cymru yn y lluoedd arfog, o wledydd tramor yn ogystal ag o wersylloedd ym Mhrydain. (Recorded Christmas greetings in Welsh)

5.20 CHILDREN'S HOUR

Tommy Handley in 'Well, for Santa Claus': a Christmas Day Unfairy Story, by Dorothy Worsley. Cast includes Dorothy Summers, Fred Yule, Sydney Keith, Bryan Herbert, Ronald Chesney, and Barrett and Max Field. BBC Variety Orchestra conducted by Charles Shadwell. Story-Teller, Derek McCulloch. Produced by Francis Worsley. (BBC recording)

6.0 Time, Greenwich: NEWS

National and Regional announcements

6.30 'SNOW WHITE AND THE SEVEN DWARFS'

Excerpts from the sound-track of Walt Disney's fantasy

6.45 CAROLS OF THE ALLIES

sung by the BBC Chorus, conducted by Sir Adrian Boult

All rejoice now (Russian) *arr. David Stanley Smith*
Lord Jesus hath a garden (Dutch) *arr. Geoffrey Shaw*
Rocking (Czech)...........*arr. Martin Shaw*
O leave your sheep (French) *arr. Cecil Hazlehurs[t]*
I hasten early (Polish) *arr. David Stanley Smit[h]*
A Merry Christmas (English) *arr. Arthur Warre[ll]*

7.0 BBC SYMPHONY ORCHESTRA

Conductor, Sir Adrian Boult

Overture: Leonora, No. 3.......*Beethov[en]*
Scherzo: L'Apprenti Sorcier (The Sorcerer's Apprentice)........................*Du[kas]*
Pictures from an Exhibition *Mussorgsky—Ra[vel]*

8.0 'VAUDEVILLE OF 1943'

A Saturday-night entertainm[ent] featuring famous stars of Vari[ety] music, and drama. Rando[lph] Sutton, Mr. Murgatroyd and [Mr.] Winterbottom, Robert Donat, A[nne] Ziegler and Webster Booth, [...] Elsie and Doris Waters. R[...] Chorus and augmented BBC R[...] Orchestra, conducted by Ch[...] Groves. Producers, John Shar[...] and Harry S. Pepper. (BBC re[cord]ing)

8.55 'WIRELESS FOR THE BLIND'

Appeal on behalf of the [...] 'Wireless for the Blind' Fund [...] tered under the Blind Person[s Act] 1920), by the Rt. Hon. the [...] Woolton, C.H.

Contributions will be gratefully [...] ledged, and should be addressed [...] Woolton, British 'Wireless for the [Blind'] Fund, 224, Gt. Portland Place, W[...]

9.0 BIG BEN MINUTE

NEWS

9.20 'ALICE'S ADVENTU[RES IN] WONDERLAND'

by Lewis Carroll, dramat[ised by] Herbert M. Prentice. Radio [adapta]tion by Cynthia Pughe. [...] by Howard Rose

10.10 SCHUBERT

Sonata in D, Op. 5[...]

played by Clifford Curzon

10.45 'THE CRADL[E ...]'

Verse and carols for Ch[...]

11.0 CHRISTMAS CA[...]

Carroll Gibbons, at the pi[ano ...] you to join the party at [...] chant Navy Club. You [...] Kent, Esther Coleman, [...] Billy Mayerl, Jack Ja[...] Debroy Somers, and—re[...] the U.S.A.—Rudy Vall[ée ...] music played by Carr[oll ...] and his Orchestra. P[...] Alick Hayes. (BBC rec[ording])

12.0 midnight-12.20 a.[m.]

Time, Greenwich [...]

RADIO TIMES

THE WAR YEARS

1939–1946

War is declared

Supplementary issue

4 September 1939

"Broadcasting Carries On" – the declaration of war on 3 September may have forced the BBC to revise its schedules and issue a supplementary edition of *Radio Times*, but the Corporation was not caught entirely unprepared. An editorial made clear it had been planning for the outbreak of war for a year and laid out its plans to serve up a daily schedule of programmes from 7.00am to midnight comprising plays, music, features, talks, religious services and comedy – with news on the hour, every hour.

It was just as well *Radio Times* was prepared, too – this was the second of three issues that staff had to produce in just one week, a phenomenal effort. The editorial also stressed that *Radio Times* would soldier on, albeit in reduced form whenever paper supplies were short, stating simply that, "We shall do our best to bring you the full and correct information about all the doings and plans of the BBC."

1939–1946

The gruelling years of war: patriotism, stoicism, a new role for women, Nazi plans to blow *Radio Times* off the map and, finally, victory

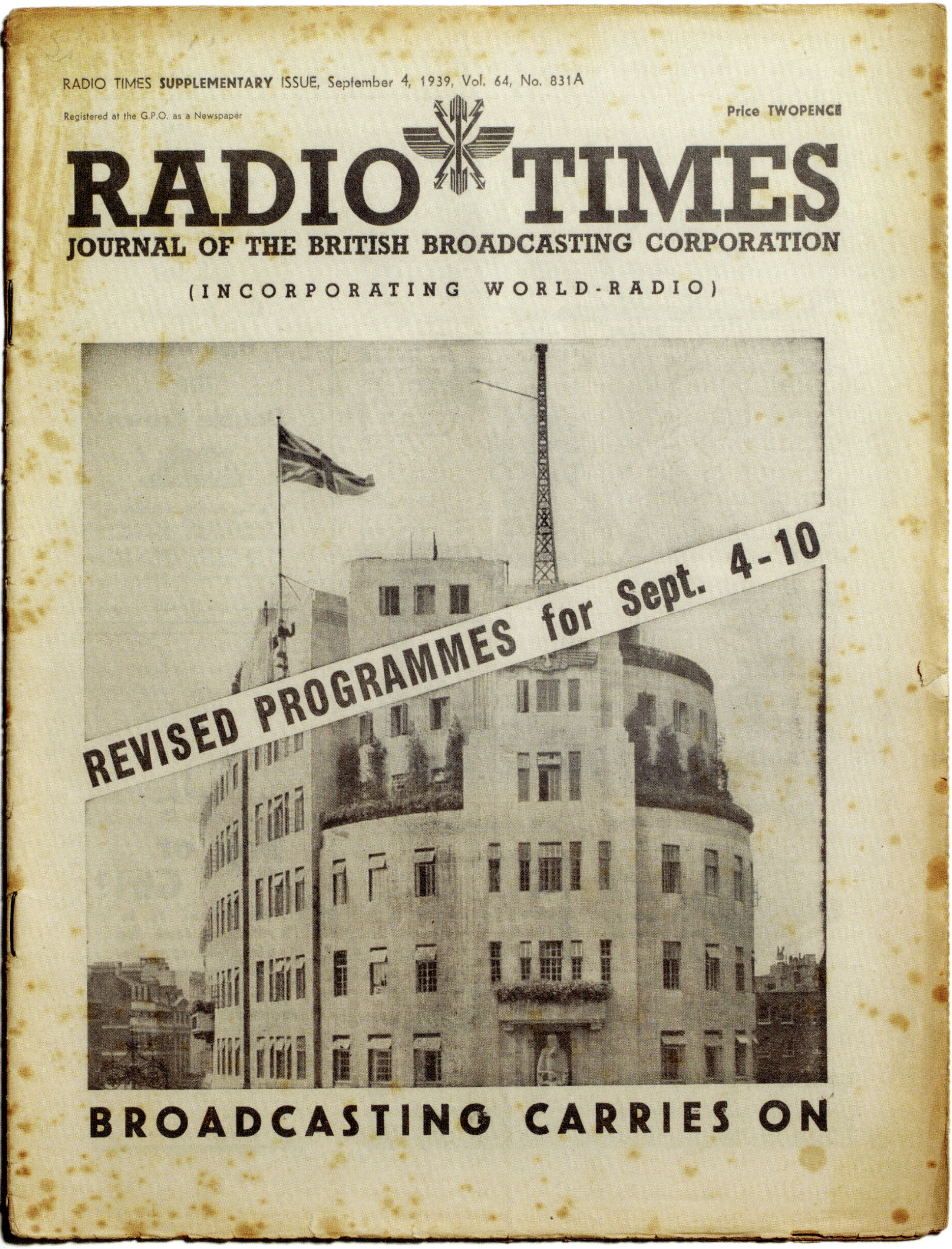
RADIO TIMES **SUPPLEMENTARY** ISSUE, September 4, 1939, Vol. 64, No. 831A

Registered at the G.P.O. as a Newspaper

Price TWOPENCE

RADIO TIMES

JOURNAL OF THE BRITISH BROADCASTING CORPORATION

(INCORPORATING WORLD-RADIO)

REVISED PROGRAMMES for Sept. 4-10

BROADCASTING CARRIES ON

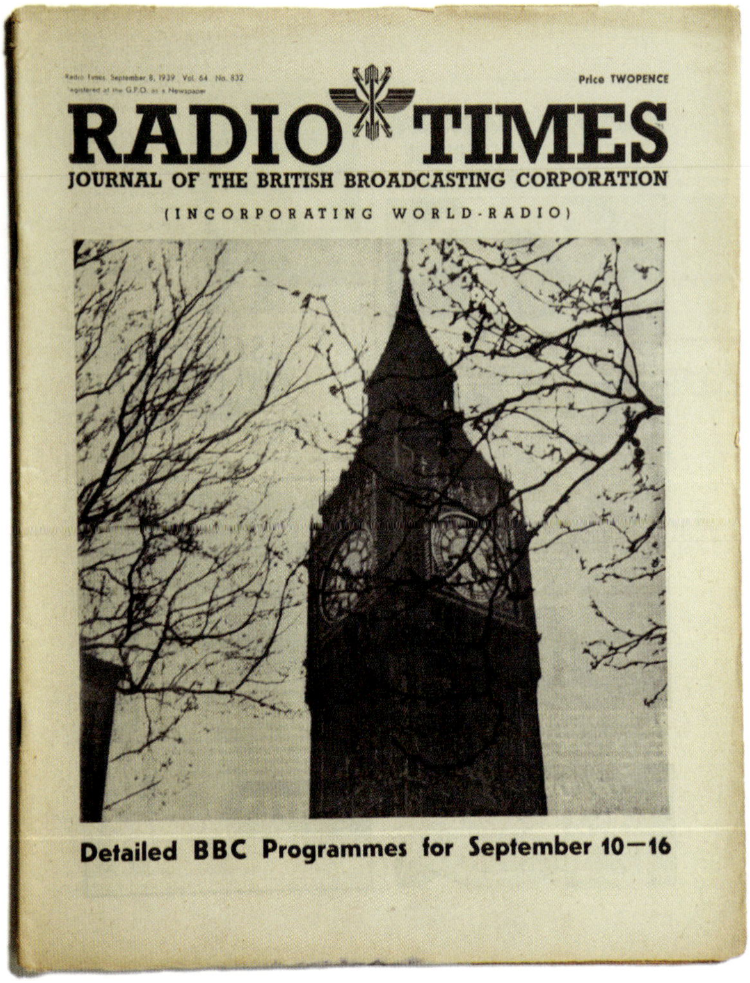

The second week *(left)*

8 September 1939

The image of the Clock Tower (now Elizabeth Tower) with the Big Ben bells inside continued the theme of patriotic defiance from the previous issue, while much of the editorial covered the mood of national anxiety, the hunger for news – and the BBC's role. Of particular note is "a short-wave service to the whole world, which runs for nearly 22 hours; the other a short-wave service meant primarily for Europe... going out in many different languages – French, Afrikaans, German, Italian, Spanish and Portuguese... representing an unprecedented effort to bring the voice of Britain to the world."

Woman's number *(right)*

Illustration by Clixby Watson

17 November 1939

To help women adjust to new circumstances and new roles in wartime this issue gave tips on how to eke out food and clothing. But there was a broader message, too – "You will not inspire your family (nor help to win the war) by looking dowdy."

The evacuation of women and children to the countryside split families apart, so housewives were advised on how they could fill the lonely evenings. The central message: "It's a mistake to brood."

But it wasn't all about winning the war with a dab of lipstick. There were also hints of women's increasing responsibility, with tales of secretaries setting up offices in school changing rooms, or training as fire-fighters and air-raid wardens.

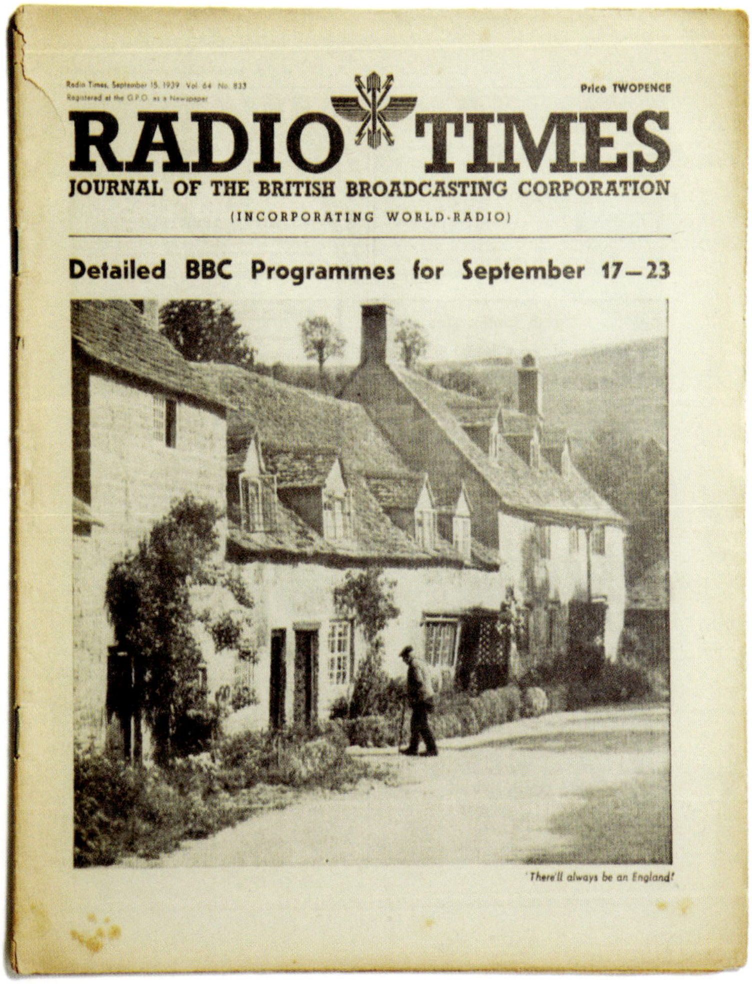

The third week *(left)*

15 September 1939

Week three of war, and the run of patriotic covers continues – "There'll always be an England!" reads the coverline. The man in the picture is Dick Newman, who was born in 1847, and the photograph was probably taken in 1938, as he died in February 1939. The cottages are in Snowhill in Gloucestershire and are now owned by the National Trust.

Inside, the listings offered up classical music and broadcasts such as *Bee-keeping: Preparations for Winter* and light entertainment programmes with Gracie Fields and Arthur Askey. The editorial also pointed out that the magazine now carried listings for foreign broadcasts, particularly those from American short-wave stations.

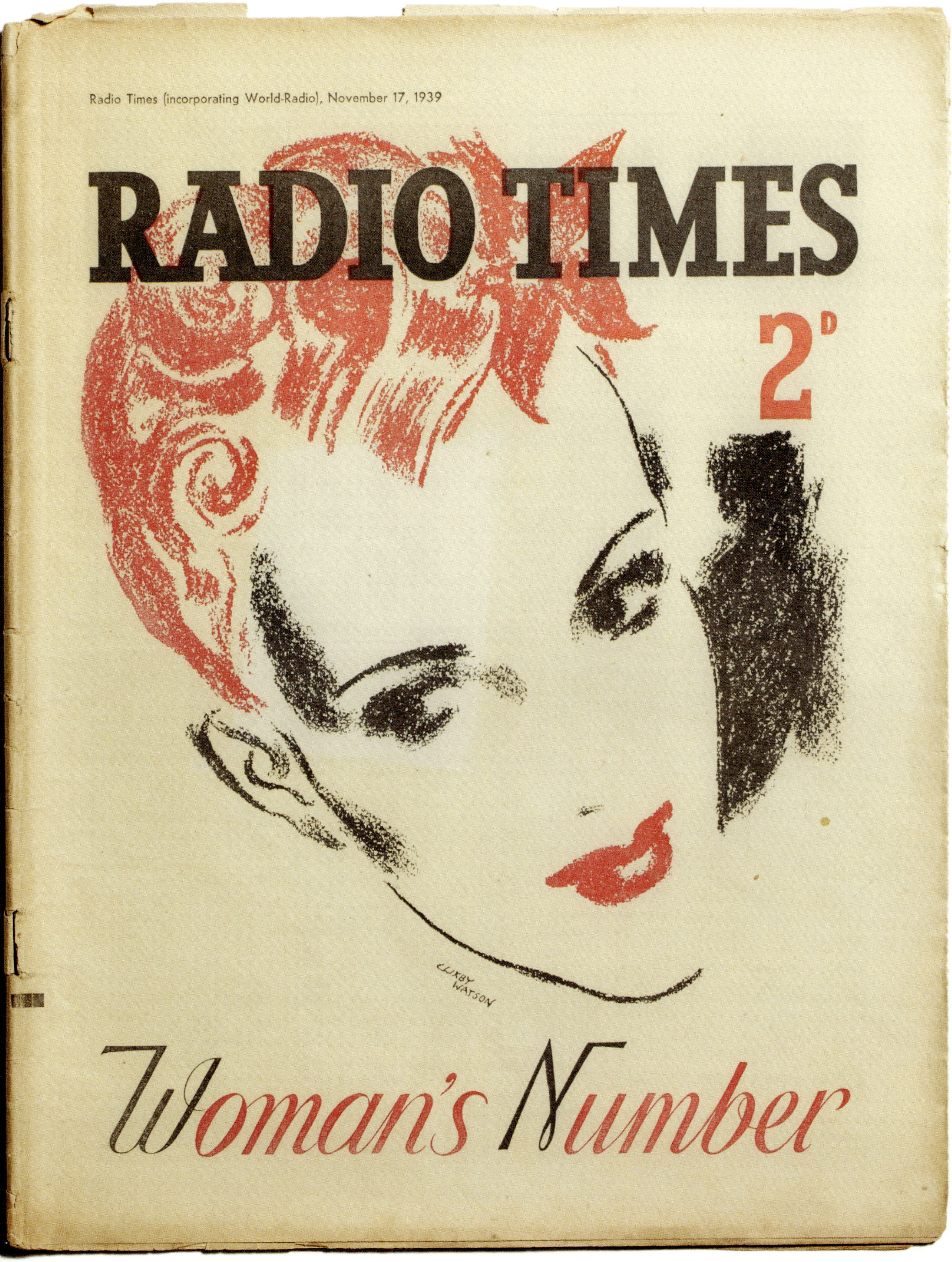
Radio Times (incorporating World-Radio), November 17, 1939
RADIO TIMES
2D
WATSON
Woman's Number

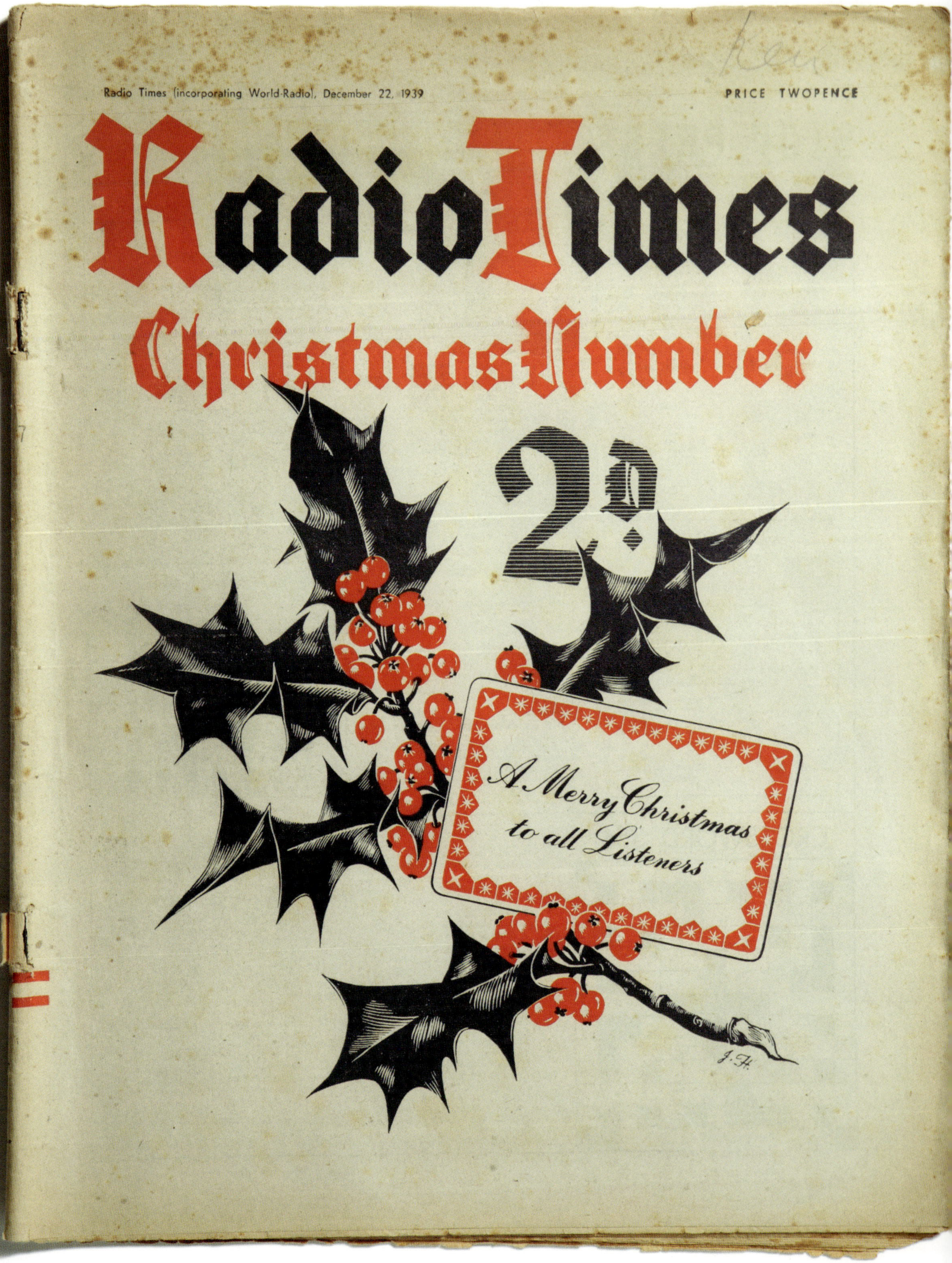
Radio Times (incorporating World-Radio), December 22, 1939
PRICE TWOPENCE
Radio Times
Christmas Number
2d
A Merry Christmas
to all Listeners
J.H.

The BBC at the front *(right)*

26 January 1940

This issue marked the launch of a radio weekly despatch from France by Richard Dimbleby (in the centre of the photograph, wearing an overcoat). Dimbleby had been with the British Expeditionary Force since October 1939 and wrote in his letter to readers: "We hope listeners will agree that so far we have succeeded in acting as some sort of link between the Army here and its families at home."

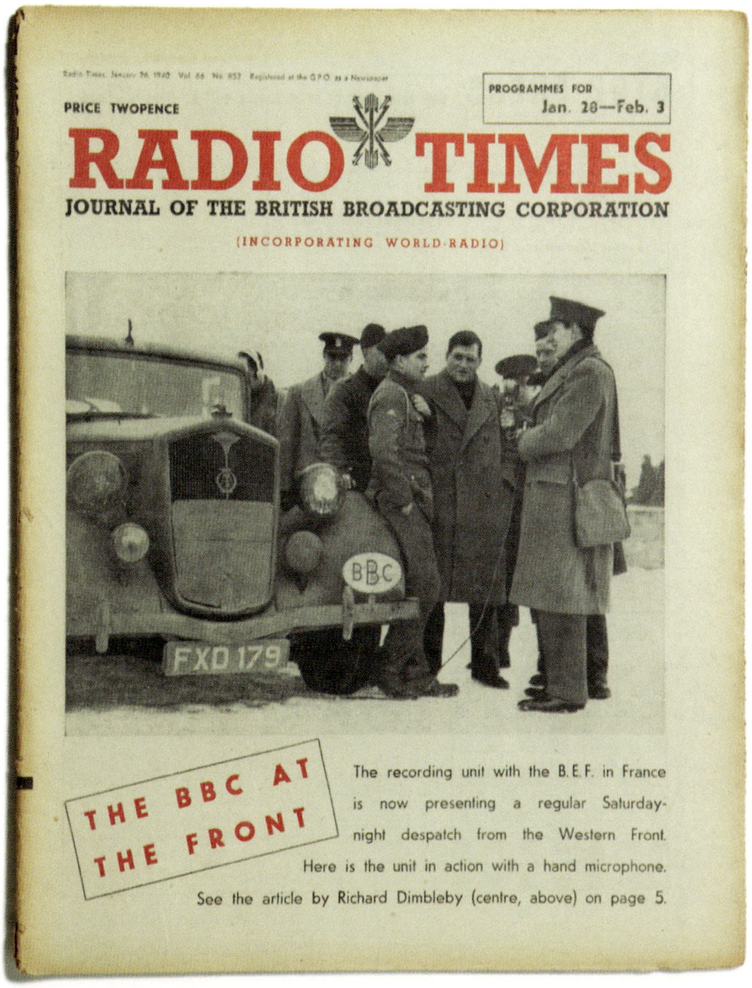
PRICE TWOPENCE

PROGRAMMES FOR Jan. 28—Feb. 3

RADIO TIMES

JOURNAL OF THE BRITISH BROADCASTING CORPORATION

(INCORPORATING WORLD-RADIO)

THE BBC AT THE FRONT

The recording unit with the B.E.F. in France is now presenting a regular Saturday-night despatch from the Western Front. Here is the unit in action with a hand microphone. See the article by Richard Dimbleby (centre, above) on page 5.

Christmas 1939 *(left)*

Illustration by JH

22 December 1939

The first Christmas issue of the Second World War is a morale-boosting exercise in festive bonhomie. AA Thomson's poem *In Spite of All That* appears in place of the usual editorial. It's a gentle exhortation to good humour:

"Things are not as bad as that; let's have it clearly stated,
The spirit of the real thing is not evacuated
In spite of all, I promise you that there will be this year
no black-out of benevolence, no censor of good cheer"

For the Forces *(right)*

Illustration by Clixby Watson

16 February 1940

This issue marked the start of the For the Forces schedule for those serving in the Navy, Army and Air Force, which ran daily for 12 hours a day starting at 11.00am. The new programmes were aimed at squads of "at least half-a-dozen men grouped round one loudspeaker", rather than "a single listener sitting in solitary concentration by his own fireside".

Light-hearted variety, popular music and sport dominated – commentary on the second half of a football match between the French and British armies from Lille was a highlight on 18 February. But the service wasn't just for British troops. The first month's schedules included summaries of the weekend's ice hockey games, especially for Canadians.

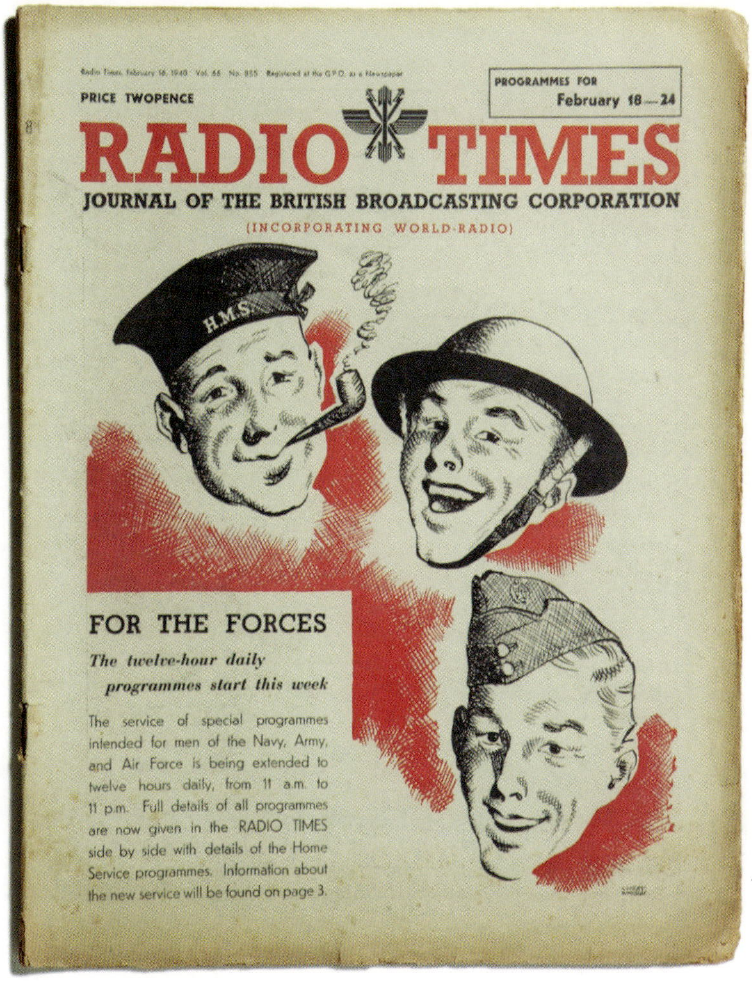
PRICE TWOPENCE

PROGRAMMES FOR February 18—24

RADIO TIMES

JOURNAL OF THE BRITISH BROADCASTING CORPORATION

(INCORPORATING WORLD-RADIO)

FOR THE FORCES

The twelve-hour daily programmes start this week

The service of special programmes intended for men of the Navy, Army, and Air Force is being extended to twelve hours daily, from 11 a.m. to 11 p.m. Full details of all programmes are now given in the RADIO TIMES side by side with details of the Home Service programmes. Information about the new service will be found on page 3.

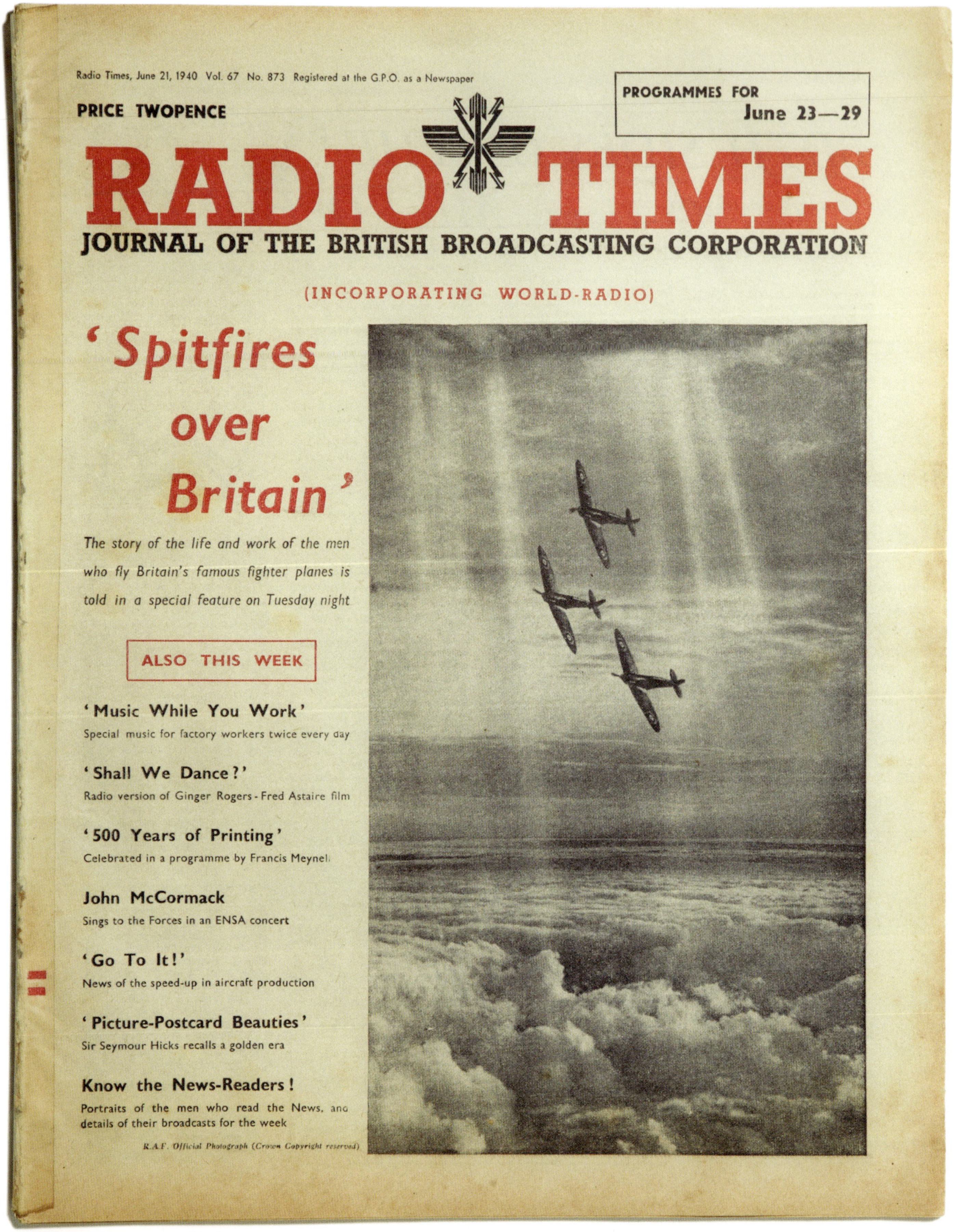

Radio Times, June 21, 1940 Vol. 67 No. 873 Registered at the G.P.O. as a Newspaper

PRICE TWOPENCE

PROGRAMMES FOR
June 23—29

RADIO TIMES

JOURNAL OF THE BRITISH BROADCASTING CORPORATION

(INCORPORATING WORLD-RADIO)

'Spitfires over Britain'

The story of the life and work of the men who fly Britain's famous fighter planes is told in a special feature on Tuesday night

ALSO THIS WEEK

'Music While You Work'
Special music for factory workers twice every day

'Shall We Dance?'
Radio version of Ginger Rogers-Fred Astaire film

'500 Years of Printing'
Celebrated in a programme by Francis Meynell

John McCormack
Sings to the Forces in an ENSA concert

'Go To It!'
News of the speed-up in aircraft production

'Picture-Postcard Beauties'
Sir Seymour Hicks recalls a golden era

Know the News-Readers!
Portraits of the men who read the News, and details of their broadcasts for the week

R.A.F. Official Photograph (Crown Copyright reserved)

Spitfires over Britain *RAF official photograph* *21 June 1940*

This formation of three Spitfires appeared on the cover to draw listeners' attention to *Spitfires over Britain*, a programme that the cover proclaimed would tell "the story of the life and work of the men who fly Britain's famous fighter planes". It was produced by Cecil McGivern, who made several acclaimed radio documentaries during the war years and went on to become director of programmes for the BBC Television Service.

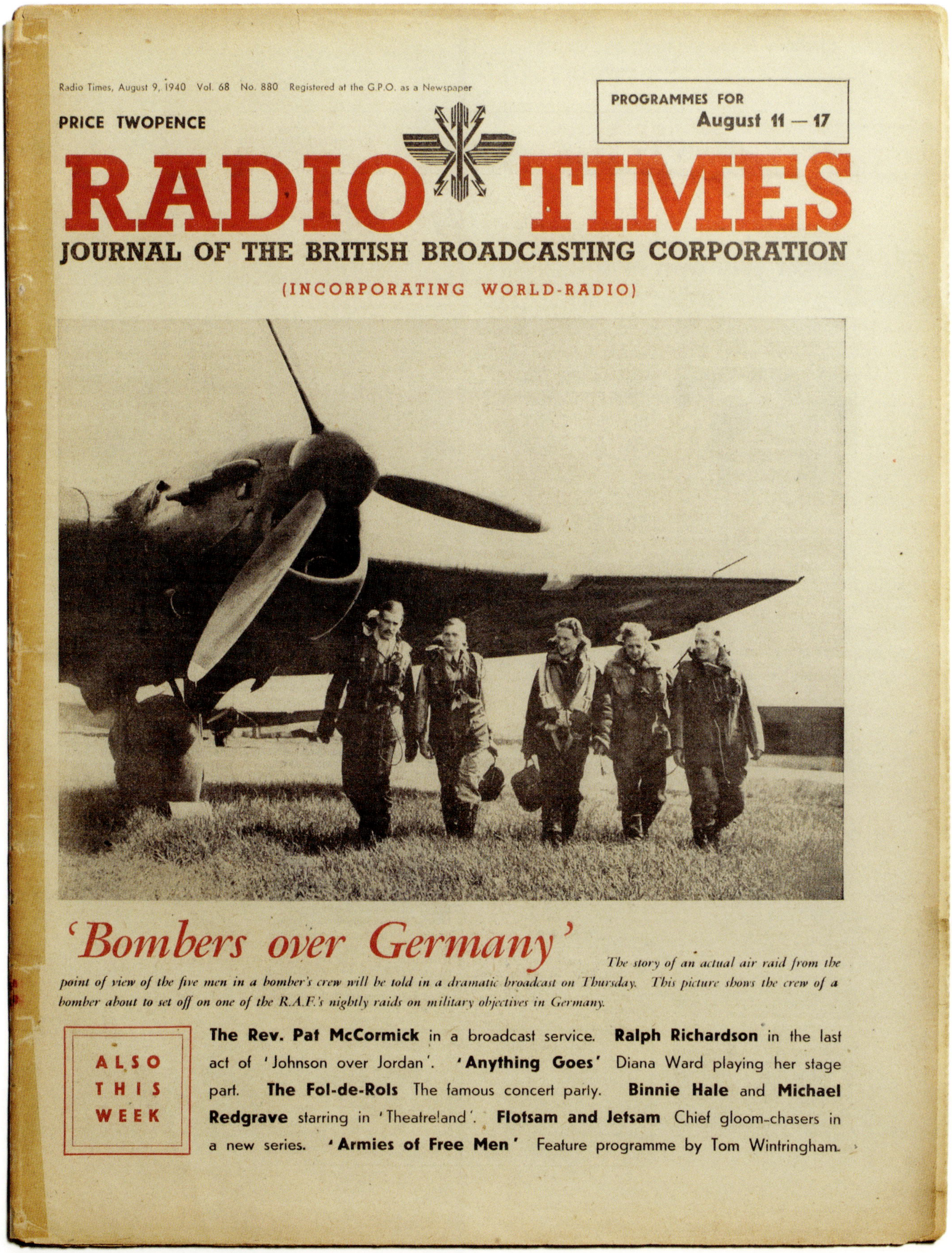

Radio Times, August 9, 1940 Vol. 68 No. 880 Registered at the G.P.O. as a Newspaper

PRICE TWOPENCE

PROGRAMMES FOR
August 11 — 17

RADIO TIMES

JOURNAL OF THE BRITISH BROADCASTING CORPORATION

(INCORPORATING WORLD-RADIO)

'Bombers over Germany' *The story of an actual air raid from the point of view of the five men in a bomber's crew will be told in a dramatic broadcast on Thursday. This picture shows the crew of a bomber about to set off on one of the R.A.F.'s nightly raids on military objectives in Germany.*

ALSO THIS WEEK

The Rev. Pat McCormick in a broadcast service. **Ralph Richardson** in the last act of 'Johnson over Jordan'. **'Anything Goes'** Diana Ward playing her stage part. **The Fol-de-Rols** The famous concert party. **Binnie Hale** and **Michael Redgrave** starring in 'Theatreland'. **Flotsam and Jetsam** Chief gloom-chasers in a new series. **'Armies of Free Men'** Feature programme by Tom Wintringham.

Bombers over Germany *9 August 1940*

Soon after the cover featuring Spitfire pilots (left), this issue shone a light on the role of RAF bomber pilots in *Bombers over Germany*. The billing for the programme, which was again produced by Cecil McGivern, said, "Listeners will be told exactly what happened from the moment the Whitley bombers took off, to the moment they landed after their trip to Bremen." The trip in question was a bombing raid on an oil refinery.

Flanagan and Allen *(right)*

Chesney Flanagan (left) and Bud Allen

24 May 1940

Hugely popular double-act Bud Flanagan and Chesney Allen featured in three programmes this week. All together now: "We're Going to Hang out the Washing on the Siegfried Line..."

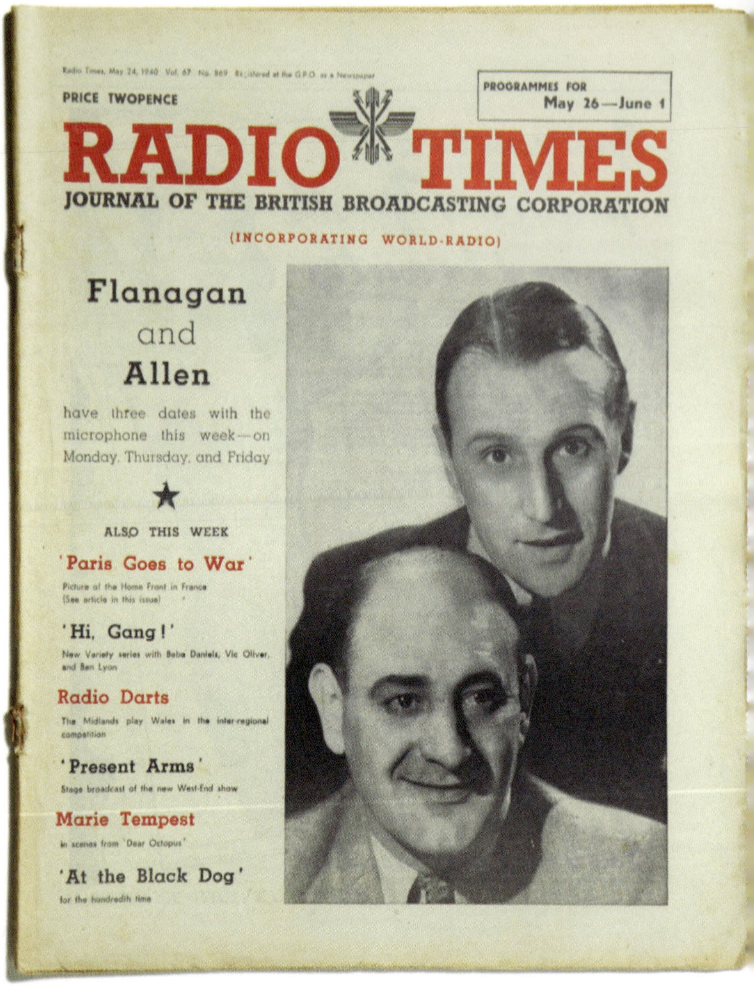

Grow your own food *(below left)*

20 September 1940

Self-sufficiency was an important part of the war effort. The experts for the programme *Backs to the Land* included Cedric Drewe, chairman of the Small Pigkeepers' Council (second right, holding a large piglet), and Alan Thompson, editor of *The Feathered World* (centre, with hen)

Hamlet *(below right)*

John Gielgud *4 October 1940*

Radio Drama Week was launched with John Gielgud's *Hamlet* the star attraction. The privations of war had led to the closure of theatres and cinemas so, as an article inside said, "This, heaven knows, is a moment when we need broadcast drama."

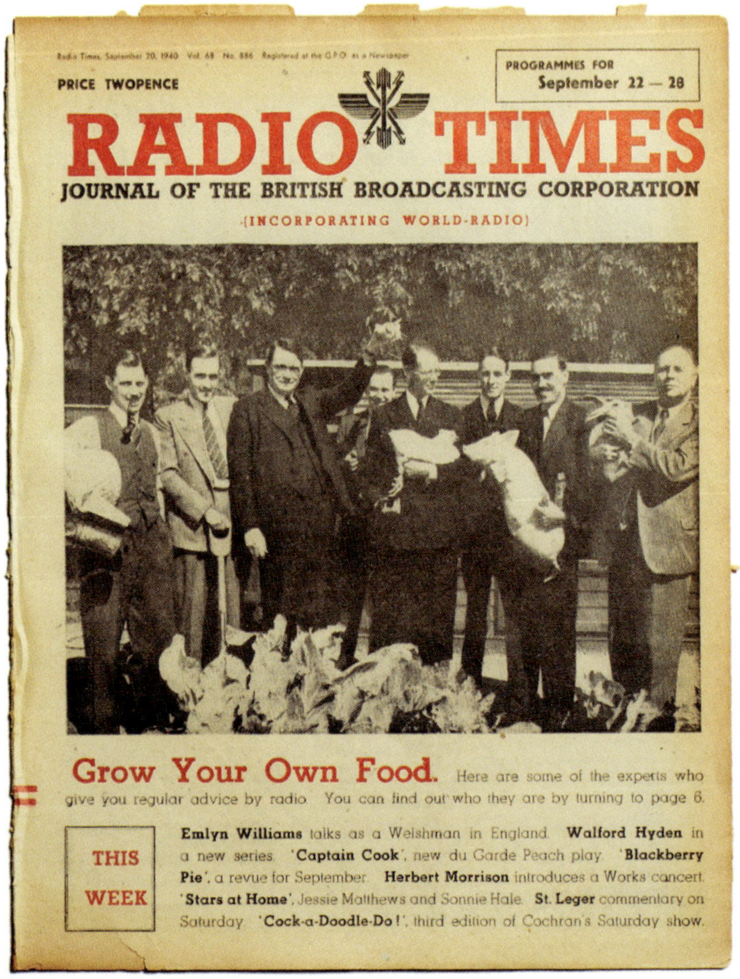

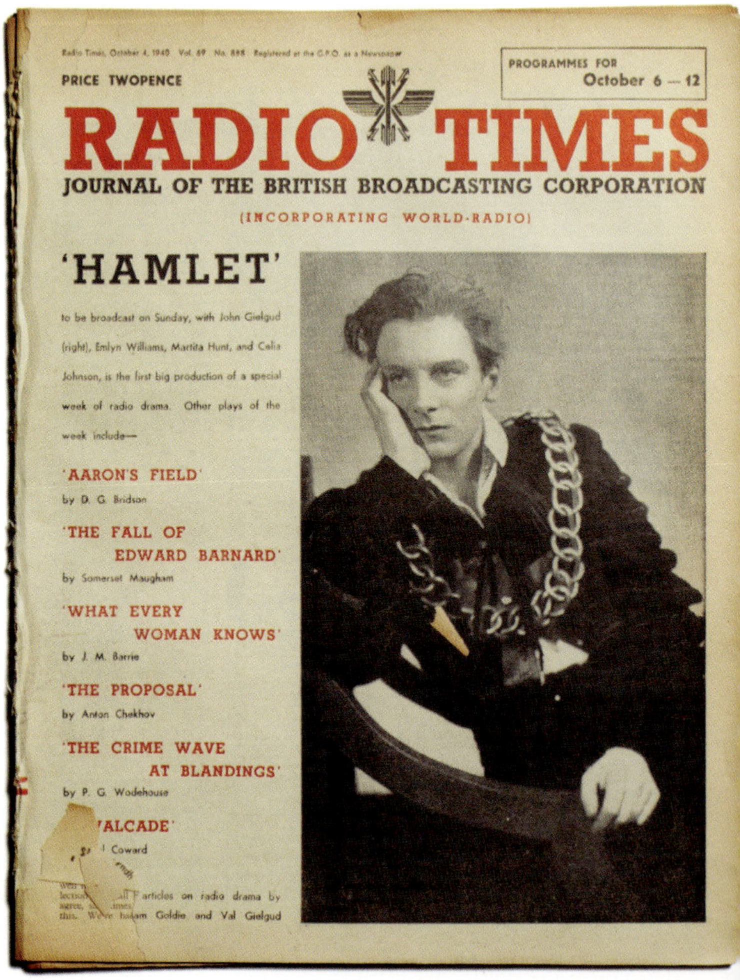

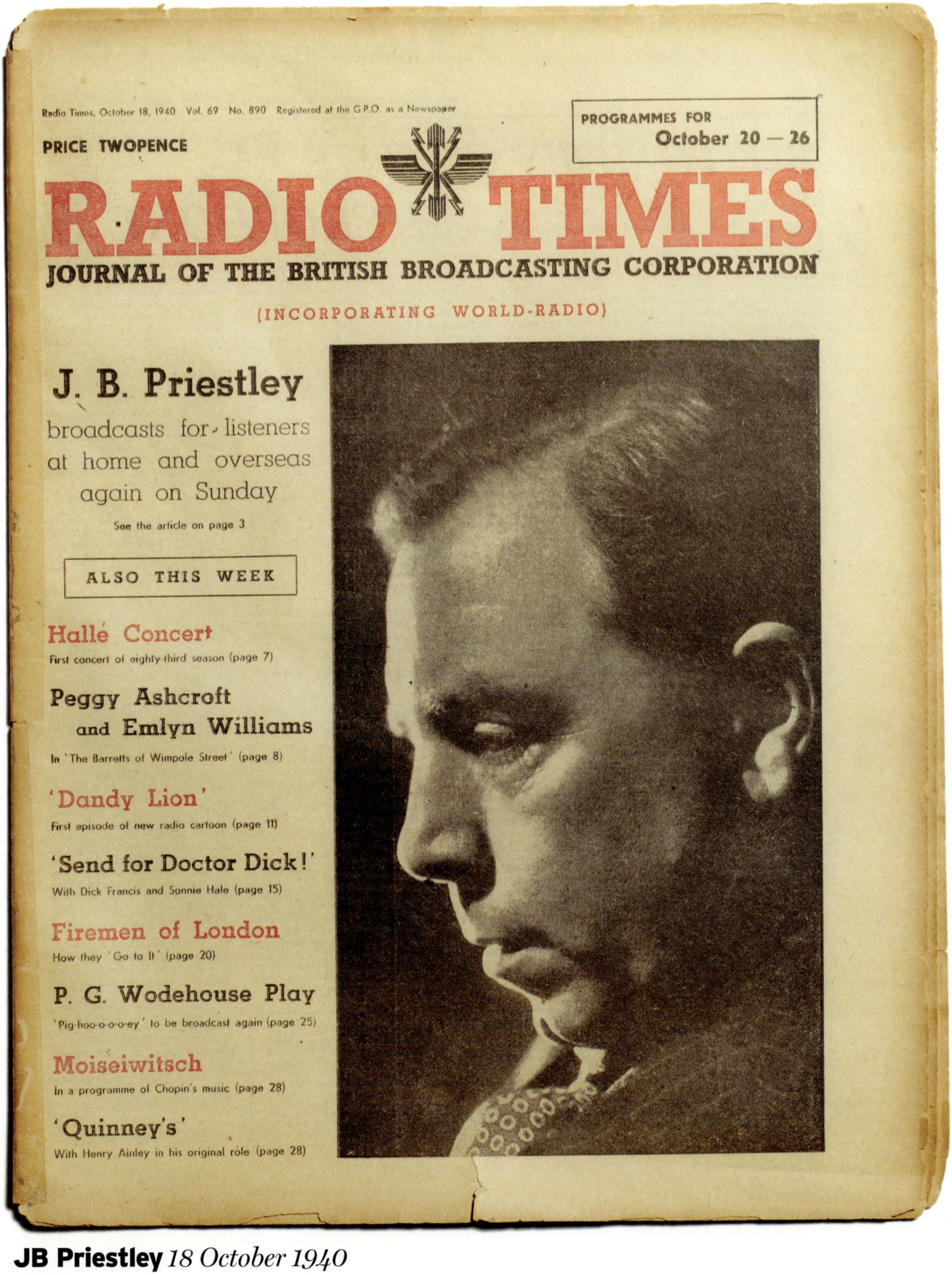

Radio Times, October 18, 1940 Vol. 69 No. 890 Registered at the G.P.O. as a Newspaper

PRICE TWOPENCE

PROGRAMMES FOR October 20 — 26

RADIO TIMES

JOURNAL OF THE BRITISH BROADCASTING CORPORATION

(INCORPORATING WORLD-RADIO)

J. B. Priestley

broadcasts for listeners at home and overseas again on Sunday

See the article on page 3

ALSO THIS WEEK

Hallé Concert

First concert of eighty-third season (page 7)

Peggy Ashcroft and Emlyn Williams

In 'The Barretts of Wimpole Street' (page 8)

'Dandy Lion'

First episode of new radio cartoon (page 11)

'Send for Doctor Dick!'

With Dick Francis and Sonnie Hale (page 15)

Firemen of London

How they 'Go to It' (page 20)

P. G. Wodehouse Play

'Pig-hoo-o-o-o-ey' to be broadcast again (page 25)

Moiseiwitsch

In a programme of Chopin's music (page 28)

'Quinney's'

With Henry Ainley in his original rôle (page 28)

JB Priestley *18 October 1940*

A leading cultural figure of the time and a regular broadcaster on the BBC during the war, novelist and playwright JB Priestley's weekly programme *Postscript* attracted up to 16 million listeners in 1940 and 1941. His broadcasts were also very popular on the other side of the Atlantic, describing wartime London to a rapt audience.

“How to bring Britain to its knees?… Destroy Radio Times!”

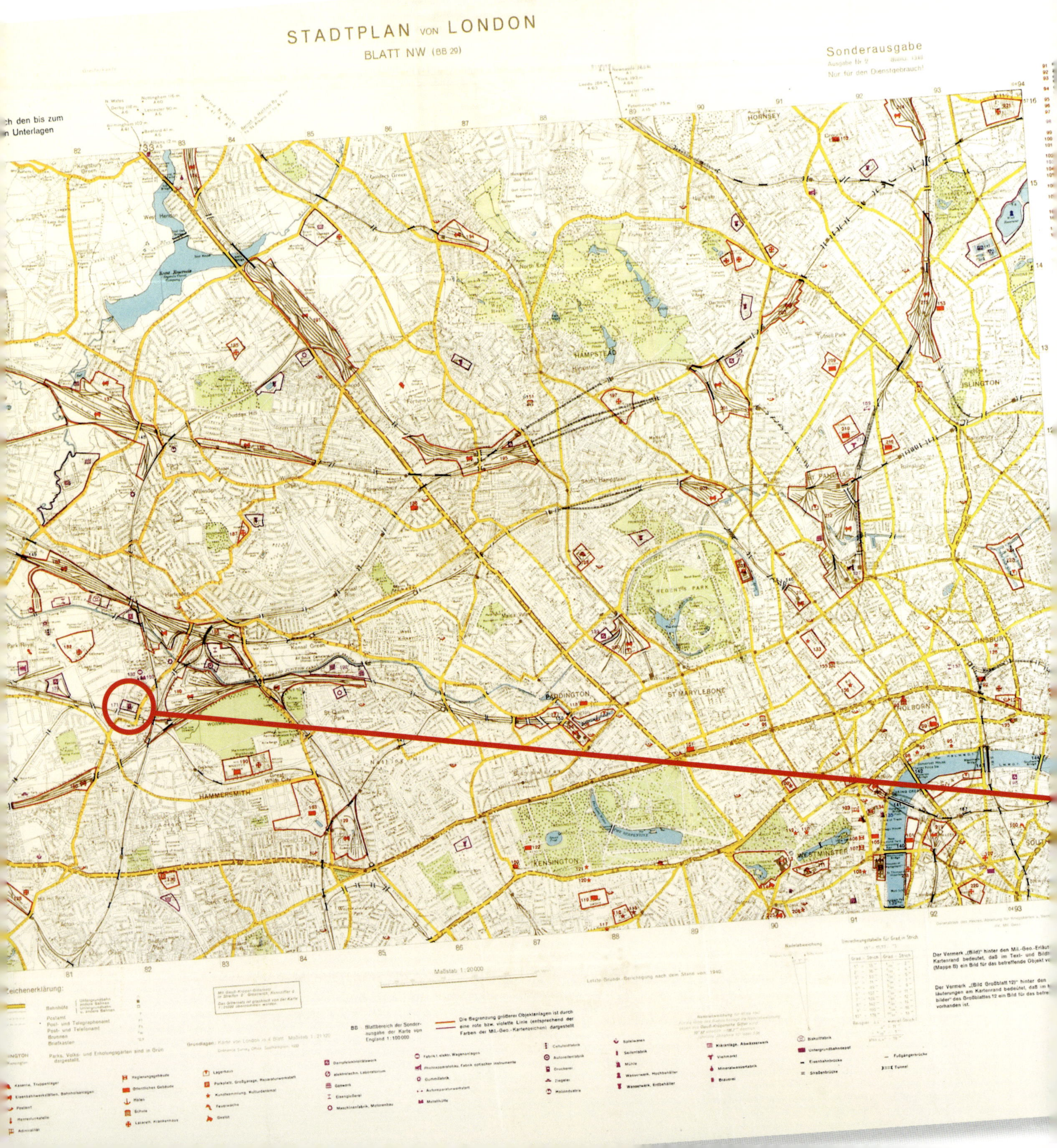

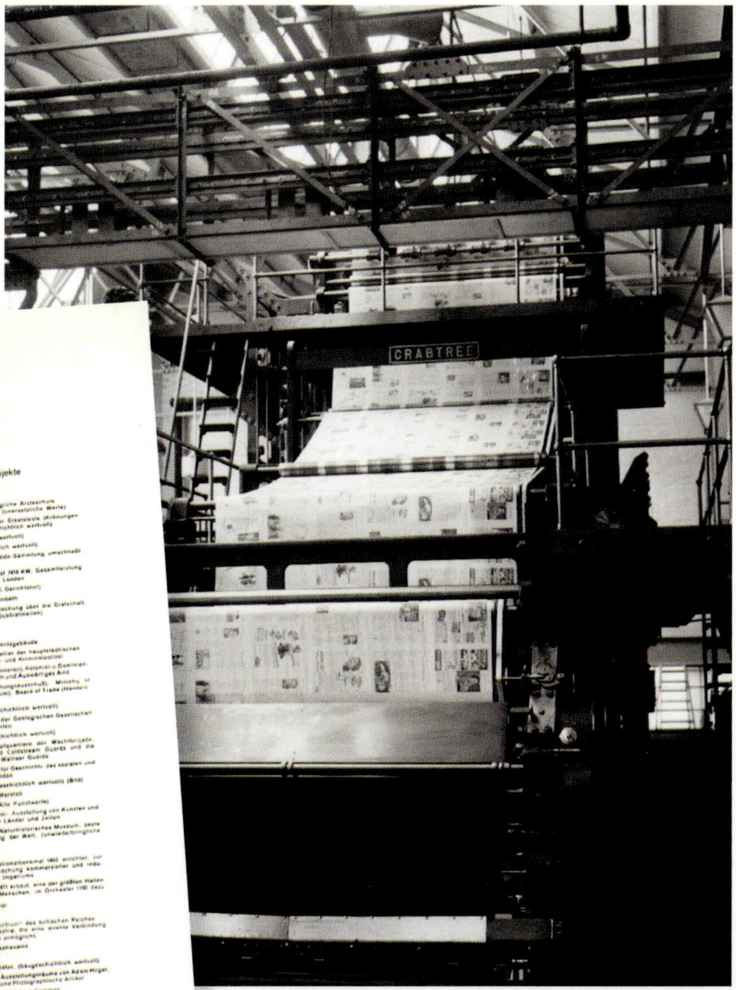

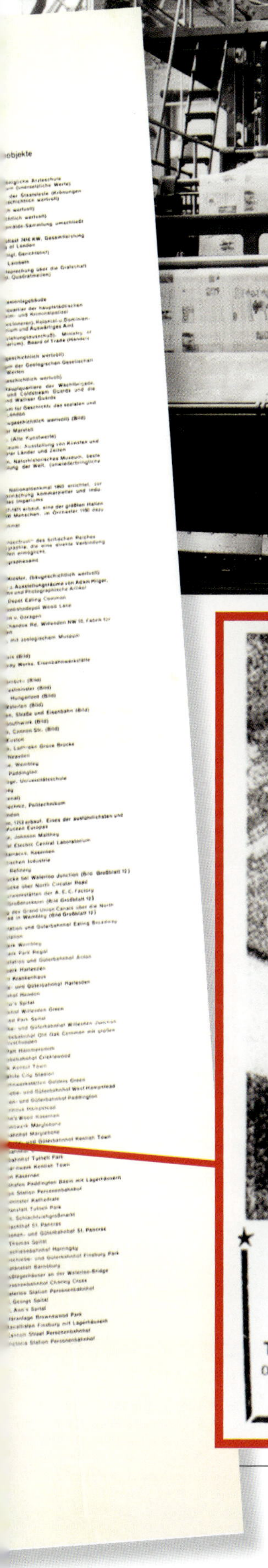

When war was declared on 3 September 1939, the BBC moved its operations from Broadcasting House in central London to Wood Norton near Evesham in Worcestershire. *Radio Times* followed suit. While the editor Maurice Gorham remained at Broadcasting House, staff were evacuated to what was felt to be the relative safety of the Waterlows print works at Park Royal in north-west London.

Little did the BBC know that the Luftwaffe had already earmarked the *Radio Times* print site as a potential target. This was confirmed after the war when maps and photographs identifying Waterlows were found at Luftwaffe headquarters in Berlin. The Germans would have known all about the importance of the BBC to the British war effort and to morale in the event of war, and the embassy staff in London would have explained the part *Radio Times* played in that. So while they couldn't bomb the BBC off the air, the Germans could certainly try to deprive the British of *Radio Times*.

Production of the magazine became hazardous during the Blitz, and Gorham was visiting the plant when German bombers struck. He wrote, "We were nearly all of us in the trench shelters when Waterlows was bombed. Two of the canteen staff were not, and I had the experience I had always imagined and never really expected – running out to give a hand with the casualties and then returning to the shelter and going on passing the page proofs."

The Luftwaffe *Stadtplan*, far left, and German aerial photograph, below, showing Waterlows, the printing works specially built for the production of *Radio Times*, left.

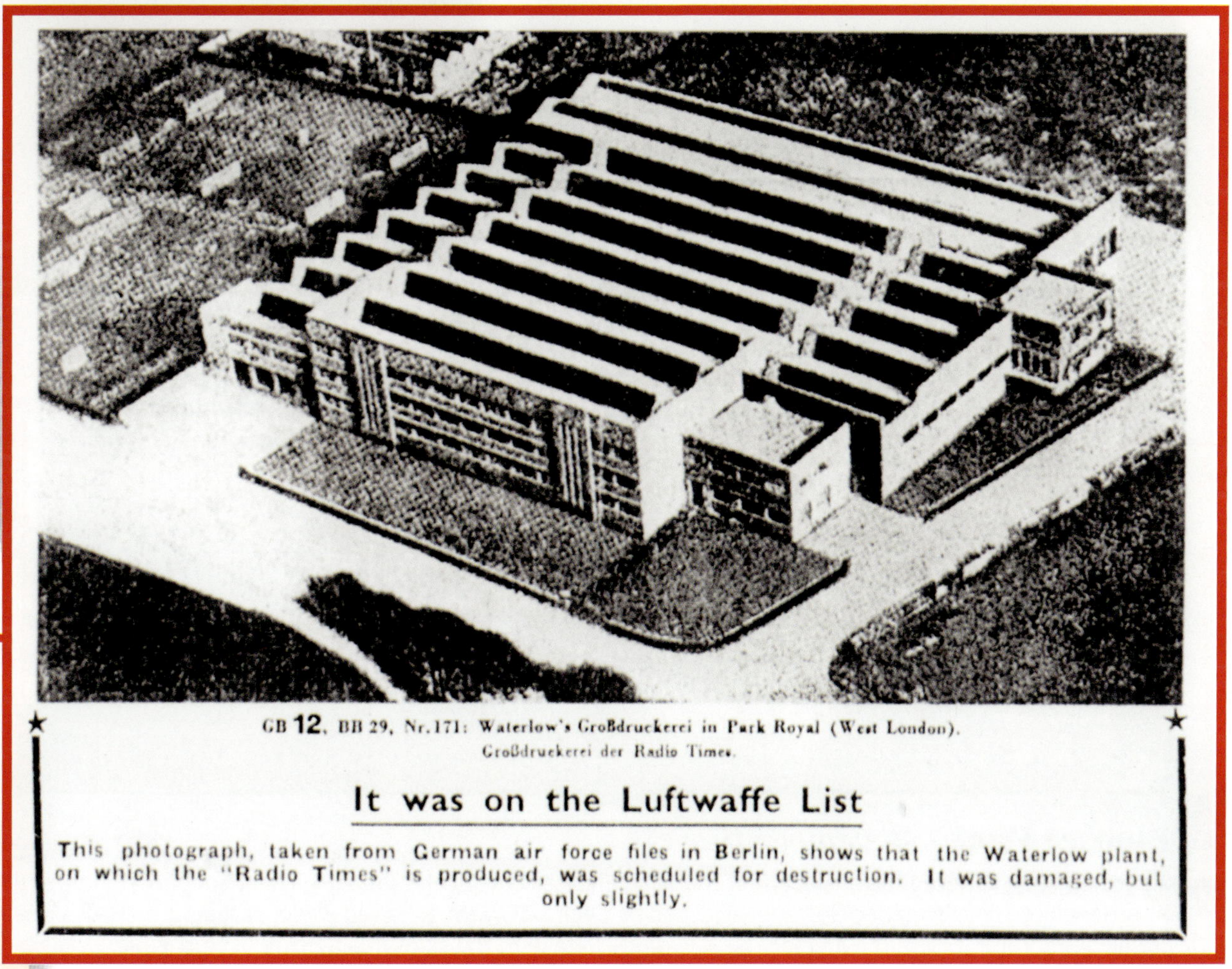

GB 12, BB 29, Nr. 171: Waterlow's Großdruckerei in Park Royal (West London).
Großdruckerei der Radio Times.

It was on the Luftwaffe List

This photograph, taken from German air force files in Berlin, shows that the Waterlow plant, on which the "Radio Times" is produced, was scheduled for destruction. It was damaged, but only slightly.

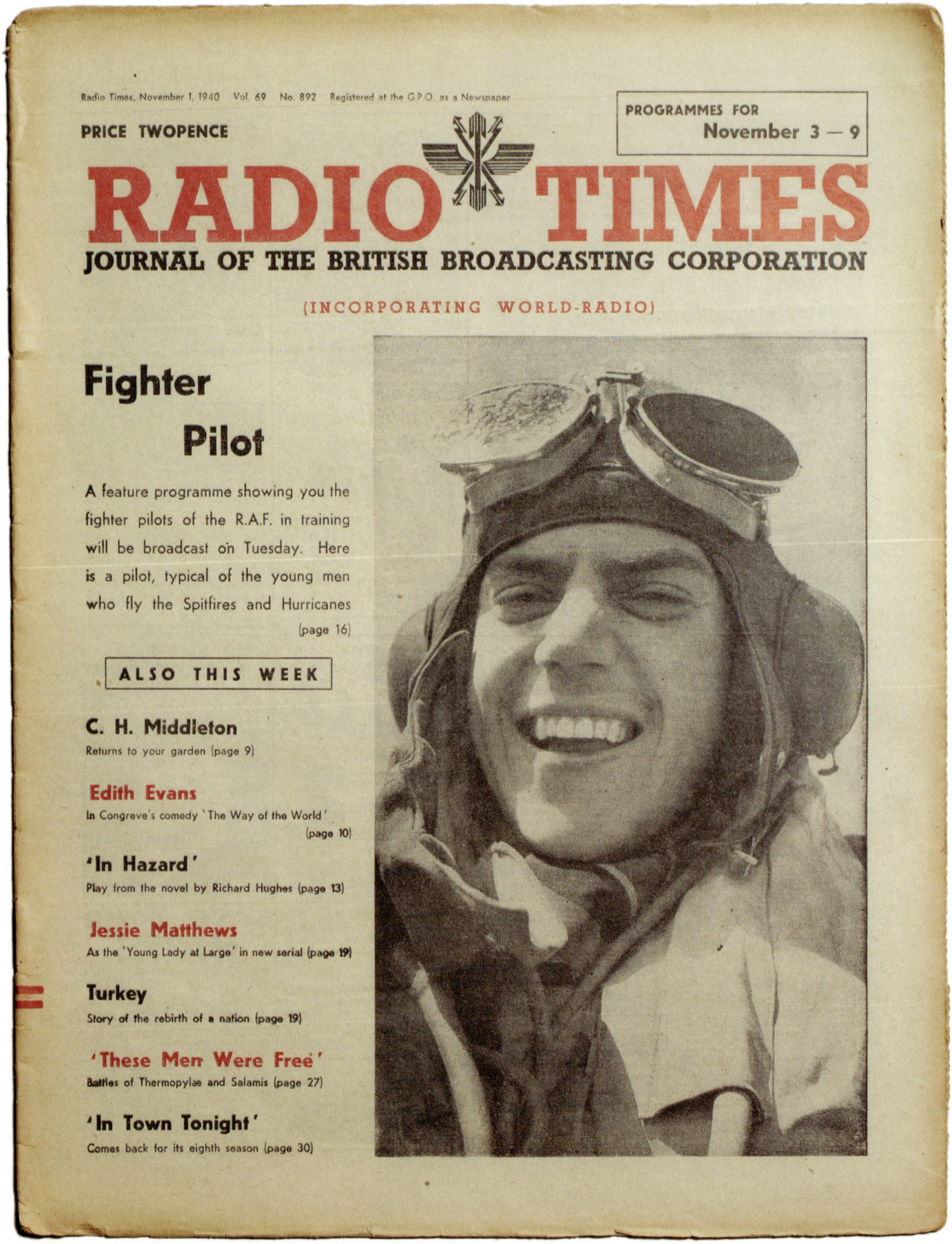

Radio Times, November 1, 1940 Vol. 69 No. 892 Registered at the G.P.O. as a Newspaper

PRICE TWOPENCE

PROGRAMMES FOR
November 3 — 9

RADIO TIMES

JOURNAL OF THE BRITISH BROADCASTING CORPORATION

(INCORPORATING WORLD-RADIO)

Fighter Pilot

A feature programme showing you the fighter pilots of the R.A.F. in training will be broadcast on Tuesday. Here is a pilot, typical of the young men who fly the Spitfires and Hurricanes (page 16)

ALSO THIS WEEK

C. H. Middleton
Returns to your garden (page 9)

Edith Evans
In Congreve's comedy 'The Way of the World' (page 10)

'In Hazard'
Play from the novel by Richard Hughes (page 13)

Jessie Matthews
As the 'Young Lady at Large' in new serial (page 19)

Turkey
Story of the rebirth of a nation (page 19)

'These Men Were Free'
Battles of Thermopylae and Salamis (page 27)

'In Town Tonight'
Comes back for its eighth season (page 30)

Fighter Pilot *1 November 1940*

As the country suffered the onslaught of the Blitz, another cover celebrating the heroism of RAF fighter pilots. The 30-minute broadcast, written and produced by Cecil McGivern, followed a pilot through the RAF's intensive training programme until the moment he was ready to take to the skies in a Spitfire or Hurricane.

Christmas 1941 *(right)*

19 December 1941

There was a sober, religious tone to this truncated festive edition. The editorial read: "There can be no fat Christmas Number this year... No need to stress the obvious fact that Christmas 1941 will be, in a material sense, only a shadow of the Christmases most of us have known."

BBC news map *(below left)*

5 March 1943

Radio Times provided a reference map on the cover to enable listeners to keep abreast of news bulletins from the Eastern Front. "Keep it near your set," urged the coverline.

BBC news map No. 3 *(below right)*

8 October 1943

Following the Allied invasion of Italy, another map appeared to help listeners follow events. Inside, an advert from the Cake & Biscuit Manufacturers Wartime Alliance celebrated the importance of cake to a nation at war – but noted, "Supplies are limited, so don't buy more than your fair share."

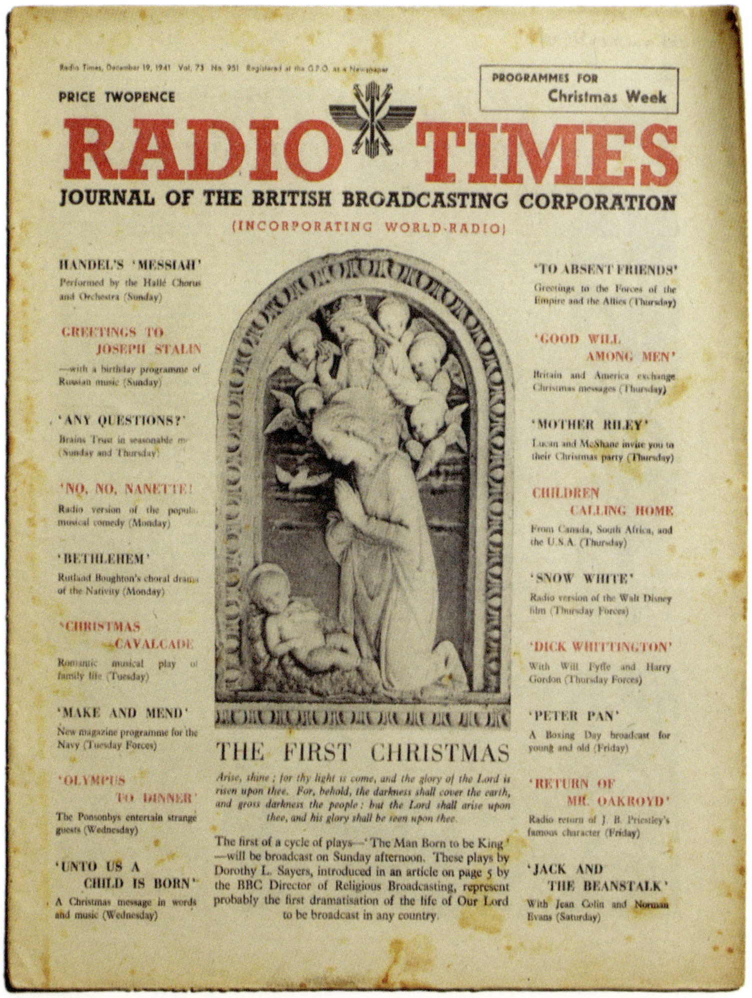

Radio Times, December 19, 1941 Vol. 73 No. 951 Registered at the G.P.O. as a Newspaper

PRICE TWOPENCE

PROGRAMMES FOR Christmas Week

RADIO TIMES

JOURNAL OF THE BRITISH BROADCASTING CORPORATION

(INCORPORATING WORLD-RADIO)

HANDEL'S 'MESSIAH'
Performed by the Hallé Chorus and Orchestra (Sunday)

GREETINGS TO JOSEPH STALIN
—with a birthday programme of Russian music (Sunday)

'ANY QUESTIONS?'
Brains Trust in seasonable m— (Sunday and Thursday)

'NO, NO, NANETTE!'
Radio version of the popula— musical comedy (Monday)

'BETHLEHEM'
Rutland Boughton's choral dram— of the Nativity (Monday)

'CHRISTMAS CAVALCADE'
Romantic musical play of family life (Tuesday)

'MAKE AND MEND'
New magazine programme for the Navy (Tuesday Forces)

'OLYMPUS TO DINNER'
The Ponsonbys entertain strange guests (Wednesday)

'UNTO US A CHILD IS BORN'
A Christmas message in words and music (Wednesday)

THE FIRST CHRISTMAS

Arise, shine ; for thy light is come, and the glory of the Lord is risen upon thee. For, behold, the darkness shall cover the earth, and gross darkness the people : but the Lord shall arise upon thee, and his glory shall be seen upon thee.

The first of a cycle of plays—'The Man Born to be King'—will be broadcast on Sunday afternoon. These plays by Dorothy L. Sayers, introduced in an article on page 5 by the BBC Director of Religious Broadcasting, represent probably the first dramatisation of the life of Our Lord to be broadcast in any country.

'TO ABSENT FRIENDS'
Greetings to the Forces of the Empire and the Allies (Thursday)

'GOOD WILL AMONG MEN'
Britain and America exchange Christmas messages (Thursday)

'MOTHER RILEY'
Lucan and McShane invite you to their Christmas party (Thursday)

CHILDREN CALLING HOME
From Canada, South Africa, and the U.S.A. (Thursday)

'SNOW WHITE'
Radio version of the Walt Disney film (Thursday Forces)

'DICK WHITTINGTON'
With Will Fyffe and Harry Gordon (Thursday Forces)

'PETER PAN'
A Boxing Day broadcast for young and old (Friday)

'RETURN OF MR. OAKROYD'
Radio return of J. B. Priestley's famous character (Friday)

'JACK AND THE BEANSTALK'
With Jean Colin and Norman Evans (Saturday)

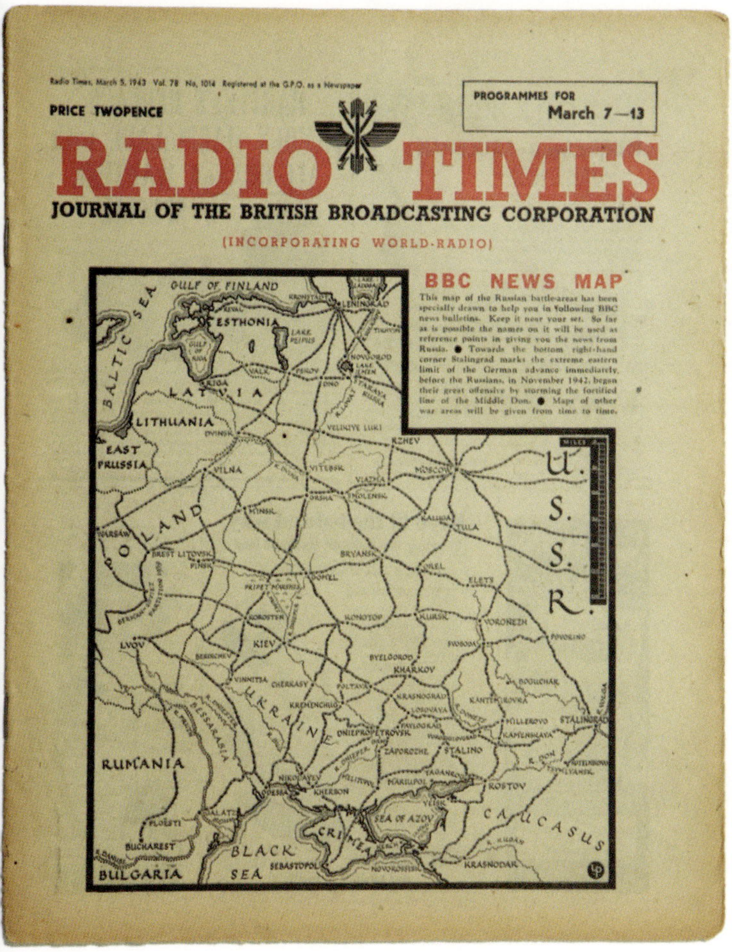

PRICE TWOPENCE

PROGRAMMES FOR March 7—13

RADIO TIMES

JOURNAL OF THE BRITISH BROADCASTING CORPORATION

(INCORPORATING WORLD-RADIO)

BBC NEWS MAP

This map of the Russian battle-areas has been specially drawn to help you in following BBC news bulletins. Keep it near your set. So far as is possible the names on it will be used as reference points in giving you the news from Russia. ● Towards the bottom right-hand corner Stalingrad marks the extreme eastern limit of the German advance immediately before the Russians, in November 1942, began their great offensive by storming the fortified line of the Middle Don. ● Maps of other war areas will be given from time to time.

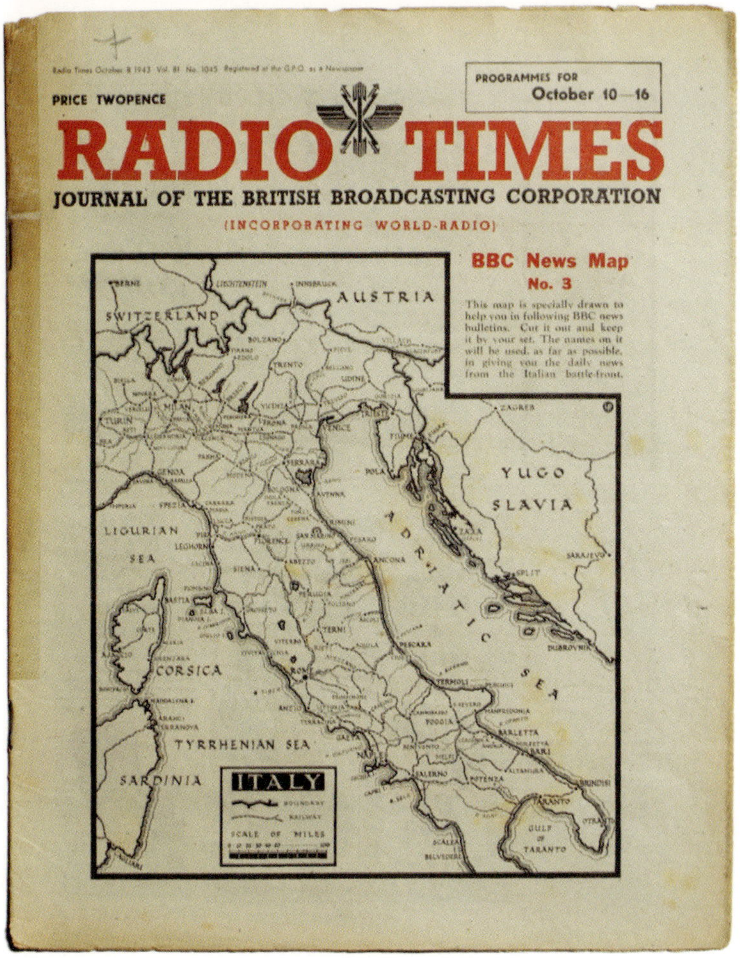

PRICE TWOPENCE

PROGRAMMES FOR October 10—16

RADIO TIMES

JOURNAL OF THE BRITISH BROADCASTING CORPORATION

(INCORPORATING WORLD-RADIO)

BBC News Map
No. 3

This map is specially drawn to help you in following BBC news bulletins. Cut it out and keep it by your set. The names on it will be used, as far as possible, in giving you the daily news from the Italian battle-front.

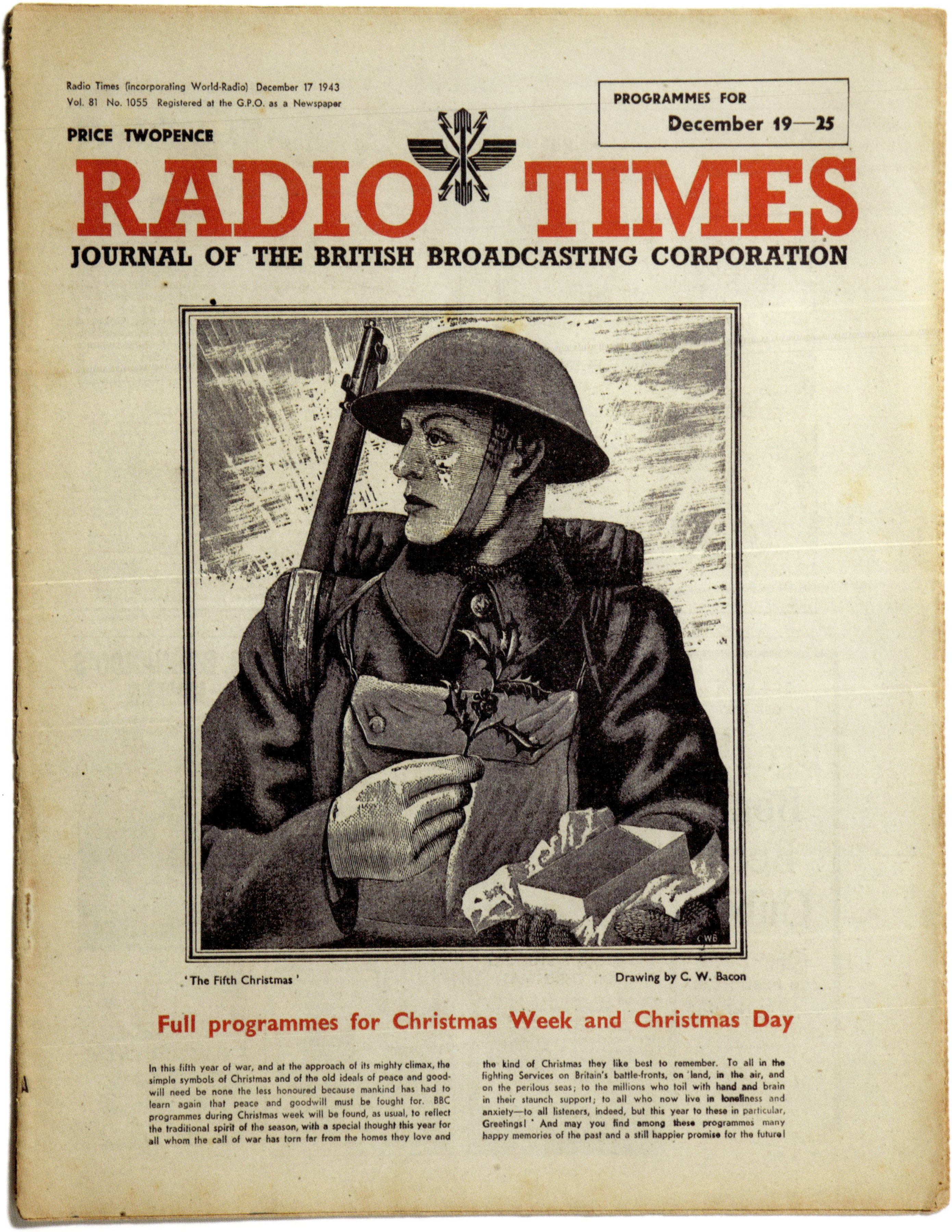

Radio Times (incorporating World-Radio) December 17 1943
Vol. 81 No. 1055 Registered at the G.P.O. as a Newspaper

PRICE TWOPENCE

PROGRAMMES FOR
December 19—25

RADIO TIMES
JOURNAL OF THE BRITISH BROADCASTING CORPORATION

'The Fifth Christmas' — Drawing by C. W. Bacon

Full programmes for Christmas Week and Christmas Day

In this fifth year of war, and at the approach of its mighty climax, the simple symbols of Christmas and of the old ideals of peace and goodwill need be none the less honoured because mankind has had to learn again that peace and goodwill must be fought for. BBC programmes during Christmas week will be found, as usual, to reflect the traditional spirit of the season, with a special thought this year for all whom the call of war has torn far from the homes they love and the kind of Christmas they like best to remember. To all in the fighting Services on Britain's battle-fronts, on land, in the air, and on the perilous seas; to the millions who toil with hand and brain in their staunch support; to all who now live in loneliness and anxiety—to all listeners, indeed, but this year to these in particular, Greetings! And may you find among these programmes many happy memories of the past and a still happier promise for the future!

Christmas 1943 **Illustration by Cecil W Bacon** *17 December 1943*

As the war dragged on, an appropriately sombre Christmas edition. But the message of the centrepiece broadcast on Christmas Day was: "We are advancing towards victory, towards understanding." Meanwhile, Mrs E Holmes of Bradford wrote to complain about an episode of *Kitchen Front*, where "a mere man" advised housewives on how to grill a steak. "We would be more grateful if we were told how to procure one," said Mrs Holmes.

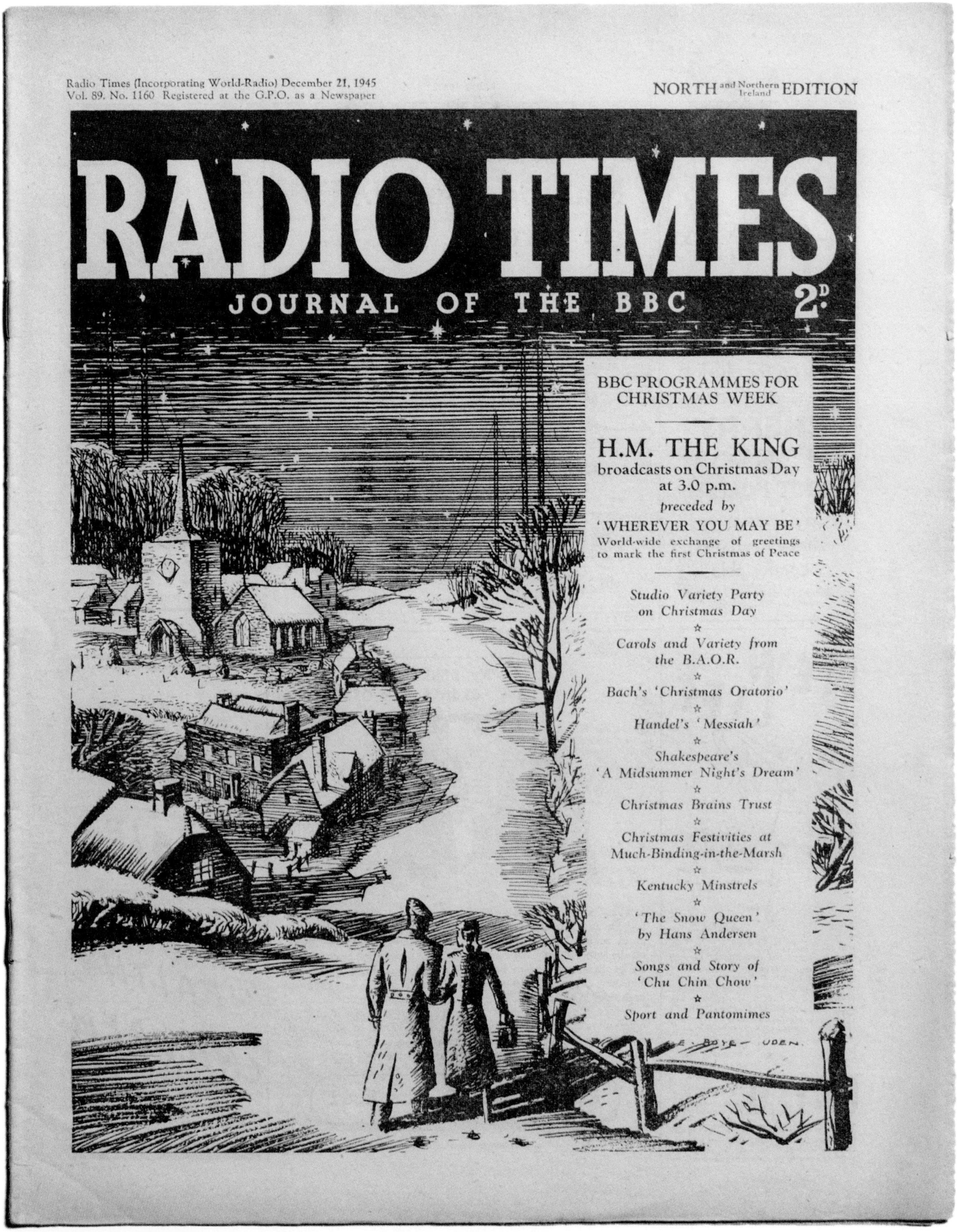

Christmas 1945 **Illustration by Ernest Boye Uden** *21 December 1945*

War was over, but hardships continued – as reflected in JB Priestley's Christmas message: "Let us face the fact that in some ways this first post-war Christmas will seem less satisfactory than some of our war Christmases... we shall naturally expect more, and are therefore more likely to be disappointed." The simple, monochrome cover was by Ernest Boye Uden, an official war artist who later produced artwork for the likes of Daimler, Dunlop and ICI.

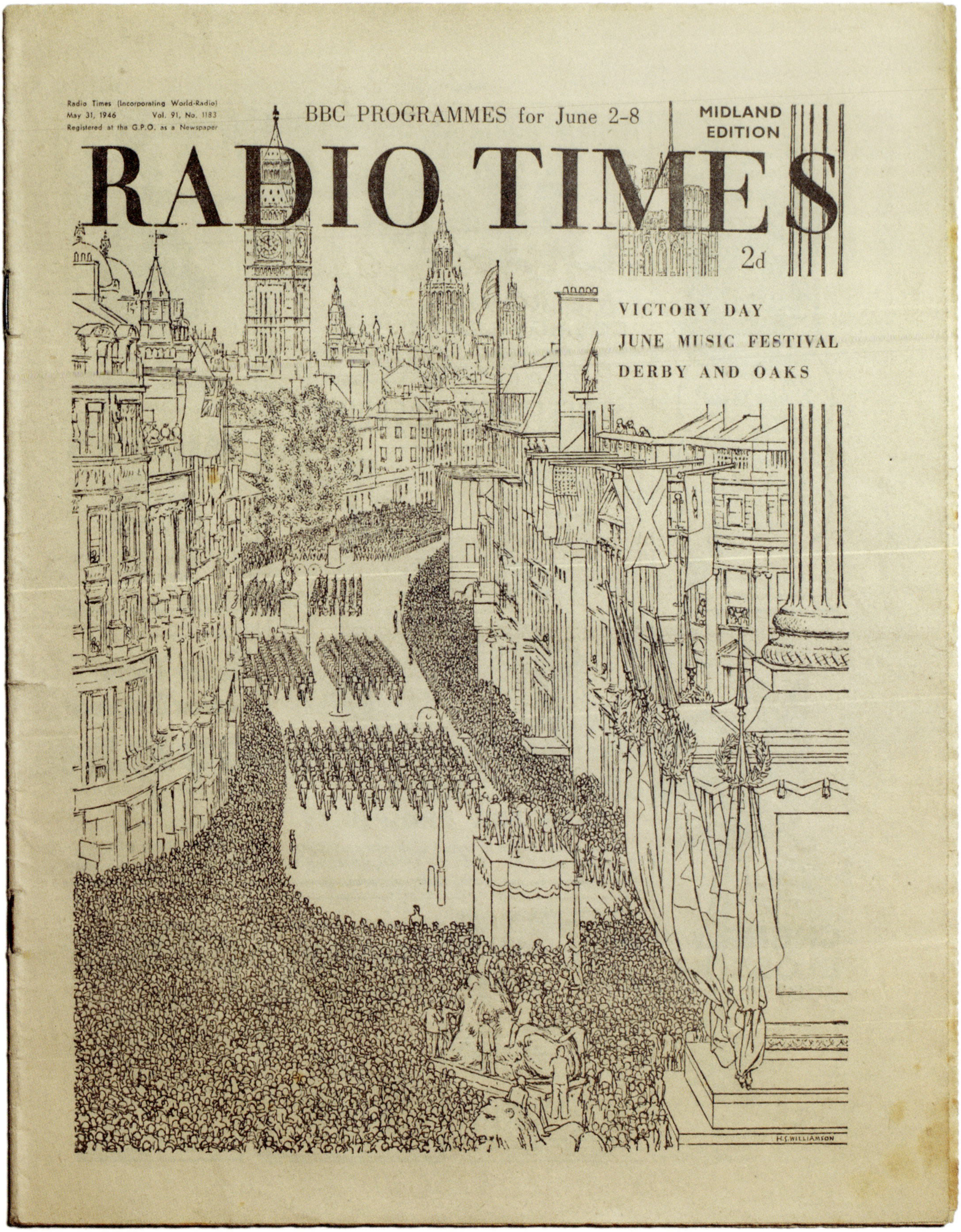

Victory Day Parade **Illustration by Harold S Williamson** *31 May 1946*

The official celebration of victory in the Second World War saw a four-mile procession comprising 20,000 troops and 18 marching bands take to the streets of London, while in the sky above there was a fly-past by 34 squadrons. For the first time since the beginning of the war BBC Television resumed broadcasting, with Richard Dimbleby stationed in the Mall, adding "his word-pictures to the televised impression of the march-past".

British Zone *(right)*
Photograph by Crown Film Unit

12 July 1946

It may have been summer 1946 but the war still featured heavily on BBC radio. The documentary *British Zone* was about the BAOR (the British Army of the Rhine) helping to rebuild postwar Germany. Reporter Robert Barr told stories of hunger and suffering: a family of seven living in a one-room cellar; and graveyards that had been turned into allotments.

A London garden *(below left)*

2 August 1946

Monkey-puzzle or rhododendrons? That was the question posed by Geoffrey Grigson, the man behind the Home Service programme *The English Garden*. The owners of the garden on the cover had neither, but nonetheless had created their own Eden outside their pre-fab in Lambeth, south London.

Christmas 1946 *(below right)*
Illustration by John S Goodall

20 December 1946

The war was long over, but in his message, the Archbishop of York urged readers: "Do not forget those millions across the channel, both who were allies and our foes, who are now near starvation and many of whom are homeless." The cover was by John Goodall, who illustrated Dora Saint's *Miss Read* series of books in the 1950s.

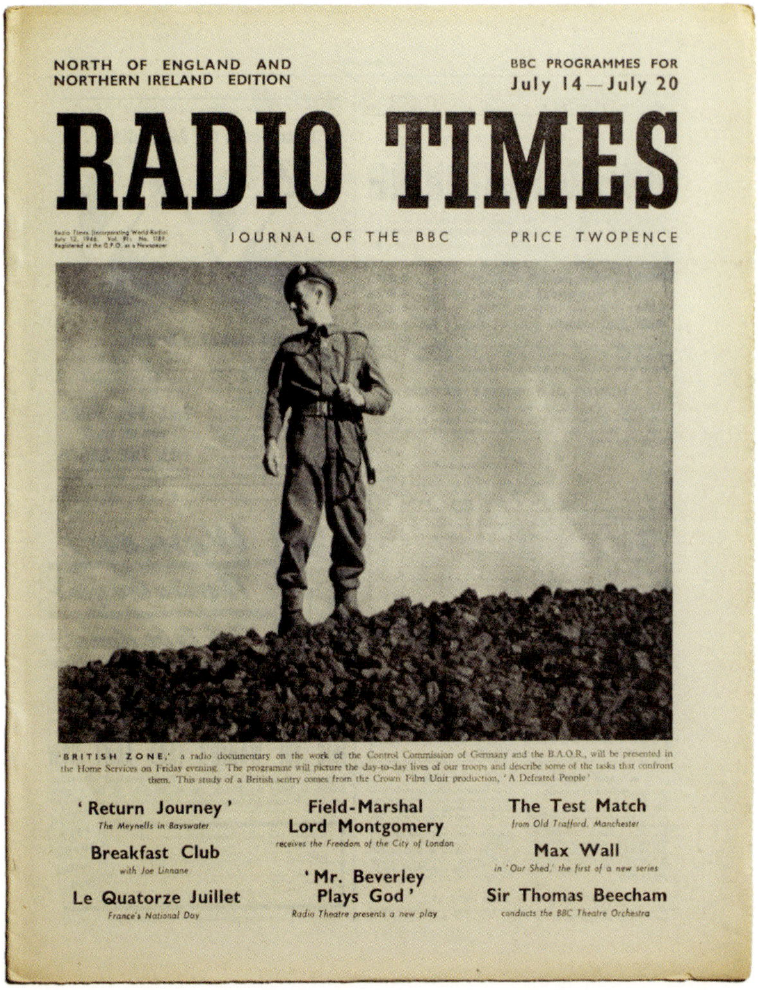

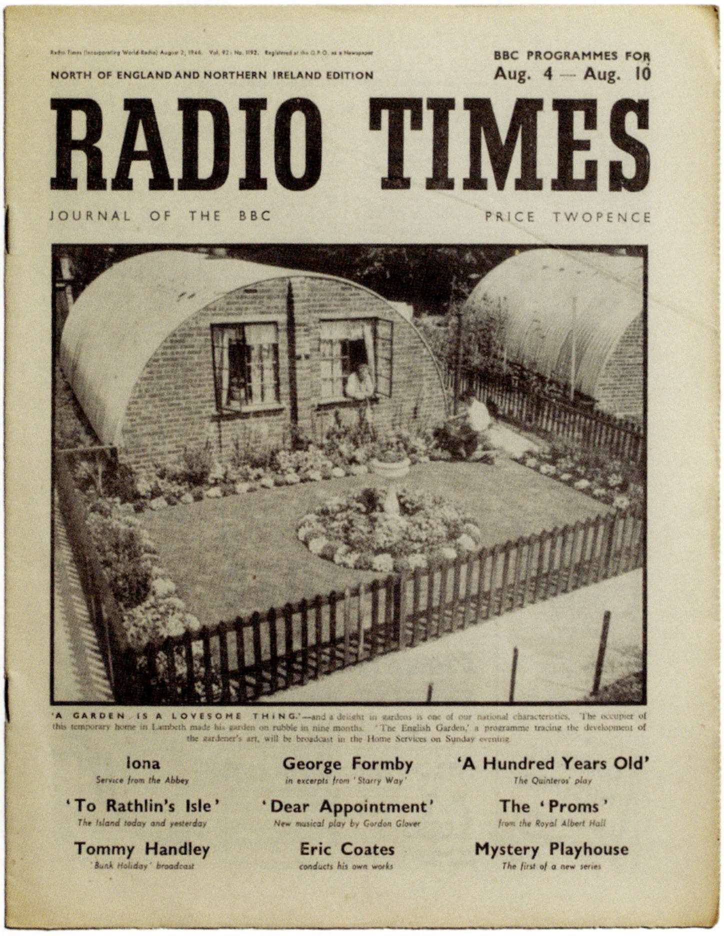

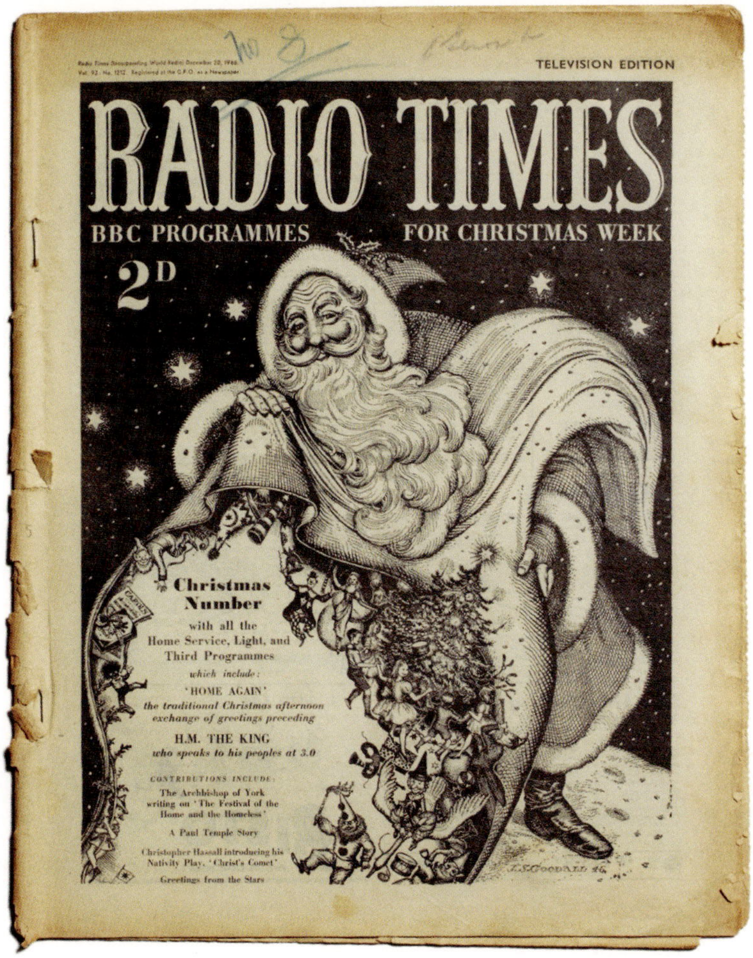

CHRISTMAS

Robin Jacques

Scottish Home Service

371 m. (809 kc/s) VHF: Kirk o' Shotts 94.3: Meldrum 93.1 Mc/s

6.55 The Weather
Forecast for land areas

7.0 Big Ben
O come, all ye faithful
NEWS

7.10 **Programme Parade**

7.15 MORNING MUSIC
See Light Programme

7.40 MARKET TRENDS
(BBC recording)

7.50 LIFT UP YOUR HEARTS
An anthology
of readings and carols by
Olive Gregg and choir of the
Royal School of Church Music

7.55 The Weather
Forecast for land areas

8.0 Greenwich Time Signal
O come, all ye faithful
NEWS

8.10 **Programme Parade**

8.15 'BORN THIS JOYFUL MORNING'
Alexander Young (tenor)
and the BBC Midland Chorus
sing favourite
Christmas hymns and carols
accompanied by the
BBC Midland Light Orchestra
Conducted by John Lowe
Reader, Anthony Jacobs
(BBC recording)

9.0 Greenwich Time Signal
NEWS

9.10 CHRISTMAS STOCKINGS
Brian Johnston visits 'the Jones family' at Dr. Barnardo's Home, Woodford Bridge, near London, and watches the children as they open their presents and Christmas stockings

9.20 CHRISTMAS BELLS
Greetings from the Parish Church of St. George, Doncaster; St. Andrew's, Plymouth; St. Mark's, Dundela, Belfast; St. Peter's Colchester; the West Church of St. Nicholas, Aberdeen; St. Mary's, Brecon; the Parish Church of St. Edburgha, Yardley, Birmingham; and the recorded bells of the Church of the Nativity at Bethlehem
See page 6

9.30 'O COME, LET US ADORE HIM'
A Service
for Christmas Morning
Children in Dunforth Home, Newhaven, Edinburgh, listen again to the Christmas story, and join in the Christmas hymns. Led by the Rev. Lewis L. L. Cameron, O.B.E., D.D., Director of Social Service in the Church of Scotland
Call to Worship
Prayer
O come, all ye faithful (First Form) (C.H. 55: Tune, Adeste Fideles)
Lesson: St. Luke 2, vv. 1-7
While humble shepherds watched their flocks (C.H. 42: Tune, Winchester)
Lesson: St. Matthew 2, vv. 1-12
In the bleak mid-winter (C.H. 50: Tune, Cranham)
Story
Still the night, holy the night (C.H. 49: Tune, Stille Nacht)
Prayer
As with gladness men of old (C.H. 63: Tune, Dix)
Blessing
Accompanist,
T. M. McCourt, Mus.Doc.

10.15 A CONCERT
on gramophone records
Overture, Tantalusqualen (*Suppé*)
Serenade (Rustic Wedding Symphony) (*Goldmark*)
Ballet Suite, Souvenirs (*Barber*)
Polka (Schwanda the Bagpiper) (*Weinberger*)
Emperor Waltz (*Johann Strauss*)

11.0 Greenwich Time Signal
'SING CHRISTMAS AND THE TURN OF THE YEAR'
A Call at your Door
in carol and custom
skiffle and folk song
from the seven sides of Britain
linked by radio
and joined in Birmingham
by the ballad-hunting American
Alan Lomax
Production by Charles Parker
See page 6

12.0 MUSIC FOR DANCING
played by Victor Silvester
and his Ballroom Orchestra

12.30 NEWS FOR SCOTTISH FARMERS

12.42 app. **FISHING NEWS**

12.55 The Weather
Forecast for land areas, followed by a detailed forecast for Scotland

1.0 Greenwich Time Signal
NEWS

1.10 Ted Ray
rings up the curtain on
a Christmas edition of
VARIETY PLAYHOUSE
presenting Cicely Courtneidge
and Jack Hulbert
Harry Worth, Thomas Round
Ronnie Barker, Patricia Hayes
Tollefsen, Julia Shelley
The Western Brothers
(Shortened version of last Saturday's recorded broadcast)
(*Cicely Courtneidge is in 'The Bride and the Bachelor' at the Duchess Theatre, London*)

2.0 COMMONWEALTH CHRISTMAS OVERTURE
by Malcolm Arnold
played by the
BBC Symphony Orchestra
(Leader, Paul Beard)
Conductor, Rudolf Schwarz
(BBC recording)
This Overture has been specially commissioned by the BBC to mark the Silver Jubilee of the Christmas Day Commonwealth programme.

2.15 THE COMMONWEALTH REMEMBERS
See foot of page and page 7

3.0 Her Majesty
THE QUEEN

3.15 BBC SYMPHONY ORCHESTRA
(Leader, Paul Beard)
Conductor, Rudolf Schwarz
Richard Lewis (tenor)
Crown Imperial: A Coronation March (1937)..........*Walton*
Aria: Dalla sua pace la mia dipende (Don Giovanni)..........*Mozart*
Suite No. 3..........*Gordon Jacob*
Aria: Il mio tesoro intanto (Don Giovanni)..........*Mozart*
Symphony No. 5, in C minor *Beethoven*
(BBC recording)

4.30 THESE FOOLISH THING
Remind you of what?
Roy Plomley
invites a reply from
Joyce Grenfell, Lady Pakenha
Michael Ayrton, Geoffrey Grigs
Ivan Staff
Wynford Vaughan Thomas
Based on an idea by Nancy Spa
(BBC recording)
Repeated on Thursday at 10.30 a

In Other Home Services

LONDON (330 m.; 908 kc/s)
7.40-7.50 Morning Music.*
9.30-10.15 Service from Nunton Parish Church near Salisbury.
12.0-12.40 Victor Silvester and his Ballroom Orchestra.
12.40-12.55 Popular songs on records.

WELSH (341 m.; 881 kc/s)
9.30-10.0 Welsh Service conducted by the Rev. John Owen Jones.
10.0-10.15 Helen Watts (contralto).*
* *Recorded programme*

SILVER JUBILEE OF

At 2.15

The Commonwealth Remembe

The people of the Commonwealth celebrat
twenty-fifth Christmas reunion by radio by exc
memories and hopes inspired by the momentous
of the quarter century since its inaugurati
by King George V in 1932

NARRATOR:
Howard Marshall

REPORTERS:
Louis MacNeice, Maurice Brown
Willy Richardson

PRODUCED BY
Laurence Gilliam and Alan Burgess

IN THE HOME

RADIO TIMES

JOURNAL OF THE BBC

The Rise of Television

1947–1959

The Coronation

Illustration by Eric Fraser

31 May–6 June 1953

The coronation of Queen Elizabeth II on Tuesday 2 June 1953 was a day that established television in the national consciousness. With over 20 million viewers (almost twice the radio audience) tuning in to see the grainy black-and-white images beamed live from Westminster Abbey, and the subsequent procession through the streets of London, this was a television event like no other before it. There were only 2.7 million TV sets in existence, which meant that, on average, between seven and eight people squeezed in front of each set – and that doesn't include children, who were not included in the statistics.

The broadcast began at 10.15am, much earlier in the day than ever before, and continued until 5.20pm. *Radio Times* sold more than nine million copies of this issue, which provided exhaustive coverage of the event – detailing, among other things, the finer points of constitutional protocol during the ceremony.

1947–1959

The King is dead, long live Queen Elizabeth II; radio grows and grows and television comes of age with Tony Hancock, the Goons and David Attenborough

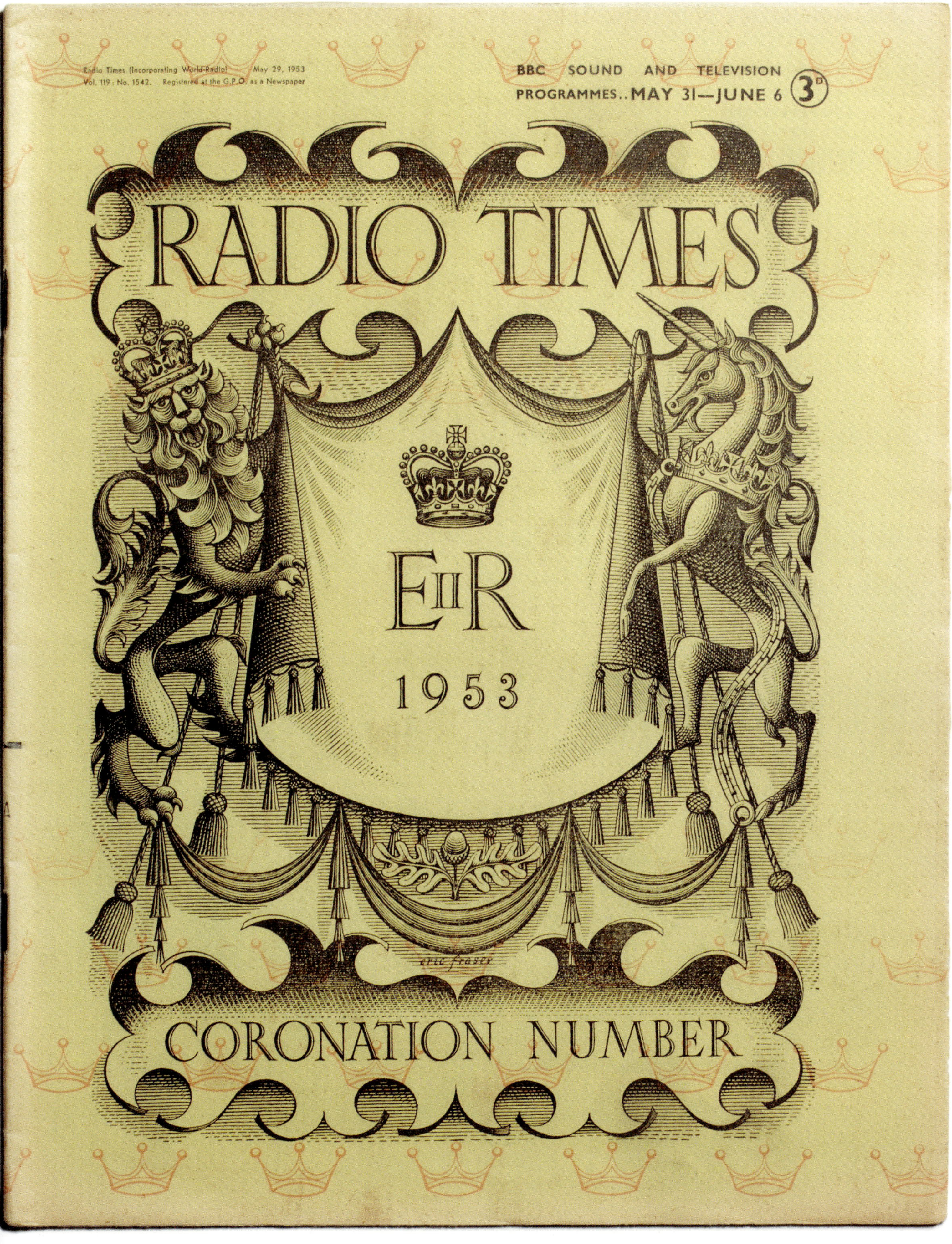
Radio Times (Incorporating World-Radio) May 29, 1953
Vol. 119 : No. 1542. Registered at the G.P.O. as a Newspaper
BBC SOUND AND TELEVISION
PROGRAMMES.. MAY 31—JUNE 6
3D
RADIO TIMES
EIIR
1953
eric fraser
CORONATION NUMBER

25th anniversary of broadcasting *(right)*

9–15 November 1947

To celebrate the BBC's silver jubilee the cover displayed the Corporation's coat of arms on the cover, while the editorial extolled the achievements of the past 25 years. Television, first broadcast in 1936, had returned after the war, and there were now three radio channels: the Home Service, the Light Programme and the Third Programme.

The Royal Wedding *(below left)*

16–22 November 1947

The marriage of HRH Princess Elizabeth and Lieutenant Philip Mountbatten was brought to the nation on radio and television. Cameras captured the pomp of the processions to and from Westminster Abbey but the wedding service itself was broadcast only on radio.

XIV Olympiad London 1948 *(below right)*

Illustration by CW Bacon

25–31 July 1948

The 1948 Olympic Games were the first to be broadcast on television, but compared to the marathon of London 2012 it was a modest undertaking for the BBC. Sports fans could follow the action on radio through a mix of live broadcasts on special-interest events and regular round-ups.

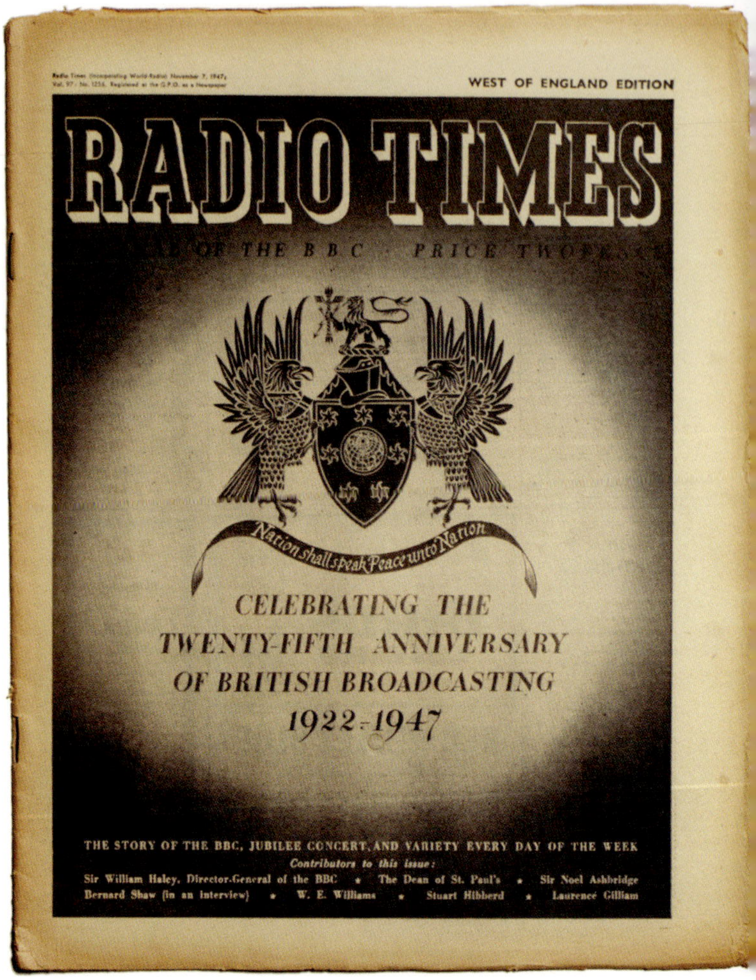

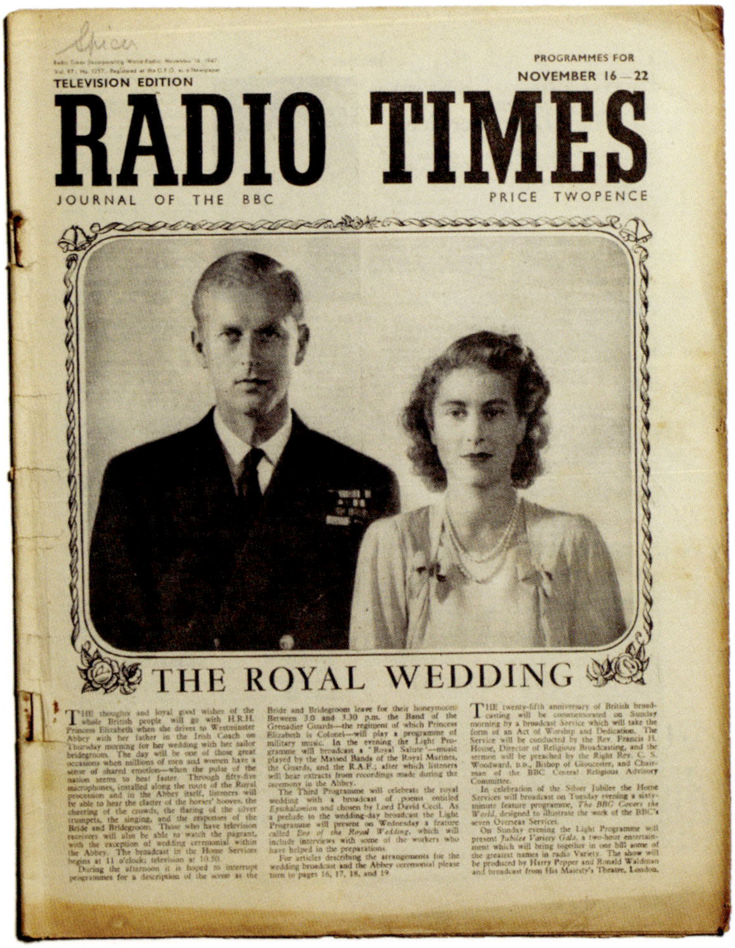

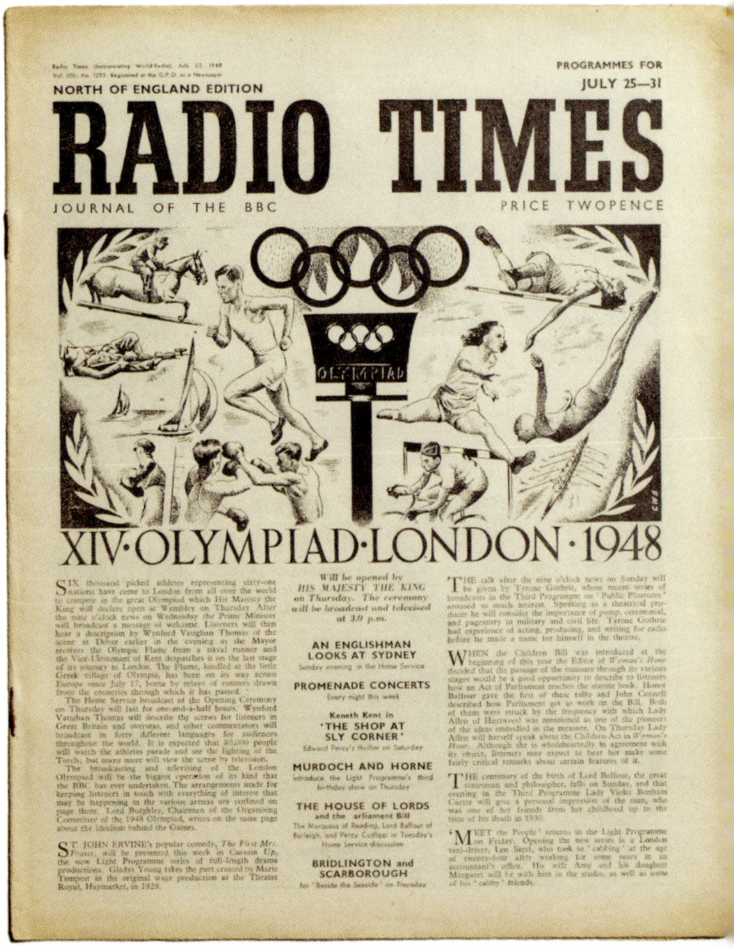

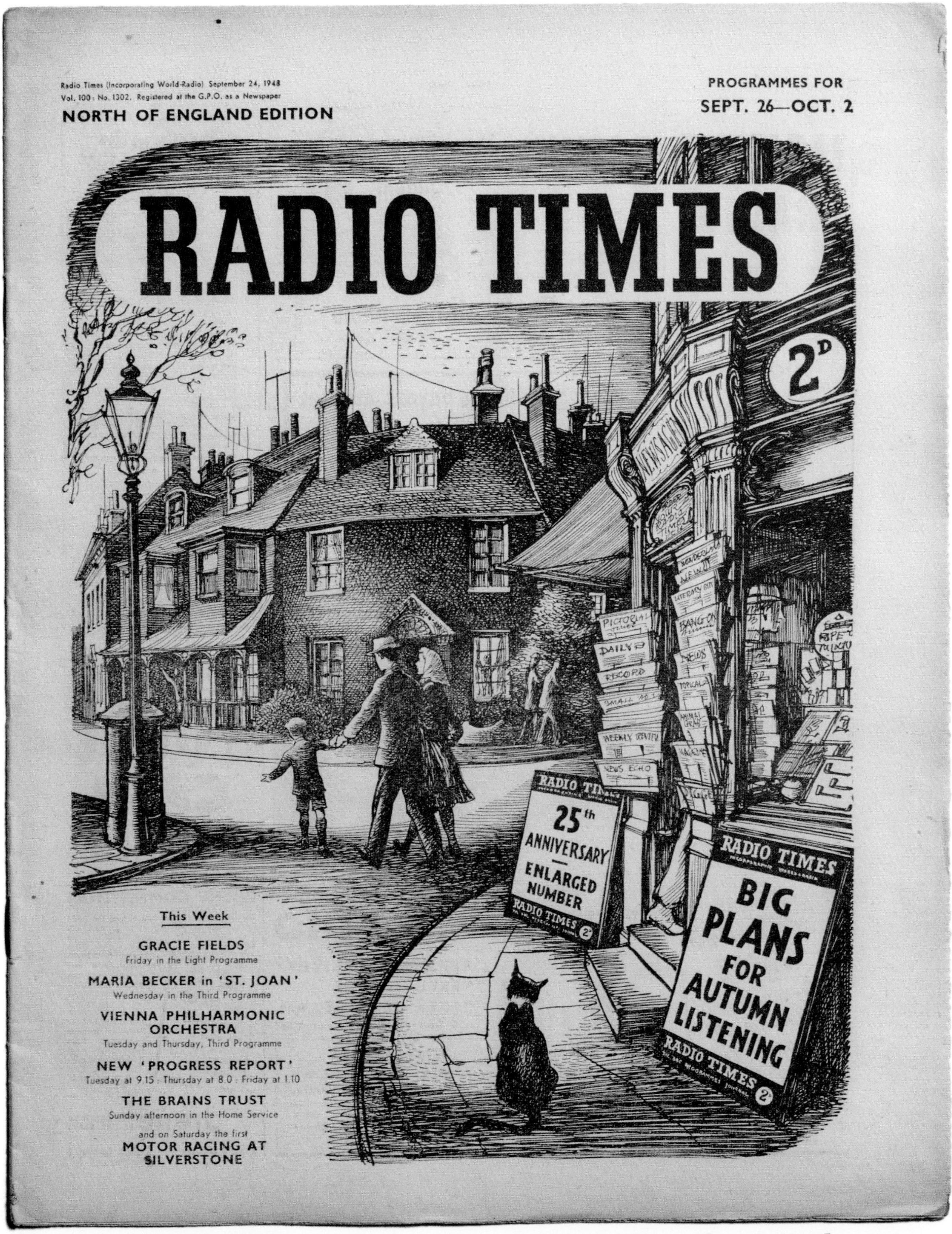

25 years of Radio Times **Illustration by Geoffrey Whittam** *26 September–2 October 1948*

Ten months after the BBC's 25th anniversary, *Radio Times* marked its own silver jubilee. The editorial tracked the magazine's growth in tandem with that of broadcasting, but there was the recognition that austerity still prevailed: "There is not enough paper to provide the sort of *Radio Times* which the present scope of broadcasting demands."

Radio Times (Incorporating World-Radio)
May 26, 1950. Vol. 107: No. 1389
Registered at the G.P.O. as a Newspaper

PROGRAMMES FOR
MAY 28—JUNE 3

RADIO TIMES

JOURNAL OF THE BBC

PRICE TWOPENCE

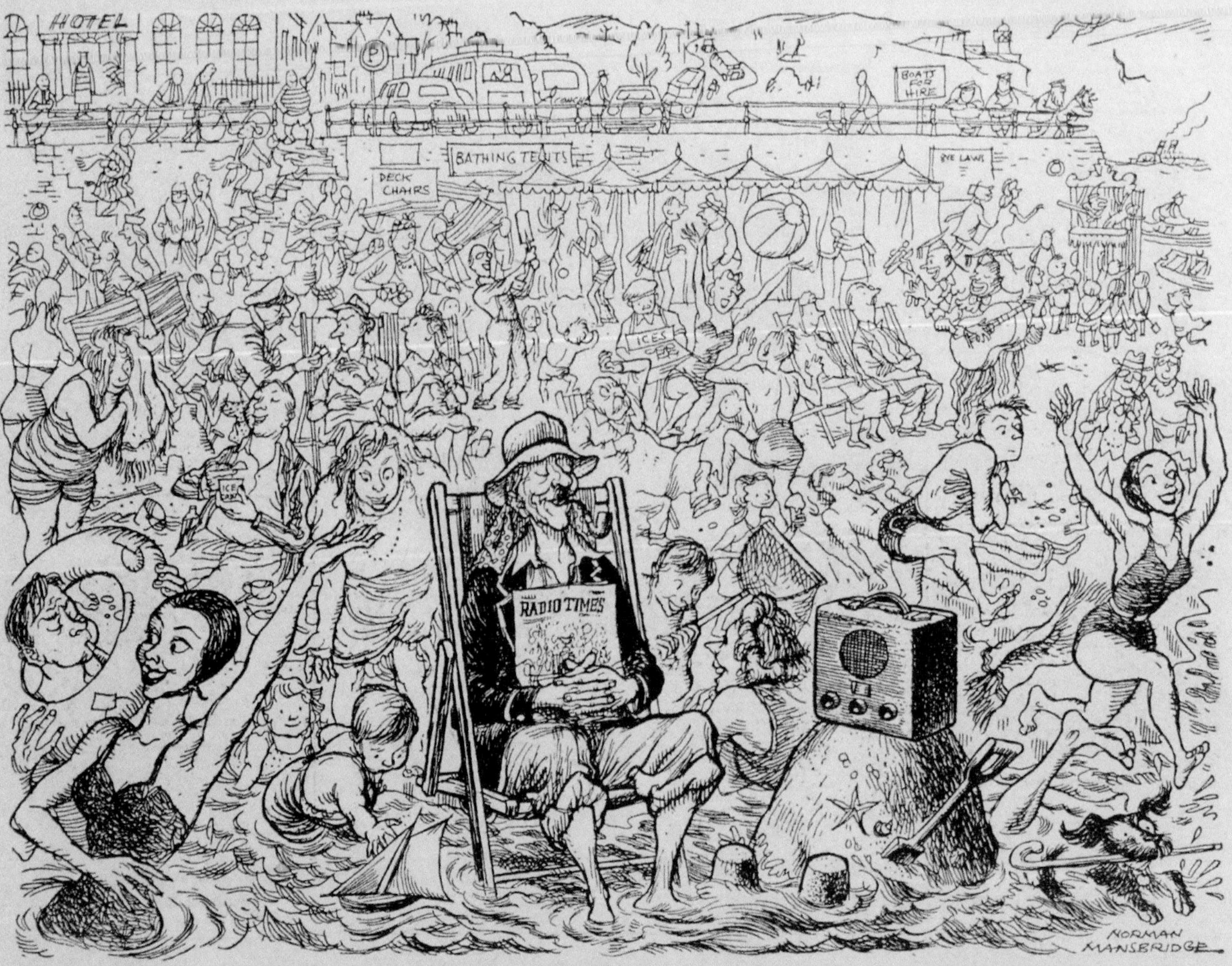

All the Whitsun Holiday Programmes

BING CROSBY
presents a record show in the Light Programme on Monday

GREGORY PECK
in a radio version of 'Twelve O'Clock High' (Wednesday)

SERGE KOUSSEVITZKY
conducts the London Philharmonic Orchestra at the Royal Albert Hall (Thursday)

'PRIDE AND PREJUDICE'
Jane Austen's novel as the new Sunday-evening serial play

'THE WAR OF THE WORLDS'
The famous H. G. Wells story opens as a serial play on Tuesday

'THE LIGHT OF OTHER DAYS'
Chekhov's 'Cherry Orchard' in an Irish setting (Monday)

'THE WELL OF THE SAINTS'
J. M. Synge's play on Sunday and Wednesday (Third)

Strike special *(right)*

Illustration by LP

15–23 September 1950

The 8 September issue of *Radio Times* failed to appear in the shops because of a printers' strike. That had happened only three times previously: during the General Strike of 1926 and for two weeks during the fuel crisis of 1947. With the printing dispute temporarily resolved, this special nine-day issue was hurriedly published but had eight pages fewer than normal. The dispute resurfaced in the following month, resulting in the cancellation of three consecutive issues.

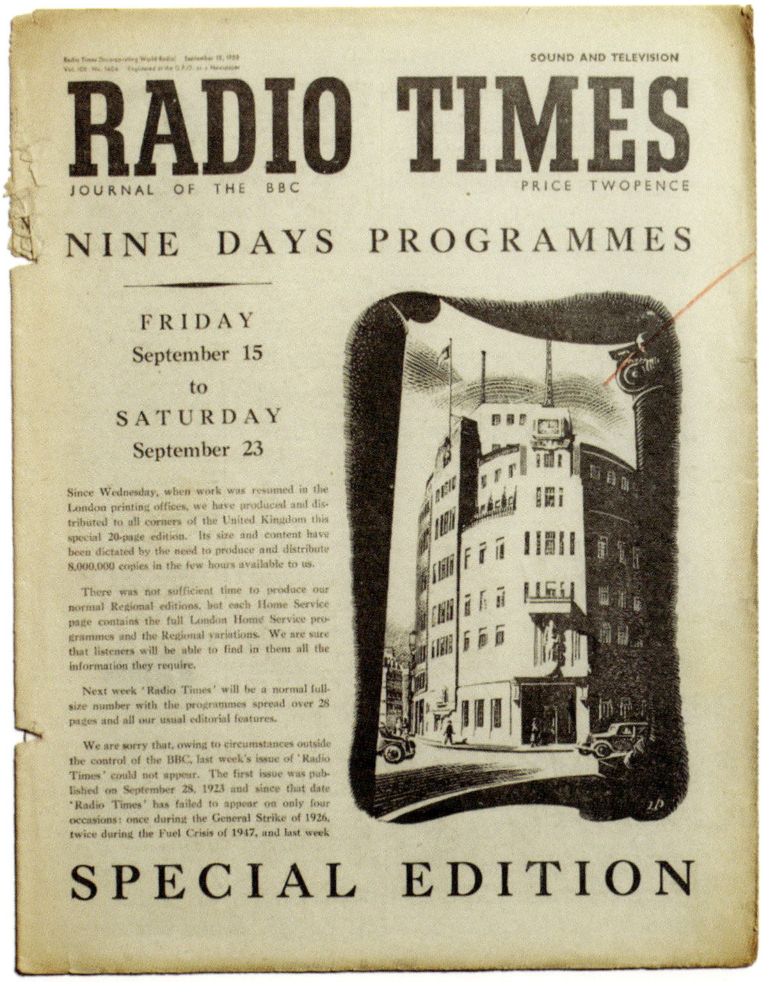
SOUND AND TELEVISION
RADIO TIMES
JOURNAL OF THE BBC
PRICE TWOPENCE
NINE DAYS PROGRAMMES
FRIDAY
September 15
to
SATURDAY
September 23

Since Wednesday, when work was resumed in the London printing offices, we have produced and distributed to all corners of the United Kingdom this special 20-page edition. Its size and content have been dictated by the need to produce and distribute 8,000,000 copies in the few hours available to us.

There was not sufficient time to produce our normal Regional editions, but each Home Service page contains the full London Home Service programmes and the Regional variations. We are sure that listeners will be able to find in them all the information they require.

Next week 'Radio Times' will be a normal full-size number with the programmes spread over 28 pages and all our usual editorial features.

We are sorry that, owing to circumstances outside the control of the BBC, last week's issue of 'Radio Times' could not appear. The first issue was published on September 28, 1923 and since that date 'Radio Times' has failed to appear on only four occasions: once during the General Strike of 1926, twice during the Fuel Crisis of 1947, and last week

SPECIAL EDITION

Whitsun holiday *(left)*

Illustration by Norman Mansbridge

28 May–3 June 1950

The Whitsun holiday cover by cartoonist Norman Mansbridge is perhaps a nod to the fact that the country was beginning to move away from the hardship of war and the austerity years. On page five there was a short news item on the planned construction of the BBC Television Centre at White City in west London, with its radical central "doughnut". The building finally opened almost exactly ten years later in June 1960.

Christmas 1950 *(right)*

Illustration by C Walter Hodges

24–30 December 1950

Television treats this festive season included Laurel and Hardy, an adaptation of *A Christmas Carol*, pantomime in the shape of *Cinderella*, and *Muffin the Mule* and *Larry the Lamb* for the children. Cyril Walter Hodges, who provided the cover's Nativity scene, is best known as an illustrator of children's books: his breakthrough came when he received a commission from *Radio Times* in 1931.

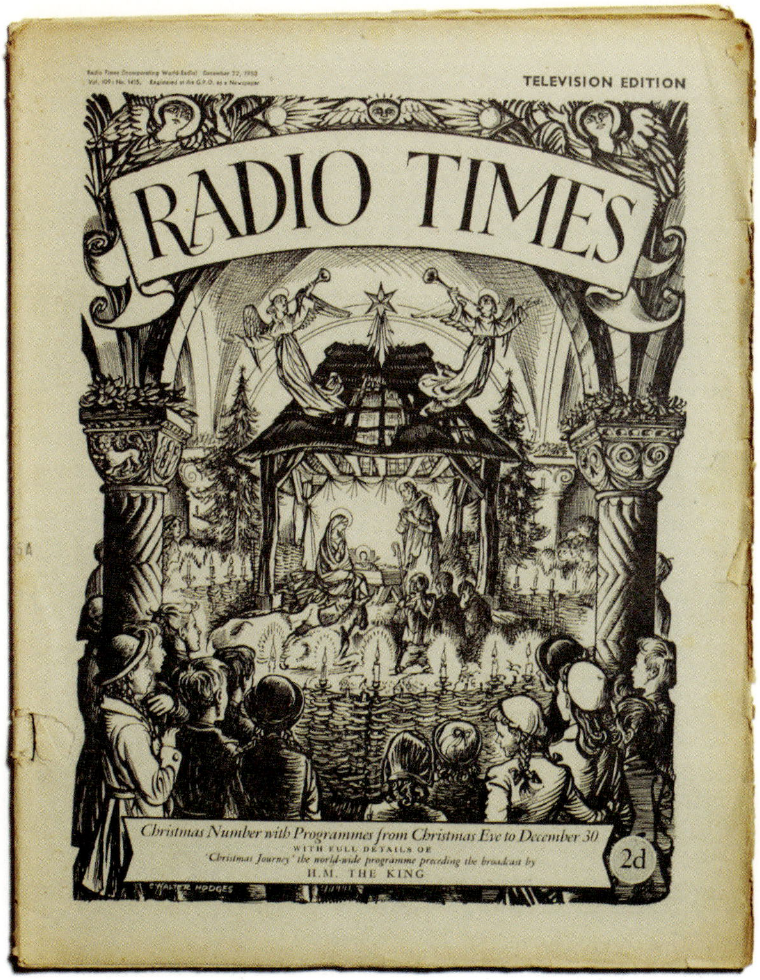
Radio Times (Incorporating World-Radio) December 22, 1950
Vol. 109: No. 1415. Registered at the G.P.O. as a Newspaper
TELEVISION EDITION
RADIO TIMES
Christmas Number with Programmes from Christmas Eve to December 30
WITH FULL DETAILS OF
'Christmas Journey' the world-wide programme preceding the broadcast by
H.M. THE KING
2d
C WALTER HODGES

Easter 1951 *(right)*

Illustration by CF Tunnicliffe

25–31 March 1951

This pastoral scene is by Charles Tunnicliffe, famous for his illustrations for *Tarka the Otter*. Inside, *All the Fun of the Fair* on Easter Monday – with Arthur Askey and Norman Wisdom – was a television highlight.

Christmas 1951 *(below left)*

Illustration by Rowland Hilder

23–29 December 1951

This simple snowy scene is by Rowland Hilder, who was celebrated for the stark beauty of his winter landscapes and in particular his watercolours of the Kentish Weald.

BBC and French TV combine *(below right)*

Illustration by C Walter Hodges

6–12 July 1952

A broadcasting landmark as the BBC and French broadcaster RTF combined to give viewers a week of programmes from Paris. Among the highlights dotted through the schedules were the Tour de France, fashion, a French housewife shopping and art in the Louvre.

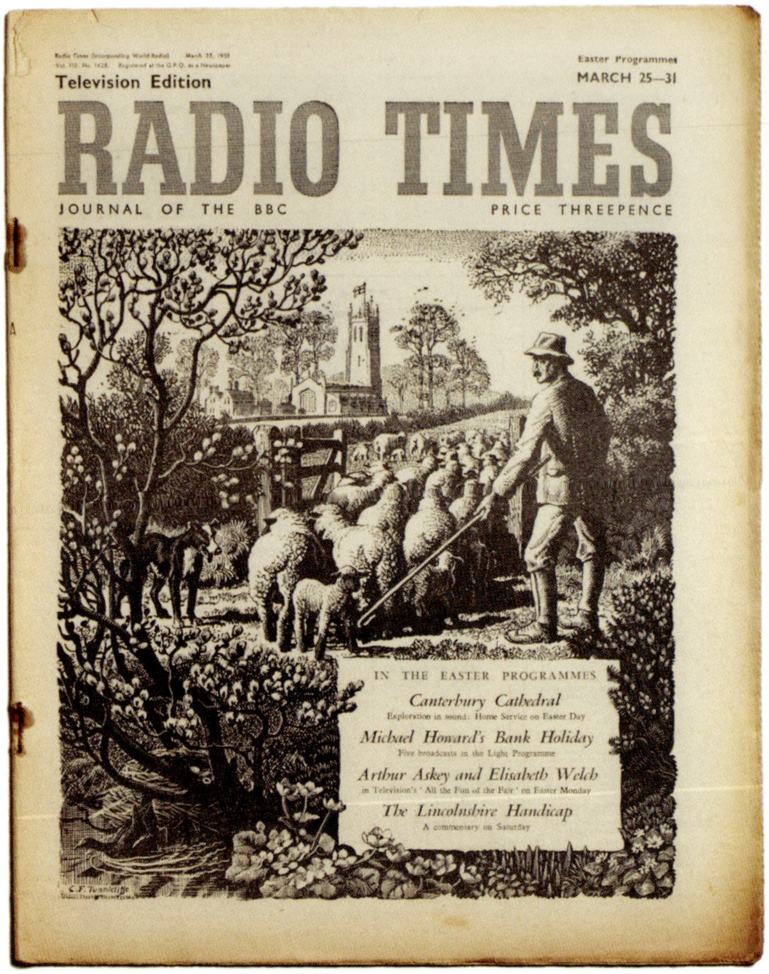

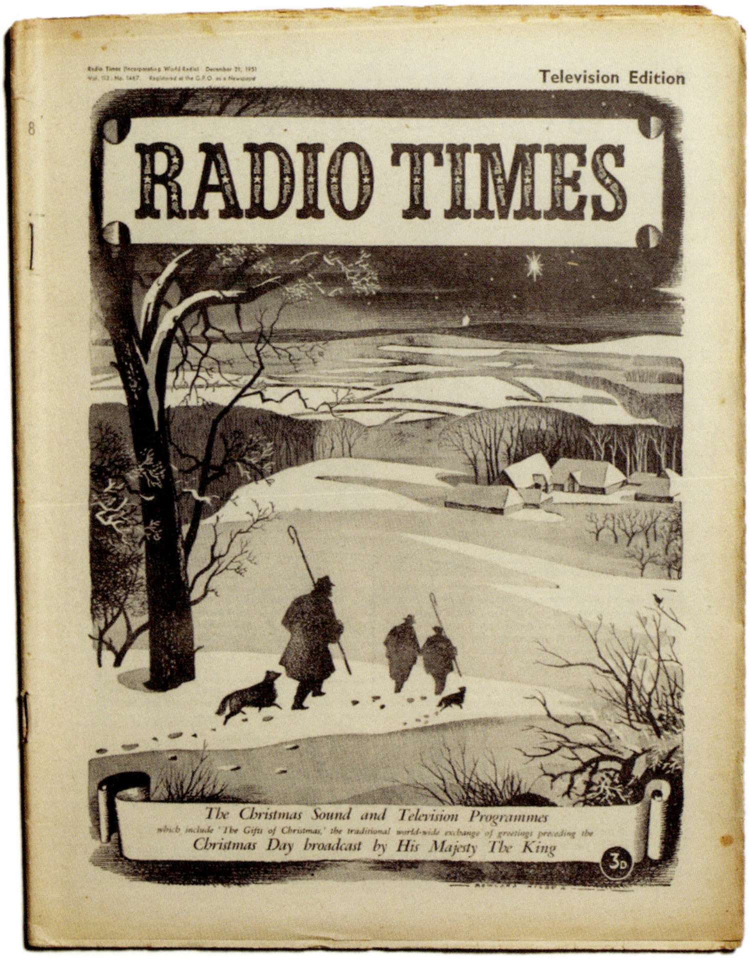

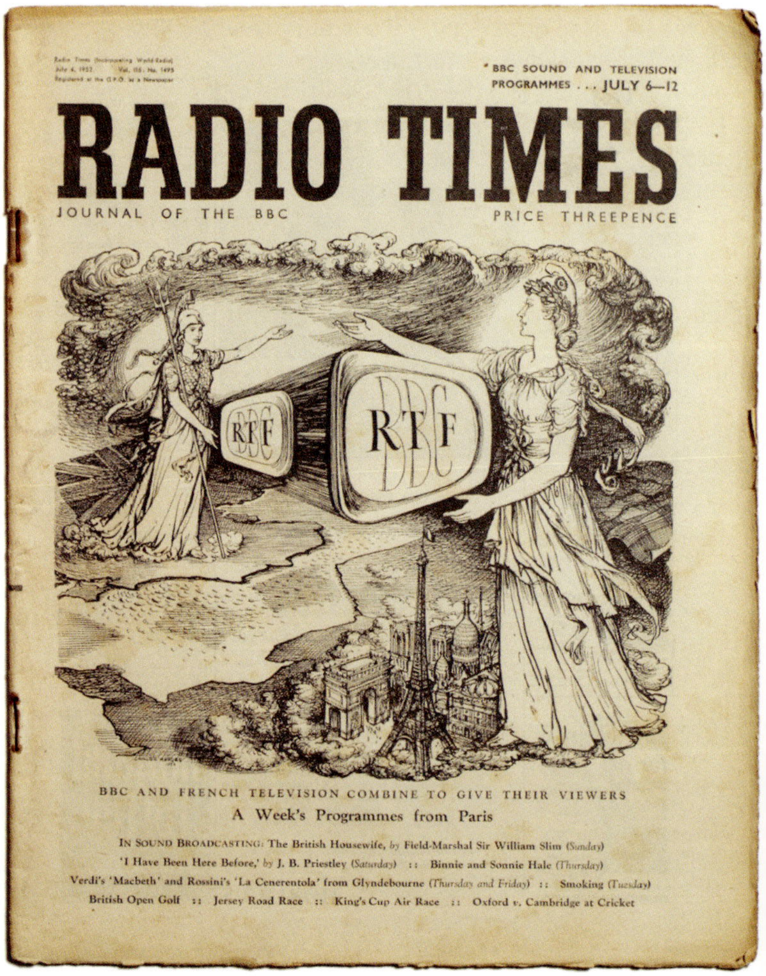

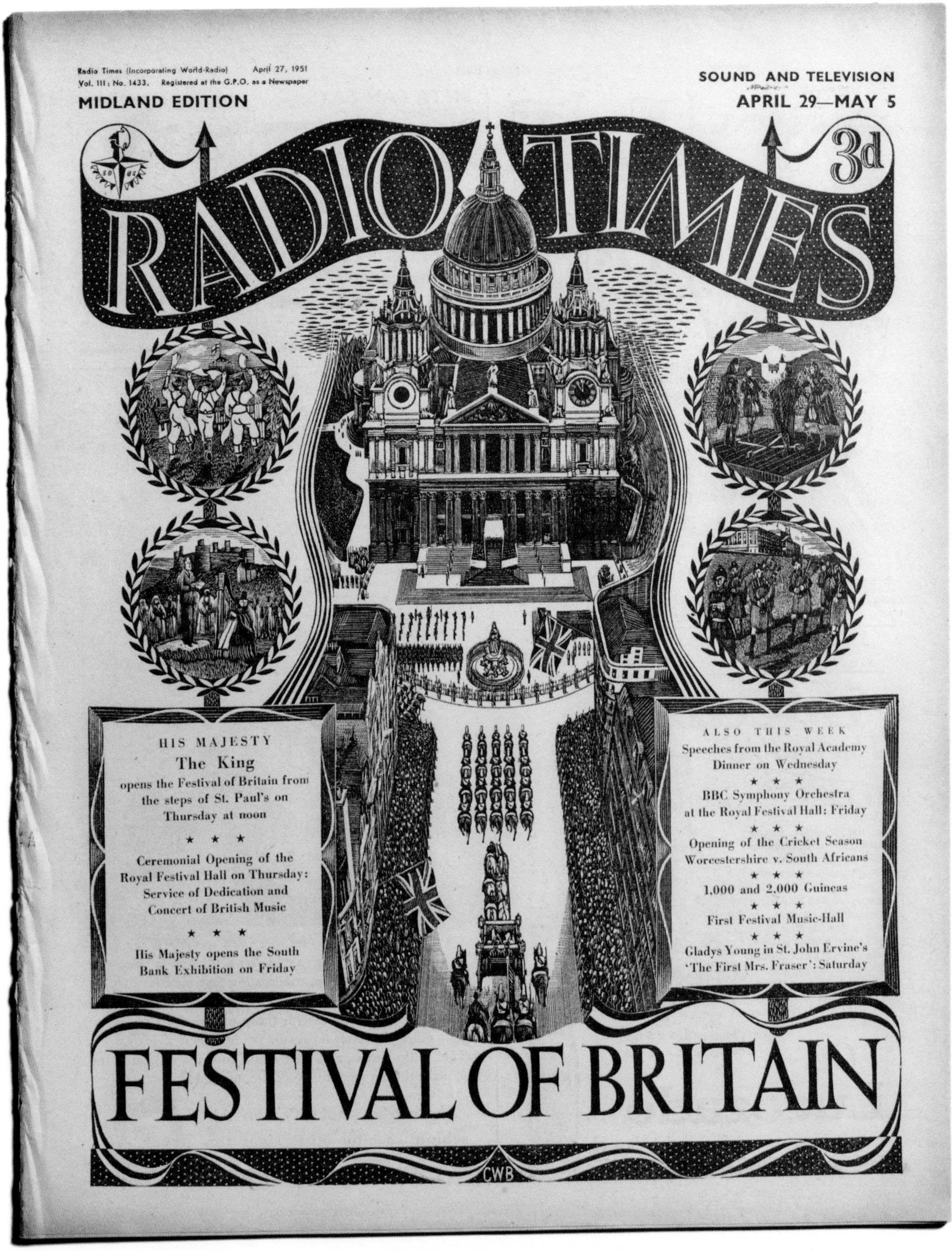

Festival of Britain **Illustration by CW Bacon** *29 April–5 May 1951*

The festival on London's South Bank was a celebration of British culture, industry and the recovery from the dark days of war. The role of broadcasting was vital to its success, said festival director, Gerald Barry. "All the high spots will be brought to the listener by actuality broadcasts, concerts and opera, and I don't know what else," he ended, somewhat lamely.

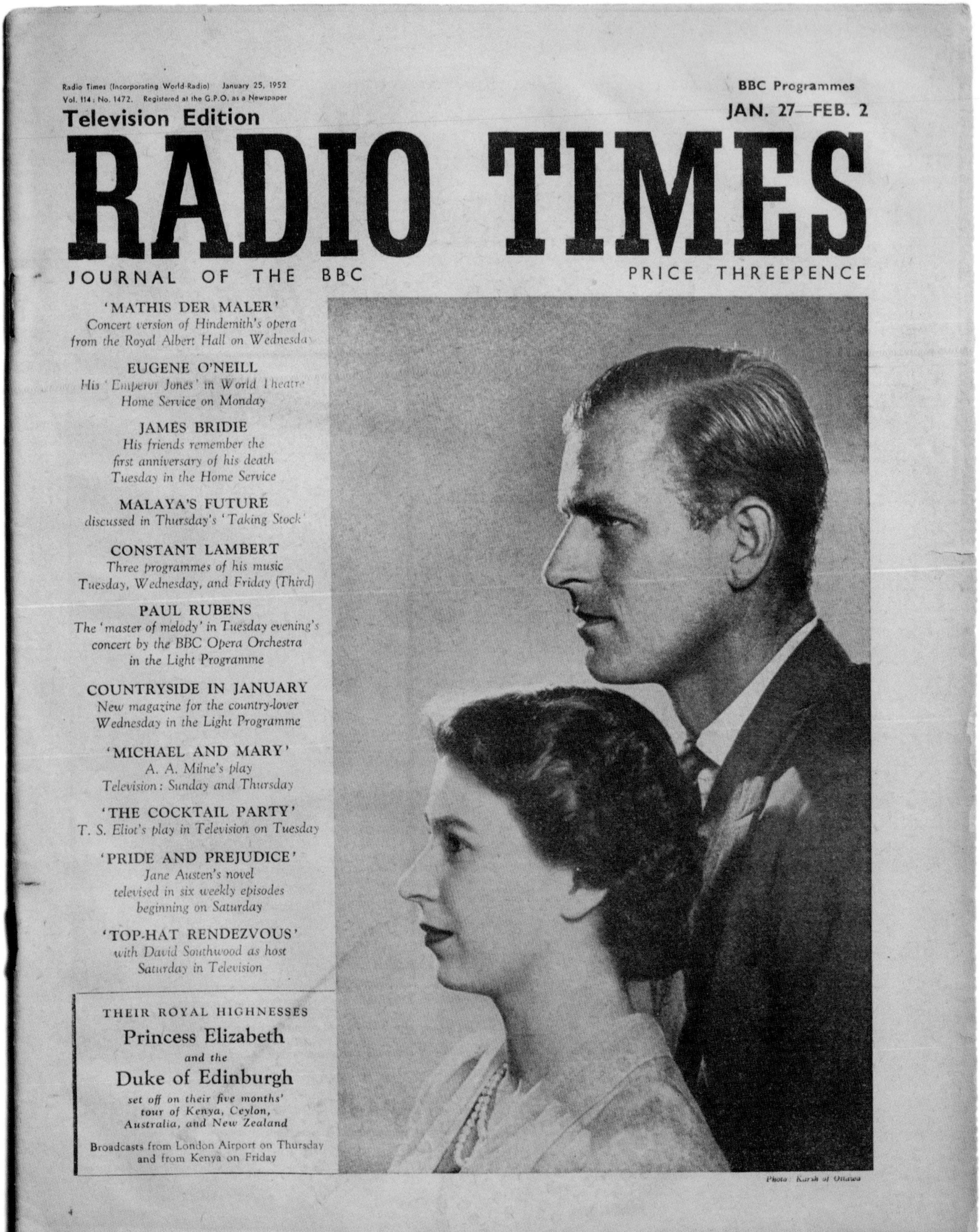
Radio Times (Incorporating World-Radio) January 25, 1952
Vol. 114 : No. 1472. Registered at the G.P.O. as a Newspaper

BBC Programmes
JAN. 27—FEB. 2

Television Edition

RADIO TIMES

JOURNAL OF THE BBC PRICE THREEPENCE

'MATHIS DER MALER'
Concert version of Hindemith's opera from the Royal Albert Hall on Wednesday

EUGENE O'NEILL
His 'Emperor Jones' in World Theatre
Home Service on Monday

JAMES BRIDIE
His friends remember the first anniversary of his death
Tuesday in the Home Service

MALAYA'S FUTURE
discussed in Thursday's 'Taking Stock'

CONSTANT LAMBERT
Three programmes of his music
Tuesday, Wednesday, and Friday (Third)

PAUL RUBENS
The 'master of melody' in Tuesday evening's concert by the BBC Opera Orchestra in the Light Programme

COUNTRYSIDE IN JANUARY
New magazine for the country-lover
Wednesday in the Light Programme

'MICHAEL AND MARY'
A. A. Milne's play
Television: Sunday and Thursday

'THE COCKTAIL PARTY'
T. S. Eliot's play in Television on Tuesday

'PRIDE AND PREJUDICE'
Jane Austen's novel televised in six weekly episodes beginning on Saturday

'TOP-HAT RENDEZVOUS'
with David Southwood as host
Saturday in Television

THEIR ROYAL HIGHNESSES
Princess Elizabeth
and the
Duke of Edinburgh
set off on their five months' tour of Kenya, Ceylon, Australia, and New Zealand

Broadcasts from London Airport on Thursday and from Kenya on Friday

Photo: Karsh of Ottawa

Royals on tour **Princess Elizabeth and the Duke of Edinburgh**
(photograph by Karsh of Ottawa) 27 January–2 February 1952

As the royal couple departed on a five-month tour of Kenya, Ceylon (as Sri Lanka was then known), Australia and New Zealand, Richard Dimbleby and Raymond Baxter were stationed at London Airport to describe the scenes. The BBC had great plans to follow the tour, but as we know things didn't work out according to plan...

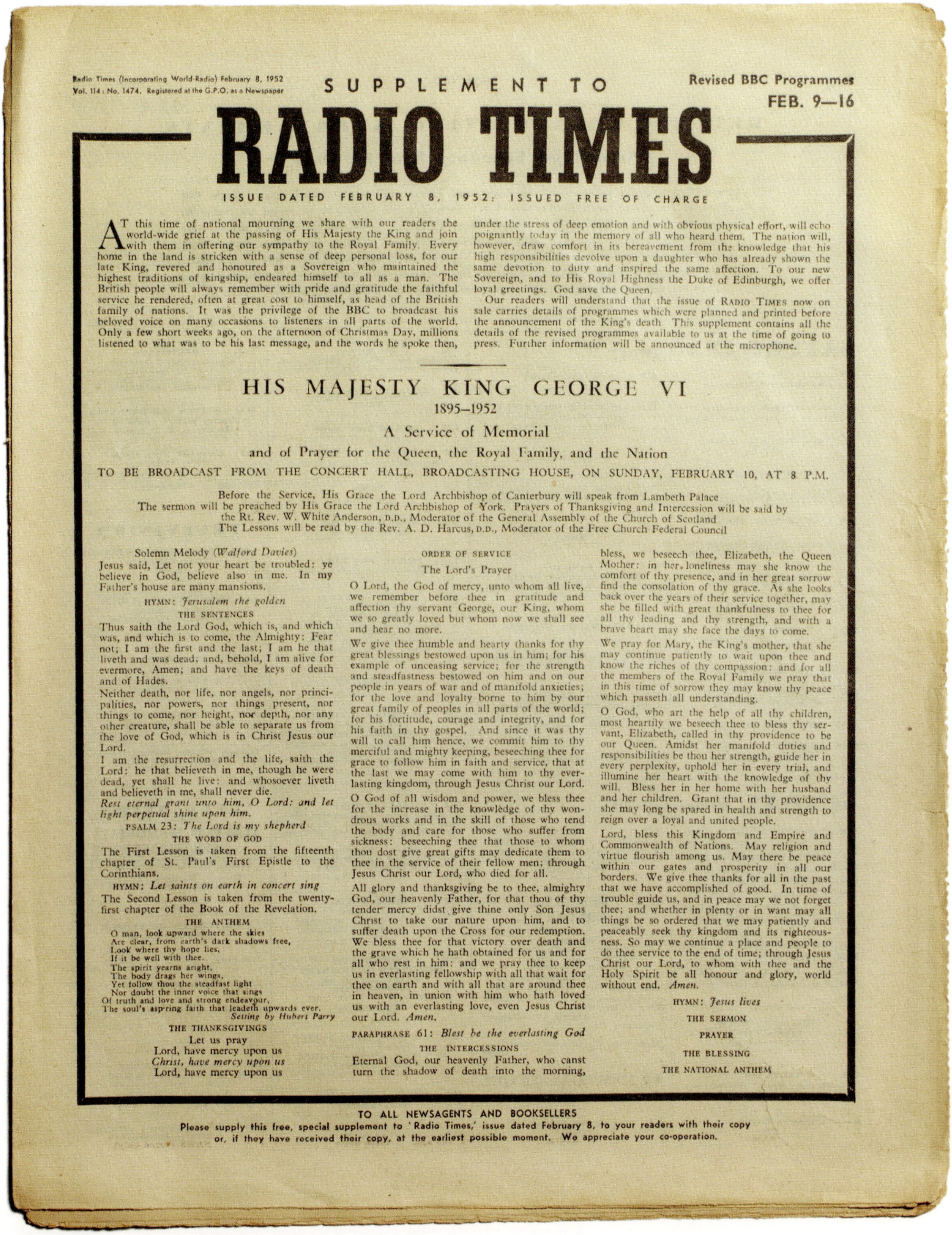

Radio Times (Incorporating World-Radio) February 8, 1952
Vol. 114 : No. 1474. Registered at the G.P.O. as a Newspaper

SUPPLEMENT TO

Revised BBC Programmes
FEB. 9—16

RADIO TIMES

ISSUE DATED FEBRUARY 8, 1952: ISSUED FREE OF CHARGE

At this time of national mourning we share with our readers the world-wide grief at the passing of His Majesty the King and join with them in offering our sympathy to the Royal Family. Every home in the land is stricken with a sense of deep personal loss, for our late King, revered and honoured as a Sovereign who maintained the highest traditions of kingship, endeared himself to all as a man. The British people will always remember with pride and gratitude the faithful service he rendered, often at great cost to himself, as head of the British family of nations. It was the privilege of the BBC to broadcast his beloved voice on many occasions to listeners in all parts of the world. Only a few short weeks ago, on the afternoon of Christmas Day, millions listened to what was to be his last message, and the words he spoke then, under the stress of deep emotion and with obvious physical effort, will echo poignantly today in the memory of all who heard them. The nation will, however, draw comfort in its bereavement from the knowledge that his high responsibilities devolve upon a daughter who has already shown the same devotion to duty and inspired the same affection. To our new Sovereign, and to His Royal Highness the Duke of Edinburgh, we offer loyal greetings. God save the Queen.

Our readers will understand that the issue of RADIO TIMES now on sale carries details of programmes which were planned and printed before the announcement of the King's death. This supplement contains all the details of the revised programmes available to us at the time of going to press. Further information will be announced at the microphone.

HIS MAJESTY KING GEORGE VI

1895–1952

A Service of Memorial

and of Prayer for the Queen, the Royal Family, and the Nation

TO BE BROADCAST FROM THE CONCERT HALL, BROADCASTING HOUSE, ON SUNDAY, FEBRUARY 10, AT 8 P.M.

Before the Service, His Grace the Lord Archbishop of Canterbury will speak from Lambeth Palace
The sermon will be preached by His Grace the Lord Archbishop of York. Prayers of Thanksgiving and Intercession will be said by the Rt. Rev. W. White Anderson, D.D., Moderator of the General Assembly of the Church of Scotland
The Lessons will be read by the Rev. A. D. Harcus, D.D., Moderator of the Free Church Federal Council

Solemn Melody (*Walford Davies*)

Jesus said, Let not your heart be troubled: ye believe in God, believe also in me. In my Father's house are many mansions.

HYMN: *Jerusalem the golden*

THE SENTENCES

Thus saith the Lord God, which is, and which was, and which is to come, the Almighty: Fear not; I am the first and the last; I am he that liveth and was dead; and, behold, I am alive for evermore, Amen; and have the keys of death and of Hades.

Neither death, nor life, nor angels, nor principalities, nor powers, nor things present, nor things to come, nor height, nor depth, nor any other creature, shall be able to separate us from the love of God, which is in Christ Jesus our Lord.

I am the resurrection and the life, saith the Lord: he that believeth in me, though he were dead, yet shall he live: and whosoever liveth and believeth in me, shall never die.

Rest eternal grant unto him, O Lord: and let light perpetual shine upon him.

PSALM 23: *The Lord is my shepherd*

THE WORD OF GOD

The First Lesson is taken from the fifteenth chapter of St. Paul's First Epistle to the Corinthians.

HYMN: *Let saints on earth in concert sing*

The Second Lesson is taken from the twenty-first chapter of the Book of the Revelation.

THE ANTHEM

O man, look upward where the skies
Are clear, from earth's dark shadows free,
Look where thy hope lies,
If it be well with thee.
The spirit yearns aright,
The body drags her wings,
Yet follow thou the steadfast light
Nor doubt the inner voice that sings
Of truth and love and strong endeavour,
The soul's asp'ring faith that leadeth upwards ever.

Setting by Hubert Parry

THE THANKSGIVINGS

Let us pray
Lord, have mercy upon us
Christ, have mercy upon us
Lord, have mercy upon us

ORDER OF SERVICE

The Lord's Prayer

O Lord, the God of mercy, unto whom all live, we remember before thee in gratitude and affection thy servant George, our King, whom we so greatly loved but whom now we shall see and hear no more.

We give thee humble and hearty thanks for thy great blessings bestowed upon us in him; for his example of unceasing service; for the strength and steadfastness bestowed on him and on our people in years of war and of manifold anxieties; for the love and loyalty borne to him by our great family of peoples in all parts of the world; for his fortitude, courage and integrity, and for his faith in thy gospel. And since it was thy will to call him hence, we commit him to thy merciful and mighty keeping, beseeching thee for grace to follow him in faith and service, that at the last we may come with him to thy everlasting kingdom, through Jesus Christ our Lord.

O God of all wisdom and power, we bless thee for the increase in the knowledge of thy wondrous works and in the skill of those who tend the body and care for those who suffer from sickness: beseeching thee that those to whom thou dost give great gifts may dedicate them to thee in the service of their fellow men; through Jesus Christ our Lord, who died for all.

All glory and thanksgiving be to thee, almighty God, our heavenly Father, for that thou of thy tender mercy didst give thine only Son Jesus Christ to take our nature upon him, and to suffer death upon the Cross for our redemption. We bless thee for that victory over death and the grave which he hath obtained for us and for all who rest in him: and we pray thee to keep us in everlasting fellowship with all that wait for thee on earth and with all that are around thee in heaven, in union with him who hath loved us with an everlasting love, even Jesus Christ our Lord. *Amen.*

PARAPHRASE 61: *Blest be the everlasting God*

THE INTERCESSIONS

Eternal God, our heavenly Father, who canst turn the shadow of death into the morning, bless, we beseech thee, Elizabeth, the Queen Mother: in her loneliness may she know the comfort of thy presence, and in her great sorrow find the consolation of thy grace. As she looks back over the years of their service together, may she be filled with great thankfulness to thee for all thy leading and thy strength, and with a brave heart may she face the days to come.

We pray for Mary, the King's mother, that she may continue patiently to wait upon thee and know the riches of thy compassion: and for all the members of the Royal Family we pray that in this time of sorrow they may know thy peace which passeth all understanding.

O God, who art the help of all thy children, most heartily we beseech thee to bless thy servant, Elizabeth, called in thy providence to be our Queen. Amidst her manifold duties and responsibilities be thou her strength, guide her in every perplexity, uphold her in every trial, and illumine her heart with the knowledge of thy will. Bless her in her home with her husband and her children. Grant that in thy providence she may long be spared in health and strength to reign over a loyal and united people.

Lord, bless this Kingdom and Empire and Commonwealth of Nations. May religion and virtue flourish among us. May there be peace within our gates and prosperity in all our borders. We give thee thanks for all in the past that we have accomplished of good. In time of trouble guide us, and in peace may we not forget thee; and whether in plenty or in want may all things be so ordered that we may patiently and peaceably seek thy kingdom and its righteousness. So may we continue a place and people to do thee service to the end of time; through Jesus Christ our Lord, to whom with thee and the Holy Spirit be all honour and glory, world without end. *Amen.*

HYMN: *Jesus lives*

THE SERMON

PRAYER

THE BLESSING

THE NATIONAL ANTHEM

TO ALL NEWSAGENTS AND BOOKSELLERS

Please supply this free, special supplement to 'Radio Times,' issue dated February 8, to your readers with their copy or, if they have received their copy, at the earliest possible moment. We appreciate your co-operation.

The death of King George VI *9–16 February 1952*

This simple, four-page supplement was issued following the death on 6 February of King George VI. The week's schedules were revised to reflect the mood of national mourning, with the usual three radio channels reduced to one, and sombre broadcasts throughout the week, culminating in the funeral on 15 February. Normal broadcasts resumed on Saturday 16 February.

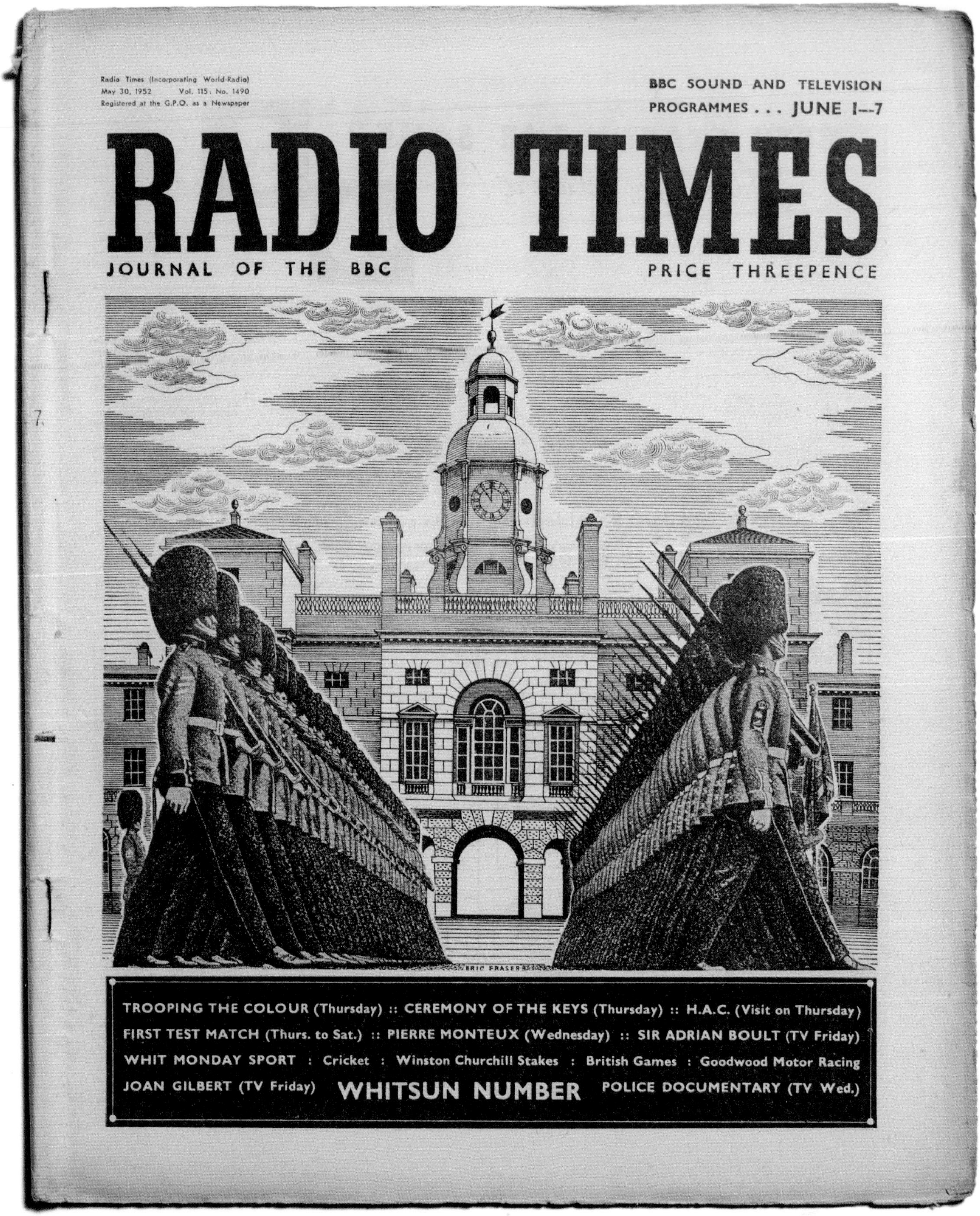

Trooping the Colour **Illustration by Eric Fraser** *1–7 June 1952*

We all know what the Trooping the Colour ceremony is, surely. Not according to Nigel Nicolson MP, who pointed out in a lengthy and informative feature that the event "should be called The Queen's Birthday Parade, of which Trooping the Colour forms only a very important part". This was the Queen's first parade as sovereign, although she had deputised for her father, George VI, the previous year.

Archie Andrews *(left)*

14–20 September 1952

Ventriloquism on the radio? Strange but true... Archie Andrews was a massive hit on *Educating Archie* on the Light Programme, thanks to the deft hands of Peter Brough, although the child on the cover looked unconvinced. But Archie had pulling power. His guests this week included Max Bygraves, Harry Secombe and Beryl Reid.

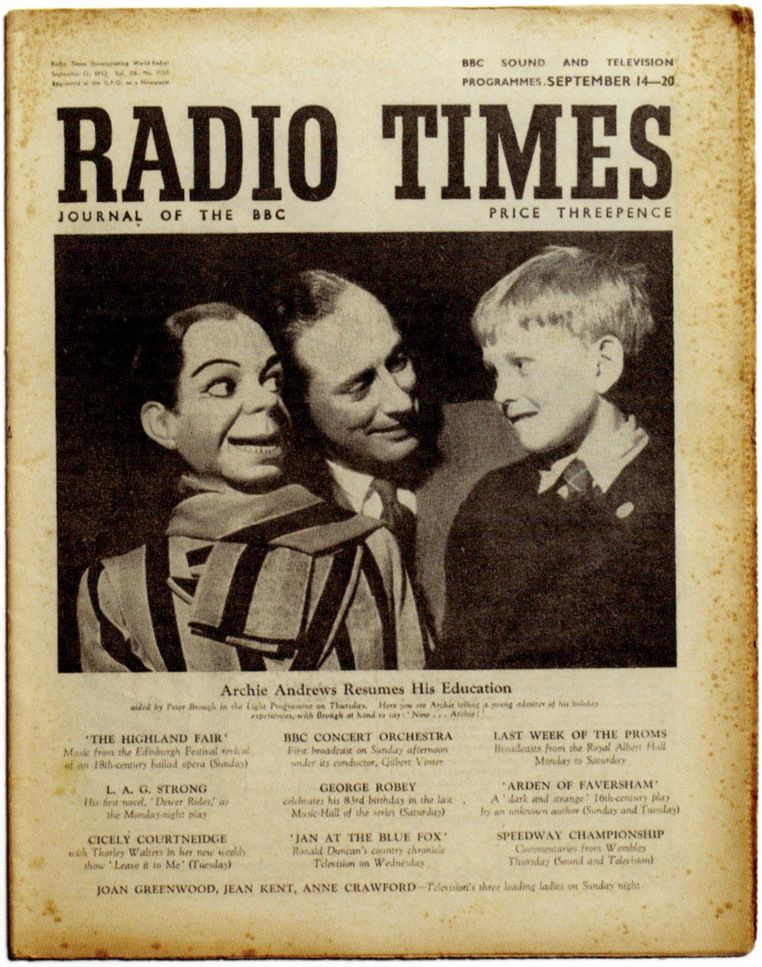

Autumn broadcasting plans *(below left)*

Illustration by Geoffrey Whittam

28 September–4 October 1952

The season of "trees without leaves and a fire in the fireplace". Radio had some heavyweight drama in store, including *Henry VI*, Kipling's *The Brushwood Boy* and *The Great Gatsby*. Television highlights included a new series of *What's My Line?*, and new playmates for Andy Pandy in *Watch with Mother* – Bill and Ben the Flowerpot Men.

Christmas 1952 *(below right)*

Illustration by FR Exell

21–27 December 1952

1952 saw the first Christmas broadcast to the Nation and Empire by Queen Elizabeth II. She hasn't missed a year since.

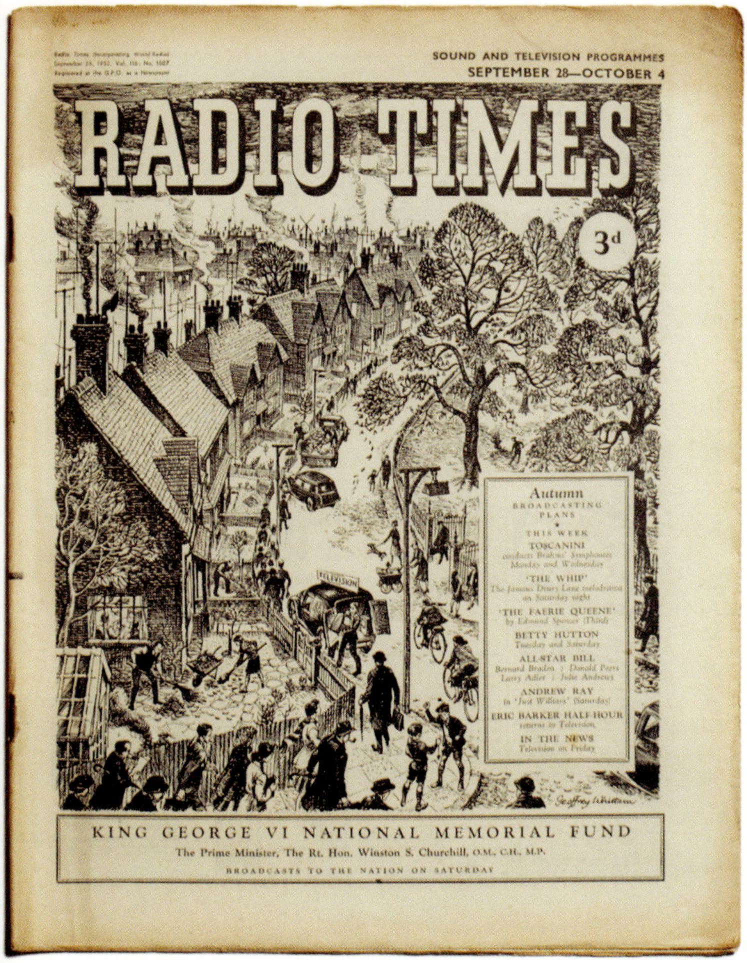

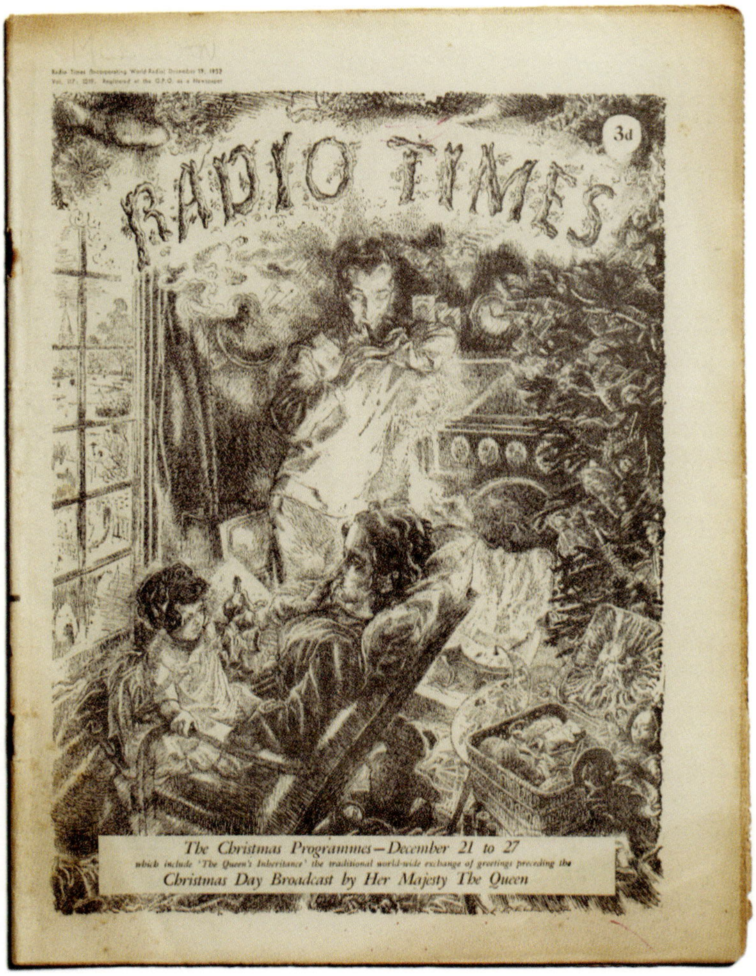

Letter from America *(right)*

Alistair Cooke

15–21 February 1953

Alistair Cooke broadcast his *Letter from America* from March 1946 to February 2004. So when this picture of the commentator was taken in the CBS TV studios in New York, he was just getting into his stride...

Whitsun number *(middle right)*

Illustration by C Walter Hodges

24–30 May 1953

Excitement was mounting in the country at the prospect of the Queen's coronation. *Radio Times* captured the flavour of the moment with a guided tour of the route the royal procession would take on the day itself.

The Weekly Bind *(far right)*

Kenneth Horne (left) and Richard Murdoch

26 July–1 August 1953

Horne and Murdoch of radio favourite *Much Binding* were pictured while on a trip to *Radio Times's* printers. The reason for the visit? The story was that it was a fact-finding mission linked to their new venture into newspaper publishing for the team's new show, *The Weekly Bind*.

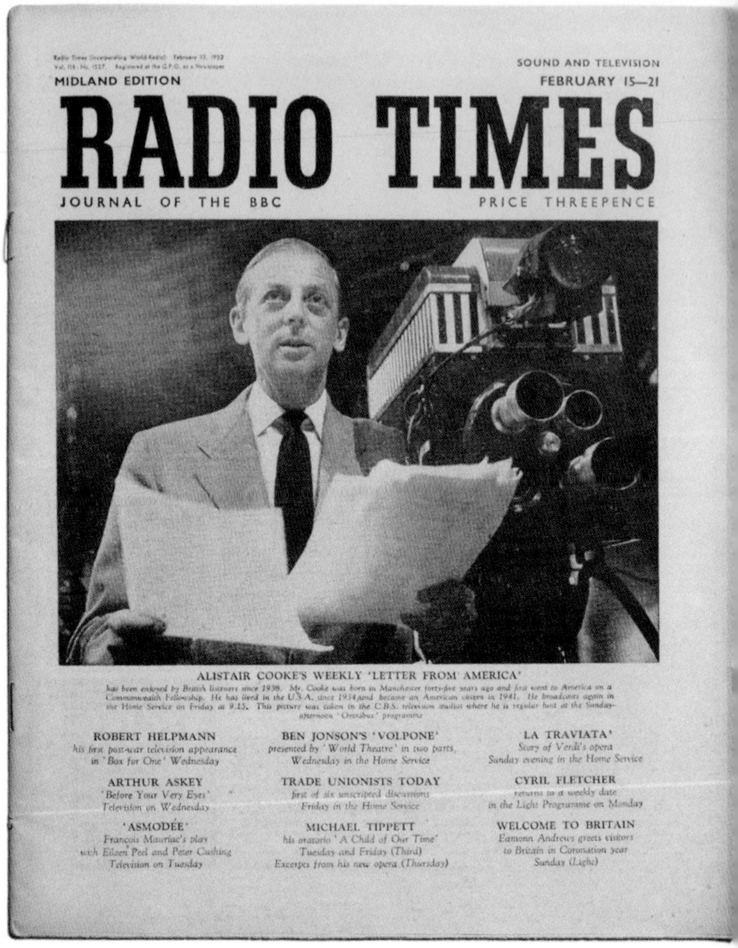

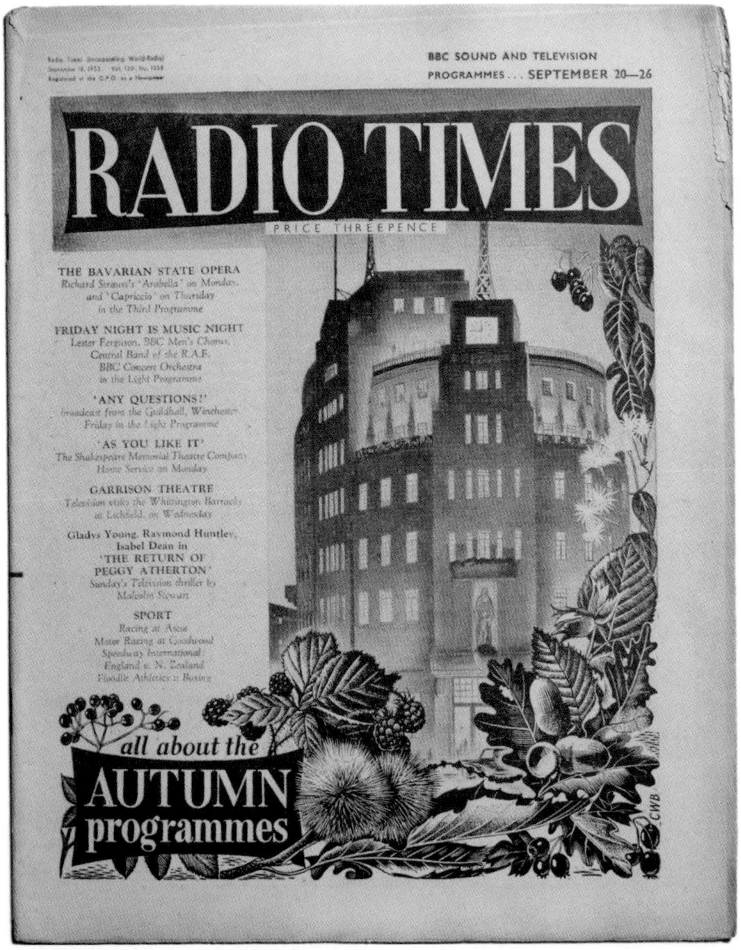

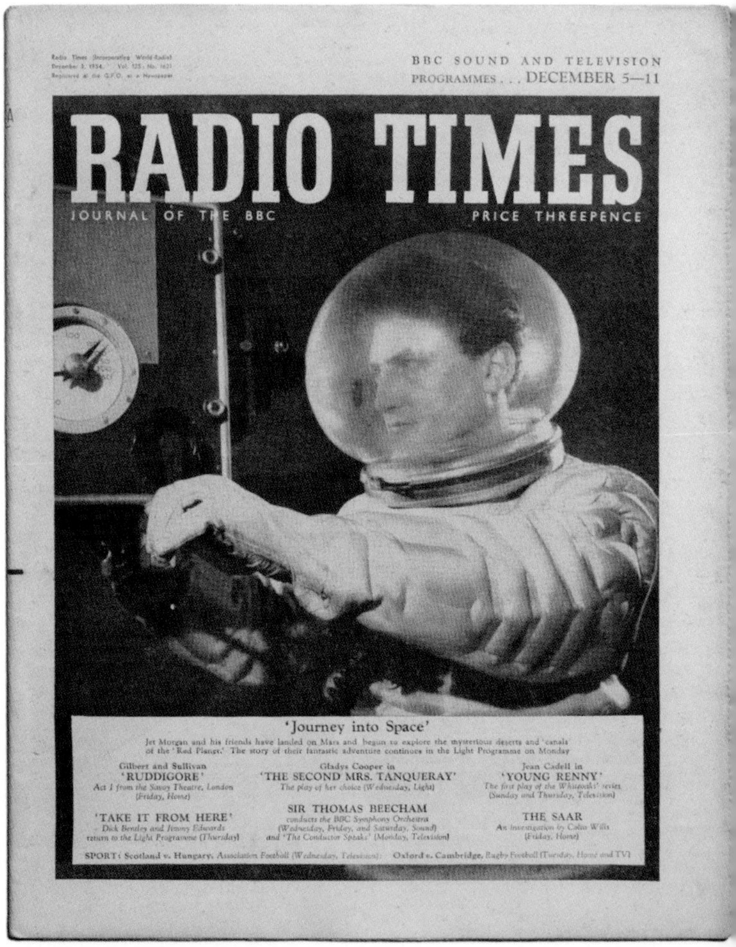

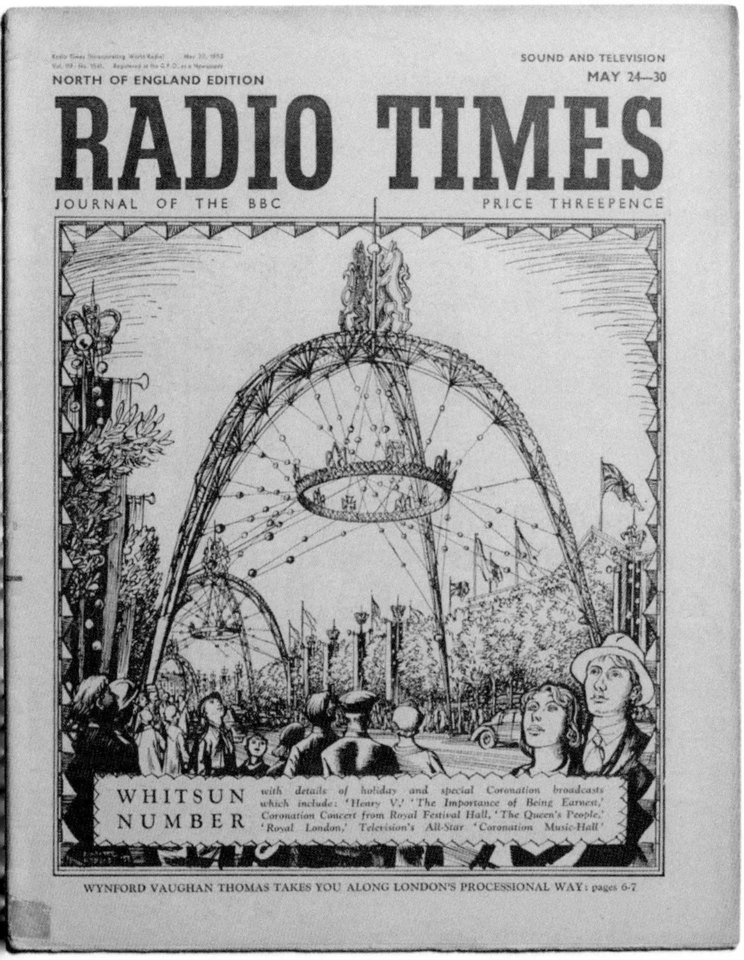

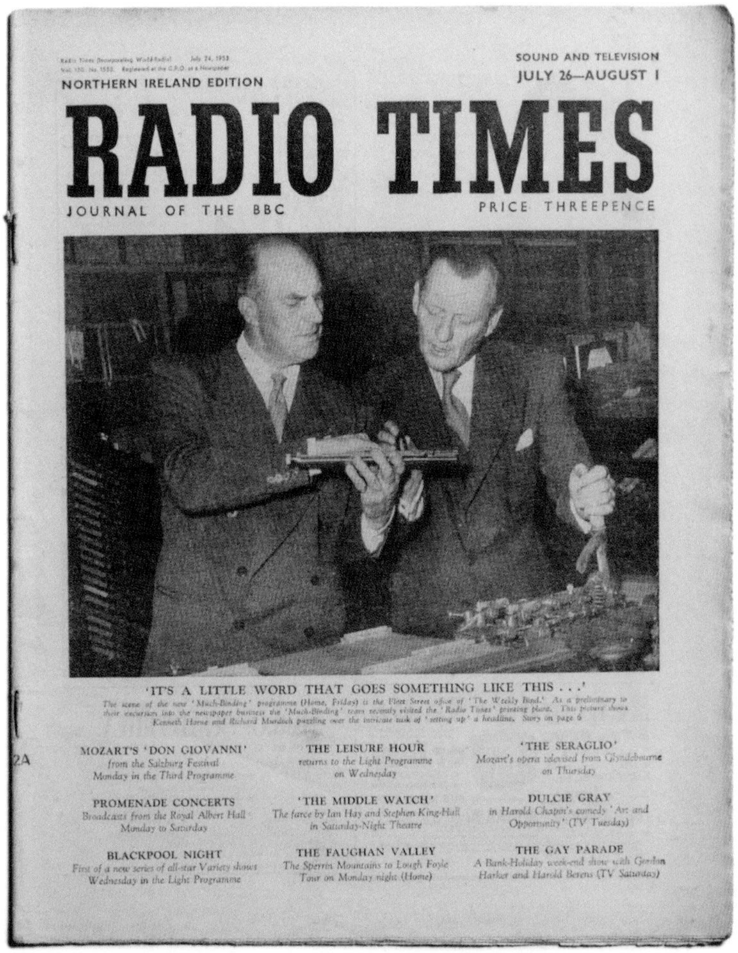

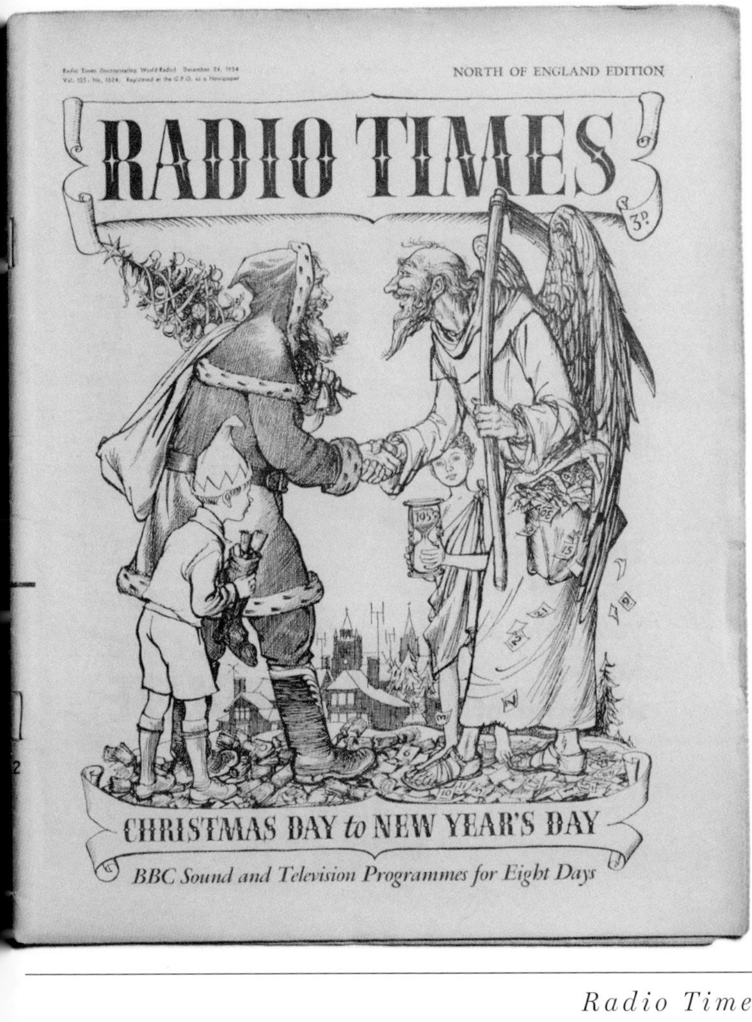

Autumn programmes *(far left)*

Illustration by CW Bacon

20–26 September 1953

This week saw the start of the sixth series of the Radio 4 stalwart, *Any Questions?* The very first question, posed on 12 October 1948, was: "What effect would it have if women were able to exert more power in politics and diplomacy?"

Journey into Space *(middle left)*

5–11 December 1954

Andrew Faulds played the exotically named Jet Morgan in *Journey into Space*, an adventure series set on Mars. An equally exotic highlight for TV viewers was coverage of a football match between Italy and Argentina from Rome. Commentator: Kenneth Wolstenholme.

Christmas 1954 *(left)*

Illustration by C Walter Hodges

25 December 1954–1 January 1955

A cover by *Radio Times* favourite CW Hodges that skilfully spanned Christmas and New Year in an eight-day edition. The TV highlight on Christmas Day was a party with Arthur Askey, Petula Clark, Tommy Cooper, Bob Monkhouse, Wilfred Pickles, Harry Secombe and Sooty (and Harry Corbett).

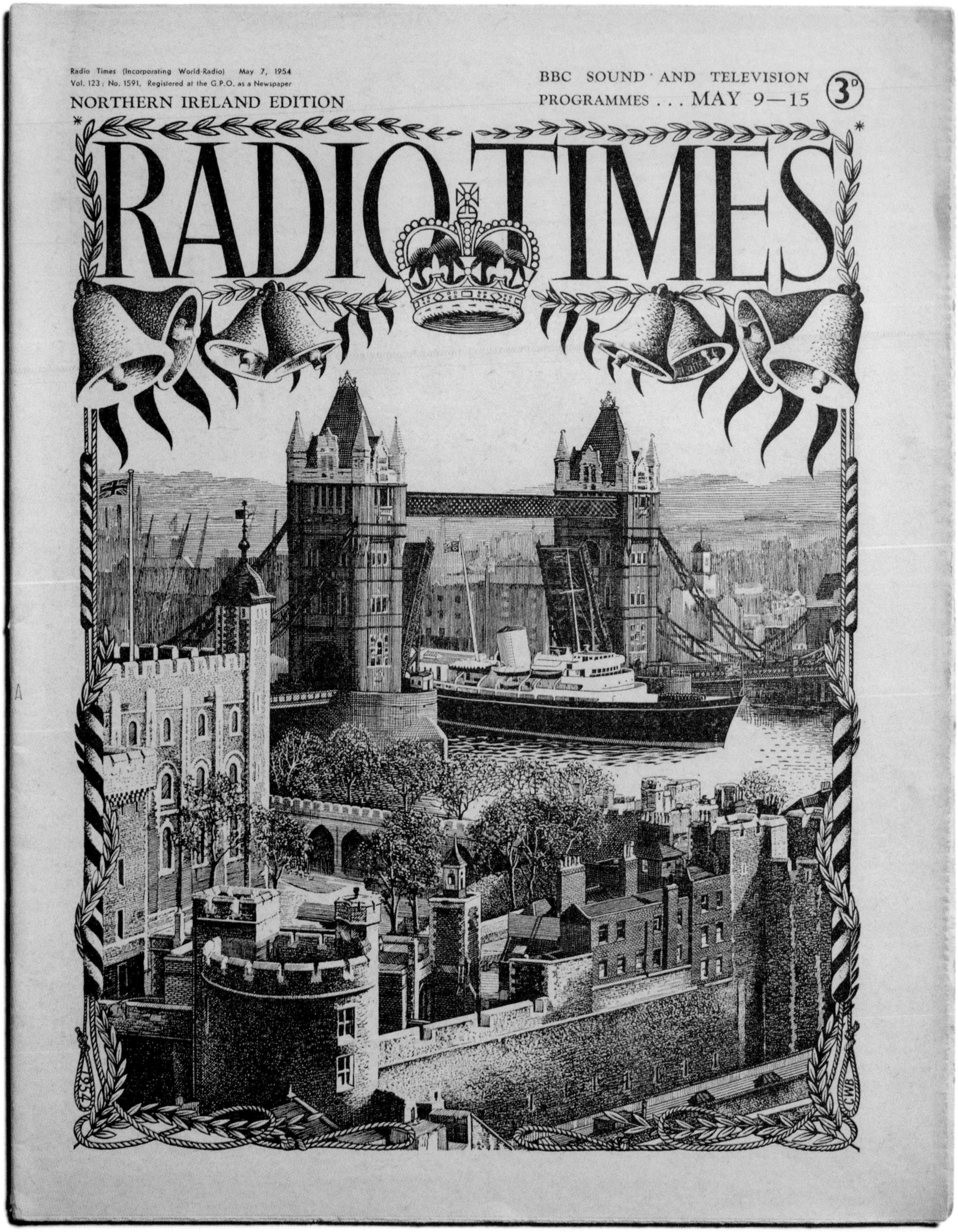

A royal return Illustration by CW Bacon *9–15 May 1954*

The cover showed Royal yacht *Britannia* under Tower Bridge and marked the return of the Queen and Prince Philip from a long tour of Australia – the first to that country by a reigning monarch. The homecoming was quite an event with crowds lining the river, bells ringing out from St Paul's Cathedral, Westminster Abbey and St Martin-in-the-Fields and the roar of a fly-past by 200 jet aircraft of the RAF and Royal Canadian Air Force.

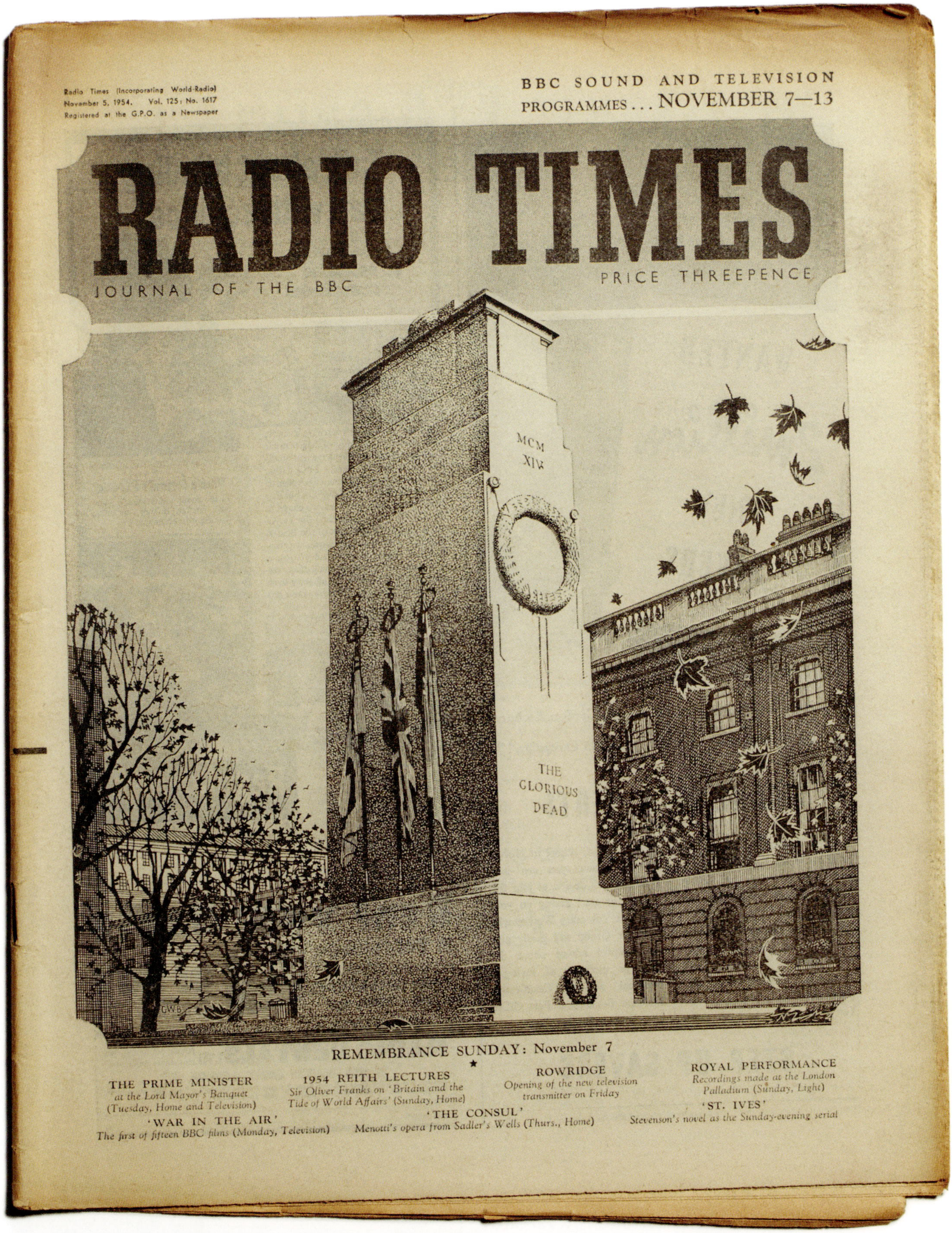
Radio Times (Incorporating World-Radio)
November 5, 1954. Vol. 125: No. 1617
Registered at the G.P.O. as a Newspaper

BBC SOUND AND TELEVISION
PROGRAMMES . . . NOVEMBER 7—13

RADIO TIMES
JOURNAL OF THE BBC
PRICE THREEPENCE

REMEMBRANCE SUNDAY: November 7

★

THE PRIME MINISTER
at the Lord Mayor's Banquet (Tuesday, Home and Television)

1954 REITH LECTURES
Sir Oliver Franks on 'Britain and the Tide of World Affairs' (Sunday, Home)

ROWRIDGE
Opening of the new television transmitter on Friday

ROYAL PERFORMANCE
Recordings made at the London Palladium (Sunday, Light)

'WAR IN THE AIR'
The first of fifteen BBC films (Monday, Television)

'THE CONSUL'
Menotti's opera from Sadler's Wells (Thurs., Home)

'ST. IVES'
Stevenson's novel as the Sunday-evening serial

Remembrance Sunday **Illustration by CW Bacon** *7–13 November 1954*

The service of remembrance in Whitehall was covered by both radio and television. Wynford Vaughan-Thomas described the scene for Home Service listeners, while Richard Dimbleby was the television commentator. Later in the week on radio, *The Adventures of Sherlock Holmes* – starring John Gielgud as Holmes and Ralph Richardson as Dr Watson – was followed by coverage of the second half of a game between Arsenal and Spartak Moscow, and then *Hancock's Half-Hour*.

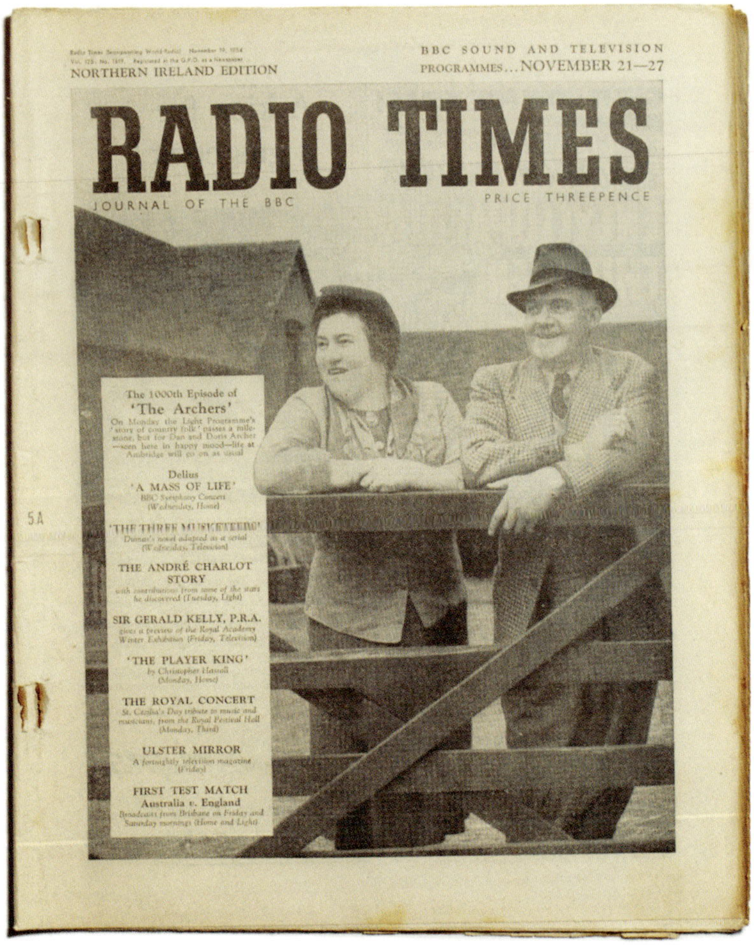

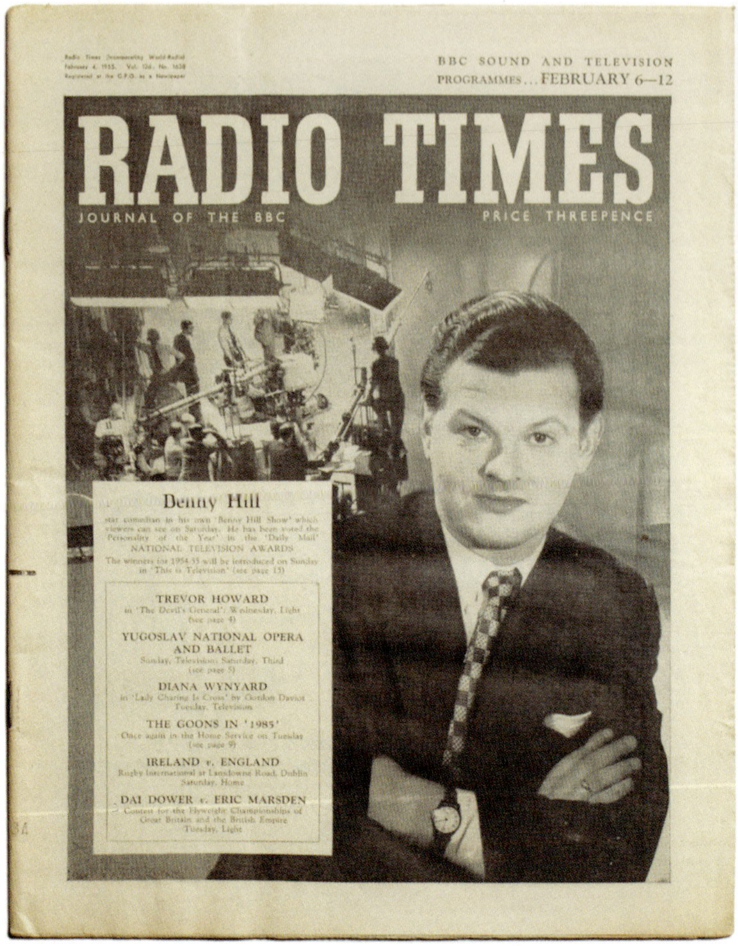

Terry-Thomas *(right)*

(photograph by Don Smith) 8–14 January 1956

Comedy actor Terry-Thomas, with his trademark twinkle, gap-toothed smile and cigarette holder, made the cover for his new television series *Strictly T-T*. Tongue firmly in cheek, he wrote: "For some reason I appear almost bald on screen – remember, the camera can lie."

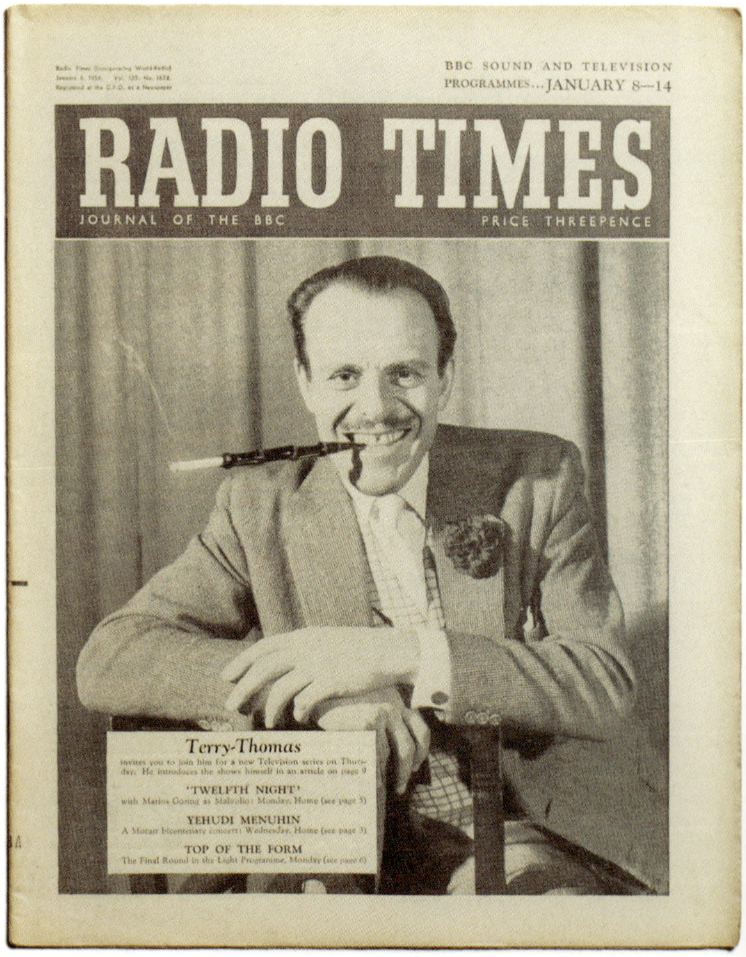

Richard Burton as Henry V *(middle right)*

22–28 April 1956

On the eve of St George's Day the Home Service broadcast a sequence from Shakespeare's *Henry V* entitled *Henry at Agincourt* (concentrating on the meaty bits before, during and after the battle), with Richard Burton playing the monarch.

At the Turn of the Year *(far right)*

Illustration by Val Biro

30 December 1956–5 January 1957

The television highlights as 1956 became 1957 were many and varied: in Dundee there was music from Jimmy Shand; in the Midlands, the bustle of a busy transport café; and in London a West Indian party with the Trinidad All-Stars Steel Band.

1,000 episodes of The Archers *(far left)*

Doris Archer (Gwen Berryman), Dan Archer (Harry Oakes)

21–27 November 1954

A big moment for Ambridge, and *Radio Times* celebrated with a picture of Dan and Doris Archer on the cover. But producer Tony Shryane was unmoved: "There will be nothing special about Monday's broadcast," he wrote. Sixty years on, there have been more than 17,100 broadcasts of *The Archers*.

Benny Hill *(middle left)*

(photograph by Don Smith) 6–12 February 1955

Fresh-faced comedian Benny Hill – he was 29 at the time – graced the cover, his reward for being named Personality of the Year at the National Television Awards. Episode two of *The Benny Hill Show* was broadcast on Saturday 12 February and featured Alma Cogan and Beryl Reid.

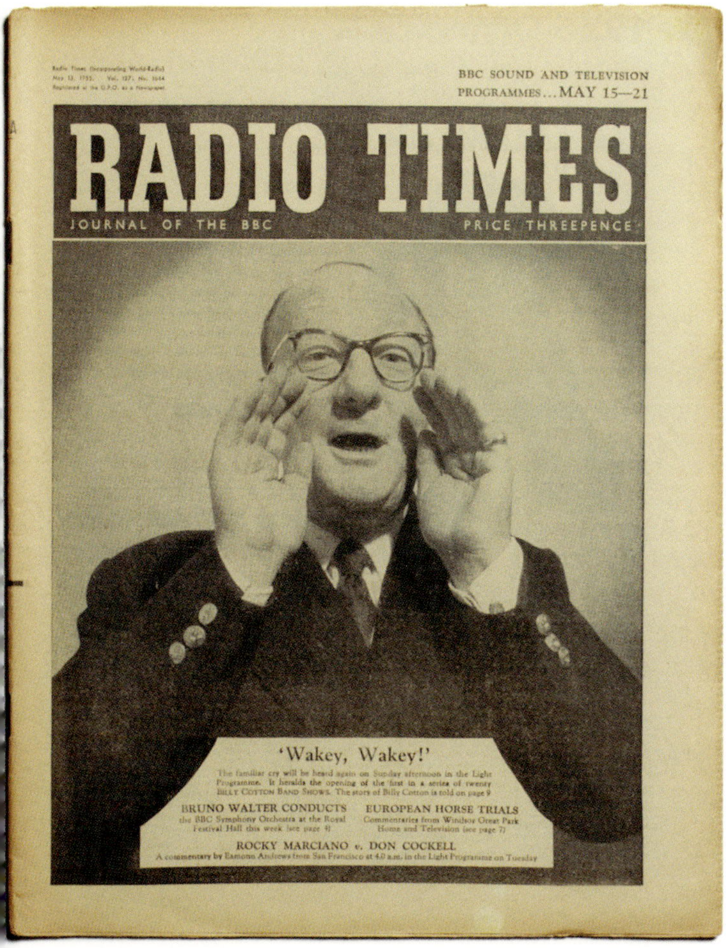

Billy Cotton *(left)*

(photograph by Don Smith) 15–21 May 1955

Another broadcasting landmark – series 20 of *The Billy Cotton Band Show*. A profile revealed that Cotton had been a boxer, a member of the Royal Flying Corps, was a keen sailor and flew his own Gypsy Moth. The secret of his success as a bandleader? "Corn – good, clean corn, simple as that."

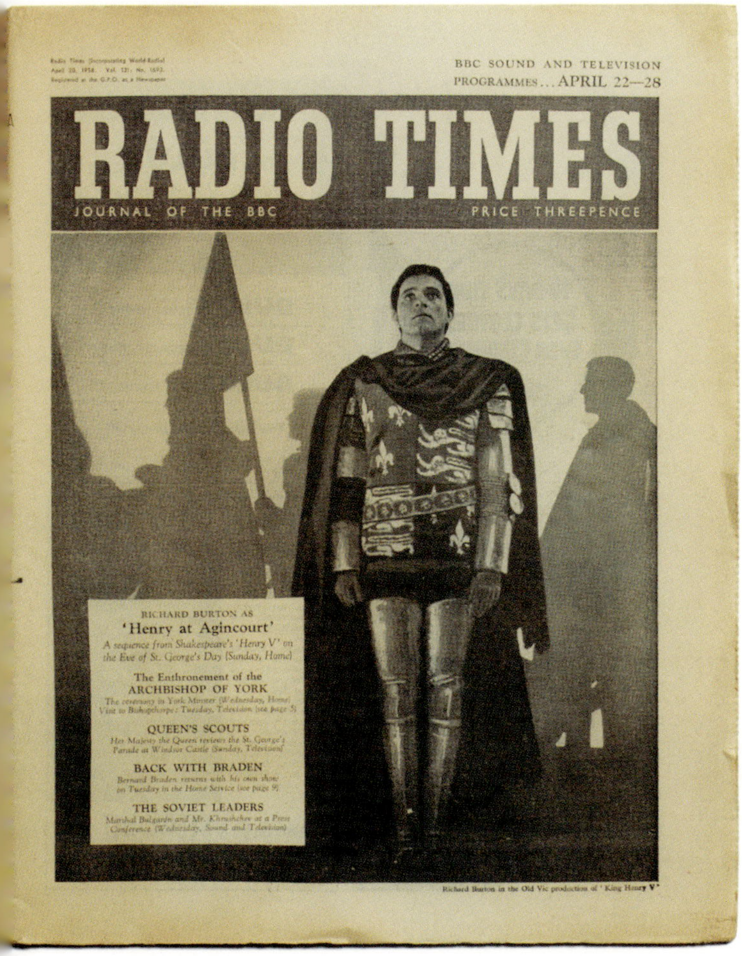

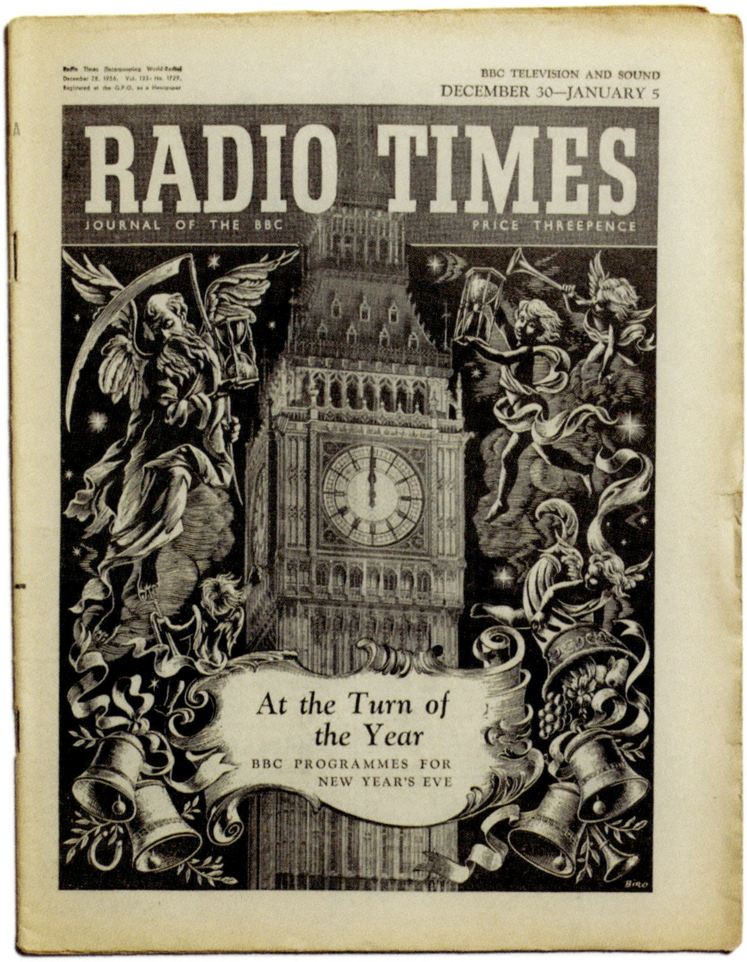

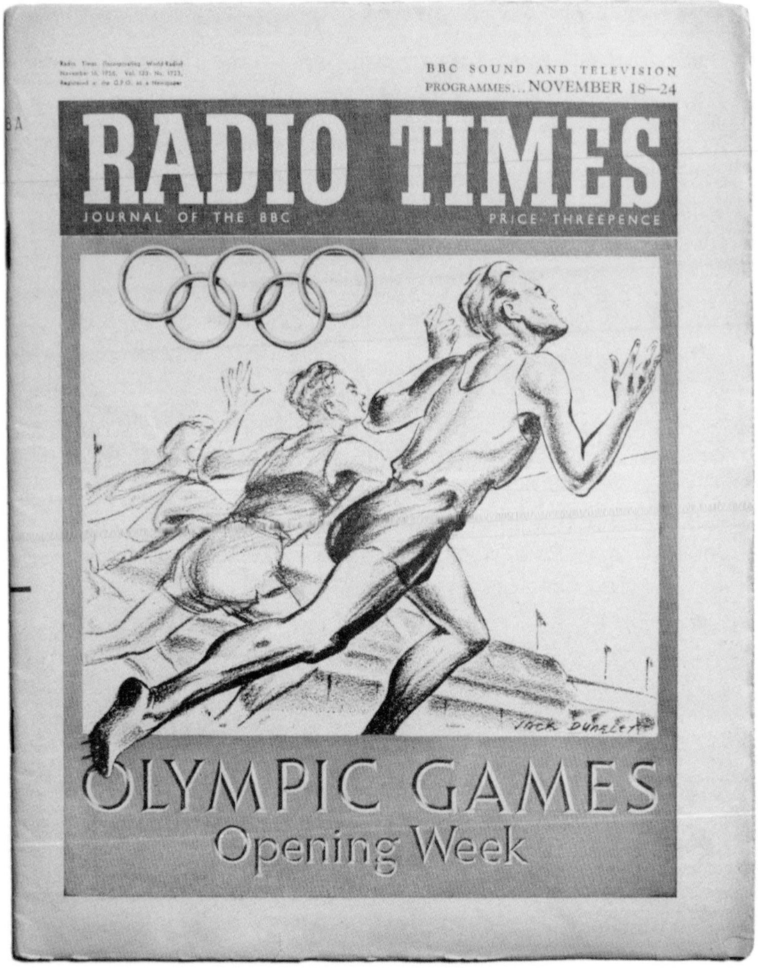

The 1956 Olympics Games *(left)*

Illustration by Jack Dunkley

18–24 November 1956

The Games were taking place in Melbourne on the other side of the world but the BBC strove to provide comprehensive coverage of events on radio. Readers were treated to a day-to-day pick of the action by Harold Abrahams.

Between Six and Seven *(below left)*

Illustration by CW Bacon

17–23 February 1957

The BBC began regular broadcasts between 6.00pm and 7.00pm in what had been a one-hour gap known as "Toddlers' Truce", when mums (and dads?) put the kids to bed. The first programme in the new slot was called *Tonight* and was presented by Cliff Michelmore.

Test Match Special *(below right)*

Peter May *26 May–1 June 1957*

Cover star Peter May had been appointed England captain for the five-Test series against West Indies. More significantly, the series marked the beginning of ball-by-ball commentary on radio (and limited television coverage). Among the commentators was John "Voice of Cricket" Arlott.

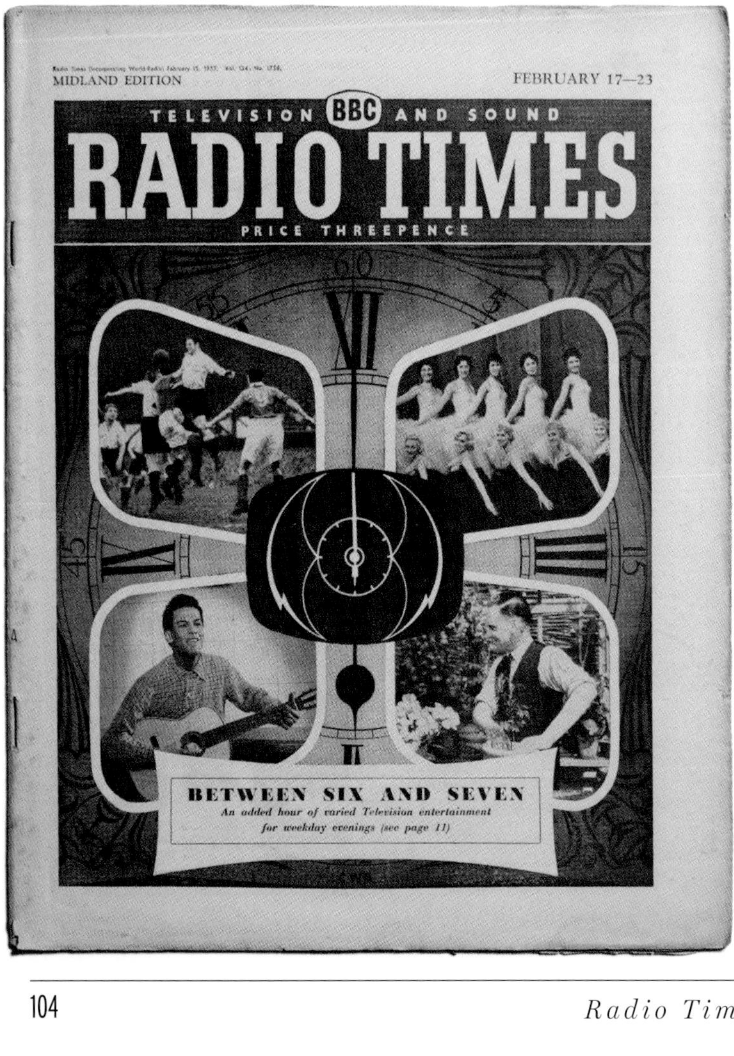

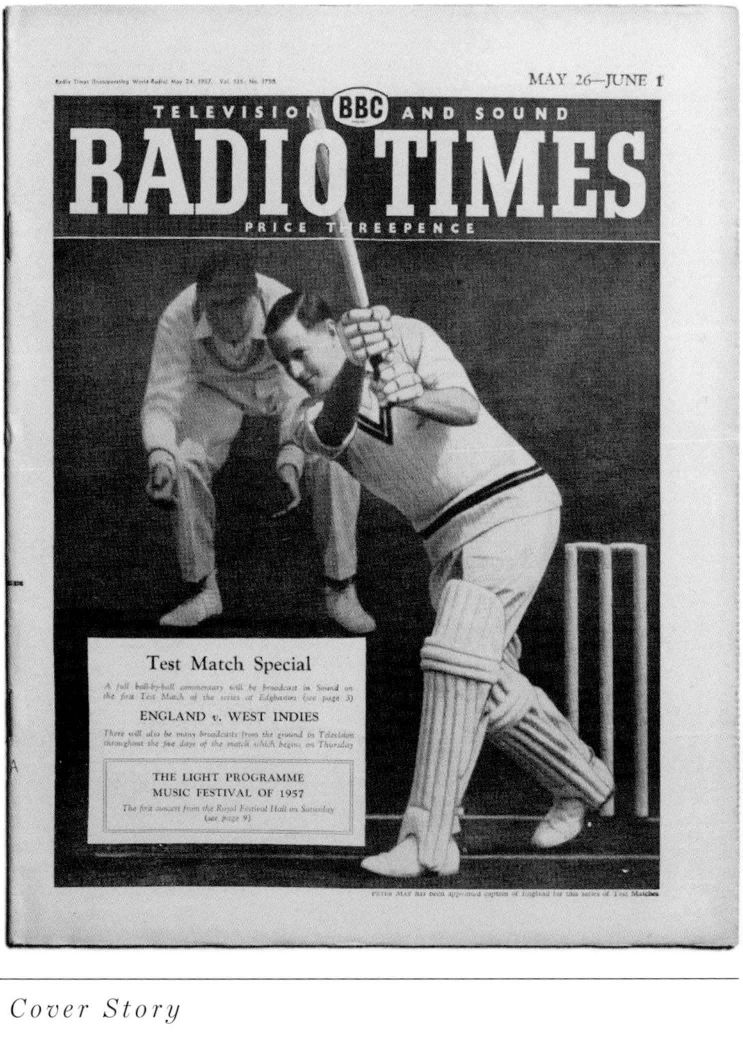

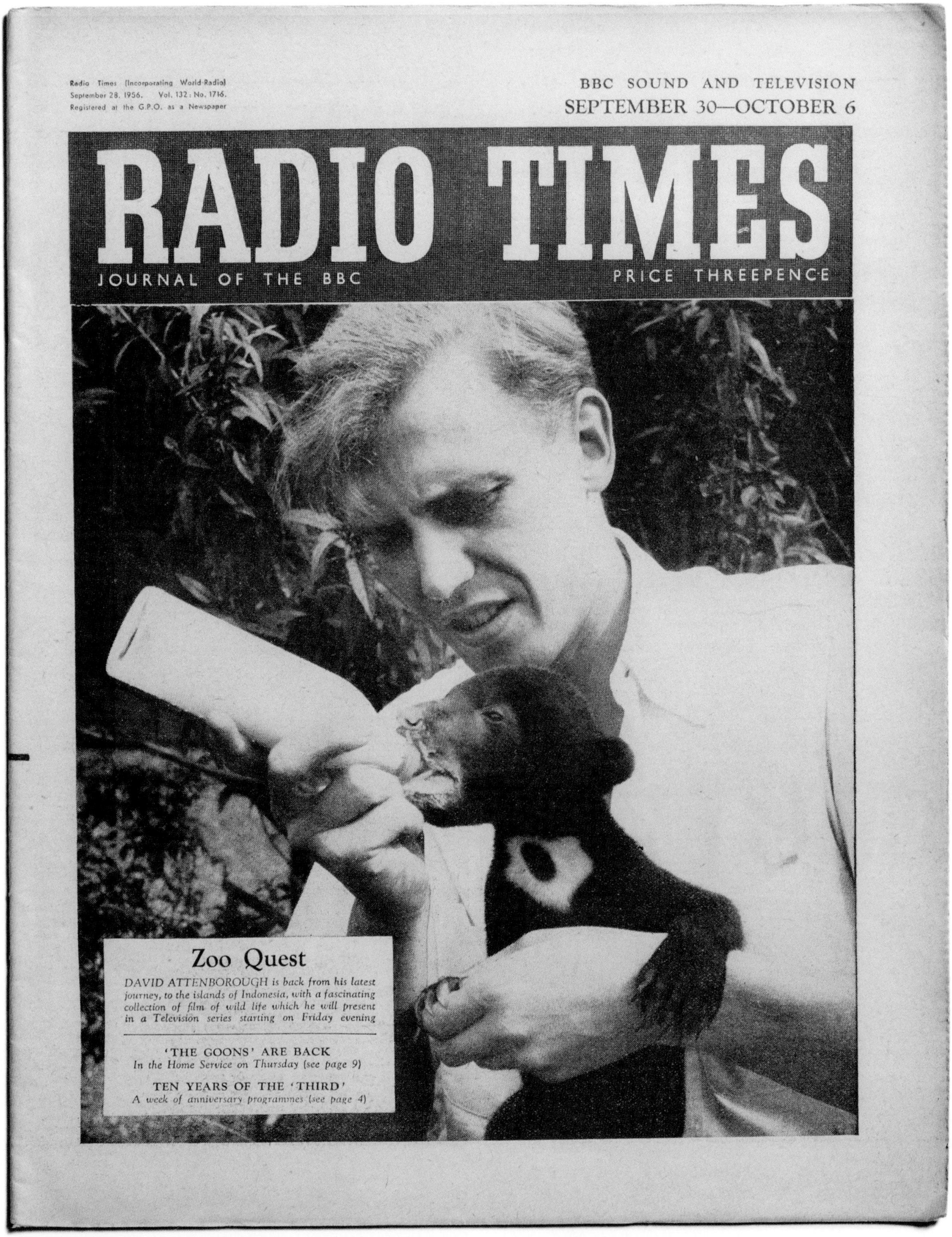

Zoo Quest **David Attenborough** *30 September–6 October 1956*

A new series of *Zoo Quest* and David Attenborough's first appearance on the cover of *Radio Times*. He was keen to tell readers about his three-month trip to Indonesia, seeking out exotic wildlife in Borneo, Java, Bali and Sumbawa. "We returned to London bringing back with us not only many thousands of feet of film but also a collection of animals including the delightful Malaysian bear we've christened Benjamin, whom you can see on the cover."

All change on radio *(right)*
Illustration by CW Bacon

29 September–5 October 1957

A revolution in the airwaves as three radio services became four: Home Service, Network Three, Third Programme and Light Programme. Director of programmes Lindsay Wellington wrote about the changes: "I hope you will agree that the BBC is offering a richness and variety of sound, and radio programmes that are the equal of any in the world."

21 years of BBC Television *(middle right)*
Illustration by CW Bacon *(photograph by Don Smith)*

27 October–2 November 1957

Another landmark was celebrated with a 90-minute programme on 2 November that included outside broadcasts from Germany, America and France as well as "experimental colour television from Alexandra Palace".

The Goon Show *(far right)*
From left: Spike Milligan, Harry Secombe, Peter Sellers *(photograph by Don Smith)*

24–30 November 1957

Goon Show stars Spike Milligan, Harry Secombe and Peter Sellers did a bit of pointing for the camera. On a more serious note, this issue carried a DIY supplement with step-by-step guides to making a pelmet, a flap table and shelves.

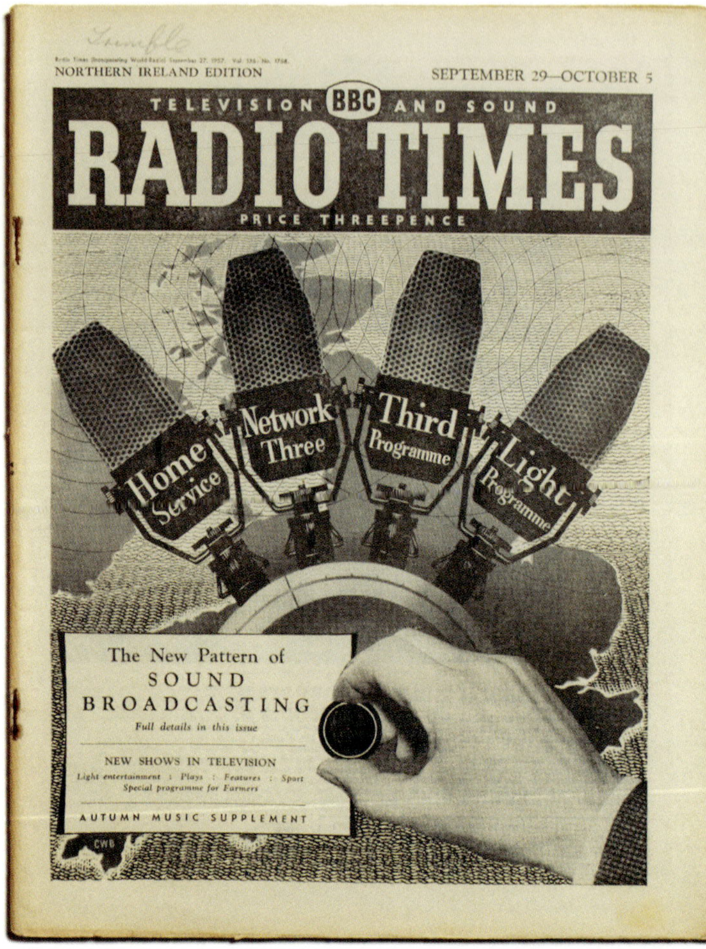

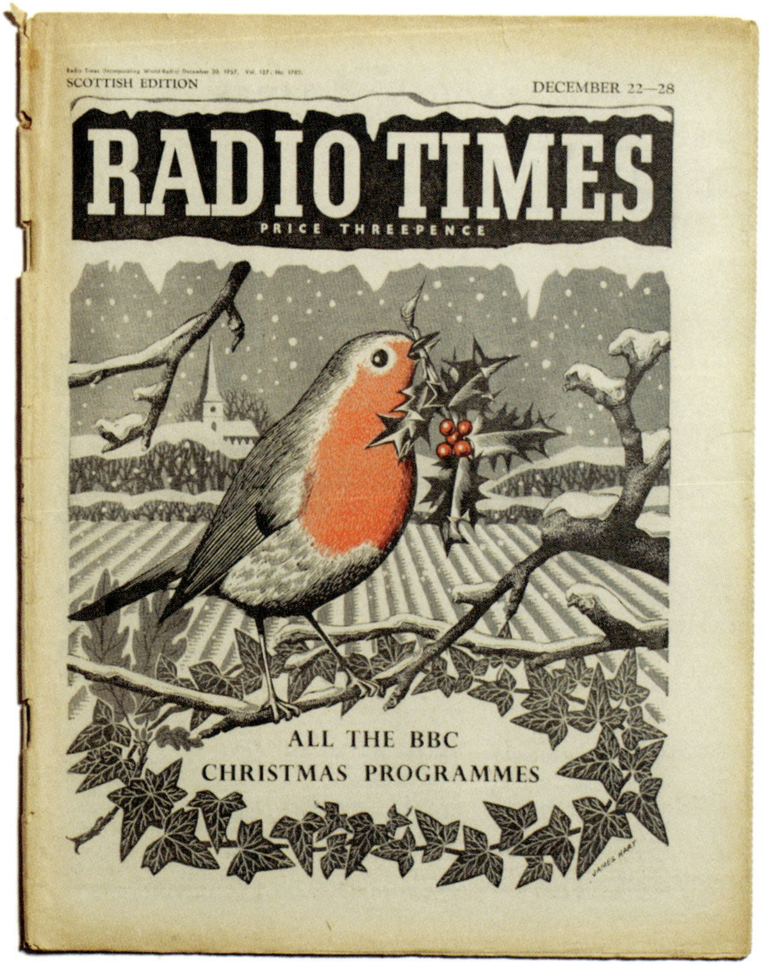

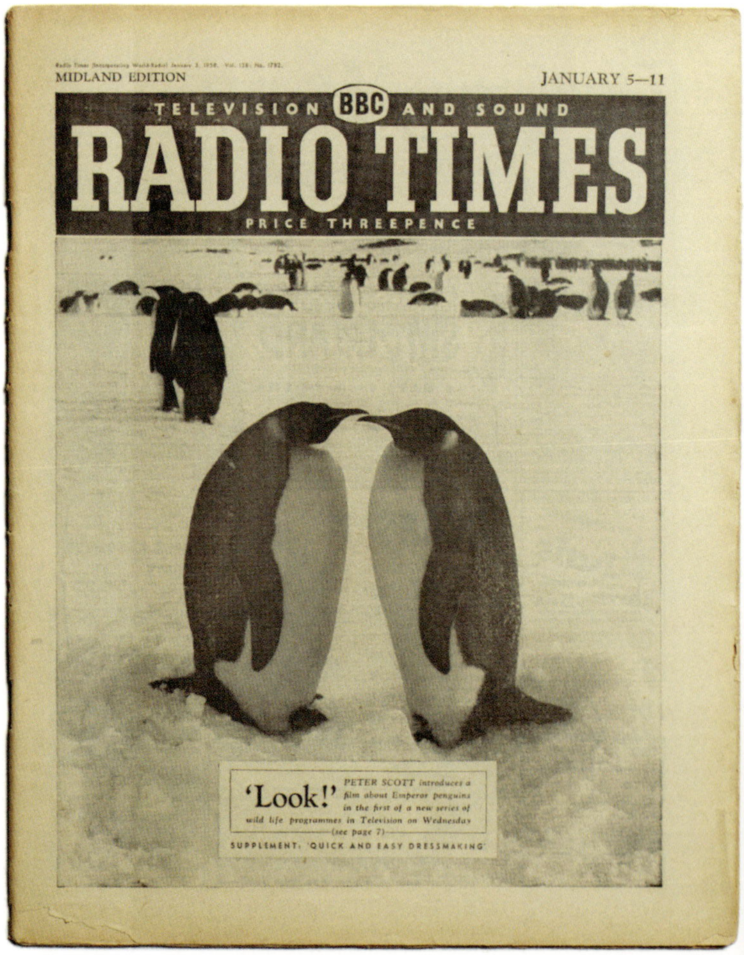

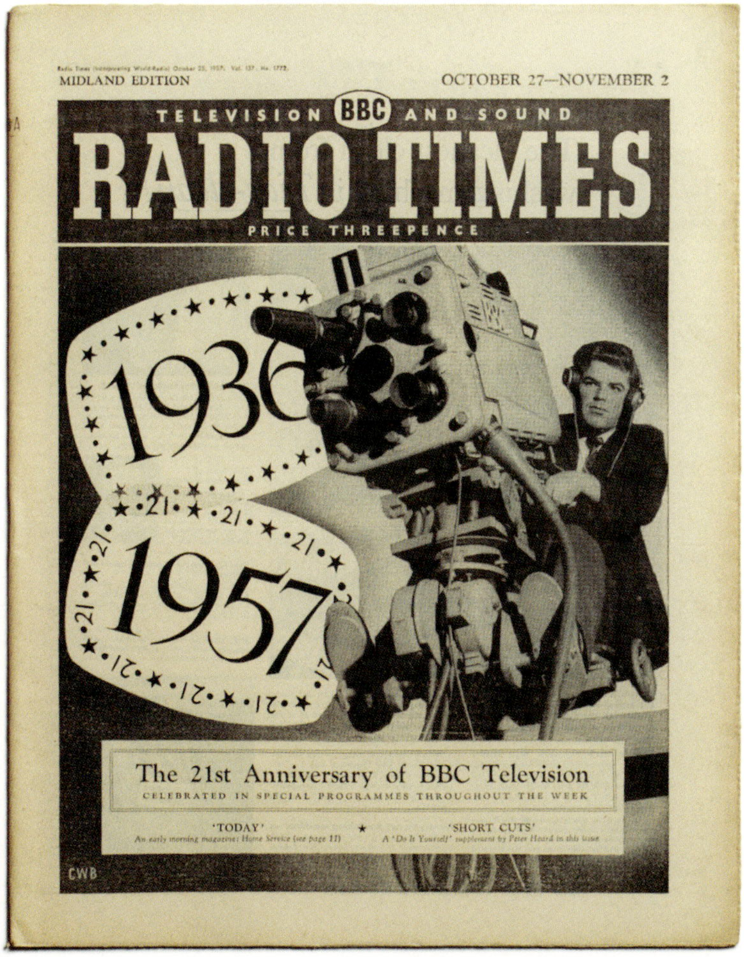

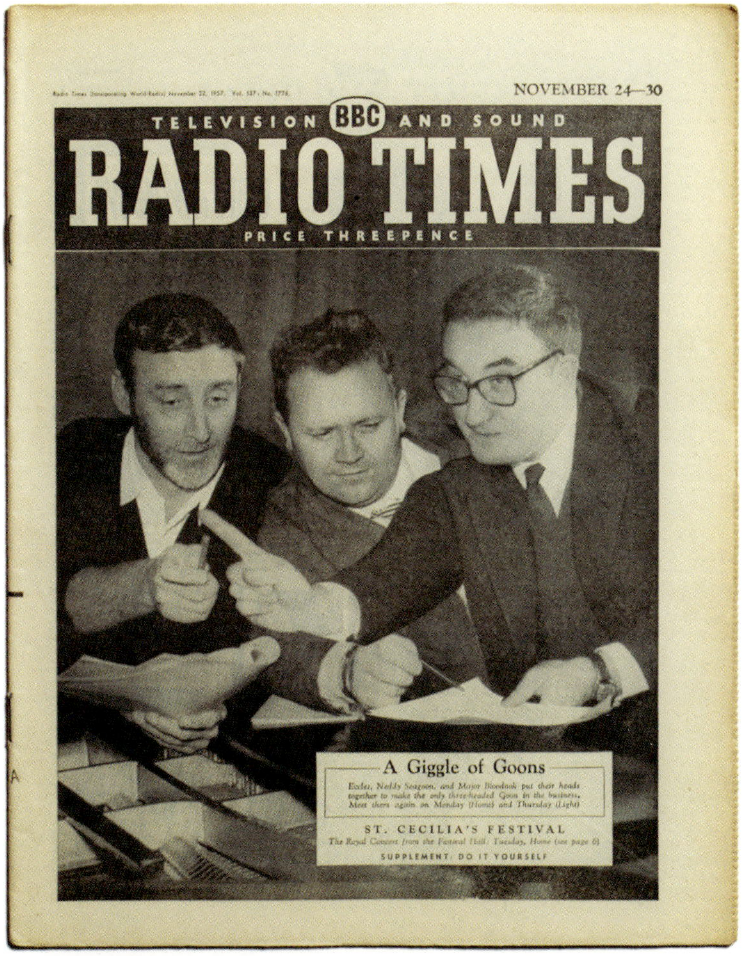

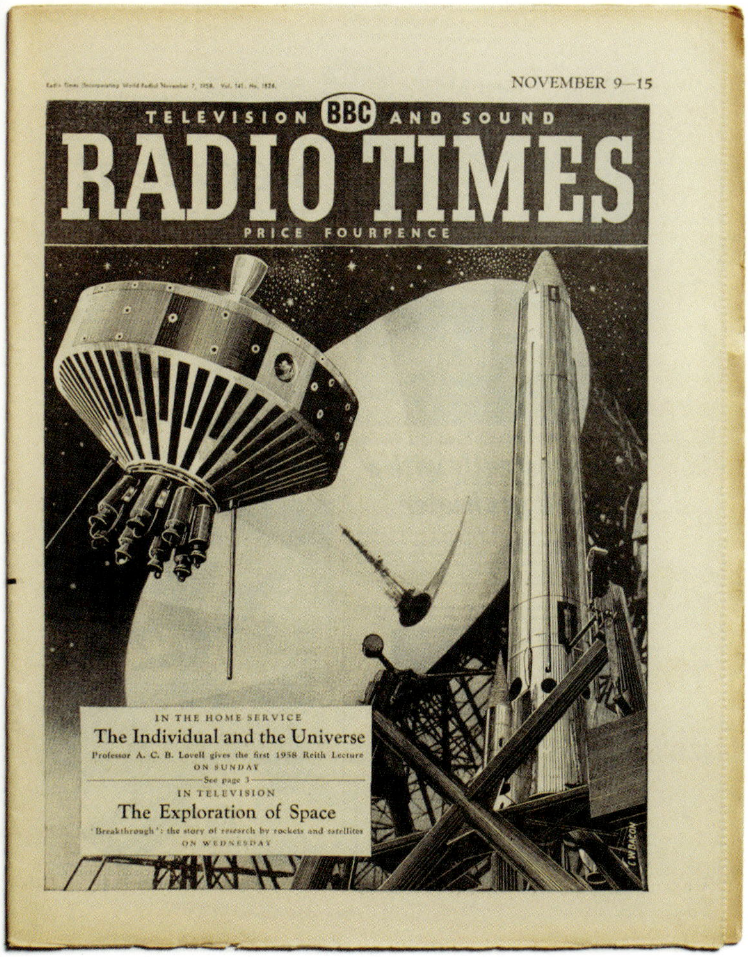

Christmas 1957 *(far left)*

Illustration by James Hart

22–28 December 1957

How's this for Christmas Day TV: the Queen's Speech, Billy Smart's Circus, *Don Juan* sung in German, clips of Gene Kelly films and *Babes in the Wood* featuring the Beverley Sisters, Charlie Drake and Tony Hancock?

Look! *(middle left)*

5–11 January 1958

Nature documentaries have always been important to the BBC. The presenter of *Look!*, Peter Scott, explained to readers that the series was about "enjoying animals, of delighting in and wondering at their appearance and behaviour". Episode one was a study of emperor penguins in Antarctica by French explorer Paul-Emile Victor.

The Individual and the Universe *(left)*

Illustration by CW Bacon

9–15 November 1958

This issue went space crazy: radio offered the Reith Lecture by Bernard Lovell, director of the Jodrell Bank Experimental Station, on the subject The Individual and the Universe. TV countered with *Breakthrough* – the story of how rockets and satellites were being used to explore space, with reports from Britain, Australia, the USA and the Soviet Union.

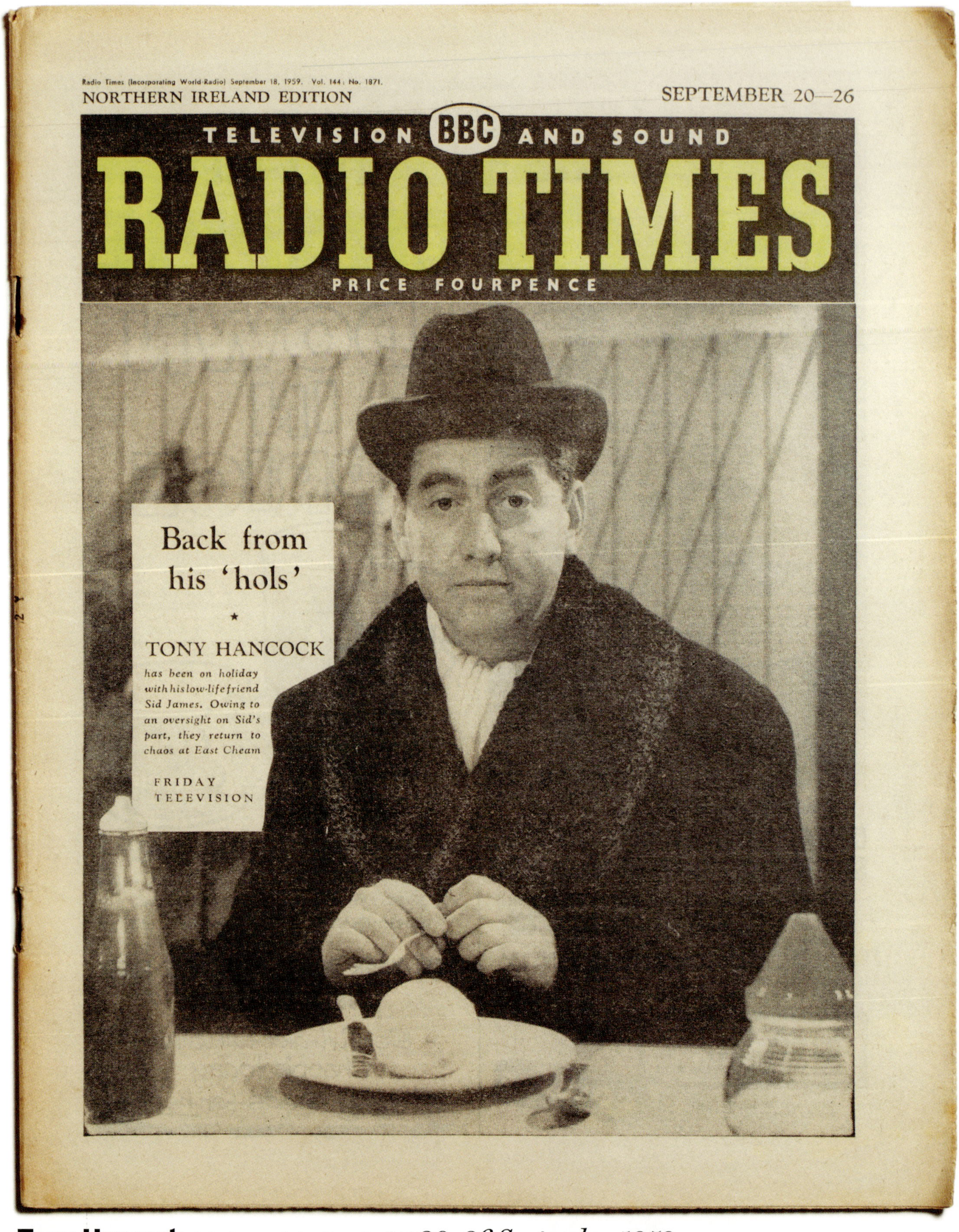

Tony Hancock *(photograph by Don Smith)* *20–26 September 1959*

Hancock wrote a beautifully comic piece to introduce the fifth series of *Hancock's Half-Hour*. "The programmes, against all advice, are once again being written by Alan Simpson and Ray Galton, who can always be relied upon to turn out a neat job, cheaply. They have informed me that they intend to portray me in a more retrospective light, within the framework and syntax of the Chekovian influence in characterisation. This means they will be dishing me up with the same old rubbish."

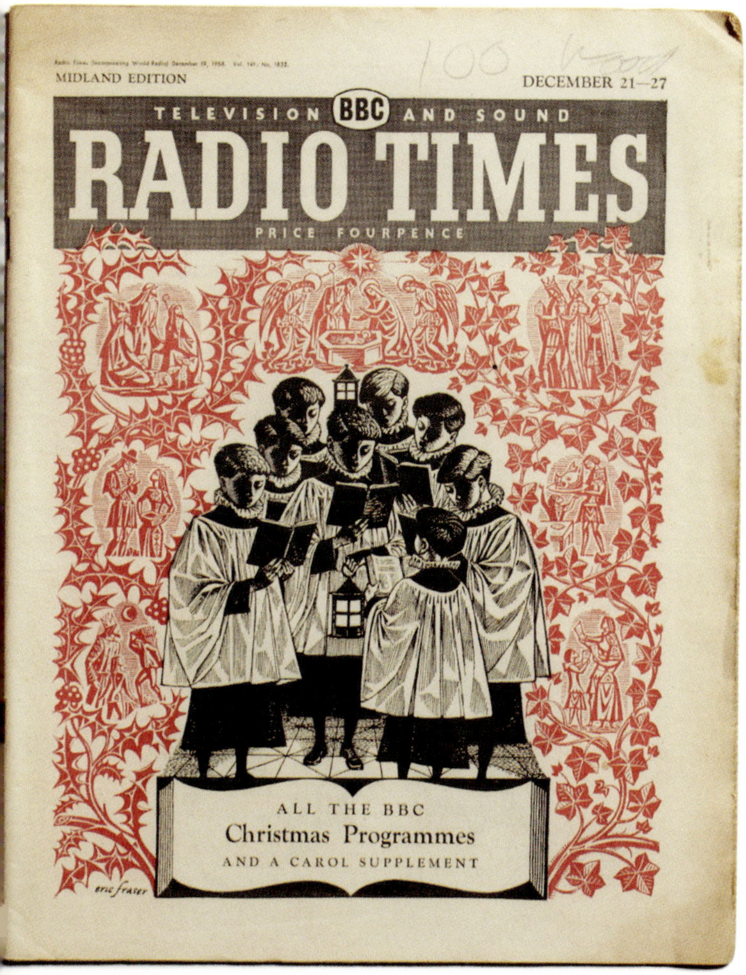

Christmas 1958 *(left)*

Illustration by Eric Fraser

21–27 December 1958

A pre-Christmas highlight was the first episode of a new six-part sci-fi adventure, *Quatermass and the Pit*, starring Andre Morell as Professor Quatermass. On Christmas Day there was a much more comforting proposition – *Top Hat* starring Fred Astaire and Ginger Rogers.

Phil Silvers *(below left)*

14–20 June 1959

American comedy actor Phil Silvers made his first live appearance on British television this week. He was the star guest on *Trinder Box*, a new variety show presented by radio comedy legend Tommy Trinder. His other guests in that first programme were Dickie Valentine and Pat Coombs.

Christmas 1959 *(below right)*

Illustration by Victor Reinganum

20–26 December 1959

On the cusp of the 60s, familiar names were to the fore. *Grandstand's* roster of commentators featured Raymond Baxter, Peter O'Sullevan and Harry Carpenter. Jack Warner was PC George Dixon in *Dixon of Dock Green*, and Frankie Howerd was the star of *Mother Goose*. And topping the bill of the Christmas edition of *The Good Old Days* was a promising comedy duo – Morecambe and Wise.

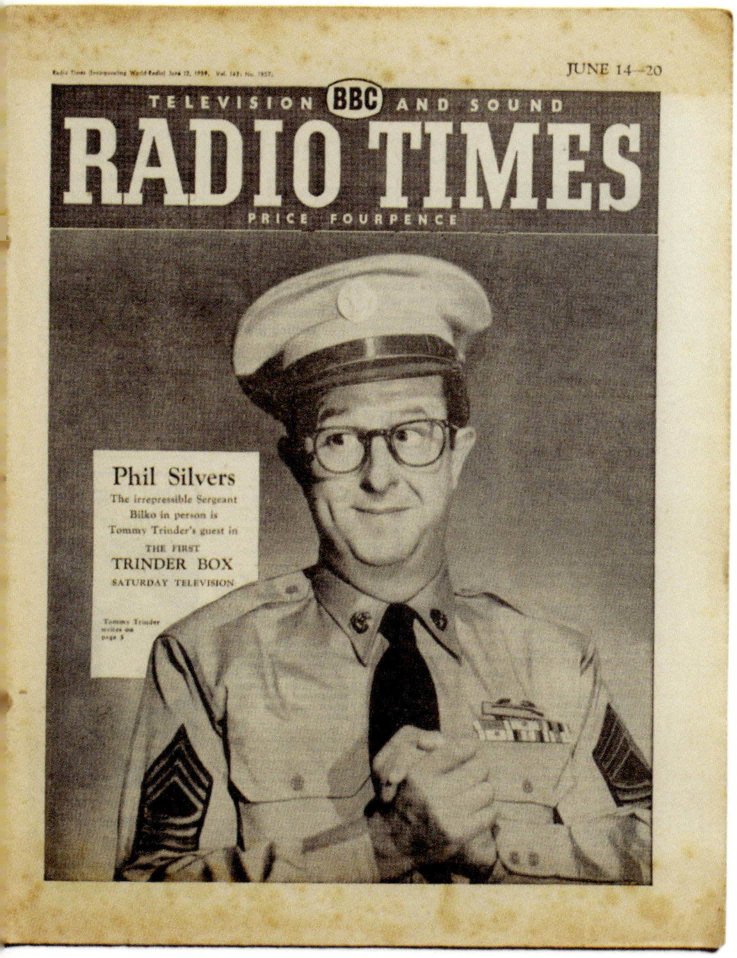

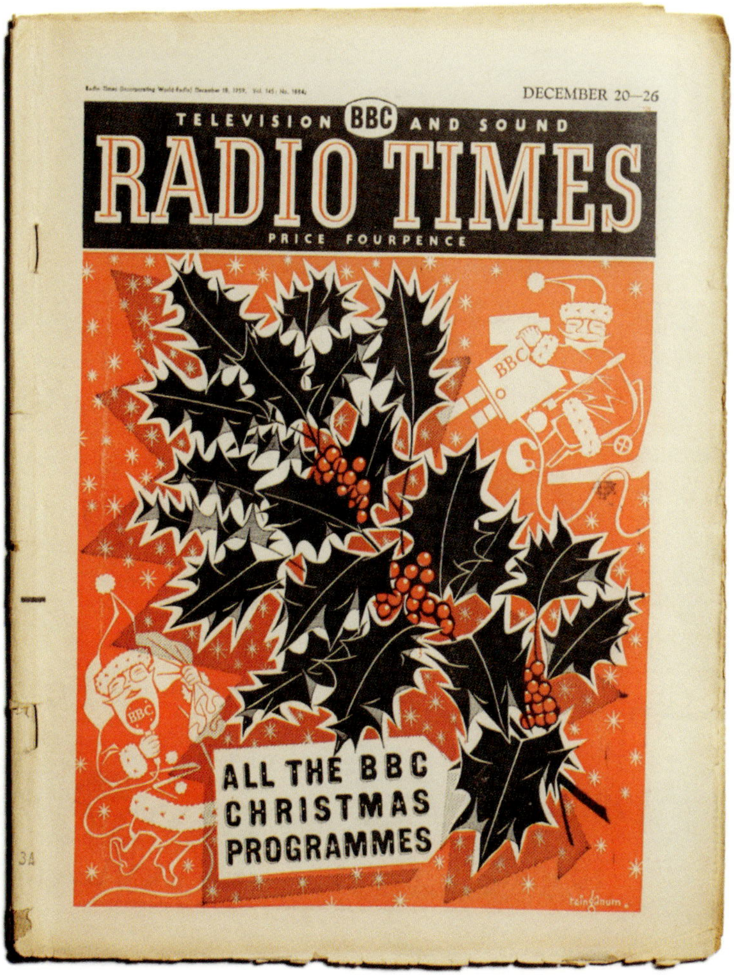

TELEVISION MORNING AND AFTERNOON

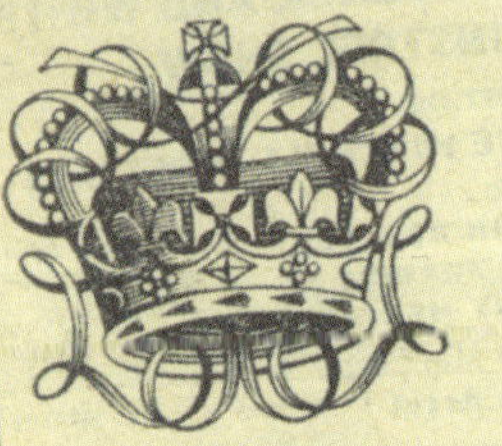

3.0 THE QUEEN

Her Majesty's Christmas Message to the Commonwealth

BBC RECORDING

ALSO ON BBC-2

The Queen's Message is preceded on BBC-1 by a programme about The Royal Palaces of Britain. Their history and their art treasures will be presented for the first time on television

SEE SPECIAL SUPPLEMENT IN CENTRE PAGES

12.45 THE LUCY SHOW

A comedy film series with never a dull moment

starring **LUCILLE BALL** *as* Lucy Carmichael and **GALE GORDON** *as* Mr. Mooney

If it's laughter you're after . . . *Lucy and George Burns* . . . are the tops!

1.10 THE ANDY WILLIAMS SHOW

Christmas greetings from the series featuring song, music, and comedy and the best from the world of entertainment

starring **ANDY WILLIAMS** and his family

with **THE OSMOND BROTHERS**
THE GOOD TIME SINGERS
THE NICK CASTLE DANCERS

A programme recorded in the U.S.A.

2.0 THE ROYAL PALACES OF BRITAIN

The Royal Palaces of Britain, their history, and their art treasures, are presented for the first time on television

In this hour **Sir Kenneth Clark** tells the story of the Kings and Queens who built these palaces and filled them with the greatest private collection of art in the world

Music composed and arranged by SIR ARTHUR BLISS
Master of the Queen's Musick
Sinfonia of London
Conducted by **Muir Mathieson**

Photographed by Arthur Englander, F.R.P.S.
Camera operator, Ken MacMillan
Stills photographer, Mike Sanders
Film editor, Roy Fry
Dubbing mixer, Brian Watkins
Recordist, Stan Nightingale
Research, Simon Buxton
Executive producer, DAVID WINDLESHAM
Directed by ANTHONY DE LOTBINIÈRE
Produced by BBC Television and Independent Television

3.5 BILLY SMART'S CIRCUS

A gala performance from the Big Top of the world's greatest touring circus

where
Father Christmas walks the wire
Elephants dance
Horses fly
and
Master of Song
David Hughes
as Britain's first singing ringmaster welcomes viewers from ten European countries

and introduces

WALKING ON AIR
Miracles of balance higher than a house
The four daring **Cimarros**

BALLERINA ON THE SILVER WIRE
On the points of her toes she dances on a single thread
At only sixteen she's **Katharina** the great

BLOOMERS ON A HORSE
It's laughter they're after
Brilliant clowning on horseback by **The Ascots**

BEDTIME FOR CHIMPS
On stilts, on bicycles, or in bed **Willi Meyer's Chimps** steal the show

ACROBATICS ON PNEUMATICS
Stars of the Czechoslovakian State Circus, the excitingly mobile **Valla-Bertini Troupe**

CLOWNING GLORY
From Brussels with a boxing machine the hilarious Belgian clowns **Les French**

SUPERB HIGH-SCHOOL RIDING
From Portugal with his wonderful stallion Toro comes the world-famous exponent of haute école **Don Meyaro**

AERIAL REVOLUTION
A death-defying toehold at the top of a forty-foot revolving mast by Sweden's star aerialists **The Aeristos**

FIFTEEN ELEPHANTS AND BILLY SMART JR.
The world's finest trained elephants in a brand-new routine

THE CIRCUS IS A WORLD OF ENTERTAINMENT
Flying horses, scores of performers, and our singing ringmaster in a fantastic
FIREWORK FINALE

Circus direction by Mr. Billy Smart's sons: RONNIE, DAVID, BILLY JR.
Musical director, KEN GRIFFIN
Assistant producer, Mary David
† Produced by DEREK BURRELL-DAVIS

See facing page

4.0 DISNEY TIME

Rolf Harris with the help of **Coojeebear** introduces this year's Christmas programme of Walt Disney films, in which the accent is on comedy and music

with scenes from
LADY AND THE TRAMP
PETER PAN
WIND IN THE WILLOWS
FOLLOW ME BOYS
BALLERINA
FIGHTING PRINCE OF DONEGAL
MARY POPPINS
WINNIE THE POOH AND THE HONEY TREE

Films by courtesy of Walt Disney
† Produced for TV by RICHARD EVANS

See facing page

4.40 ALADDIN and his Wonderful Lamp

starring **ARTHUR ASKEY** and **ROY CASTLE**
featuring **CHARLIE CAIROLI**
with
Alan Curtis *as* Abanazar
Angela Richards *as* Aladdin
Ian Wallace *as* The Emperor
Mary Millar *as* the Princess
and
Peter Grant *as* The Vizier
Pat Goh *as* So Shy
Christine Child *as* The Genie of the Ring
David Davenport *as* The Slave of the Lamp
The Douglas Squires Dancers
The George Mitchell Singers

Choreography by DOUGLAS SQUIRES
Musical associate, ART DAY
Orchestra directed by **Harry Rabinowitz**
Directed by PETER WHITMORE
† Written and produced by DAVID CROFT

Arthur Askey and Roy Castle are appearing in 'Babes in the Wood' at the Wimbledon Theatre, London; Alan Curtis is in 'Babes in the Wood' at the Palace Theatre, Manchester; Charlie Cairoli in 'Merry King Cole' at the Empire Theatre, Liverpool; Mary Millar is appearing at The Poor Millionaire, London

See facing page

Part 7 of 'The Three Musketeers' will be shown tomorrow at 5.30 p.m.

6.5 THE NEWS and THE WEATHER MAN

† BBC recording
‡ Repeat broadcast
* *Approximate time*

BBC-2

3.0 p.m. THE QUEEN

Her Majesty's Christmas Message

See BBC-1

3.5 THE WORLD OF JACQUES-YVES COUSTEAU

The incredible world of th famous French underwater e plorer and inventor—55 fathoi beneath the Mediterranean

Produced by the NATIONAL GEOGRAPHIC SOCIETY and DAVID L. WOLPER
Written by JAMES DUGAN and IRWIN ROSTEN
Music by LALO SCHIFRIN
Filmed by PHILIPPE COUSTEAU
Narrated by **Orson Welles**

See page 11

4.0 OH MR. PORTER

The comedy film classic starri **WILL HAY** *as* William Porter
with
MOORE MARRIOTT *as* Jeremiah Harbottle
GRAHAM MOFFATT *as* Albert
Directed by MARCEL VARNEL
Fraud and blustering incomp but a trainload of laughter order of the day when William takes over as Stationmaster.

5.20 THE LENINGRAD STA KIROV BALLET

Three pieces from the pro danced by the oldest bal pany in the world durir recent visit to
The Royal Opera House Covent Garden

SWAN LAKE: Act 2
Music by TCHAIKOVSKY
Choreography by PETIPA and
New choreography by KONSTANTIN SERGEYEV
with
Natalia Makarova *as* Odette
Sergei Vikulov *as* Prince S
Magician........................AN
Cygnets....................NINA S
NINA SOLDUN, LYUDMIL
TAM
Swans.....................TATIANA
MARGUERITA ALFIMOVA, N
INESS

THE CORSAIR
Classical duet
Music by RICCARDO DRIC
Choreography by ALEXAND
Kaleriya Fedicheva and

TARAS BULBA
Zaporozhtse Dance
Vsevolod Uchov, Oleg So and Alexander Pavlovsk

Orchestra of the Royal Opera House C
Leader, CHARLES TAYLOR
Conducted by **Victor and Victor Shirokov**
Artistic director, KONS
Introduced by James
† TV presentation by Jo
Televised by arrangem Hochhauser Ltd. and House Covent Garden

Radio Times

FIVEPENCE

BBC tv Sound

THE BOX IN THE CORNER GROWS UP

1960–1969

25 years of BBC TV

Illustration by Victor Reinganum

28 October–3 November 1961

The cover by Victor Reinganum celebrated the silver jubilee of BBC Television and its new home in Television Centre in west London. The cover feature took a tour of the building with its paint shop, wardrobe and prop rooms, the runways where stagehands delivered scenery to studios and the "discreet, disciplined and curiously attractive" control suite for receiving live foreign broadcasts.

There were also hints of a second TV channel, and the point was made that the building's air-conditioning could deal with the technical demands "if colour television were ever allowed".

But that was for the future: the highlights on the single black-and-white channel available to viewers were *Just Gracie* – a half-hour of songs and stories with Gracie Fields – and the first TV production of *Anna Karenina*, starring Claire Bloom and Sean Connery.

1960-1969

The decade that brought us the Beatles, Doctor Who, That Was the Week That Was, colour TV and the first man on the Moon…

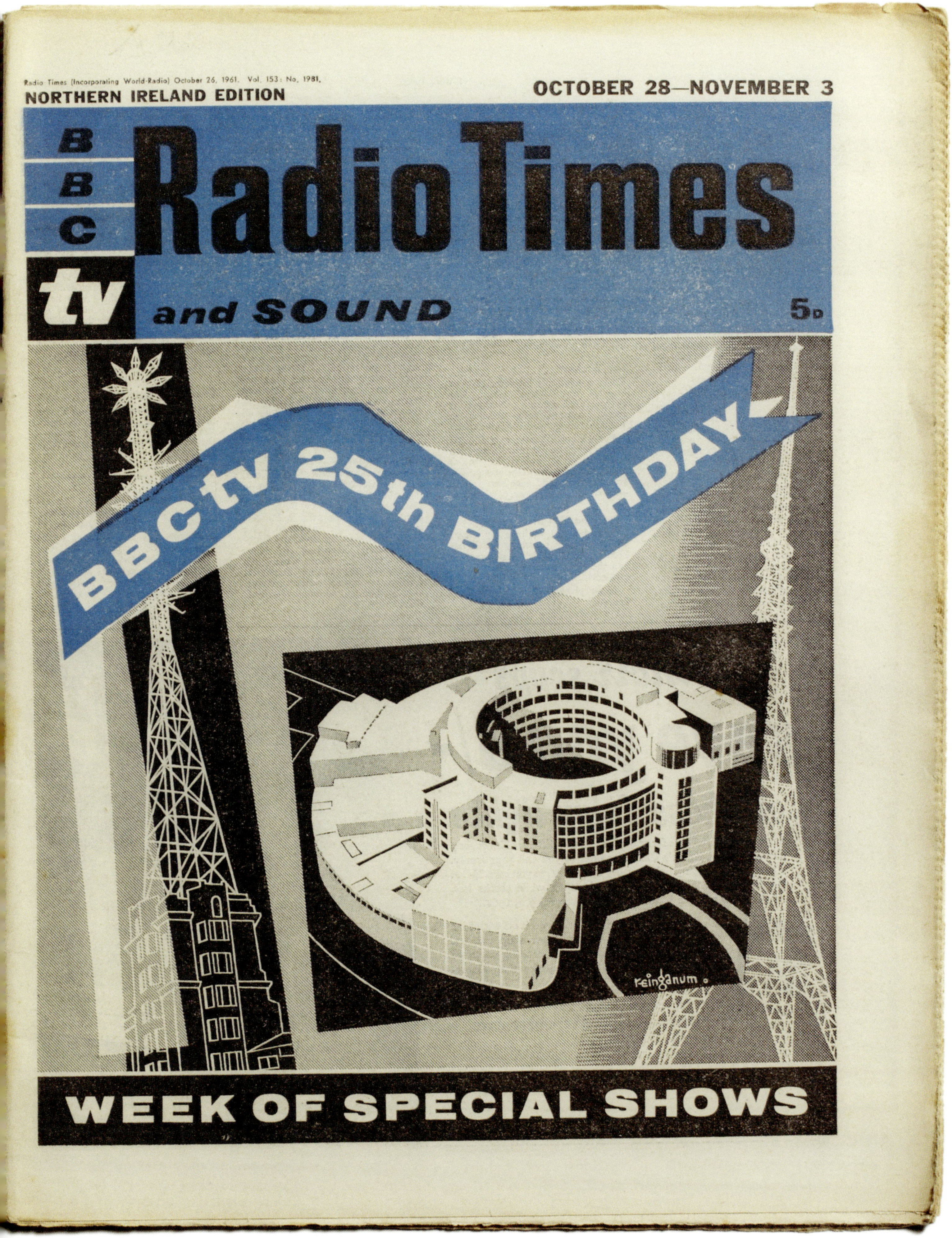
Radio Times (Incorporating World-Radio) October 26, 1961. Vol. 153: No. 1981.
NORTHERN IRELAND EDITION
OCTOBER 28—NOVEMBER 3
BBC
Radio Times
tv
and SOUND
5D
BBC tv 25th BIRTHDAY
WEEK OF SPECIAL SHOWS

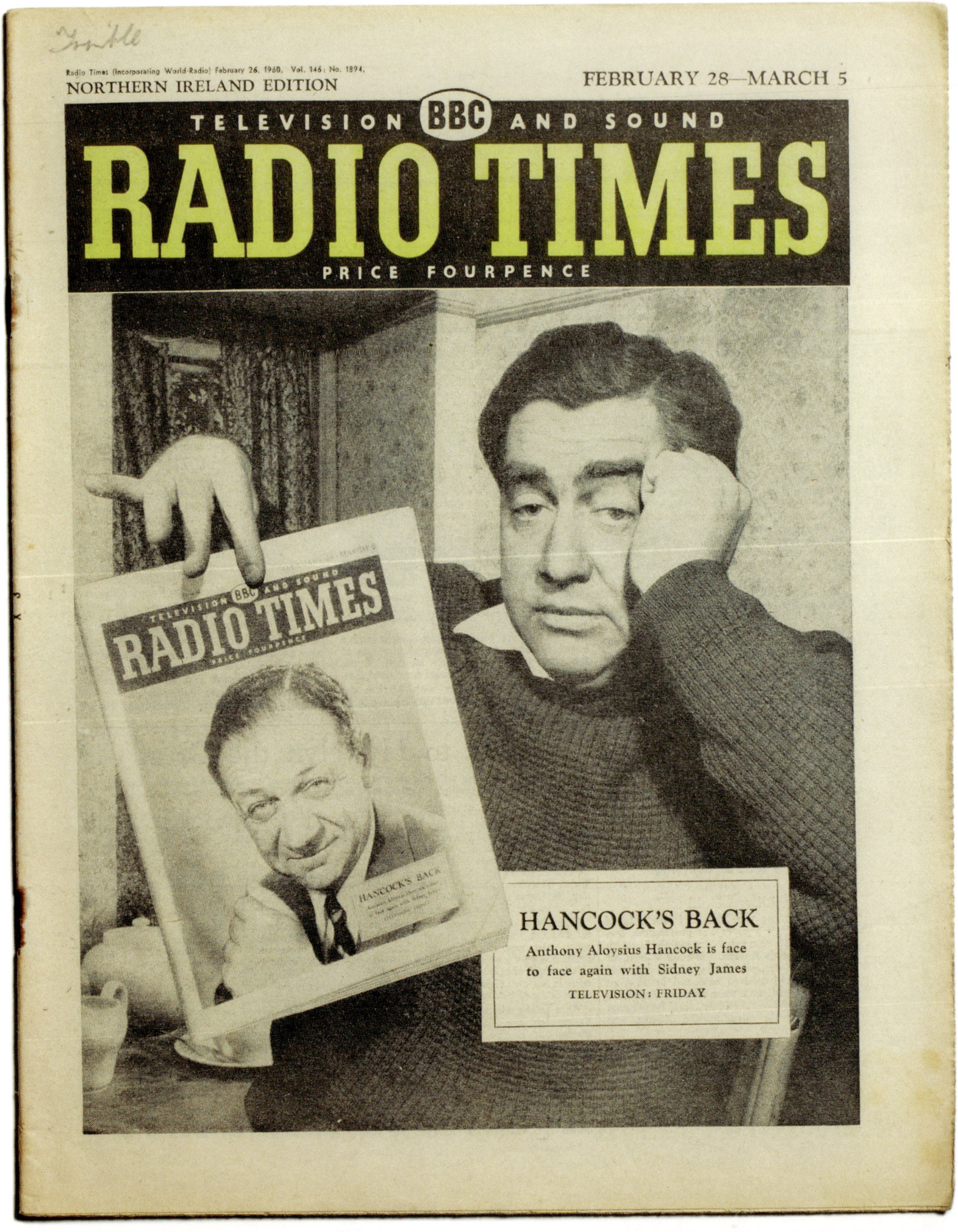

Hancock's Half-Hour **Tony Hancock** *(photograph by Don Smith)* *28 February–5 March 1960*

The seven-year comic partnership of Tony Hancock and Sidney James on radio and television was almost over by the time this series of *Hancock's Half-Hour* was broadcast. By the following year the show would be called simply *Hancock*, without James, and the final series would include the classic episodes *The Blood Donor* and *The Radio Ham* before Hancock also parted company with his writers, Ray Galton and Alan Simpson. This cover also made an appearance in 1985 – see page 229.

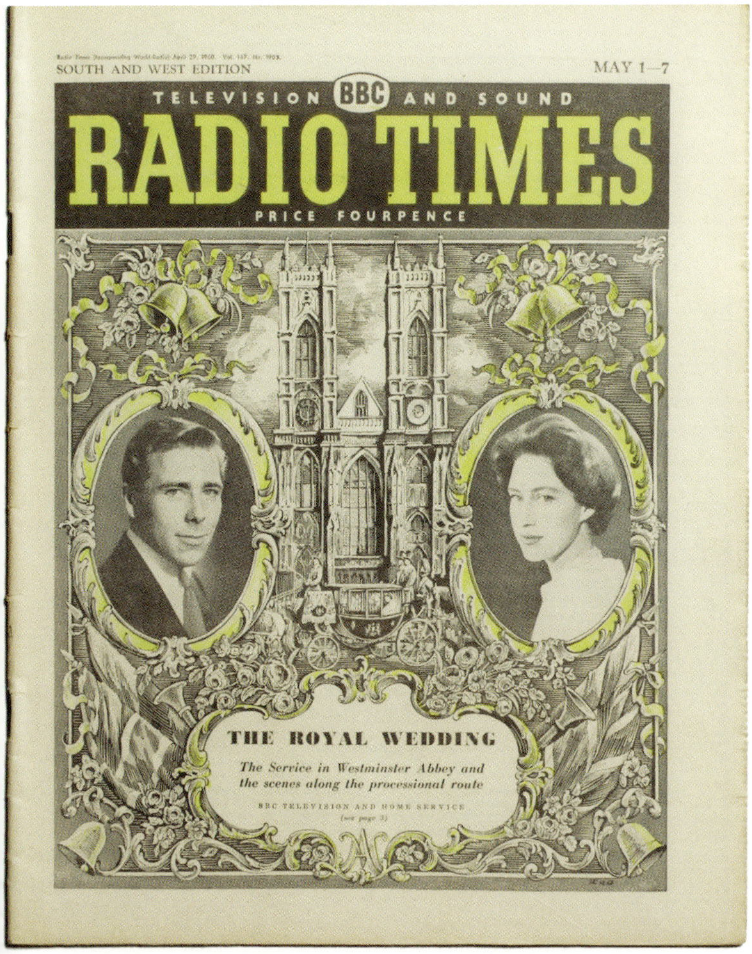

The Royal Wedding *(left)*
Illustration by Val Biro

1–7 May 1960

Richard Dimbleby headed the commentary team at Westminster Abbey as Princess Margaret married Antony Armstrong-Jones on Friday 6 May. The wedding was the most complex outside broadcast since the Coronation, with worldwide radio coverage as well as 25 cameras along the processional route.

Wimbledon *(below left)*

19–25 June 1960

The 1947 champion Jack Kramer joined the commentary team and David Coleman was installed to provide a rolling results and news service. There was great excitement at the introduction of a "second vision circuit", which meant that viewers could watch highlights from neighbouring courts during intervals in live broadcasts of the major matches.

Television Centre – First Night *(below right)*
From left: David Nixon, Richard Hearne, Arthur Askey *(photograph by Don Smith)*

26 June–2 July 1960

Nixon, Hearne and Askey topped the bill of a variety show that was the first production to be broadcast from Television Centre. *This Is the BBC*, a film of an imaginary day in the life of the Corporation and its staff, was shown the same evening.

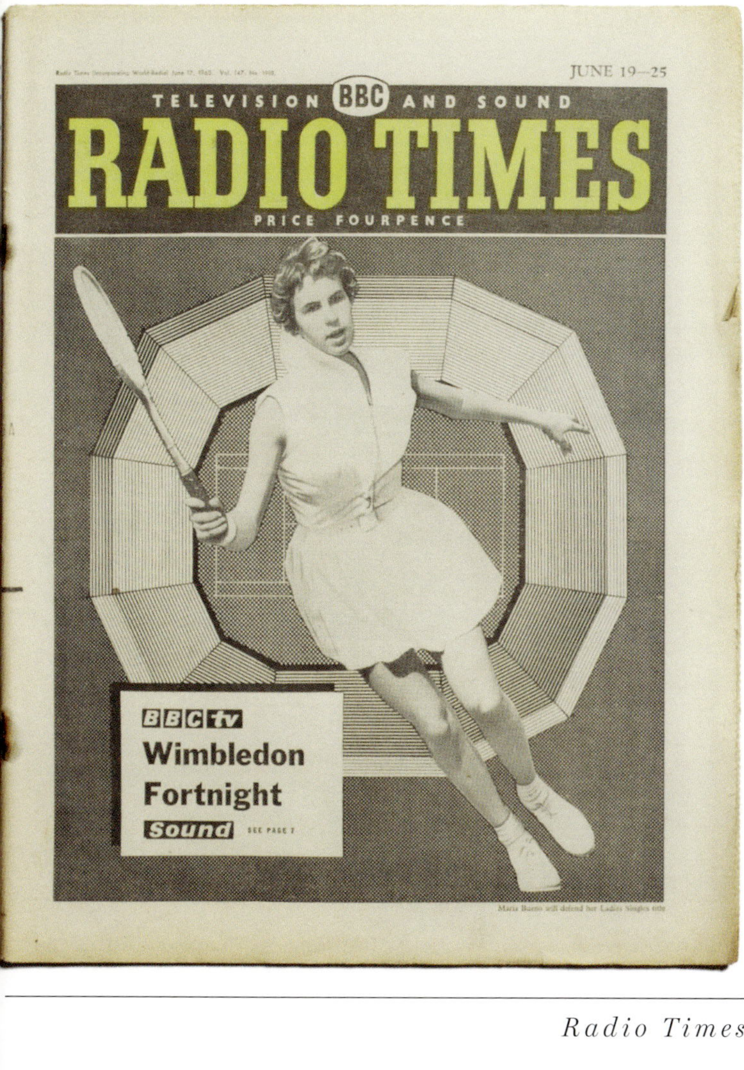

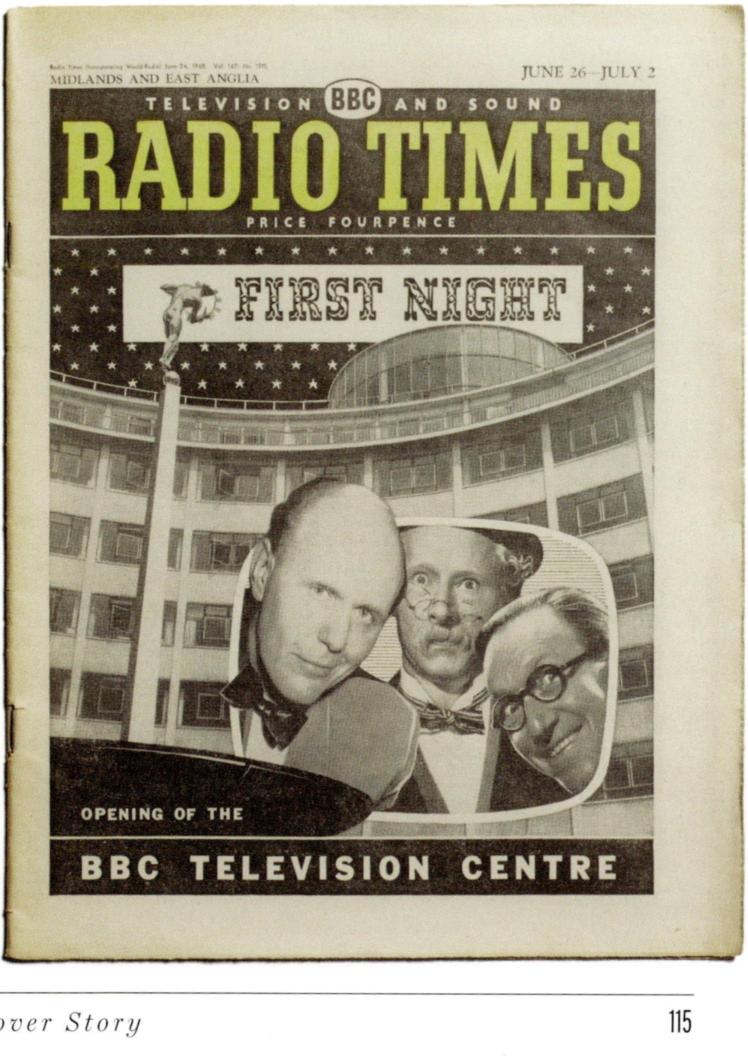

Dixon of Dock Green *(right)*

PC George Dixon (Jack Warner) ***(photograph by Don Smith)***

6–12 March 1960

Dixon of Dock Green ran from 1955 to 1976 and starred Jack Warner as PC George Dixon, who was more of an old-school copper, adept at helping schoolchildren to cross roads, rather than an anti-crime crusader.

Face to Face *(below left)*

Gilbert Harding ***(photograph by Don Smith)***

18–24 September 1960

The first subject for a new run of the interview series *Face to Face* was the notoriously grumpy broadcaster Gilbert Harding. The interview with host John Freeman became infamous for two reasons: Harding broke down in tears when he was asked about his mother; and he died just weeks after the programme was recorded – on the pavement outside Broadcasting House.

Beyond Our Ken *(below right)*

Kenneth Horne (centre), Kenneth Williams and Betty Marsden ***(photograph by Don Smith)***

15–21 October 1960

Kenneth Horne's radio sketch show *Beyond Our Ken* was midway through its lifespan, launching its fourth series with co-conspirators Kenneth Williams and Betty Marsden. Both went on to appear in *Round the Horne*: Williams as half of Julian and Sandy, and Marsden as Dame Celia Molestrangler.

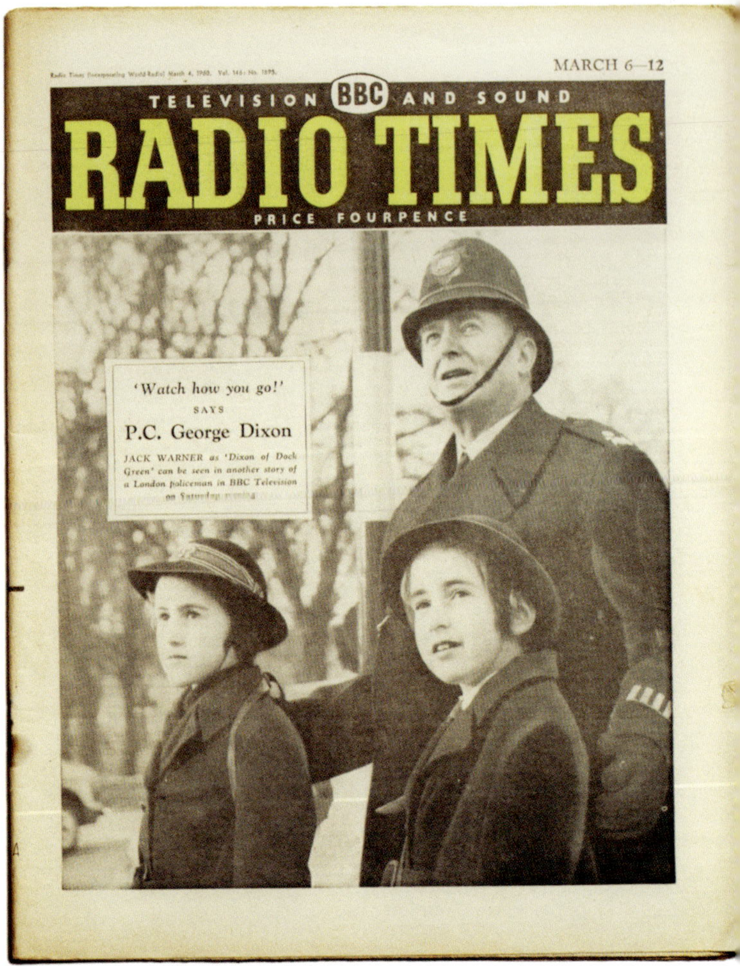

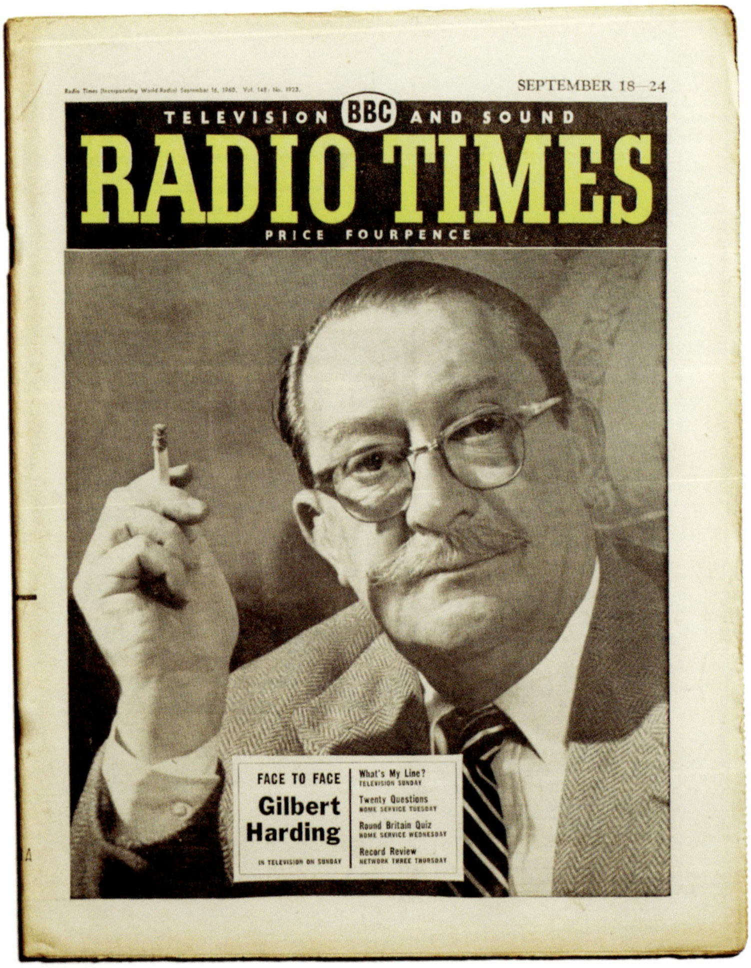

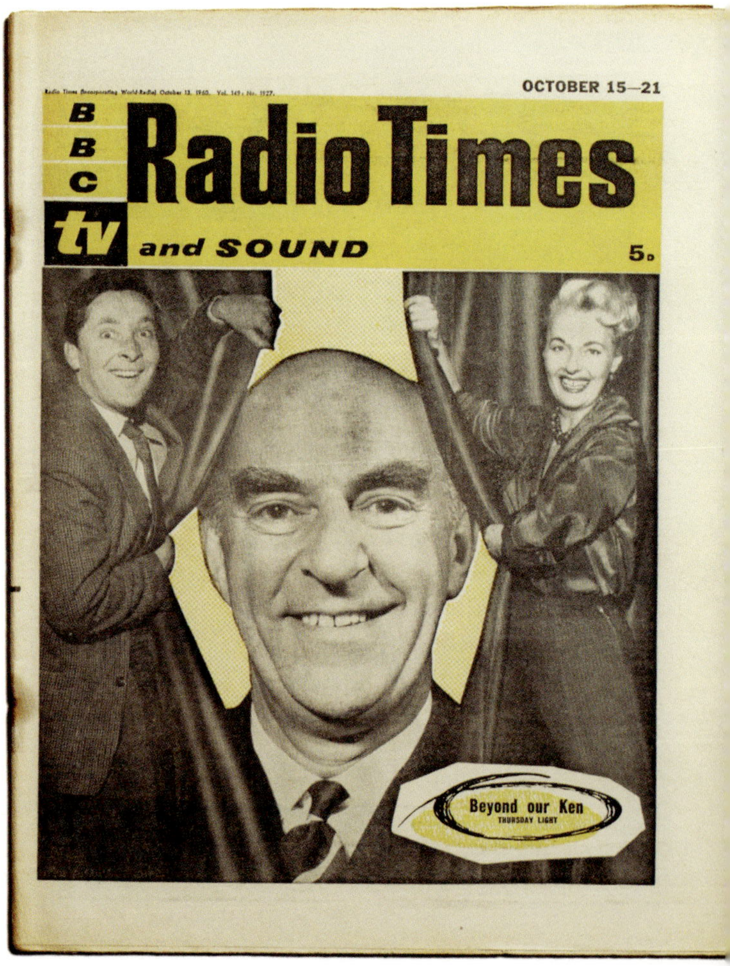

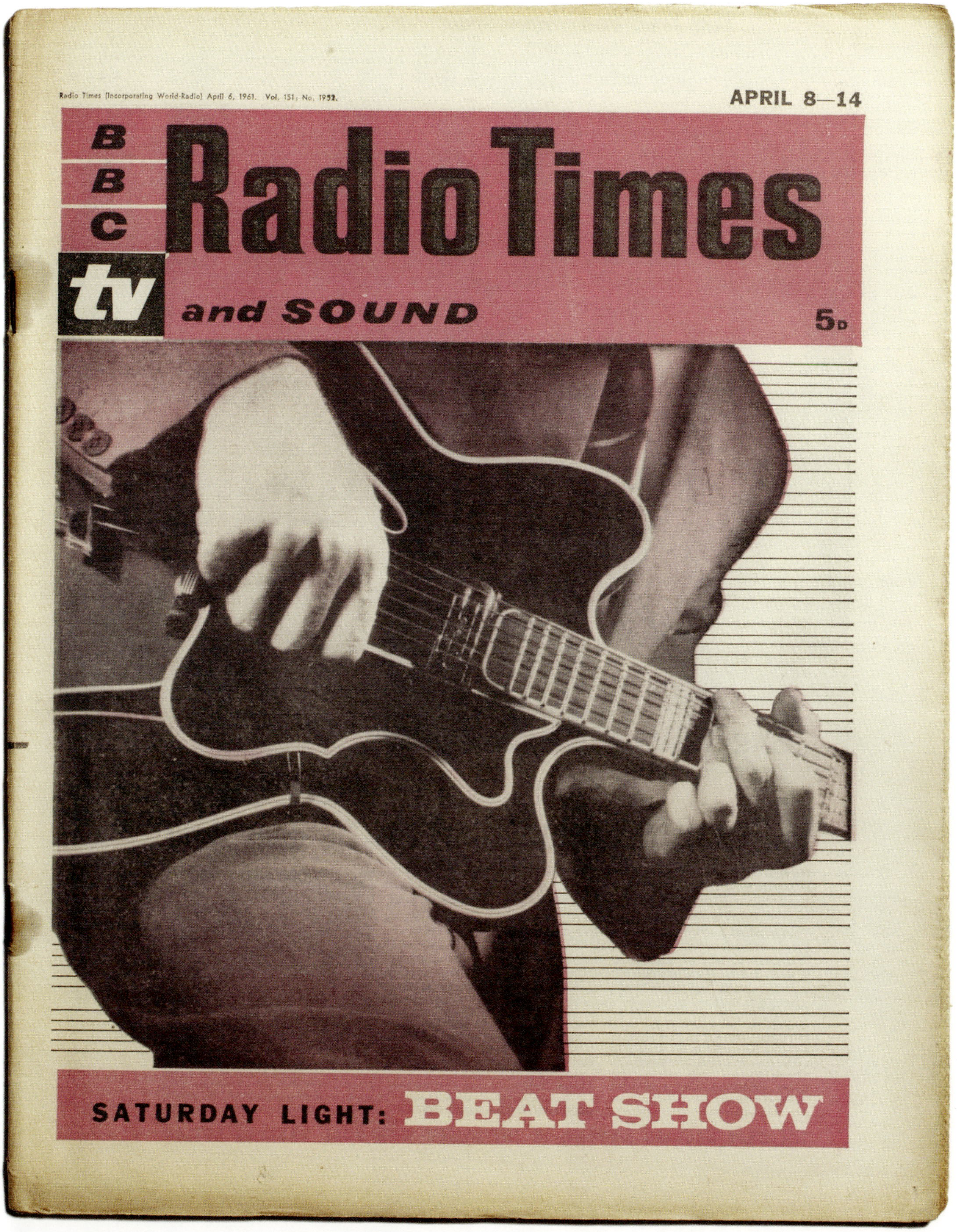

Beat Show *(photograph by Don Smith)* 8–14 April 1961

Cliff Richard and Lonnie Donegan were among the stars of *The BBC Beat Show*, the first of two concerts from the Royal Albert Hall. Brian Matthew compered the programme, which drew on the output of three of the BBC's 38 live weekly pop programmes: *Saturday Club*, *Go Man Go* and *Sing It Again!* The model on the cover is *Radio Times* staff photographer Don Smith, posing with a guitar that he borrowed from a friend.

The Trad Fad *(right)*

(photograph by Don Smith)

2–8 September 1961

The Trad Fad set out to counter the seedy reputation that had become attached to jazz and its followers, showing that even "square" mums and dads could appreciate the talents of (this week) Kenny Ball and Mick Mulligan. And the 15- to 25-year-olds who queued for tickets to dance on camera were clearly having good, clean, harmless fun.

Dr Kildare *(middle right)*

Left: Dr Gillespie (Raymond Massey) and Dr Kildare (Richard Chamberlain)

14–20 October 1961

Teen idol Richard Chamberlain caused many a heart to flutter in his role as idealistic medical intern Dr Kildare when he did the rounds of the wards of Blair General in New York. Raymond Massey played his tough-but-fair boss.

Christmas 1961 *(far right)*

Paper sculptures by Bruce Angrave

(photograph by Don Smith)

23–29 December 1961

Bruce Angrave didn't use glue to construct his paper sculptures: his secret weapon was sticky tape. His trademark was satirical portraits of politicians, but for this Christmas number he depicted the Magi.

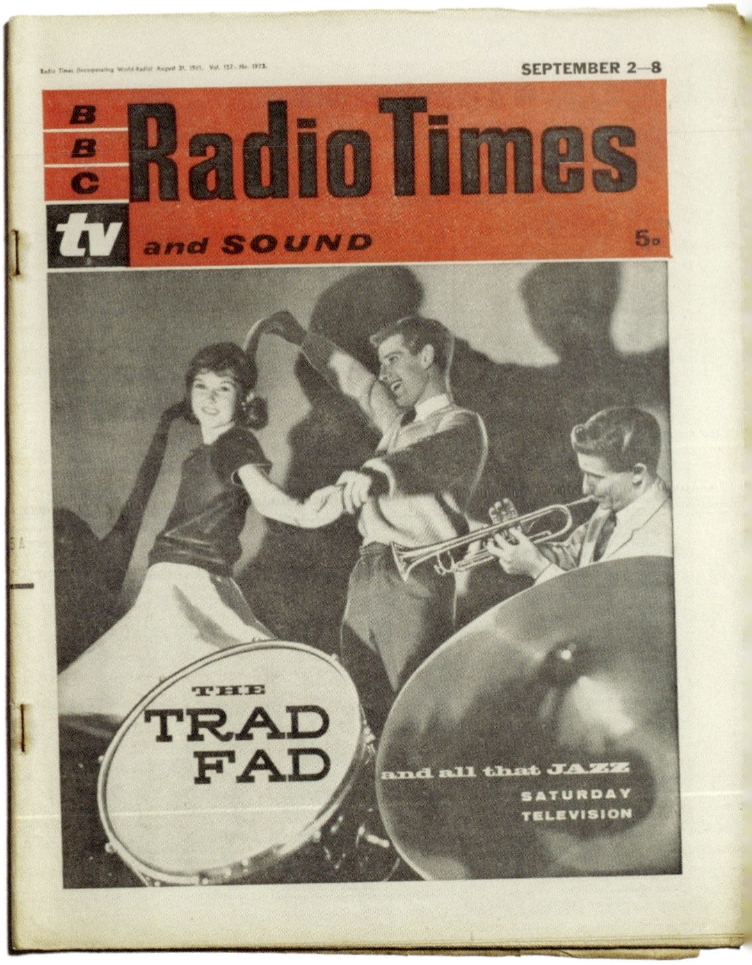

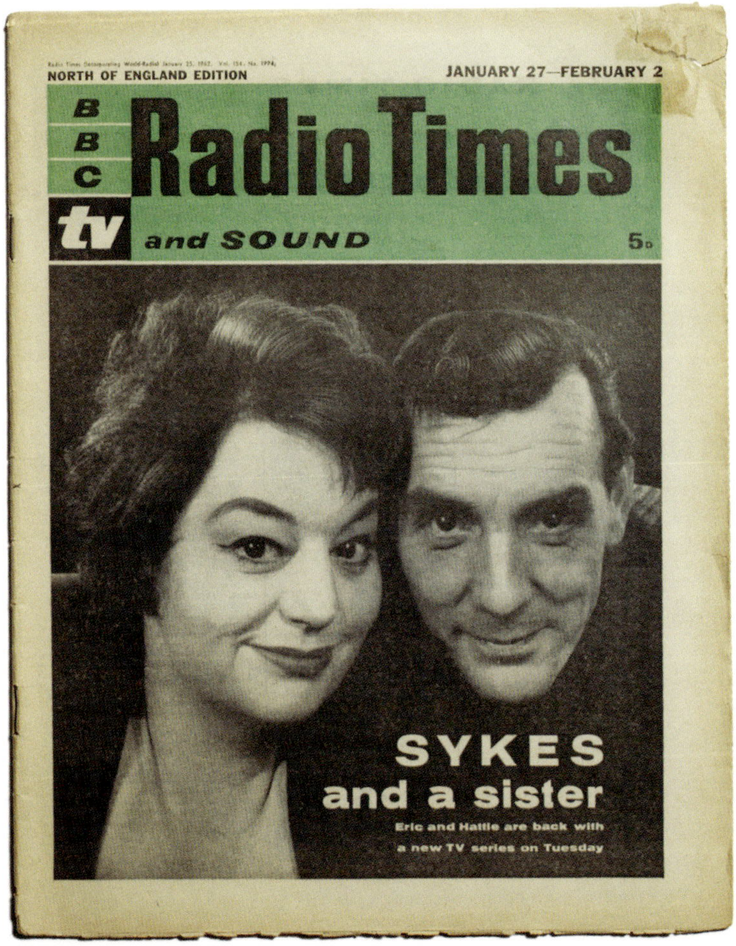

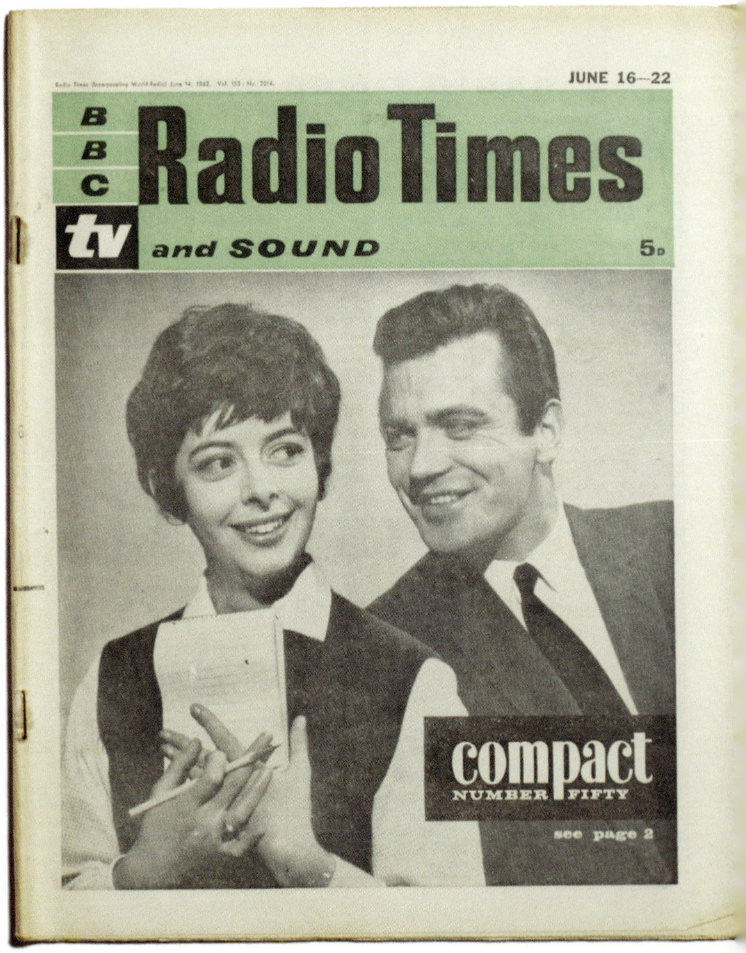

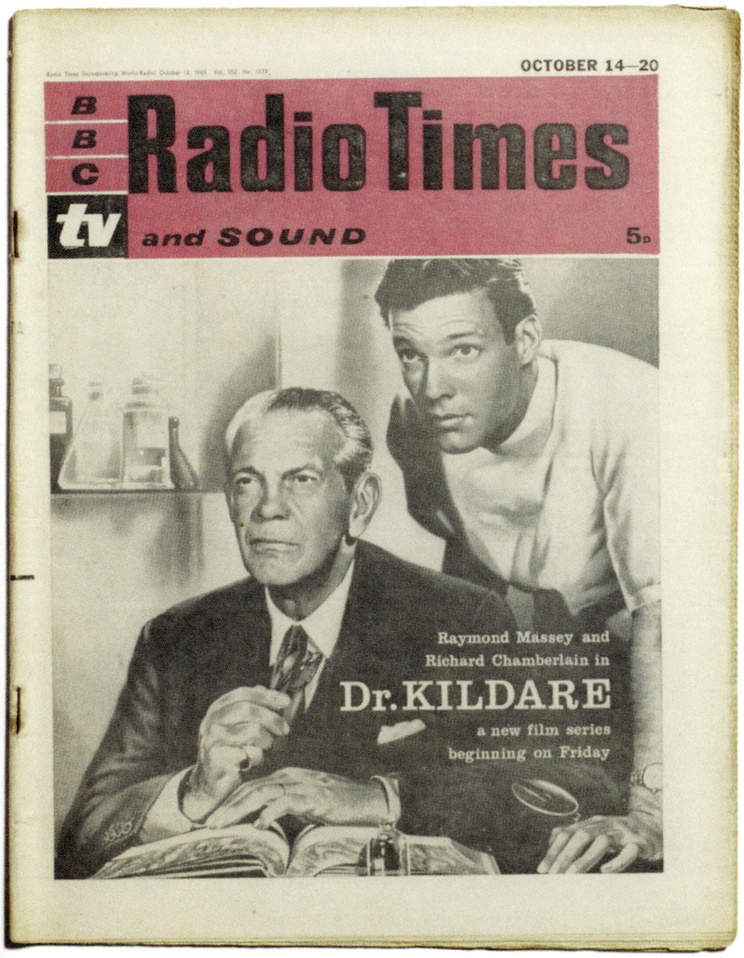

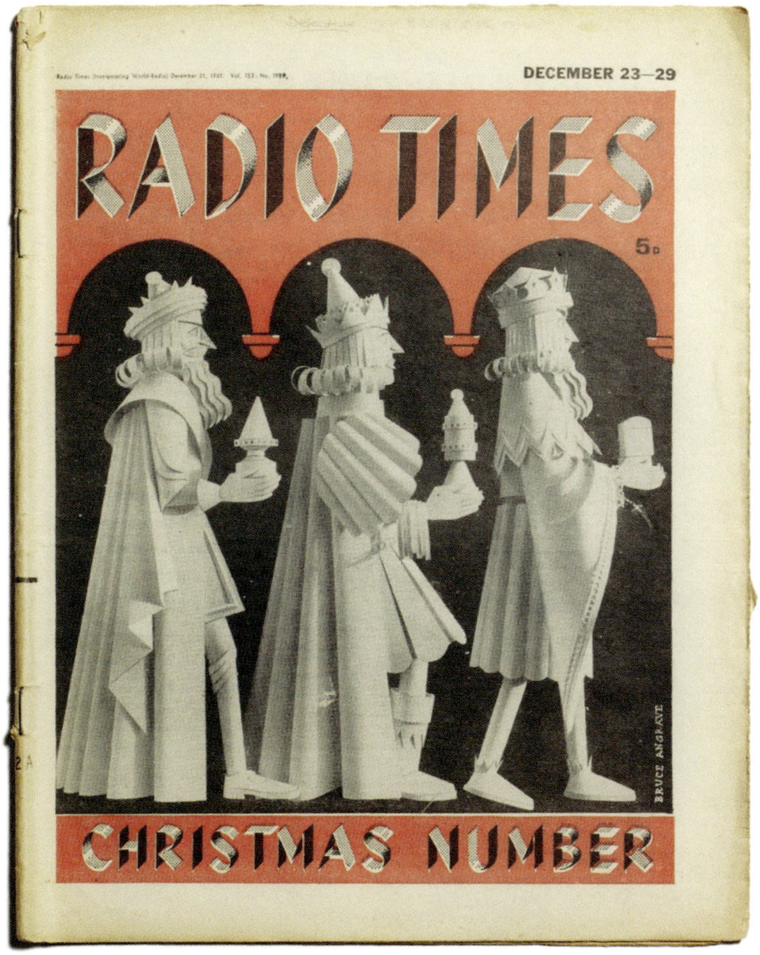

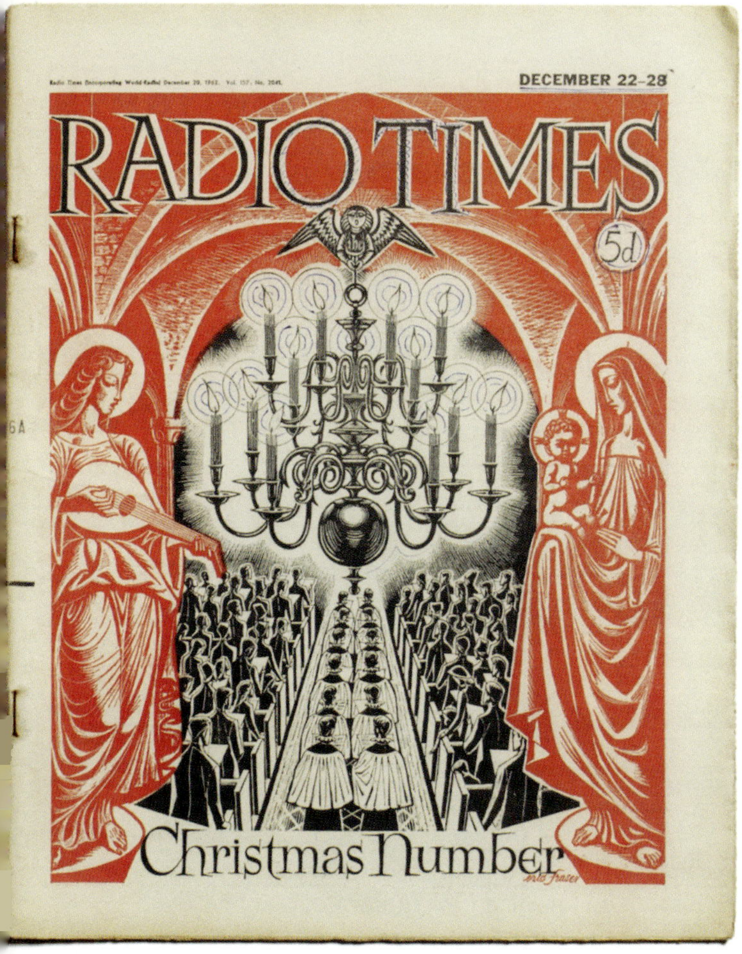

Sykes and a... *(far left)*

Eric Sykes, Hattie Jacques *(photograph by Don Smith)*

27 January–2 February 1962

This was Eric Sykes and Hattie Jacques's sixth TV series together. But what to call it? The regular title was *Sykes and a...* whatever the situation he found himself in. To simplify matters, the production team came up with the idea of referring to the show as *Sykes and a Sister*.

Compact *(middle left)*

Sally Henderson (Monica Evans) and Ian Harmon (Ronald Allen)

16–22 June 1962

The twice-weekly soap *Compact* was set in the glamorous world of magazine publishing. The cover celebrating the 50th episode showed office secretary Sally Henderson and editor Ian Harmon, played by Ronald Allen, who went on to star in *Crossroads* as David Hunter.

Christmas 1962 *(left)*

Illustration by Eric Fraser

22–28 December 1962

The cover by *Radio Times* regular Eric Fraser referred to *Carols across Europe*, a programme on Christmas Eve in which the Vienna Boys' Choir joined the choristers of Wells Cathedral and choirs from Sweden and Switzerland to usher in Christmas.

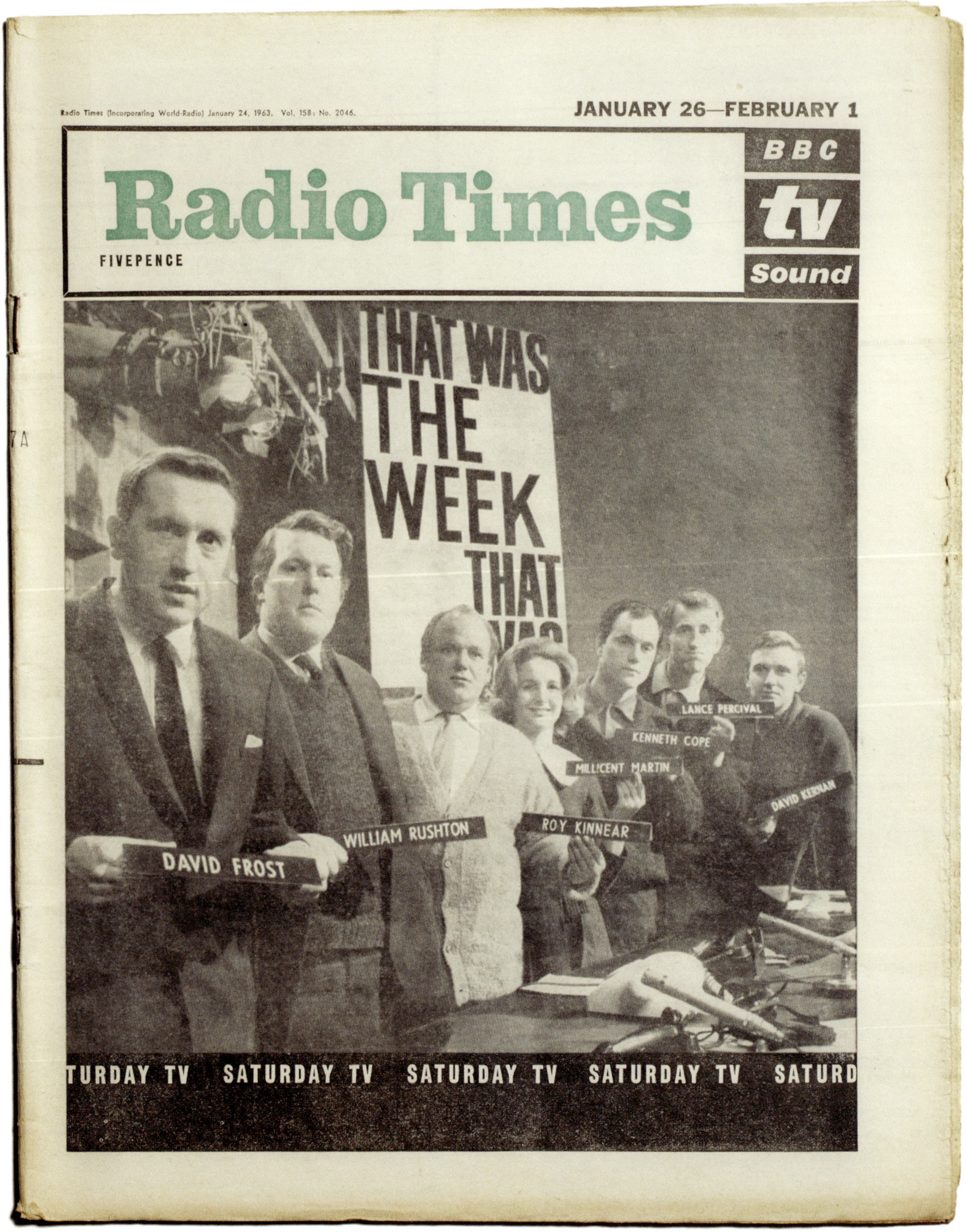

That Was the Week That Was **Starring: see nameplates above** *(photograph by Don Smith)*

26 January–1 February 1963

With its sketches lampooning everything from politicians to class, apartheid to religion, and Millicent Martin's news round-up delivered in song, *TW3* is credited with inventing political satire on television. Presenter David Frost liked to end the most blistering attacks with the phrase: "But seriously, he's doing a grand job."

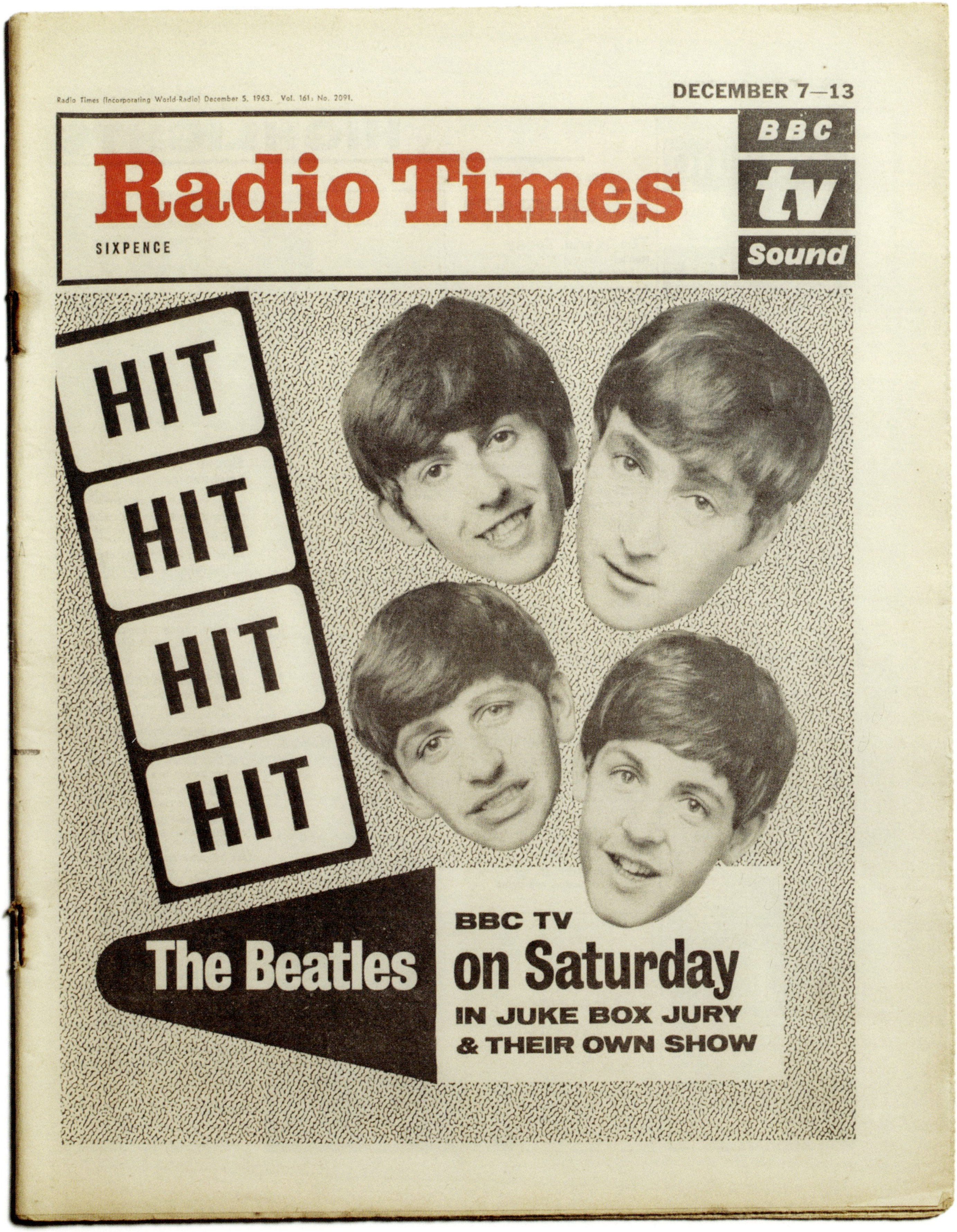

The Beatles **Clockwise from top left: George Harrison, John Lennon, Paul McCartney and Ringo Starr** *(photograph by Don Smith)* *7–13 December 1963*

The Fab Four featured twice on TV on Saturday: at 6.50pm they were the judges in *Juke Box Jury* and at 8.10pm *It's the Beatles!* was a recording of a concert at Liverpool Empire. The preview noted: "The programmes will be virtually a study in Beatlemania. Parents with teenagers are advised to sit well back from the TV."

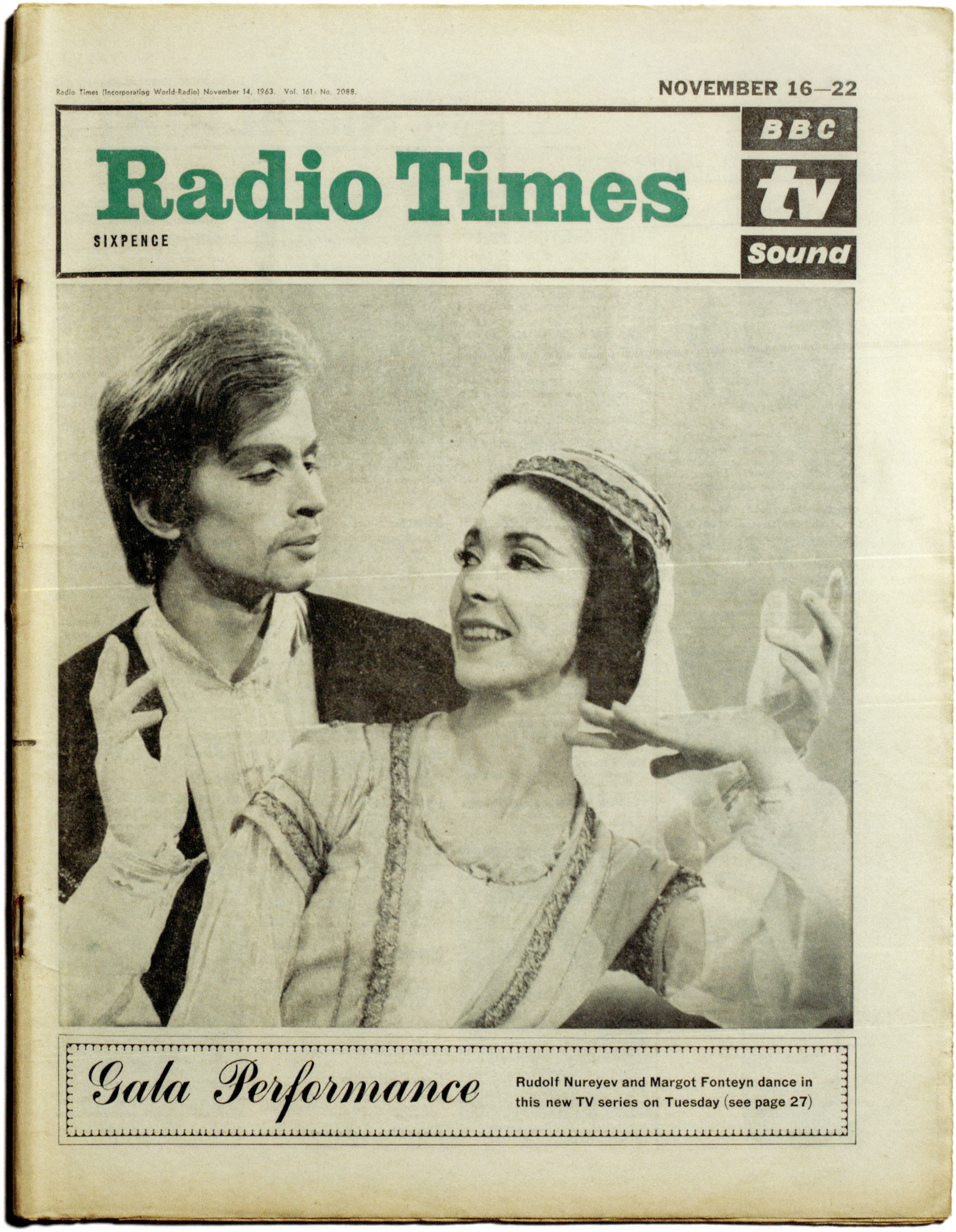

Gala Performance **Rudolph Nureyev and Margot Fonteyn** *16–22 November 1963*

Rudolph Nureyev and Margot Fonteyn were the star attraction of *Gala Performance*, a new series presented by Richard Attenborough that was all about making music fun – "Why treat good music as sacred?" asked Attenborough. "Why not *enjoy* it? Let's knock out the pomposity and have fun." Nureyev and Fonteyn performed a *pas de deux* from *Gayaneh* by Khachaturian and the *pas de deux* from Act 2 of *Swan Lake*.

Miss World *(right)*

2–8 November 1963

The irony-free preview noted: "In picking a beauty queen one doesn't need to know her speed over a given distance. It is enough to have fifty-fifty vision and a TV set that can be trusted not to blow a fuse at the wrong moment." The cover shows Miss Holland, Catharina Lodders, being crowned Miss World 1962.

Christmas 1963 *(below left)*

Illustration by Victor Reinganum

21–27 December 1963

Reinganum's cover featured a modernist angel carrying a mobile of Christmas scenes. Victor Reinganum was a perfectionist. In a later interview he expressed disappointment in the quality of the colour work he did for *Radio Times*. "I was delighted to have the commissions and I enjoyed doing them, but I was always very disappointed by the final result."

Z Cars *(below right)*

Foreground: PC "Fancy" Smith (Brian Blessed) and PC "Jock" Weir (Joseph Brady). Background: Sgt Lynch (James Ellis) and PC Graham (Colin Welland) *(photograph by Don Smith)*

29 February–6 March 1964

The 100th edition of *Z Cars*, a series loved by audiences for its portrayal of the gritty reality of crimefighting in the north of England. It also launched many careers...

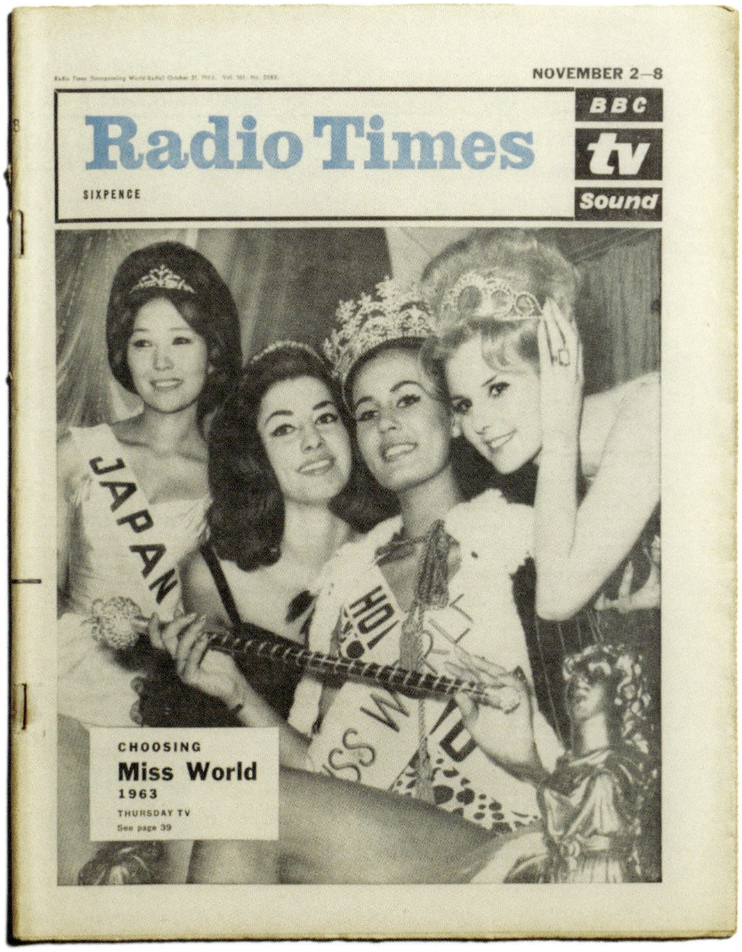

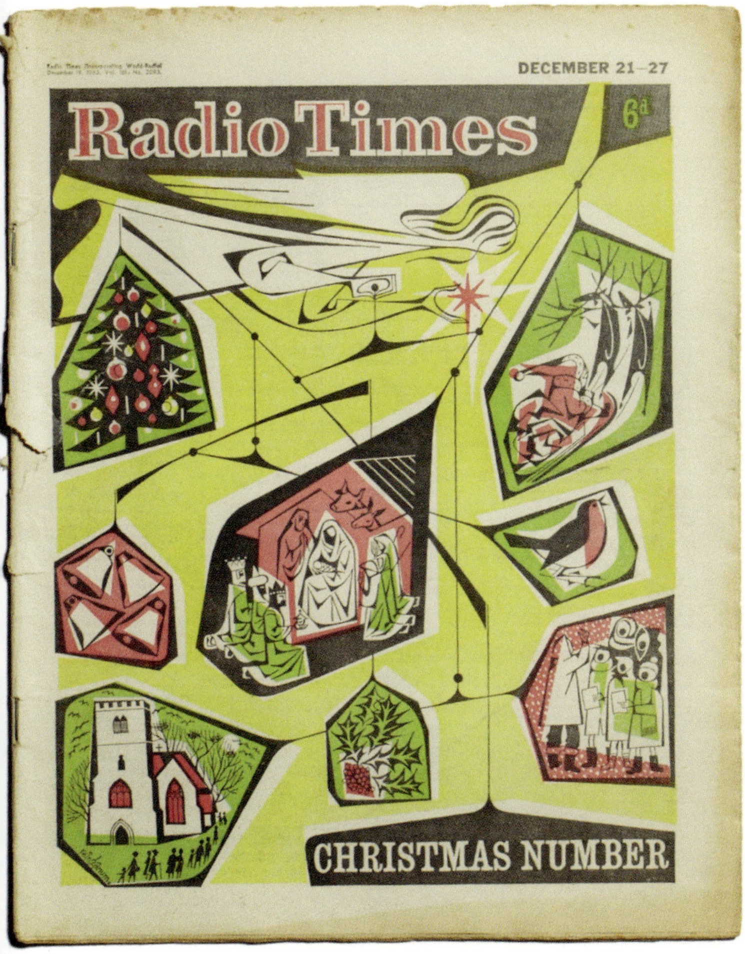

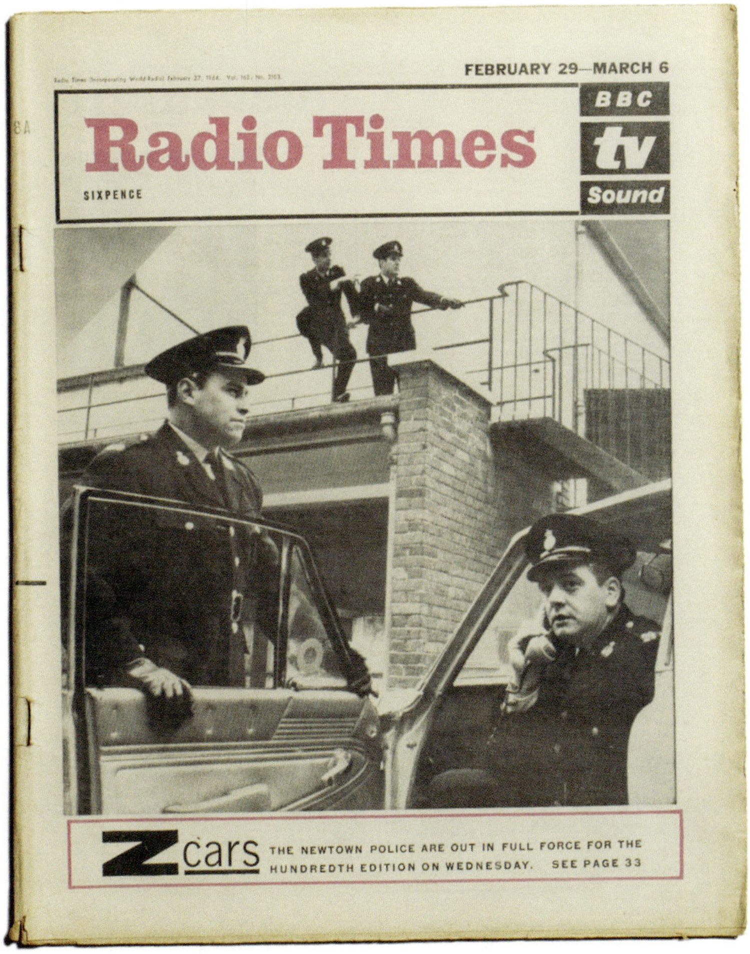

The Great War *(right)*

30 May–5 June 1964

To mark the 50th anniversary of the start of the First World War, BBC2 launched *The Great War*, a 26-part documentary that brought together archive footage from 20 countries, some of it never previously seen on TV.

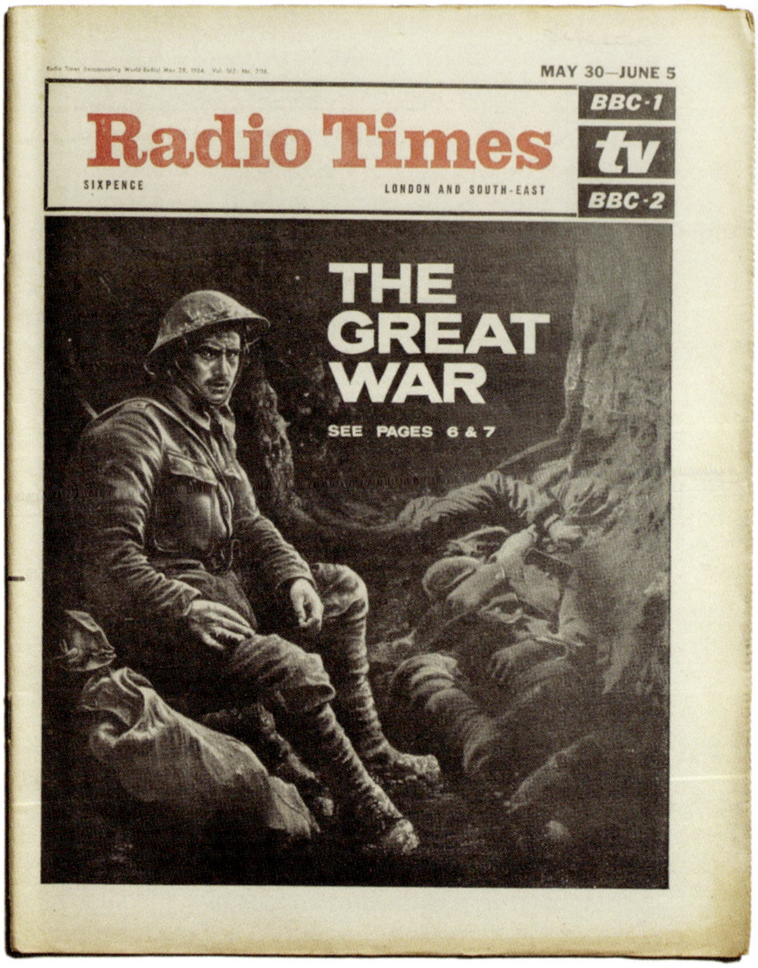

Top Gear *(below left)*

From left: Paul McCartney, John Lennon, Ringo Starr, George Harrison and Dusty Springfield

11–17 July 1964

The Beatles were fresh from conquering America and Australia when they joined Dusty Springfield for the launch of late-night radio pop show, *Top Gear*.

Dixon of Dock Green *(below right)*

Sergeant Dixon (Jack Warner)

(photograph by Don Smith)

19–25 September 1964

After a decade on the beat, George Dixon finally accepted promotion to sergeant in this week's episode. Inside, the show's creator, Ted Willis, supported the programme-makers' intention to concentrate on smaller, everyday crimes and keep violence to a minimum.

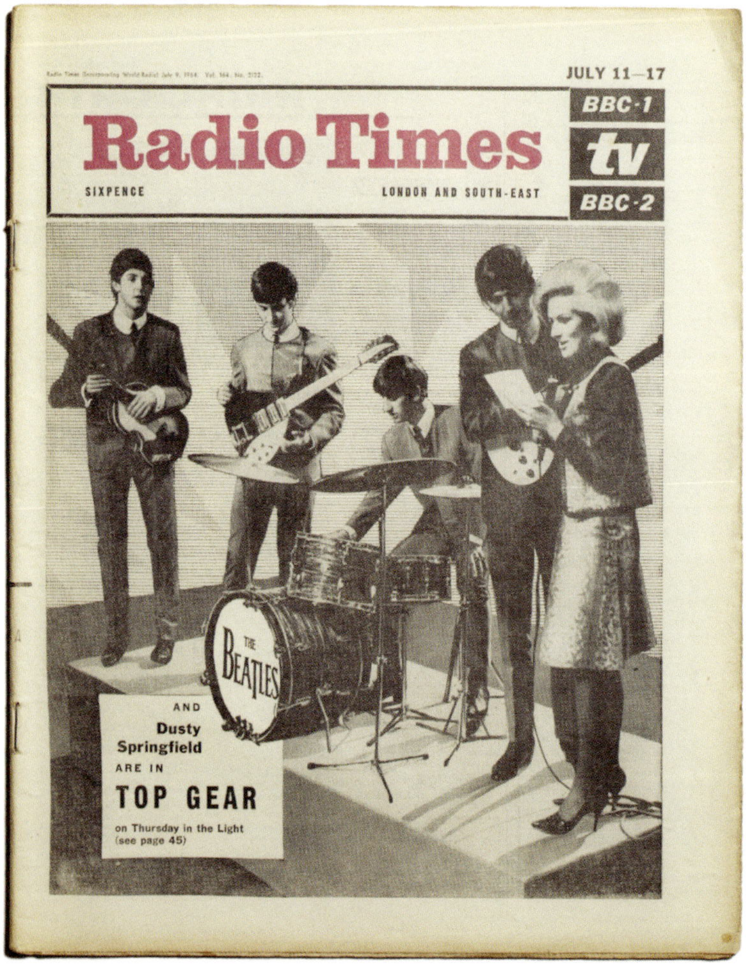

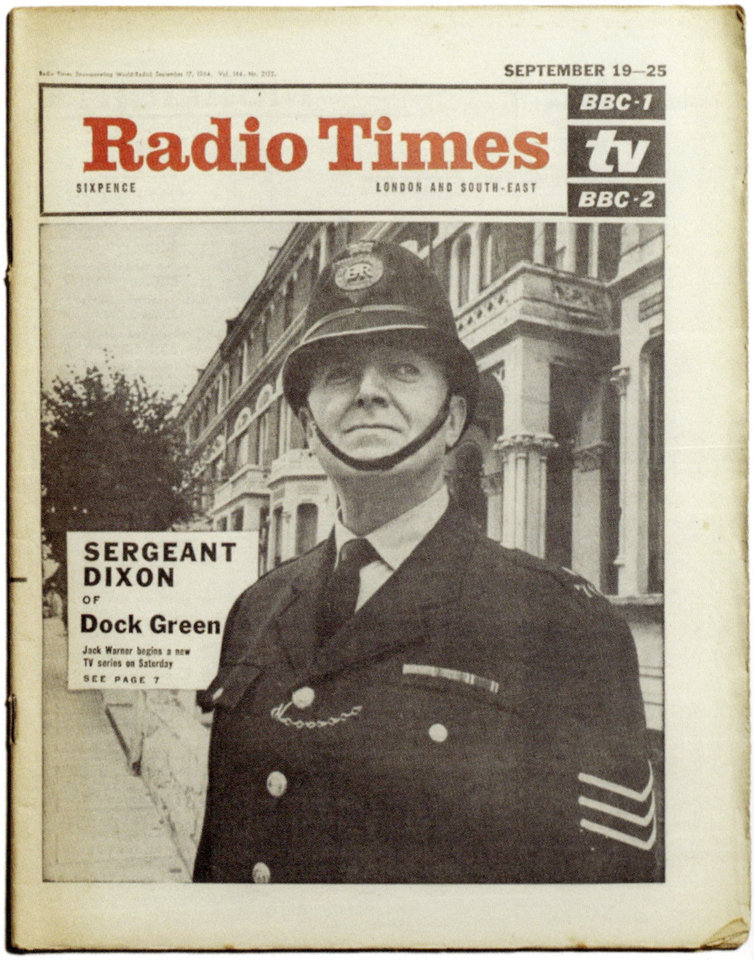

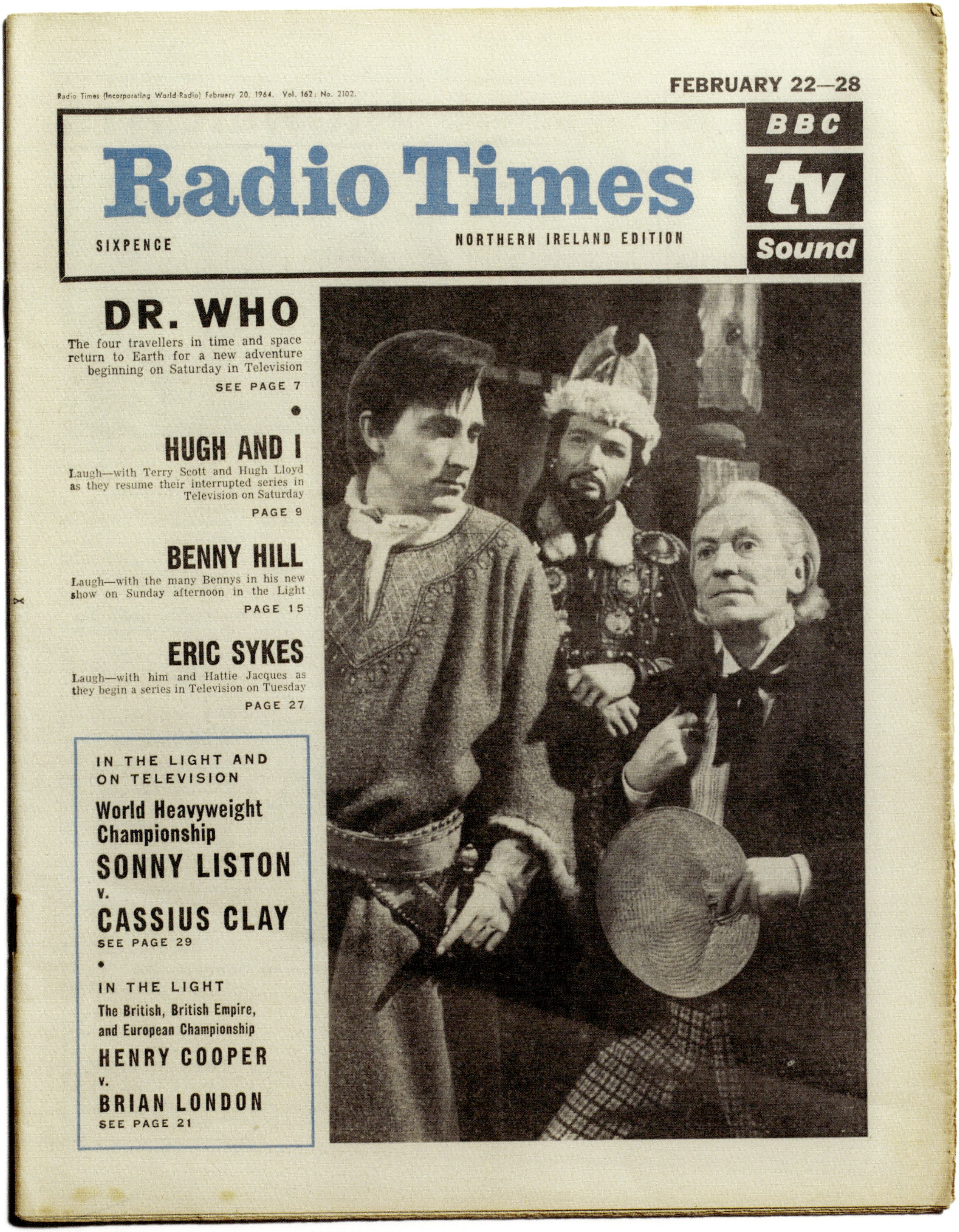

Radio Times (Incorporating World-Radio) February 20, 1964. Vol. 162: No. 2102.

FEBRUARY 22—28

BBC tv Sound

Radio Times

SIXPENCE

NORTHERN IRELAND EDITION

DR. WHO

The four travellers in time and space return to Earth for a new adventure beginning on Saturday in Television

SEE PAGE 7

•

HUGH AND I

Laugh—with Terry Scott and Hugh Lloyd as they resume their interrupted series in Television on Saturday

PAGE 9

BENNY HILL

Laugh—with the many Bennys in his new show on Sunday afternoon in the Light

PAGE 15

ERIC SYKES

Laugh—with him and Hattie Jacques as they begin a series in Television on Tuesday

PAGE 27

IN THE LIGHT AND ON TELEVISION

World Heavyweight Championship

SONNY LISTON

v.

CASSIUS CLAY

SEE PAGE 29

•

IN THE LIGHT

The British, British Empire, and European Championship

HENRY COOPER

v.

BRIAN LONDON

SEE PAGE 21

Doctor Who **From left: Marco Polo (Mark Eden), Tegana (Derren Nesbitt) and the Doctor (William Hartnell)** *(photograph by Don Smith)* *22–28 February 1964*

The good Doctor made his cover debut with his fourth serial, a historical escapade featuring Marco Polo.
And in boxing, a young man called Cassius Clay was about to take the world heavyweight title for the first time.

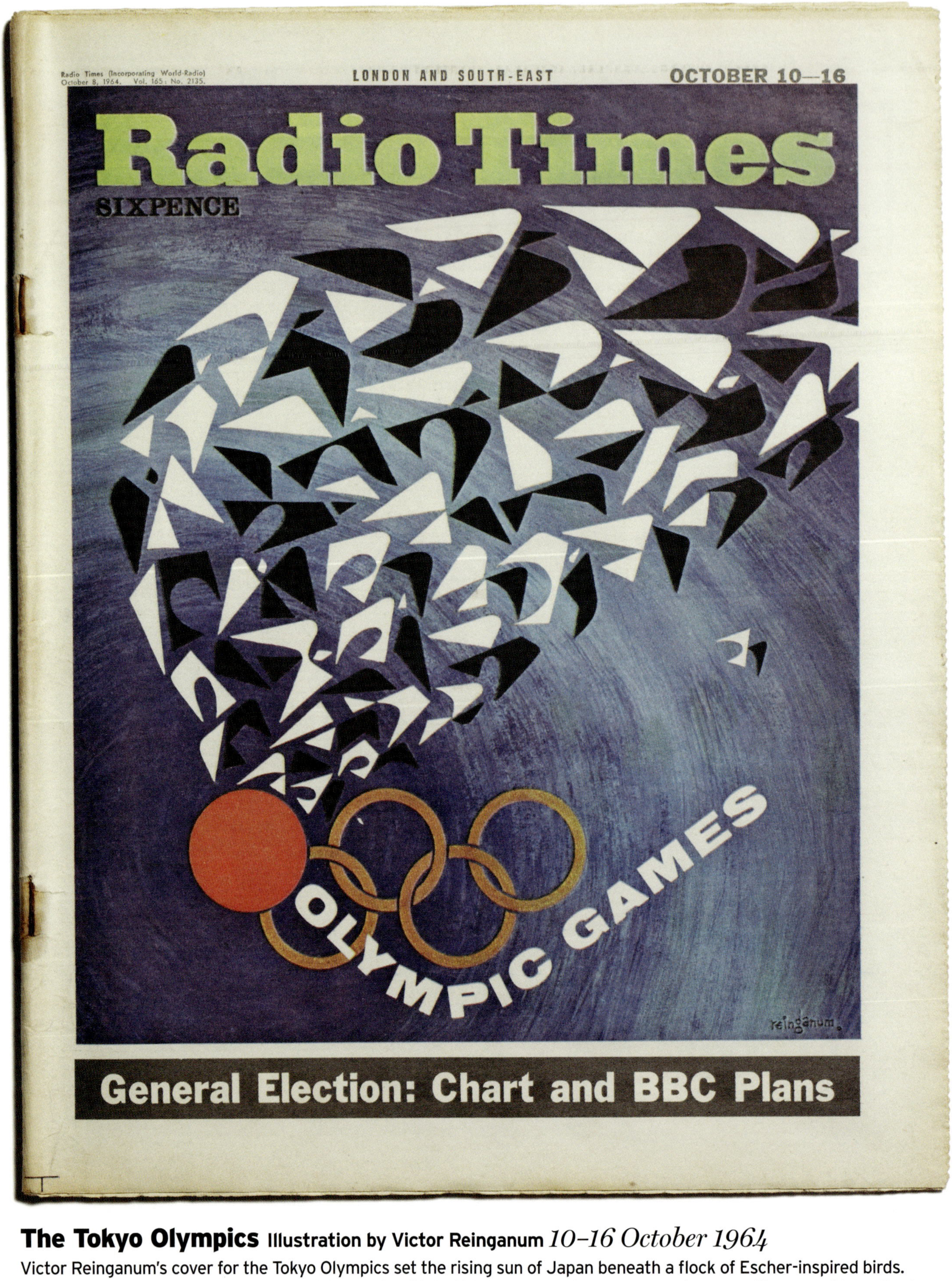

The Tokyo Olympics **Illustration by Victor Reinganum** *10–16 October 1964*

Victor Reinganum's cover for the Tokyo Olympics set the rising sun of Japan beneath a flock of Escher-inspired birds. Inside, Ross and Norris McWhirter predicted that British athletes Ann Packer, Mary Rand, Ken Matthews and Lynn Davies had the potential to win gold medals and, remarkably, they all did. In a different type of competition entirely, *Radio Times* provided a chart for recording the result of every seat in the general election.

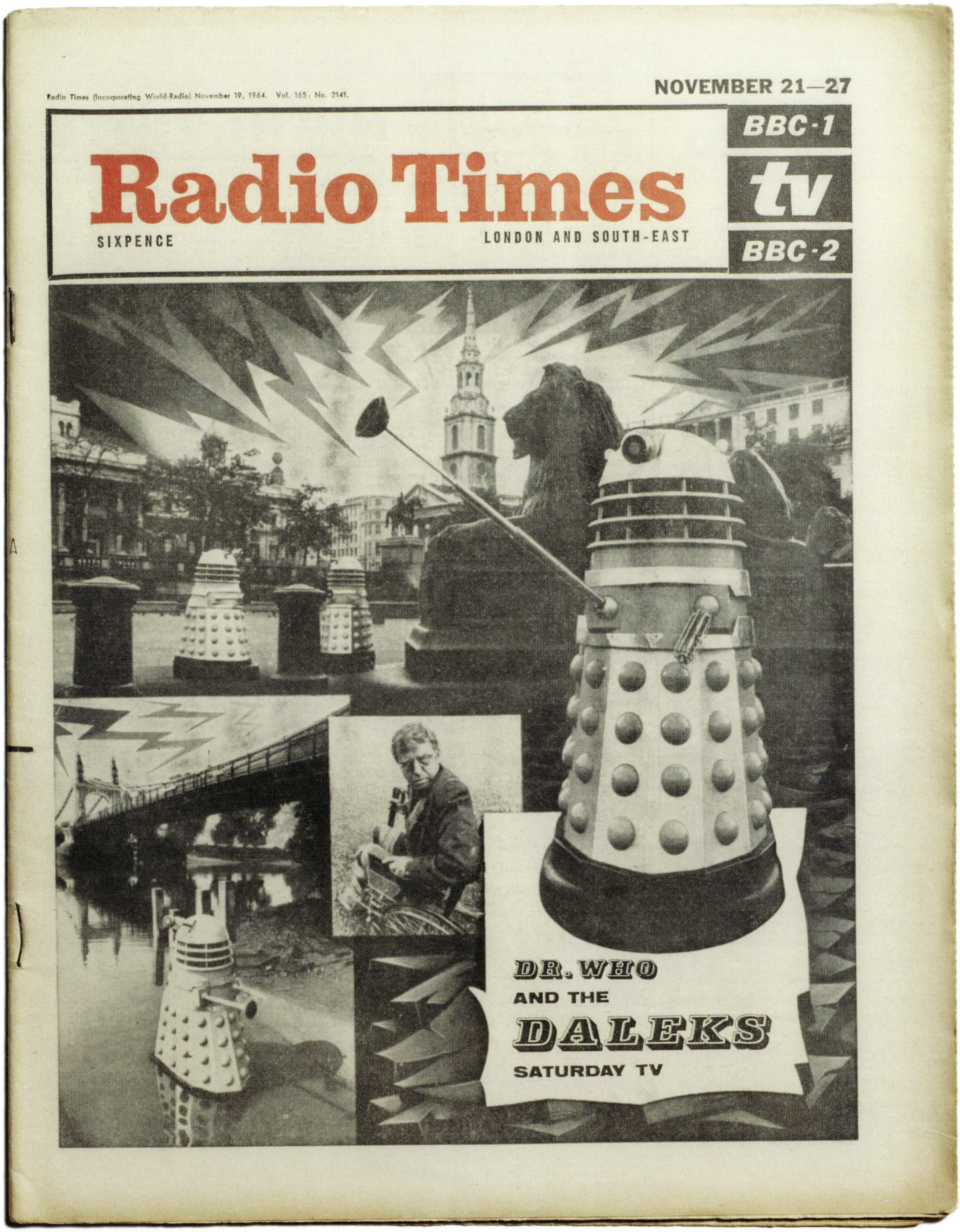

Doctor Who *(photographs by Don Smith) 21–27 November 1964*

For their second outing in *Doctor Who*, the Daleks invaded Earth in the 22nd century, plotting to extract the planet's core via a mine in Bedfordshire. In a montage surrounding Dortmun (Alan Judd), a wheelchair-using resistance leader, it was their first appearance on the cover. This serial showed remarkable scenes of Daleks over-running London landmarks, shots being restaged in 2013 for the BBC2 drama *An Adventure in Space and Time*.

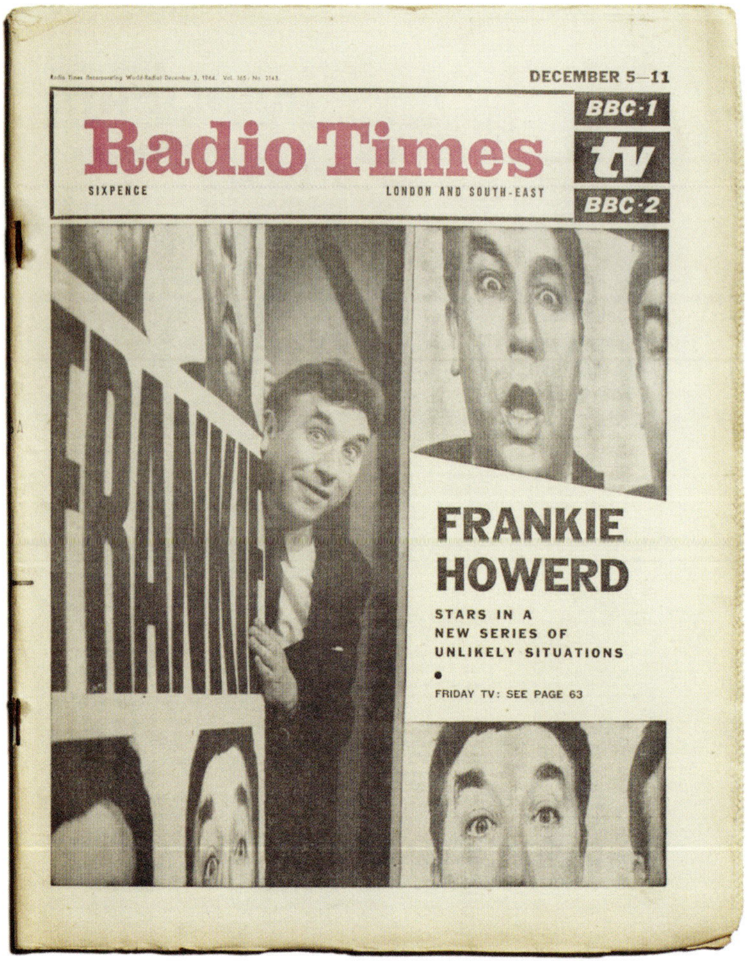

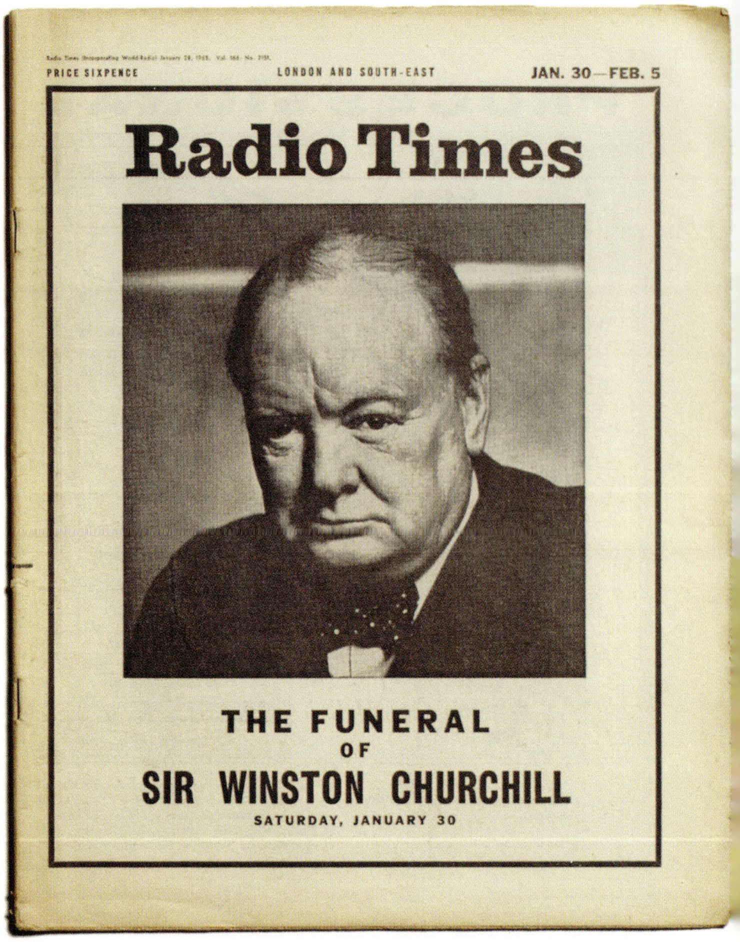

Sherlock Holmes *(right)*

Sherlock Holmes (Douglas Wilmer) and Doctor Watson (Nigel Stock) *(photograph by Don Smith)*

20–26 February 1965

A 1964 pilot led to this distinguished 12-part series. Douglas Wilmer was a lifelong enthusiast of Arthur Conan Doyle and bore an "uncanny resemblance" to the Holmes depicted in the original *Strand Magazine* illustrations.

Not Only... But Also *(middle right)*

Peter Cook and Dudley Moore

6–12 March 1965

Not Only... But Also with Peter Cook and Dudley Moore helped to define and sharpen British satire. The programme richly deserved a *Radio Times* cover but, curiously, theissue had no accompanying feature, interview or preview.

Debussy *(far right)*

Claude Debussy (Oliver Reed)

15–21 May 1965

Oliver Reed was the suitably intense star of Ken Russell's film about French composer Claude Debussy. Russell introduced the BBC1 project, explaining how he had tried to replicate Debussy's hallucinatory state of mind and the dreamlike quality of his music.

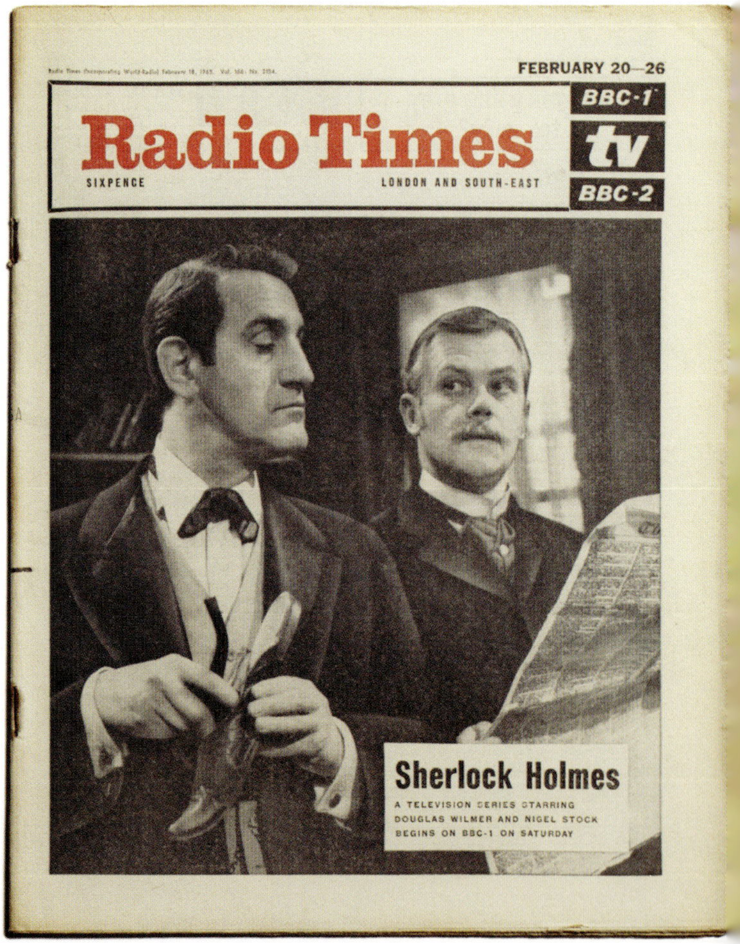

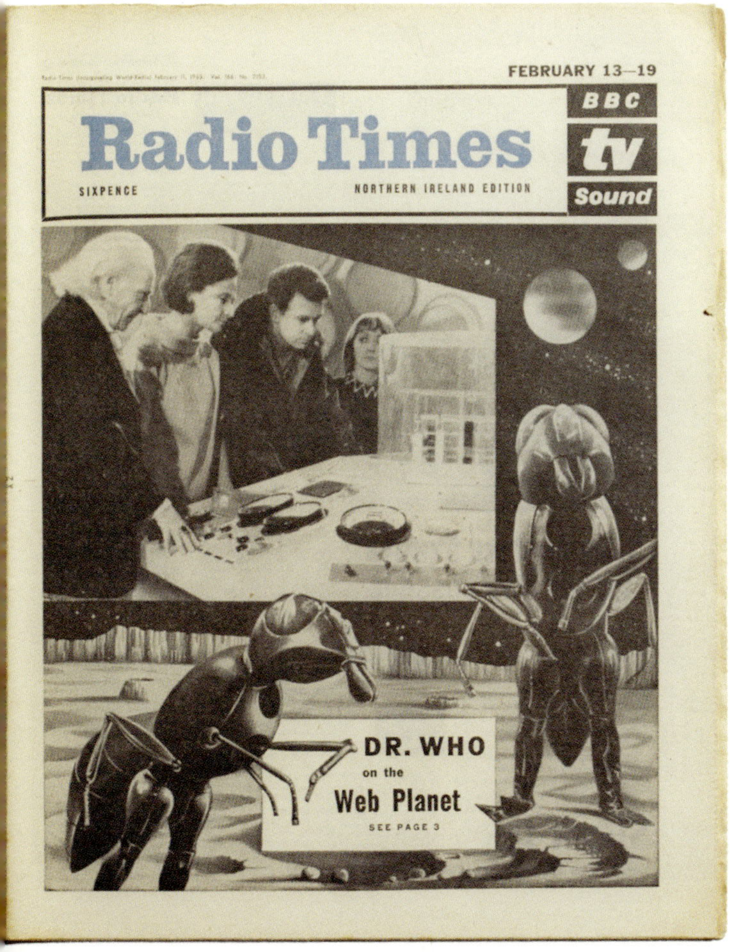

The Frankie Howerd Show *(far left)*

Frankie Howerd ***(photograph by Don Smith)***

5–11 December 1964

Frankie Howerd was tickling the nation in *The Frankie Howerd Show* on BBC1 (or BBC-1 as it was displayed on the cover and listings pages inside). And note the discreet but important change to the masthead with the addition of the new television channel BBC2 – or, to be faithful to the cover, BBC-2.

Churchill's funeral *(middle left)*

30 January–5 February 1965

The state funeral on 30 January of Britain's wartime leader was covered in full on BBC1 and on radio, with *Radio Times* providing a map of the processional route and the full order of service in St Paul's Cathedral. Richard Dimbleby wrote a piece for the magazine setting the scene for the funeral and explaining Churchill's decision to be buried at Bladon near Blenheim Palace rather than Westminster Abbey or St Paul's.

Doctor Who *(left)*

The Doctor (William Hartnell), Barbara (Jacqueline Hill), Ian (William Russell) and Vicki (Maureen O'Brien) ***(photograph by Don Smith)*** *13–19 February 1965*

The Tardis crew faced the ant-like Zarbi on planet Vortis. The first episode of this ambitious six-part serial was watched by 13.5m, the highest audience for any 1960s *Doctor Who.*

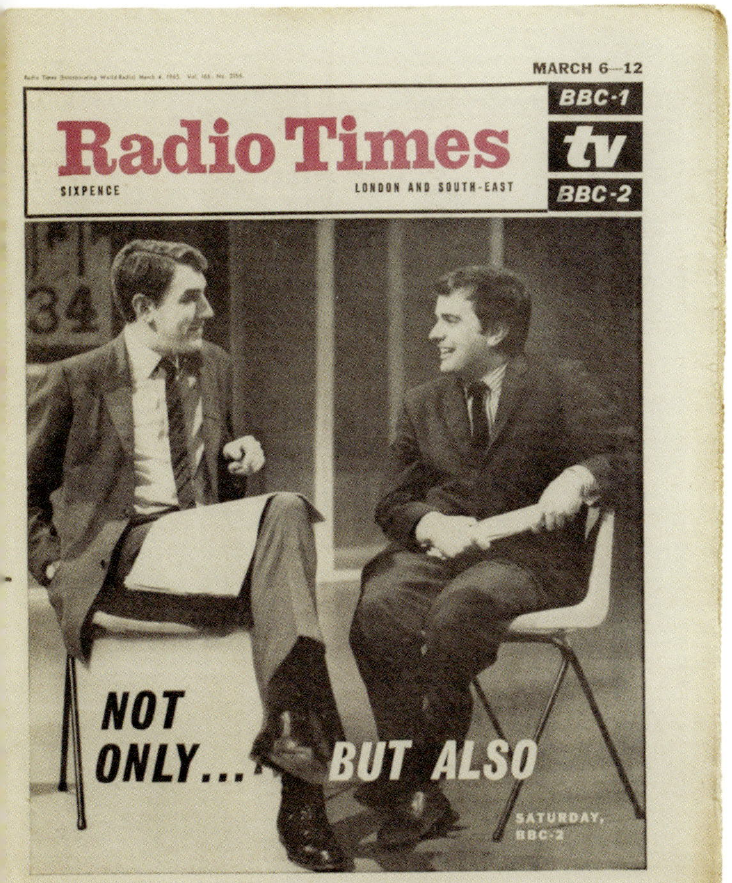

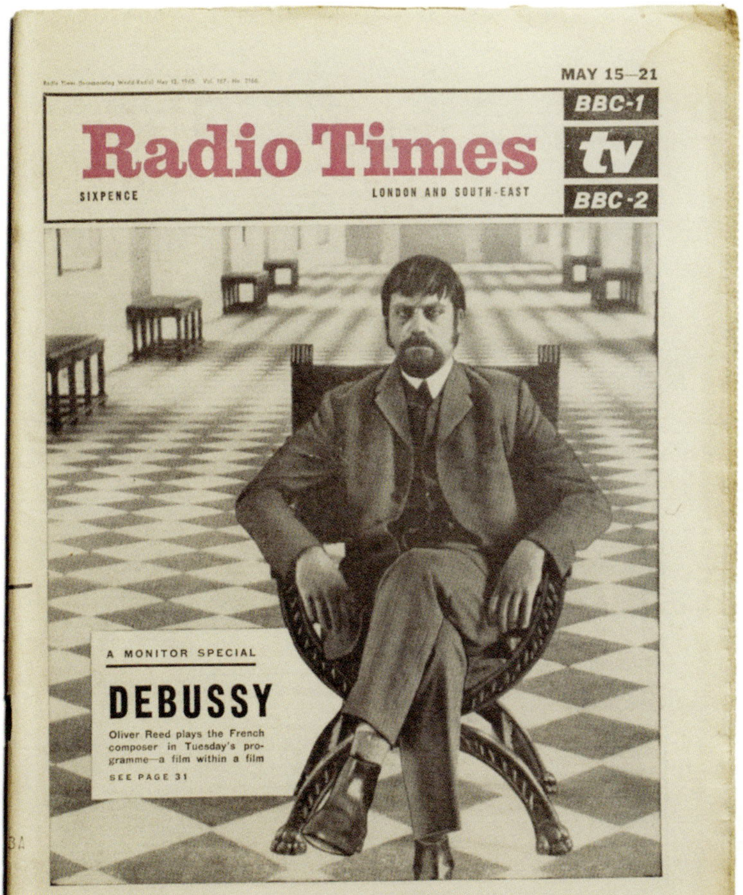

Blue Peter *(right)*
Christopher Trace and Valerie Singleton with Petra the dog and Jason the cat *(photograph by Don Smith)*
24–30 July 1965

Blue Peter presenters Christopher Trace and Valerie Singleton had packed their bags for a summer trip to Norway, leaving the pets behind and providing younger readers with a fun-packed supplement to help fill the gap.

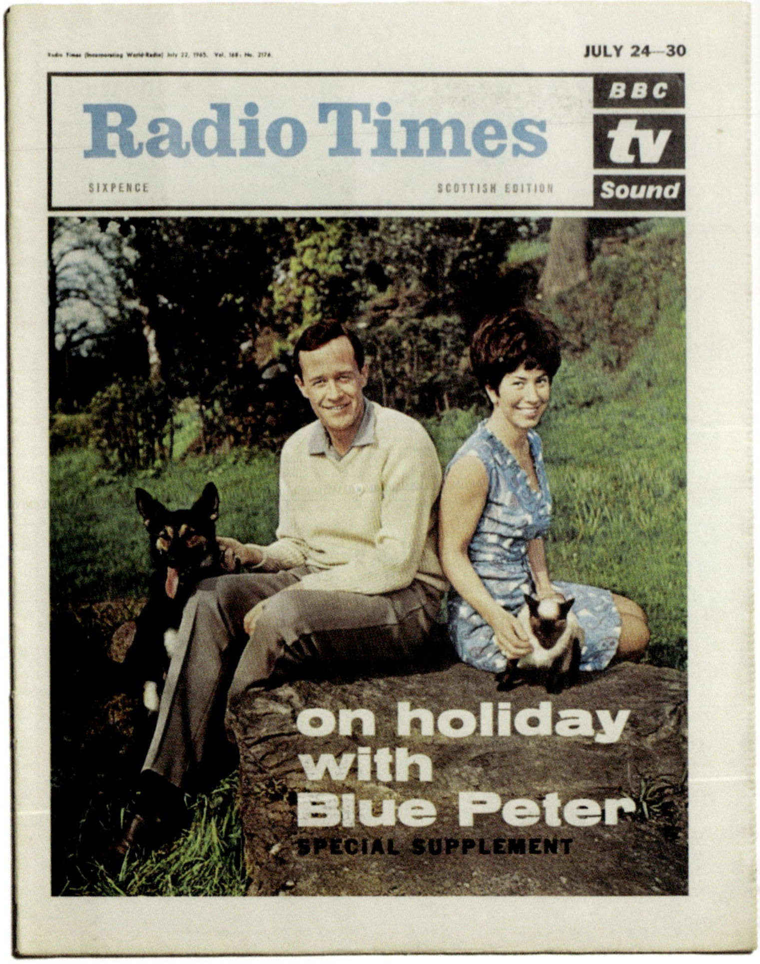

Ken Dodd *(below left)*
30 October–5 November 1965

Ken Dodd, Liverpool's favourite comic son, was the inspired choice for the cover in the week that viewers in the North West were able to pick up BBC2 programmes for the first time. The number of people in the country who could watch BBC2 was now 18 million.

Christmas 1965 *(below right)*
Illustration by Gaynor Chapman
25–31 December 1965

Gaynor Chapman's vibrant, abstract cover must have been well received by readers and the editor of *Radio Times* – she was also commissioned to create the Christmas cover for the following year.

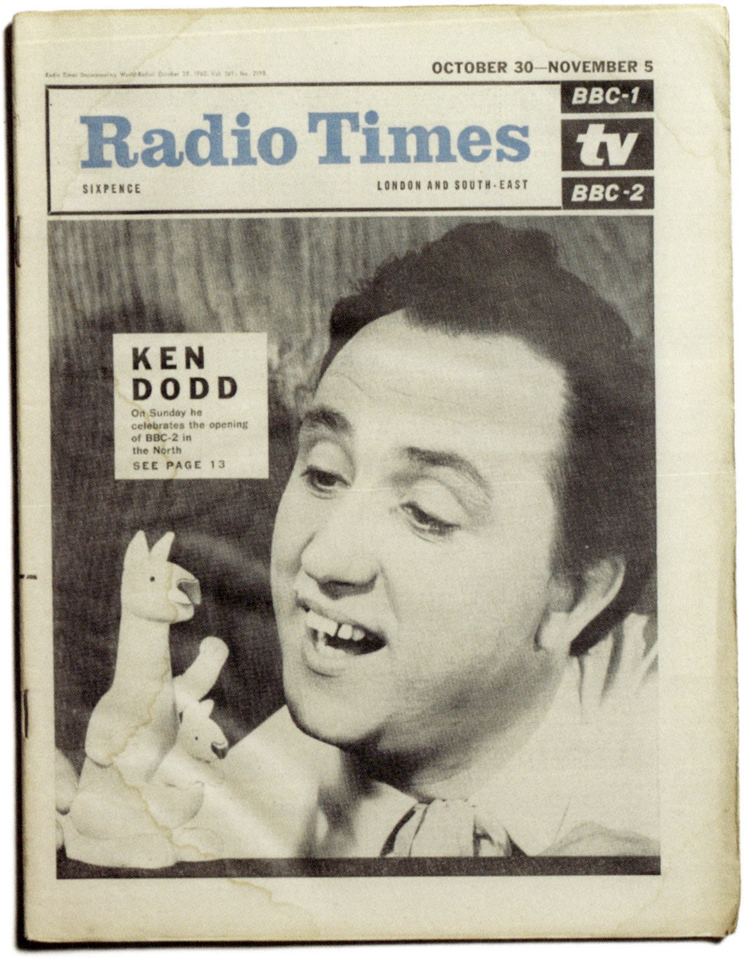

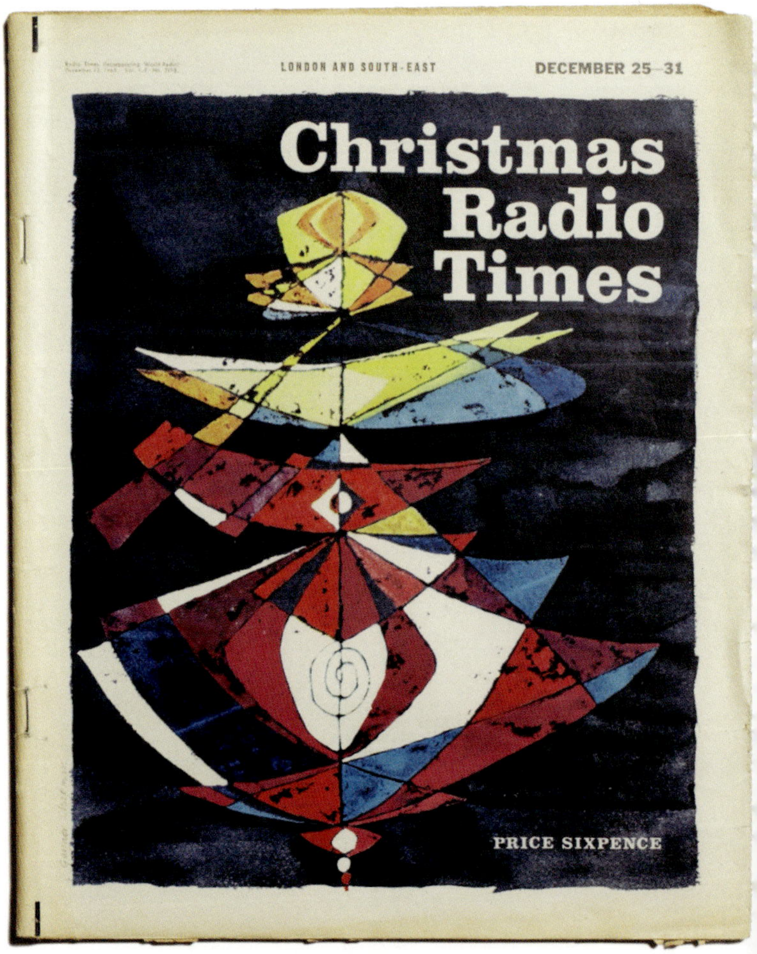

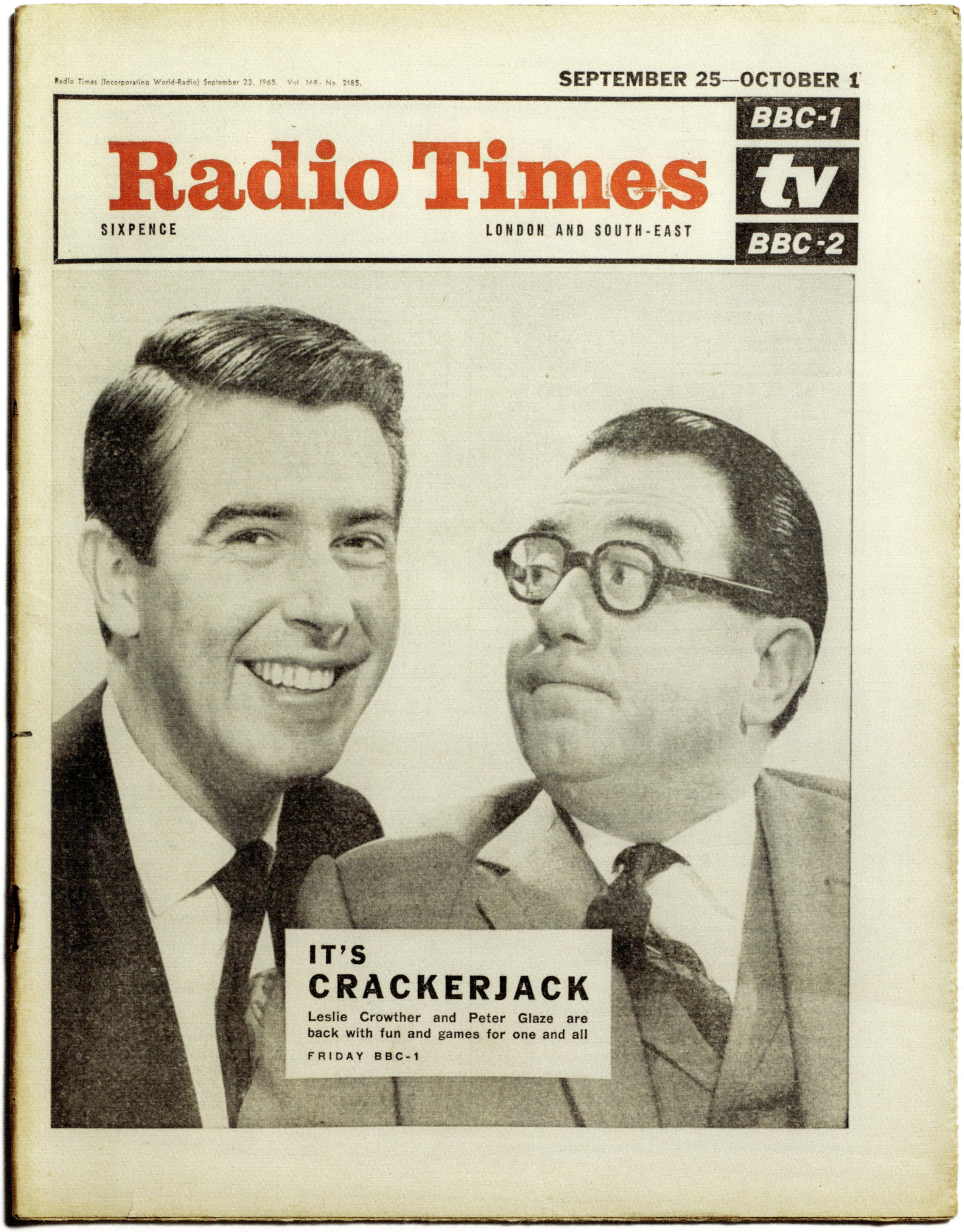

Crackerjack **Leslie Crowther and Peter Glaze** *25 September–1 October 1965*

Friday teatimes meant manic stand-up from Crowther and Glaze, cheered on by 500 children in the BBC Television Theatre. Regular games included Double or Drop in which contestants who gave wrong answers were awarded cabbages. This week, Crowther and Glaze and regular host Jillian Comber welcomed Valerie Walsh to the team.

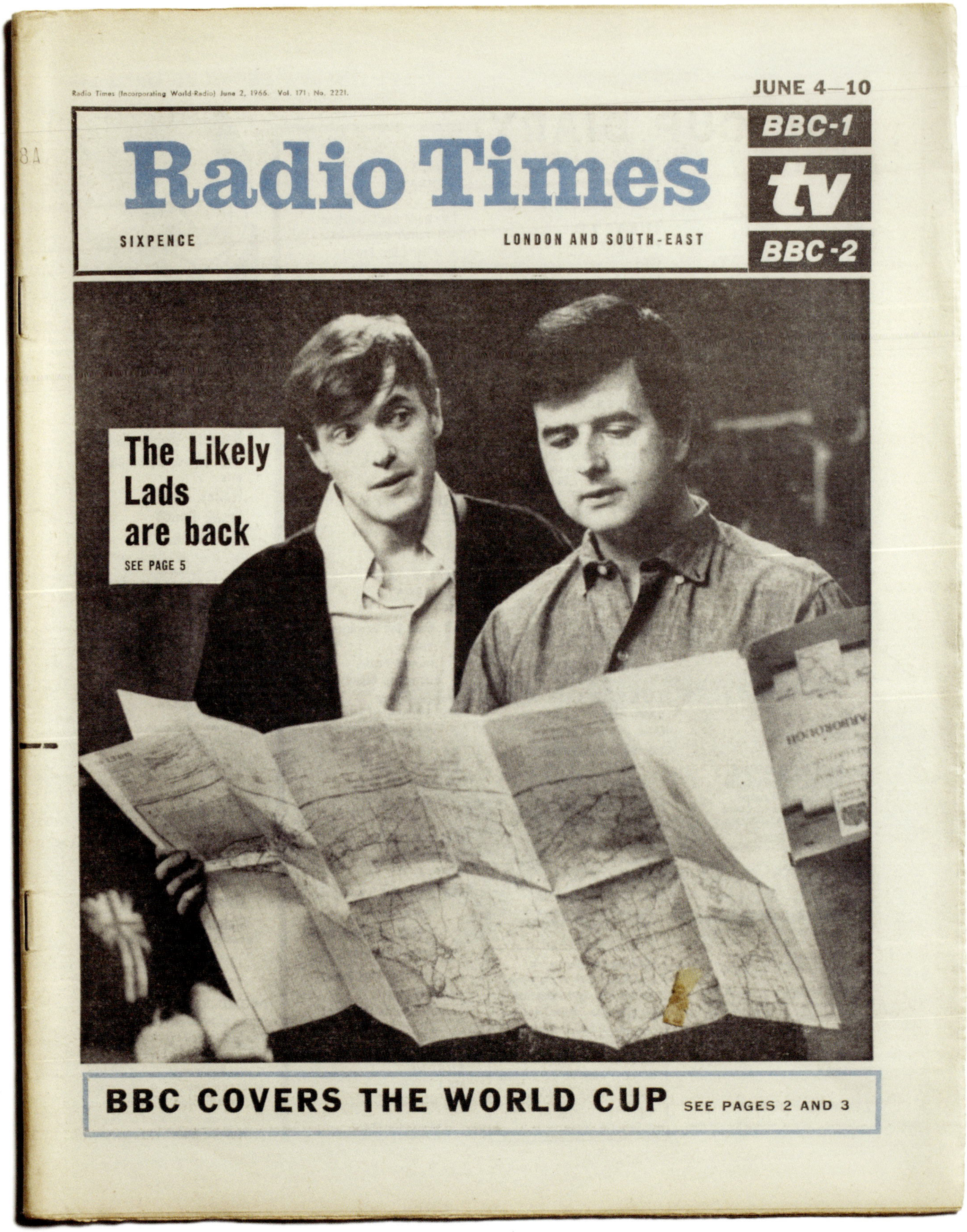
Radio Times (Incorporating World-Radio) June 2, 1966. Vol. 171: No. 2221.

JUNE 4—10

Radio Times

BBC-1 tv BBC-2

SIXPENCE

LONDON AND SOUTH-EAST

The Likely Lads are back

SEE PAGE 5

BBC COVERS THE WORLD CUP SEE PAGES 2 AND 3

The Likely Lads **Terry (James Bolam) and Bob (Rodney Bewes)**
(photograph by Don Smith) *4–10 June 1966*

The third series of Dick Clement and Ian Le Frenais's sitcom made the cover while, inside, in an episode of *Whicker's World*, Alan Whicker investigated "anonymous societies that seek to help alcoholics and gamblers, neurotics and divorcees". The coverline at the bottom hints at a football competition that would occupy the country until the end of July...

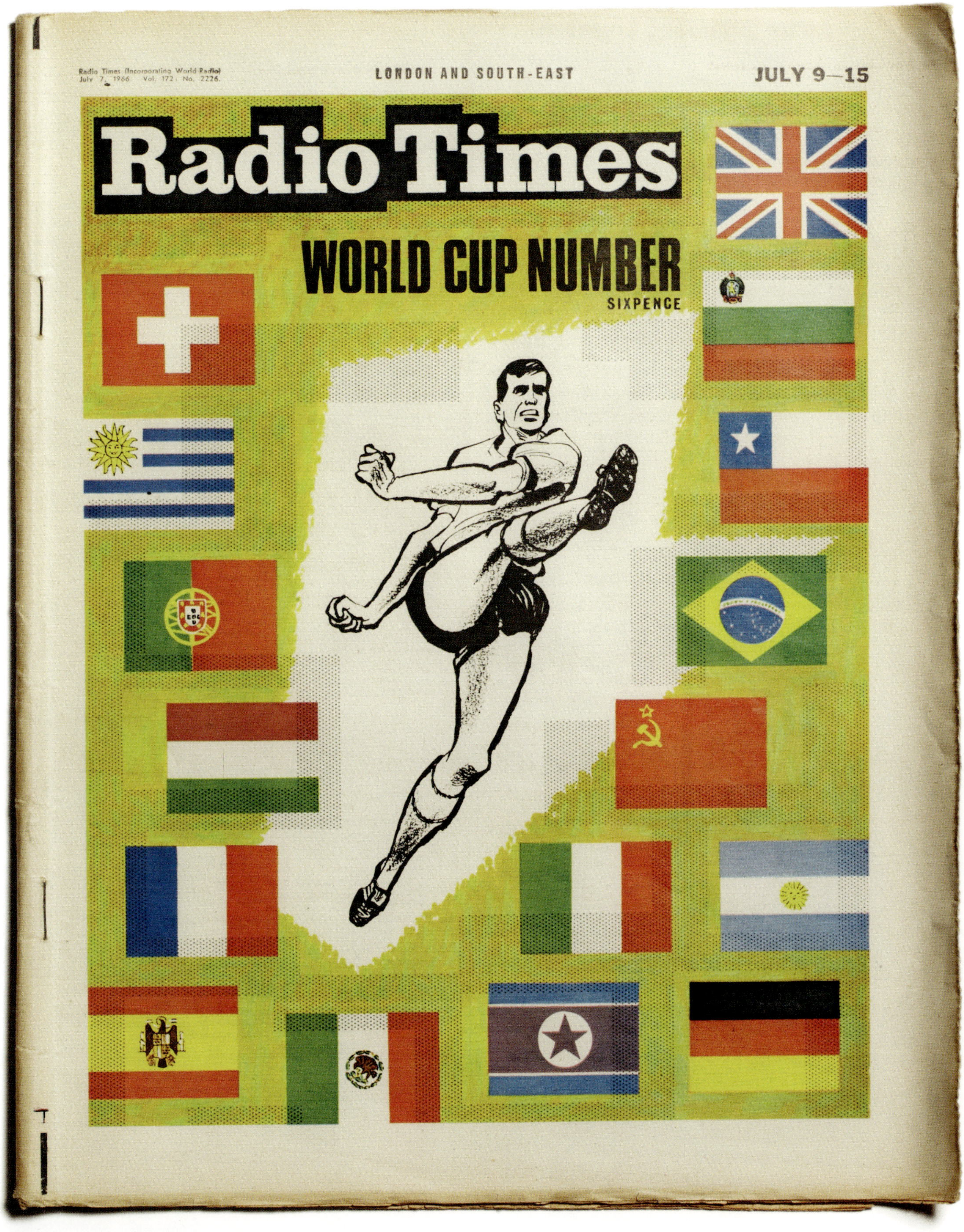

The 1966 World Cup *9–15 July 1966*

As the 16 teams who would play for the Jules Rimet Trophy began their final preparations, Kenneth Wolstenholme and Brian Moore delivered their analysis of each team's chances. "England have made too little use of their chances in front of goal," they warned as they mused on Alf Ramsey's promise that his team would win the World Cup. On the cover, England was represented by the Union flag rather than the St George's Cross.

Adam Adamant Lives! *(right)*

Adam Adamant (Gerald Harper)
Illustration by Robert Blaney

18–24 June 1966

Gerald Harper played Victorian adventurer Adam Adamant, who had been imprisoned in ice in 1902 and then released, bewildered, into the Swinging Sixties.

The Man from U.N.C.L.E *(middle right)*

Illya Kuryakin (David McCallum), Napoleon Solo (Robert Vaughn), Mr Waverly (Leo G Carroll)
Inset: April Dancer (Stefanie Powers)

15–21 October 1966

From this week international crimebusters Napoleon Solo and Ilya Kuryakin had a new recruit to help in their fight against crime – April Dancer, star of *The Girl from U.N.C.L.E.* The two series were broadcast on alternate Thursdays on BBC1.

Doctor Who *(far right)*

Dalek montage (photographs by Don Smith)

5–11 November 1966

The Daleks provided a draw for viewers reeling from *Doctor Who's* first change in lead actor, with Patrick Troughton debuting this week as the second Doctor.

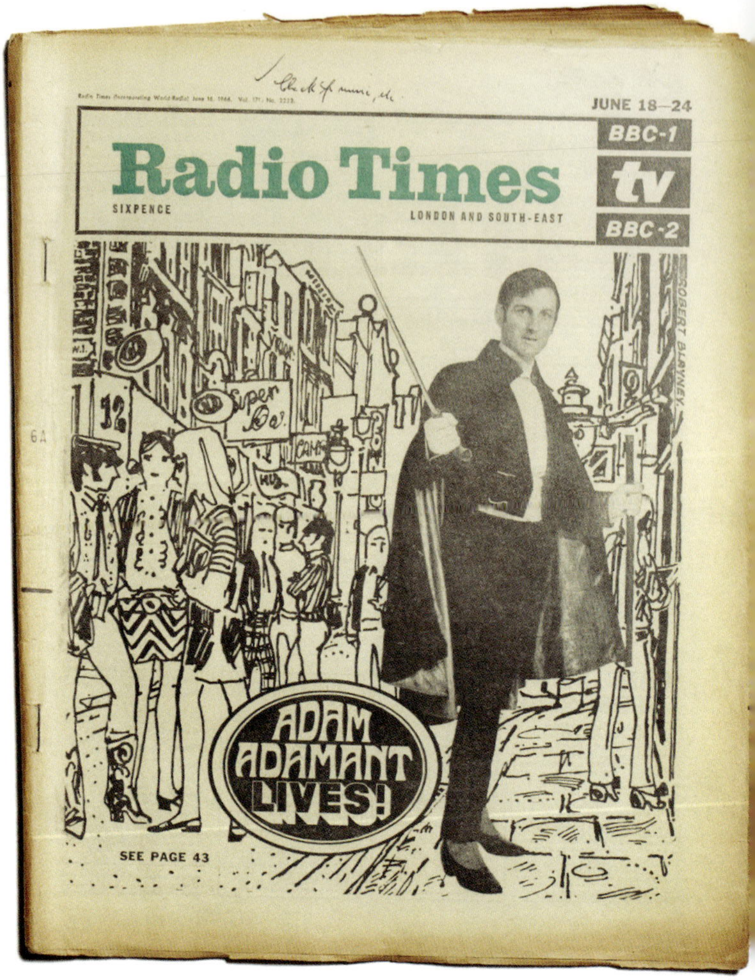

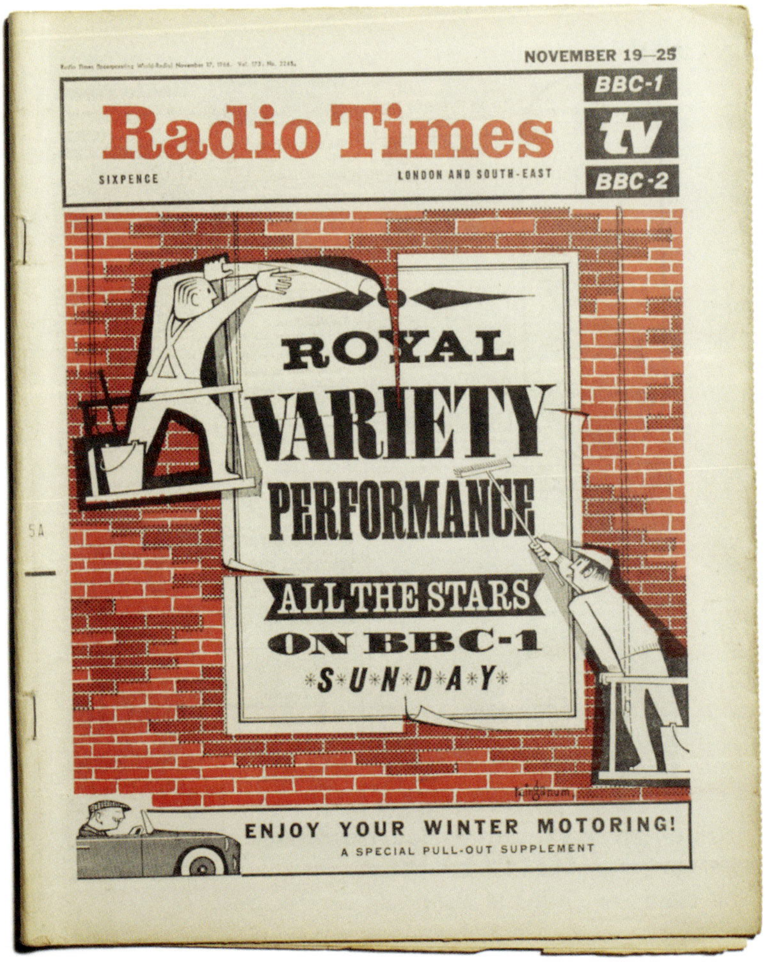

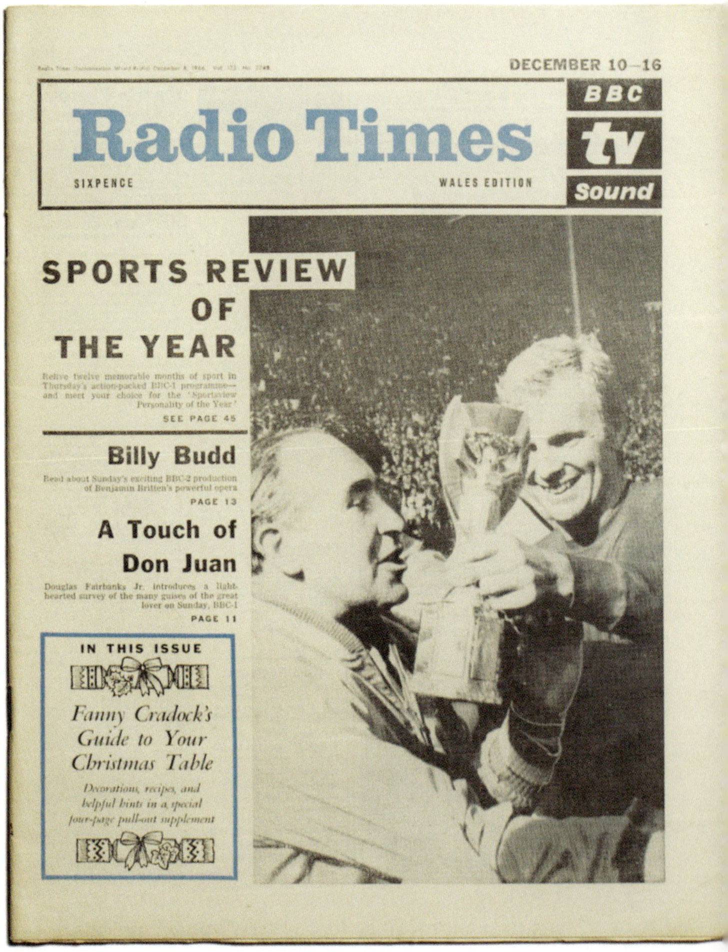

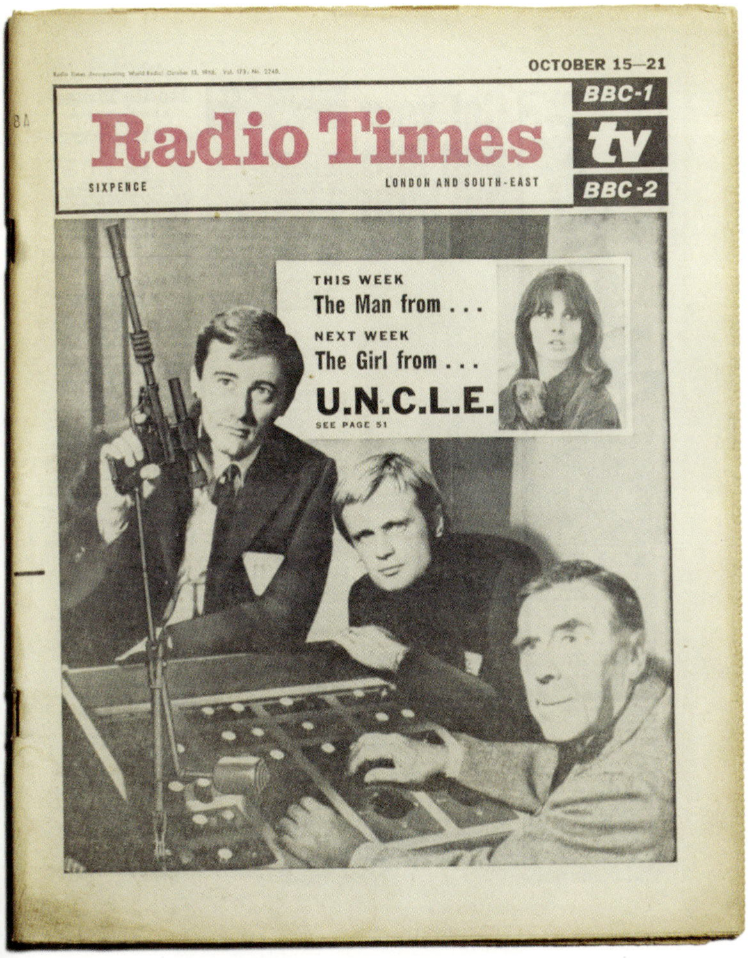

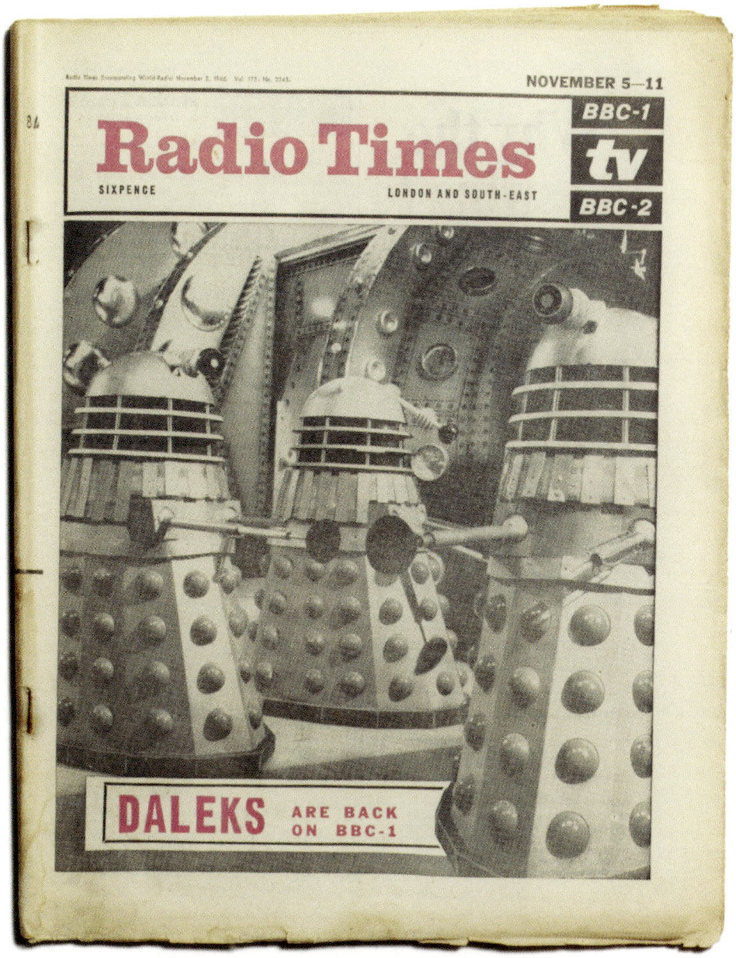

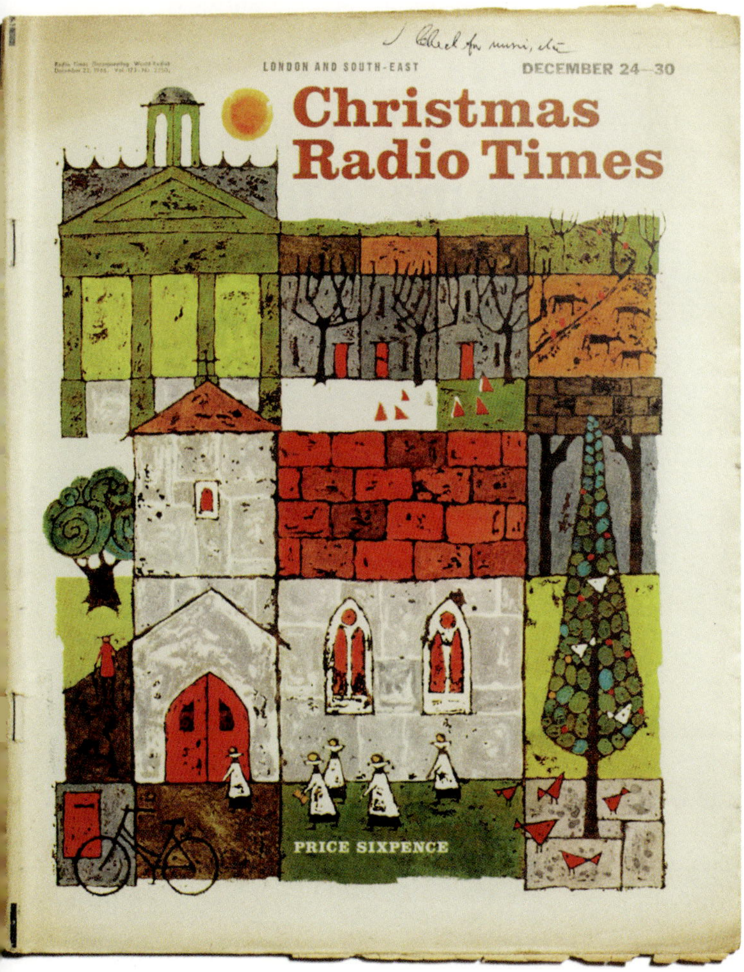

Royal Variety Performance *(far left)*

Illustration by Victor Reinganum

19–25 November 1966

The Bachelors, Eric and Ernie, Frankie Howerd, Sammy Davis Jr, Kenneth McKellar, Matt Monro and Gene Pitney were among the stars who entertained the Queen Mother at the London Palladium. The show was broadcast in full from 7.25pm to 10.50pm, with a ten-minute break for the news at 9.00pm.

Sports Review of the Year *(middle left)*

Alf Ramsey (left) and Bobby Moore

10–16 December 1966

This was the 13th edition of the BBC's *Sports Review of the Year* and the England football team were predictable winners of the Team of the Year award for winning the World Cup. Team captain Bobby Moore was voted Sports Personality of the Year, while hat-trick hero Geoff Hurst came third.

Christmas 1966 *(left)*

Illustration by Gaynor Chapman

24–30 December 1966

A second consecutive Christmas cover by Gaynor Chapman, who lit a scene of pastoral charm with patches of ruby red. On Christmas Day, Kenneth Clark presented a one-hour documentary *The Royal Palaces of Britain* and *Radio Times* published an eight-page supplement to accompany it, complete with illustrations and colour pictures.

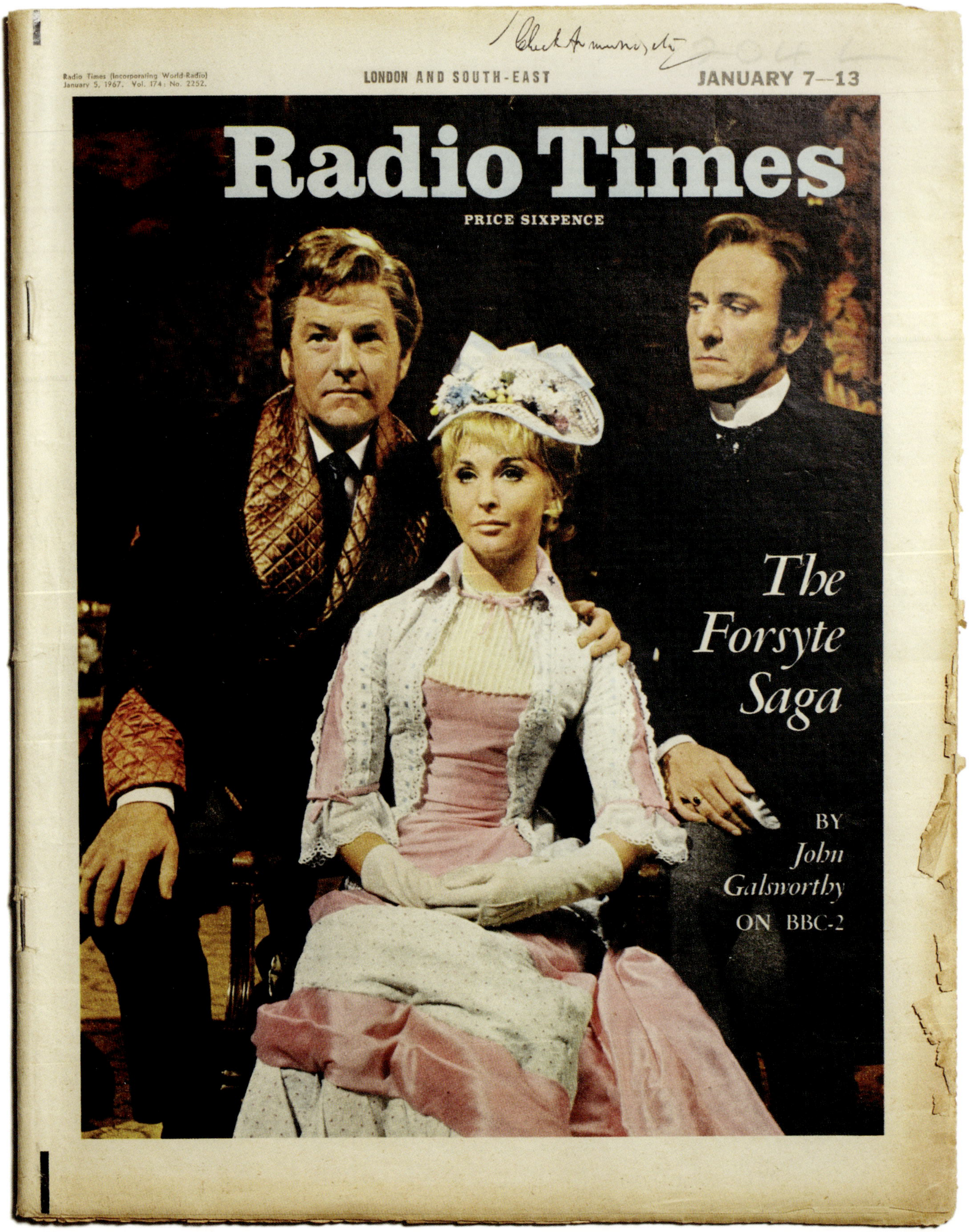

The Forsyte Saga **Jo (Kenneth More), Irene (Nyree Dawn Porter) and Soames (Eric Porter)**
(photograph by Don Smith) *7–13 January 1967*

The dramatisation of John Galsworthy's Forsyte novels was broadcast on Saturday nights on BBC1 over 26 weeks (with a repeat on the same channel on Tuesday nights) and was a huge hit for the BBC. Inside the issue, the producer, Donald Wilson, explained why three episodes of backstory were needed to get to the first page of the first novel...

Rolf Harris *(left)*

(photograph by Don Smith)

21–27 January 1967

The Rolf Harris Show was Rolf's first solo show for adults. Readers were told to expect comedy songs, yarns and huge sploshy paintings. His guests included Sandie Shaw, who was representing Britain in that year's Eurovision Song Contest.

The Monkees *(below left)*

From left: Peter Tork, Mike Nesmith, Davy Jones and Micky Dolenz

11–17 February 1967

The American pop group sent their young British fans a cable from the US: "You can watch our quiet restrained show every week. Cheerio and stay real cool man."

The Black and White Minstrel Show *(below right)*

"Jolson" (Dai Francis) ***(photograph by Don Smith)***

15–21 April 1967

The preview article announced with enthusiasm that this new series was the 87th appearance of the Mitchell Minstrels, with Dai Francis, John Boulter and Tony Mercer. It was also the year that the BBC received petitions objecting to the blackface make-up and stereotypical mannerisms of the white singers. The show was cancelled in 1978.

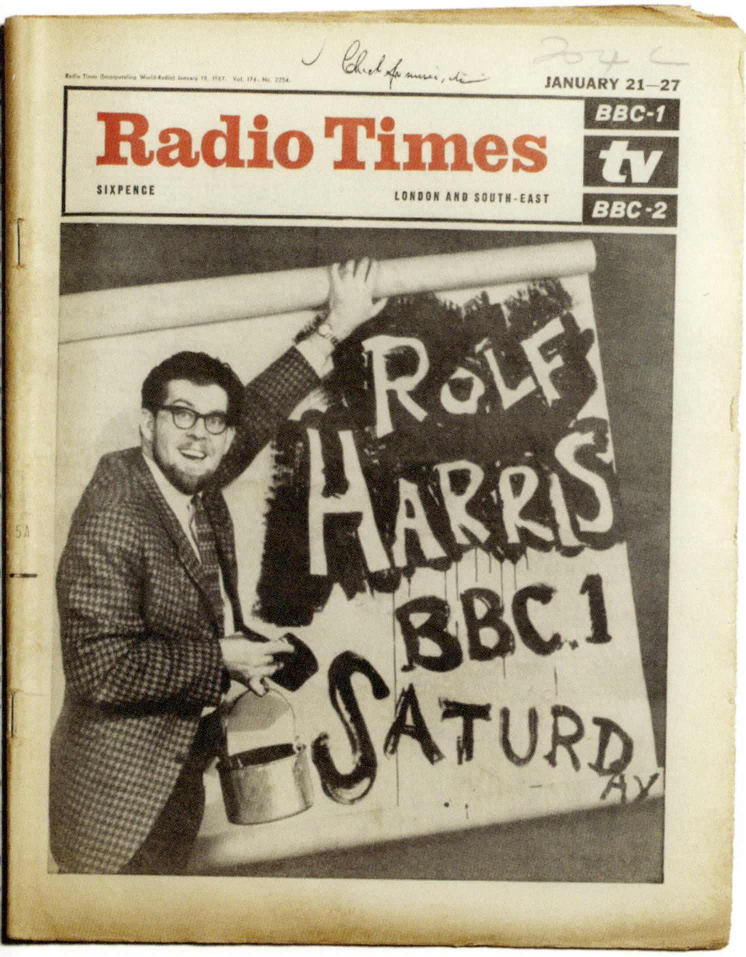

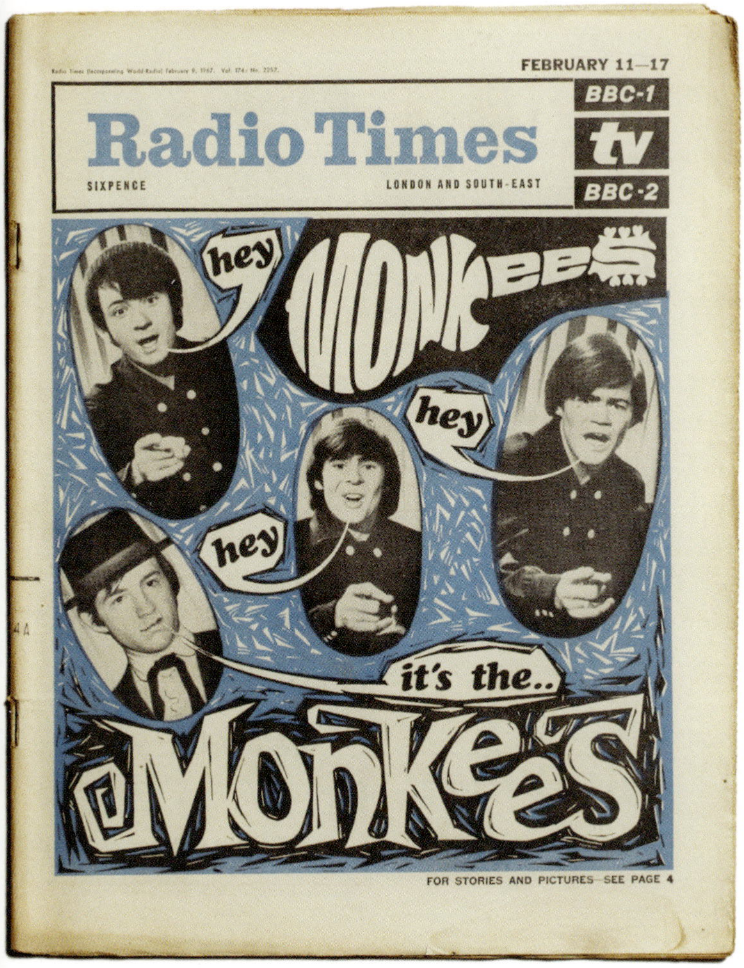

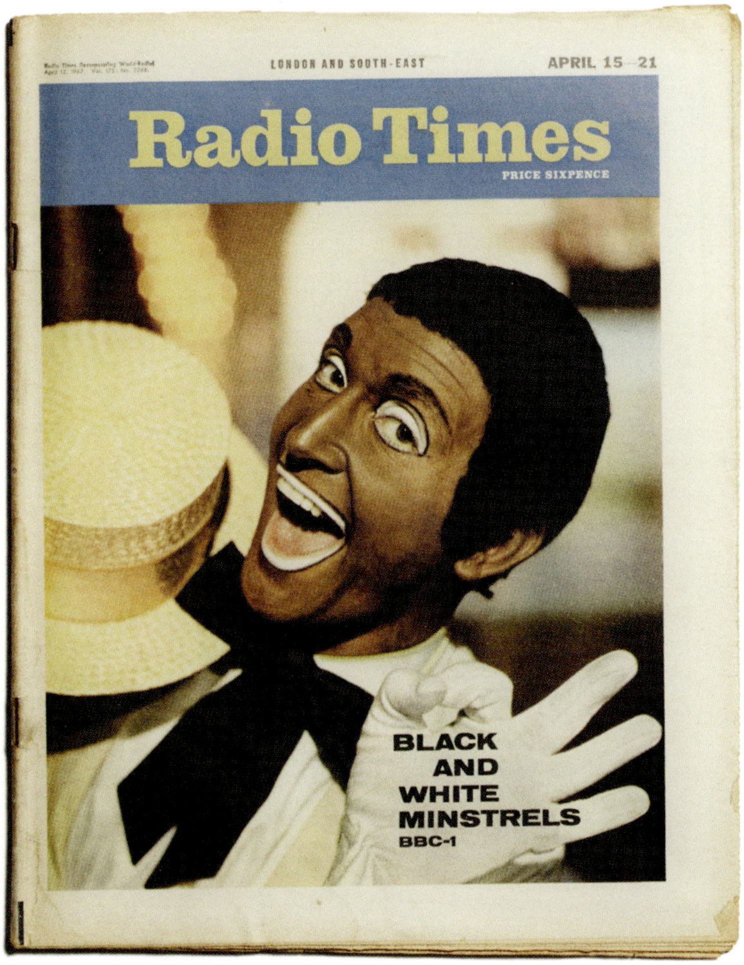

It's a Knock-out! *(right)*

Illustration by Victor Reinganum

19–25 August 1967

David Vine was the host, Blackpool was the venue and it was Cheltenham Spa representing Britain in this round of *Jeux sans Frontières*, the international version of the competition that featured hapless amateurs engaging in games involving foam, water and humiliation.

Doctor Who *(below left)*

(photograph by Don Smith) *2–8 September 1967*

"Today we have landed on Telos... Somewhere on this planet lie the remains of the Cybermen. They are supposed to be extinct, but I wonder if they really are?" So read an extract from the Doctor's diary, as *Radio Times* prepared readers for a third deadly encounter with the Cybermen, lying dormant in their "tomb".

The Val Doonican Show *(below right)*

Val Doonican *(photograph by Don Smith)*

7–13 October 1967

The Star Story feature, with its glimpses of the lives of BBC celebrities, was printed in colour to lend added glamour. Irish singer Val Doonican was pictured in his element on the golf course and at home with his family, and talked frankly about his long slog to TV success.

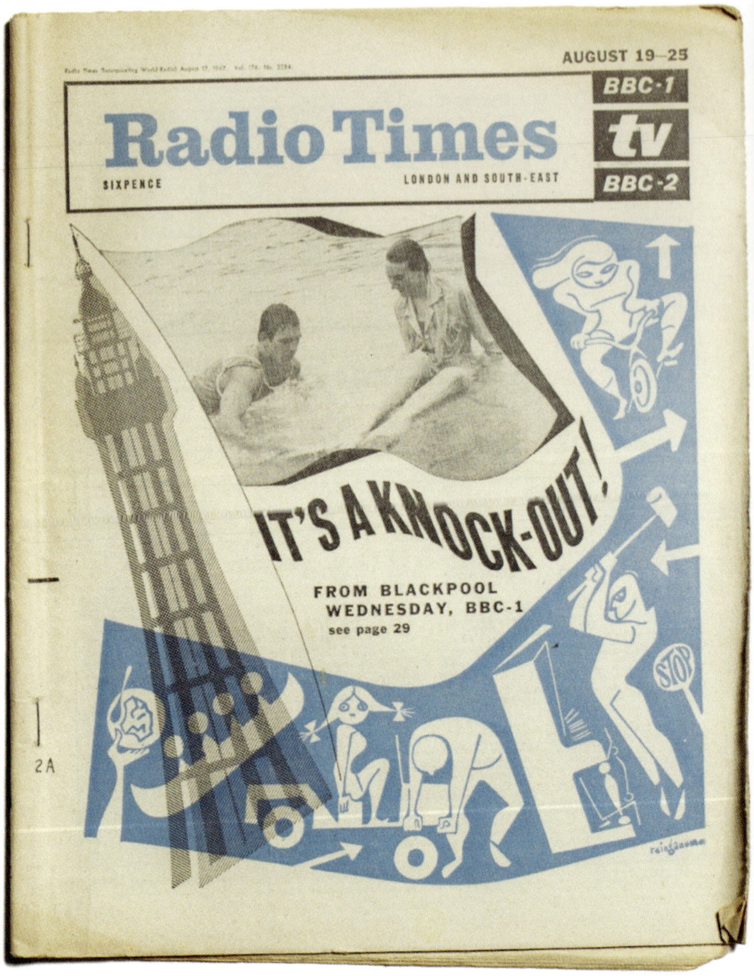

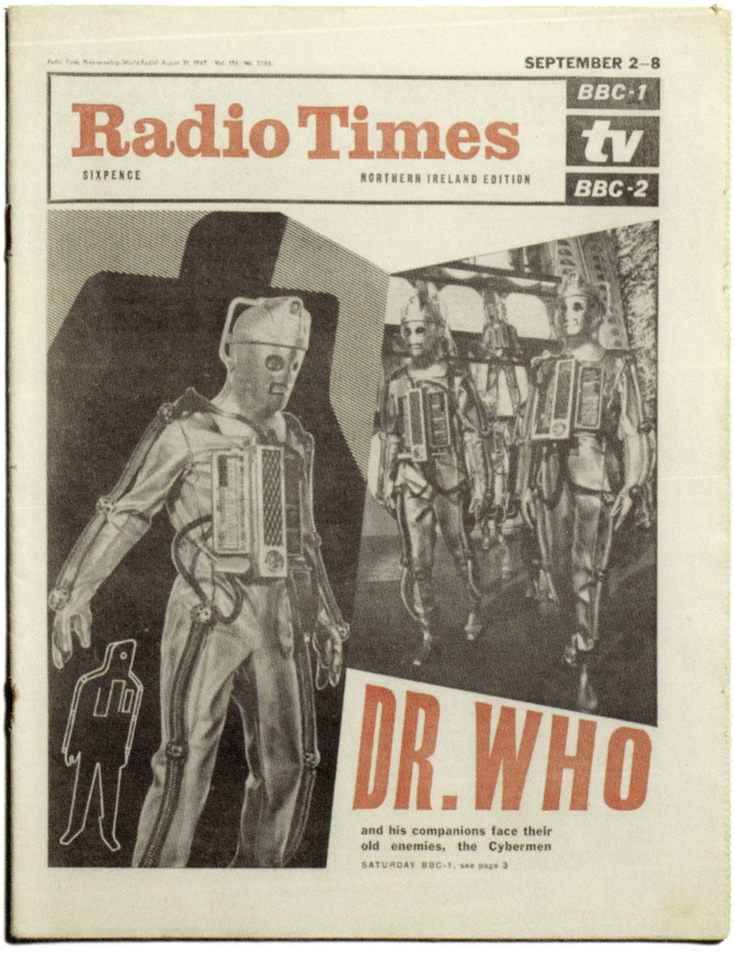

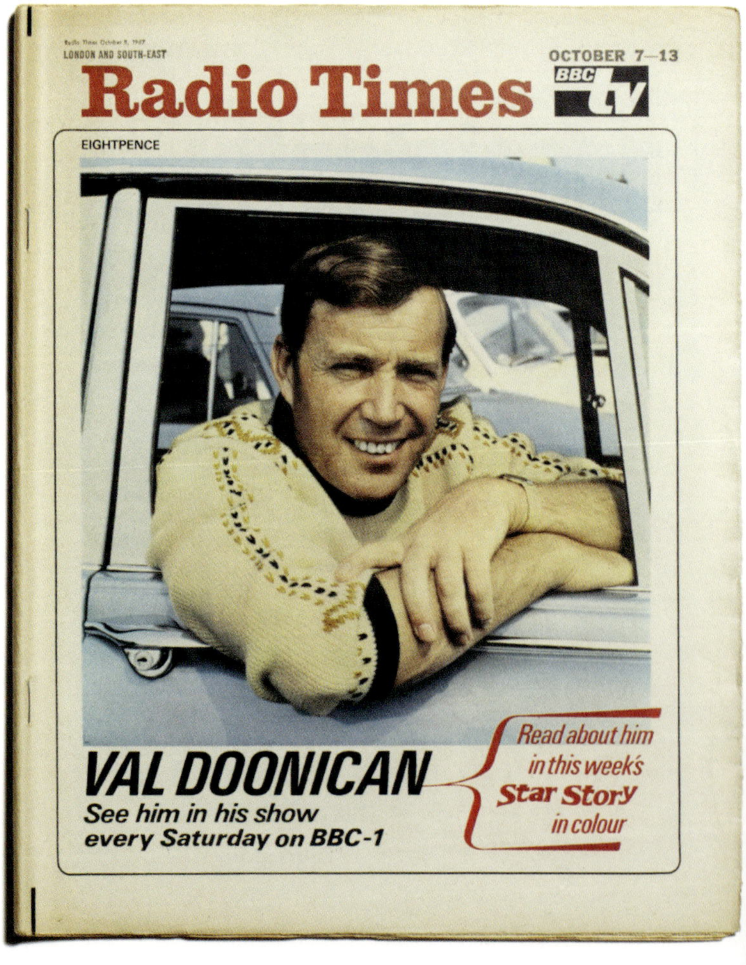

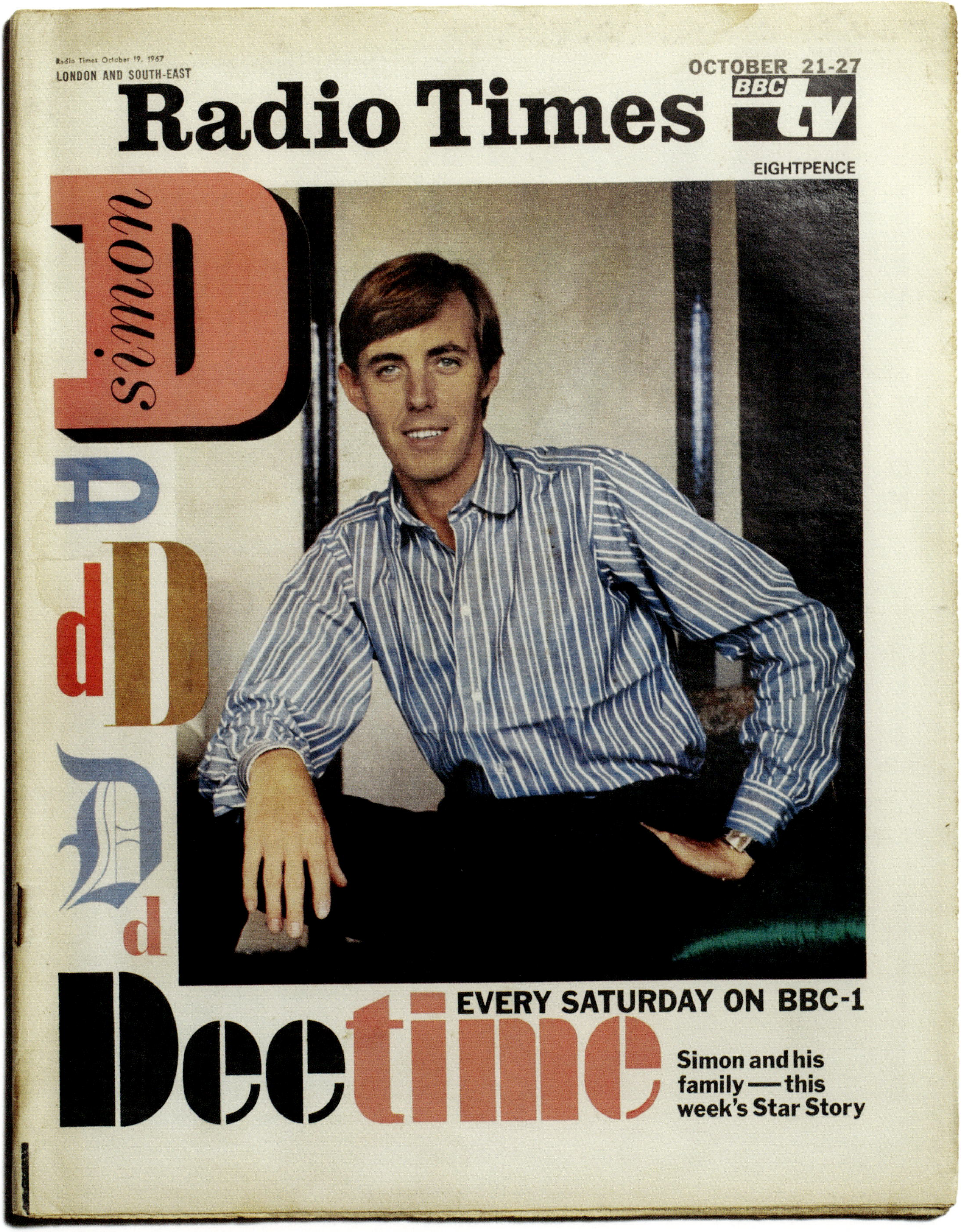

Dee Time Simon Dee *21–27 October 1967*

In the Star Story feature 32-year-old Simon Dee looked back on the six months he'd been presenting his BBC1 chat show *Dee Time* and said he just wanted to be taken seriously. "I'm as interested in things like Vietnam, birth control, abortion, the church, politics as anybody else. But because I look 22, the audience don't take it from me."

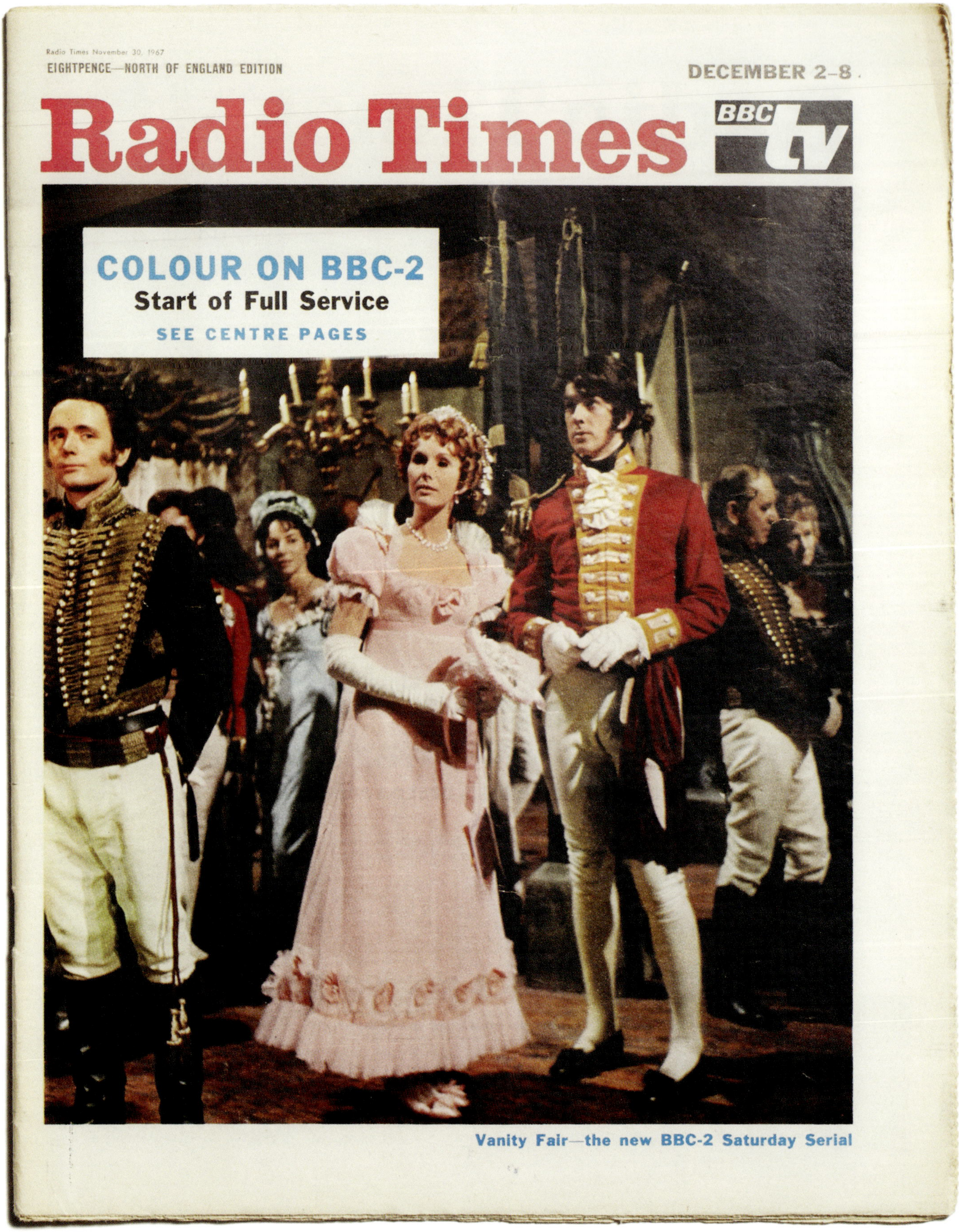

Vanity Fair **Becky Sharp (Susan Hampshire)** *(photograph by Don Smith)* *2–8 December 1967*

A suitably vibrant cover to mark the first week of colour progammes on BBC2. "From today everybody who can get BBC2 programmes will be able to see them in colour – if they have a colour set," ran the editorial on page three. Susan Hampshire was the star of the adaptation of William Makepeace Thackeray's novel, and was already familiar to viewers as she's played Fleur in the other 1960s period drama hit, *The Forsyte Saga*.

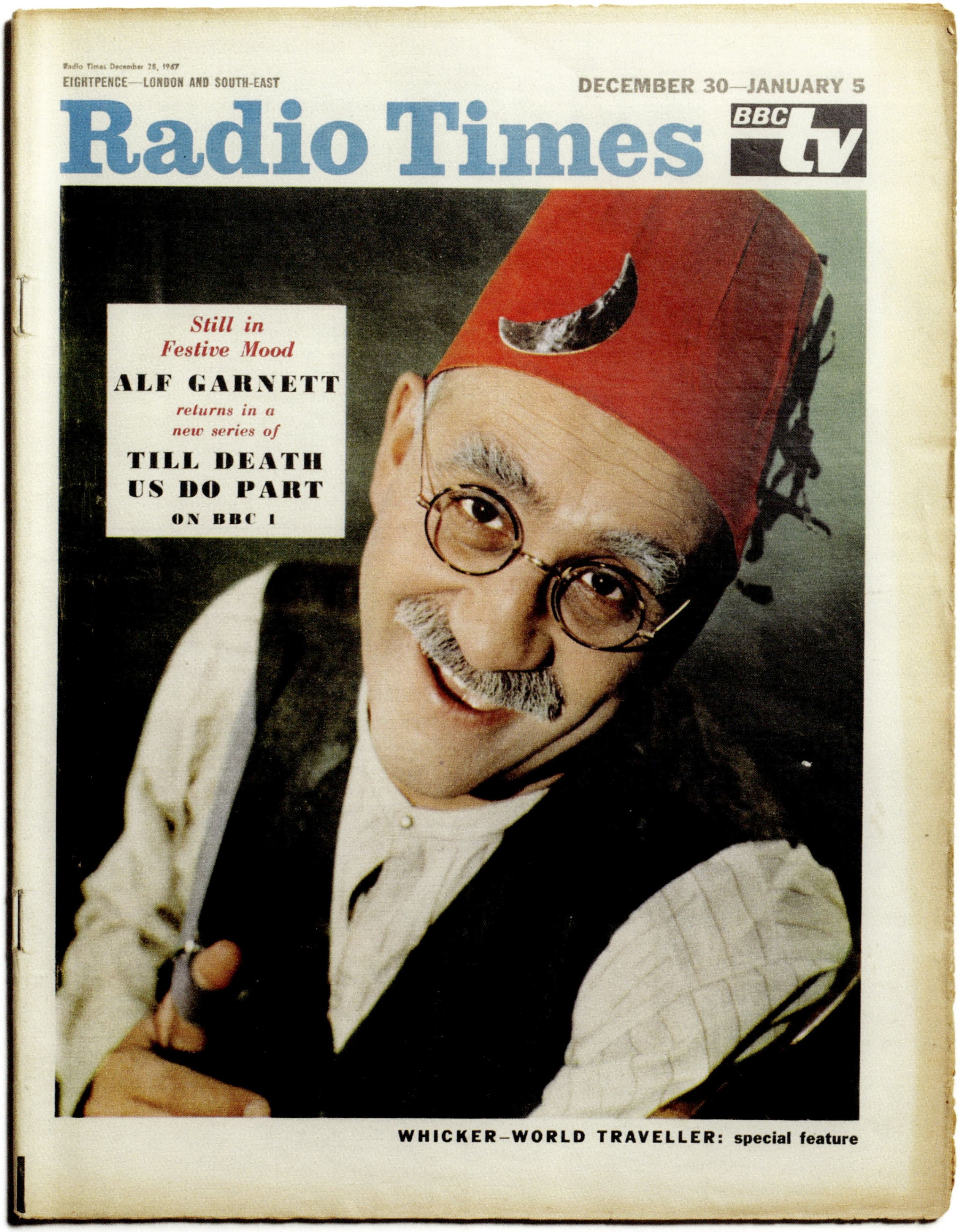

Till Death Us Do Part **Alf Garnett (Warren Mitchell)** *30 December 1967–5 January 1968*

This was the third series of the hugely popular sitcom starring Warren Mitchell as Cockney bigot Alf Garnett. Dennis Main Wilson, the producer, wrote in his introduction: "Johnny Speight [the writer] is able to hold the reactionary Alf Garnett up to public ridicule – and so the radicals of this world laugh at Alf. On the other hand, there are millions who seem to agree with Alf and rather than laugh *at* him, laugh *with* him."

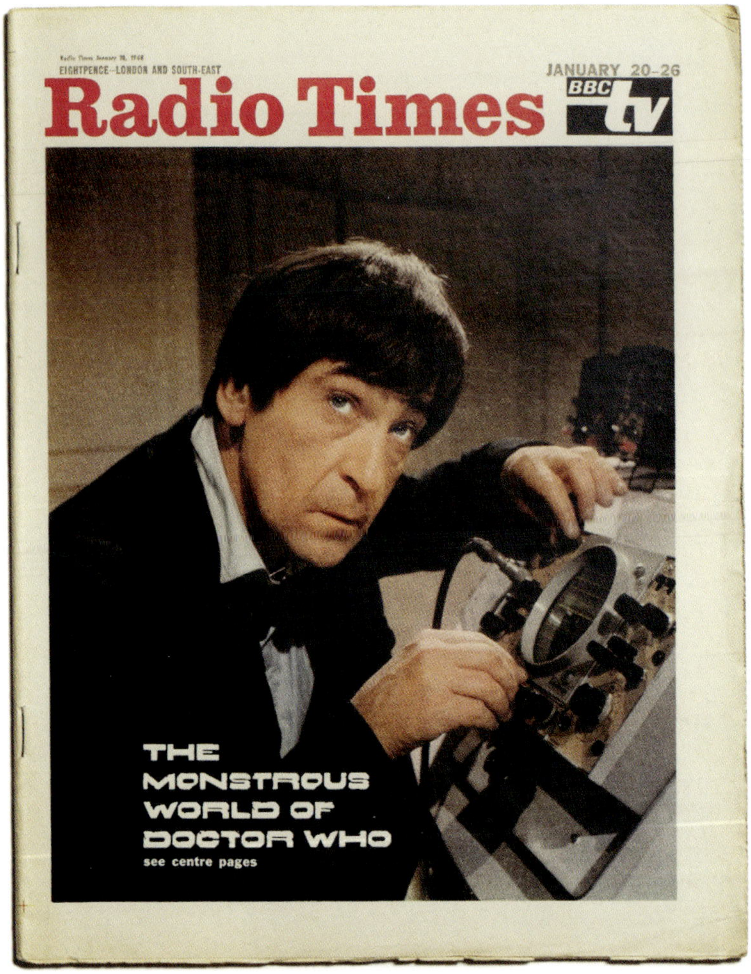

Doctor Who *(left)*
The Doctor (Patrick Troughton) *(photograph by Don Smith)*
20–26 January 1968

Almost halfway through his tenure, the second Doctor, Patrick Troughton, garnered his first cover – and *Doctor Who's* first full-colour cover. Inside, reporter Gay Search met the costume and visual-effects designers who made the Daleks, Cybermen, Ice Warriors and Yeti.

Newsroom *(below left)*
9–15 March 1968

Newsroom was BBC2's weekday news programme and *Radio Times* sent a reporter to its HQ at Alexandra Palace to find out what impact the arrival of colour broadcasting had made. "We might spend a little longer at the Chelsea Flower Show," joked joint editor Ken Callaway.

Come Dancing *(below right)*
23–29 March 1968

It was Home Counties South v West Scotland in the final of BBC1's ballroom dancing competition. The Home Counties South team boasted a celebrity of sorts – by day, Ray Rouse was a policeman who stood guard outside 10 Downing Street. The cover was in colour but dance fans had to be content with watching the action in black and white.

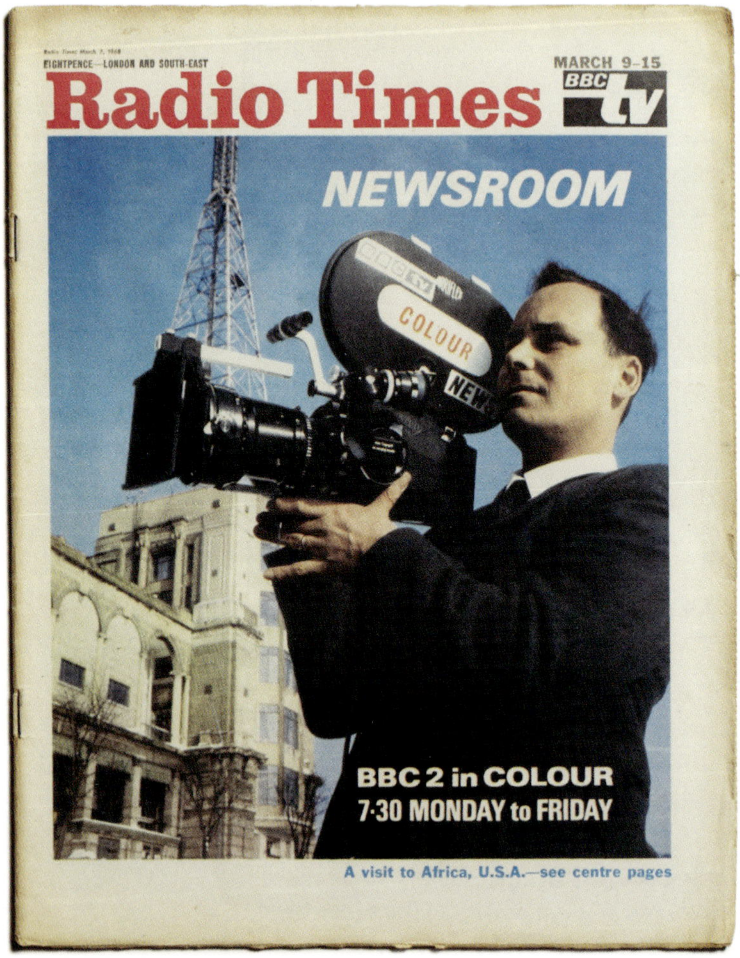

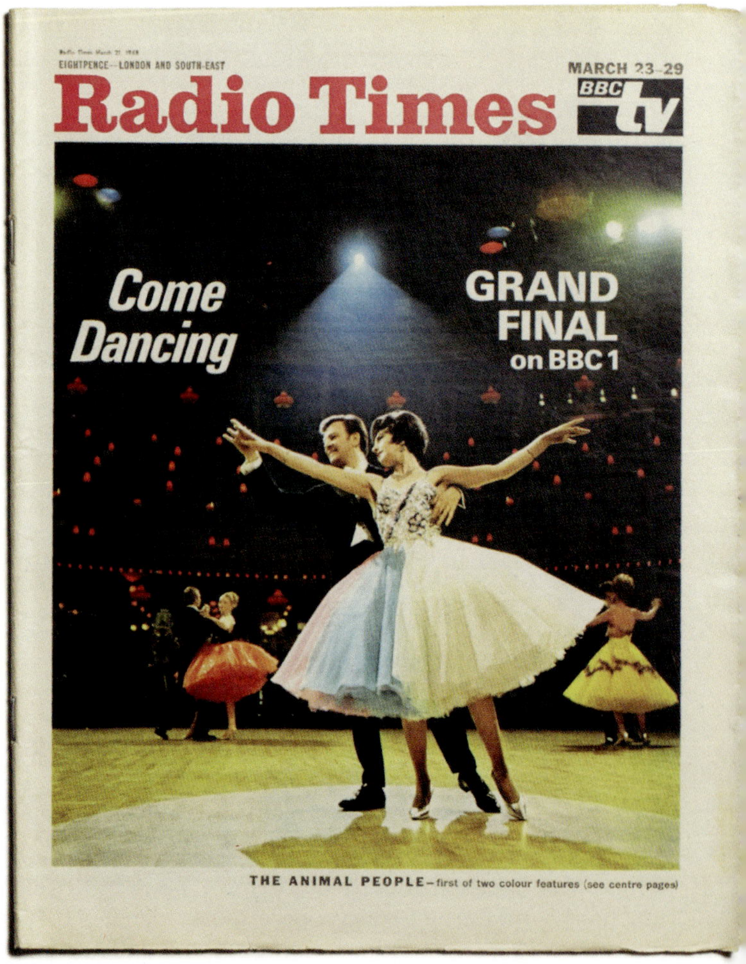

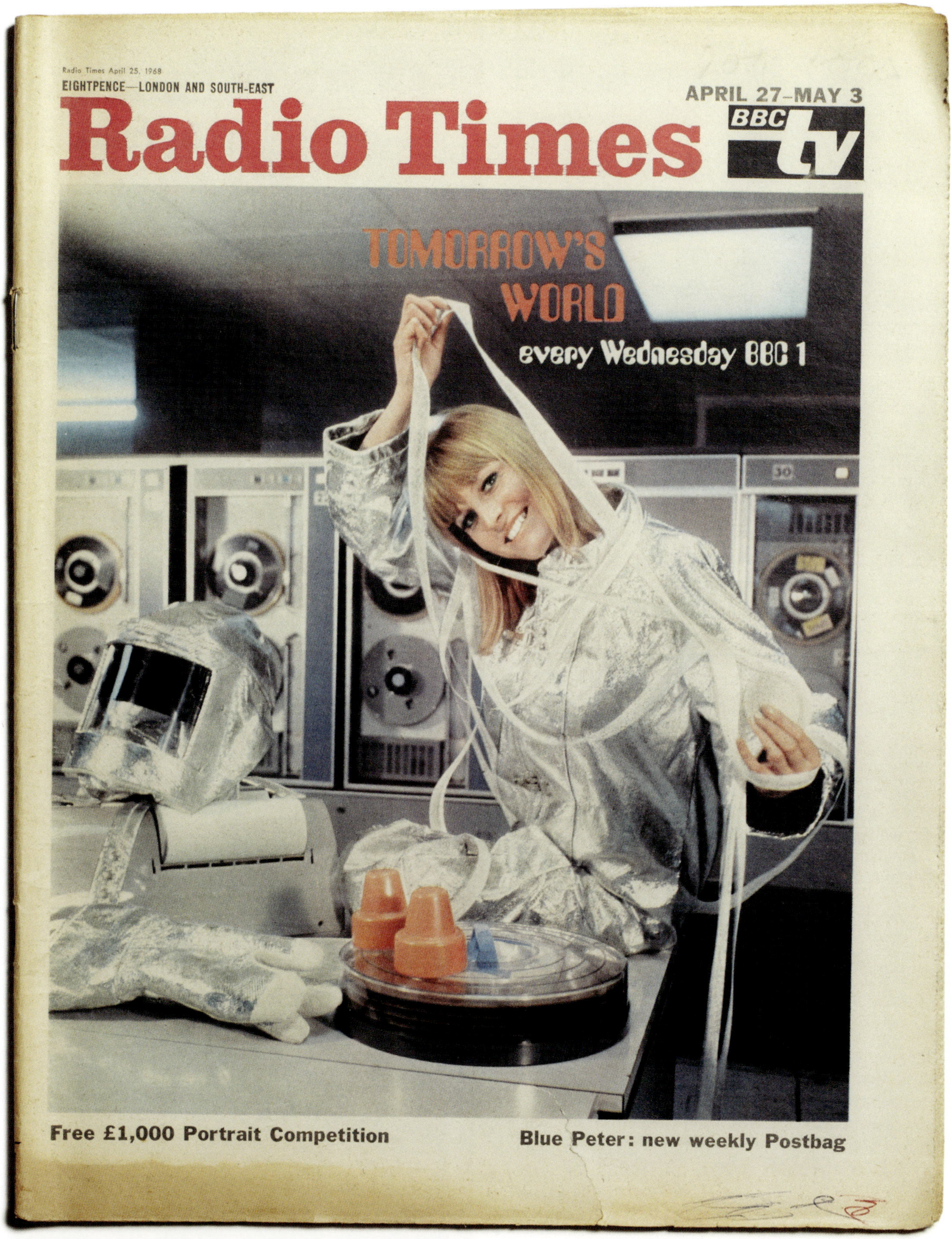

Tomorrow's World *27 April–3 May 1968*

The focus of the series was science and technology, but as its editor Michael Latham made clear, the aim was "to entertain. *Tomorrow's World* doesn't set out to teach." The cover was also potentially misleading – the presenting team was all-male, comprising Raymond Baxter, James Burke and John Parry.

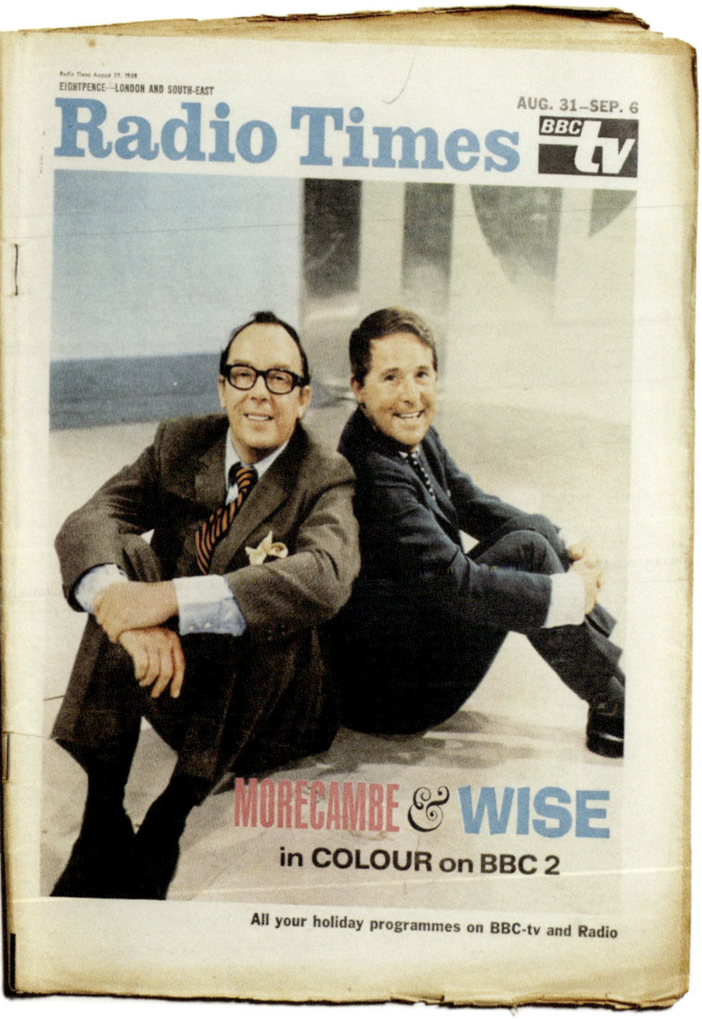

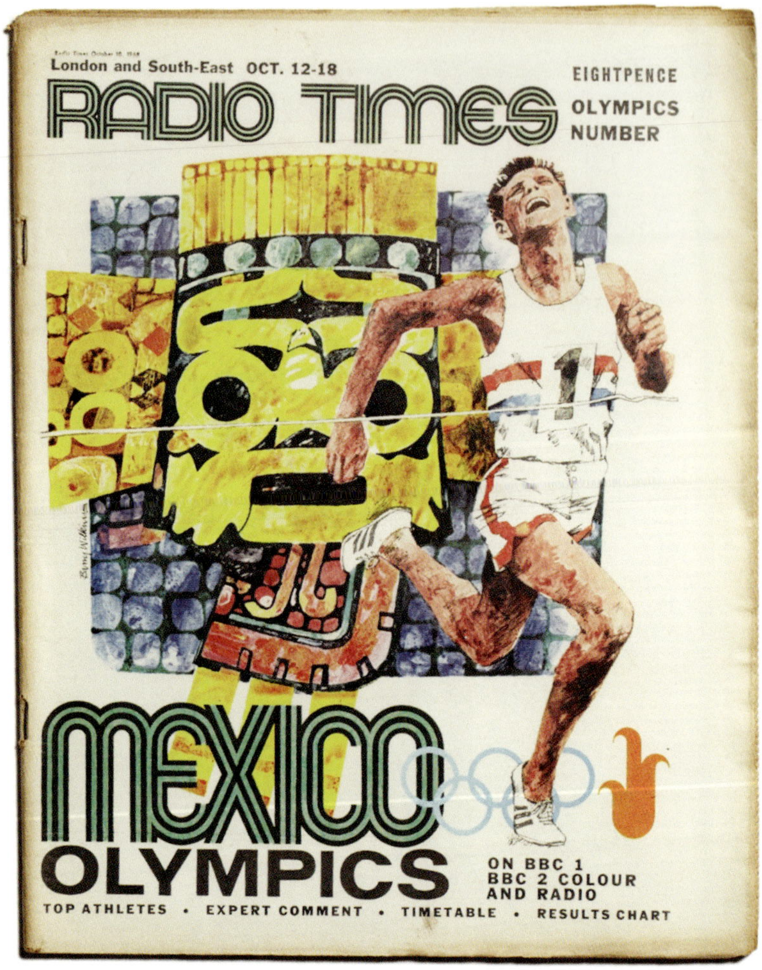

Rolf Harris *(right)*
(photograph by Barry Redman)

4–10 January 1969

By now a mainstream entertainer, Rolf had integrated his giant paintings into his TV show: "I feel I'm giving a tremendous number of people a greater insight than they've had before into the way a painting is developed."

Maigret at Bay *(middle right)*
Maigret (Rupert Davies)

8–14 February 1969

Rupert Davies had starred as Georges Simenon's maverick police detective in four series (1960–63). Returning for this *Play of the Month*, Davies told *Radio Times*: "*Maigret* still has a considerable grip on me – the stories, the atmosphere... I guess it's got me for life in one form or another."

Eurovision Song Contest *(far right)*
Lulu

29 March–4 April 1969

Eurovision fever was fuelled by Sandie Shaw's win with *Puppet on a String* in 1967, followed by Cliff Richard's second place for *Congratulations*. Lulu was thought to have nailed her "Song for Europe" with *Boom Bang-a-Bang*, but she shared first place with Spain, France and the Netherlands.

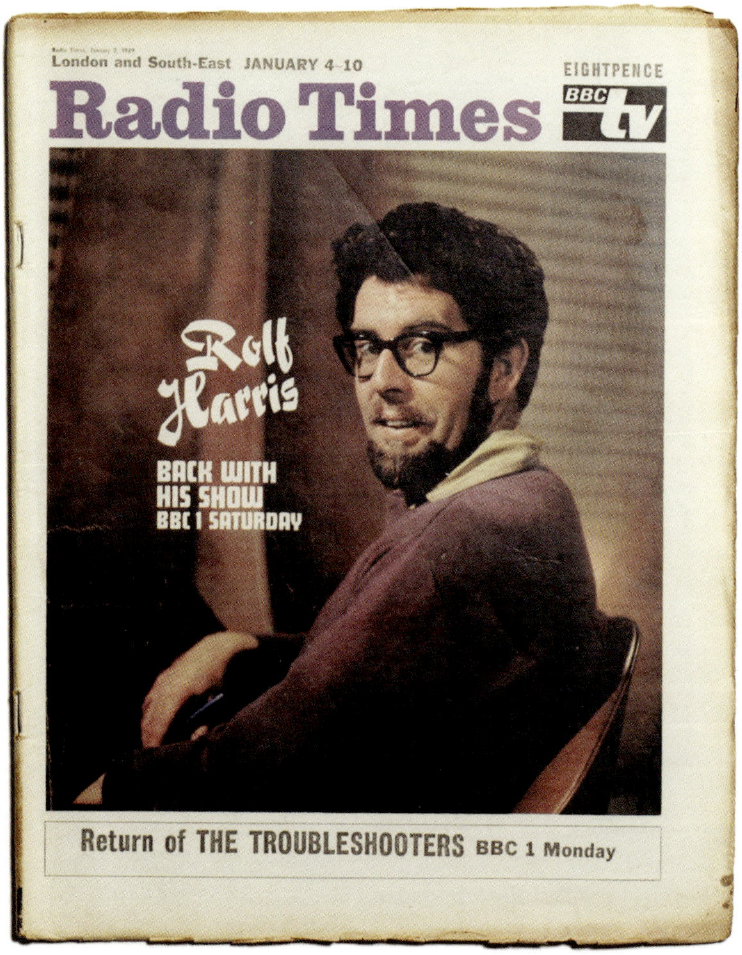

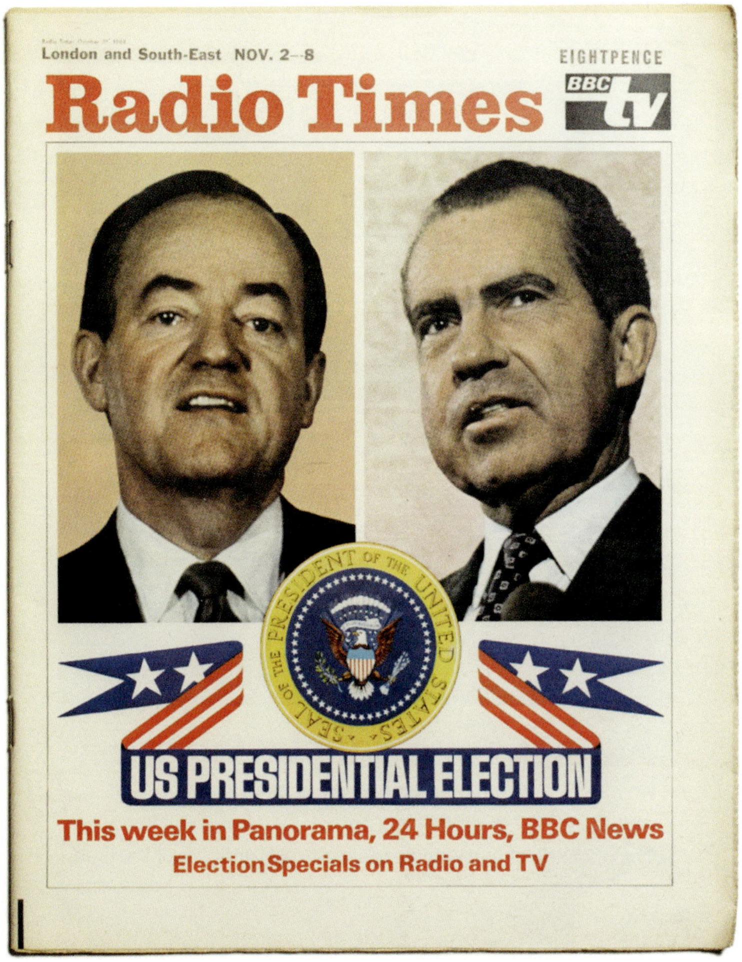

Morecambe & Wise *(far left)*

Eric Morecambe, Ernie Wise ***(photograph by Don Smith)***

31 August–6 September 1968

Back on BBC TV after a long spell at ITV, the pair talked to Gay Search about their 28-year showbiz "marriage". "I'm thinking of divorcing him, he talks too much," said Eric. "We split everything down the middle," said Ernie. "Sixty per cent for me and forty per cent for Eric."

The Mexico Olympics *(middle left)*

Illustration by Barry Wilkinson

12-18 October 1968

The graphics inside the 24-page Olympics section echoed the Mayan iconography of the cover. The issue included a results scorecard and analysis of the effects of the stadium's altitude. Mary Rand, a gold medallist at the 1964 Olympics, joined the commentary team.

US Presidential Election *(left)*

Hubert Humphrey and Richard Nixon

2–8 November 1968

For the first time, viewers in Britain could watch the US election results live by satellite. A preview by Robert McKenzie predicted the victory of Richard Milhous Nixon over Democrat nominee Hubert Humphrey.

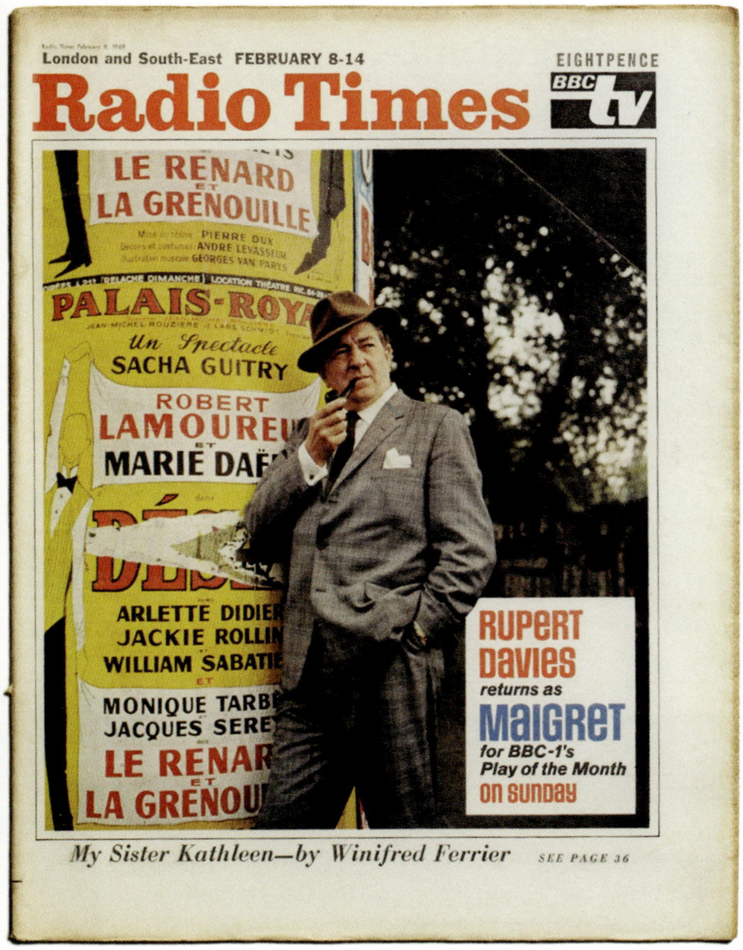

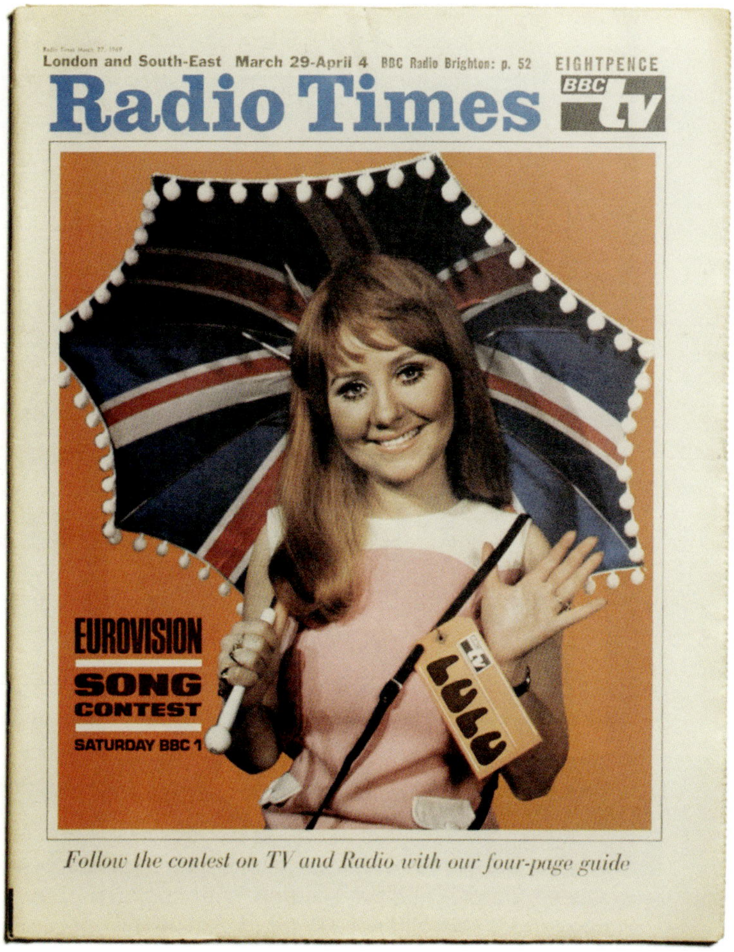

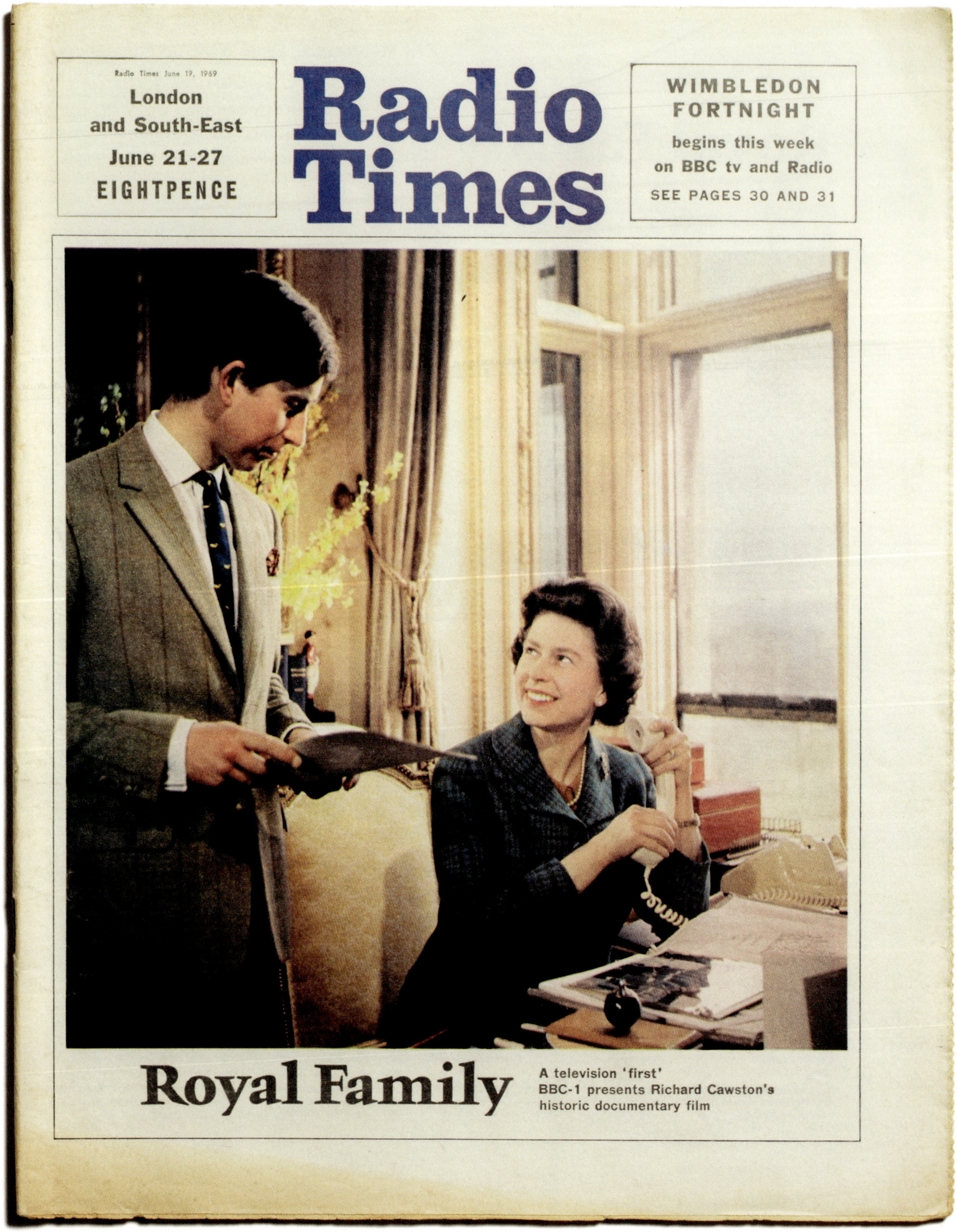

The Royal Family **Prince Charles and the Queen** *(photograph by Joan Williams)* *21–27 June 1969*

Richard Cawston described his fly-on-the-wall documentary about a year in the life of the Queen and her immediate family as "an incredible historical opportunity. Think of what it would be like to be able to pull from the vaults film of Queen Victoria and her children." Although the programme-makers retained editorial control, the Palace had right of veto. They did not ask for any changes, but the film was withdrawn after six months.

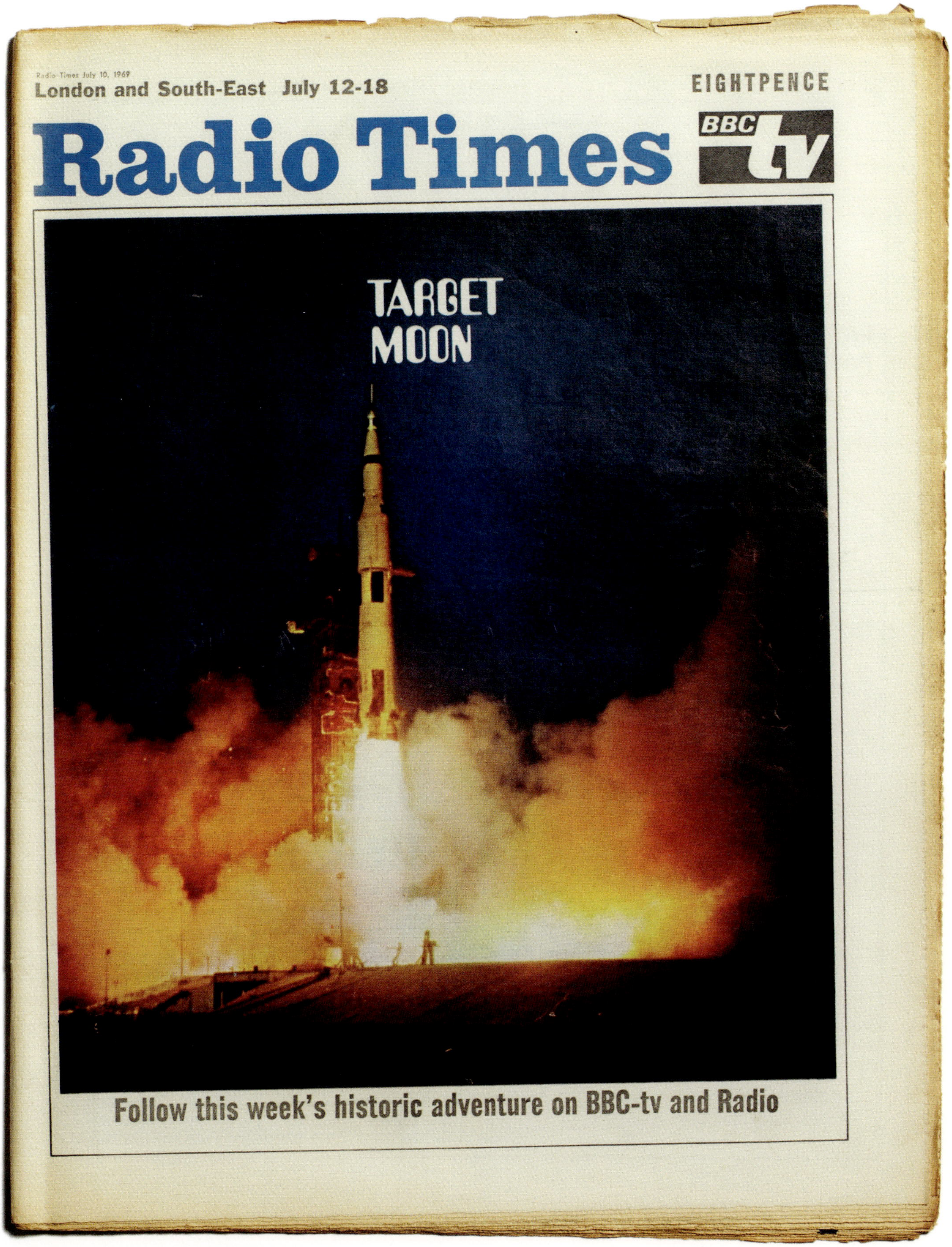

Apollo 11: Target Moon *(photograph courtesy of Nasa)* *12–18 July 1969*

"The wonder of the *Apollo 11* mission is incredible enough," ran the *Radio Times* editorial, "but as well as being the threshold of the space age, this is also the television age. You at home will be able to follow the moon mission stage by stage, right up to the climax." Inside, James Burke introduced "the men, the mooncraft and the mission". On BBC1 – with perfect timing – the US sci-fi series, *Star Trek,* debuted in the Saturday teatime slot.

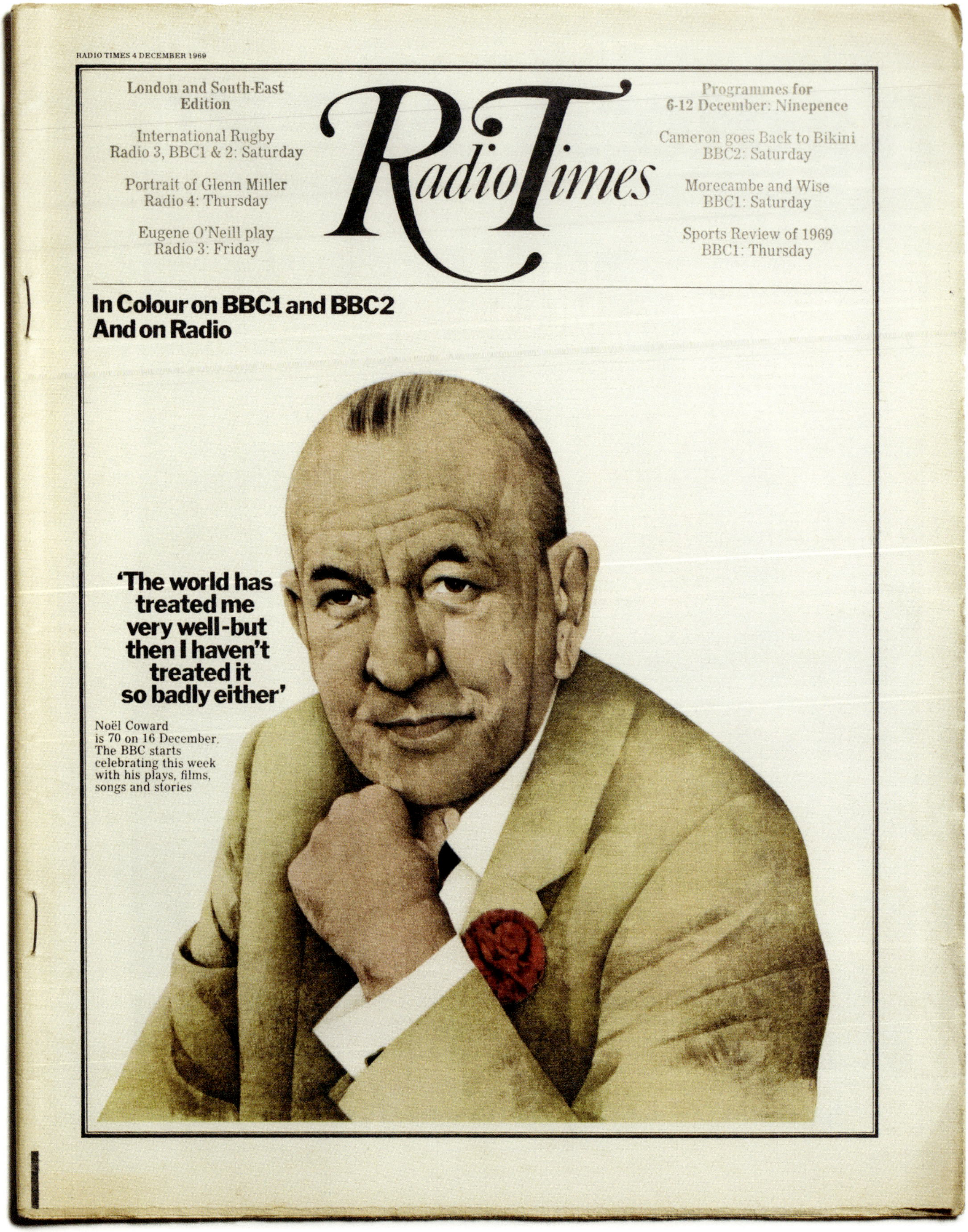

Noël Coward at 70 **Illustration by Charles Raymond** *6–12 December 1969*

"Writing is an art and a craft and if you can combine the two, you can make a living at it," playwright Noël Coward told Patrick Garland in the *Omnibus* documentary that opened a two-week birthday season of his plays and films. He cocked a snook at the upper middle classes but reserved his most barbed and brittle witticisms for the theatrical folk he knew so well.

Investiture of the Prince of Wales *(right)*

Prince Charles

28 June–4 July 1969

Prince Charles had just been interviewed for the first time on BBC television by Cliff Michelmore and this week's issue was almost entirely devoted to the heir to the throne, the celebrations in the principality to mark his investiture and the ceremonial day itself at Caernarvon Castle.

The Golden Silents *(below left)*

Clara Bow

13–19 September 1969

The fruits of a dramatic redesign, including *Radio Times's* most enduring logo, appeared on newsstands this month. Editor Geoffrey Cannon wanted to connect the R and T in the masthead with Radio and Television in readers' minds. The cover celebrated a 26-week series featuring the stars of the silent film era introduced by Michael Bentine.

Christmas 1969 *(below right)*

Illustration by Tony Meeuwissen

20 December 1969– 2 January 1970

The first Christmas and New Year double issue saw out the 1960s in 108 pages (24 in colour) packed with lavish portraits of the Christmas stars, including Harry Secombe, Barbra Streisand, Tommy Steele and Johnny Cash. The cover squeezed as many celebrities as possible into a festive tableau.

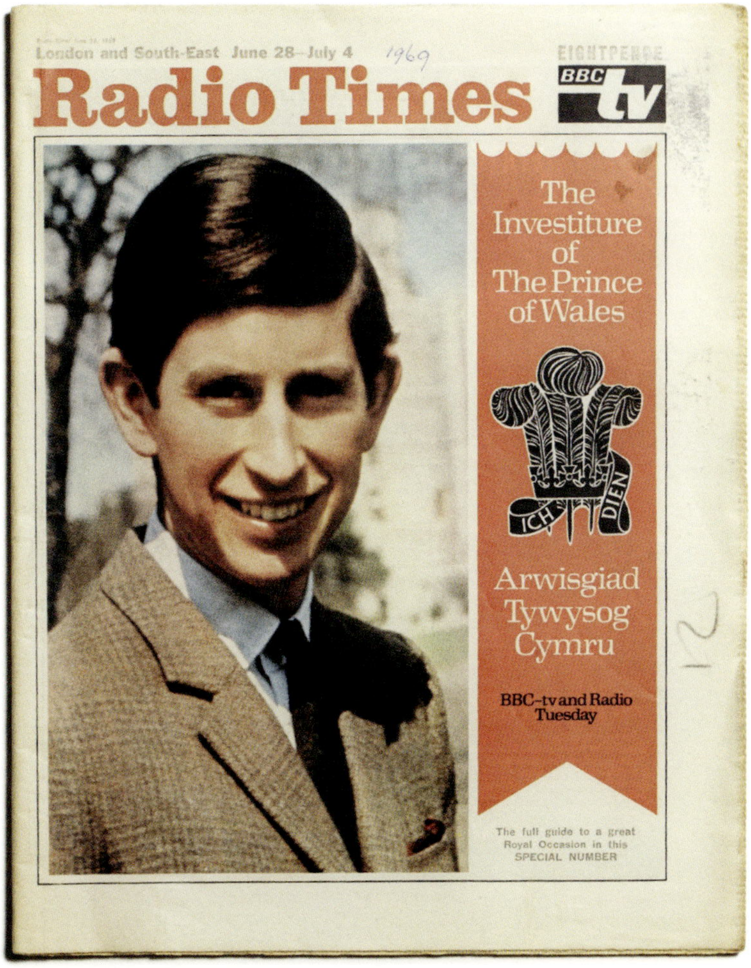

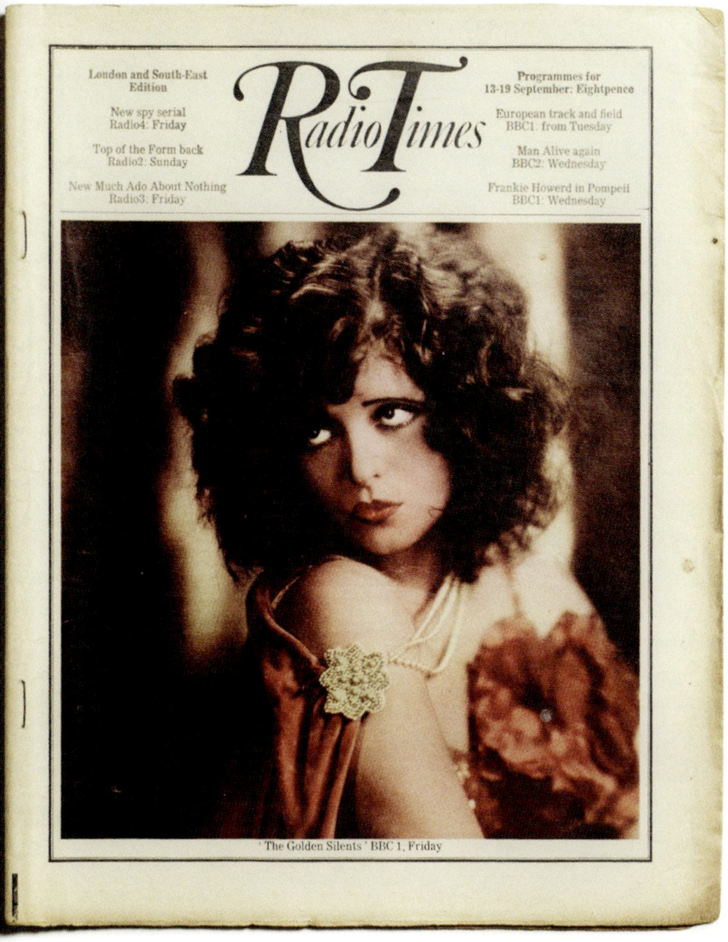

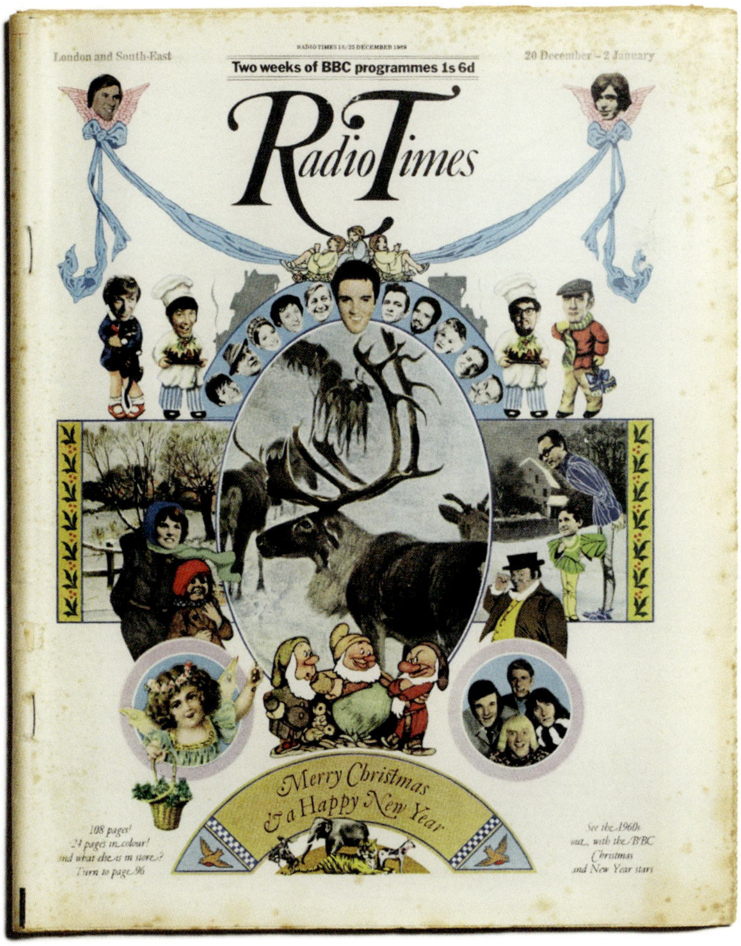

BBC1

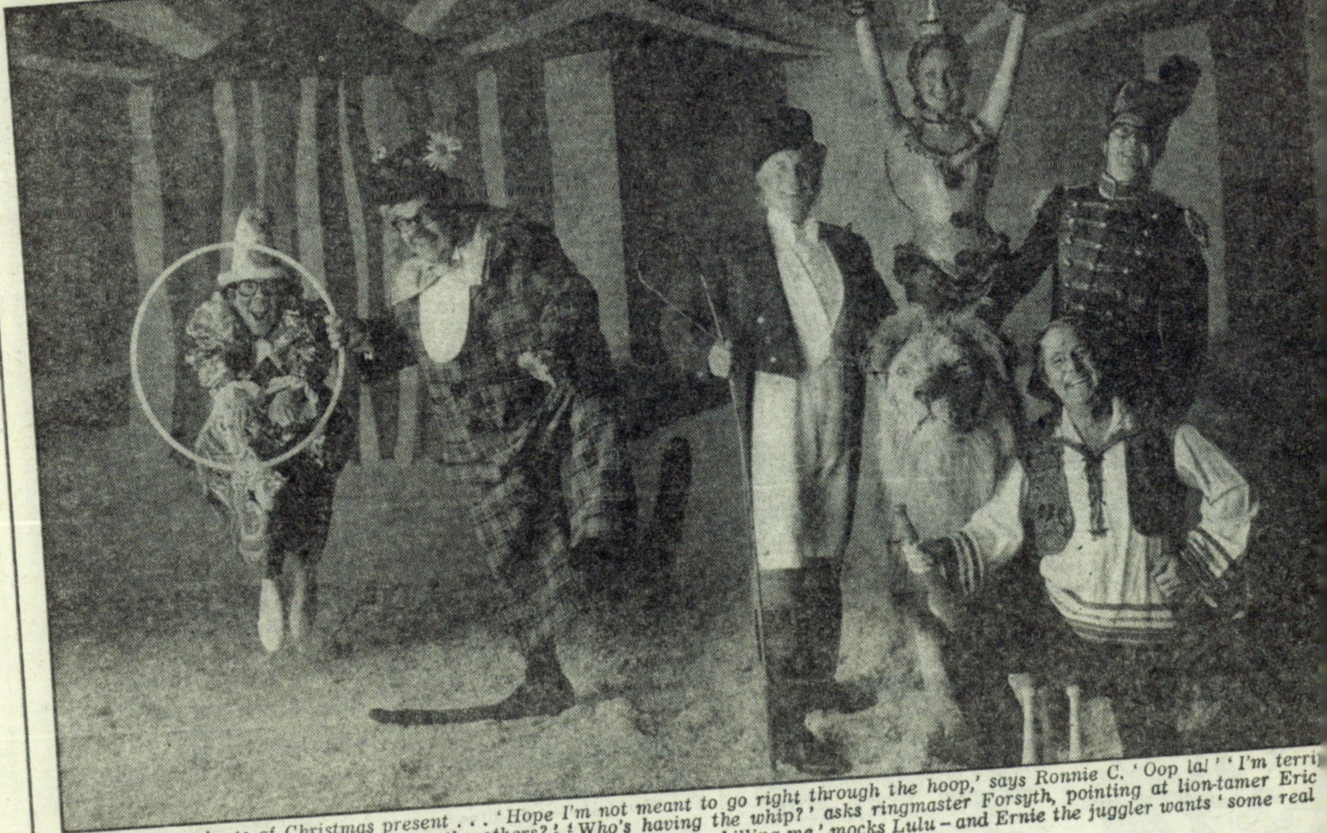

Here are your hosts of Christmas present . . . 'Hope I'm not meant to go right through the hoop,' says Ronnie C. 'Oop la!' 'I'm terri lions, myself,' says Ronnie B, 'how are the others?' 'Who's having the whip?' asks ringmaster Forsyth, pointing at lion-tamer Eric cambe – who's happy to find the lion is stuffed. 'Hurry, my feet are killing me,' mocks Lulu – and Ernie the juggler wants 'some real

5.55 pm *Colour* Bruce Forsyth and The Generation Game

starring
Bruce Forsyth
in a special Christmas programme where the wits, skill and ingenuity of both young and young-in-heart are put to a seasonal test with a tongue-in-cheek flavour.
with seven surprising dwarfs,
an amazing dancing bear,
a potted panto
and family couples from
all over the country
with hostess **Anthea Redfern**

Programme associate TONY HAWES
Designer ROBIN TARSNANE
Producers ALAN TARRANT
and JAMES MOIR
(The hosts of Christmas 1922-1972: p 100)

BBC1 Variations

WALES
5.55-6.25 Adeste Fideles: carols
6.25-6.55 Ryan a Ronnie

6.55 *Colour* Christmas Night with the Stars

Introduced by
Ronnie Corbett and **Ronnie Barker**
starring **Cilla Black**
The Young Generation, Lulu

'Dad's Army'
Script by
JIMMY PERRY and DAVID CROFT
starring **Arthur Lowe**
John Le Mesurier, Clive Dunn
featuring JOHN LAURIE, JAMES BECK
ARNOLD RIDLEY, IAN LAVENDER
Producer DAVID CROFT

'Look – Mike Yarwood!'
Script by ERIC DAVIDSON
starring
Mike Yarwood, Adrienne Posta

'The Liver Birds'
Script by CARLA LANE
starring
Polly James, Nerys Hughes
with MOLLIE SUGDEN, SHEILA FAY
Producer SID LOTTERBY
(Cilla Black is the cover star of the New Year's third issue of RADIO TIMES)

'The Goodies'
Script by
GRAEME GARDEN and BILL ODDIE
with TIM BROOKE-TAYLOR
starring **Tim Brooke-Taylor**
Graeme Garden, Bill Oddie with
DENISE DISTEL, PAUL ELLISON
Producer JIM FRANKLIN

The Young Generation
Choreography by NIGEL LYTHGOE
ALYN AINSWORTH AND HIS ORCHESTRA
ST RICHARD'S WITH ST ANDREW'S
SCHOOL CHOIR, HAM, SURREY

'The Two Ronnies' script by
GARRY CHAMBERS, BARRY CRYER
TONY HAWES, RONNIE KING
WALLY MALSTON, DAVID MCKELLAR
SPIKE MULLINS, DAVID NOBBS
MICHAEL PALIN and TERRY JONES
NEIL SHAND and JOE STEEPLES
PETER VINCENT, DICK VOSBURGH

Cilla Black and Ronnie Corbett
duet by RONNIE TAYLOR
Orchestra directed by
RONNIE HAZLEHURST
Vocal backing by THE BREAKAWAYS

Sound LARRY GOODSON
Lighting BILL MILLAR
Designer MARTIN COLLINS
Producers MICHAEL HURLL, TERRY HUGHES
(Ronnie Corbett is appearing in 'Cinderella' at the Bristol Hippodrome; Lulu in 'Peter Pan' at the Opera House, Manchester; Adrienne Posta in 'Babes in the Wood' at the London Palladium; Polly James in 'I and Albert' at the Piccadilly Theatre, London)

8.15 *Colour* Morecambe and W Christmas Show

A star-studded holiday sp
starring
Eric Morecambe and Ern
with special guests
Glenda Jackson, Jack Jo
Vera Lynn, Pete Murray
with **Kenny Ball and his J**
and guest appearances o
Shirley Bassey, Ian Carr
Fenella Fielding, Eric P
André Previn, Flora Ro
featuring ANN HAMILTON
with JANET WEBB
Written by BARRY CRYER, JOH
Reindeer sketch by
MIKE CRAIG and LAWRIE KIN
Additional material
by MORECAMBE and WISE
Musical arrangements and
directed by PETER KNIGHT
Sound MICHAEL MCCARTHY,
Costume designer VERITY
Make-up SANDRA EXELBY
Lighting PETER WESSON
Designer VICTOR MEREDITH
Producer JOHN AMMONDS
(The hosts of Christma p 100)

Radio Times

The Golden Age of Television

1970–1979

The Morecambe and Wise Show

Eric Morecambe and Ernie Wise

(photograph by Mark Gudgeon)

3–9 January 1976

A new year saw the return of *The Morecambe and Wise Show*: Eric and Ernie were now so famous their names didn't even need to appear on the cover. Inside, comedians including Max Wall, Jimmy Jewel and Elsie and Doris Waters explained the duo's magic: "What they have developed is an onstage relationship where one instinctively gets to know the movements of the other," said Wall. "They have blended into a real team." The feature also provided readers with a step-by-step guide to the double act's trademark hornpipe.

The new season of programmes included *When the Boat Comes In* with James Bolam, Jean Heywood and Susan Jameson. And as well as pages of classified ads for British holiday destinations – "Happiness is Southport '76" – *Holiday 76* was on hand to offer ideas for budget foreign destinations, including a new Pontins site in Morocco.

1970-1979

Fun with Eric & Ernie, Monty Python and Fawlty Towers; drama with Colditz, Poldark and Tinker, Tailor, Soldier, Spy. Plus two World Cups and the Queen's Silver Jubilee

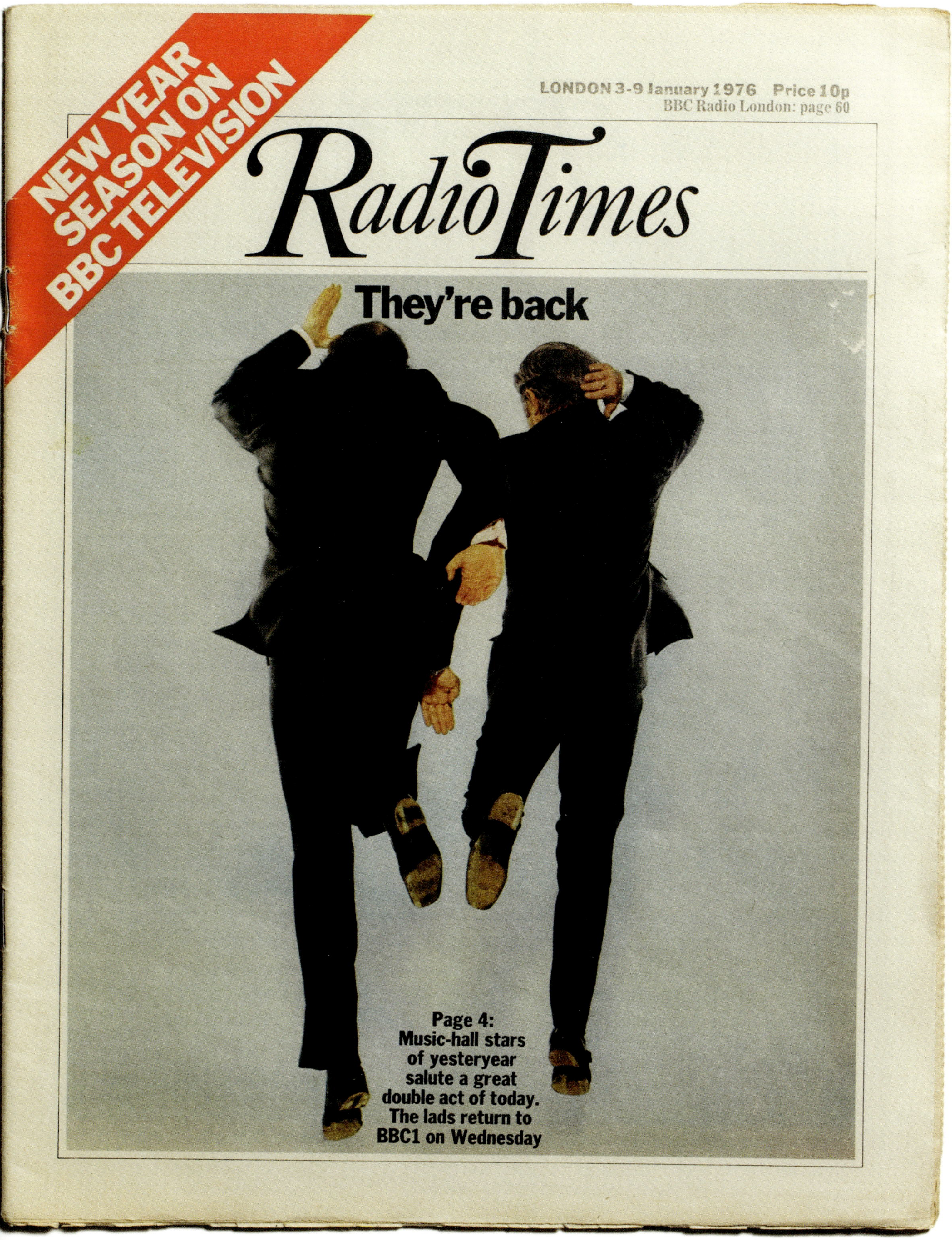
NEW YEAR SEASON ON BBC TELEVISION
LONDON 3-9 January 1976 Price 10p
BBC Radio London: page 60
Radio Times
They're back
Page 4: Music-hall stars of yesteryear salute a great double act of today. The lads return to BBC1 on Wednesday

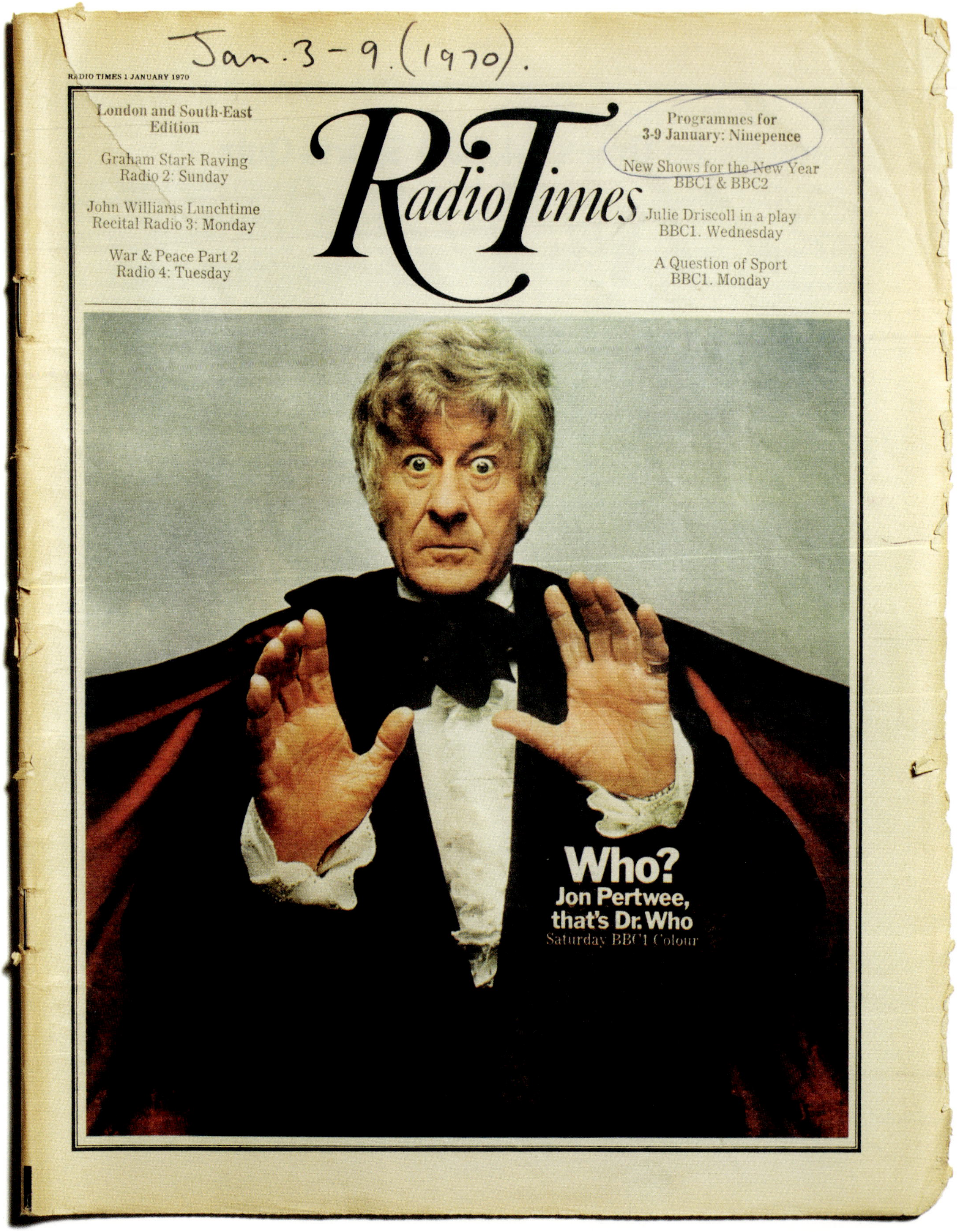

Doctor Who **The Doctor (Jon Pertwee)** *(photograph by Ray Rathborne)* *3–9 January 1970*

"A swarm of 'meteorites' lands – and so does the Tardis. From it emerges a new Doctor – or is it an impostor?" ran the BBC1 billing for *Spearhead from Space*, which welcomed the third Doctor to television, in colour for the first time. "Small children and animals are every actor's nightmare – I have to cope with monsters," Pertwee told *Radio Times*. And the new Doctor's first words? "Shoes. Must find my shoes... Unhand me, madam."

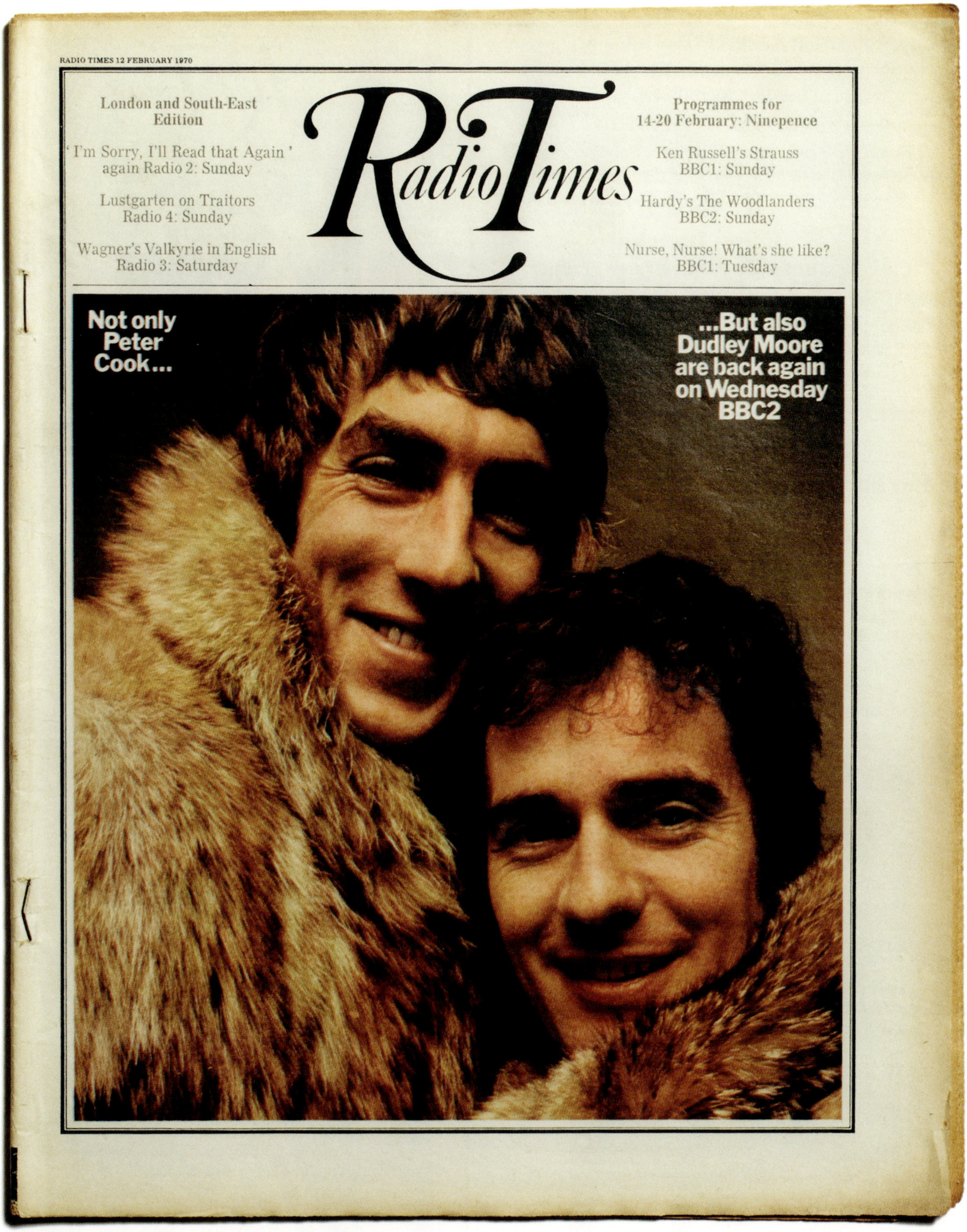

Peter Cook and Dudley Moore *(photograph by Ray Rathborne) 14–20 February 1970*

Not Only... But Also returned to BBC2 after an absence of nearly four years. Pete and Dud didn't use writers, but ad-libbed sketches into a tape recorder, then gradually ironed out the kinks on subsequent attempts. But who knows what comedy gems might have been missed: "Having dinner or a drink with somebody, you can go into a whole stream of fantasy of some kind or another, and it's all forgotten," admitted Cook.

Up Pompeii! *(right)*

From left: Ludicrus (Max Adrian), Lurcio (Frankie Howerd), Ammonia (Elizabeth Larner)
(photograph by John Perkins)

28 March–3 April 1970

Howerd was downbeat at the launch of his comedy *Up Pompeii!* "I'm living in a world of delusion. I'm being terribly serious and everyone thinks it's just madly funny."

Come Dancing *(middle right)*

Illustration by Bentley/Farrell/Burnett

18–24 April 1970

This kaleidoscopic cover was for the final of *Come Dancing* from the Palais, Nottingham. Among the coverlines are the words Big Splash!, a reference to scheduled coverage of the splashdown of the ill-fated *Apollo 13* on Tuesday 21 April. In fact, the spacecraft returned safely to Earth four days earlier.

The fun and Commonwealth team *(far right)*

Illustration by Julian Allen

23–29 May 1970

The stars of *Dad's Army*, Eric Morecambe and Ernie Wise, Cilla Black, Frankie Howerd, Vera Lynn and Dave Allen were shown in smart team blazers for a royal gala in aid of the Commonwealth Games, which were being held in Edinburgh.

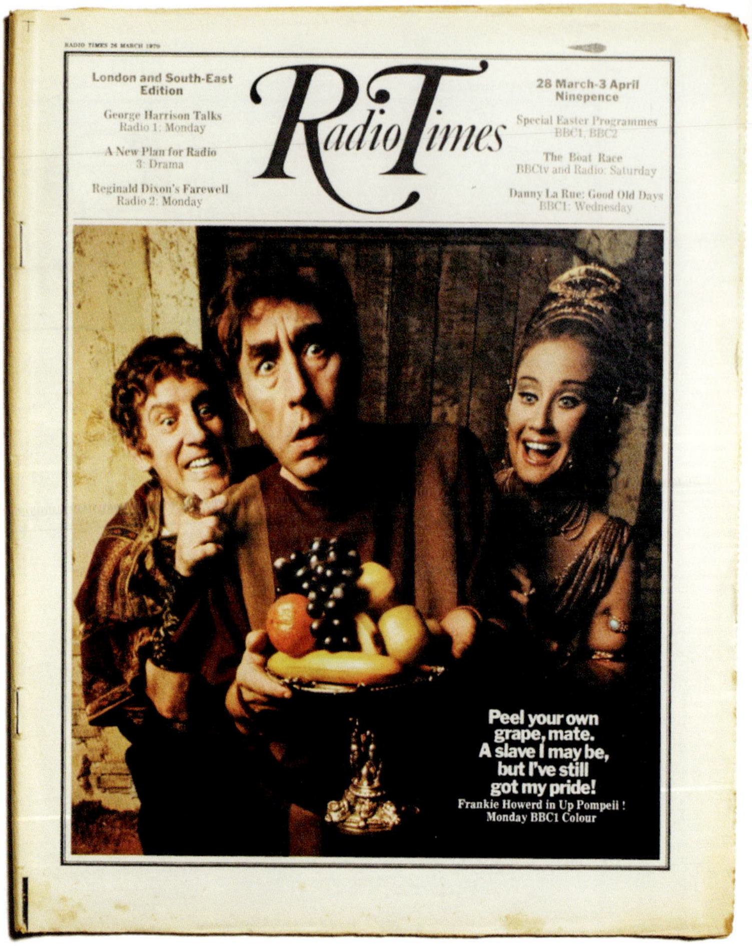

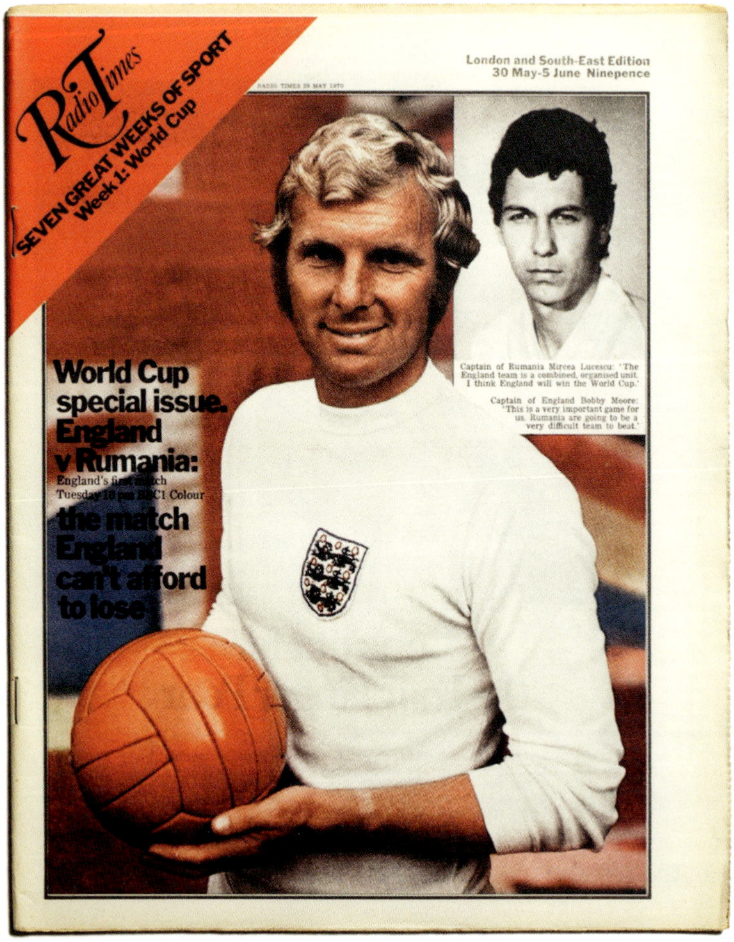

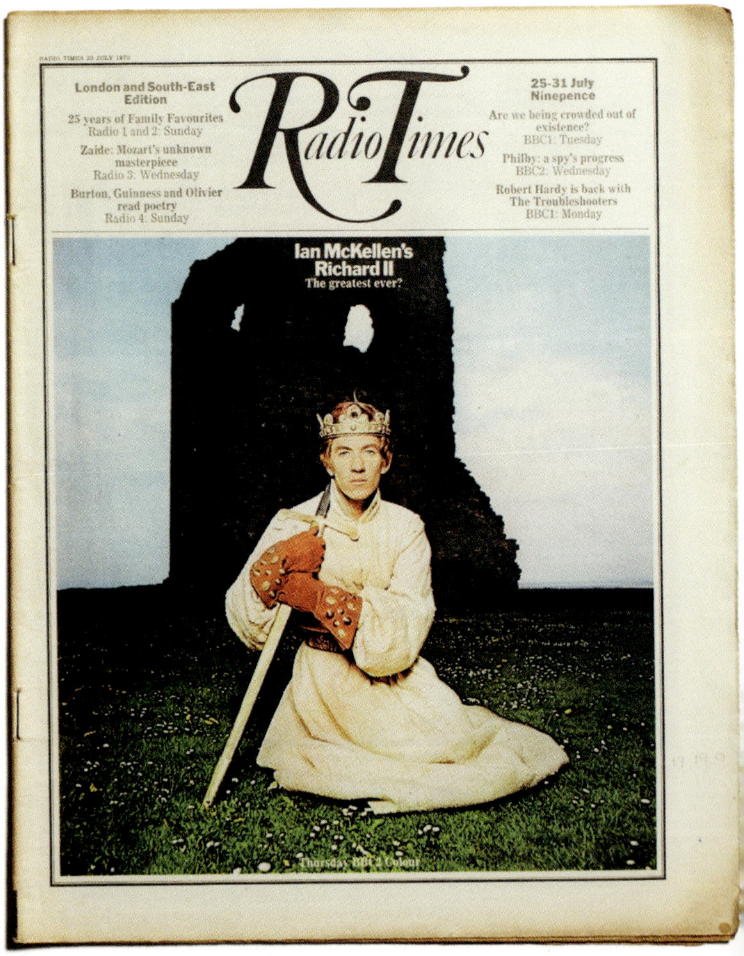

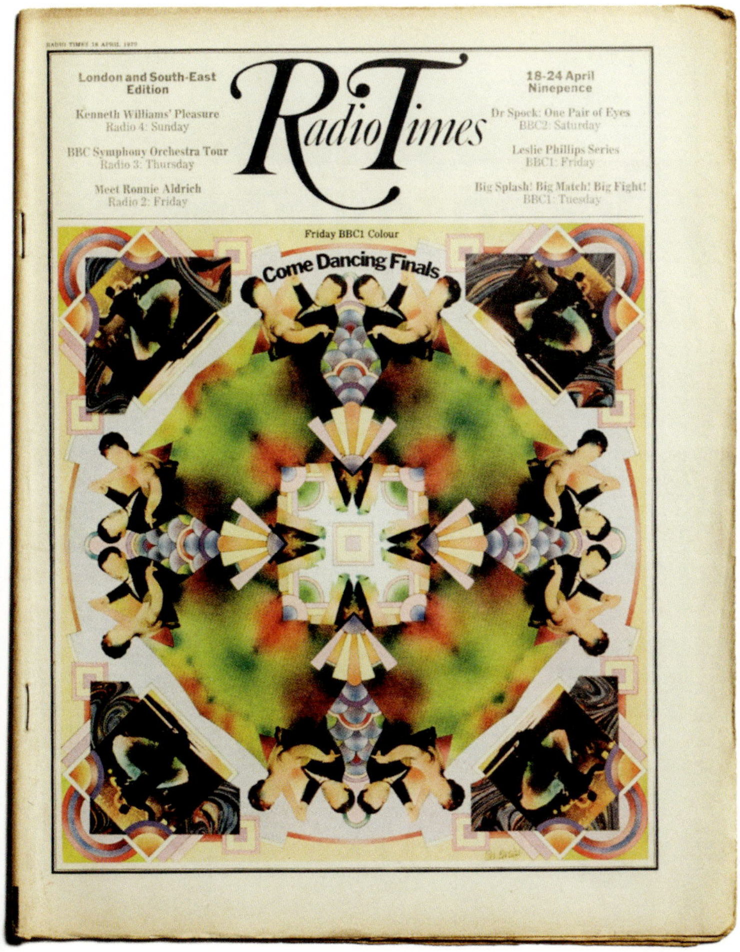

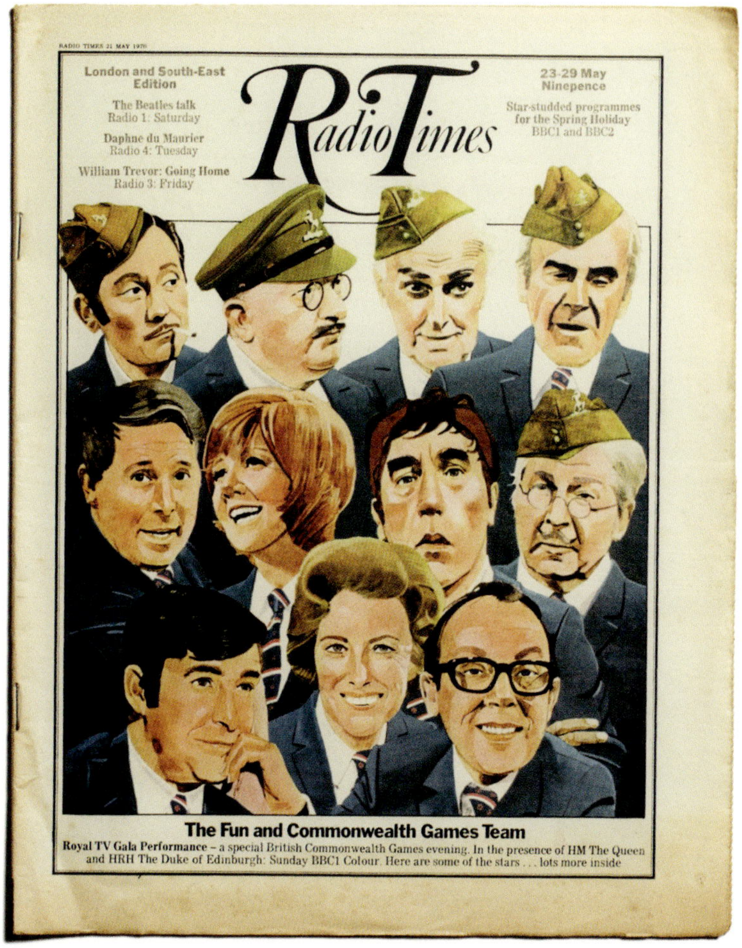

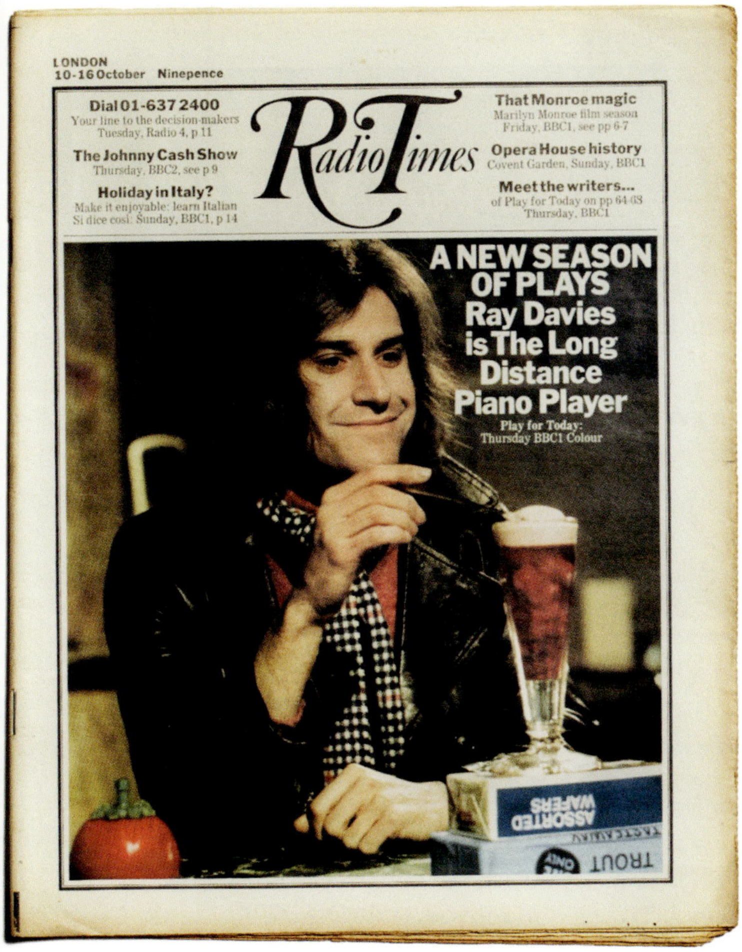

Bobby Moore *(far left)*

30 May–5 June 1970

England captain Bobby Moore was promoted to cover star as Alf Ramsay's team began their defence of the Jules Rimet Trophy in the Mexico World Cup. Their first game was against Romania, which explains the appearance of Mircea Lucescu. *Radio Times* splashed out with a 16-page supplement billed modestly as "the most comprehensive factual background to the World Cup ever published in magazine form".

Richard II *(middle left)*

Ian McKellen *(photograph by Ray Rathborne)*

25–31 July 1970

McKellen was photographed at Flint Castle in north Wales, where he sat on the battlements, reciting speeches from Shakespeare's *Richard II*, which the Prospect Theatre Company had toured around Britain and to Czechoslovakia before filming the play for BBC2.

Play for Today *(left)*

Pete (Ray Davies) *(photograph by Keith McMillan)*

10–16 October 1970

The Kinks' singer Ray Davies made his acting debut in Alan Sharp's *Play for Today*, about a man trying to set a world record for nonstop piano playing. "A nice part," said Davies. "Introverted, which is what I am, really."

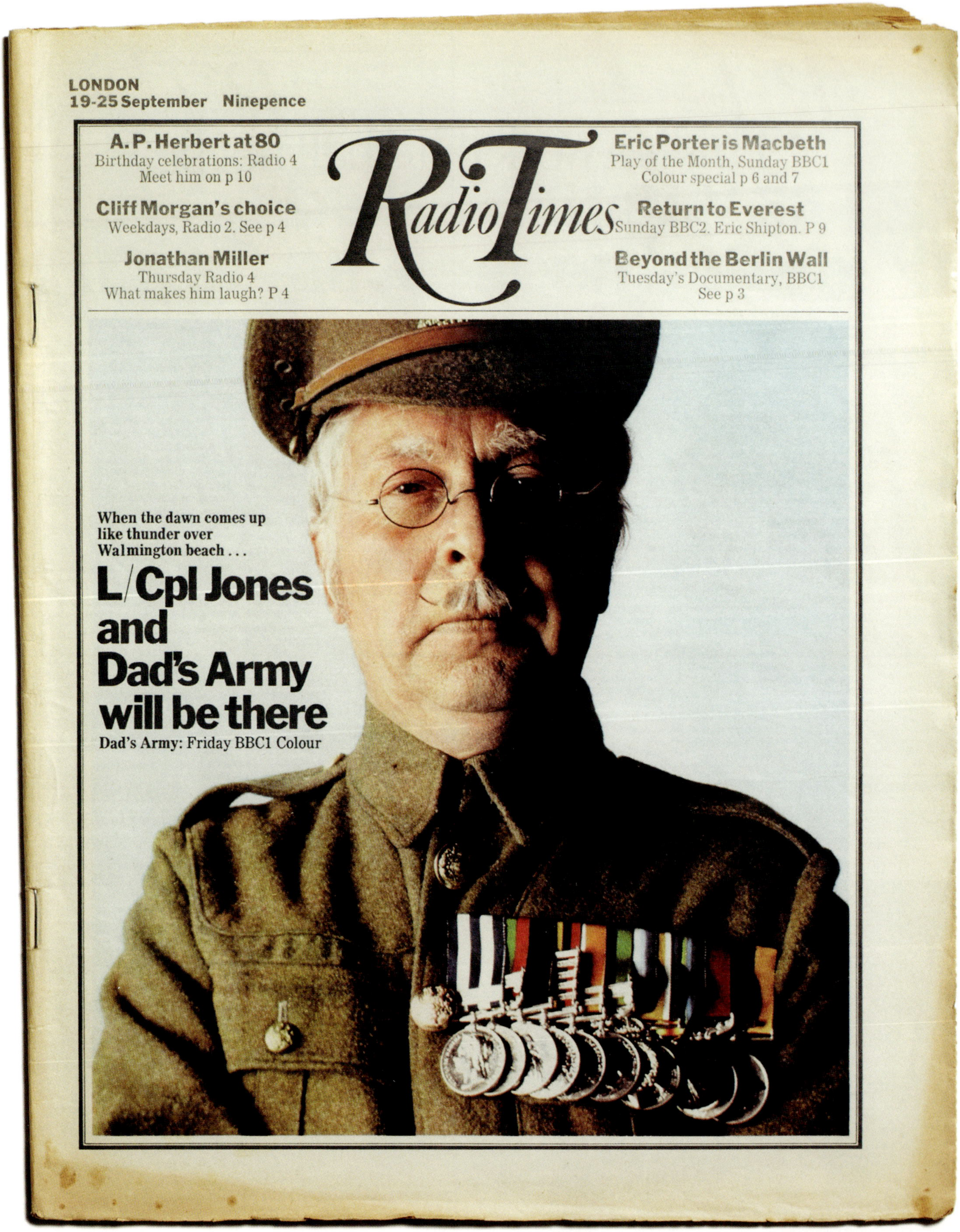

Dad's Army **L/Cpl Jones (Clive Dunn)** *(photograph by Don Smith)* 19–25 September 1970

The stars of *Dad's Army* revealed what they actually did in the war (except for Ian Lavender, of course, who was born in 1946). Cover star Clive Dunn joined the 4th Hussars in 1940 as a volunteer and remained a trooper for six years. Having spent four years as a PoW in Austria, he said, "I don't have any happy memories from the war." Arthur Lowe's experiences were somewhat different: "I rather liked it in the Army," he recalled.

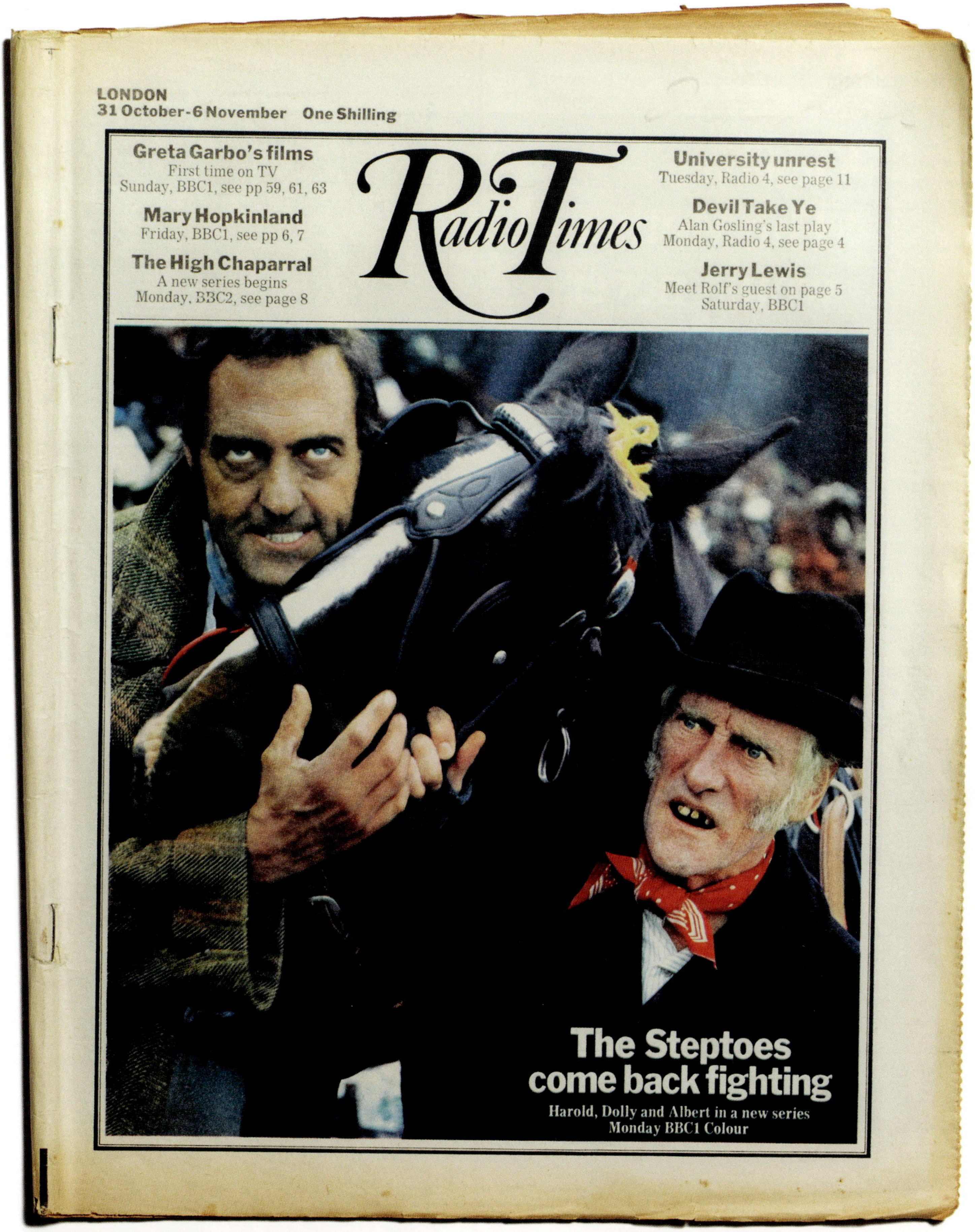

Steptoe and Son **Harold (Harry H Corbett) and Albert (Wilfrid Brambell)** *(photograph by John Perkins)*

31 October–6 November 1970

Steptoe and Son returned for a new series, with Harold and Albert (not to mention Dolly the horse, of course) still at loggerheads in Shepherd's Bush. *Radio Times* talked to rag and bone men Arthur and Chris Arnold, who provided the original carthorse, Hercules, for the show, and whose scrapyard appeared in the programme's opening credits.

The Nine O'Clock News *(right)*

Top line, from left: Robert Dougall, Richard Baker and Kenneth Kendall *(photograph by Ray Rathborne)*

5–11 December 1970

The three cover stars were asked about their jobs. Robert Dougall joked that "good eyesight and sobriety" were the only qualifications. Richard Baker said it was a steady job, but "two days are never alike". And Kenneth Kendall made the point that newsreaders "are human, not robots".

Doctor Who *(below left)*

Jo (Katy Manning) and the Master (Roger Delgado) *(cover design by David Driver; photographs by Martin Breese and Douglas Playle)*

2–8 January 1971

Two new characters joined *Doctor Who*: Roger Delgado played the Master (a baddie) and Katy Manning played the Doctor's new companion Jo Grant (a goodie). Decimalisation alert: this was the first issue on sale for 5p.

The Six Wives of Henry VIII *(below right)*

Henry VIII (Keith Michell) *(photograph by Don Smith)*

9–15 January 1971

Keith Michell's monarch had been such a hit on BBC2 the previous year (gaining the channel's biggest audience to date) that the serial merited a repeat showing on BBC1. This was also the week the Open University began broadcasting.

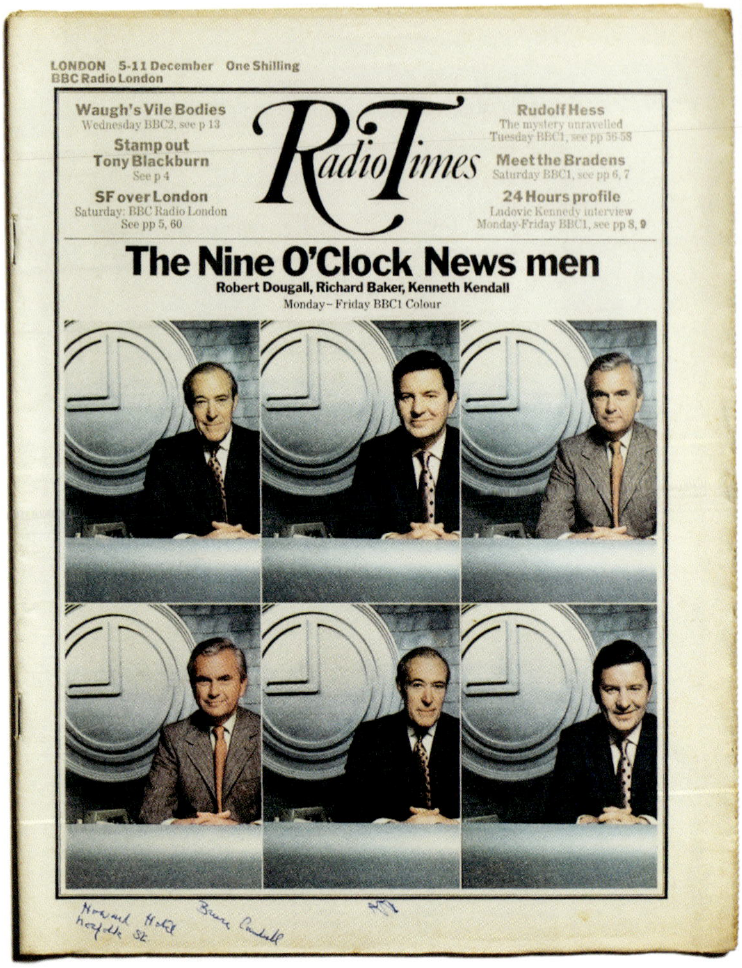

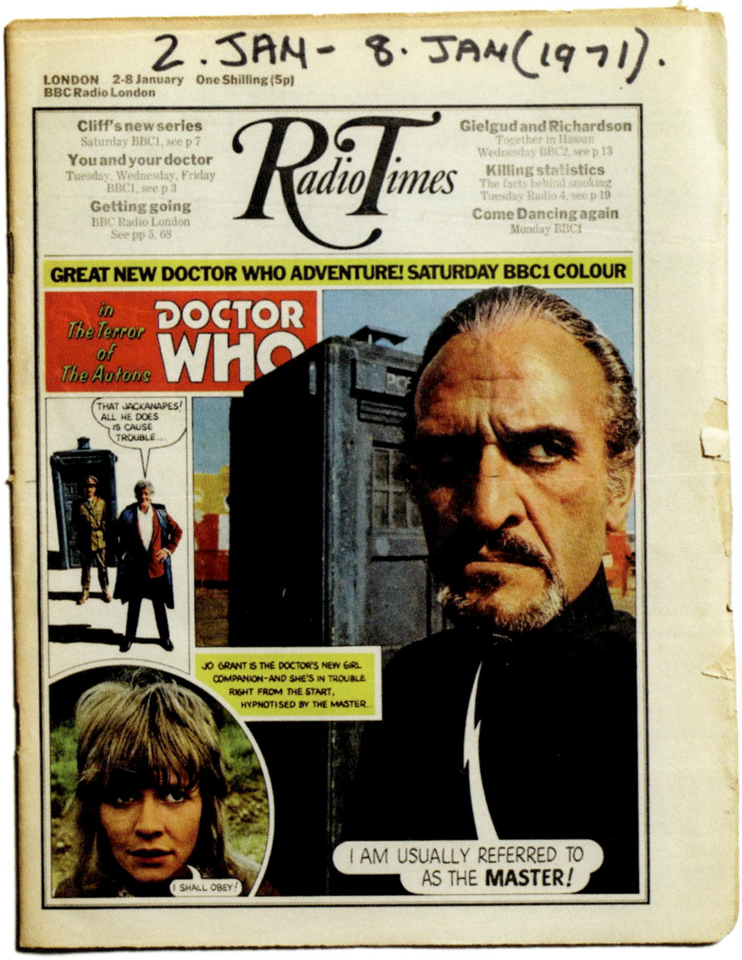

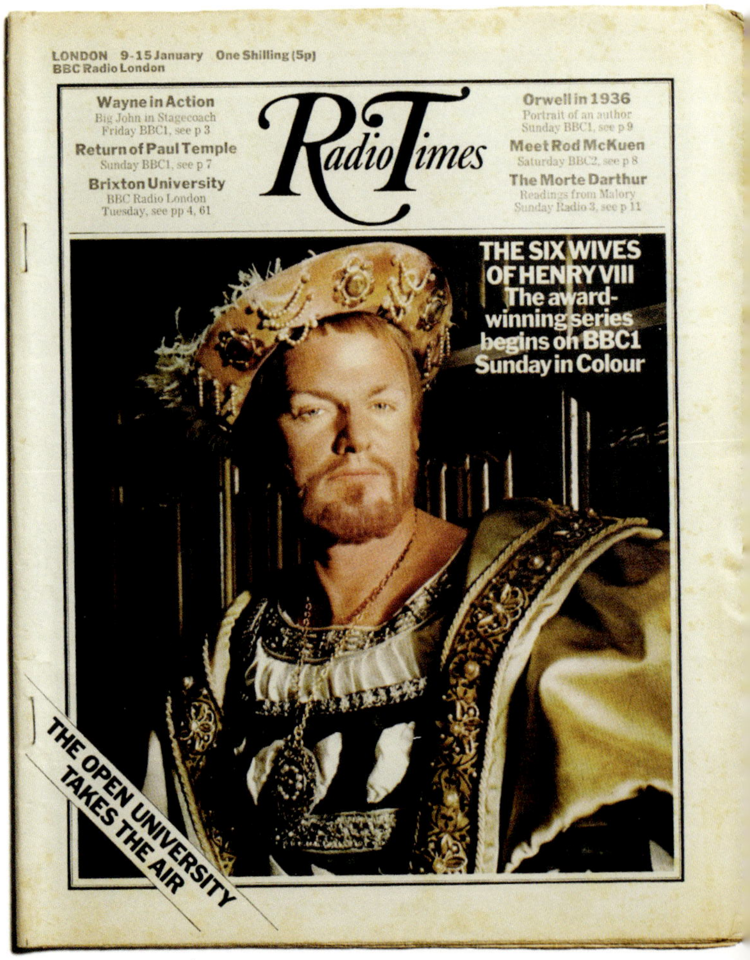

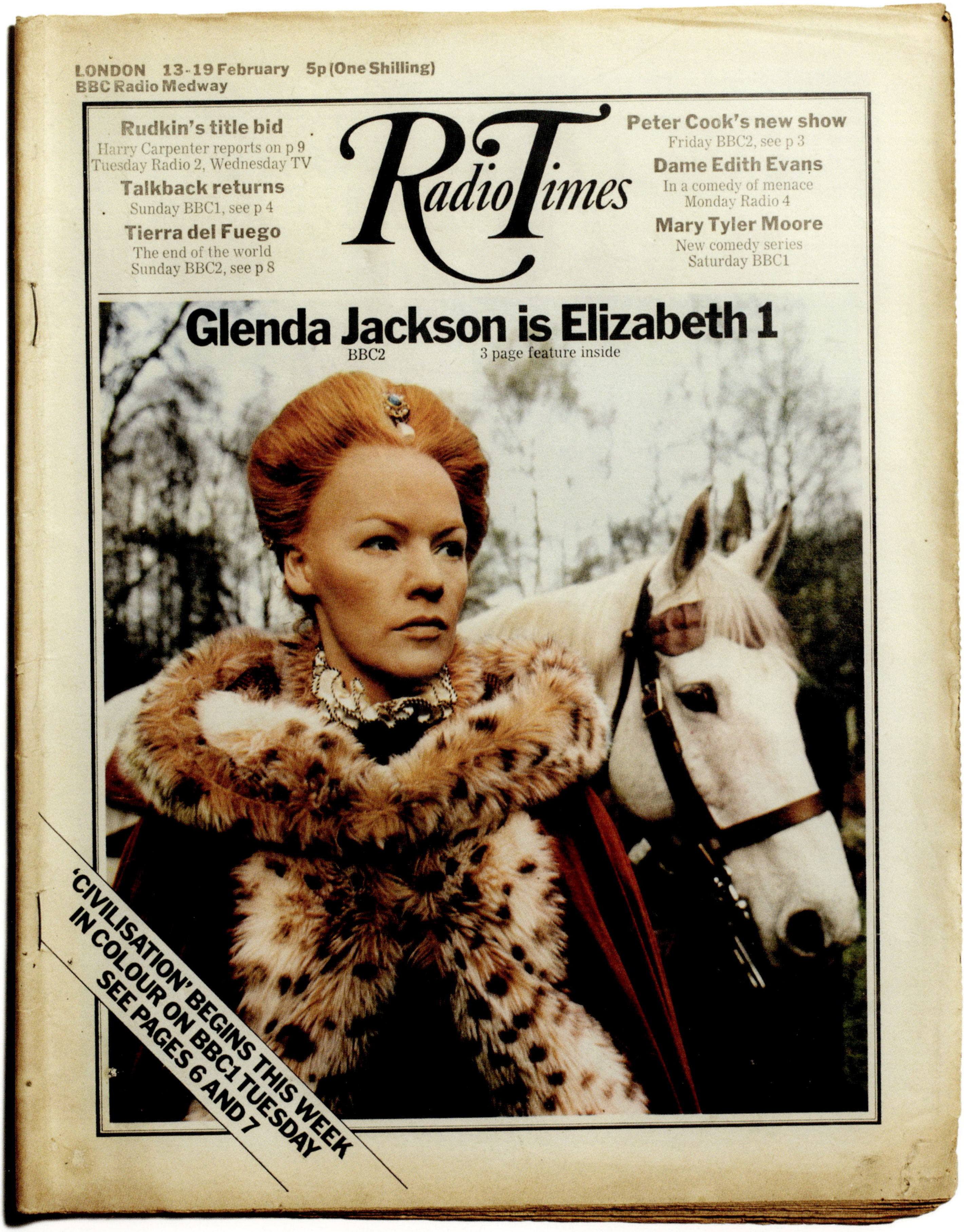

Elizabeth R **Elizabeth I (Glenda Jackson)** *(photograph by Keith McMillan) 13–19 February 1971*

Hot on Henry's heels came his daughter, as *Elizabeth R* began on BBC2. Historian Robert Lacey profiled the queen, and the actress who played her. "Developing a character over this enormous width of canvas was a challenge I couldn't resist," said Jackson. "She was like a chameleon, altering to suit the circumstances and the people she was with." Also this week: Kenneth Clark's *Civilisation* (which, like *The Six Wives of Henry VIII*, had transferred from BBC2 to BBC1).

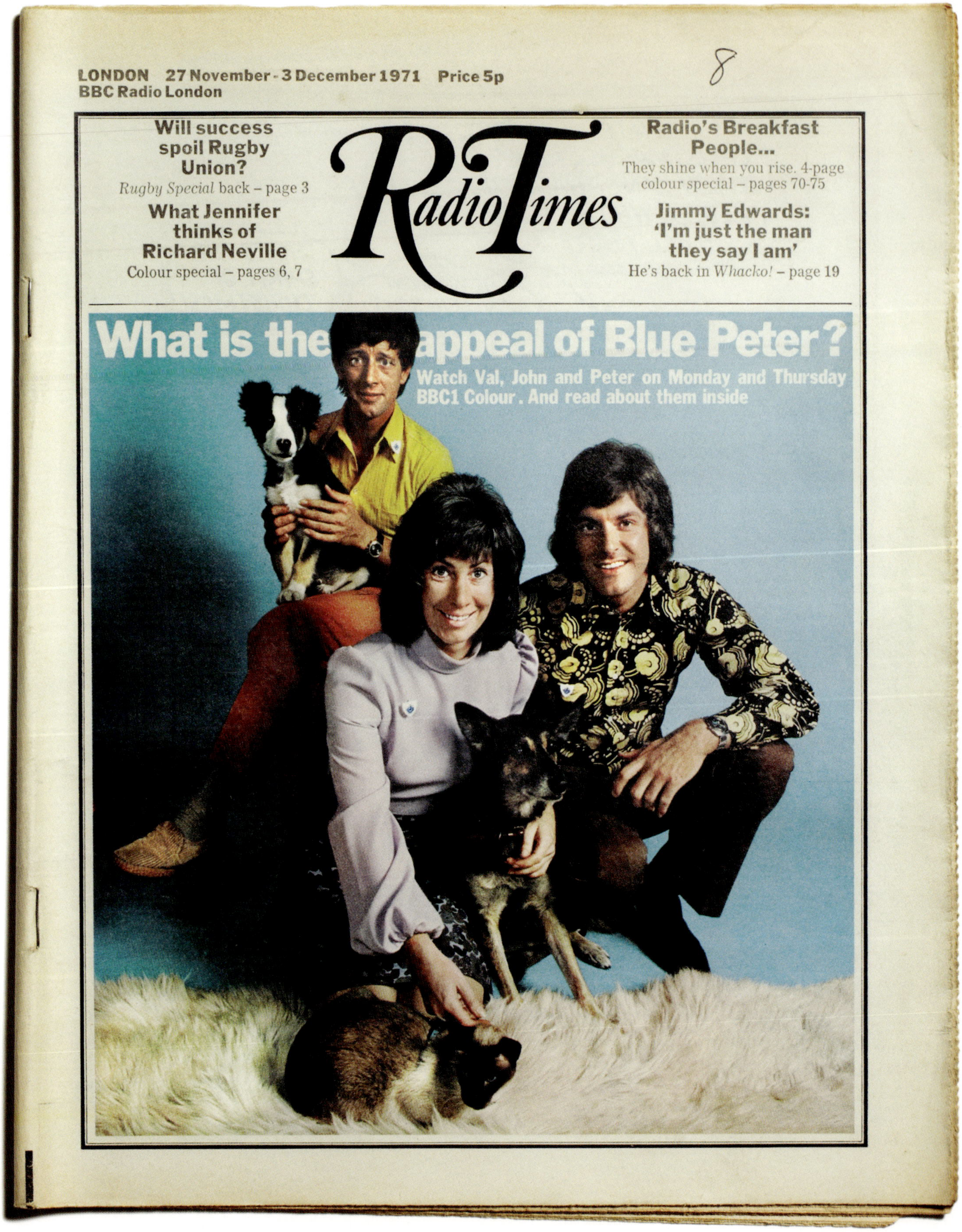

Blue Peter From left: John Noakes, Valerie Singleton and Peter Purves plus Shep the dog, with Noakes, Petra and Jason the cat *(photograph by Penny Tweedie)* *27 November–3 December 1971*

In the week that *Blue Peter* launched its Christmas appeal, novelist Margaret Drabble wondered about the secret of the programme's success: "It's more than just something to watch, it gives you things to do... we can't all go cross-Channel swimming (thank goodness) but we can all collect silver paper."

The Two Ronnies *(right)*

Ronnie Corbett and Ronnie Barker

(photographs by Ray Rathborne)

10–16 April 1971

Ronnie Corbett and Ronnie Barker were starring for the first time in their own joint series, but were keen to be seen as their own men: "We like working together and we like doing our own things – separately," said Barker.

Man Alive: the Foreign Legion *(below left)*

(photograph by Richard Farley)

18–24 September 1971

Radio Times joined Desmond Wilcox and the *Man Alive* team in Corsica for a rare chance to film the reality behind the Beau Geste legend. Training was tough and one young British recruit admitted to being drunk when he volunteered.

The Morecambe and Wise Show *(below right)*

Eric Morecambe and Ernie Wise with Keith Michell (left)

25 September–1 October 1971

Beau Geste fever was rampant, as Morecambe and Wise did a spoof with guest star Keith Michell. Inside they discussed how their work had changed since Eric's heart attack three years earlier and how they hoped to take a year off. Ernie's solution? "We'll get two much younger men who look like us and send them on tour and collect the money."

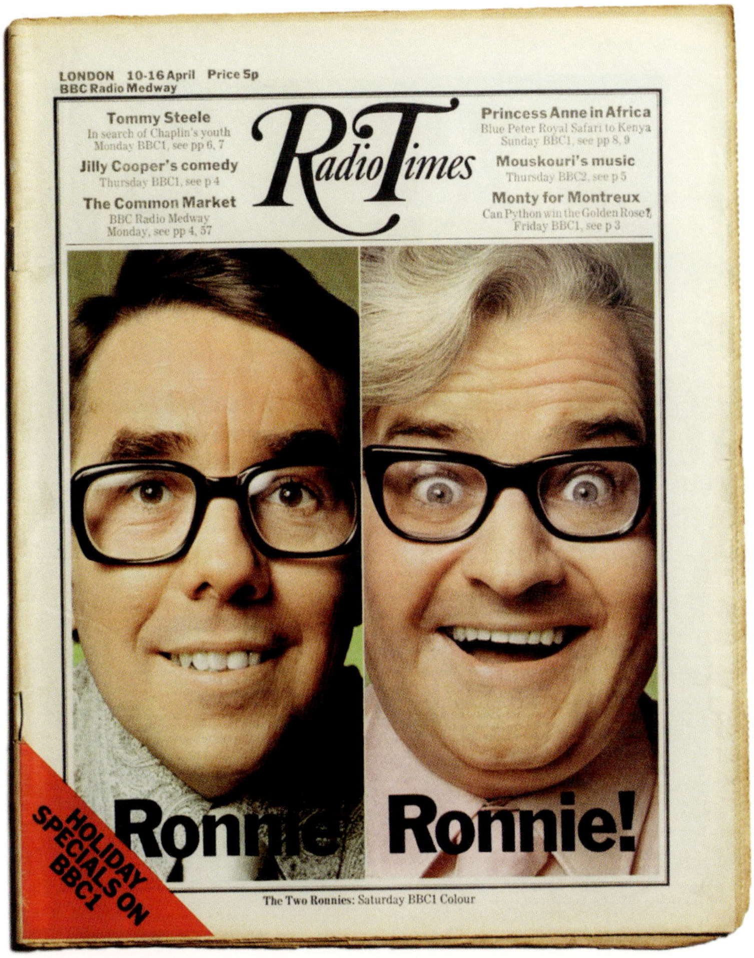

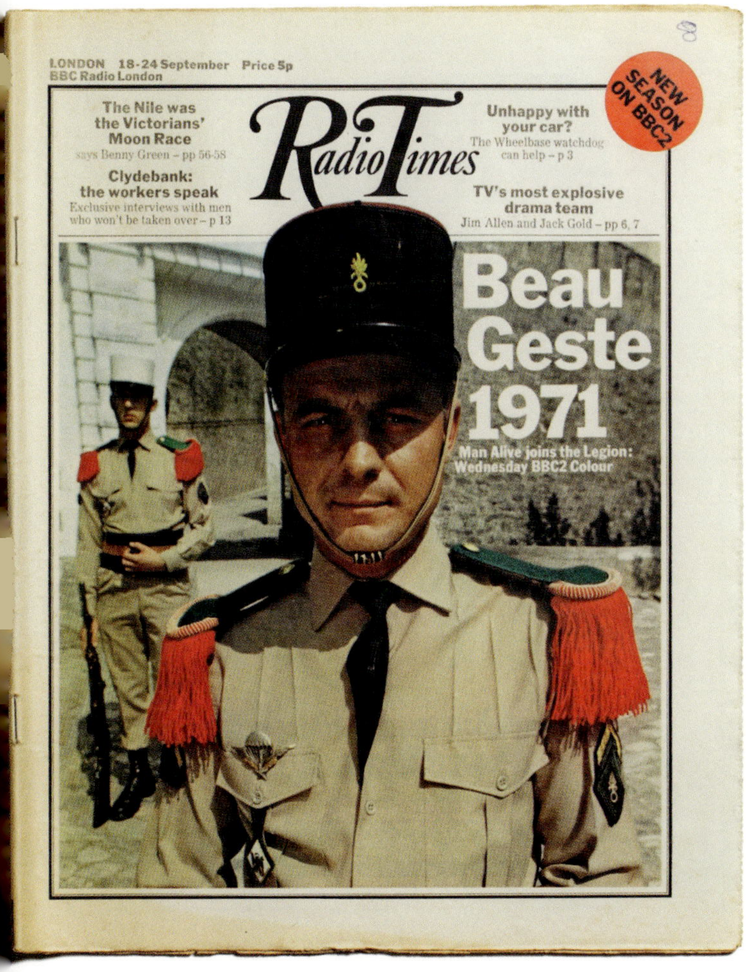

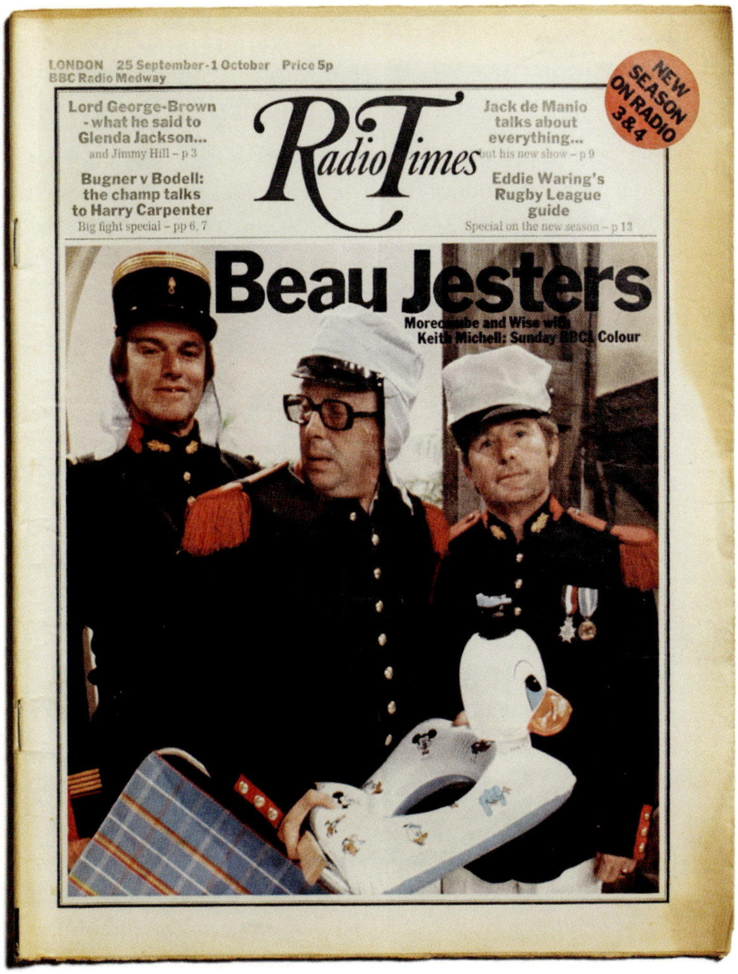

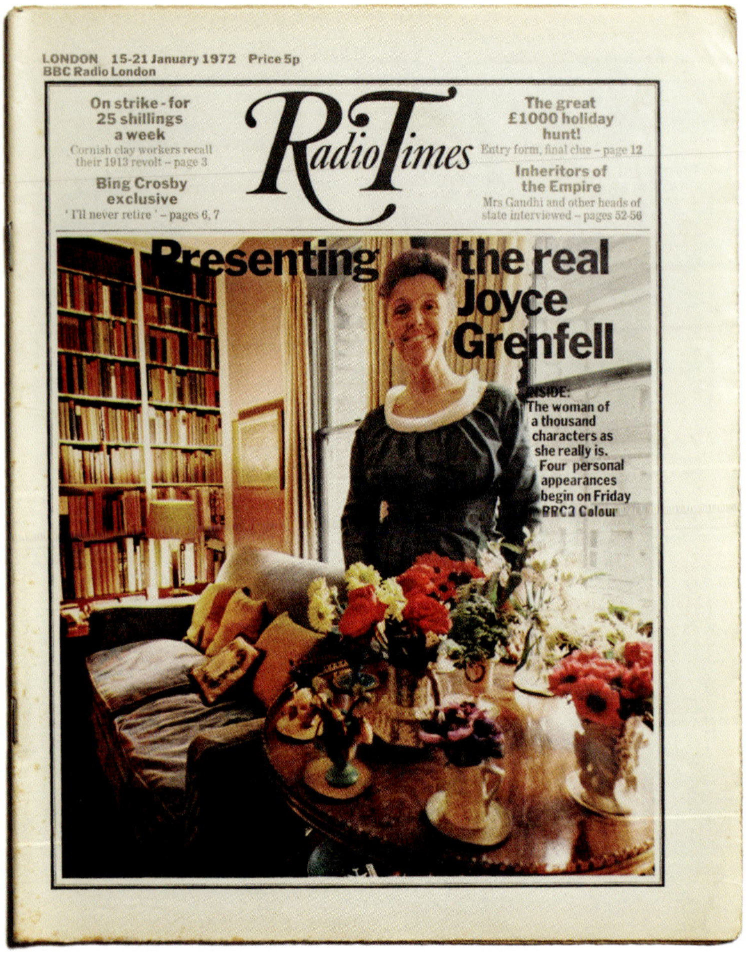

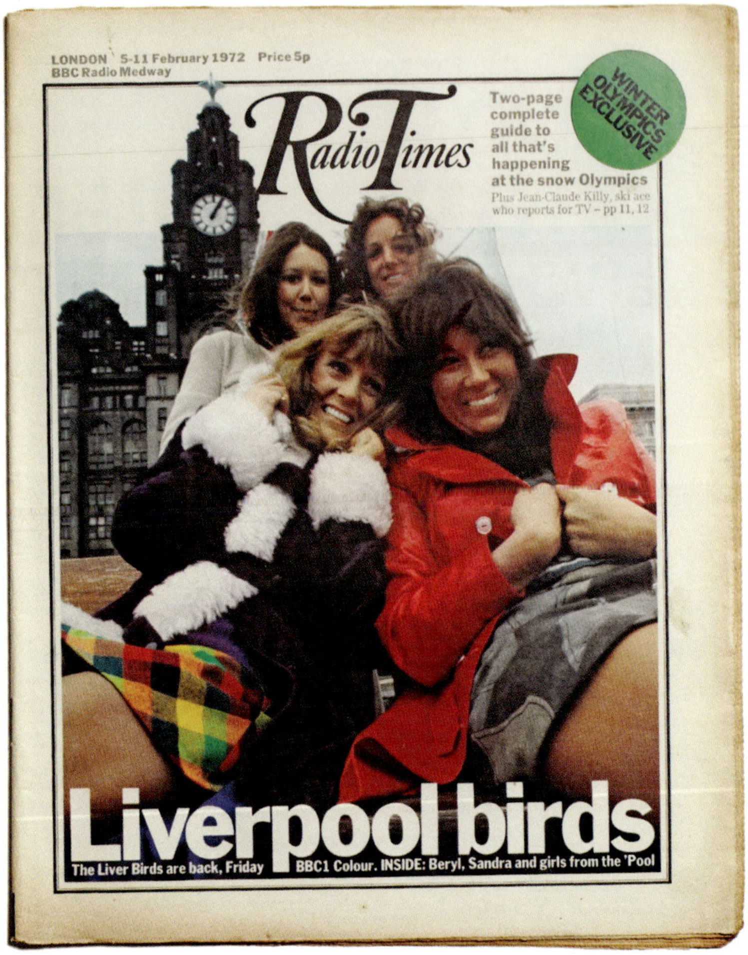

The Generation Game *(right)*

Bruce Forsyth *(photograph by Dmitri Kasterine)*

27 May–2 June 1972

At 44 years old, Bruce Forsyth had already enjoyed a career spanning three decades. He told *Radio Times*: "I've always said I'd hate to become a bitter, frustrated old showbusiness pro, jealous of other people's success, because showbusiness has been good to me."

Wimbledon *(middle right)*

Virginia Wade *24–30 June 1972*

Wade didn't win the singles title this time – she lost to Billie Jean King – but in an interview she revealed that, for her, tennis wasn't all about winning. "One of the reasons to play is to give people pleasure. What I would really like to do is play beautiful tennis. In fact, I would rather do that than win."

The Royal International Horse Show *(far right)*

Harvey Smith *22–28 July 1972*

A profile of Yorkshire showjumper Harvey Smith included little from the man himself, although he did explain how difficult he found losing: "I'm not interested in coming second." But there was much more from his rivals. "He is one of the handful of really great riders since the war," said Douglas Bunn.

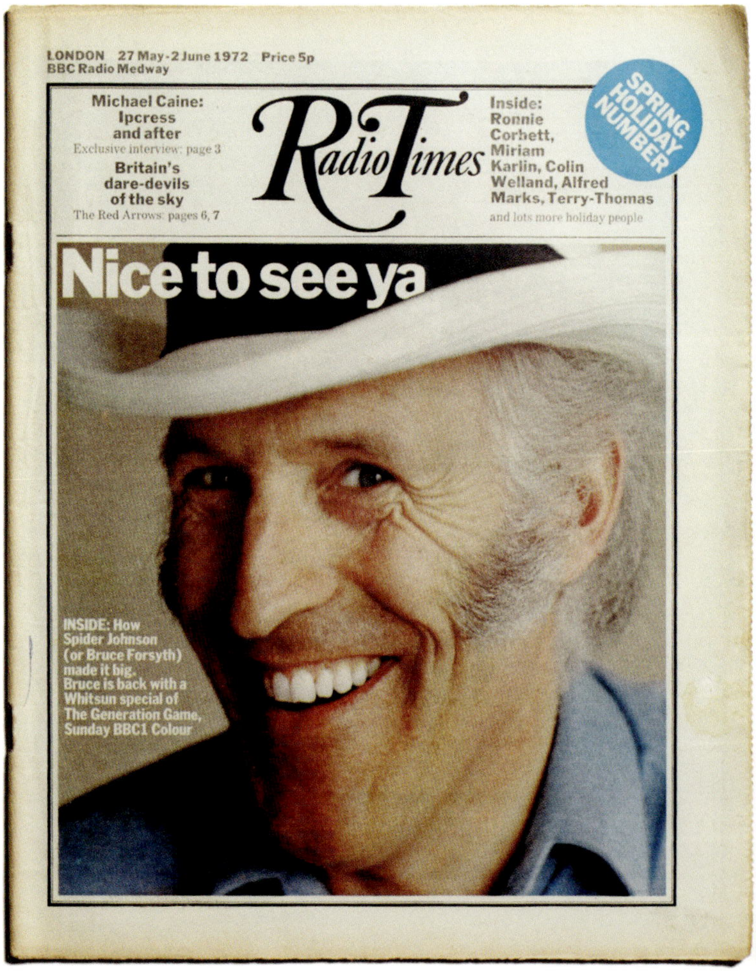

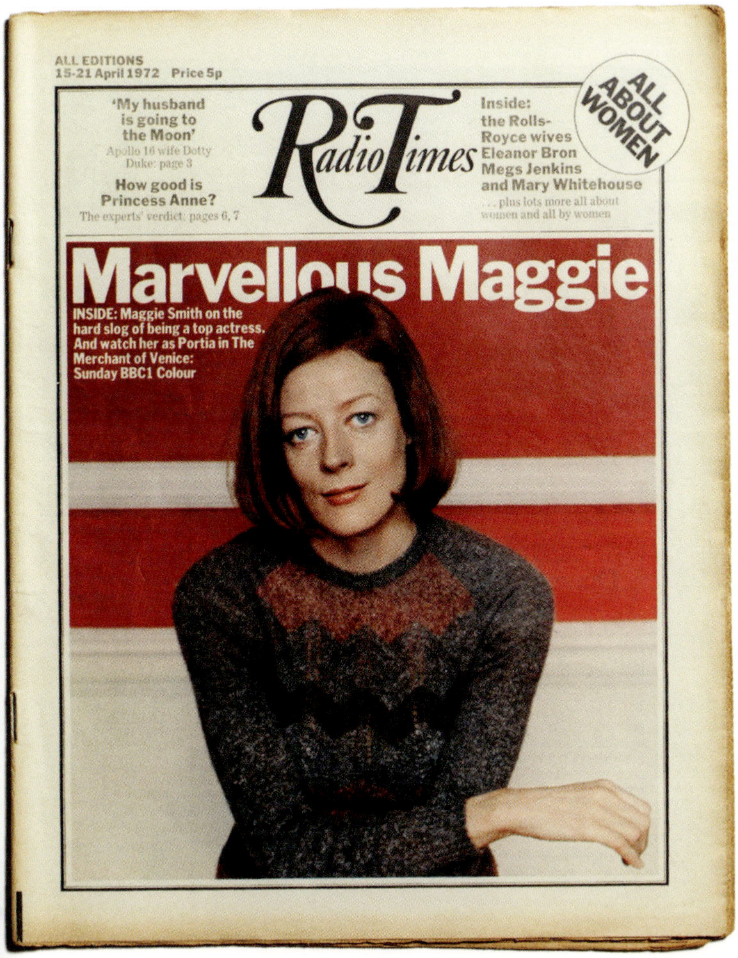

Joyce Grenfell *(far left)*

(photograph by Gordon Moore)

15–21 January 1972

To mark the start of a new series of her show *Joyce Grenfell*, the queen of the comic monologue, was interviewed at home. She had been writing letters in longhand ("I've never taken to the typewriter") and was about to dash out to lunch with Spike Milligan ("I've just read his book – filthy in parts, but so funny").

The Liver Birds *(middle left)*

Beryl (Polly James, left) and Sandra (Nerys Hughes) (the two other women are real-life Liverpudlians)

(photograph by John Perkins)

5–11 February 1972

Radio Times accompanied Polly James and Nerys Hughes on a trip to Liverpool and met the locals: "Everybody's friends, like. Down in the South they're not very sociable, are they?"

Maggie Smith *(left)*

(photograph by Richard Farley)

15–21 April 1972

Appearing in *The Merchant of Venice* on BBC1, the actress reflected on the hard work involved in being successful on stage and screen. She was also a proud – and prescient – mother. "Toby [Stephens] shows every sign of becoming an actor," she said of her young son.

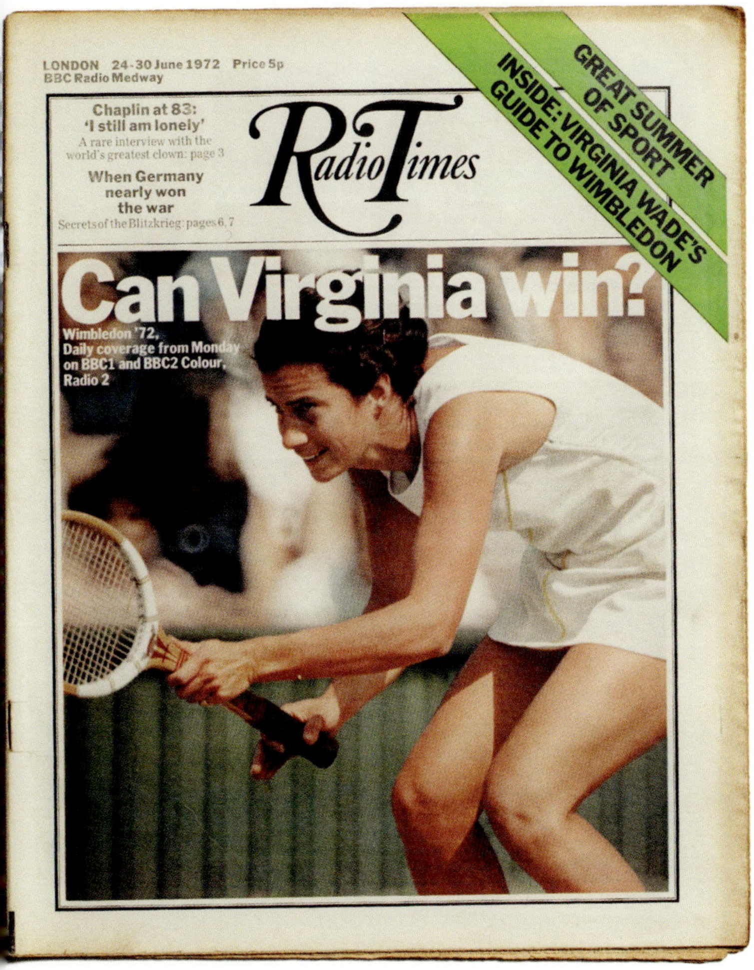

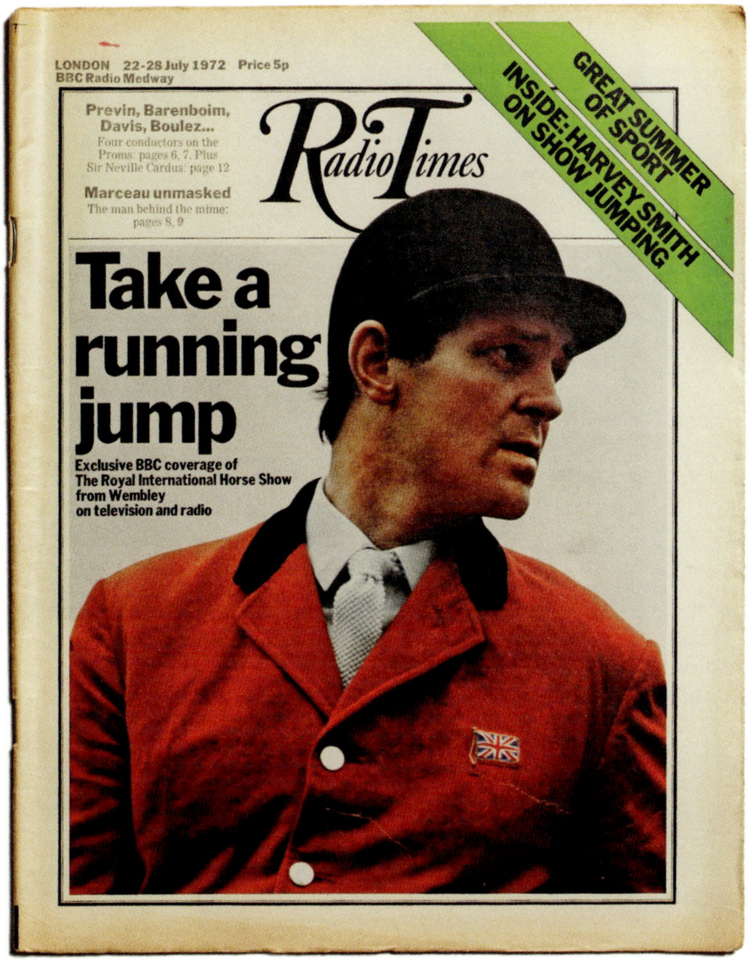

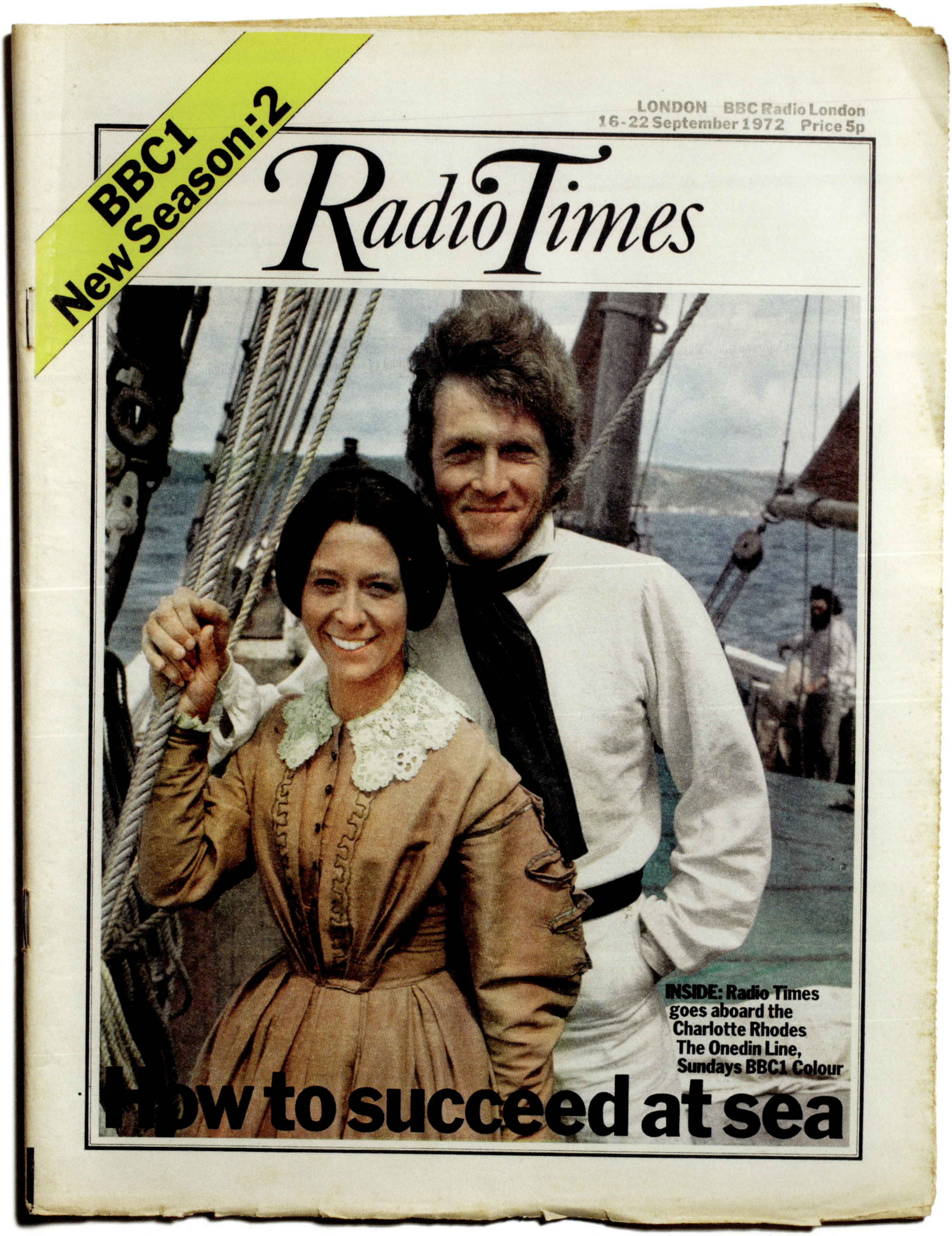

The Onedin Line **James Onedin (Peter Gilmore) and Anne Onedin (Anne Stallybrass)**
(photograph by Richard Farley) 16–22 September 1972

One of 1971's biggest hits and an icon of 1970s television drama, *The Onedin Line* returned for a second series with Peter Gilmore as the mutton-chopped 19th-century shipping magnate James Onedin. The other star was *Charlotte Rhodes*, a three-masted schooner built in 1900 that its real captain, Jim Mackreth, bought for £2,400 in the late 1960s.

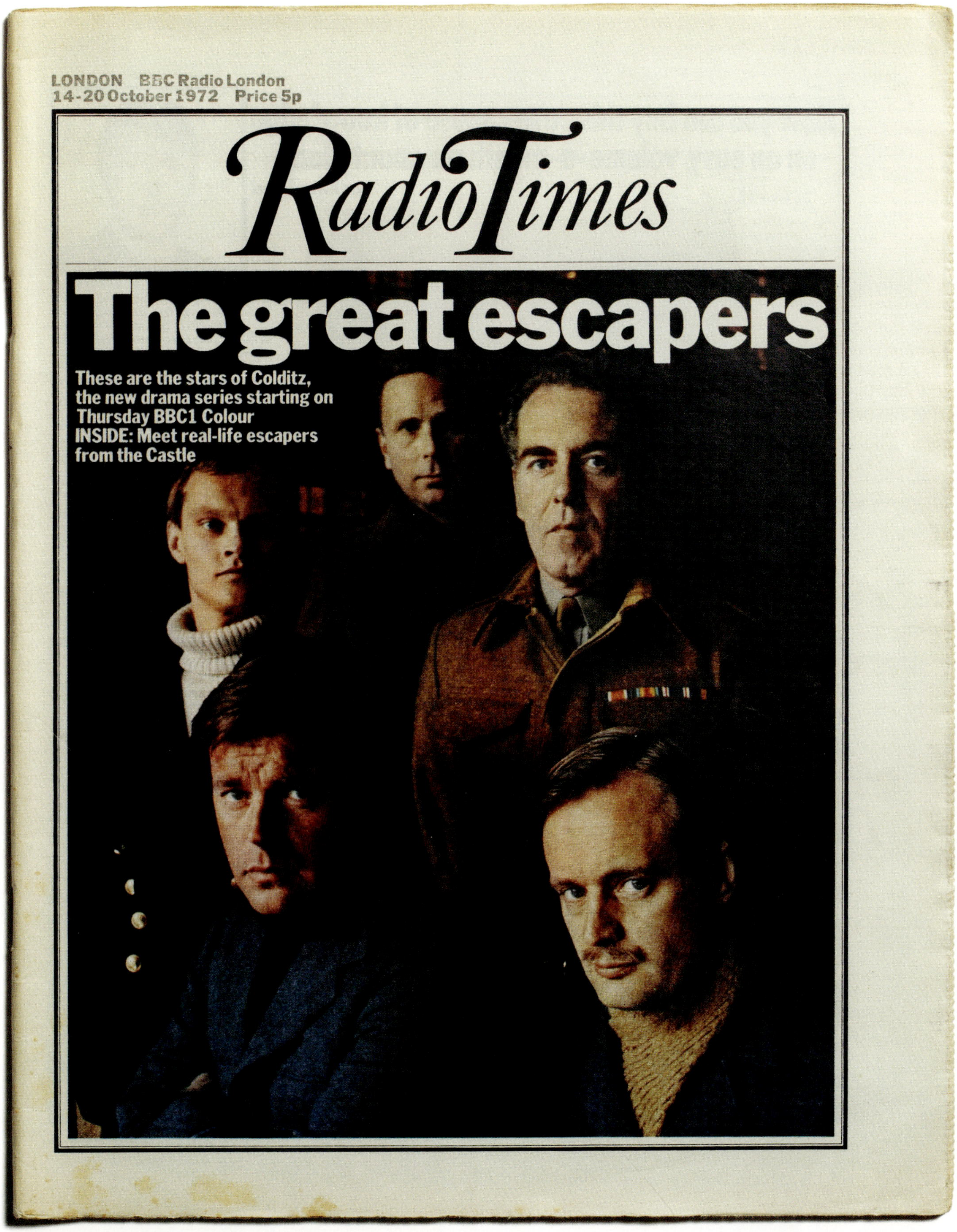
LONDON BBC Radio London
14-20 October 1972 Price 5p

Radio Times

The great escapers

These are the stars of Colditz, the new drama series starting on Thursday BBC1 Colour
INSIDE: Meet real-life escapers from the Castle

Colditz **Clockwise from top left: Lt Dick Player (Christopher Neame), Capt Pat Grant (Edward Hardwicke), Lt Col John Preston (Jack Hedley), Flt Lt Simon Carter (David McCallum), Flt Lt Phil Carrington (Robert Wagner)** *(photograph by John Perkins)* *14–20 October 1972*

The launch of another classic BBC drama. *Colditz* was a collaboration with Universal Studios, who insisted Robert Wagner be in the cast alongside the likes of David McCallum and Jack Hedley. It was more successful here than in the States.

The Royal Variety Performance *(right)*

Ken Dodd and Danny La Rue *(photograph by Tony Evans)*

4–10 November 1972

Topping the bill at *The Royal Variety Performance,* Dodd told *Radio Times*: "There have been several assassination attempts and it's been critically ill for a while, but variety will never die." As well as Ken Dodd and Danny La Rue, the Queen and Queen Mother were entertained by Elton John, the Jackson 5, Dickie Henderson and a *Till Death Us Do Part* sketch.

America *(below left)*

Alistair Cooke *(photograph by Penny Tweedie)*

11–17 November 1972

Alistair Cooke was launching his new television series *America* – and broadcasting his 1,239th *Letter from America* on Radio 4. He explained that he'd spent "35 years trying to destroy the clichés the British have" about the country and its people.

Christmas 1972 *(below right)*

Clockwise from left: Bruce Forsyth, Lulu, Eric Morecambe, Ernie Wise, a stuffed lion *(photograph by Ray Rathborne)*

16–29 December 1972

"Here's the most complete, gloriously old-fashioned Christmas possible," claimed *Radio Times*. Among the viewing highlights were a Charlie Chaplin retrospective, the opera *Falstaff* and *Billy Smart's Christmas Circus*.

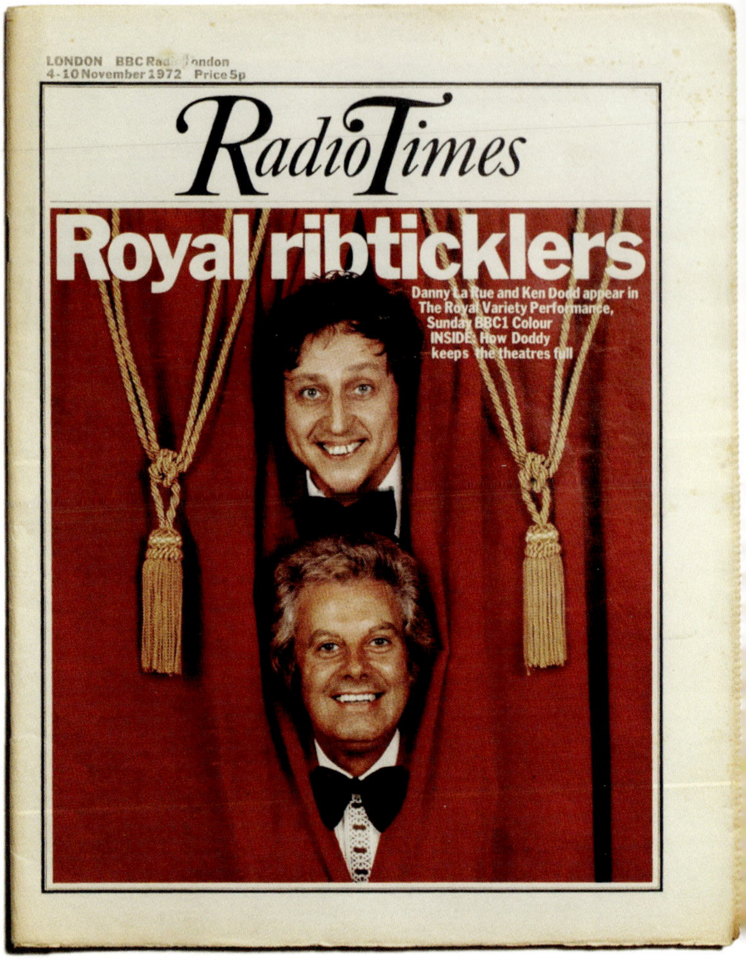

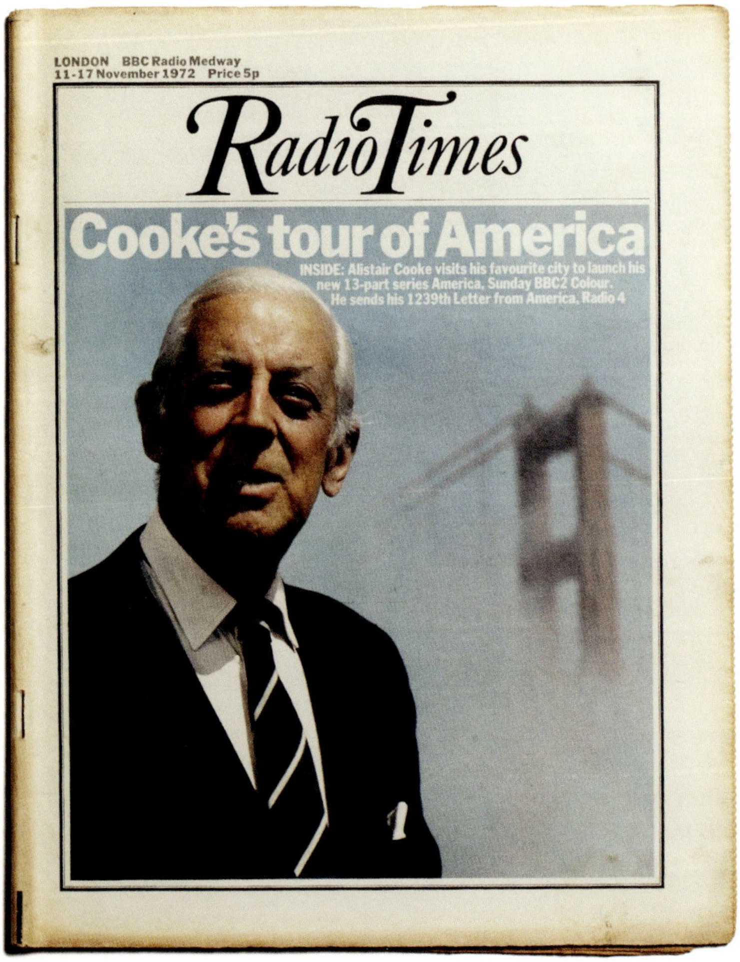

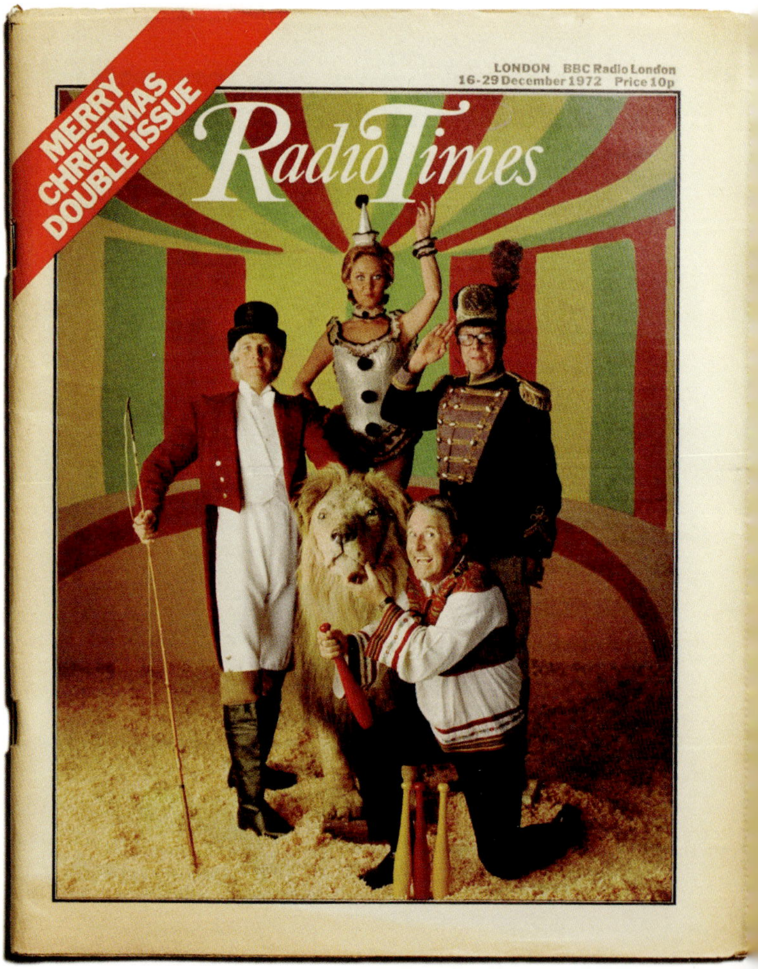

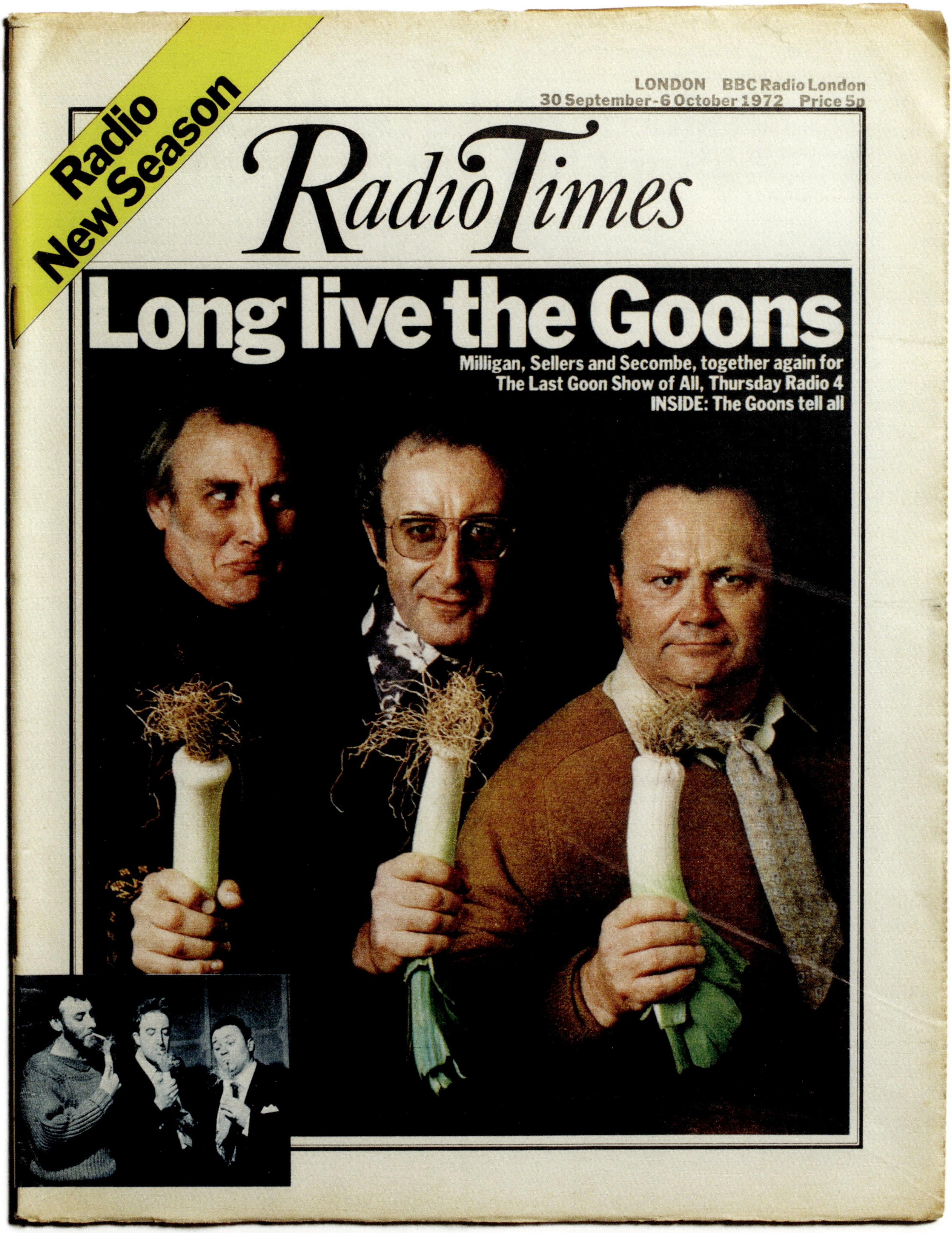

The Last Goon Show of All Spike Milligan, Peter Sellers and Harry Secombe
(photograph by Tony Evans) 30 September–6 October 1972

After 12 years, the three stars of *The Goon Show* reunited for a send-off that aired simultaneously on radio and TV. Milligan said that making *The Goons* had taken a toll: "It cost blood to put that show on. It wrecked my first marriage and my health."

Doctor Who *(right)*

From left: William Hartnell, Jon Pertwee and Patrick Troughton ***(photograph by Ray Rathborne)***

30 December 1972–5 January 1973

The Three Doctors launched the tenth series of the sci-fi show, and *Radio Times's* photoshoot (October 1972) was the first time all three actors had come together. William Hartnell said he knew the show would last: "I was universally scoffed at."

Lord Peter Wimsey *(middle right)*

Lord Peter Wimsey (Ian Carmichael) ***(photograph by Dmitri Kasterine)***

27 January–2 February 1973

Ian Carmichael played the noble sleuth created by novelist Dorothy L Sayers. Inside, *Radio Times* set out to discover if there were any remnants of Wimsey's leisurely 1920s world to be found in the London of the day.

The Goodies *(far right)*

From left: Tim Brooke-Taylor, Bill Oddie, Graeme Garden ***(photograph by Peter Howe)***

3–9 February 1973

"Ideally *The Goodies* will be great in 70 years' time," Tim Brooke-Taylor told *Radio Times*. "Although we are not writing for posterity... that would be fatal. Basically, we are trying to produce the funniest half-hour anyone has seen."

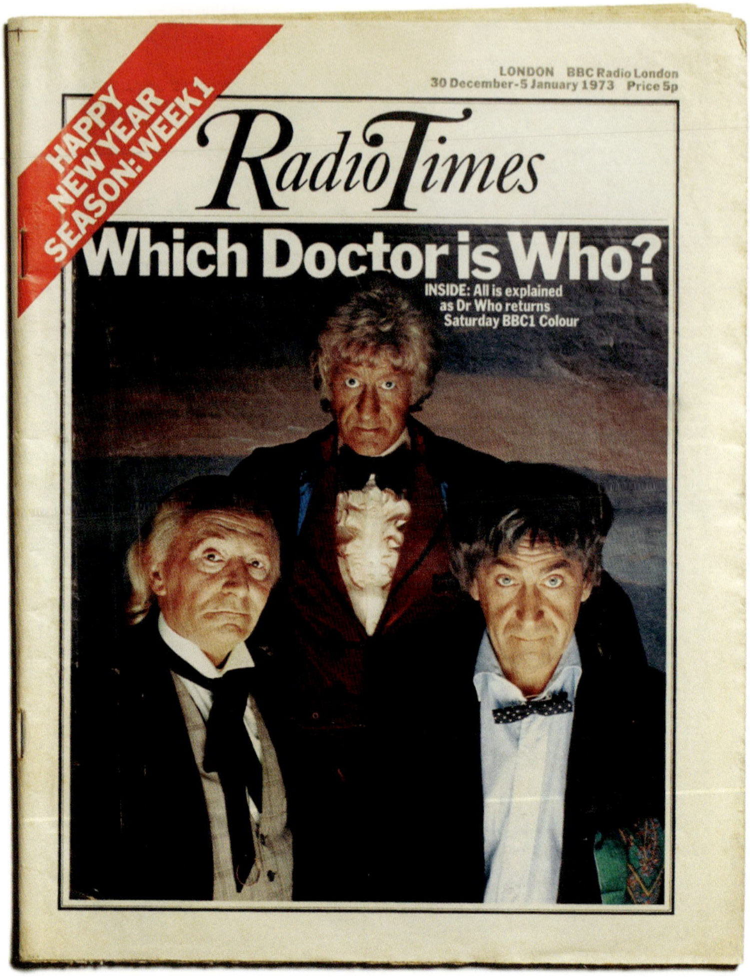

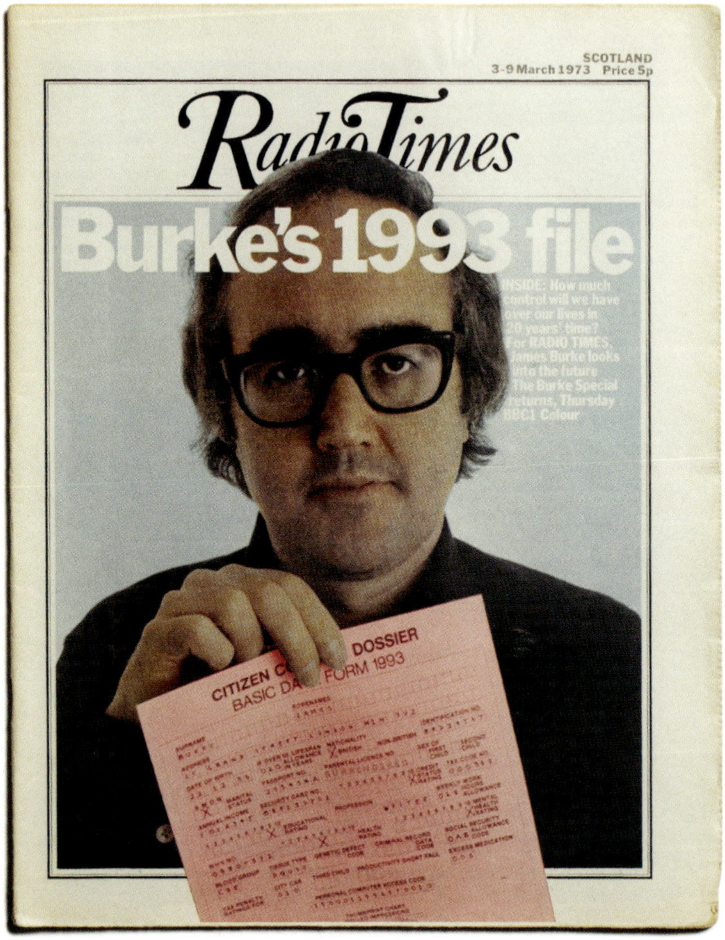

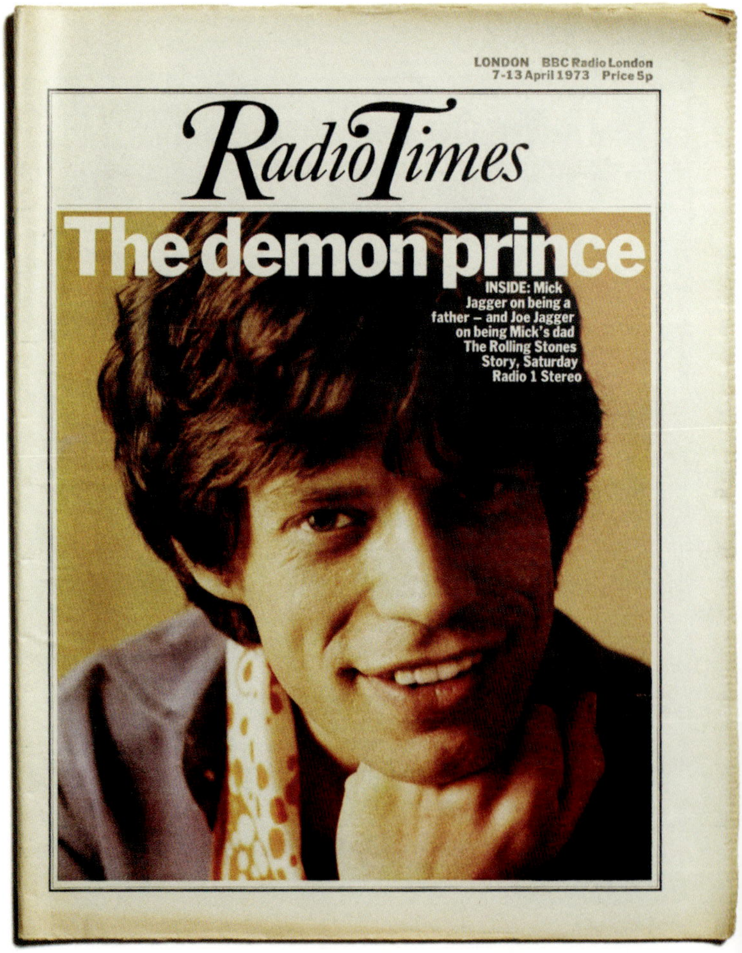

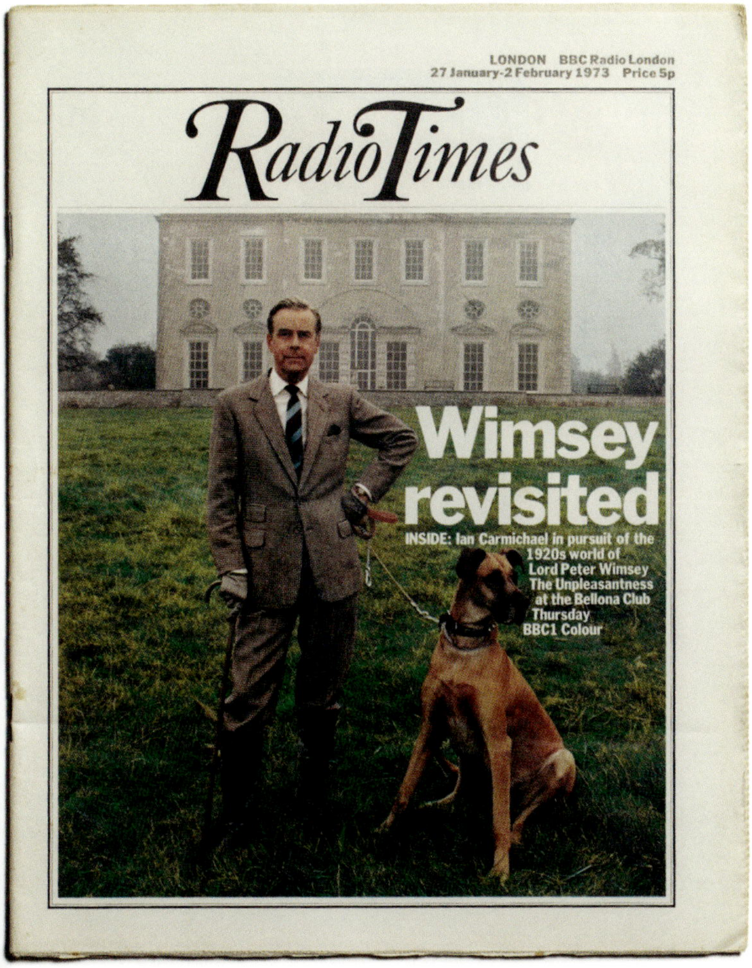

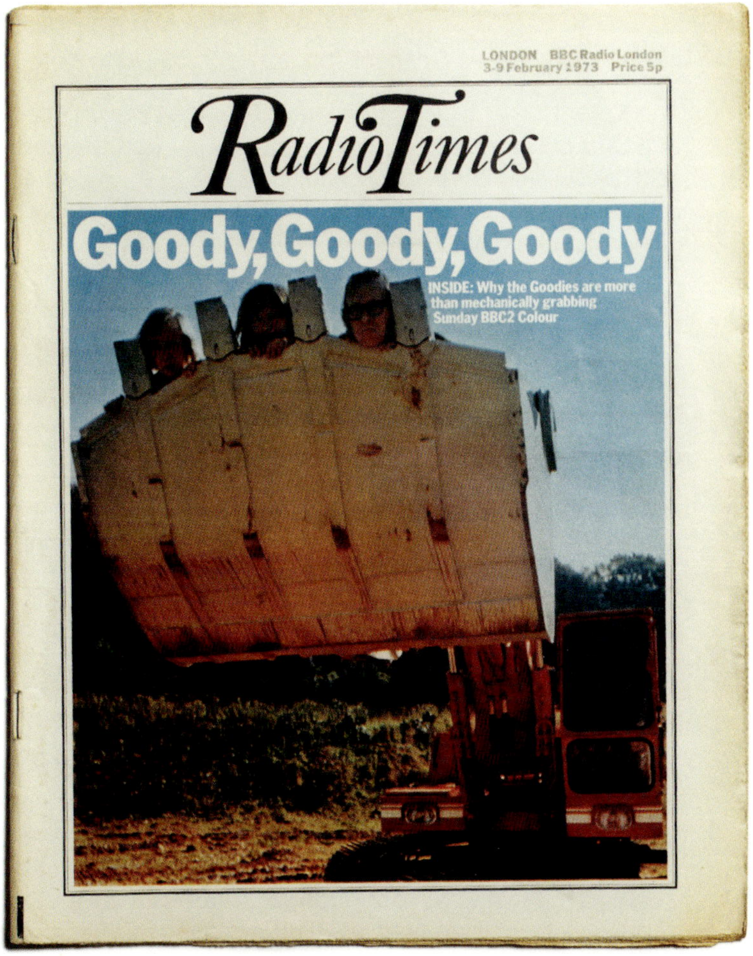

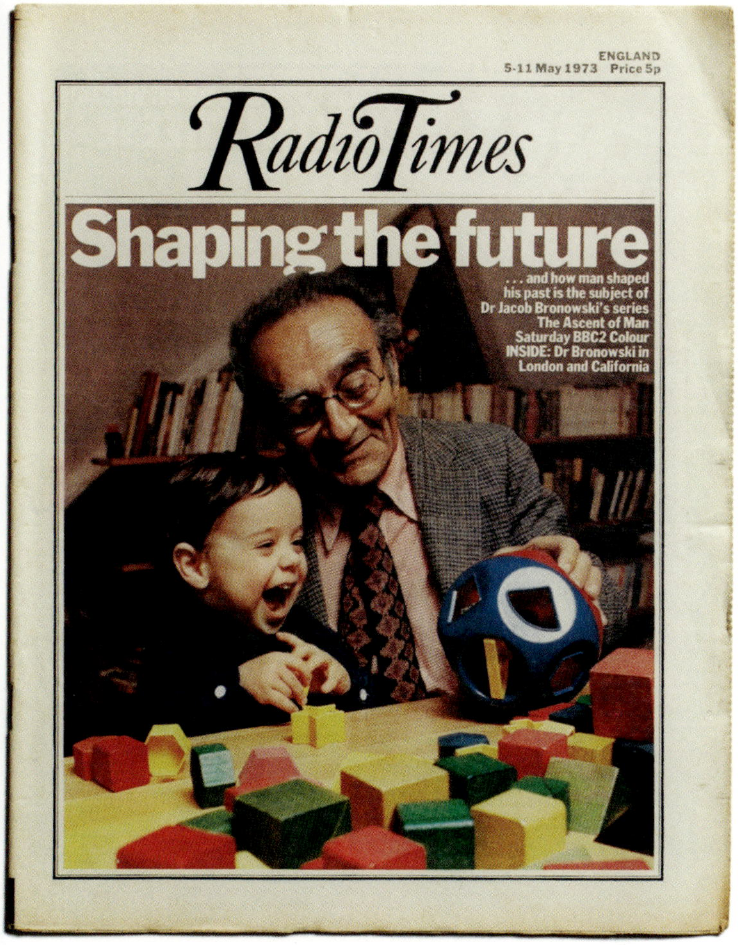

The Burke Special *(far left)*

James Burke ***(photograph by Tony Evans)***

3–9 March 1973

James Burke looked 20 years into the future and tried to predict how much control people would have over their lives in a world increasingly dominated by technology. Privacy would be a major issue, he said, because by 1993 there could be as many as 300,000 computers in the country.

The Rolling Stones Story *(middle left)*

Mick Jagger ***(photograph by Dmitri Kasterine)***

7–13 April 1973

"He is, and it seems incredible, on the brink of being 30," begins the profile of Jagger. The new dad (daughter Jade was 18 months old) revealed that he was in favour of discipline. "Everyone has to be tied down to something, but with discipline there's a lot of room to move. Maybe I'm a frustrated Army officer."

The Ascent of Man *(left)*

Dr Jacob Bronowski ***(photograph by Tony Evans)***

5–11 May 1973

As Dr Jacob Bronowski began his landmark television series, he spoke about his own rise, from struggling at school to dropping out after Cambridge and going on to become a star of *The Brains Trust*. The little boy on the cover is Bronowski's grandson, Daniel Bruno Jardine.

What's My Line? *(right)*

Lady Isobel Barnett *(photograph by John Kelly)*

18–24 August 1973

As *What's My Line?* returned for a tenth series, Lady Barnett said her success on the panel game was due to the fact that "ordinary women can identify with me. I live in the back of beyond, quite ordinary. Women know what makes me tick."

Casanova '73 *(below left)*

Henry Newhouse (Leslie Phillips) *(photograph by John Kelly)*

8–14 September 1973

The sitcom *Casanova '73*, about a womanising PR, was written by Ray Galton and Alan Simpson and was one of their rare failures. Leslie Phillips was the star and he spoke of his frustration at being cast yet again as a lothario – "If I go off and do a super television play, nobody wants to know about it."

Frost's Weekly *(below right)*

David Frost *(photograph by John Kelly)*

8–14 December 1973

In this new magazine-format show, jet-setting newsman David Frost teamed up with Eddie Braben, the comedy writer behind Moecambe and Wise's best years. Braben said he'd expected Frost to be hard-hitting but "he has a great deal of warmth and feeling, a very human person".

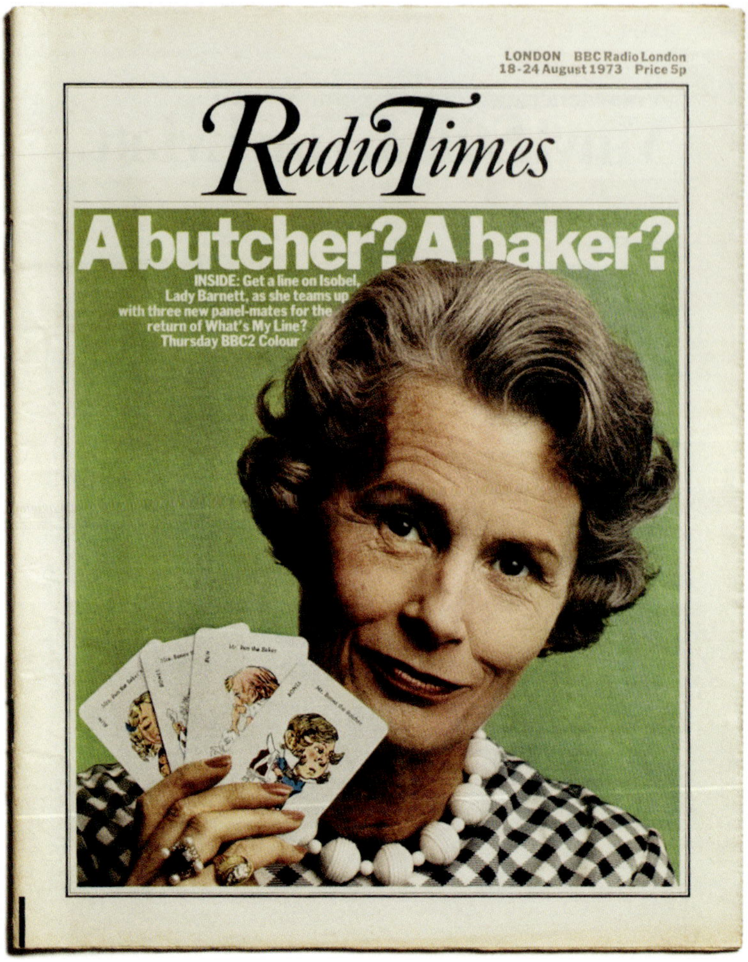

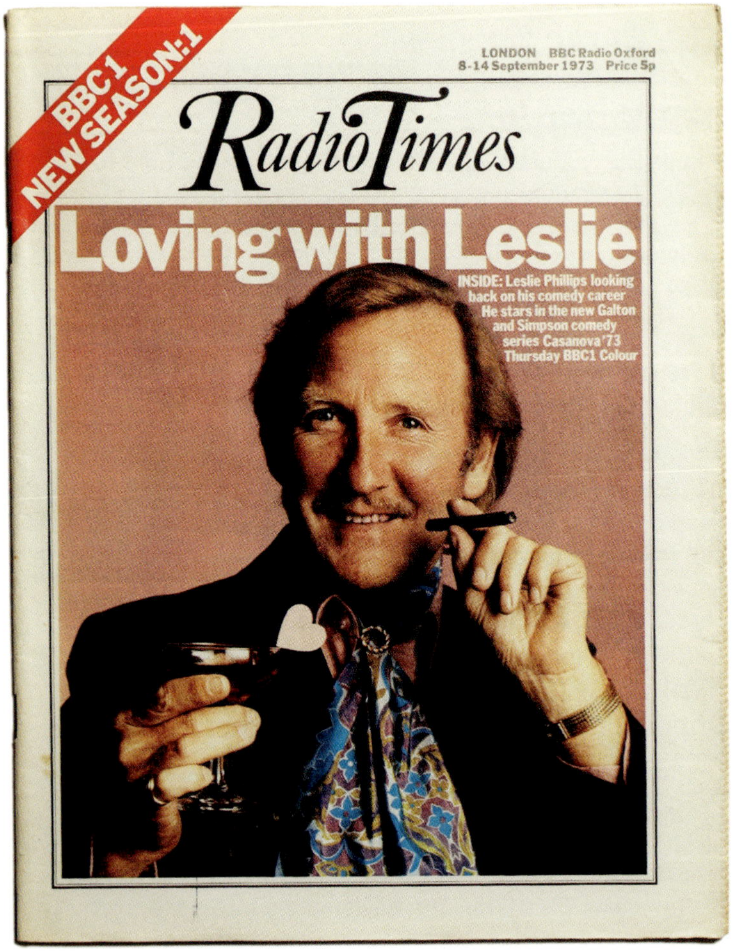

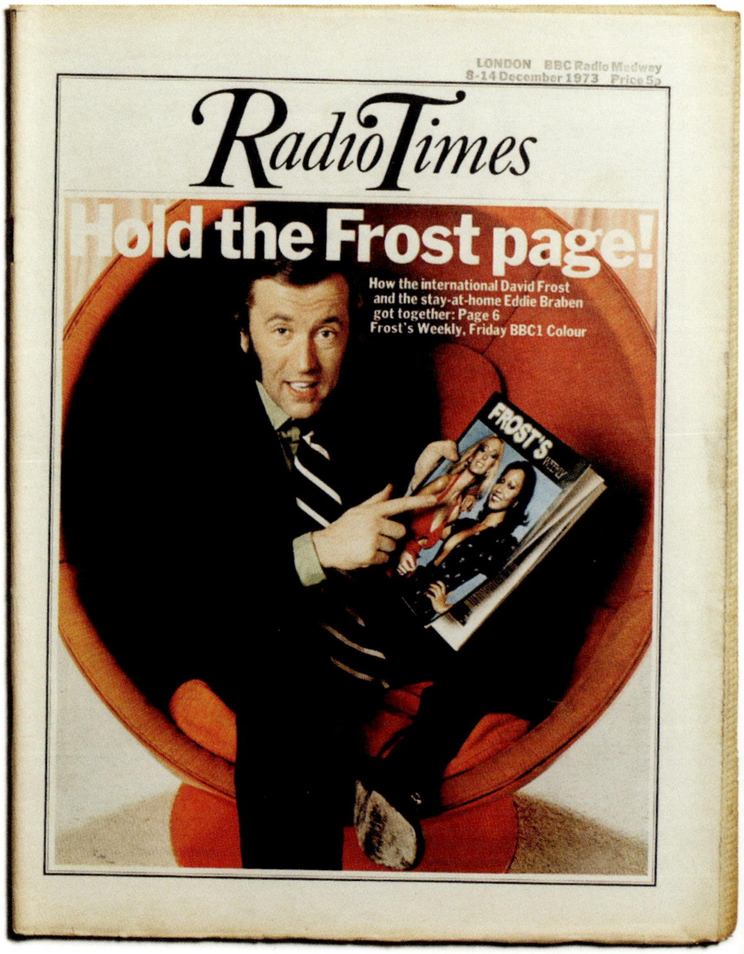

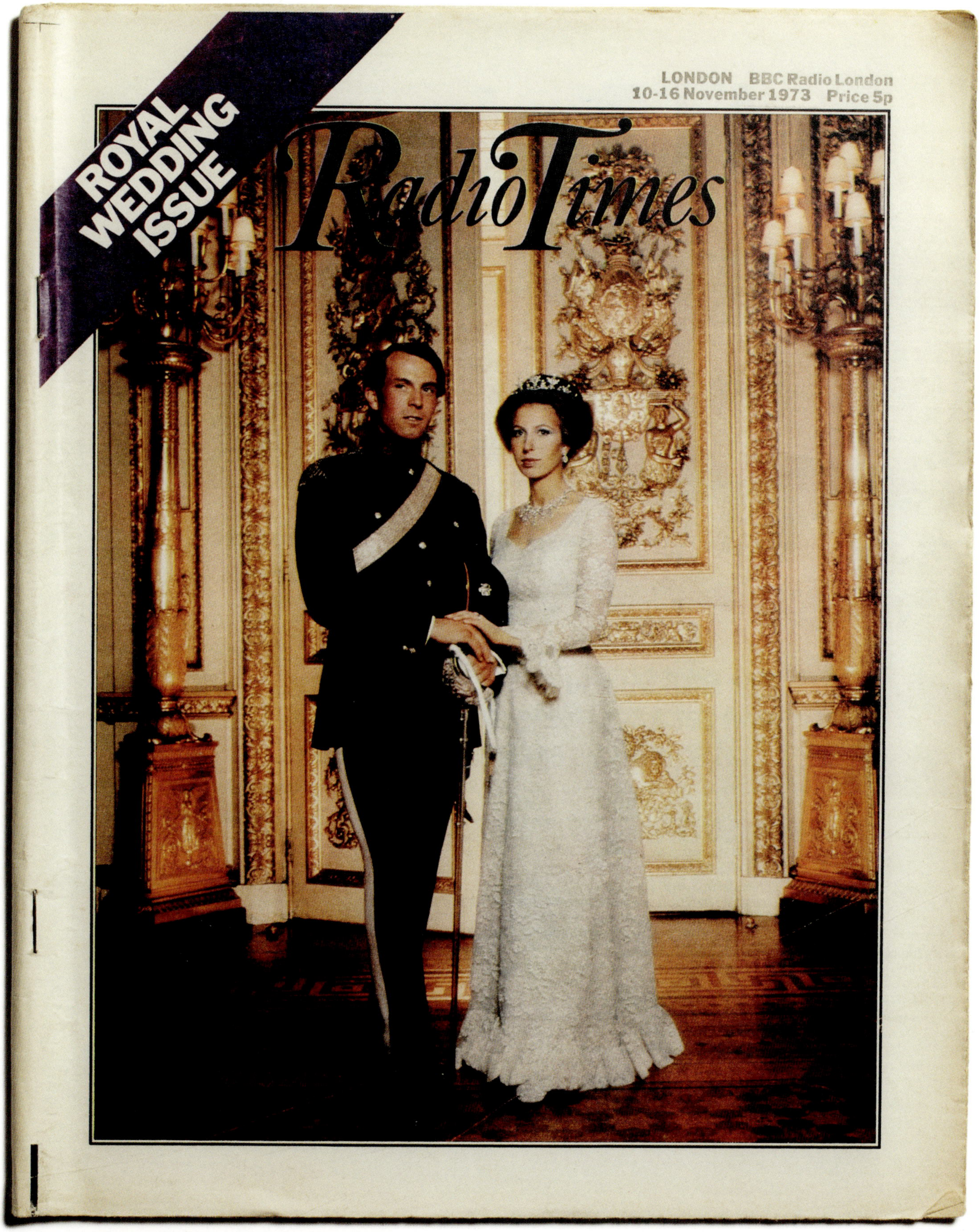

Royal Wedding Issue **Captain Mark Phillips and Princess Anne** *(photograph by Norman Parkinson)*
10–16 November 1973

Every article and 24 pages of the 92-page issue were devoted to the wedding – beginning with how the bride and groom had denied they were a couple right up to the engagement. "It was only decided over the weekend after the Badminton Horse Trials," said a royal spokesperson. Across the globe, an estimated 500 million people watched the wedding.

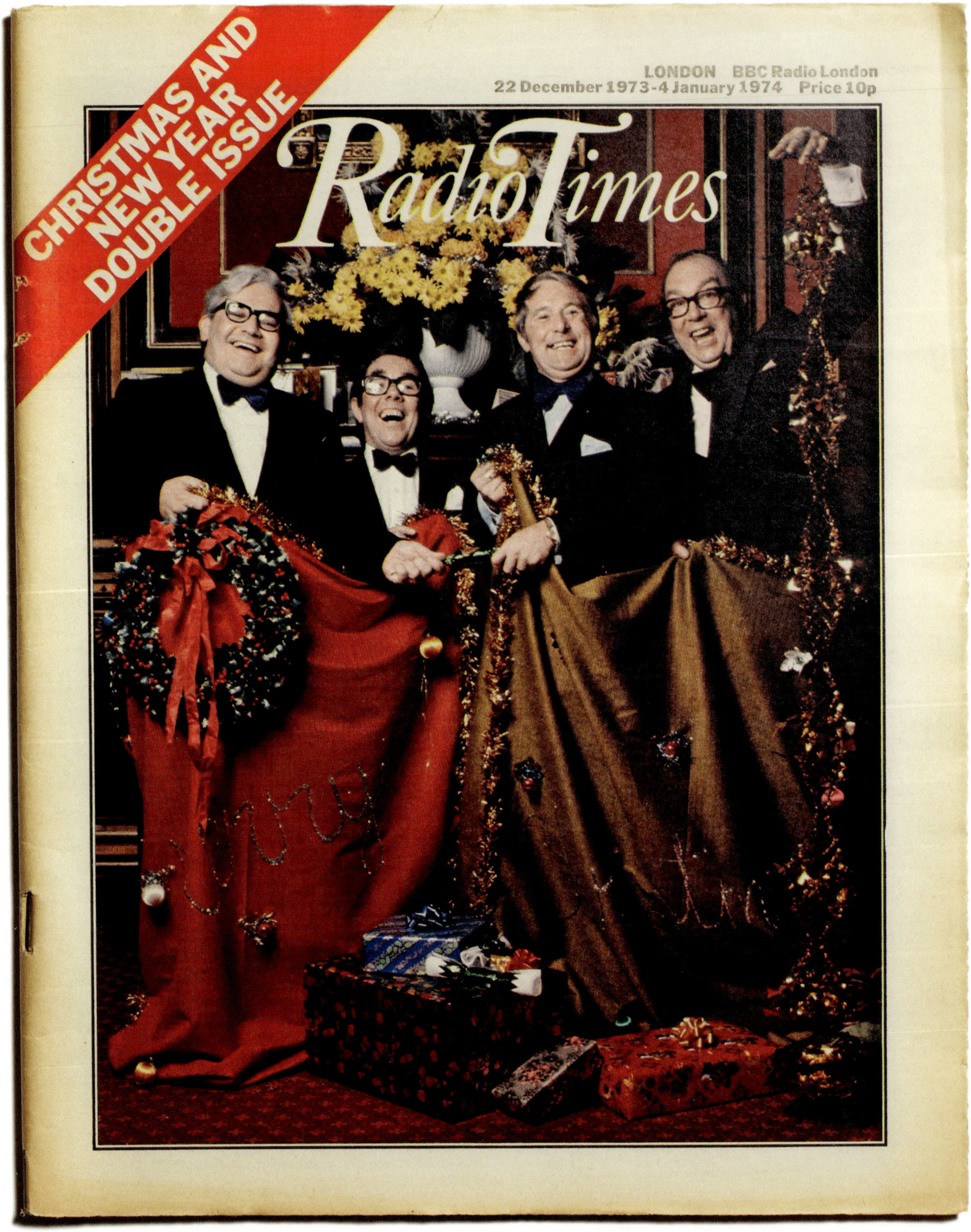

Christmas 1973 **Ronnie Barker, Ronnie Corbett, Ernie Wise and Eric Morecambe**
(photograph by John Kelly) *22 December 1973–4 January 1974*

Radio Times brought the nation's two most beloved comedy duos together for a photo and a drink at Crockford's club in London. Ernie Wise revealed that he and Eric Morecambe never met up on Christmas Day itself: "Some things must be sacred. And my face needs a rest from all that slapping." Eric said that, for him, Christmas was a time of "booze, food, telly and wild, wild women. The dames, however, are forbidden entry by my wife."

Heart Attack *(left)*

Arthur Askey *(photograph by Dmitri Kasterine)*

23–29 March 1974

The man they called Big-Hearted Arthur had suffered a heart-attack six years earlier and was on radio this week talking about coping. He'd returned to work against medical advice but said, "When the audience realised it was me, they gave me the best tonic I've ever had."

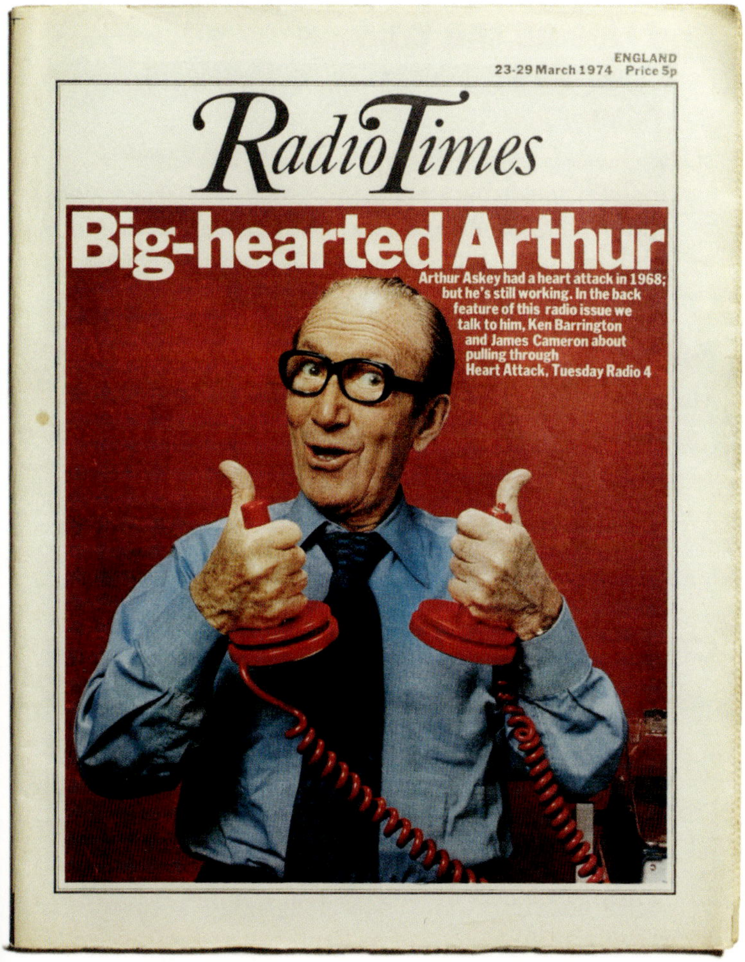

The Tender Trap *(below left)*

(photograph by Sean Morris and Peter Parks)

21–27 September 1974

Killer plants were the subject of the programme, illustrated on the cover by a striking close-up of a Venus fly-trap. Sean Morris and Peter Parks of Oxford Scientific Films were asked how they did it and the answer was with a lot of skill and time. "It can be frustrating," said Morris. "You never know whether the film is right or wrong until it comes back from being processed."

If You Think You've Got Problems! *(below right)*

Illustration by Peter Brookes

28 September–4 October 1974

As Radio 4 launched a series of programmes investigating the nation's health, *Radio Times* reported on the NHS. There were more than 25,000 GPs then – today the figure is 62,369.

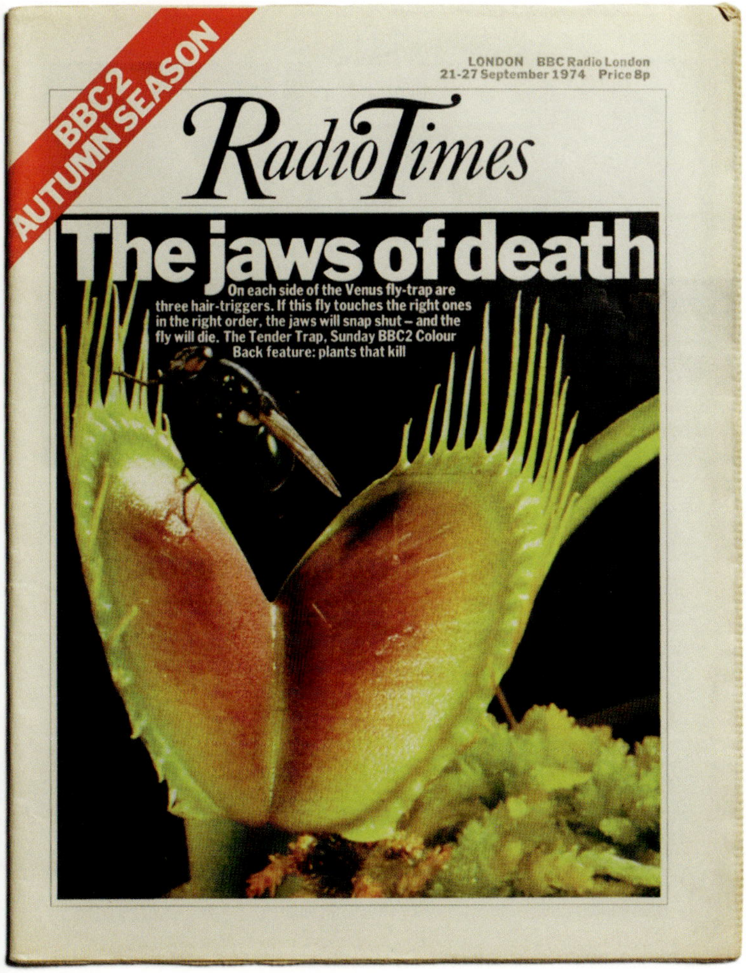

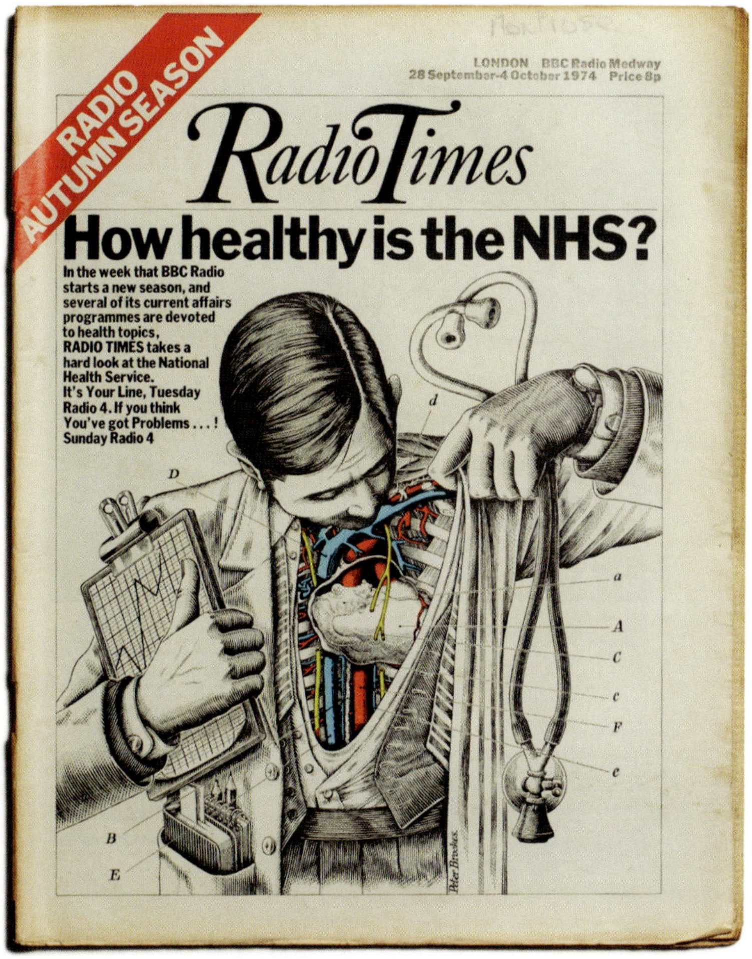

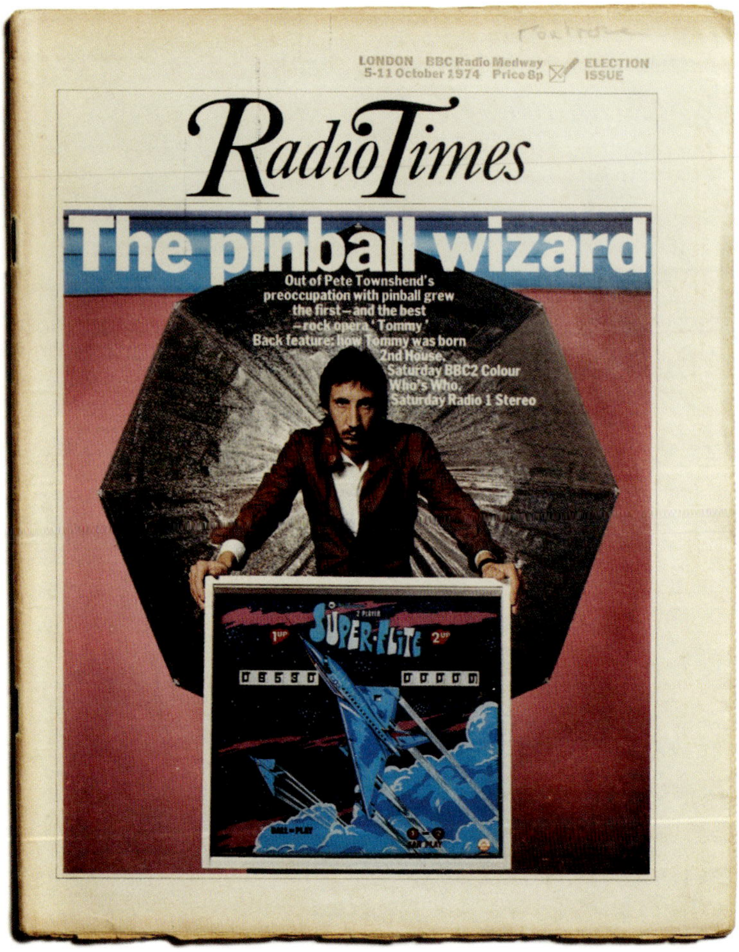

2nd House: the Who *(left)*

Pete Townshend ***(photograph by Allan Ballard)***

5–11 October 1974

The Who were profiled on BBC2 and Radio 1 to mark the band's tenth anniversary, but *Radio Times* was exasperated because the bigger news was the snap general election of 10 October. Given that colour printing took longer than black and white, the cover could not be changed in time.

Kojak *(below left)*

Theo Kojak (Telly Savalas)

(photograph by Tony Evans) 23–29 November 1974

Tough-guy, lolly-sucking New York detective Theo Kojak was a huge Saturday night hit on BBC1. Savalas said: "I can't conceive of myself ever being a police officer, but *Kojak* is my way of showing my appreciation of them."

Christmas 1974 *(below right)*

Frank Spencer (Michael Crawford)

(photograph by Tony Evans)

21 December 1974–3 January 1975

Cover star Michael Crawford told the story of how in Christmas 1963 he'd cooked lunch for fellow members of the cast of *Coriolanus* at Nottingham Playhouse. "A butcher gave us the most enormous turkey – I think it was really a small emu. It took 18 hours to cook."

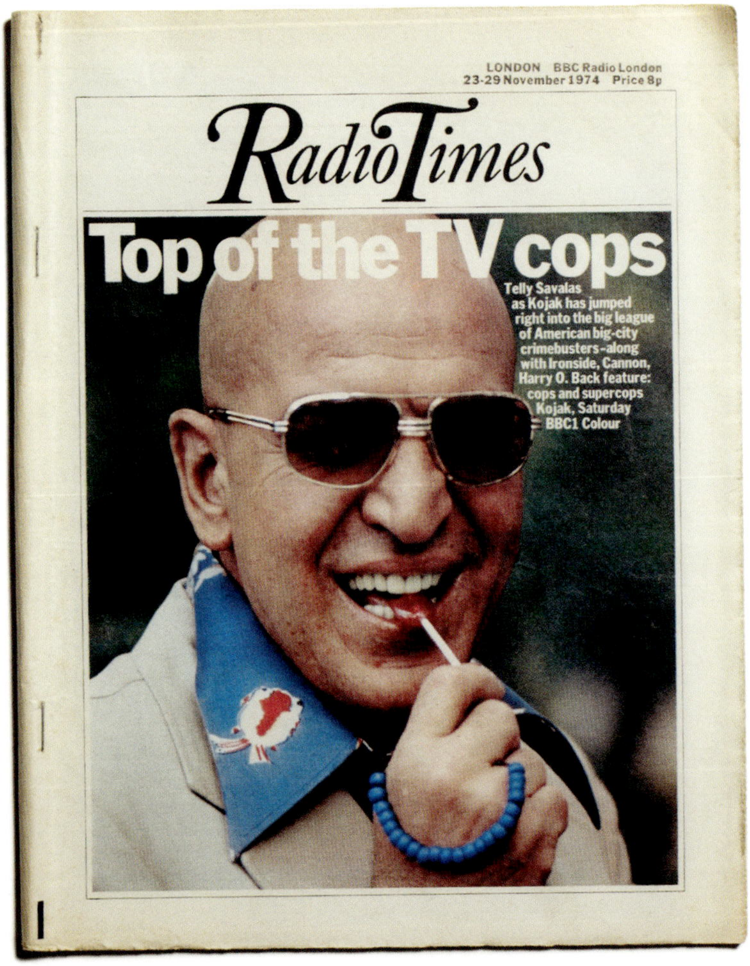

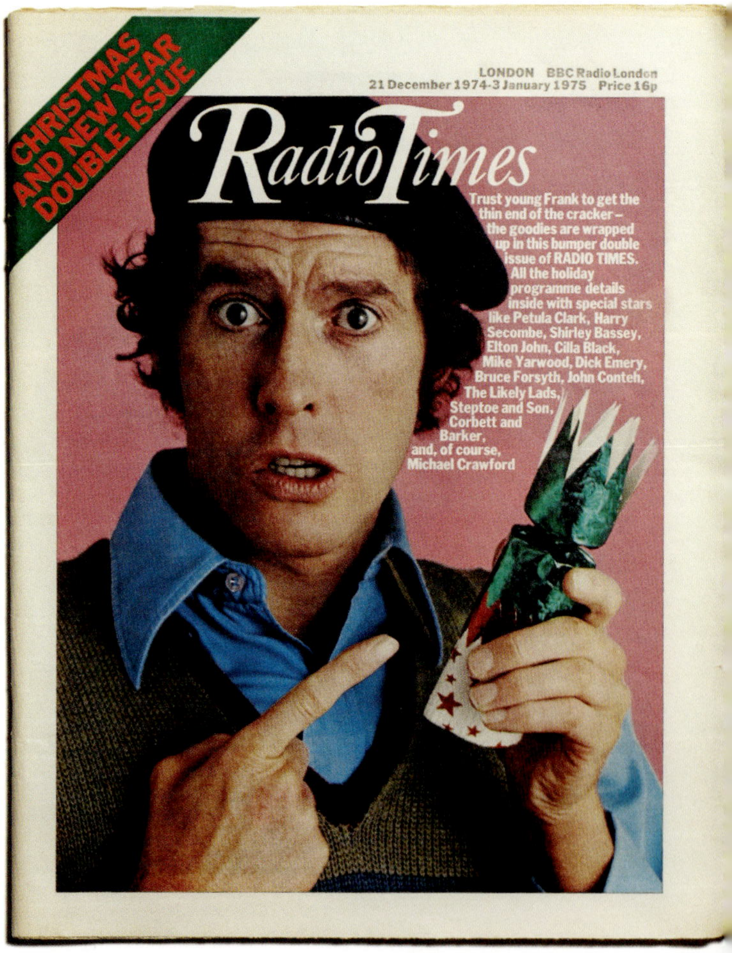

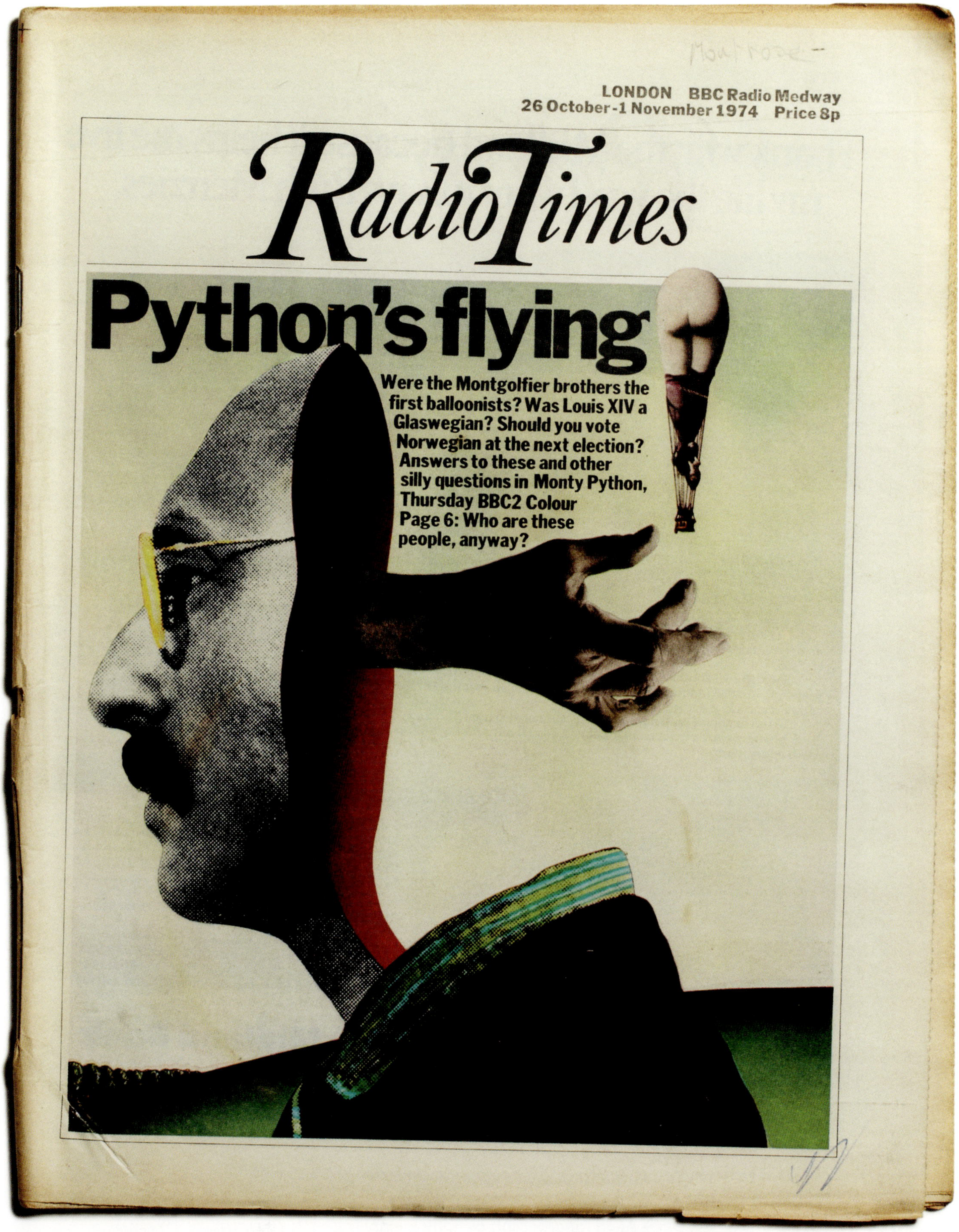

Monty Python **Illustration by Terry Gilliam** *26 October–1 November 1974*

This was the first series of *Monty Python* without John Cleese, and while Terry Jones and Graham Chapman talked enthusiastically about the new show, Terry Gilliam was more guarded. "What was nice at the beginning – and I think it really communicated – was that we were all really enjoying it. Now it's getting a bit like work." This was to be the final *Python* series.

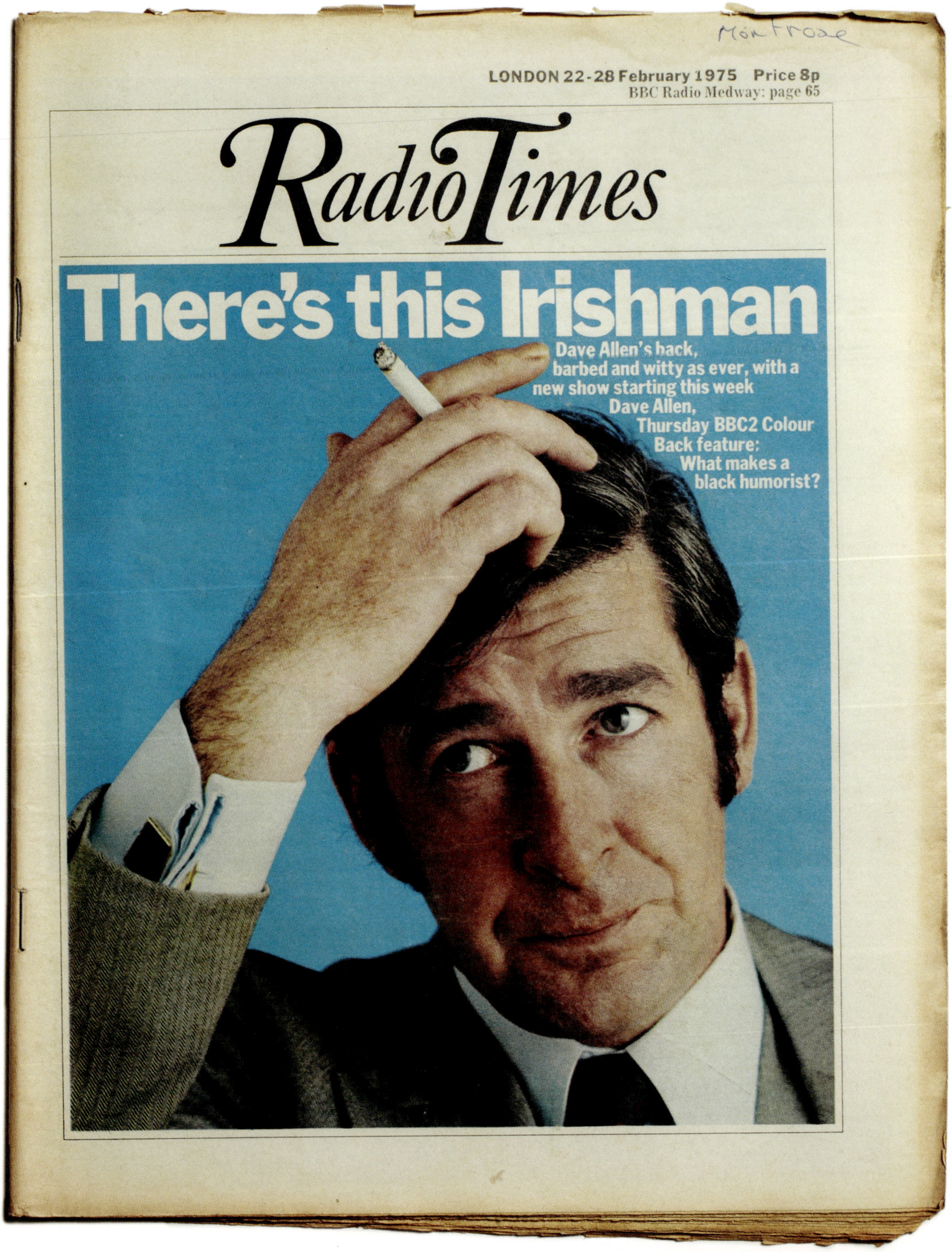

Dave Allen at Large **Dave Allen** *(photograph by Tony Evans)* *22–28 February 1975*

Radio Times tried and mostly failed to interview the comedian during the making of his new series. He was interviewed by Jack Trevor Story on location while filming one of the 300 or so sketches that were made for the series, but answered every serious question with an entirely unrelated but very funny anecdote. Yet Story noted: "Soon you are content to listen and laugh. He is an easy, relaxed man to be with."

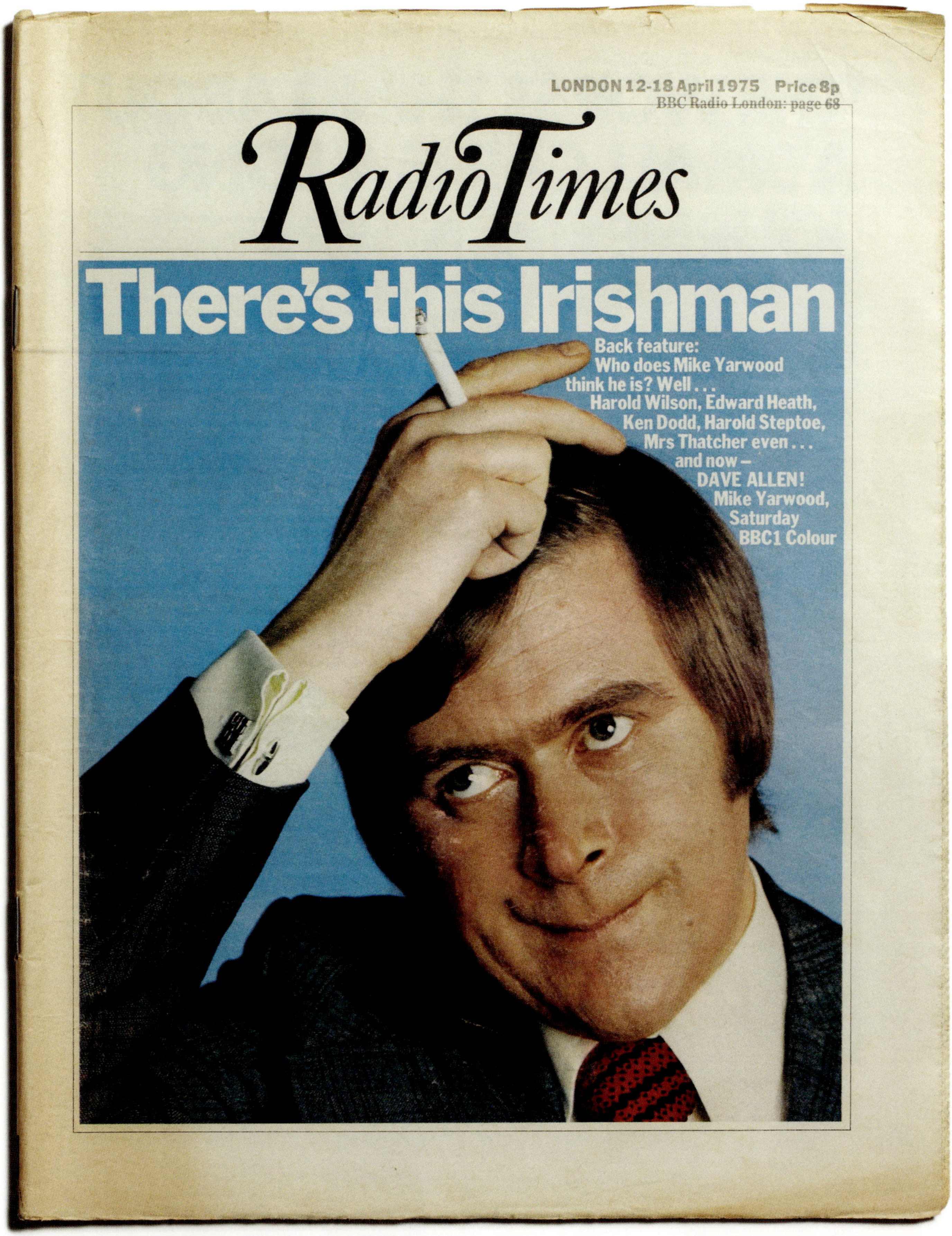

Look – Mike Yarwood Mike Yarwood *(photograph by Tony Evans)* *12–18 April 1975*

Radio Times has always been willing to use its cover to tell a good gag and the start of a new series of impressionist Mike Yarwood's show a few weeks after Dave Allen's show began was too good an opportunity to miss. At the time of the interview Yarwood was speculating who would win the vote to be the new leader of the Conservative Party. "I can do Thatcher, but I'm not happy with it yet. Pity it's not William Whitelaw, I've got him already."

Last of the Summer Wine *(right)*

From bottom left: Compo (Bill Owen), Blamire (Michael Bates) and Clegg (Peter Sallis)
(photograph by Allan Ballard)

1–7 March 1975

The second series of the long-running sitcom with the three original cast members. Michael Bates was forced to leave because of ill health after this series but the show kept going until 2010 for a total of 295 episodes.

The Grand National *(middle right)*

Red Rum *(photograph by Tony Evans)*

5–11 April 1975

Red Rum was aiming for a third consecutive win in the Grand National. However, perhaps overburdened by the nation's expectations, he came second.

Wodehouse Playhouse *(far right)*

Susan Blake (Pauline Collins) and George Mulliner (John Alderton)
(photograph by Tony Evans)

19–25 April 1975

Pauline Collins and John Alderton starred in a dramatisation of PG Wodehouse's short story *The Truth about George* – and so did PG Wodehouse, who had finished recording introductions to each story in the seven-part series a fortnight before his death.

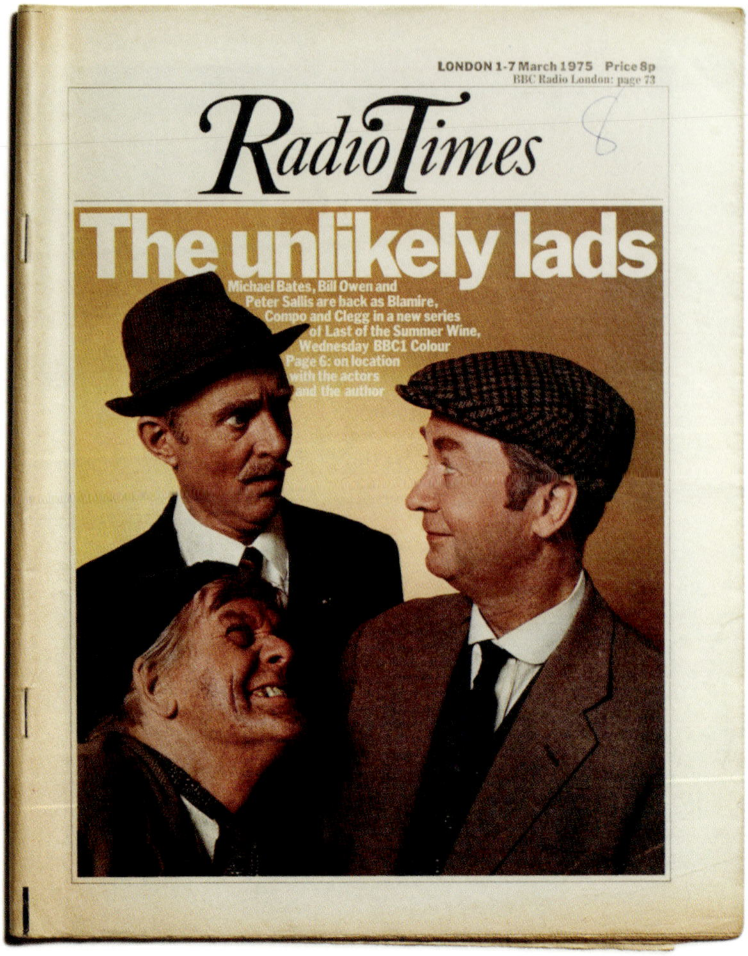

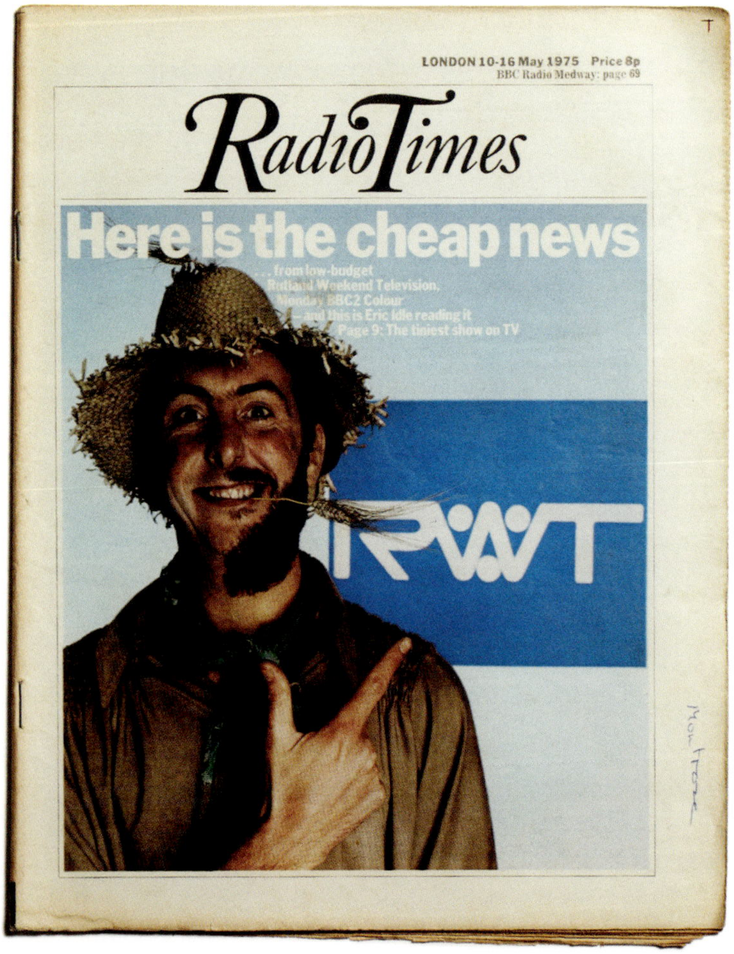

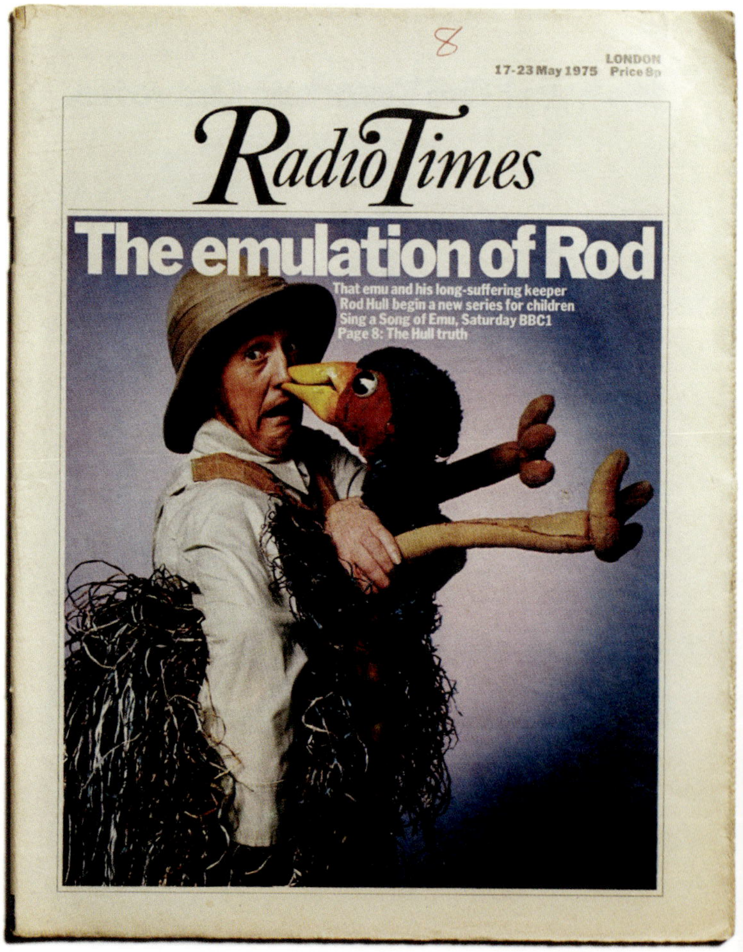

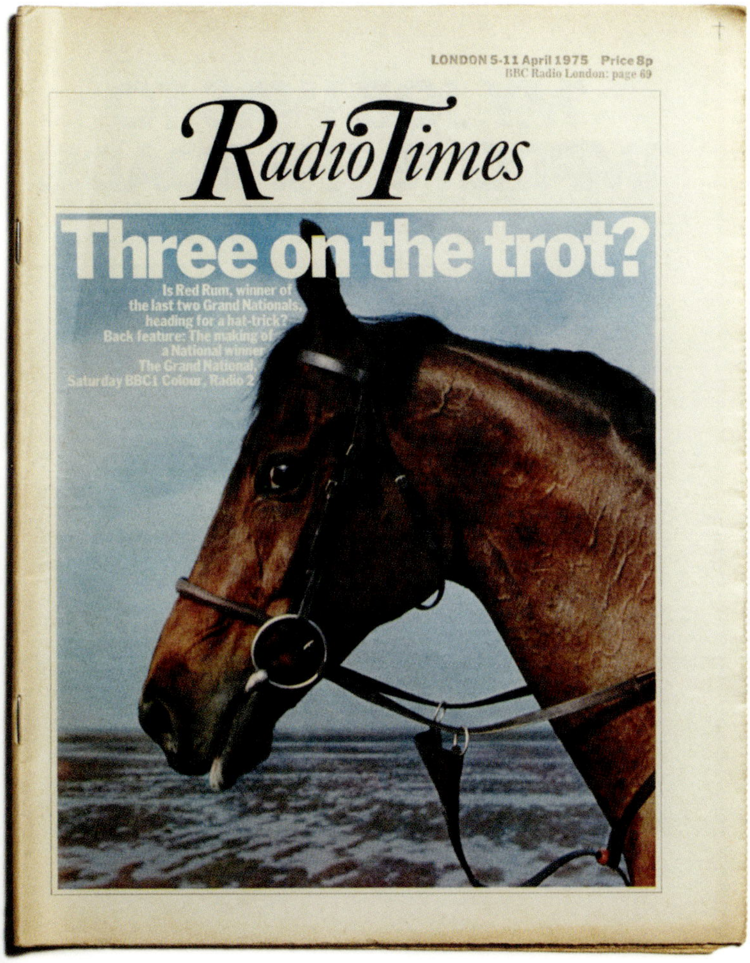

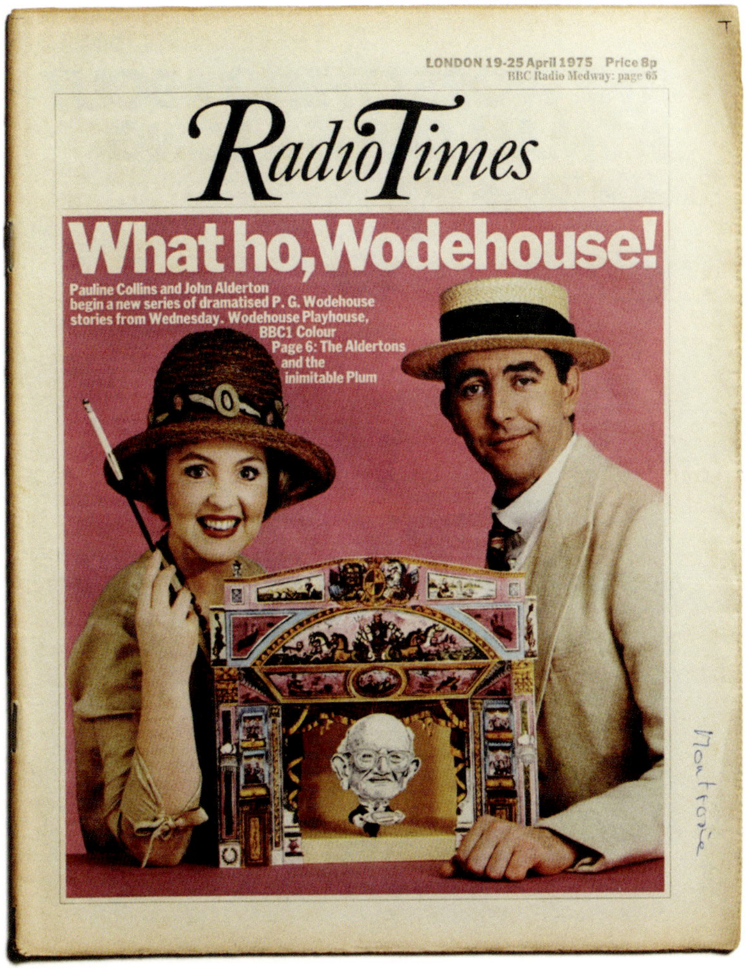

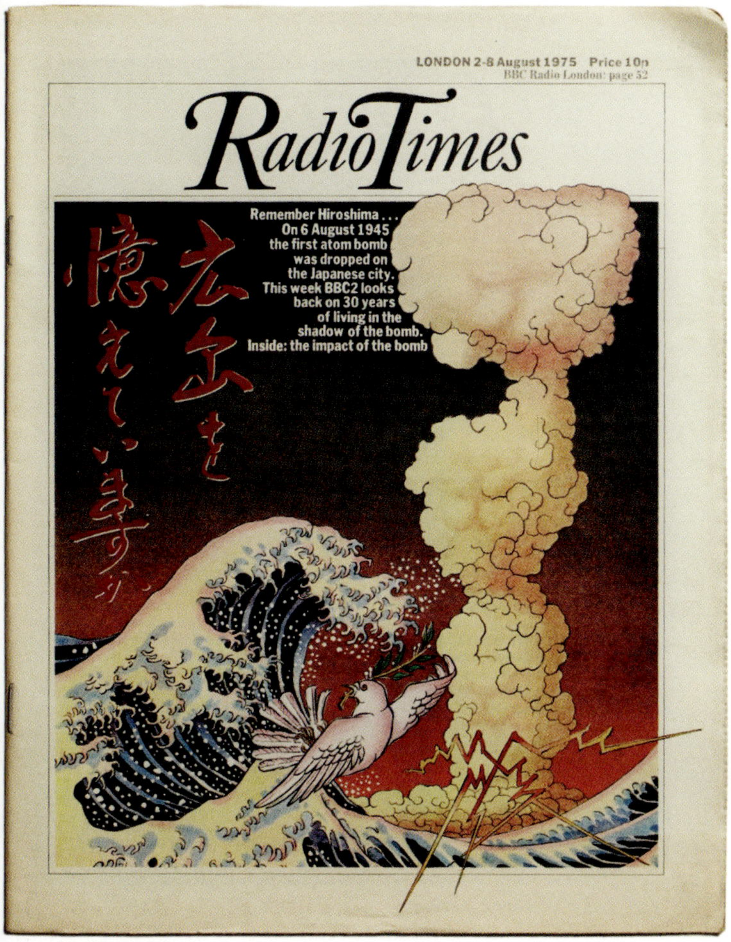

Rutland Weekend Television *(far left)*

Eric Idle ***(photograph by John Kelly)***

10–16 May 1975

A year after finishing *Monty Python*, Eric Idle brought us the sketch show *Rutland Weekend Television* – the tiniest show on TV, broadcast from a presentation studio the size of an average living room. "It was made on a shoestring budget," said Idle, "and someone else was wearing the shoe."

Sing a Song of Emu *(middle left)*

Rod Hull and Emu ***(photograph by Allan Ballard)***

17–23 May 1975

This cover was for a comparatively calm children's series called *Sing a Song of Emu* where the pair encouraged 300 kids to sing some of their favourite songs. Emu's infamous encounter with Michael Parkinson was still a year away.

The Building of the Bomb *(left)*

Illustration by Peter Brookes

2–8 August 1975

It was the 30th anniversary of the first atomic bomb – "The Japanese characters on the cover of this issue spell out the words 'Remember Hiroshima'," *said Radio Times.* "Nobody wants to remember, everyone needs to remember it."

A Taste of Britain *(right)*

(photograph by Tony Evans/cake by Sagne)

9–15 August 1975

BBC2's *A Taste of Britain* investigated cooking around the nation. Derek Cooper was the presenter and one of the first British journalists to write about food – four years later he started *The Food Programme* on Radio 4. Sagne was a cake shop around the corner from the *RT* offices in Marylebone High Street.

Tonight *(below left)*

Sue Lawley *(photograph by John Timbers)*

6–12 September 1975

Gender shouldn't matter and *Radio Times* knew it – but still managed to spend the whole feature saying how much it shouldn't matter. "I like to be treated both as a professional and a journalist," said Lawley. "I don't trade on my femininity."

Poldark *(below right)*

Ross Poldark (Robin Ellis) and Demelza (Angharad Rees)

(photograph by John Timbers)

4–10 October 1975

The dramatisation of Winston Graham's romance novels ran to just 29 episodes, but the series still helped to define the decade, set fans' hearts fluttering, showed Cornwall in a new light and made stars of Robin Ellis and Angharad Rees.

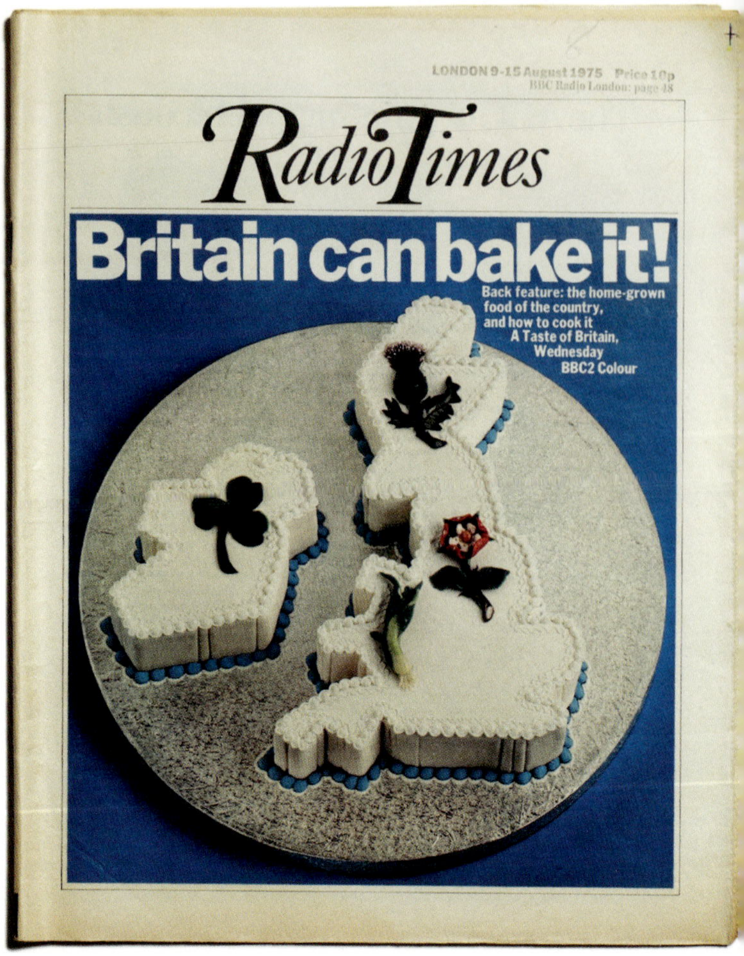

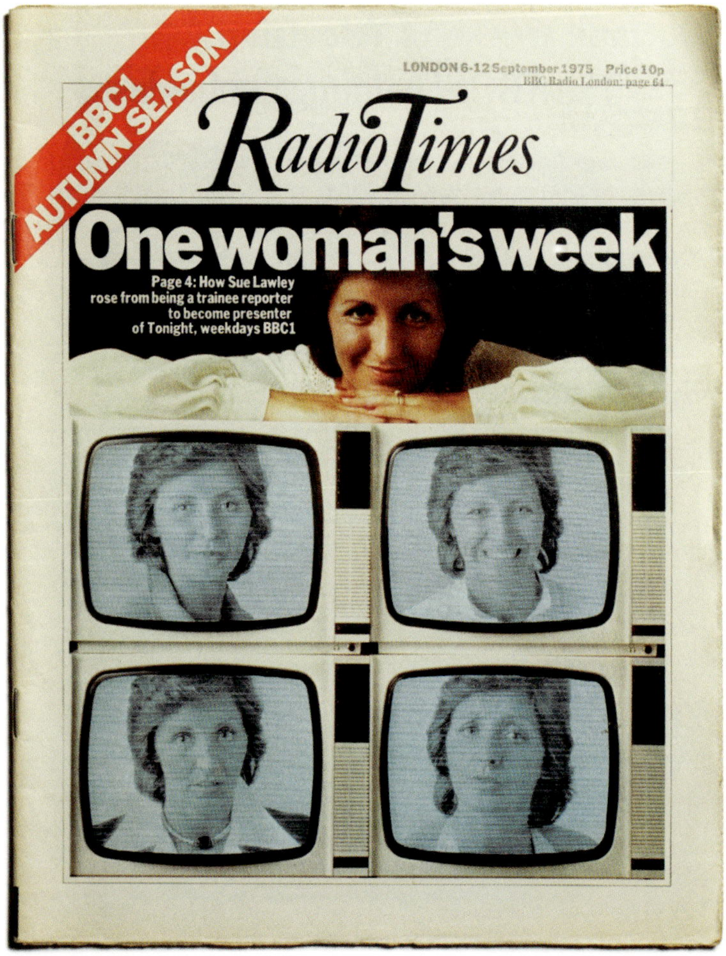

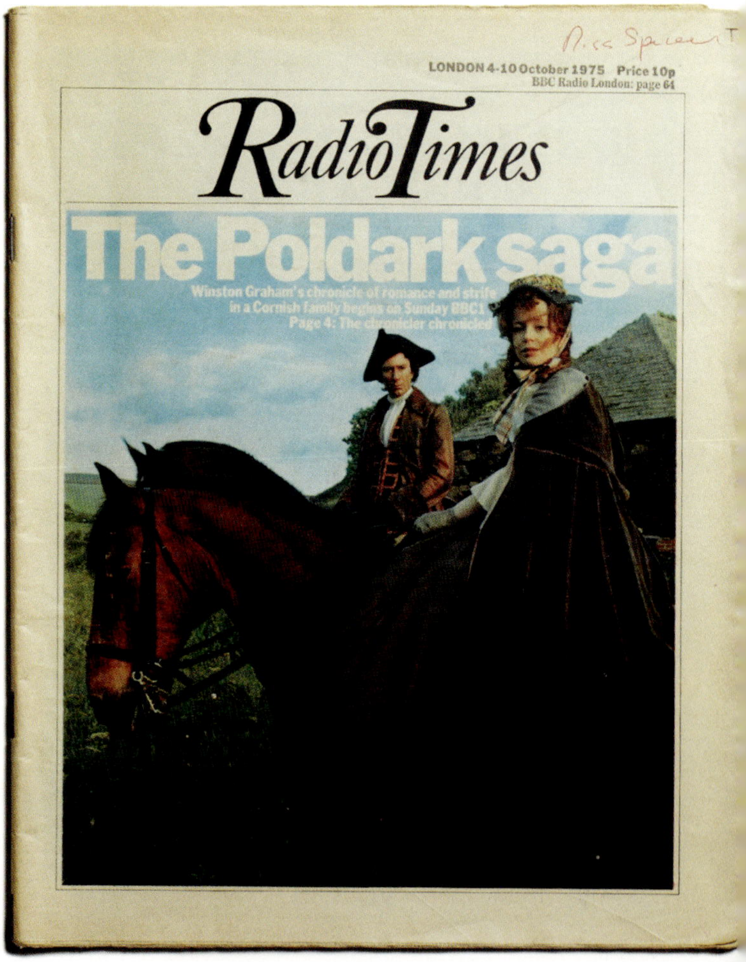

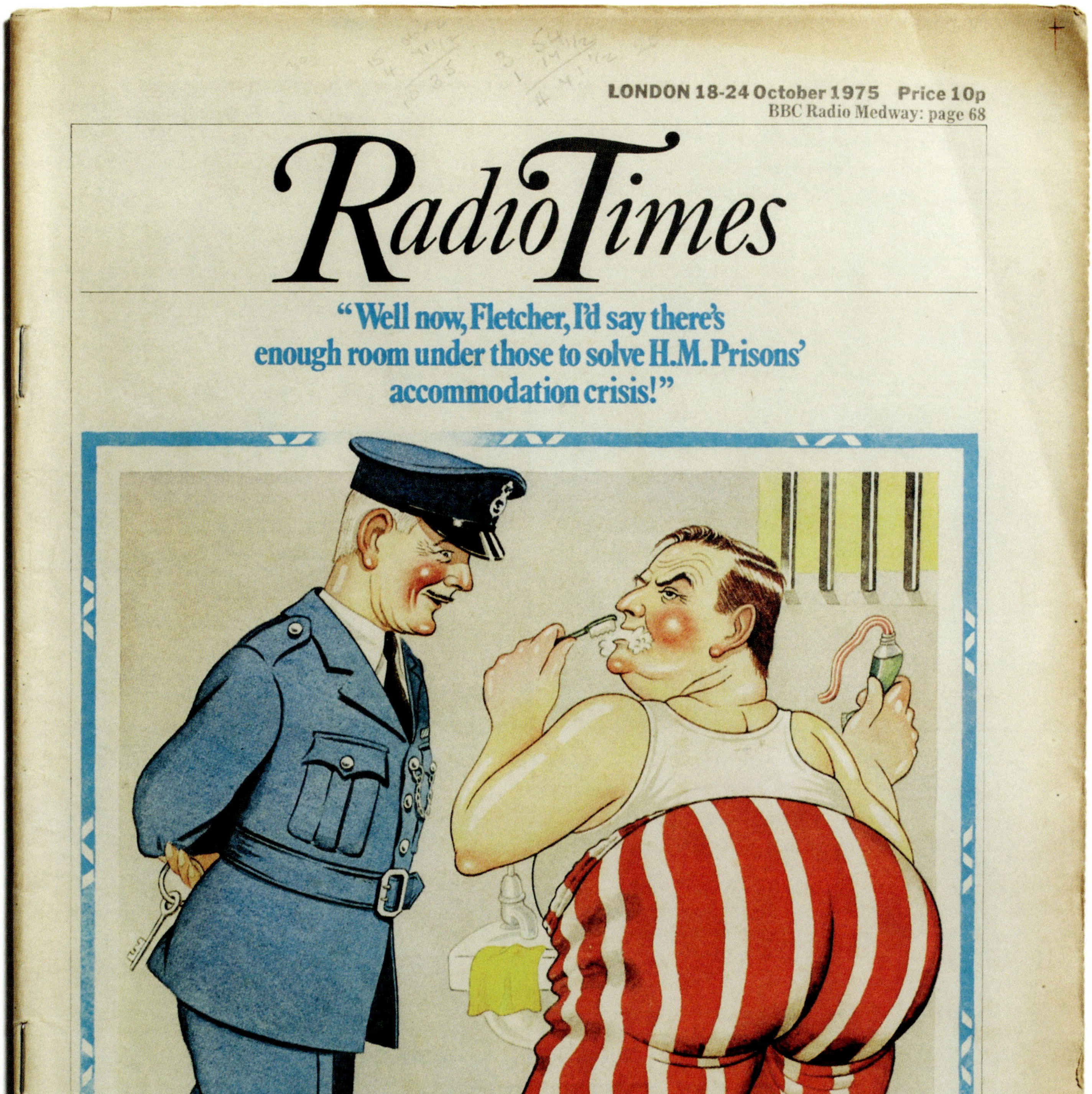

Porridge **Illustration by Peter Brookes** *18–24 October 1975*

Peter Brookes emulated the style of saucy seaside postcards drawn by artist Donald McGill to mark this second series of *Porridge*. But the prison sitcom itself was nothing like that. Ronnie Barker enthused about it but said: "In some ways it's a very claustrophobic part. Even when I'm playing to a studio audience, I sometimes feel that I'm actually in prison."

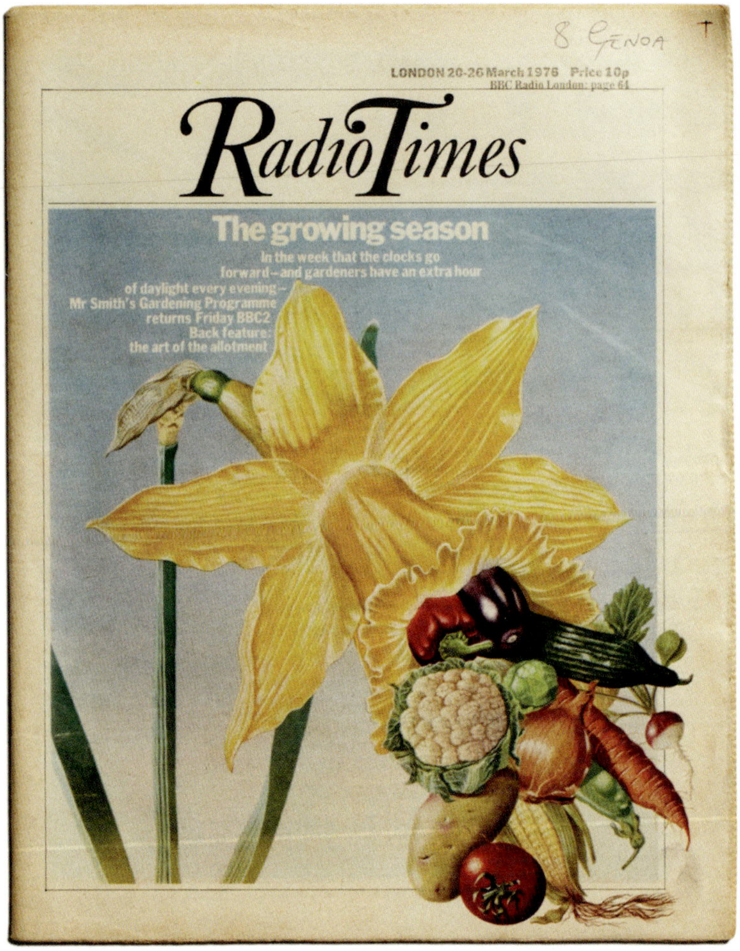

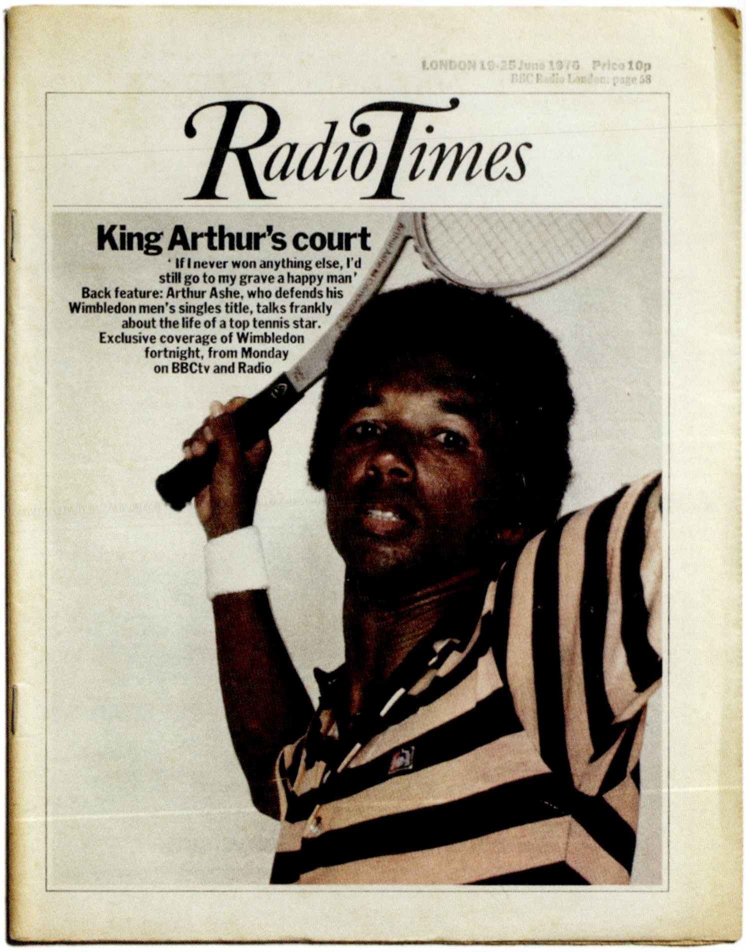

The Queen's Garden *(right)*

(photograph by Dmitri Kasterine)

10–16 July 1976

The Queen's Garden was filmed over the course of a year for BBC1 and *Radio Times* talked to the monarch's head gardener, Fred Nutbeam: "When I first came here in 1954, my idea was to introduce unusual shrubs. They said azaleas wouldn't grow and look at them now. Six to eight feet across, some of them."

Summoned by Bells *(middle right)*

Illustration of John Betjeman by Adrian George

28 August–3 September 1976

Betjeman was 70 and making a TV version of his autobiographical poem *Summoned by Bells*. He visited places he'd not seen for 50 or 60 years, including the road in Highgate in London where he was beaten up by a gang of boys who thought he was German because the original spelling of the family name was Betjemann.

The Duchess of Duke Street *(far right)*

Louisa Leyton (Gemma Jones)

(photograph by John Timbers)

4–10 September 1976

The Duchess of Duke Street was another hugely popular BBC drama. It was based on the real-life story of Rosa Lewis who, with no education and little money, established the upmarket Cavendish hotel in central London.

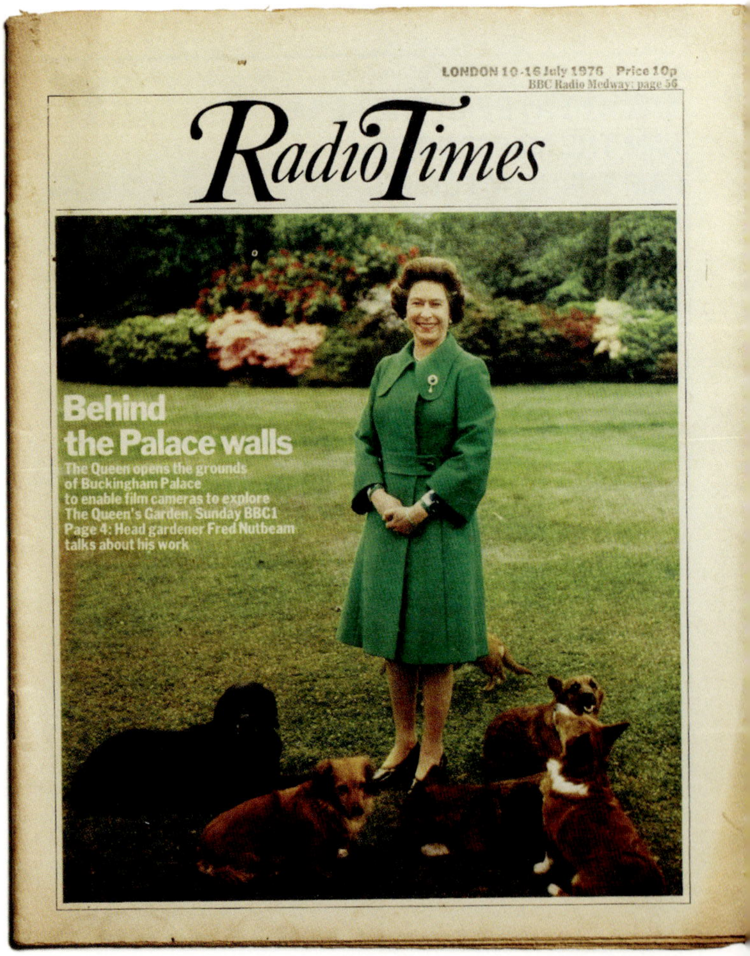

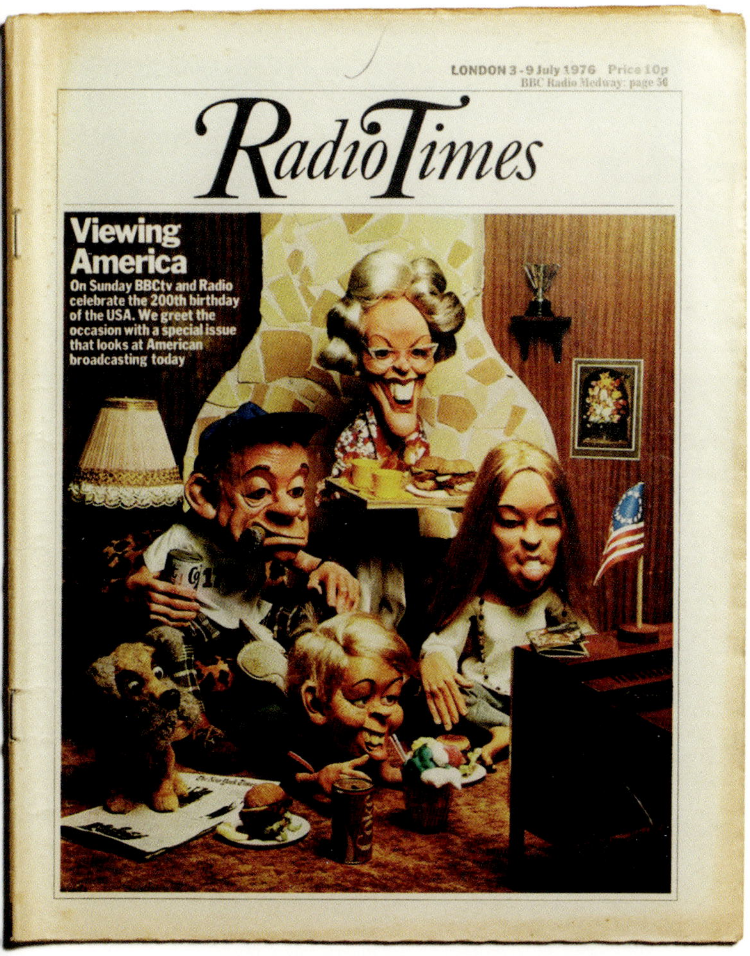

Mr Smith's Vegetable Garden *(far left)*

Illustration by Peter Brookes

20–26 March 1976

The Mr Smith in question was Geoffrey Smith whose mission in this series was to inspire the nation's gardeners to grow more vegetables. Cover artist Peter Brookes went on to take over the magazine's back-page cartoon in 1979.

Wimbledon *(middle left)*

Arthur Ashe *(photograph by Gary Heery)*

19–25 June 1976

American Arthur Ashe had won the men's singles at Wimbledon the previous year – the first black man to do so. But at the age of 33 he had one eye on retirement. "I probably have about another four years left in tennis." Sure enough, he retired in 1980.

Uncle Sam Celebrates *(left)*

Models by Fluck & Law

(photograph by John Lawrence Jones)

3–9 July 1976

Eight years before they created *Spitting Image*, Roger Law and Peter Fluck crafted this model for the US bicentennial celebrations with their brand of affectionate cruelty. Inside, *Radio Times* secured the services of Andy Warhol as a writer. His subject: American game shows.

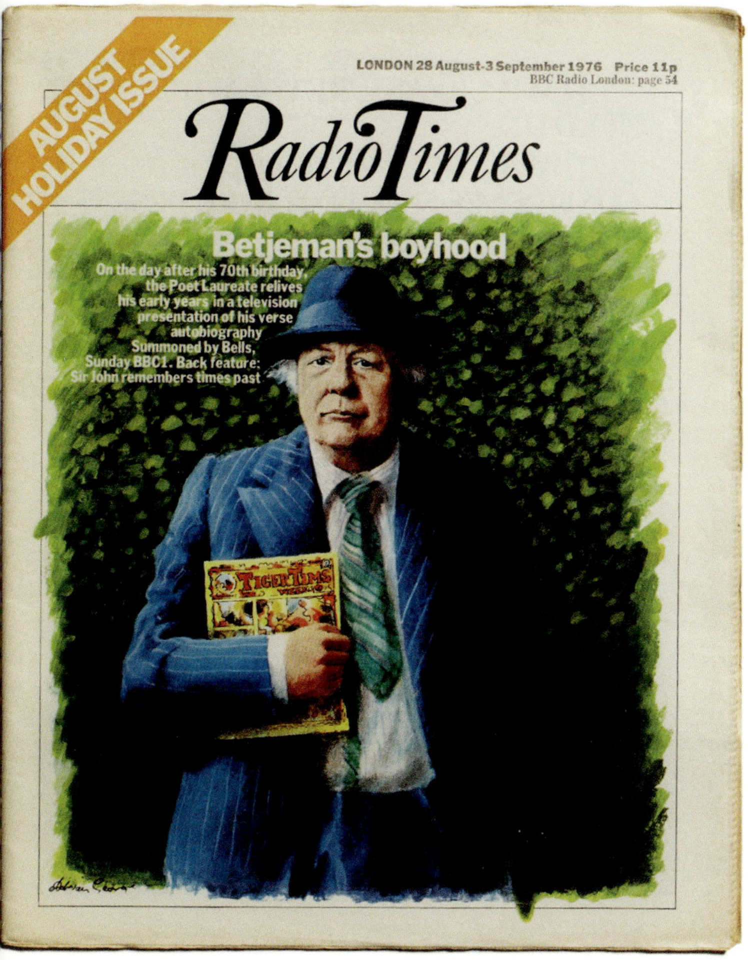

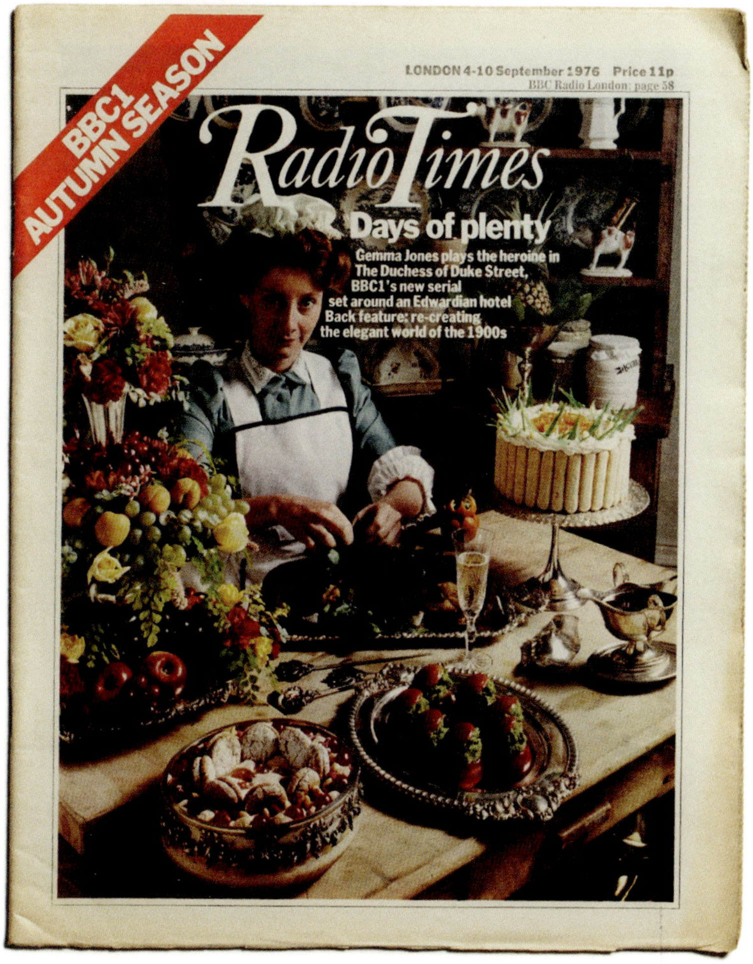

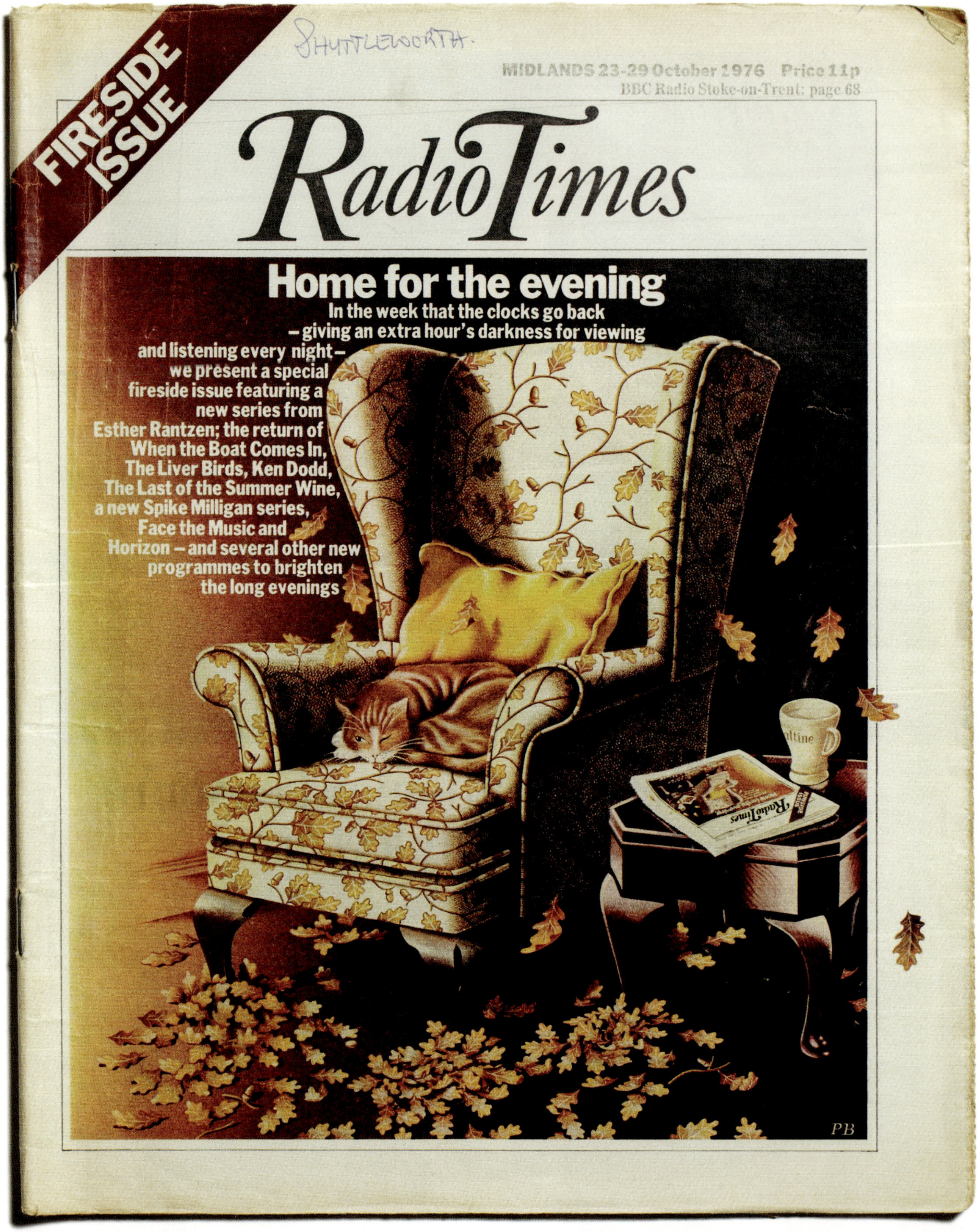

Fireside number **Illustration by Peter Brookes** *23–29 October 1976*

As the country put its clocks back at the start of British winter time, *Radio Times* offered up this tribute to its "fireside numbers" of the 1920s and 30s. The longer nights meant "an extra hour's darkness every evening to sit by your fireside and enjoy the BBC's new series". Among them were the return of *When the Boat Comes In*, *The Liver Birds* and *Last of the Summer Wine*, and new series from Esther Rantzen and Spike Milligan.

The Generation Game *(right)*

Bruce Forsyth and Anthea Redfern *(photograph by David Montgomery)*

11–17 September 1976

Anthea Redfern didn't get a syllable in the feature, which was all about the return of *The Generation Game*. Brucie said: "When people see me perform they think I look like a person who can never relax. But if I sit down, I can turn off the Bruce Forsyth who is the vitamin pill on legs."

Christmas 1976 *(below left)*

Illustration by Peter Brookes

18 December 1976–1 January 1977

This double issue ran for an extra day because of when Christmas fell to accommodate New Year's Day. It was a 15-day festive comedy season with *Porridge*, *Just a Minute*, *Are You Being Served?*, *The Liver Birds*, *It Ain't Half Hot Mum* and, of course, *The Morecambe and Wise Christmas Show*.

The Disappearance of Aimee *(below right)*

Faye Dunaway *(photograph by Patrick Lichfield)*

15–21 January 1977

Faye Dunaway starred with Bette Davis in *The Disappearance of Aimee*: a true-life movie made for American television. *RT* investigated the real tale of evangelist Aimee who vanished mysteriously and reappeared equally mysteriously.

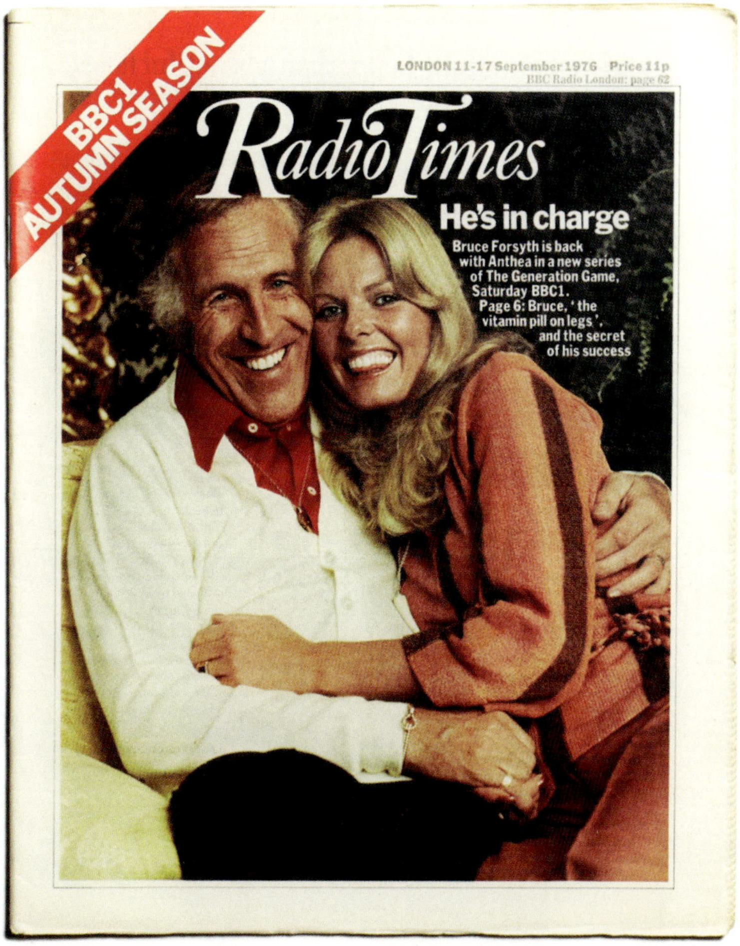

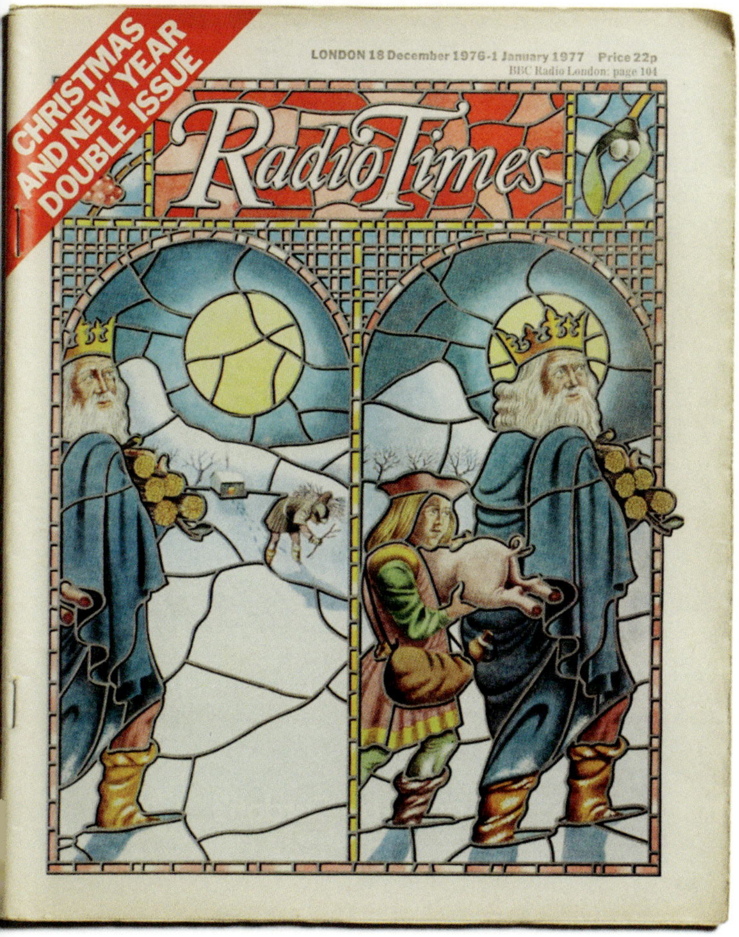

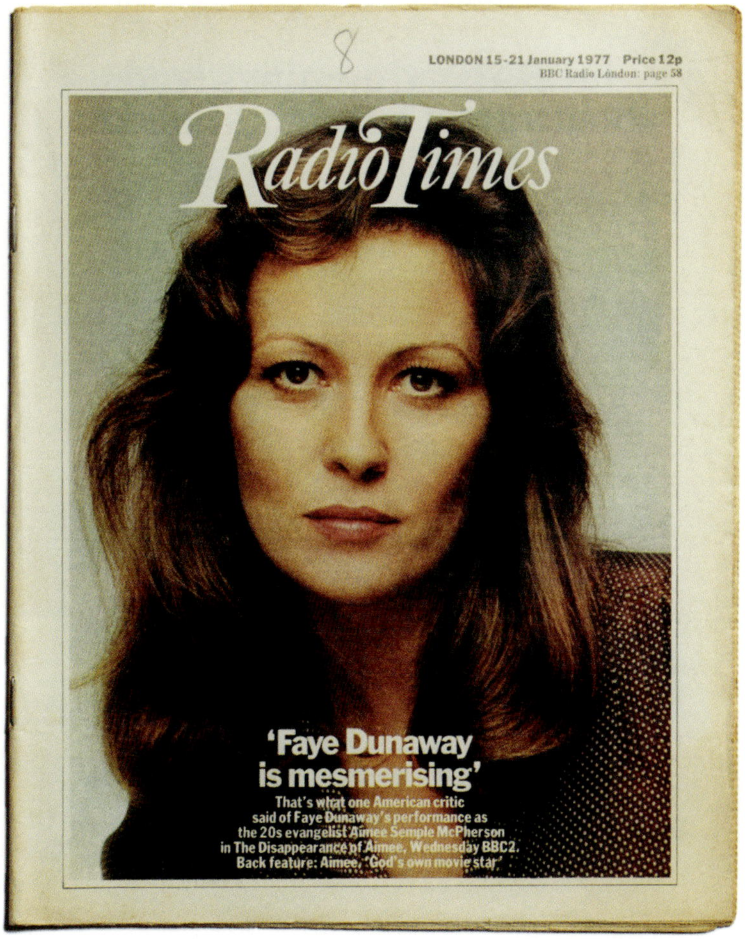

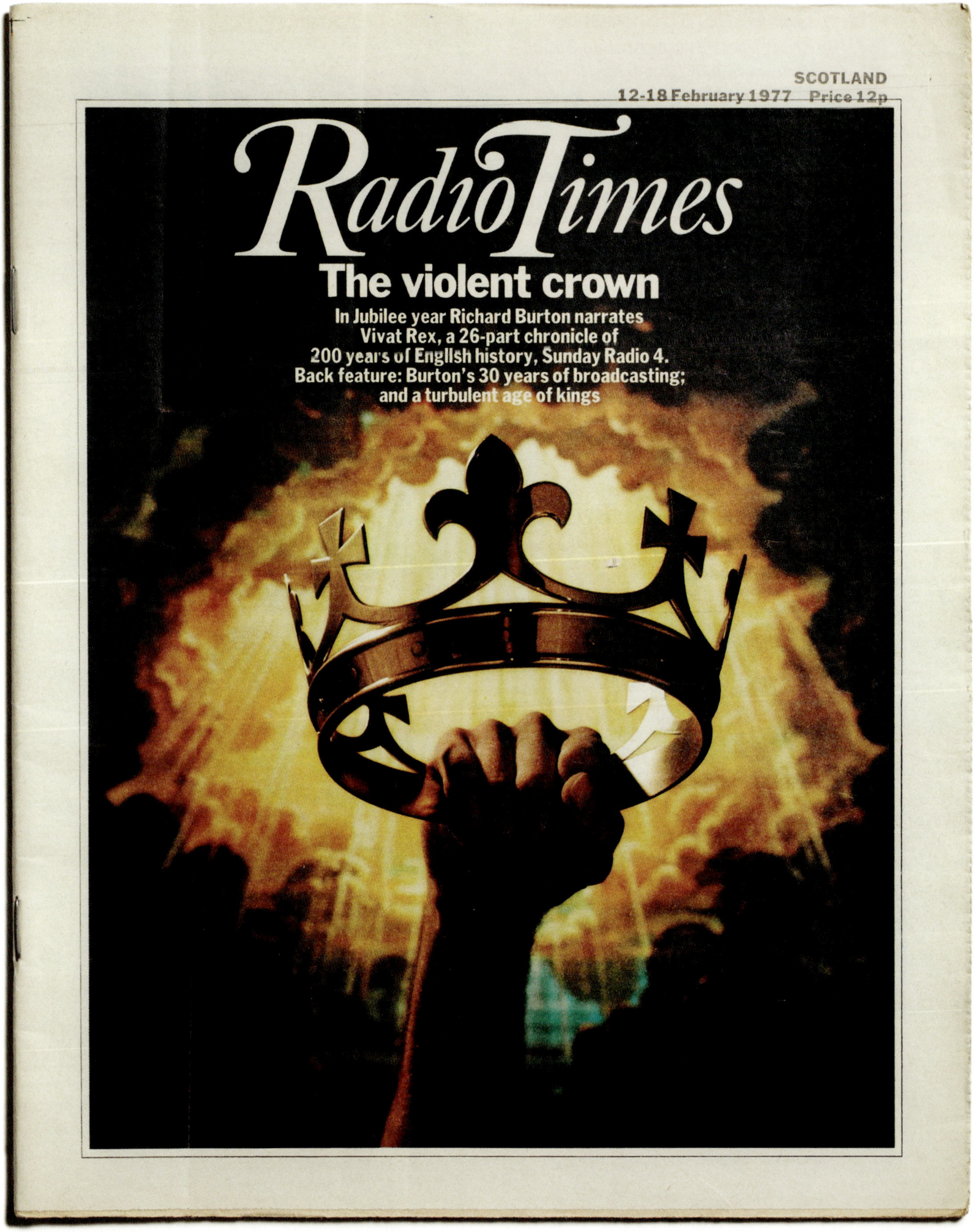

Vivat Rex *(photograph by Tony Evans) 12–18 February 1977*

BBC Radio 4 broadcast *Vivat Rex*, a series of historical plays narrated by Richard Burton, who was returning to radio after 15 years. So why had he returned? "Well, it's nice not to have to learn lines," he said. "But this is home, this is where I started. I used to work here with some of the stars of my childhood. It was glamorous, something of a university. And afterwards we'd go to the ML Club, where you could drink for hours. It was a haven of abandoned filth – you had to take a hot bath afterwards."

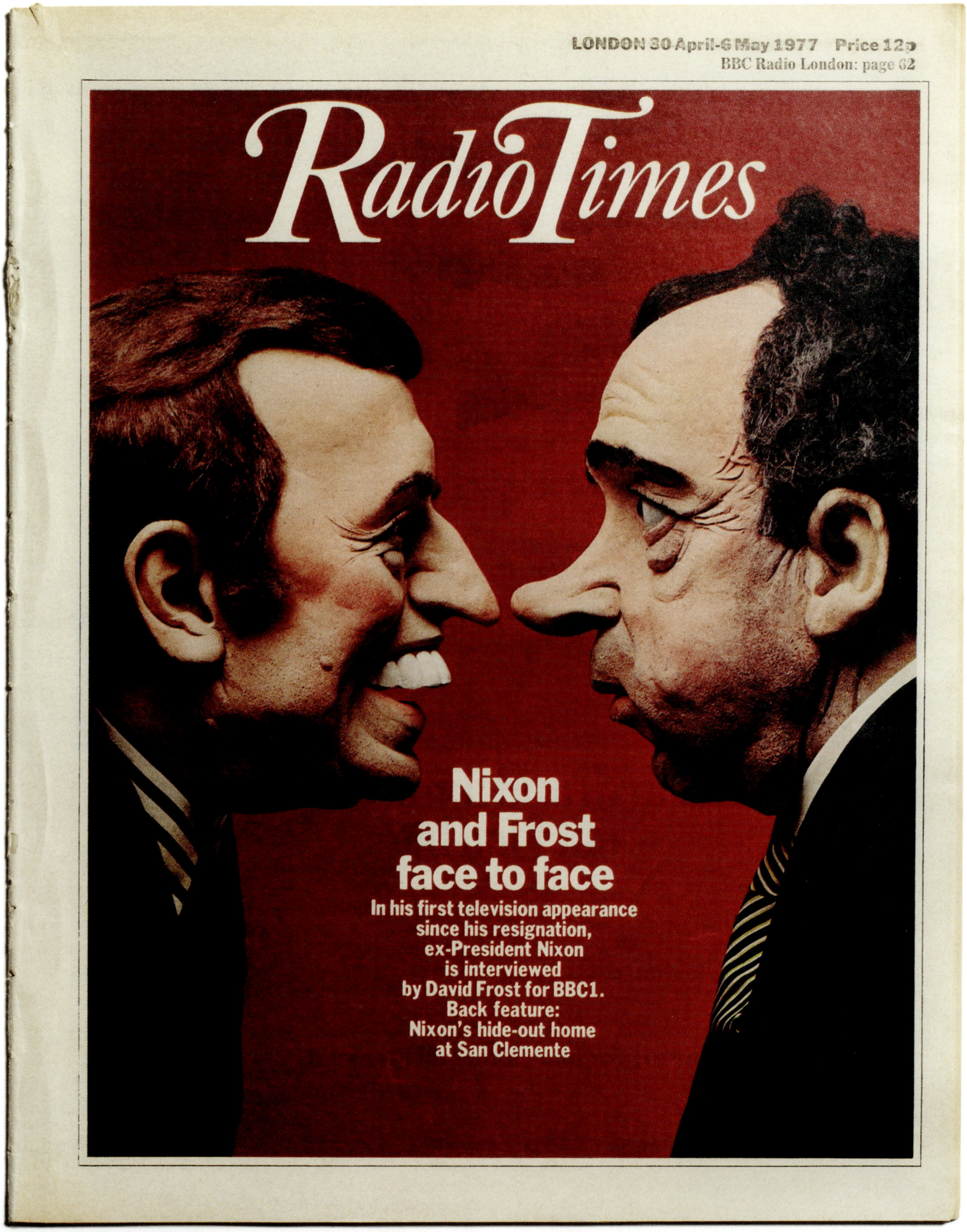

The Nixon Interviews **Models by Fluck & Law**
(photograph by John Lawrence Jones) 30 April–6 May 1977

David Frost had secured the interview everyone else wanted and nobody else could get. This was the first of four encounters between the two and they made compelling viewing. The cover set up the encounter beautifully and, inside, *RT* sent Paul Theroux to California to talk to Nixon's neighbours. "He's like a retired tycoon," one told him. "If you want to see him, you pay."

Having a Baby *(right)*

Illustration by Peter Brookes

19–25 March 1977

Peter Brookes's illustration marks the start of spring with the surreal sight of a sheep knitting a sock from its own wool. *Having a Baby* was a new documentary series all about giving birth, so *Radio Times* spoke to midwives. Sister Mary Noel of Bristol Maternity Hospital wasn't keen on men being present at births: "They ask me about all the equipment... and they faint."

The Eurovision Song Contest *(middle right)*

Angela Rippon ***(photograph by Patrick Lichfield)***

2–8 April 1977

Strike action threatened the Eurovision Song Contest, which was due to be broadcast from Wembley Conference Centre. Undaunted, *Radio Times* devoted four pages to the competition, heavy on technical details and light on quotes from the host Angela Rippon. The contest did go ahead and Lynsey de Paul and Mike Moran came ninth for Britain with *Rock Bottom*.

Jubilation! *(far right)*

Illustration by Nicola Griffin (age 5)

28 May–3 June 1977

Five-year-old Nicola Griffin was the artist who won *Blue Peter's* competition to design a cover for *Radio Times* to mark the Queen's Silver Jubilee. She is without question the youngest person to create a cover for the magazine.

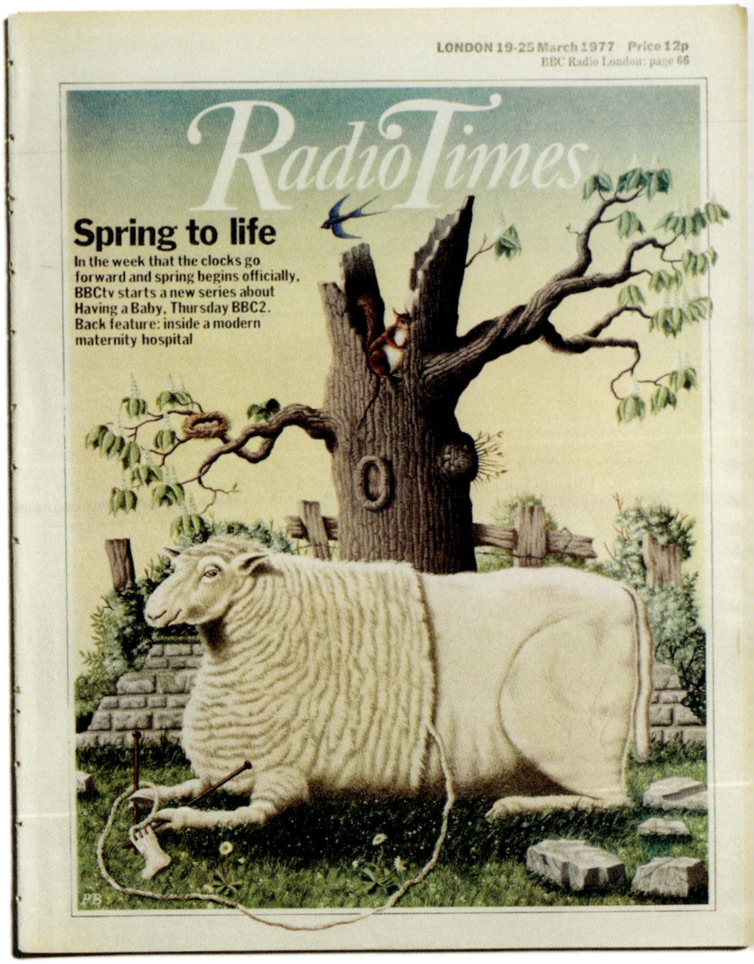

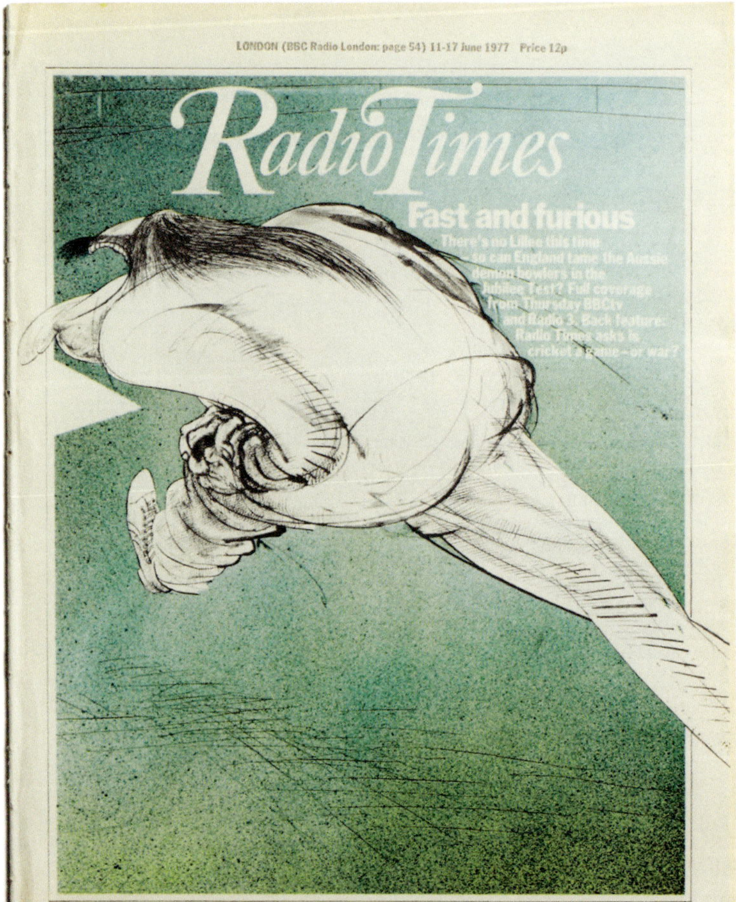

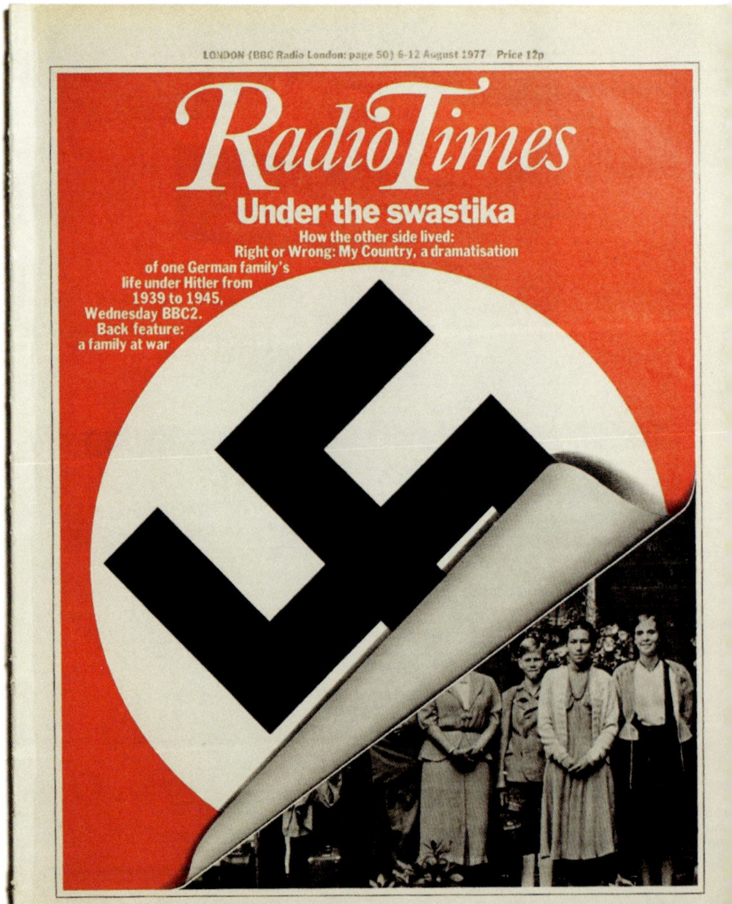

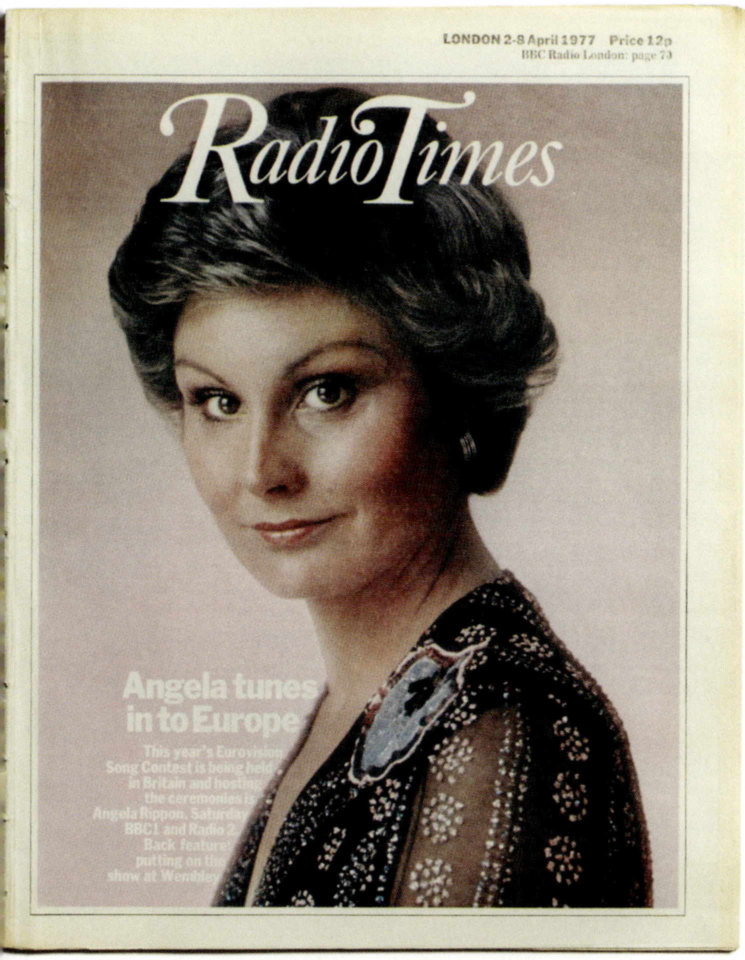

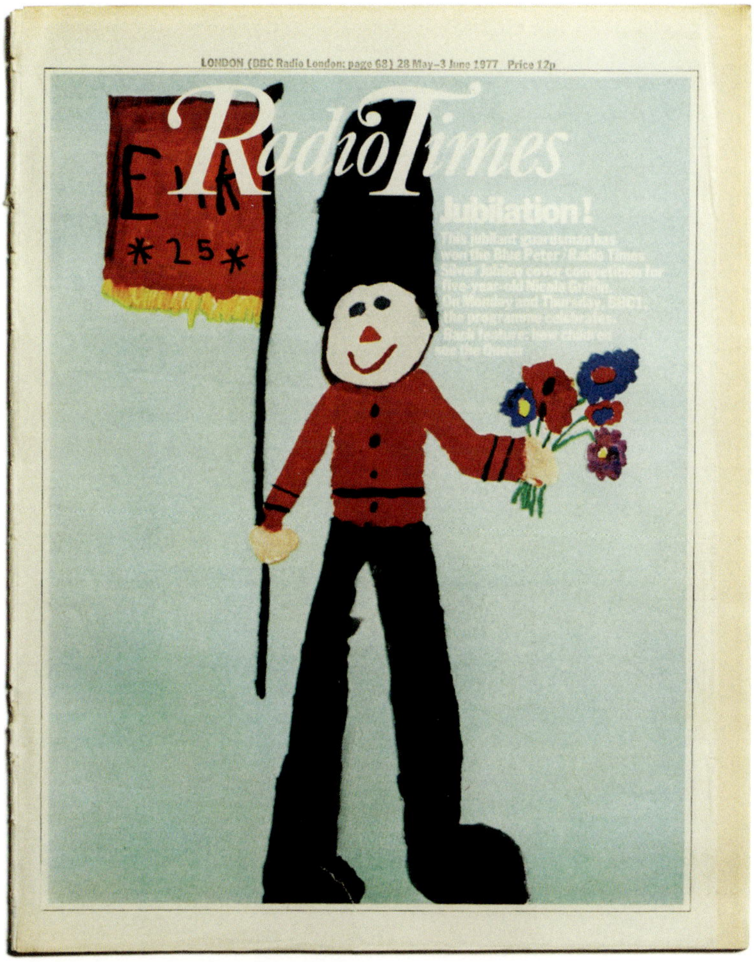

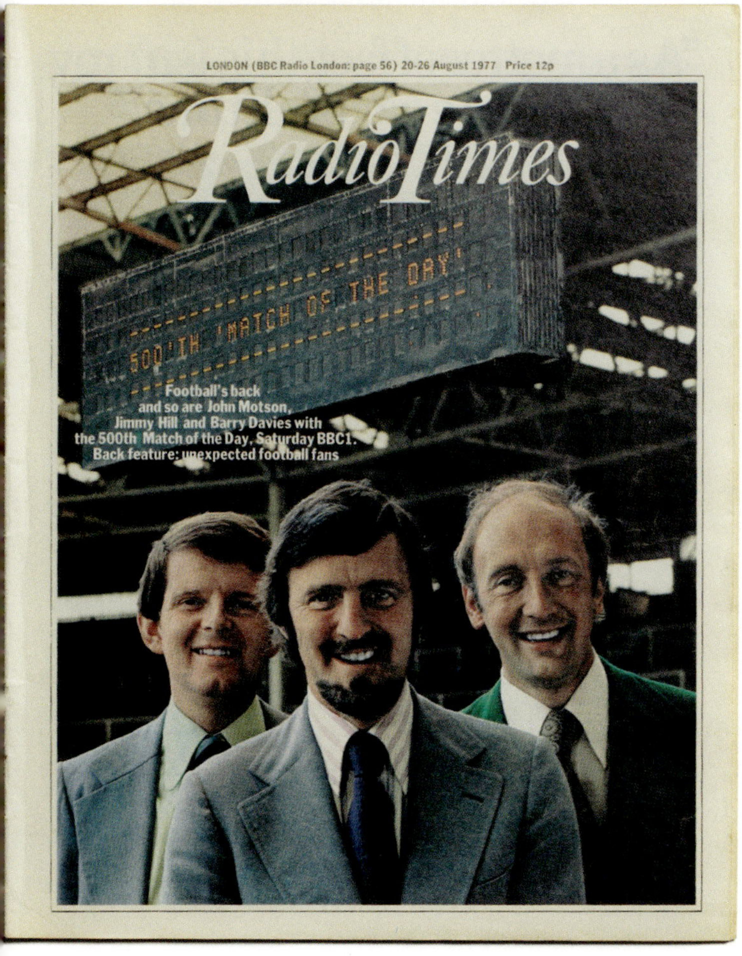

The Jubilee Test *(far left)*

Illustration of Dennis Lillee by Ralph Steadman

11–17 June 1977

Radio Times sent artist and illustrator Ralph Steadman to Melbourne to capture the likenesses of Australian cricketers Dennis Lillee, Rodney Marsh and Greg Chappell during the Centenary Test against England. Three months later they were once more in action against England in the Jubilee Test at Lord's. The match ended in a draw.

Right or Wrong: My Country *(middle left)*

6–12 August 1977

The dramatisation of the autobiographical novel by Walter Kempowski told the story of the Second World War through the eyes of a young German boy. "One question will always torment me," he told *Radio Times*. "Why should my father volunteer to fight for the Nazis, whom he couldn't stand?"

Match of the Day *(left)*

John Motson, Jimmy Hill and Barry Davies

(photograph by John Timbers)

20–26 August 1977

As *Match of the Day* celebrated its 500th edition, *Radio Times* talked to some "unexpected" football fans, among them philosopher Alfred (Freddie) Ayer who refuted the theory that football doesn't mix with brains: "One exaggerates the difference between ordinary people and intellectuals."

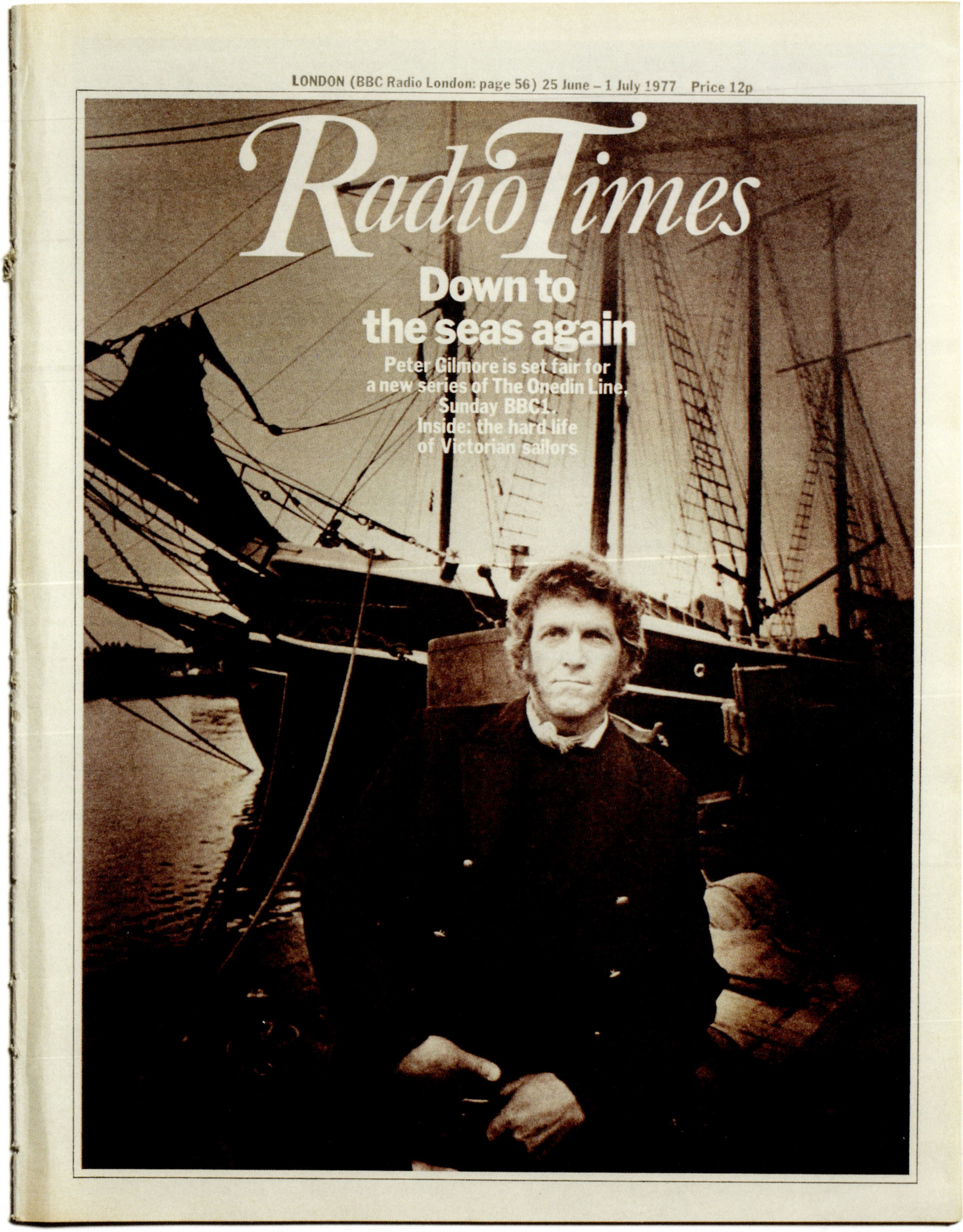

The Onedin Line **James Onedin (Peter Gilmore)** *(photograph by Phil Sayer)* *25 June–1 July 1977*

For series five of the seafaring drama *Radio Times* went for a sepia tint on the cover. *The Onedin Line* wasn't the only period drama in the schedules that week – on Friday BBC2 began a repeat run of *I, Claudius*, which had first been shown the previous year. Derek Jacobi revealed that Robert Graves had visited the set one day to watch the drama being recorded and later sent a telegram to the cast that said, "Claudius would have been very pleased."

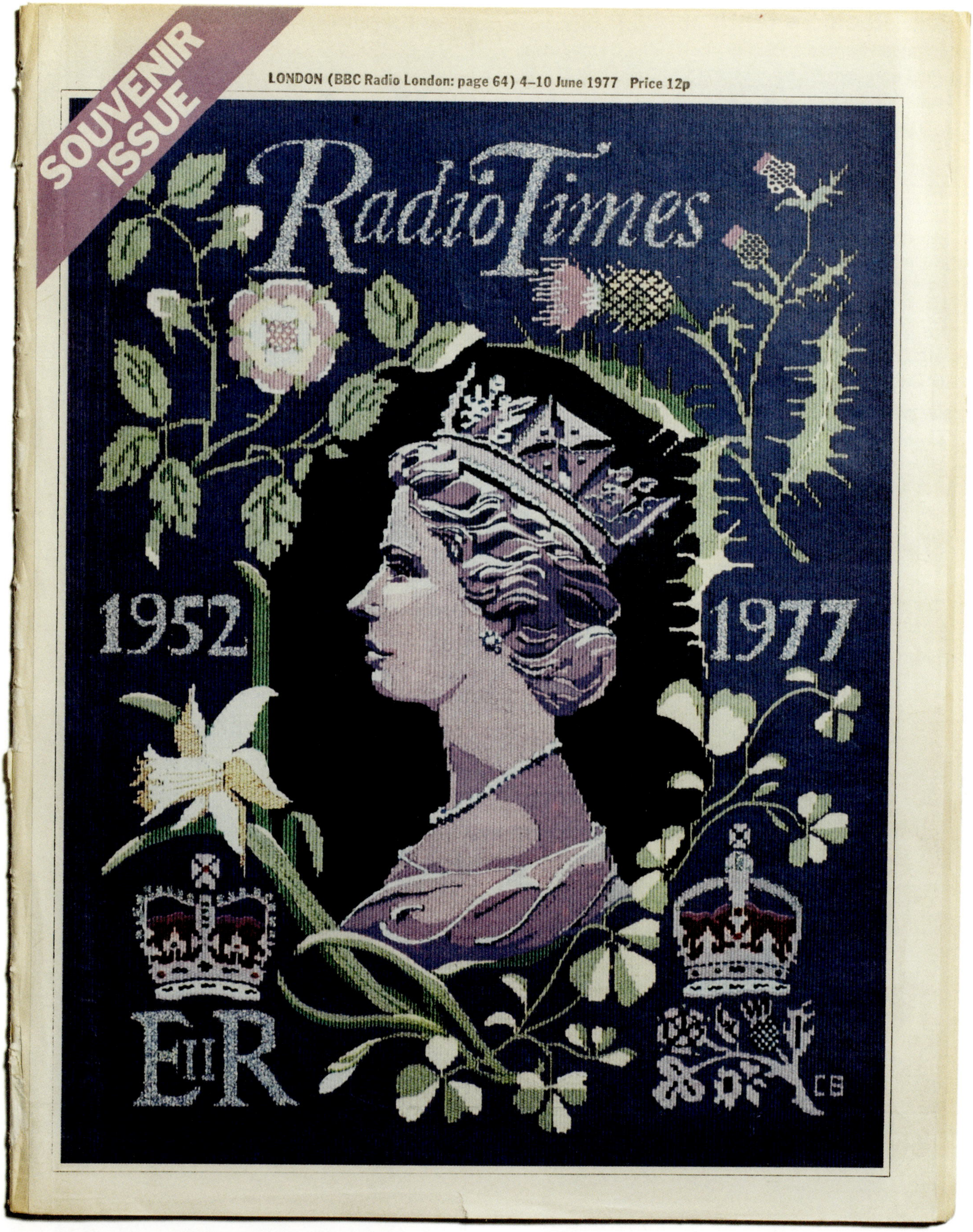

The Queen's Silver Jubilee

Tapestry by Candace Bahouth *4–10 June 1977*

Rather than mark the occasion with an illustration or a photograph, *Radio Times* art editor David Driver commissioned a tapestry from Candace Bahouth. But the magazine's illustrators hadn't been forgotten. Inside, five famous artists – Eric Fraser, Victor Reinganum, Robin Jacques, Peter Brookes and Nigel Holmes – were asked to create a new work of art.

Radio 1's tenth anniversary *(right)*

Back row **David Hamilton, Paul Burnett, Paul Gambaccini, John Peel and Tom Browne** *Middle row* **Dave Lee Travis, Annie Nightingale, Noel Edmonds and David Jensen** *Front row* **Alan Freeman, Ed Stewart, Tony Blackburn and the now disgraced Jimmy Savile** *(photograph by David Montgomery)*

1–7 October 1977

Tony Blackburn showed Radio 1 had its finger on the country's musical pulse. "Everyone's talking about punk rock. That will probably last two weeks and then be replaced by something else."

It Ain't Half Hot Mum *(below left)*

From left: Bdr Beaumont (Melvyn Hayes), BSM Williams (Windsor Davies) and Gunner "Lofty" Sugden (Don Estelle) *(photograph by Patrick Lichfield)* *22–28 October 1977*

Co-writer Jimmy Perry explained how the hit comedy was all true – the stories were based on his experiences in a Royal Artillery Concert Party in India 30 years before.

The Week Before Christmas *(below right)*

Illustration by Robin Jacques

17–23 December 1977

It was the week before Christmas, and *Radio Times* asked regular illustrator Robin Jacques to create a food-related cover.

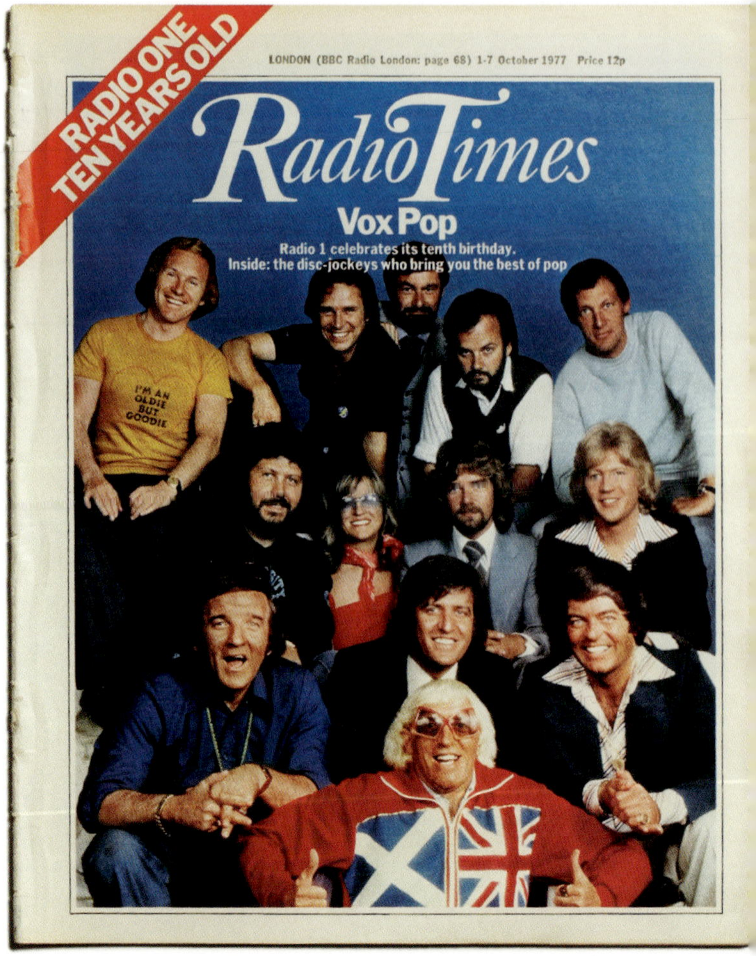

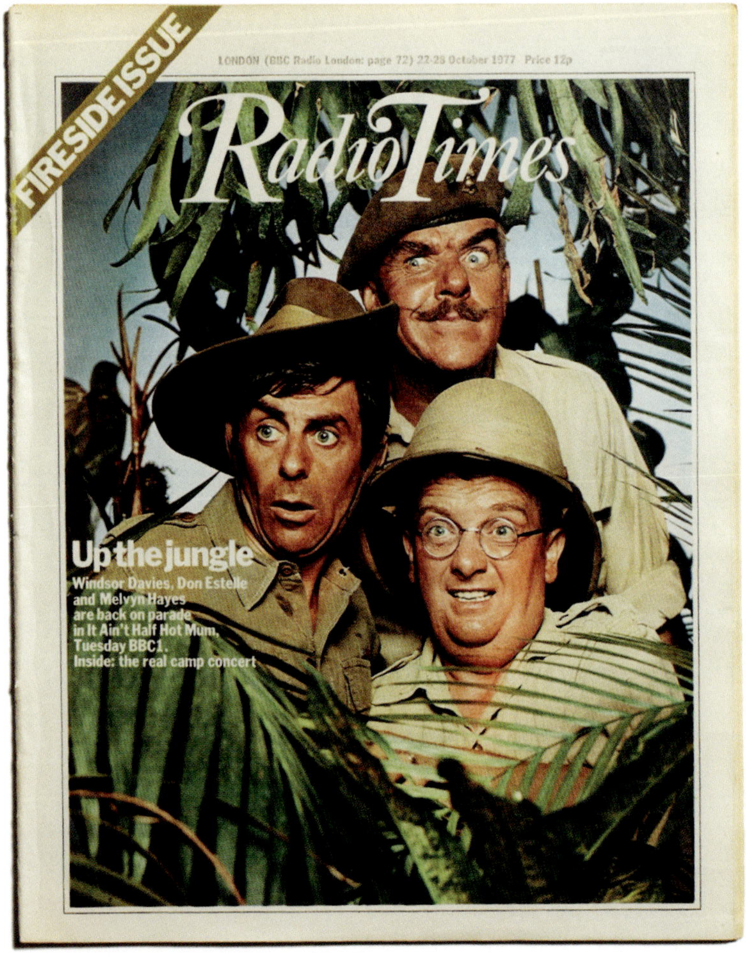

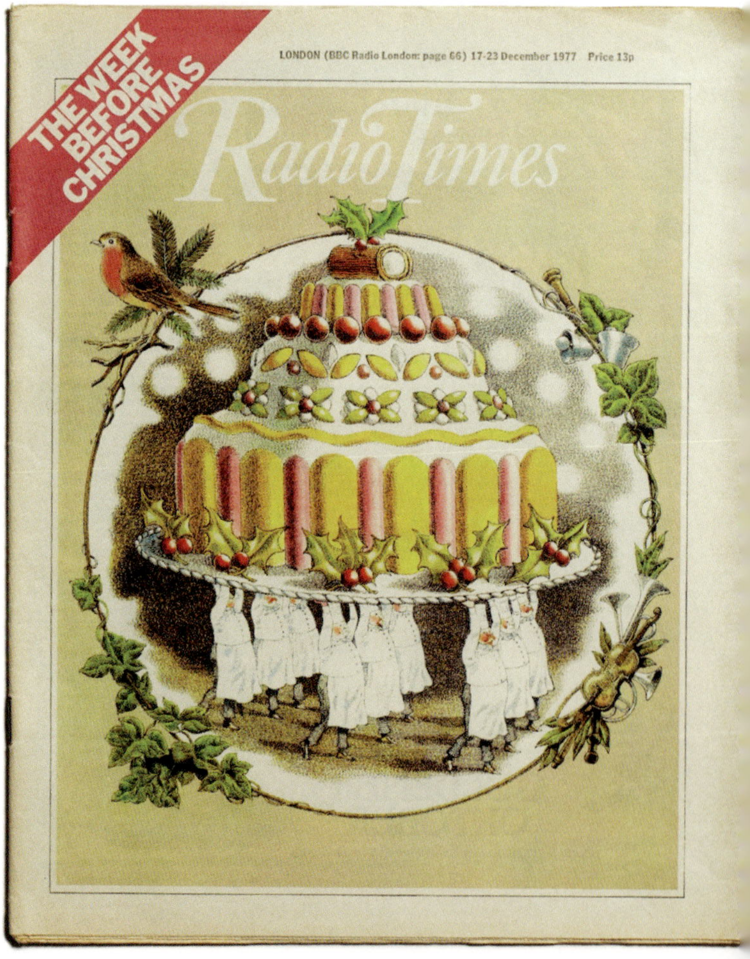

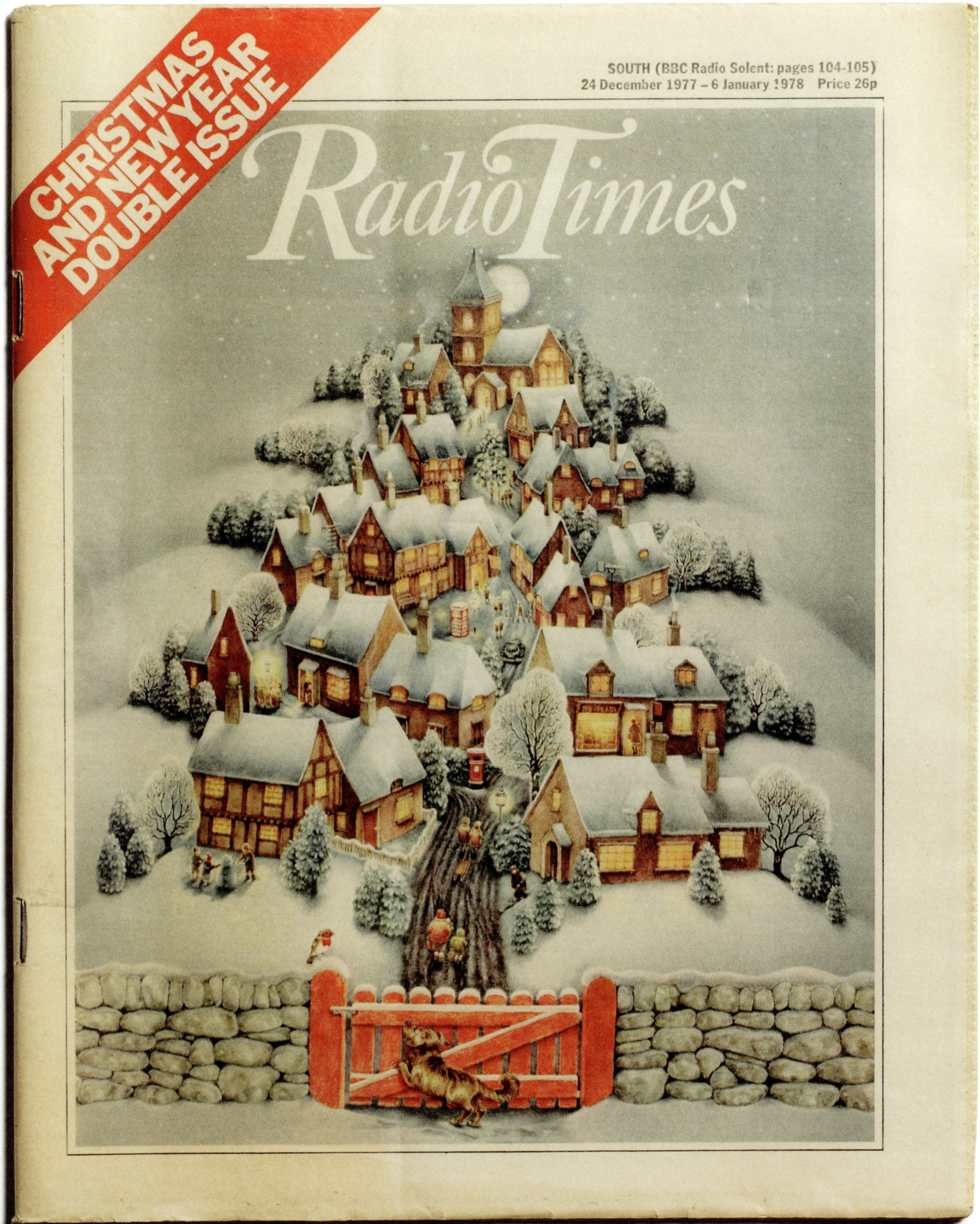

Christmas 1978 **Illustration by Pauline Ellison** *24 December 1977–6 January 1978*

From a distance, the cover looks like a Christmas tree; closer up, it's a small village. But keep looking. Ellison packs in a huge amount of delicious detail such as a phone box, a post box, shops, at least one snowman, more than 20 people, a robin and a dog. But, strangely, not many television aerials.

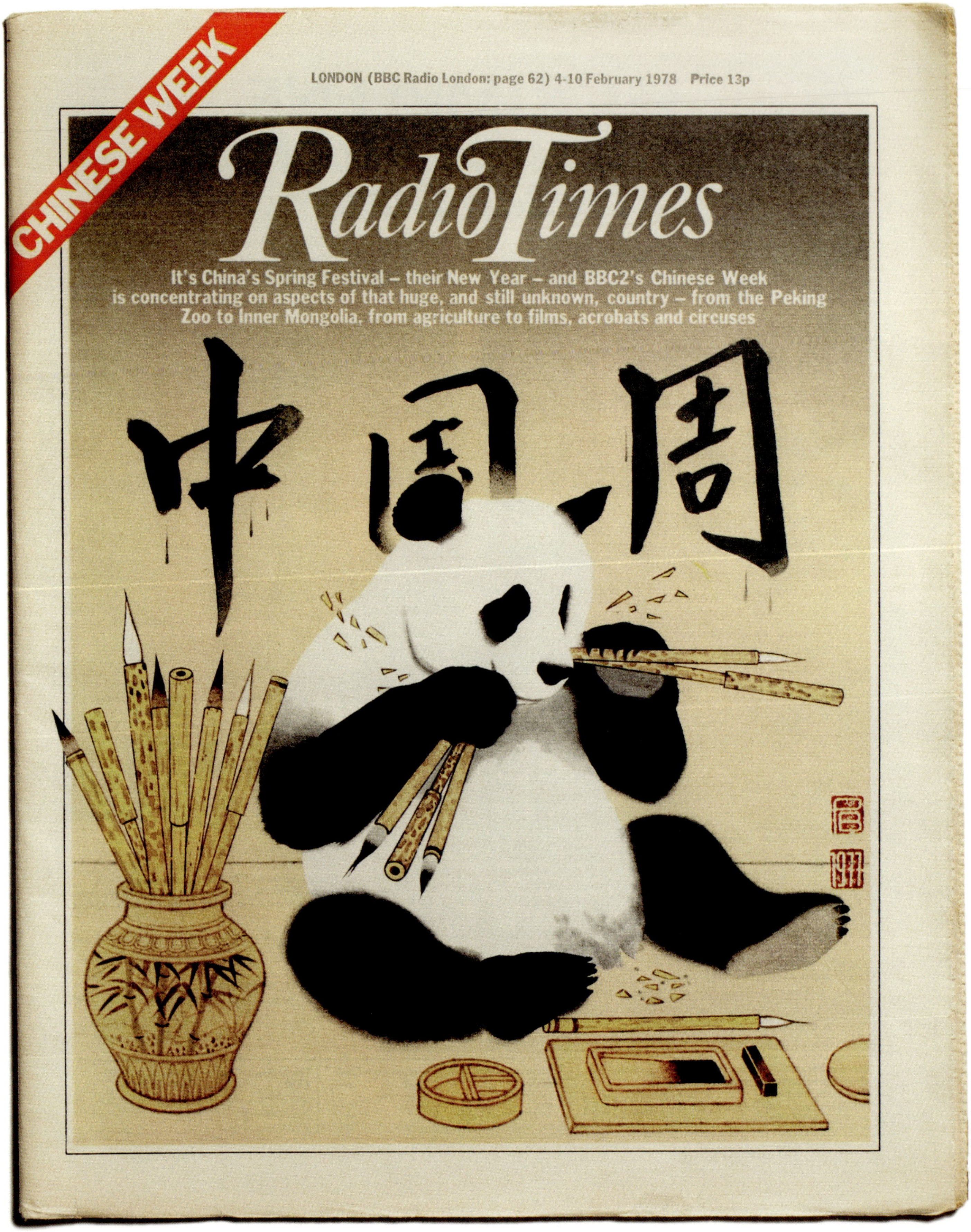

Chinese Week **Illustration by Peter Brookes** *4–10 February 1978*

BBC2 devoted a week of programmes to China and its people. The season opener was *Joris Ivens' China*, a film by the celebrated documentary-maker who was also a friend of Chairman Mao. It took the Dutch director 18 months to shoot and another 18 months to edit. More prosaically, as the World Professional Darts Championship began in Nottingham there were five pages devoted to darts – its origins, the equipment and its star players – courtesy of Sid Waddell.

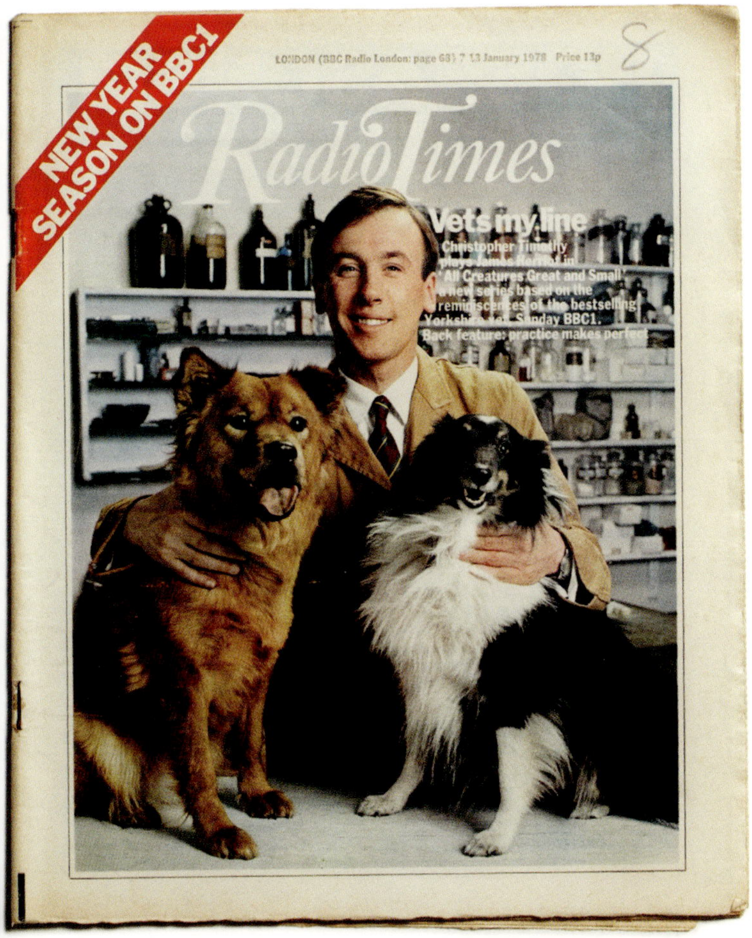

All Creatures Great and Small *(left)*

James Herriot (Christopher Timothy)
(photograph by Dmitri Kasterine)

7–13 January 1978

The TV series was a huge hit, but Alf Wright, the real James Herriot, said his books were treated badly by critics: "They say it's all rather lightweight stuff, not too taxing on the intellect. I agree with them, actually."

Pennies from Heaven *(below left)*

Arthur Parker (Bob Hoskins)
Illustration by Dan Fern *(photograph by John Timbers)*

4–10 March 1978

Dennis Potter introduced his masterpiece with these words: "*Pennies from Heaven* is a sextet with music which follows the misadventures of Arthur Parker, a commercial traveller with a song in his heart and a lie on his lips..."

Mr Smith Propagates Plants *(below right)*

(photograph by Tony Evans)

18–24 March 1978

Geoffrey Smith returned to BBC2 with a series all about raising plants from seed. "It is a fortunate man who can sit in the shadow of a tree which started as a seed under his care," he said. "But then, how often does a gardener have time to sit?"

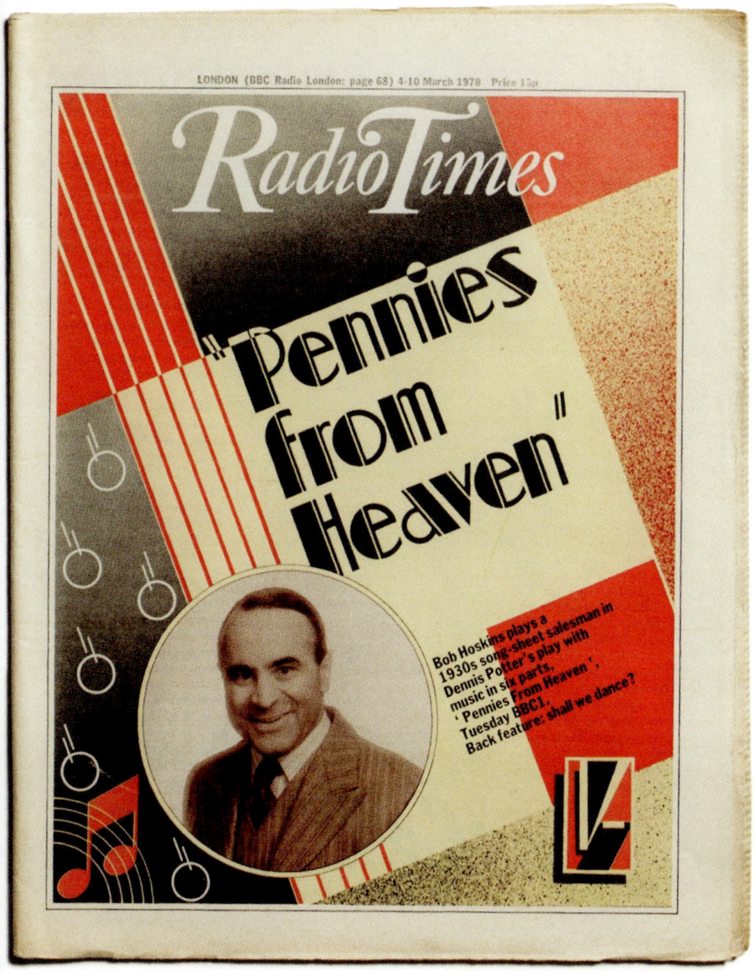

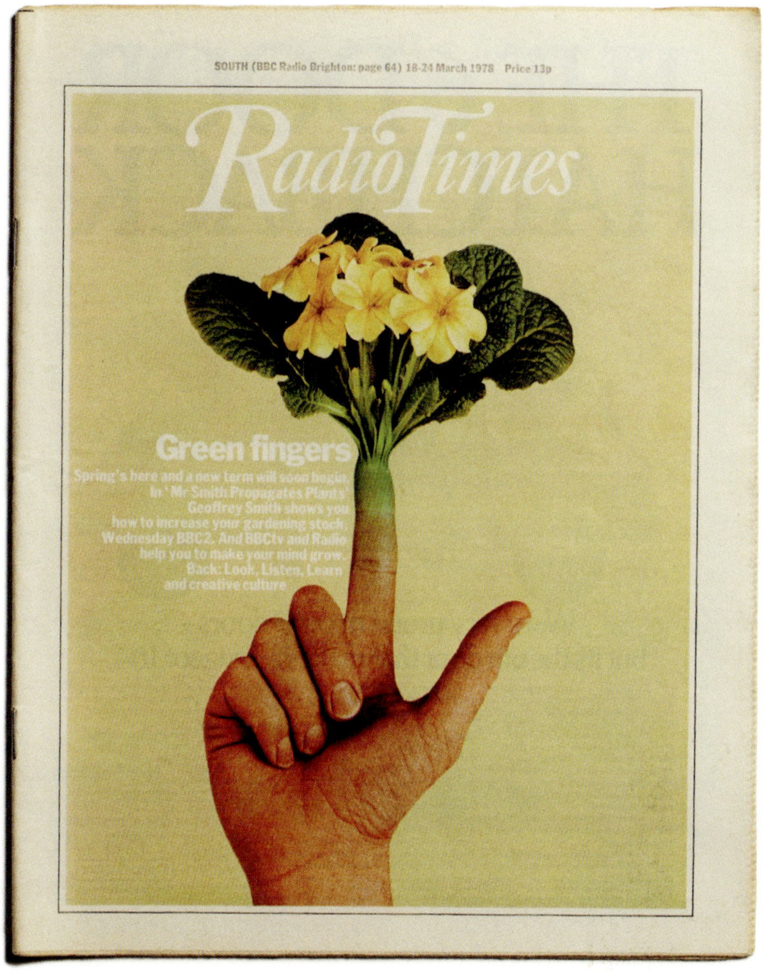

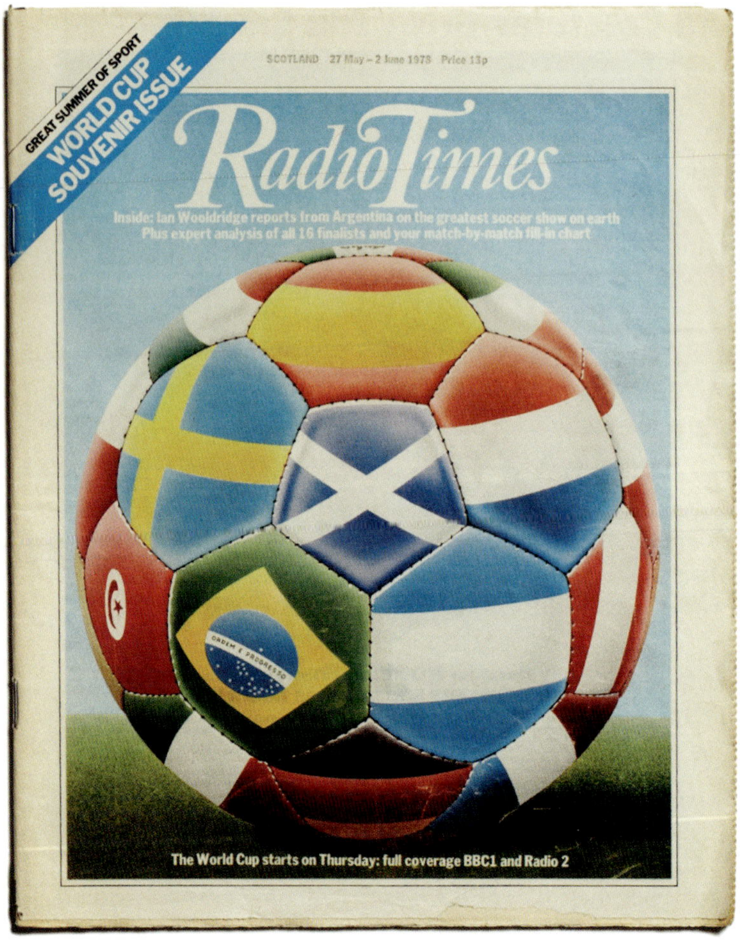

Horizon – On a Different Track *(right)*

Illustration by Adrian George

12–18 August 1978

The documentary series *Horizon* took a long, relaxed and envious look at rail journeys across France. The accompanying feature (also illustrated by Adrian George's evocative drawings) noted that "French railways are going places and in a rather different way from British Rail's".

The Fall and Rise of Reginald Perrin *(middle right)*

Leonard Rossiter ***(photograph by John Timbers)***

25 November–1 December 1978

The old-style black-and-white cover was down to a series of disputes with print unions. The return of Leonard Rossiter's sitcom prompted *Radio Times* to seek out real-life Reggie Perrins. They found Anthony Pugh, who had earned £15,000 a year in advertising and who was now happy to do "nothing".

Sports Review of 1978 *(far right)*

From left: Ian Botham, Sharron Davies and Daley Thompson ***(photograph by Tony Duffy)***

9–15 December 1978

Botham, Davies and Thompson were offered up as likely winners of the 25th Sports Personality of the Year contest. The eventual winner – Steve Ovett – was nowhere to be seen.

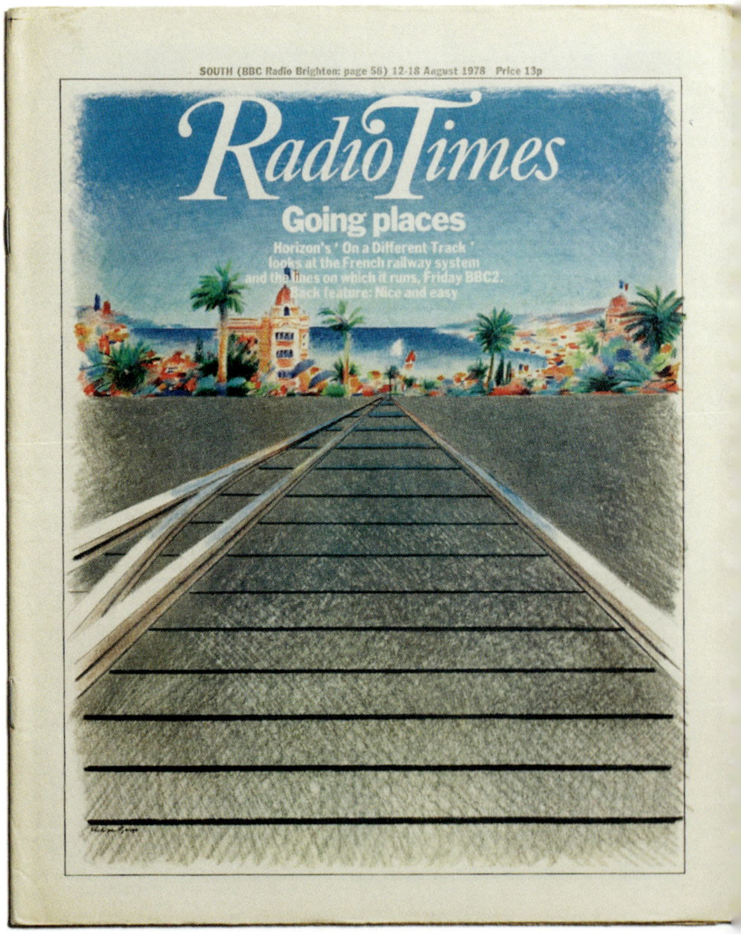

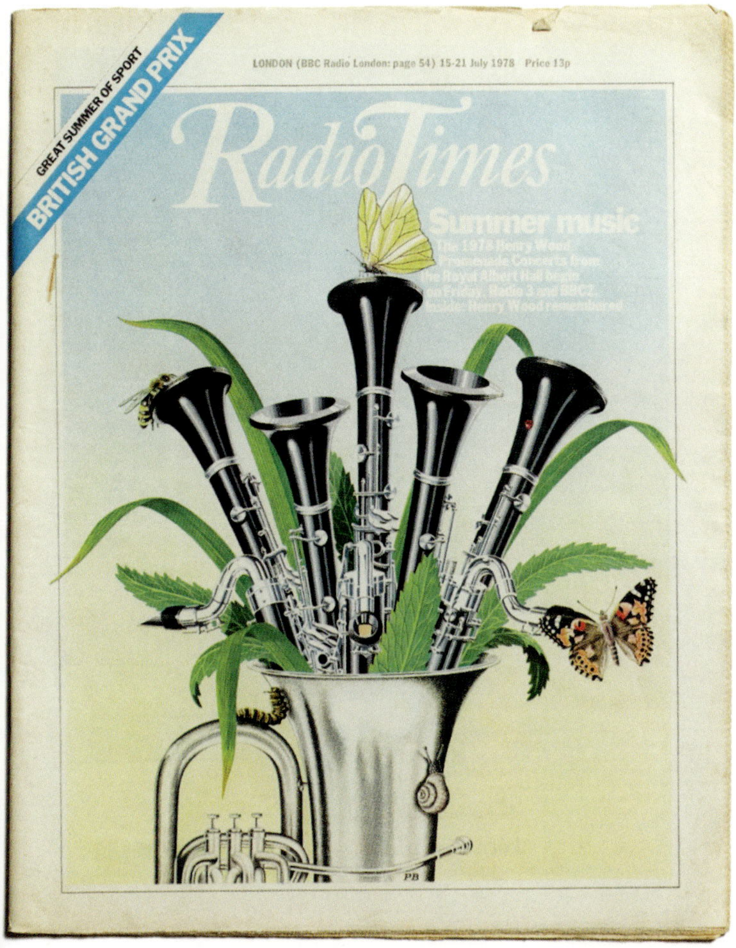

The 1978 World Cup *(far left)*

Illustration by Richard Draper and John Dower

27 May–2 June 1978

Six pages were devoted to previews and analysis, but there was also a sceptical note: Ian Wooldridge was sent to Argentina to discover how a country in the grip of raging inflation could pay 940,800,000,000 pesos (£700 million) to stage the tournament.

The Good Life *(middle left)*

Clockwise from top left: Barbara (Felicity Kendal), Tom (Richard Briers), Jerry (Paul Eddington) and Margo (Penelope Keith) *(photograph by John Timbers)*

10–16 June 1978

The cast of the hit sitcom were reunited for one last episode, which was filmed in front of the Queen. Creators Bob Larbey and John Esmonde promised there would be "no references to corgis, horses or allotments at the Palace".

Summer music *(left)*

Illustration by Peter Brookes

15–21 July 1978

The cover marked the start of 84th season of the Henry Wood Promenade Concerts, the Proms, and *Radio Times* spoke to people who remembered Wood. "He conducted the first notes of Schoenberg heard in this country, in 1912," said one, "and got hissed for it!"

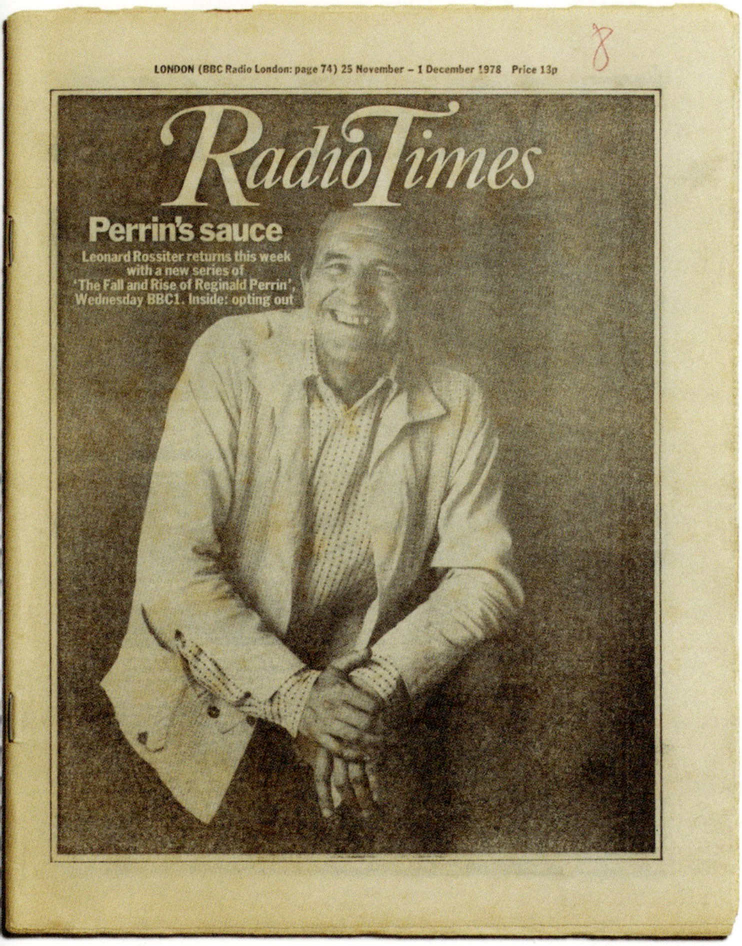

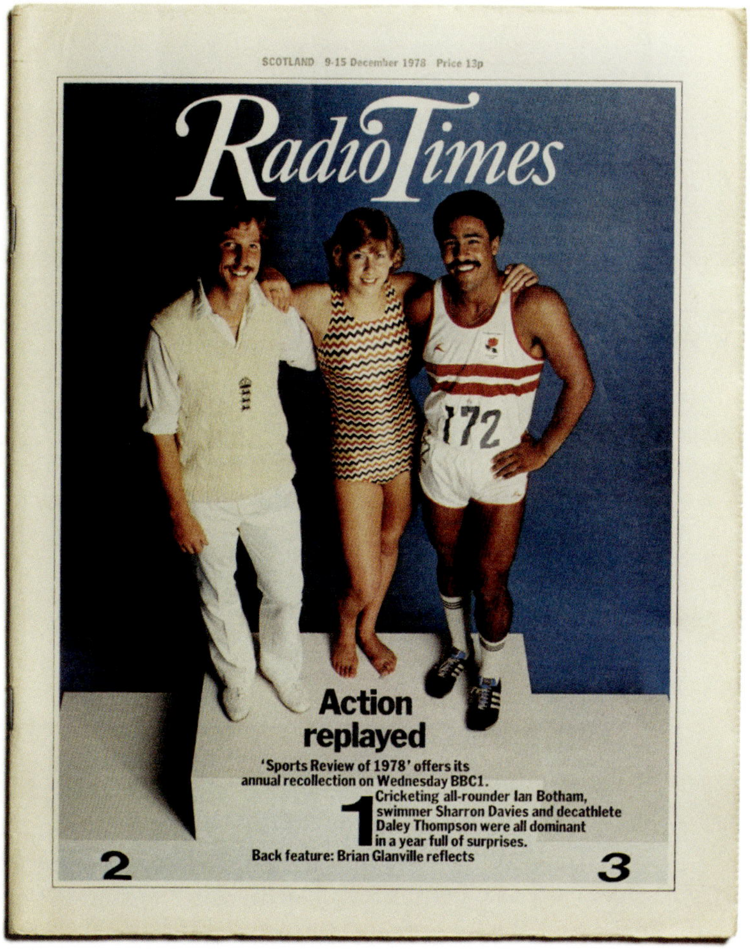

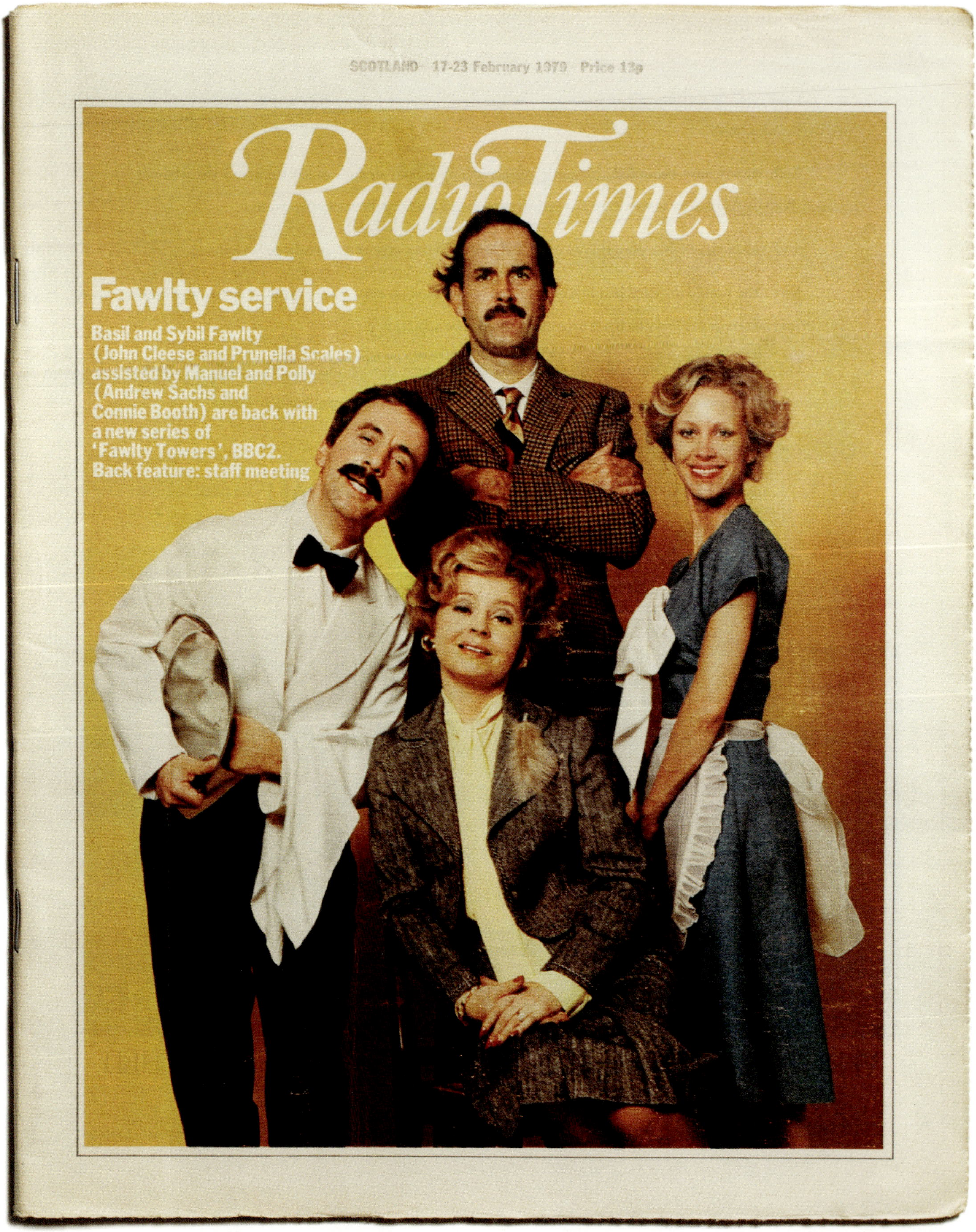

Fawlty Towers **Clockwise from left: Manuel (Andrew Sachs), Basil (John Cleese), Polly (Connie Booth) and Sybil (Prunella Scales)** *(photograph by Brian Moody)* *17–23 February 1979*

Four years after its first series, John Cleese and Connie Booth's sitcom returned for a second and final run. "Connie and I work very slowly," Cleese explained. "We started the dialogue for this series in October 1976 but there have been a lot of interruptions." One interruption was particularly key: "Connie and I split up and that slowed things."

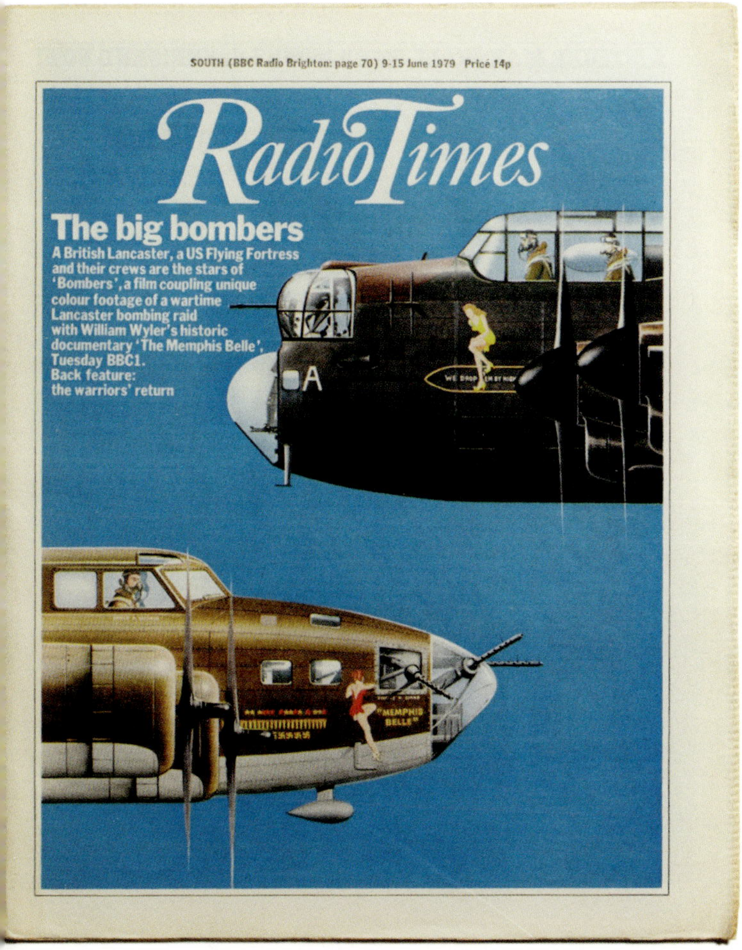

Bombers *(left)*

Illustration by Peter Endsleigh Castle

9–15 June 1979

A USAF B17 bomber, the *Memphis Belle*, and an RAF Lancaster, *V Victor*, were brought together on the cover for a documentary series *Bombers* that investigated what wartime bomber raids were really like for the young men who flew on them.

Wimbledon *(below left)*

John McEnroe *(photograph by Tony Duffy)*

23–29 June 1979

Paul Theroux interviewed the bad boy of tennis, who revealed his insecurity. "I play Bjorn Borg and the crowd goes bananas for him. Why? Because he doesn't change his expression? I want them on my side, but I don't know how to do it."

The Hollywood Greats *(below right)*

Illustration of Barry Norman by Mick Brownfield

28 July–3 August 1979

In his new series Barry Norman, who became *Radio Times's* film expert in the 1980s, profiled great Hollywood actors, starting with Edward G Robinson. The problem with any profile of Tinseltown's main players, he wrote, was "trying to sort out the probable truth from the possible truth".

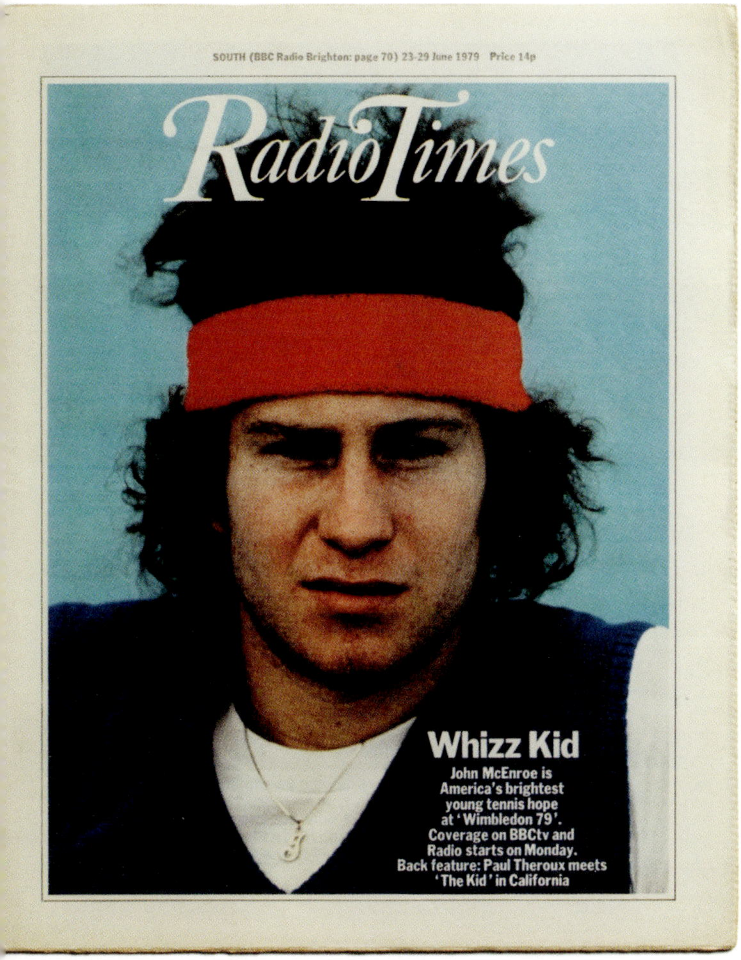

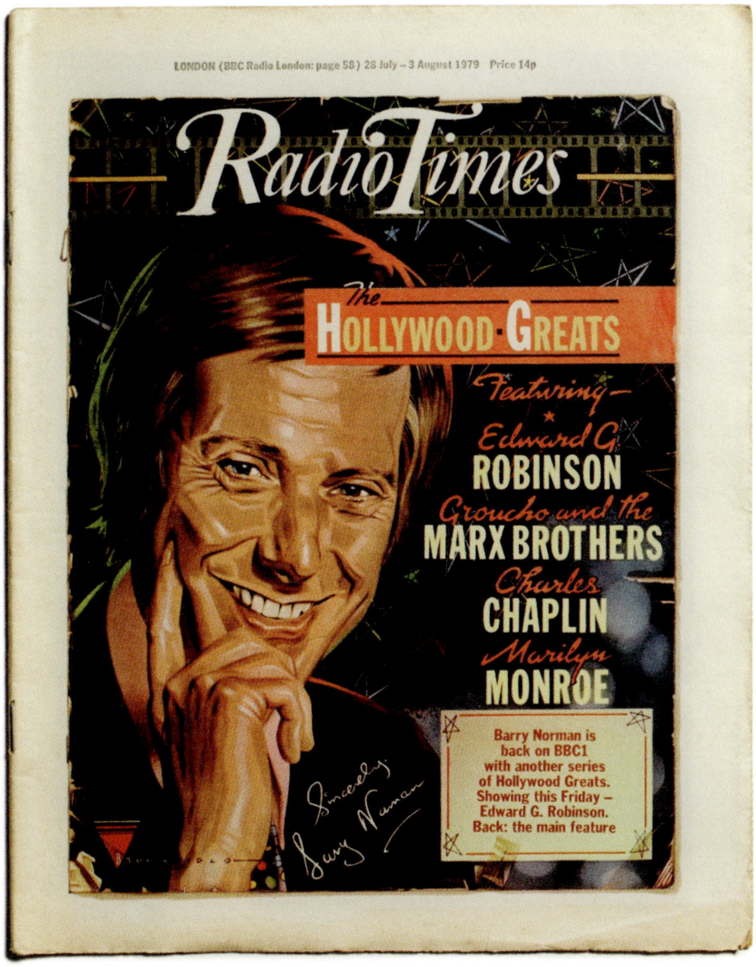

Churchill and the Generals *(right)*

Winston Churchill (Timothy West)

(photograph by John Timbers)

22–28 September 1979

Timothy West was transformed into the wartime leader by make-up that included a false nose and special contact lenses. "With Churchill you've got to fulfil the basics, otherwise they're not going to believe in you," said West.

The Magic of Dance *(below left)*

Rudolph Nureyev and Margot Fonteyn

(photograph by Zoë Dominic)

3–9 November 1979

"In dance, there is truly something for everyone," said Margot Fonteyn as she launched her BBC2 series. As presenter and co-writer, she insisted it shouldn't be a history of dance: "I was anxious to provide entertainment, not a lecture."

Miss World *(below right)*

(photograph by Dmitri Kasterine)

10–16 November 1979

Cover star Carolyn Seaward went on to win Miss World this year. The feature in *Radio Times* recalled the contest where she was crowned Miss United Kingdom and noted that Miss Scotland, Lorraine Davidson, had lost out because of a lack of sparkle. "Still, she's not hysterical. She's a brave little girl."

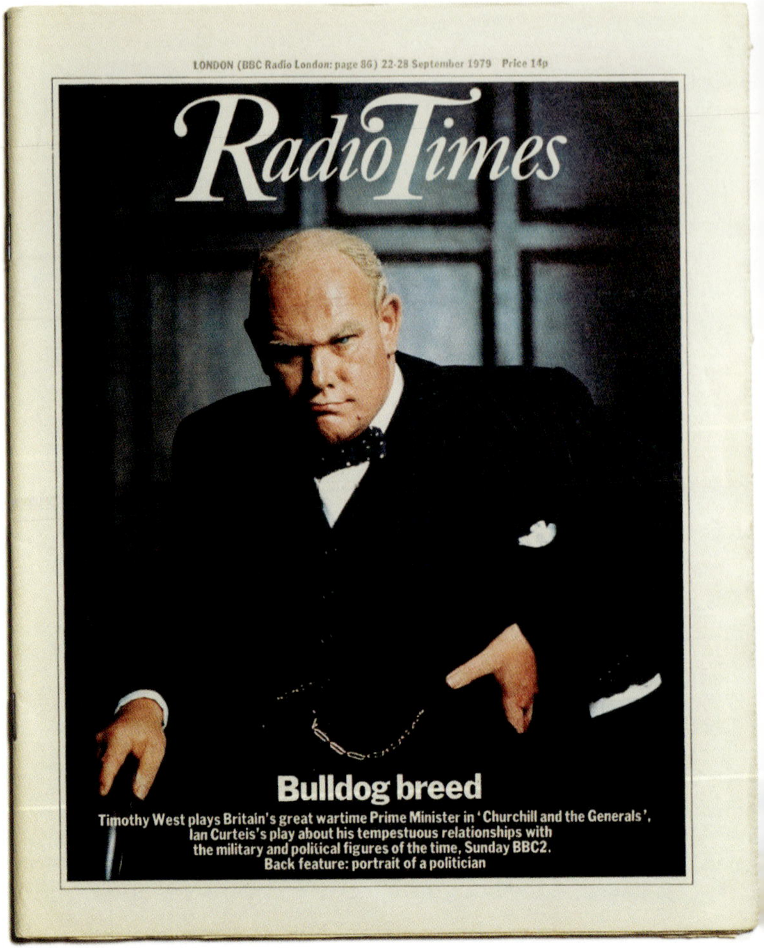

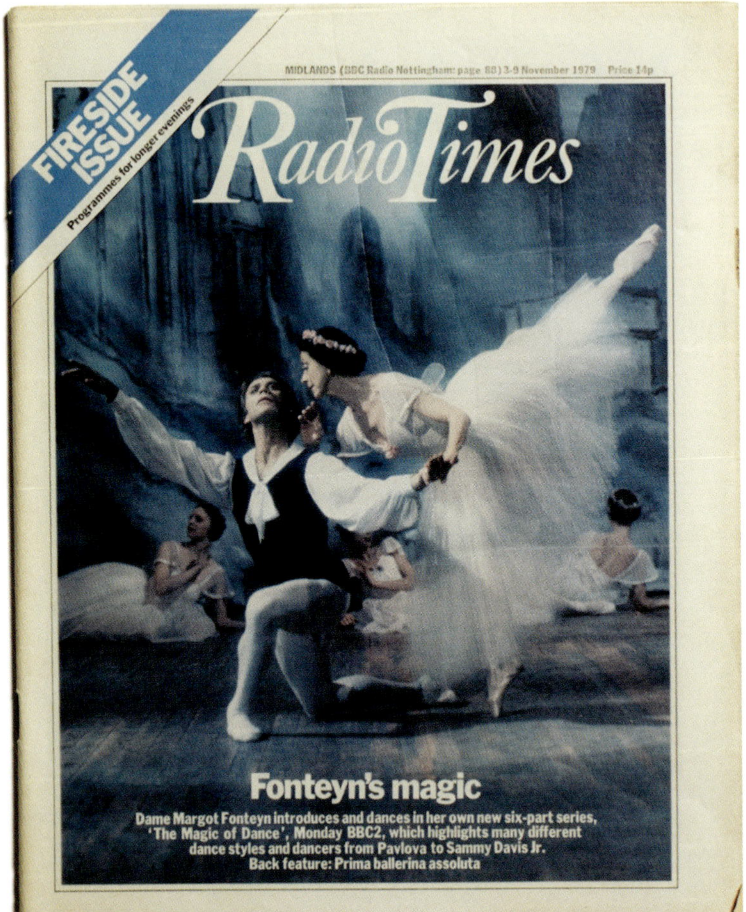

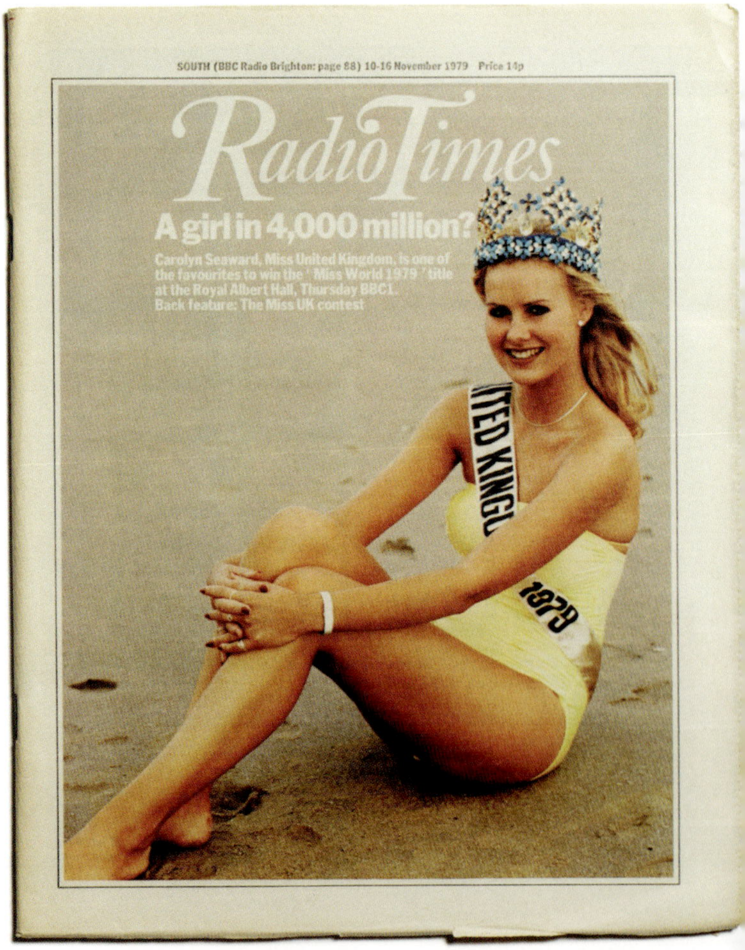

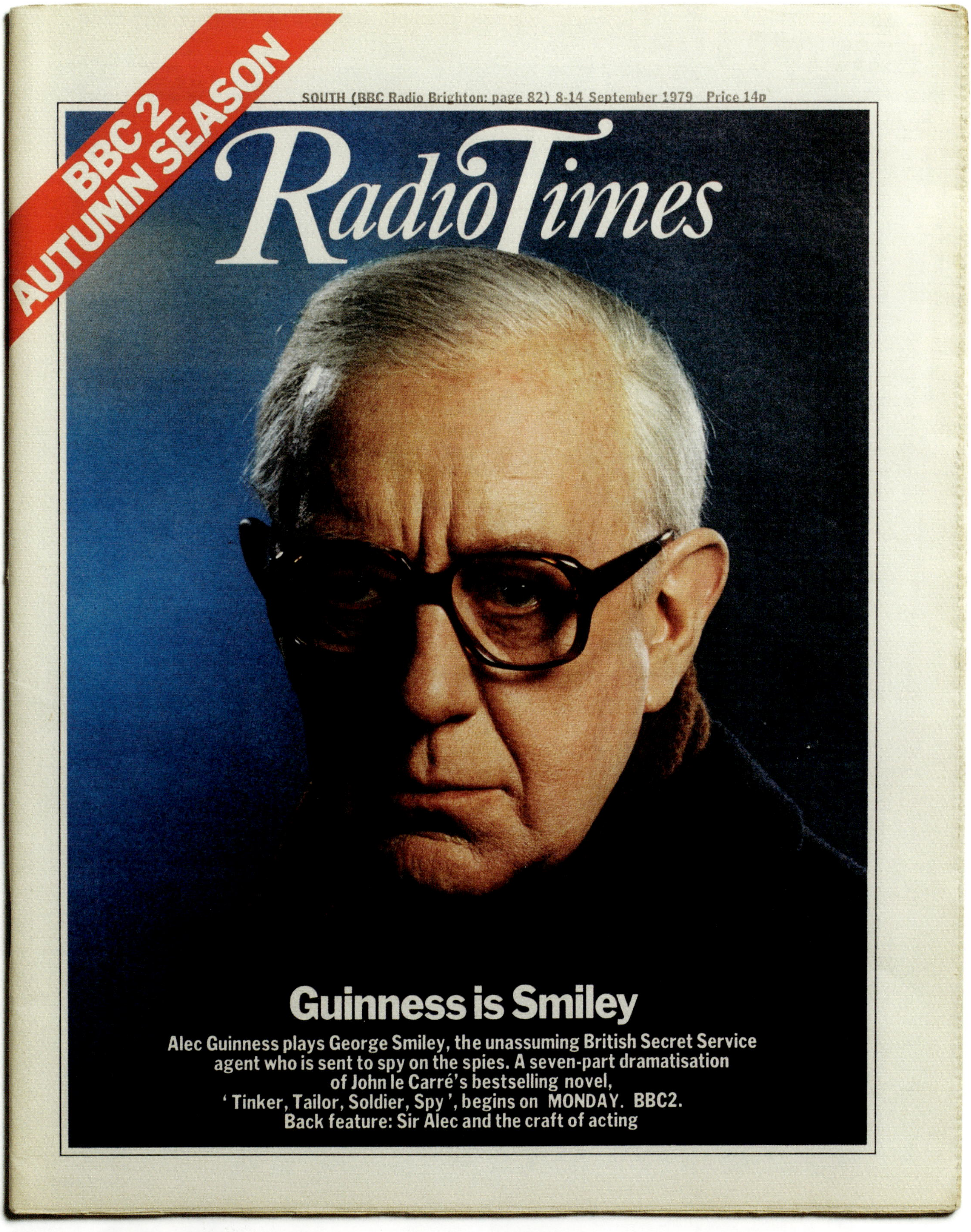

Tinker, Tailor, Soldier, Spy **George Smiley (Alec Guinness)**
(photograph by John Timbers) *8–14 September 1979*

Alec Guinness brought a powerful stillness to the role of British spy chief George Smiley in the dramatisation of John le Carré's novel. "I think the less I do the better," said Guinness. "I think maybe I've gone too far in paring things down."

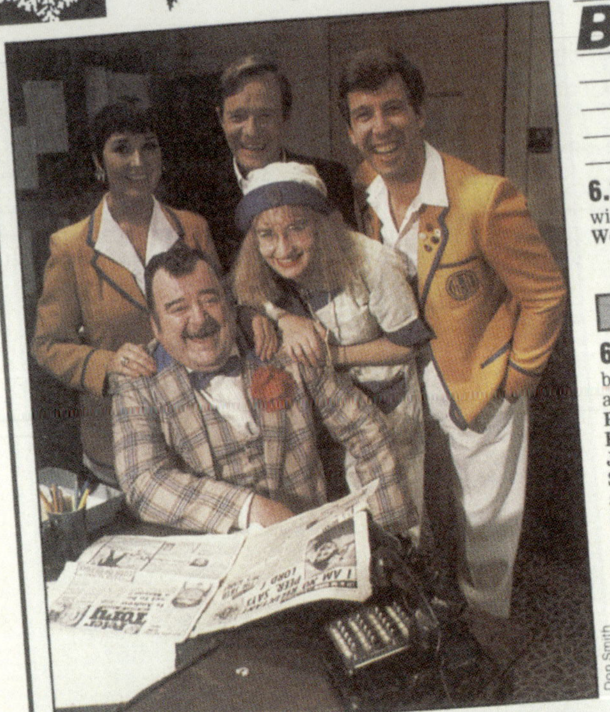

Don Smith

The entertainment staff of Maplin's warm up for Christmas
BBC1, 6.30 pm Hi-de-Hi!

'Just you wait Tuxedo Johnson. One of these days Rocky Stallone's gonna be out of this slammer . . .'
BBC1, 9.0 pm The Two Ronnies

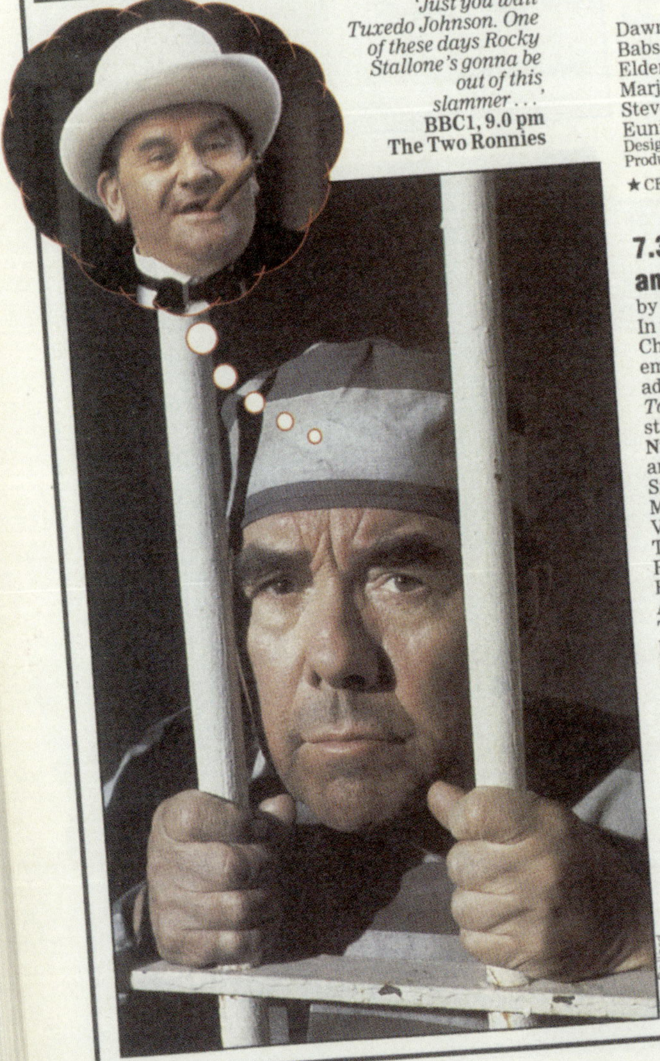

Alan Ballard

BBC 1

6.25 pm News
with Moira Stuart
Weather News

NEW SERIES

6.30 Hi-de-Hi!
by JIMMY PERRY and DAVID CROFT
Paul Shane as Ted Bovis
Ruth Madoc as Gladys Pugh
Jeffrey Holland as Spike
Su Pollard as Peggy
and **David Griffin** as Sqn Ldr Clive Dempster, DFC
Maplin's Holiday Camp, 1960
The Great Cat Robbery
The entertainment staff's troubles have only just begun when they discover there's an emerald necklace hidden somewhere on the camp.
Fred Quilly ......FELIX BOWNESS
Yvonne............DIANE HOLLAND
Barry...............BARRY HOWARD
Sylvia ....NIKKI KELLY
April ....LINDA REGAN
Yellowcoat boys
THE WEBB TWINS
CHRIS ANDREWS
Dawn..............LAURA JACKSON
Babs ....JULIE-CHRISTIAN YOUNG
Elderly man......JOHN RUTLAND
Marjorie .....JEANNE MOCKFORD
Steve ....RICHARD SPEIGHT
Eunice ....LUCY GOULD
Designer ANDREE WELSTEAD HORNBY
Produced and directed by DAVID CROFT
★ CEEFAX SUBTITLES

7.30 Only Fools and Horses . . . .
by JOHN SULLIVAN
In this special edition for Christmas, the Trotter family embark on a money-making adventure which takes them *To Hull and Back*
starring **David Jason**
Nicholas Lyndhurst
and **Buster Merryfield**
Smuggler ....JANE THOMPSON
Mike ......KENNETH MACDONALD
Vicky..................KIM CLIFFORD
Teddy ....JOHNNY WADE
Ruby....................ANNIE LEAKE
Boycie.................JOHN CHALLIS
Abdul..................TONY ANHOLT
Trigger ....ROGER LLOYD PACK
Denzil ....PAUL BARBER
Slater ....JIM BROADBENT
Hoskins
CHRISTOPHER MITCHELL
Sid ....ROY HEATHER
Colin ....MARK BURDIS
PC Parker.......JEFF STEVENSON
Bridge attendant ..ALAN HULSE
Lil.........................RACHEL BELL
Boatmen ....JOE BELCHER
JOHNNIE ALLEN
Gas rigger ...DAVID FLEESHMAN
Van Kleefe ....PHILIP BOND
Hussein ...LORENCE FERDINAND
Film cameraman CHRIS SEAGER
Sound recordist DENNIS PANCHEN
Film editor JOHN JARVIS
Designer BERNARD LLOYD-JONES
Produced and directed by RAY BUTT
★ CEEFAX SUBTITLES

NEW SERIES

9.0 The Two Ronnies
starring
Ronnie Barker
and Ronnie Corbett
The two Ronnies are back with a crackerful of jokes in the gift-wrapped first show of a new series.
Plus all the news that's fit to laugh at, and *Little Big Shot*
– a searing tale set in Chicago in the 1920s when men were men and Ronald Reagan was just an OAP.
With their special guest
Phil Collins
Also appearing:
Janet Mahoney
Elizabeth Anson
John Blythe
Howard Lew Lewis
Paul McDowell
Gerrie Raymond
Script associate IAN DAVIDSON
Written by BRYAN BLACKBURN
ROBERT A. GRAY, COLIN PEARSON
DAVID RENWICK, LAURIE ROWLEY
GERALD WILEY
Choreographer JEFF THACKER
Musical director
RONNIE HAZLEHURST
Sound MICHAEL MCCARTHY
Lighting WARWICK FIELDING
Designer JAMES GRANT
Producer MICHAEL HURLL
Director MARCUS MORTIMER
(Next programme on Saturday 4 January)
Record: The Very Best of Me and the Very Best of Him, REC/ZCM 514;
Video: The Best of the Two Ronnies, BBCV/BBCB 7017, *available from retailers.*

9.50 News
Moira Stuart presents the day's news with BBC teams at home and abroad
Weather News BILL GILES

10.0 Wogan
Terry deserts his little home on Shepherd's Bush Green to fly out to Denver for Christmas at the Carrington mansion.
He says, 'At the outset, let me point out that this is no reflection on my wife's cooking, although I feel I did get short-changed with the brown meat last Christmas. However, when the invitatior came from Denver to join the Carringtons over their groaning festive board, I felt that, for your sakes, I couldn't refuse.
'It means, of course, that my little children will not have their regular Christmas trea of seeing Daddy slump senseless into the pudding, nor burst into tears at not getting the wishbone.
But they will understand. The viewers come first.
Anyway, what red-blooded male could pass up the chance of tasting Krystle's mince pies?'
Researcher IRENE LEVIN
Producer JON PLOWMAN
Series producer FRANCES WHITAI
(Wogan can be seen again on Fri at 7.0 pm)

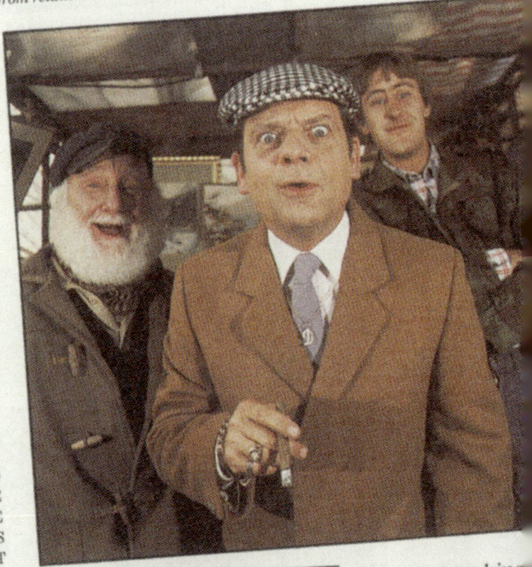

The money-makin of Del, Uncl Albert and Ro continue as they s to prove they are fools nor hor
BBC1, 7.30 Only Fools and H

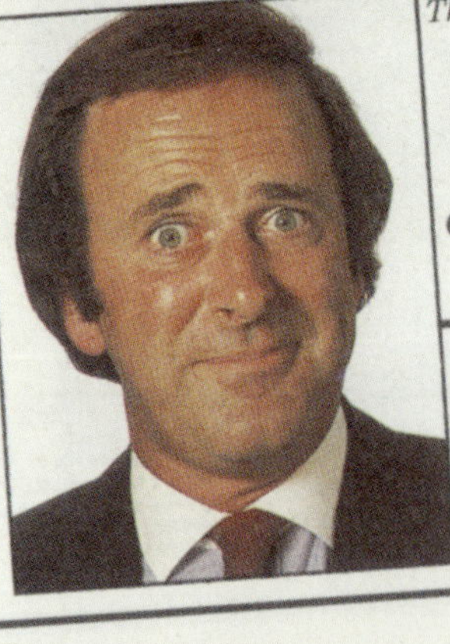

Don't miss the seeing BBCtv's sycophant imb Christmas spiri
BBC1, 10.0 pr

Radio Times

THE FUTURE STARTS HERE

1980–1989

Christmas 1988

Illustration by Lynda Gray

17–30 December 1988

You're looking at the one *Radio Times* cover to be featured in the *Guinness Book of Records*. It was the biggest-selling edition of any British magazine in history, selling 11,220,666 copies.

Lynda Gray's delicate, pantomime-themed cover set the tone for the magazine's opening feature: a photo spread with The Radio Times Players. The fictional theatre group, assembled especially for the issue, starred Tony Robinson as Robin Hood, Griff Rhys Jones and Mel Smith as the Ugly Sisters and French and Saunders as the donkey. However, not everyone was so full of festive cheer for the season. The *EastEnders* Christmas special, set during the Second World War, featured a young Lou Beale desperately awaiting the return of her soldier husband, Albert.

Other television highlights included *Unforgettable*, a BBC2 documentary about Nat "King" Cole with contributions from his widow, and more than five hours of coverage from Nelson Mandela's 70th birthday concert at Wembley six months earlier.

1980-1989

Radio celebrates its 60th birthday and breakfast TV is launched. Plus EastEnders, Live Aid and Michael Palin goes travelling

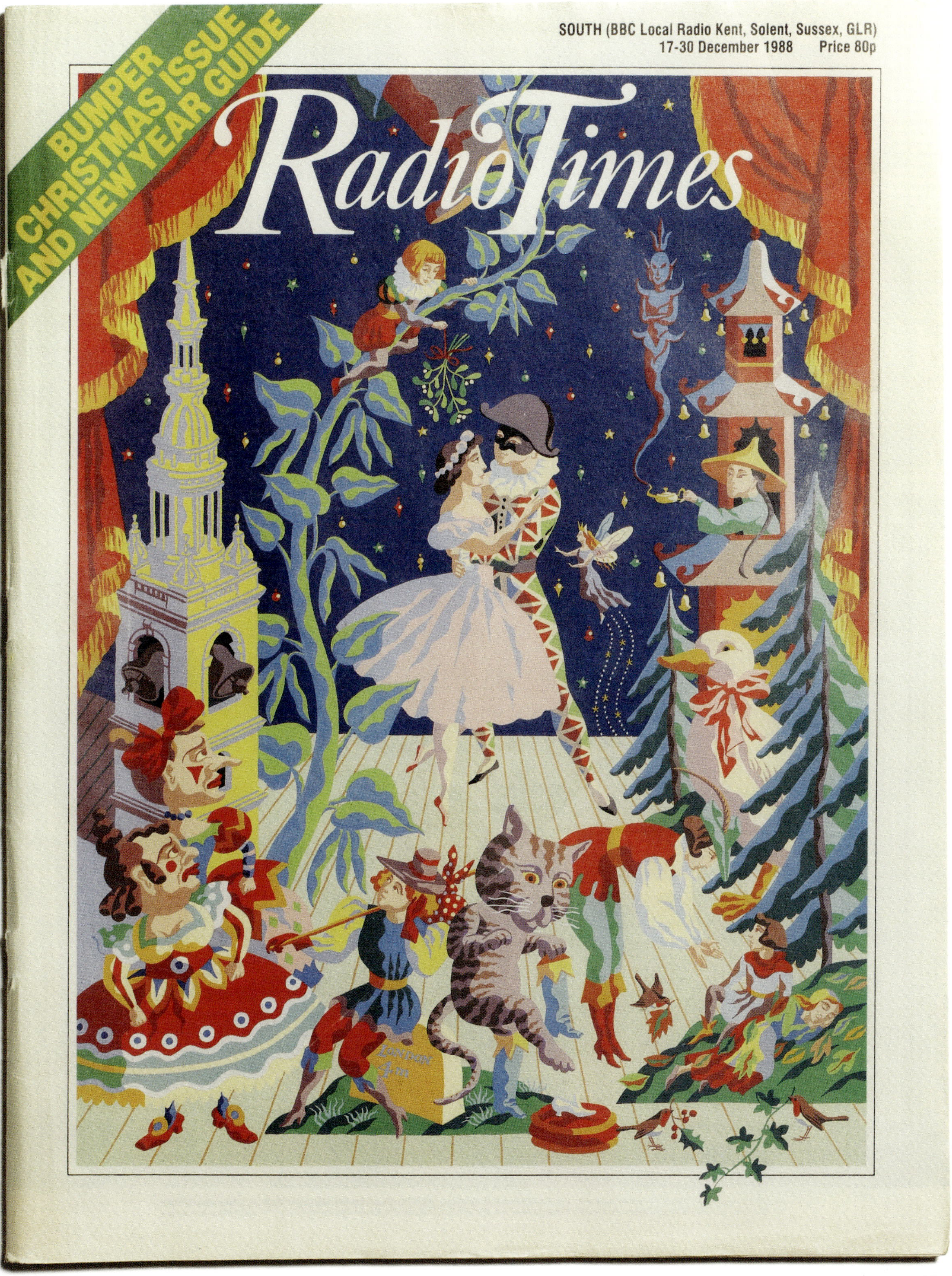
SOUTH (BBC Local Radio Kent, Solent, Sussex, GLR)
17-30 December 1988 Price 80p
BUMPER CHRISTMAS ISSUE AND NEW YEAR GUIDE
Radio Times

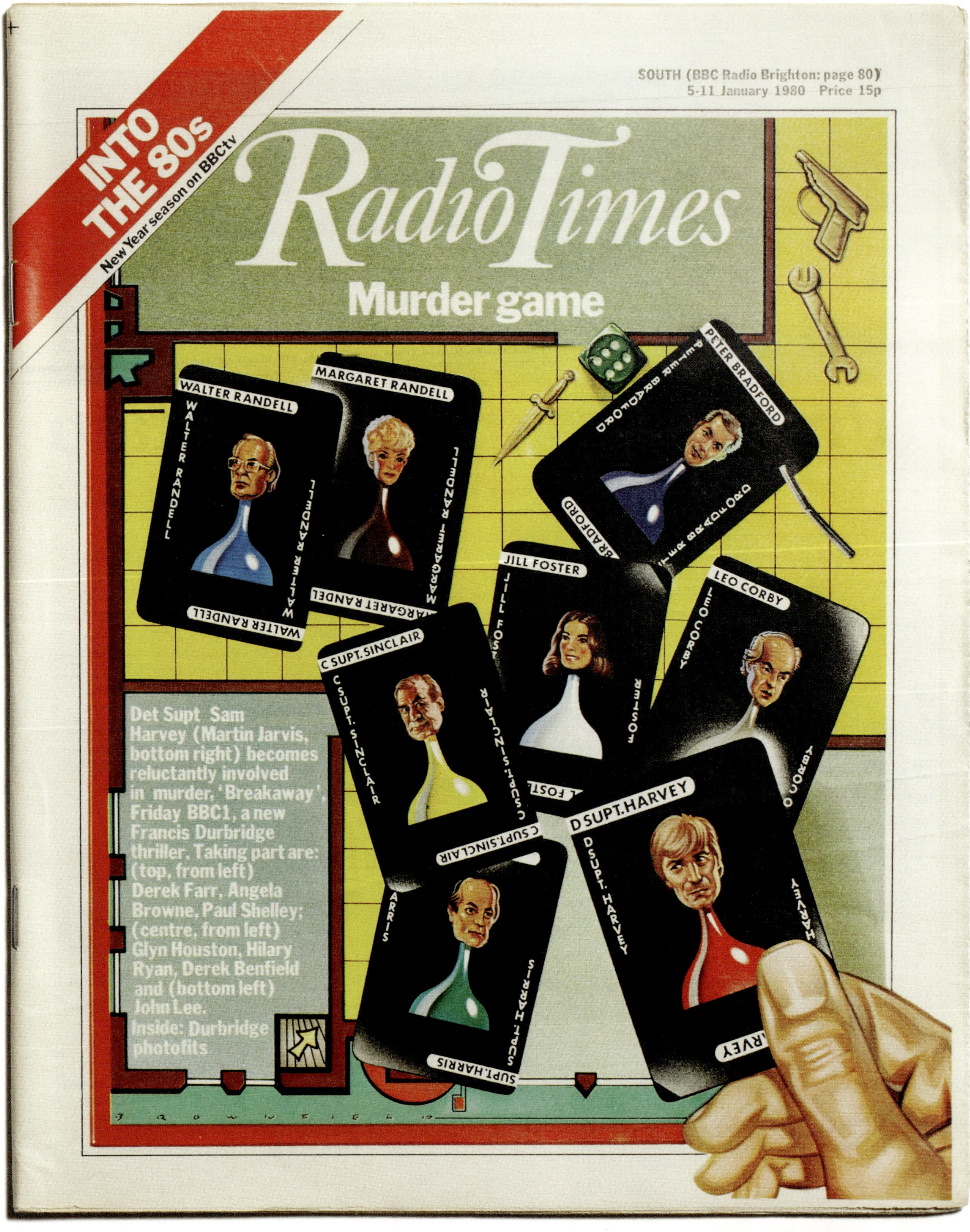

Breakaway Top row, from left: Walter Randell (Derek Farr), Margaret Randell (Angela Browne) and Peter Bradford (Paul Shelley). Middle row: Chief Supt Sinclair (Glyn Houston), Jill Foster (Hilary Ryan) and Leo Corby (Derek Benfield). Bottom row: Supt Harris (John Lee) and Det Supt Sam Harvey (Martin Jarvis) Illustration by Mick Brownfield *5–11 January 1980*

Radio Times unveiled a Cluedo theme for a new thriller by Francis Durbridge, writer of the 1950s *Paul Temple* radio series.

The Hitchhiker's Guide to the Galaxy *(right)*

Illustration by John Pasche *(photograph by Phil Jude)*

19–25 January 1980

It couldn't happen now but, in 1980, Radio 4 promised Douglas Adams the cover of *Radio Times* – but only if he got the entire second series of *Hitchhiker* ready to run nightly this week, which he duly did. Shortly before his death in 2001, Adams expressed a wish that, for his works at least, "Hitchhiker" should not be hyphenated.

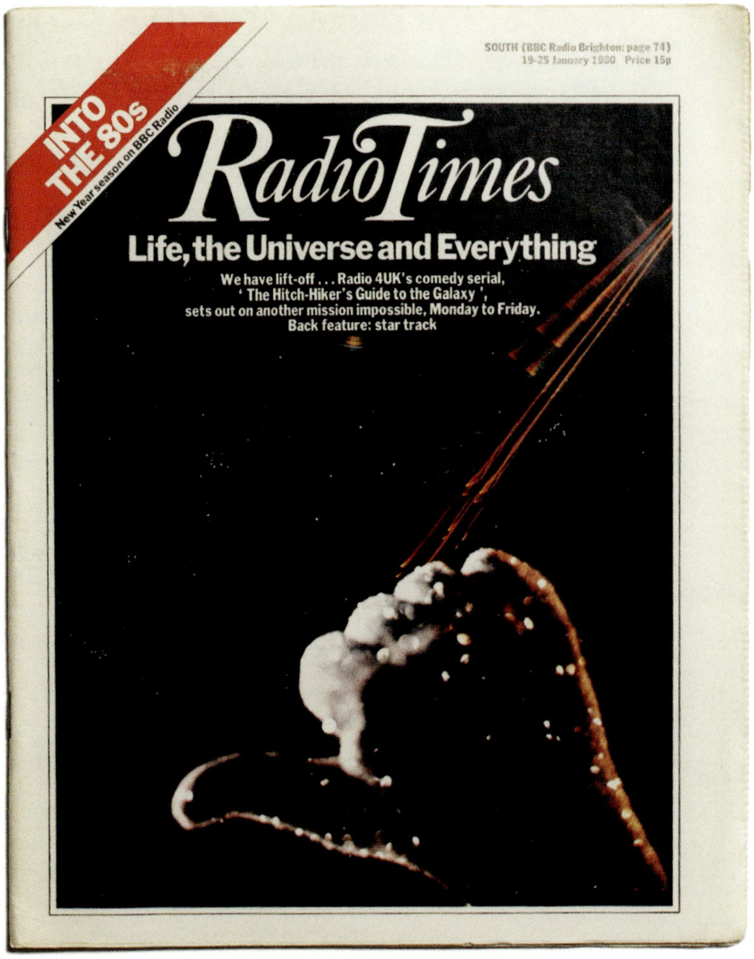

World Professional Darts Championship *(below left)*

Illustration by David Scutt

From left: Leighton Rees, John Lowe and Eric Bristow

2–8 February 1980

David Scutt, who went on to illustrate Philip Pullman's *His Dark Materials* trilogy, provided the cover for "the darts".

Daily Service *(below right)*

Illustration by Eric Fraser

29 March–4 April 1980

Eric Fraser's illustration highlights the fact that in Holy Week Radio 4's *Daily Service* was broadcast from All Souls Church, next door to Broadcasting House in London. Also this week: the start of the second series of *Not the Nine o'Clock News*.

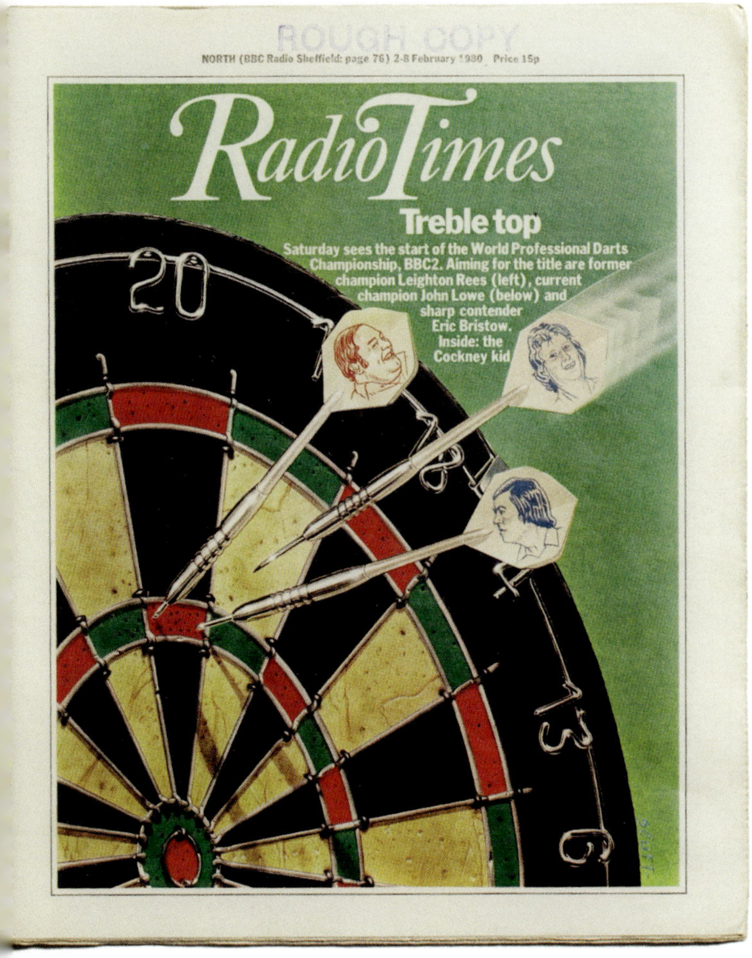

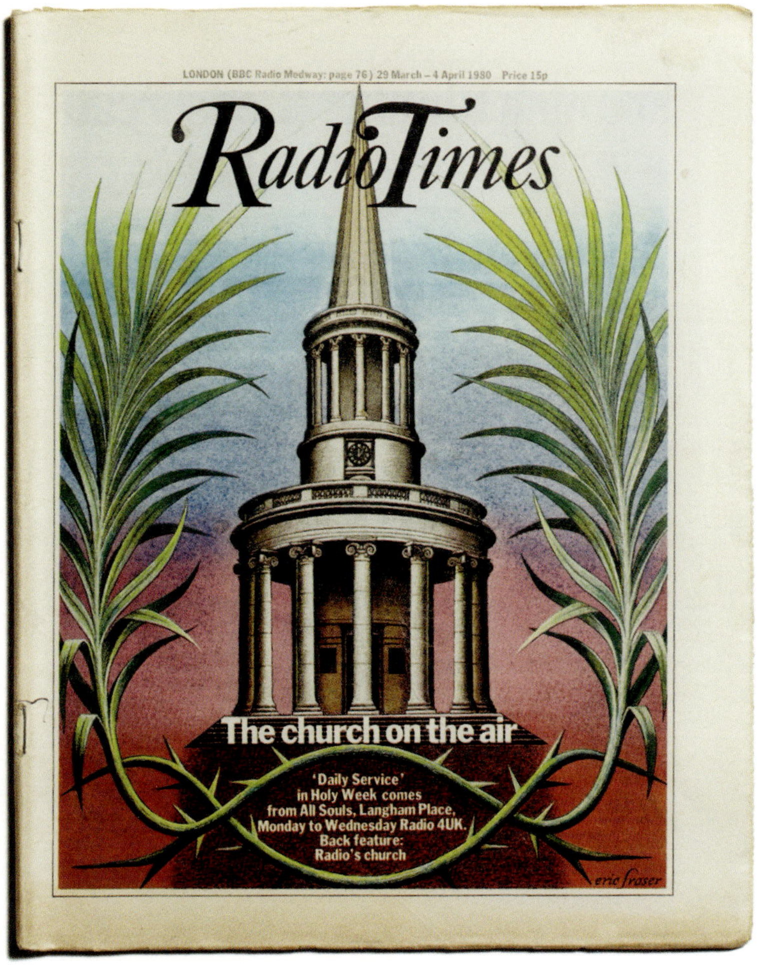

Night of the Demon/The Ghoul *(right)*

Top: John Holden (Dana Andrews), Joanna Harrington (Peggy Cummins). Bottom: Dr Lawrence (Peter Cushing), Angela (Alexandra Bastedo)
Illustration by Mark Thomas

28 June–4 July 1980

A dramatic cover for a double bill of horror movies. In his introduction to the season, film critic Geoff Brown approved of its late-night slot because "one's critical faculties are on the wane and inadequacies can be seen as virtues".

First Night of the Proms *(below left)*

Illustration by James Marsh

12–18 July 1980

James Marsh's cover heralded the start of the new Proms season and the "flowering of British music" thanks to Gennadi Rozhdestvensky, chief conductor of the BBC Symphony Orchestra.

The voice of cricket *(below right)*

John Arlott *(photograph by Denis Waugh)*

19–25 July 1980

John Arlott retired after 35 years of providing ball-by-ball cricket commentary. He said: "I've enjoyed cricket more and served it better for realising it was never the be-all and end-all of everything."

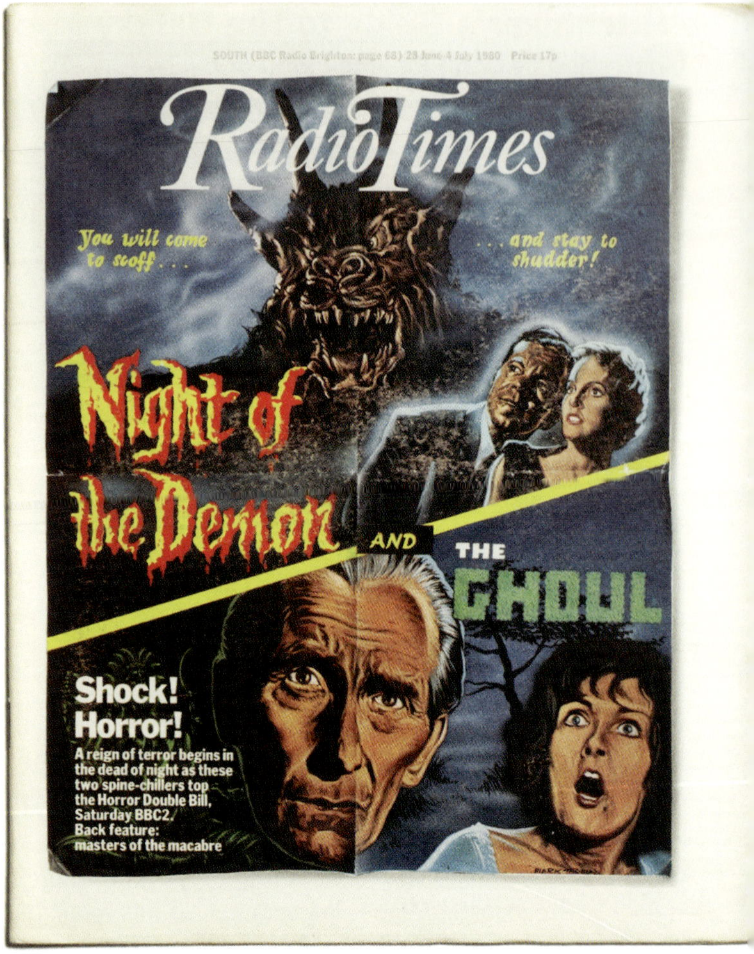

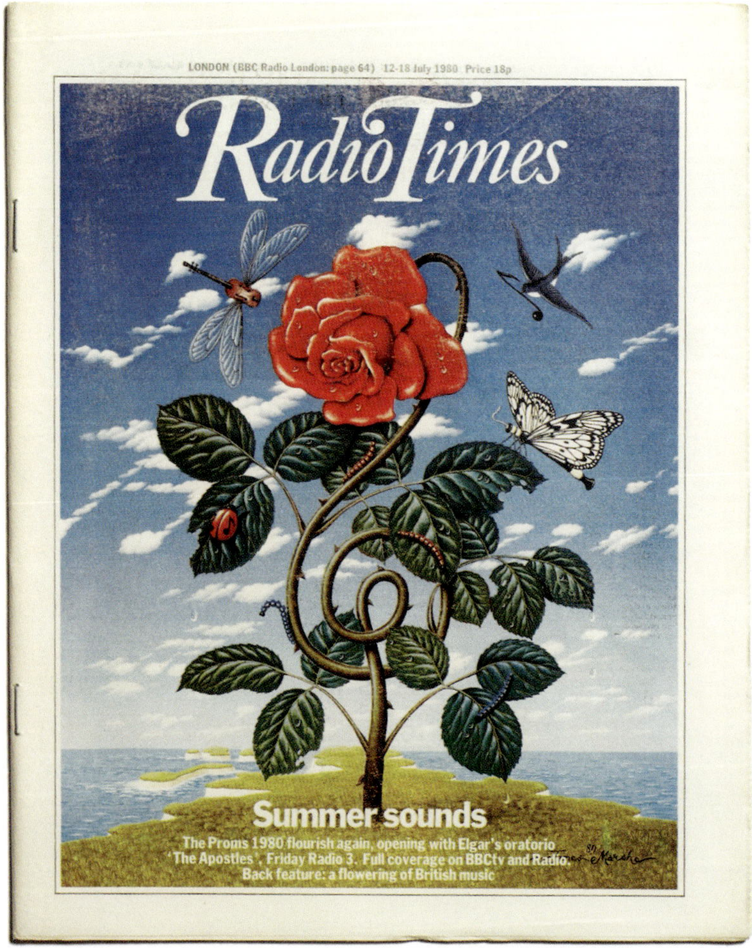

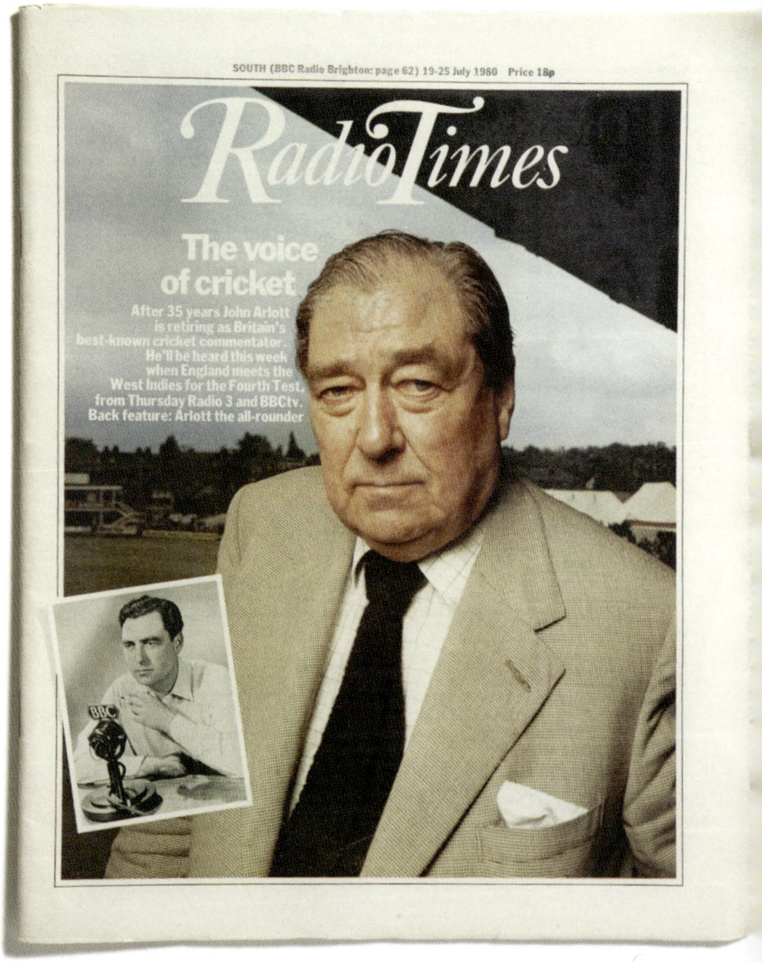

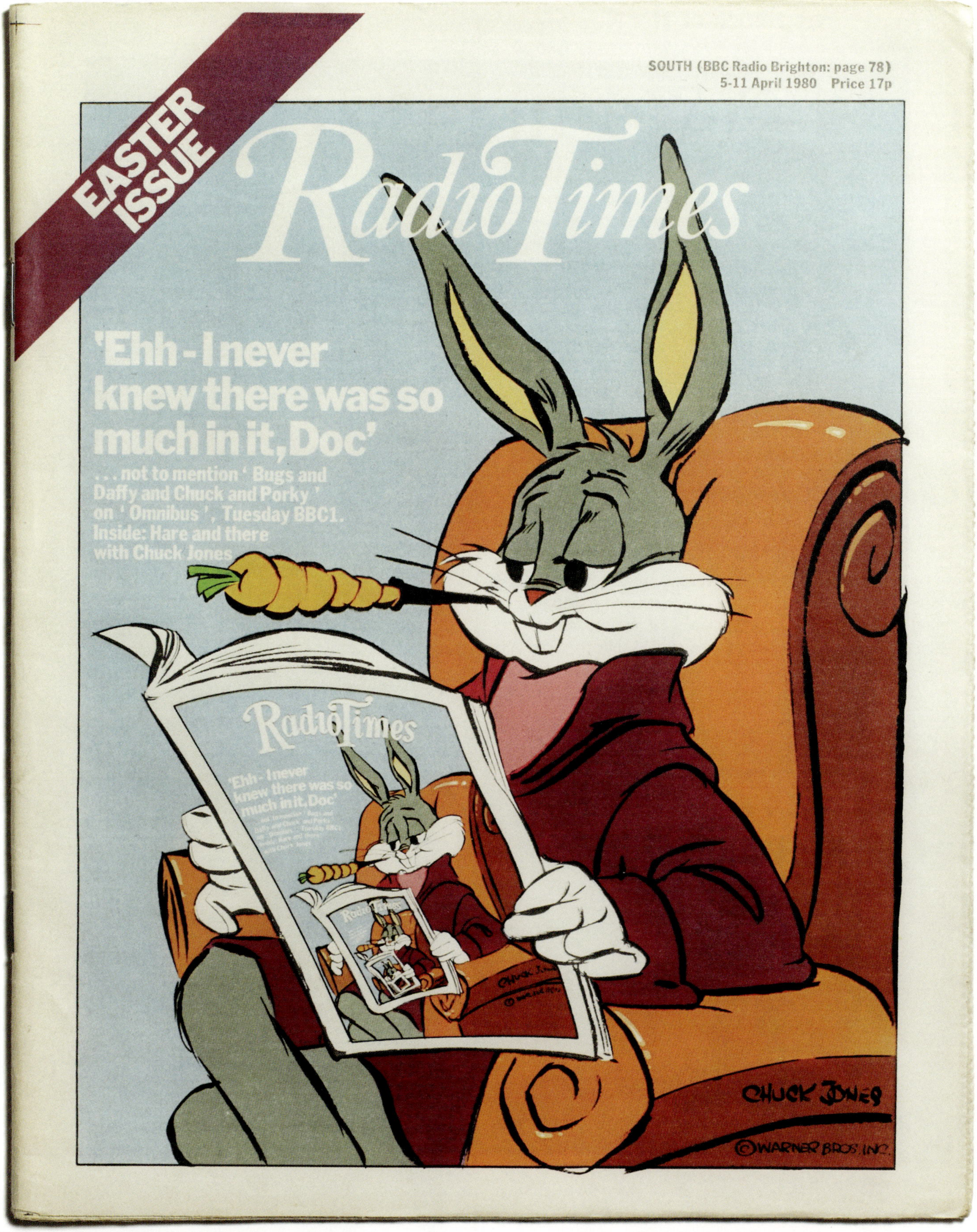

Omnibus **Bugs Bunny by Chuck Jones** *5–11 April 1980*

Warner Bros cartoon animator and director Chuck Jones provided the playfully repeating cover and was the subject of an *Omnibus* profile. He said: "Movement is the key to character. Take Bugs Bunny: he always leans his weight all on one foot, leaving the other free. He's insouciant, he's devil-may-care – his stance is the classic man-about-town's." Just as cheeky was the decision to borrow the cover line from rival magazine *TV Times*'s slogan, "I never knew there was so much in it".

The Shock of the New *(right)*

(photograph by Victor Watts, with thanks to the Brick Development Association and students of Willesden College of Technology, London)

20–26 September 1980

Australian art critic Robert Hughes had to work hard to persuade the BBC he was a suitable presenter for its landmark series on modern art. "To see if I was still the drug-sodden loon they remembered from the 60s, they presented me with the task of adapting a truly awful two-and-a-half hour Italian film on Caravaggio into a 75-minute documentary."

Question Time *(middle right)*

Robin Day *(photograph by Dmitri Kasterine)*

11–17 October 1980

Robin Day celebrated 25 years as a political broadcaster. "I would rather have been an MP than a television personality, if that's the right word," he said. "I like to think I'd have been a useful backbencher."

Ireland: a Television History *(far right)*

Illustration by Mark Reddy

29 November–6 December 1980

The 13-part documentary series gave presenter Robert Kee a chance to reflect on how television portrayed history. He concluded that, despite its shortcomings, TV depicted history "as it really was by making you feel that you were there".

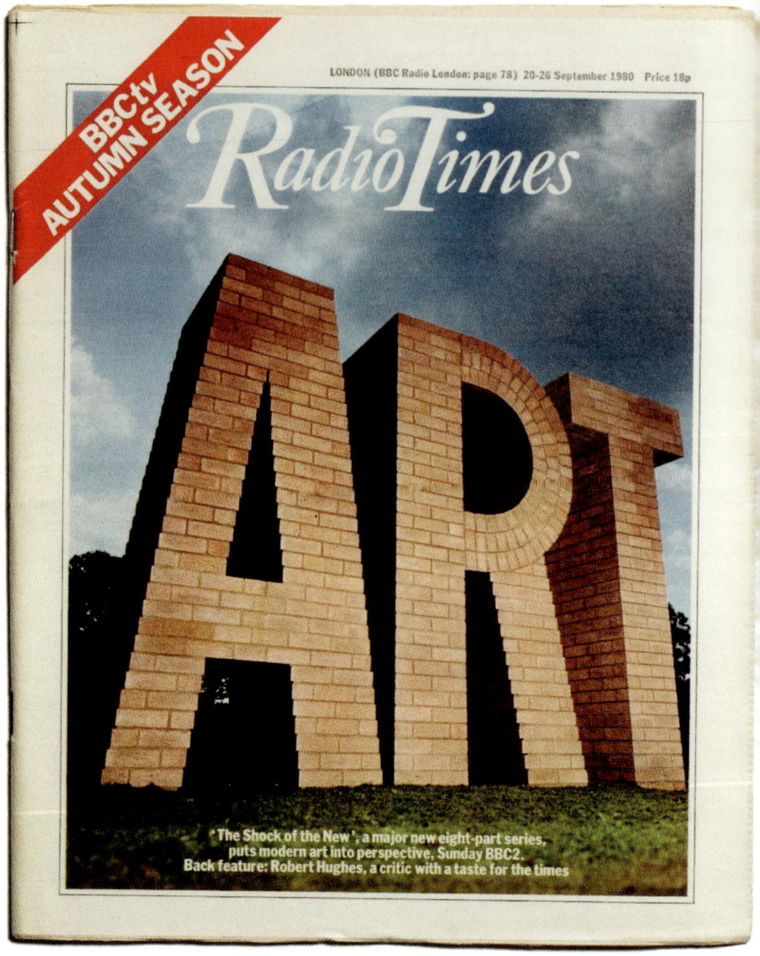

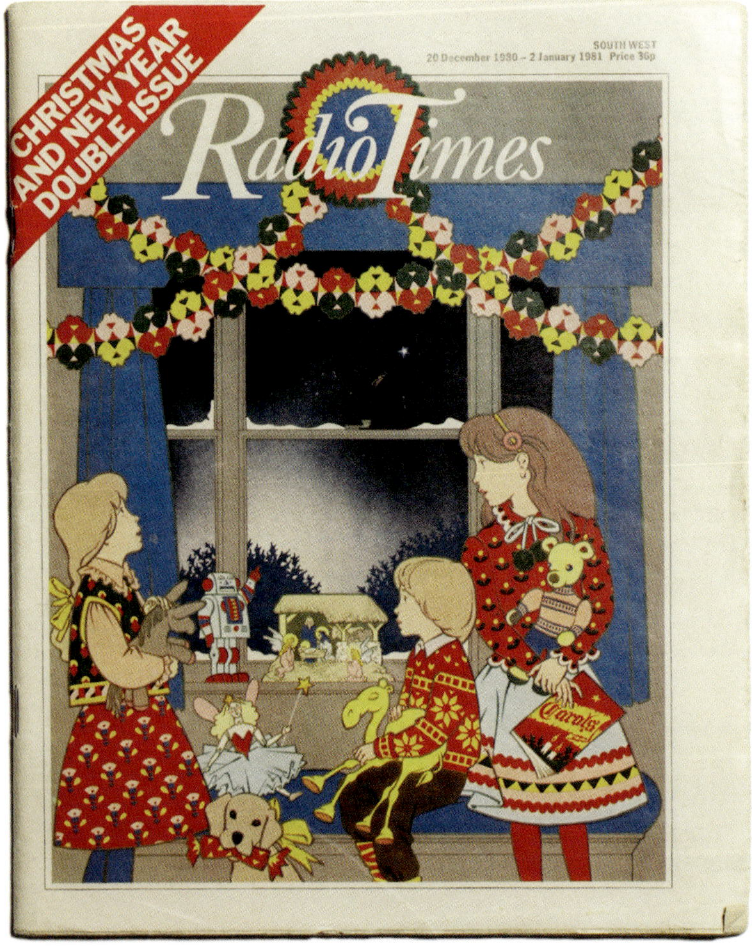

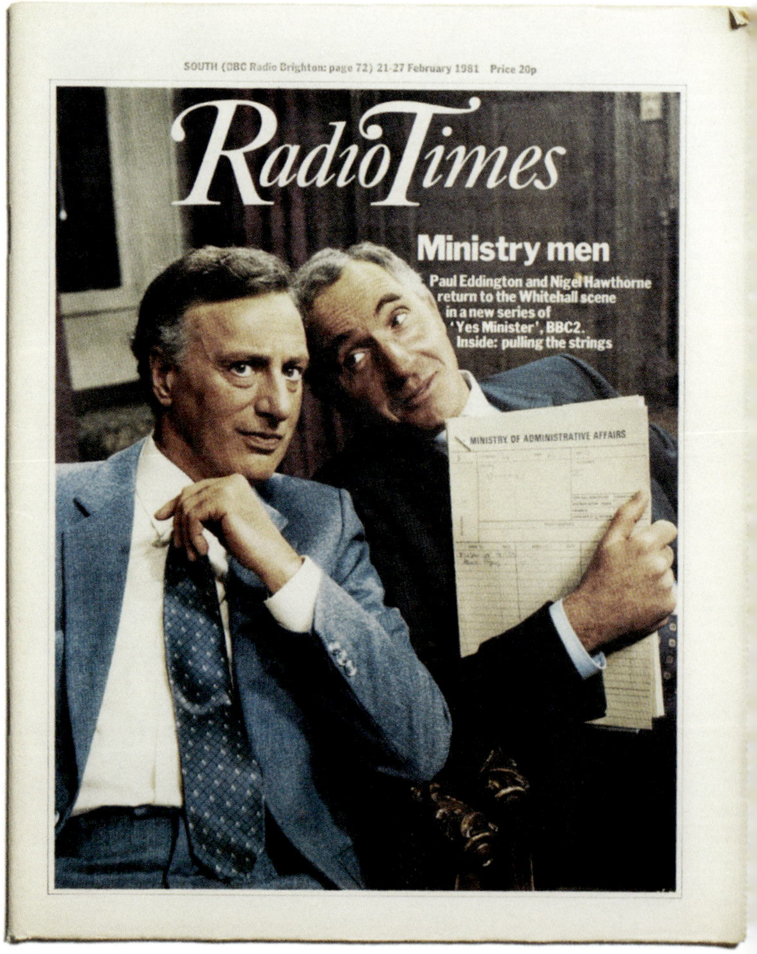

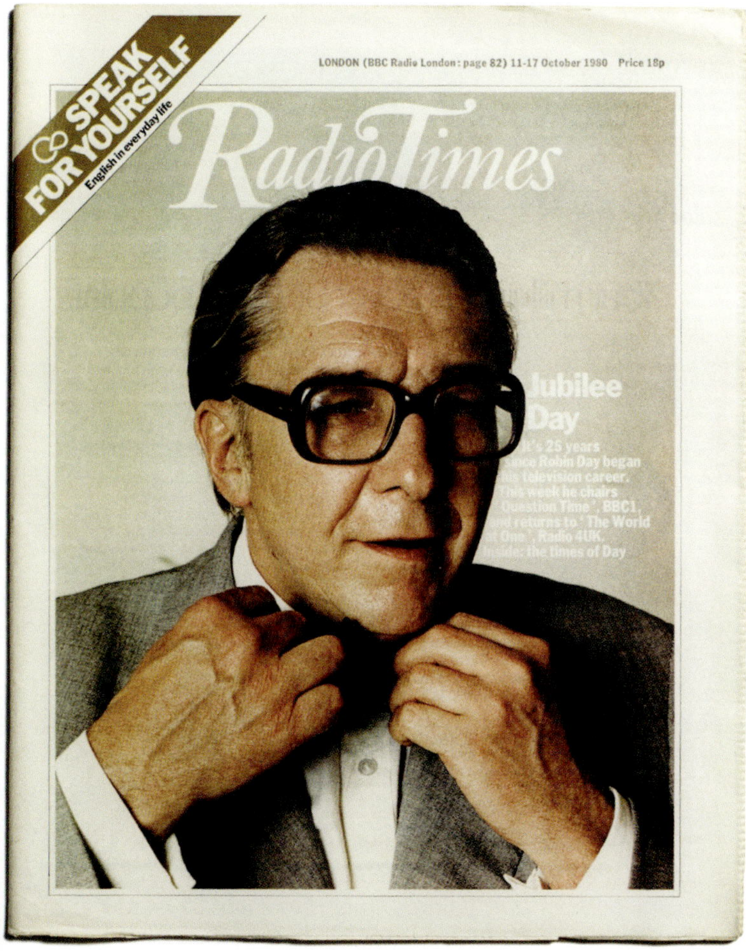

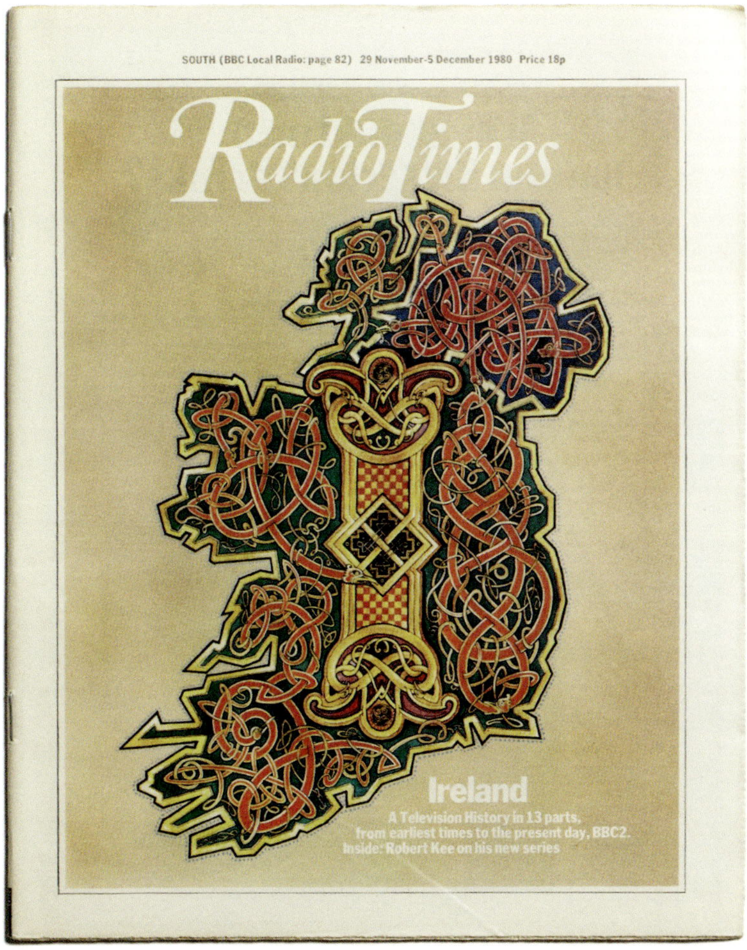

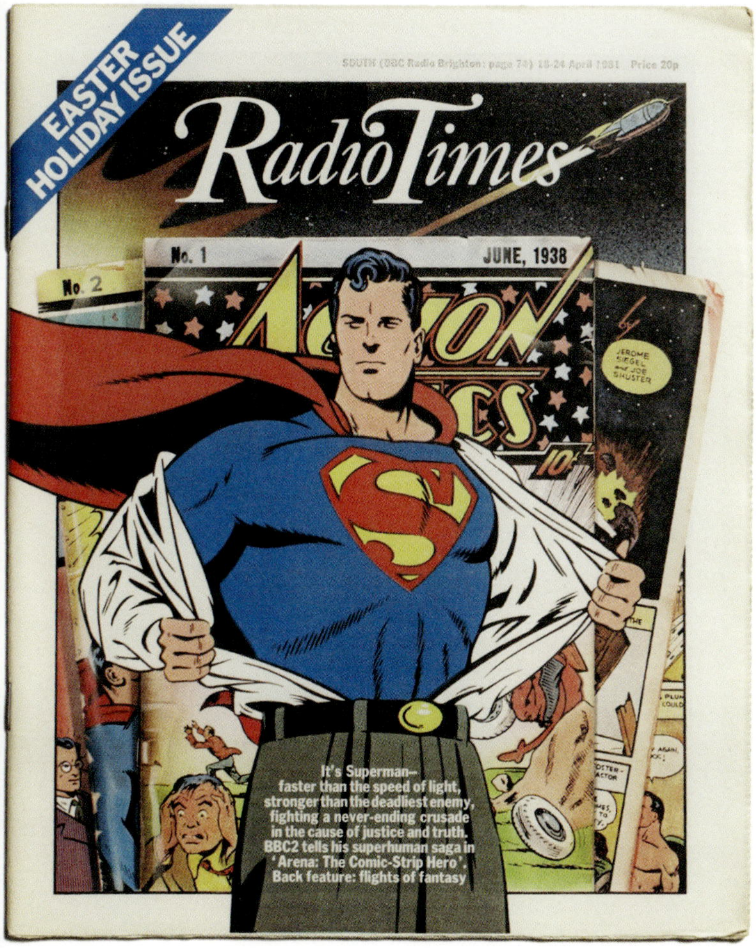

Christmas 1980 *(far left)*
Illustration by Lynda Gray

20 December 1980–2 January 1981

A Christmas cover that blended tradition with a hint of the modern world. There was nothing too taxing on BBC1 on Christmas Day: Paul Daniels, *Larry Grayson's Generation Game*, *The Mike Yarwood Christmas Show* and *Airport 1975*.

Yes Minister *(middle left)*
Jim Hacker (Paul Eddington) and Sir Humphrey Appleby (Nigel Hawthorne) ***(photograph by Don Smith)***

21–27 February 1981

As *Yes Minister* returned for a second series, *Radio Times* sent Michael White of *The Guardian* to find out from writers Antony Jay and Jonathan Lynn where they got their inside information on how politicians and civil servants tick. Jay and Lynn remained resolutely silent on the subject…

Arena: the Comic-Strip Hero *(left)*
Illustration by Mick Brownfield

18–24 April 1981

As arts strand *Arena* celebrated the Superman phenomenon, Radio 1 embarked on a 13-part adaptation of *Star Wars*. TV, meanwhile, boasted a Pam Ayres Easter special and a documentary on the evolution of jeans from workwear to a fashion must-have.

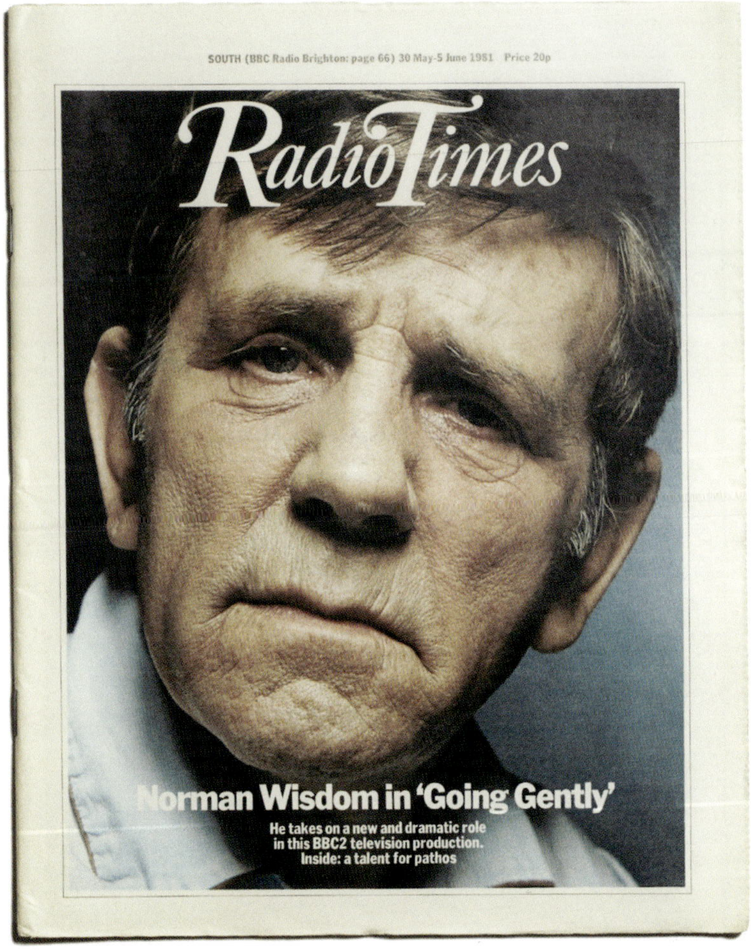

Going Gently *(left)*
Bernard Flood (Norman Wisdom)
(photograph by John Timbers)

30 May–5 June 1981

Slapstick superstar Norman Wisdom was cast as retired salesman Bernard Flood, a man with terminal cancer – a role he carried off with aplomb. "I'm a very emotional person. That's why it's easy for me to do pathos," he said.

The Borgias *(below left)*
Clockwise from top: Cesare Borgia (Oliver Cotton), Pope Alexander VI (Adolfo Celi) and Lucrezia Borgia (Anne Louise Lambert) *(photograph by Ric Gemmell)*

10–16 October 1981

A notoriously juicy BBC drama about a lively Italian dynasty. But how true was it to real life? "We don't say it's the true story," said co-writer John Prebble. "Nobody can tell that."

Arena *(below right)*

31 October–6 November 1981

As *Arena* reported on the cult of the Da Vinci portrait, *Radio Times* asked art critic Waldemar Januszczak to examine the many myths surrounding the painting. "She is the only portrait ever painted which seems to be examining you more closely than you are examining her," he concluded.

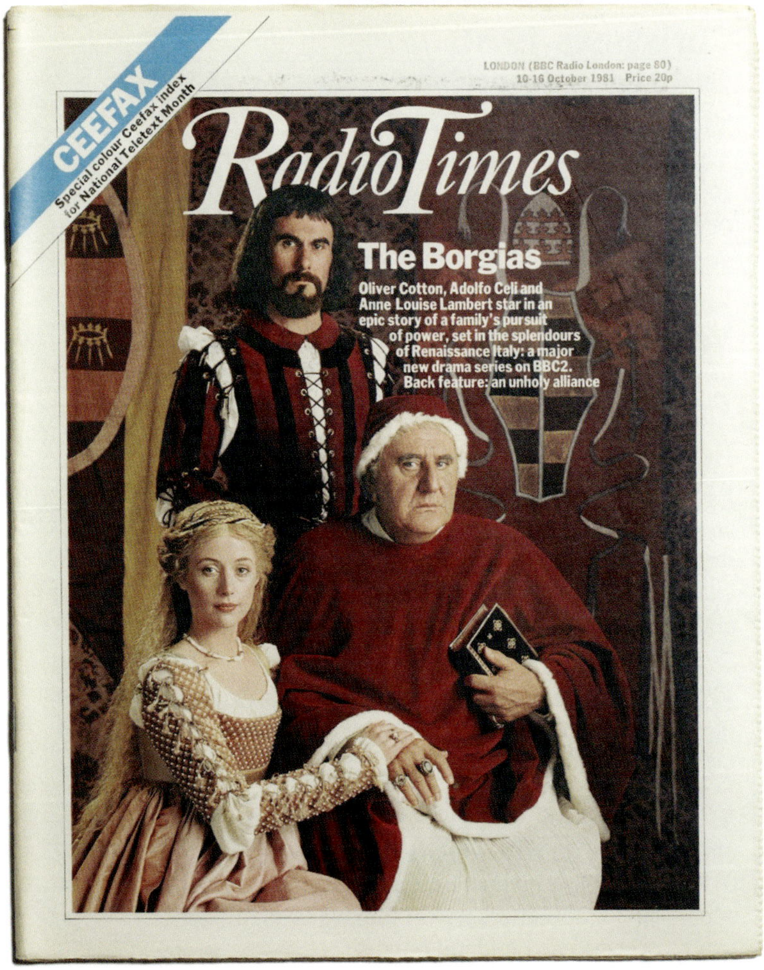

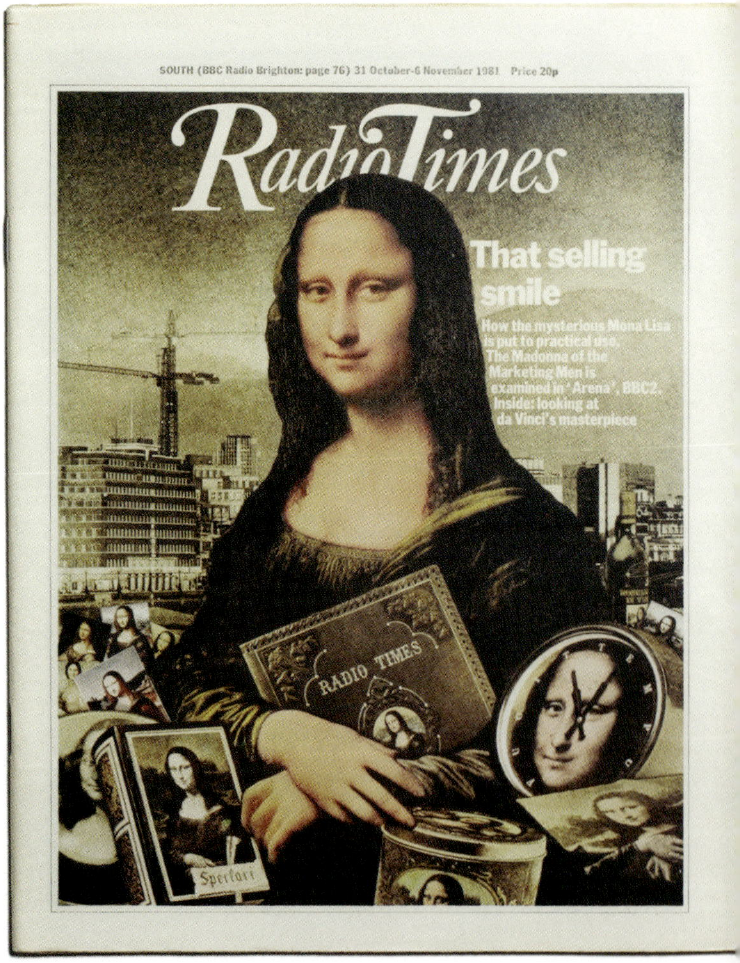

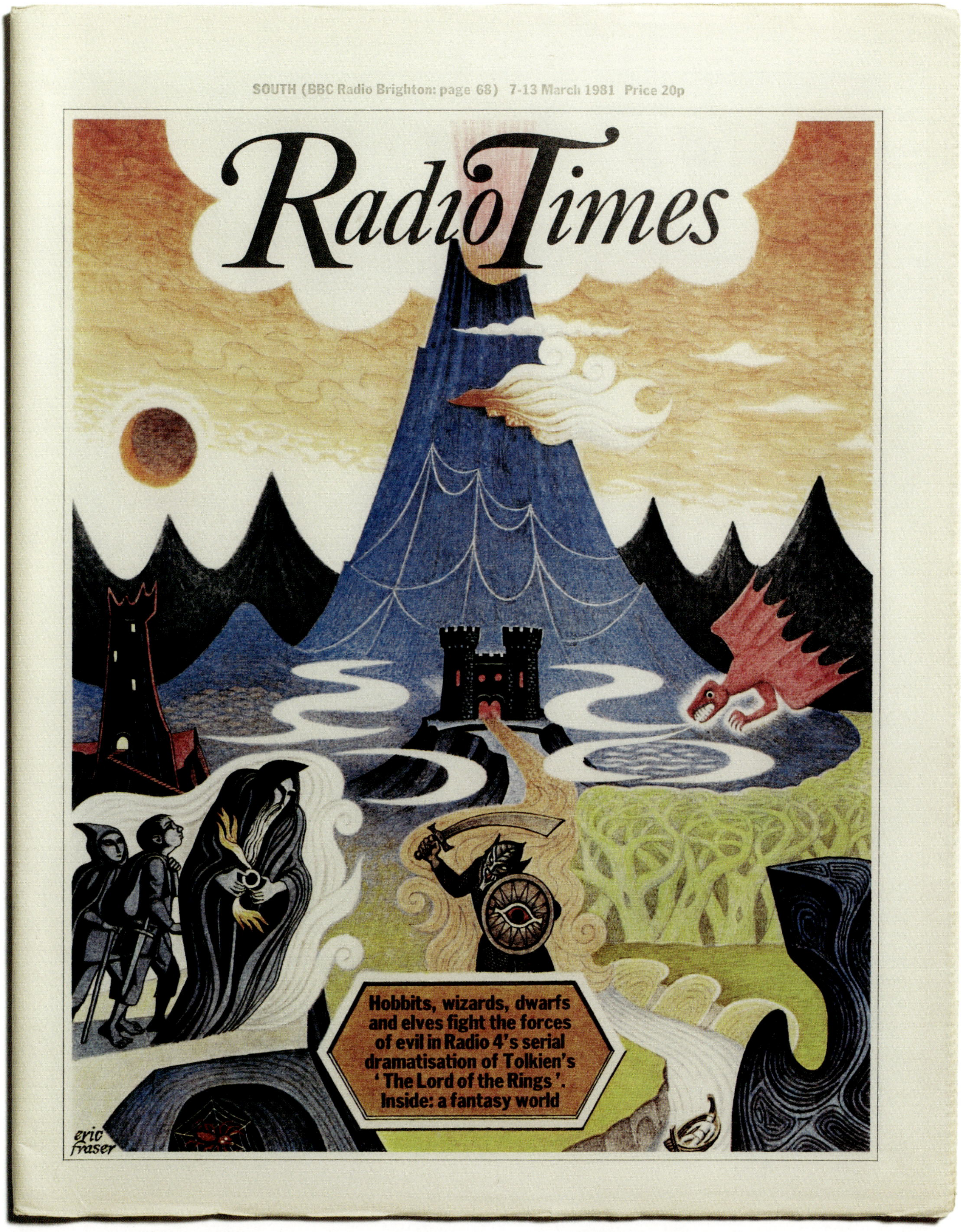

The Lord of the Rings Illustration by Eric Fraser *7–13 March 1981*

Radio 4 embarked on a 26-part adaptation of JRR Tolkien's *The Lord of the Rings*. Six months later, after it ended, Ruth T Clarke of Suffolk wrote to *Radio Times* saying the drama had been "the loveliest serial I have ever listened to". Meanwhile, on television, Ronnie Corbett and Barbara Lott starred as son and mother in the new sitcom *Sorry!*

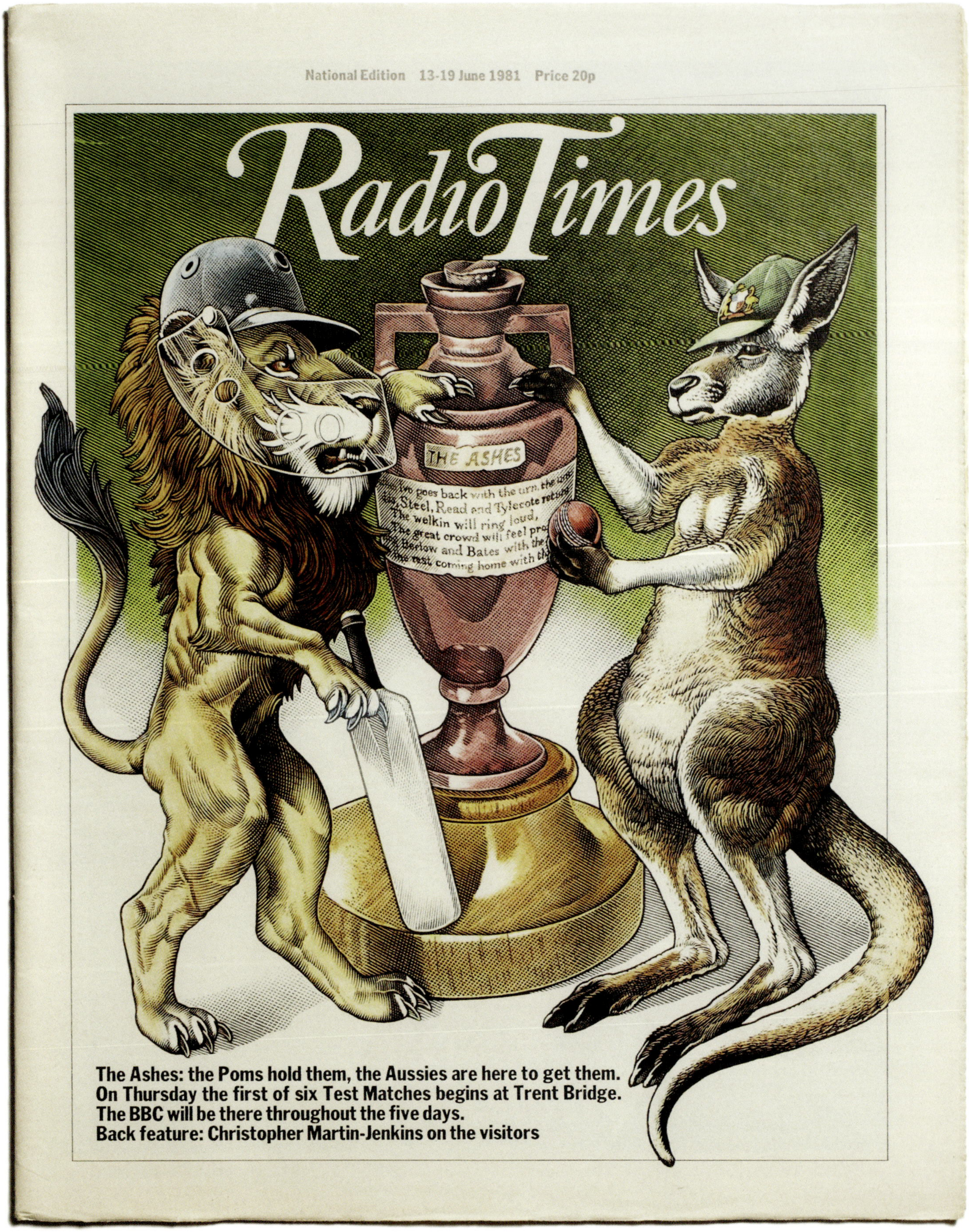

The Ashes Illustration by Bill Sanderson *13–19 June 1981*

Before the six-Test series began, it was known as the Ashes. After it was all over, and thanks to a barely imaginable England victory at Headingley inspired by all-rounder Ian Botham, it was forever known as Botham's Ashes. Looking slightly further afield, American astronomer Carl Sagan began his landmark 13-part series *Cosmos*. His aim was to explain two millennia of progress in scientific ideas. "There is nothing about science that cannot be explained to the layman," he said.

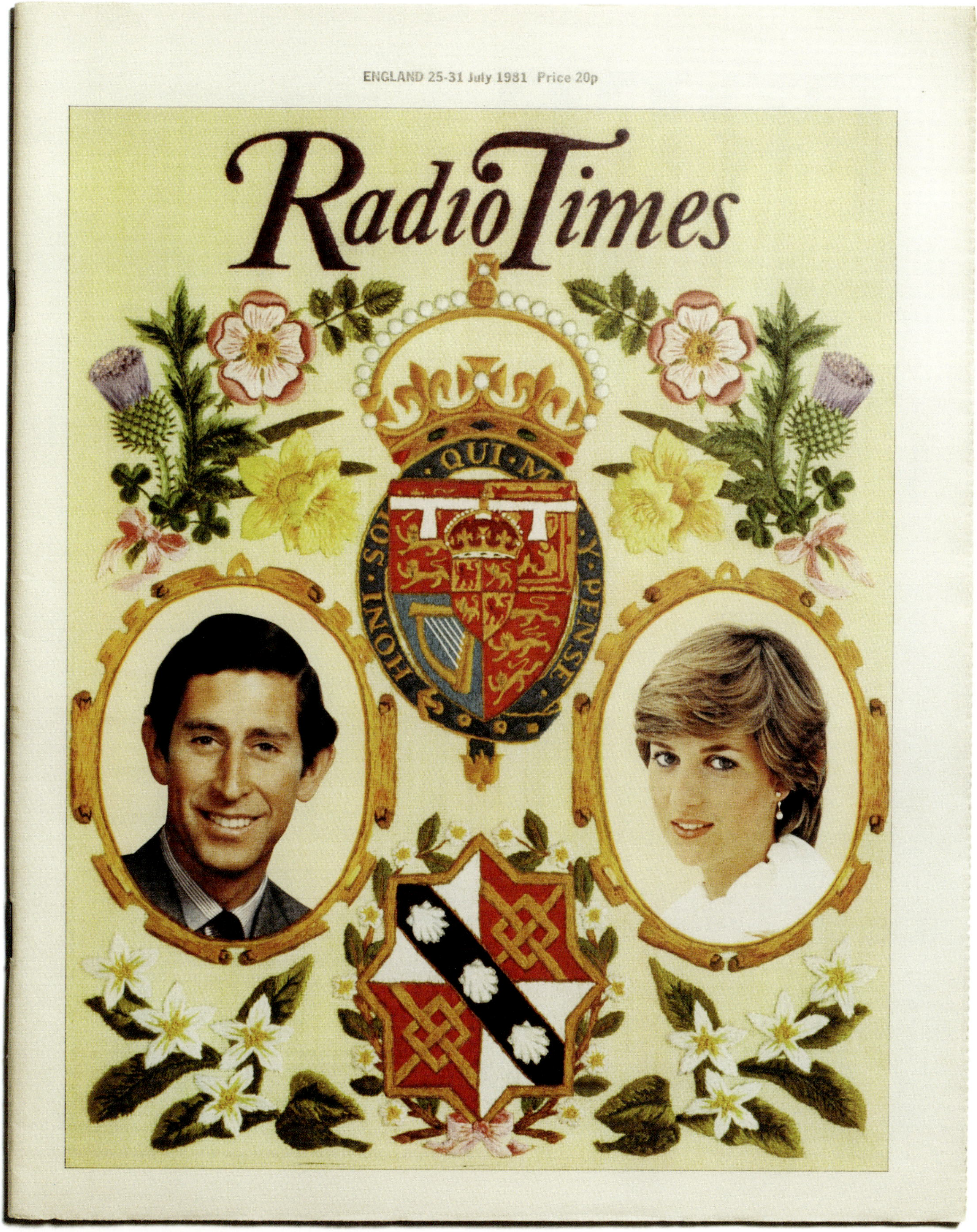

The Royal Wedding **Prince Charles and Lady Diana Spencer**
Tapestry by the Royal School of Needlework *25–31 July 1981*

It was the royal wedding the nation had been looking forward to. For Prince Charles, it was "a watershed in his life, a passage from unencumbered youth to responsible maturity," said *Radio Times*. As for Lady Diana: "Like any other fetching, butter-blonde baby, she has taken 20 years to grow into the very model of aristocratic British beauty."

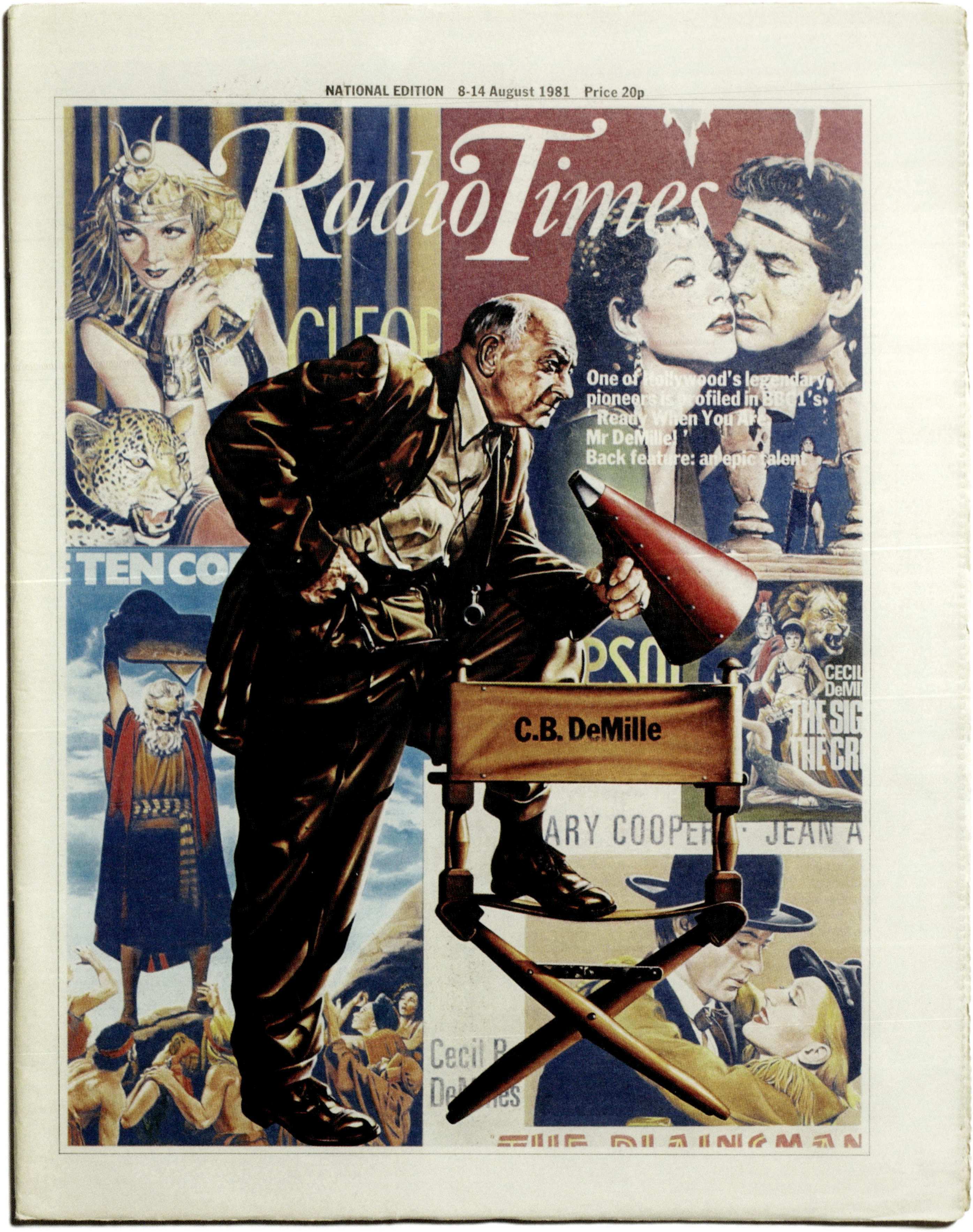

Ready When You Are, Mr DeMille!

Illustration of Cecil B DeMille by Jeff Cummins *8–14 August 1981*

A century after his birth – and 22 years after his death – film director Cecil B DeMille was celebrated on BBC1 and in *Radio Times*. His niece, Agnes DeMille, described his controversial career, saying: "He kept sex, sadism, patriotism, real estate, religion and public relations dancing in mid-air like jugglers' balls for 50 years."

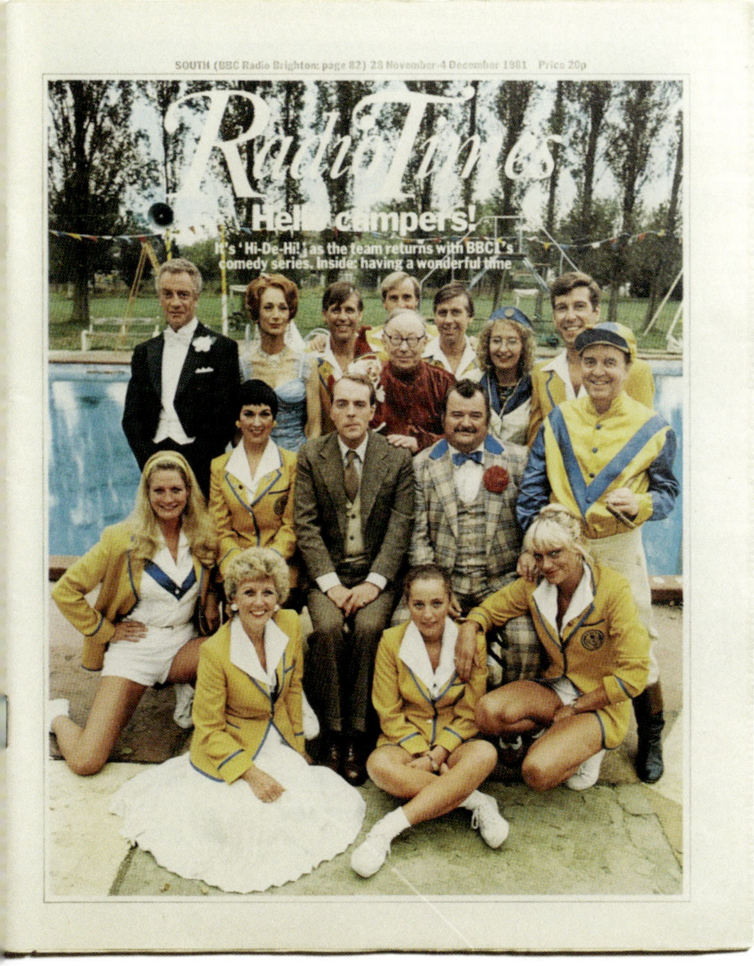

Hi-de-Hi! *(left)*

(photograph by Brian Moody)

28 November–4 December 1981

Seated from left are Gladys (Ruth Madoc), Jeffrey (Simon Cadell) and Ted Bovis (Paul Shane). Thanks to the sitcom's success, Shane became an overnight star. He said: "I thank the Lord I'm old enough to handle it, to rise so fast from oblivion, from £100 a night to telephone numbers."

The Flight of the Condor *(below left)*

(photograph by Mike Andrews)

13–19 February 1982

The World about Us producer Mike Andrews, who took the cover shot, said: "I wanted to show the scale and grandeur of the Andes, and it seemed that the best way was a sort of bird's-eye view. And if you're talking about a bird in the Andes, you're talking about the condor."

The Kenny Everett Television Show *(below right)*

Kenny Everett *(photograph by Ric Gemmell)*

20–26 February 1982

Everett had scored a hit on ITV with *The Kenny Everett Video Show;* now he was on BBC1 with a host of new characters. "It's quite distressing to be all those interesting people, go home and look in the mirror and see someone ordinary!"

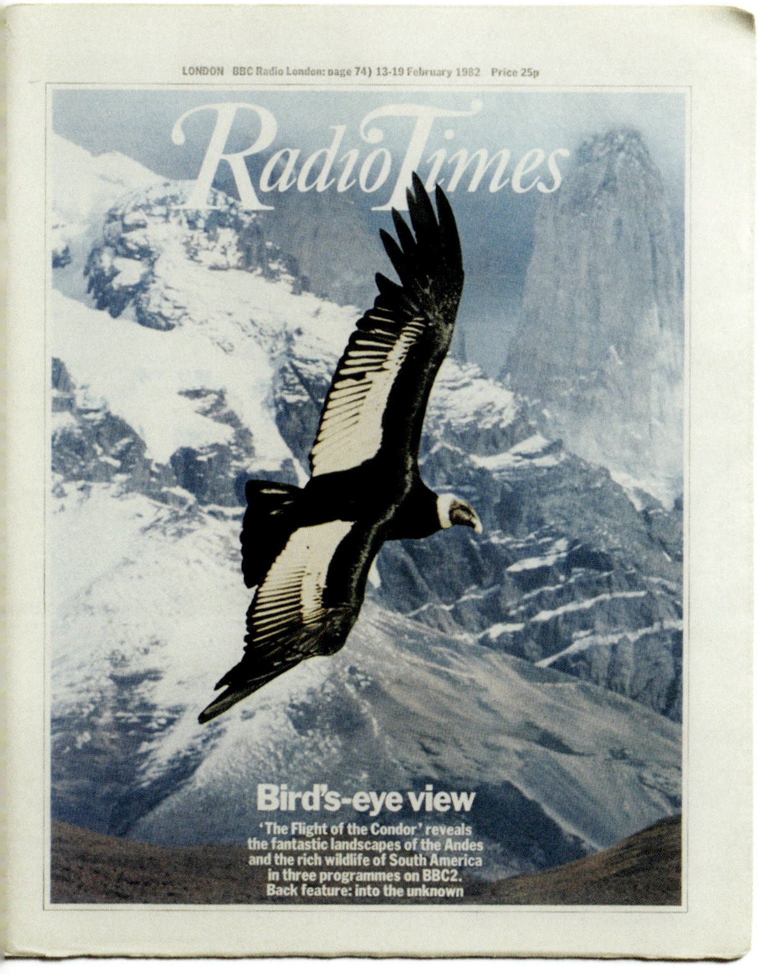

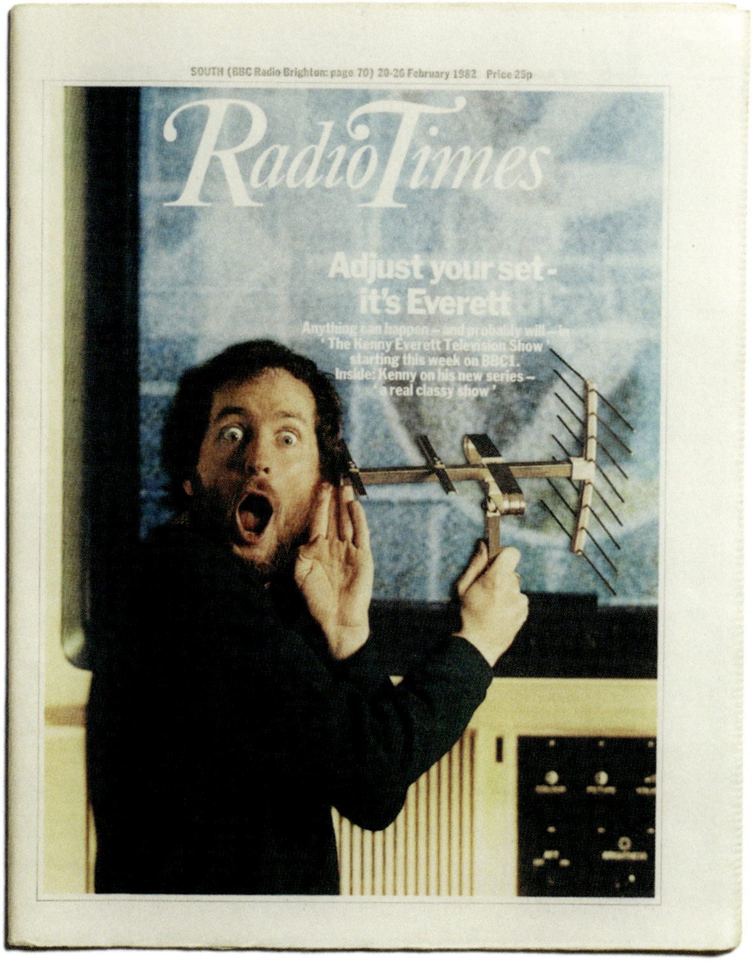

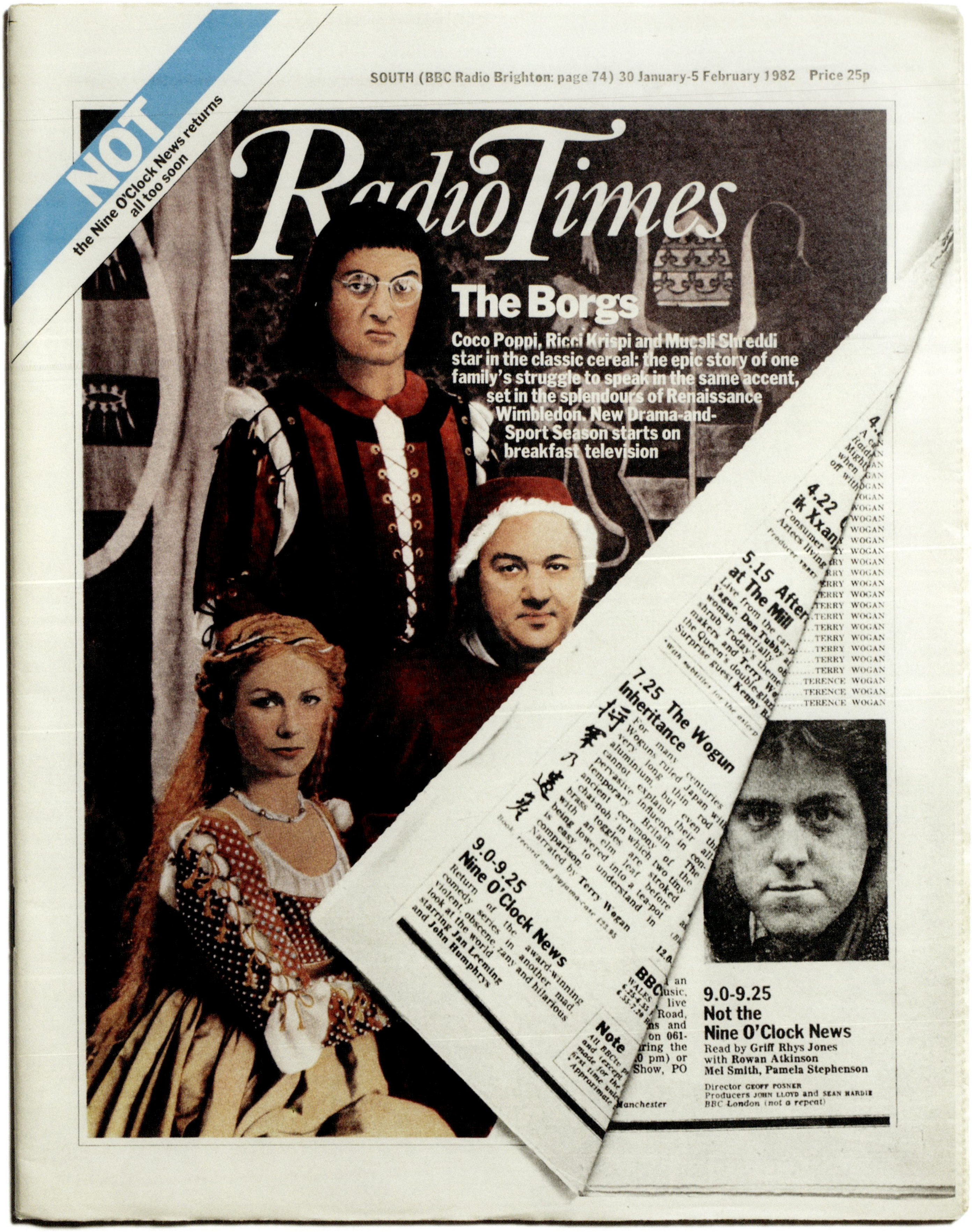

Not the Nine O'Clock News **From left: Muesli Shreddi (Pamela Stephenson), Coco Poppi (Rowan Atkinson) and Ricci Krispi (Mel Smith). Inset: Griff Rhys Jones** *(photomontage by Michael Bennett, hand-tinting by Amanda Currey)* *30 January–5 February 1982*

This was the final series of the sketch show, and the folded cover caused consternation in newsagents' across the land. It aped *The Borgias* cover (page 214). Note the faux billings on BBC1 and BBC2 at 9.00pm.

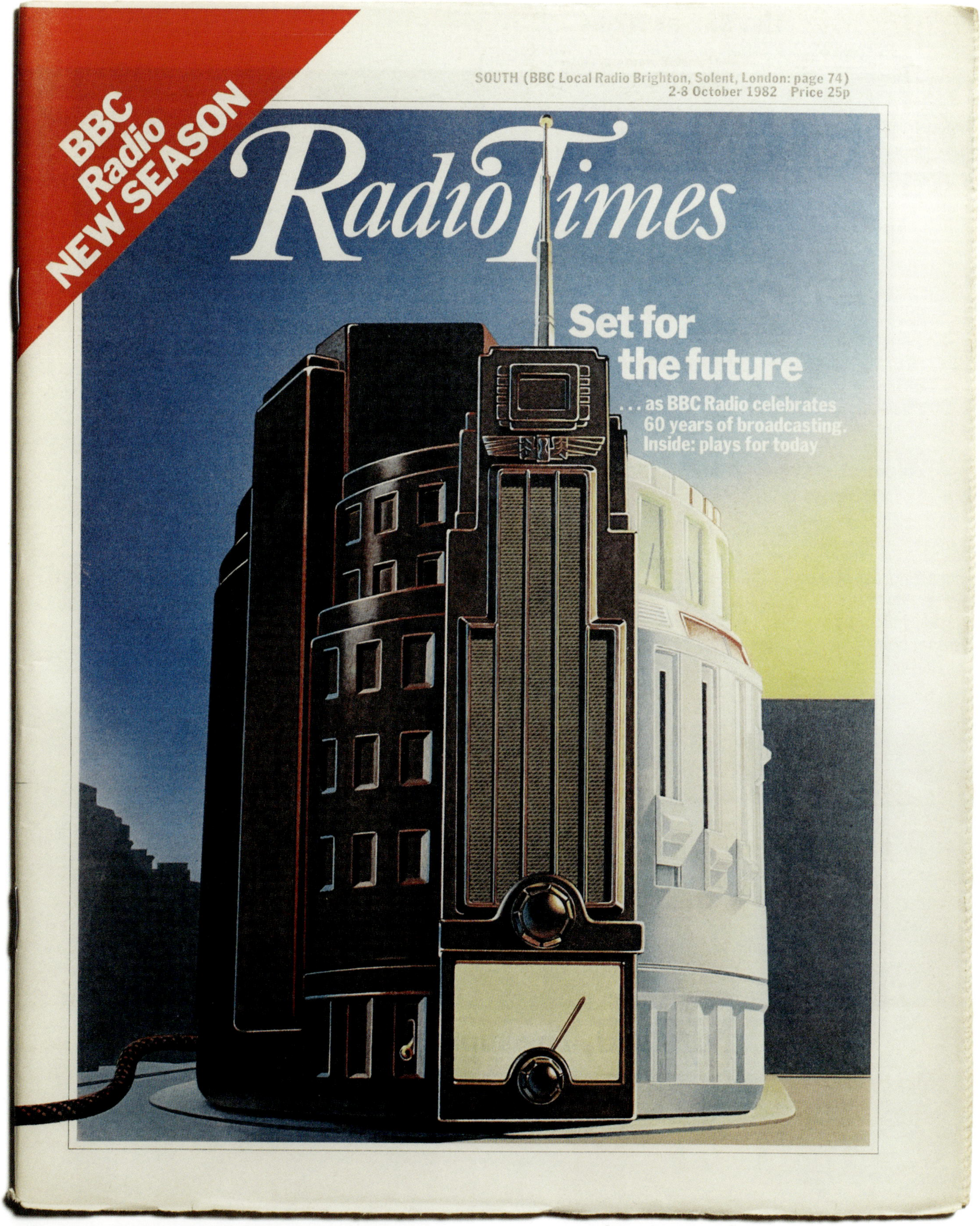

60 Years of BBC Radio **Illustration by Roy Knipe** *2–8 October 1982*

Roy Knipe's illustration made full use of Broadcasting House, showing the building in Bakelite on the left, merging into the hi-tech controls of the 1980s. Inside, radio drama presented a "rich harvest of new plays for the autumn" – including works by John Arden, John Mortimer, Alan Plater, Simon Moss, Alun Owen, James Saunders and Rhys Adrian – as well as a new version of *Twelfth Night*, the first play ever broadcast on the airwaves.

The Sky at Night *(right)*

Patrick Moore *(photograph by Victor Watts)*

24–30 April 1982

Dr Patrick Moore – he wouldn't be knighted for another six years – was 59 and *The Sky at Night* a mere 25 when *Radio Times* profiled both. Moore proved to be a self-taught everything: astronomer, typist, pianist and xylophone player.

International Athletics *(middle right)*

Sebastian Coe and Steve Ovett
Illustration by Mark Thomas

17–23 July 1982

Coe and Ovett were the big stars of British athletics and they were due to race over 3,000m at Crystal Palace. But it was not to be. "After our cover and colour pages had been printed, we learned that the big showdown would not begin after all, owing to an injury to Seb Coe."

Wogan's Guide to the BBC *(far right)*

Terry Wogan *(photograph by Brian Moody)*

28 August–3 September 1982

Wogan gave readers a tour of the BBC to mark 60 years of broadcasting, but he also had advice for "that auld rag, *Radio Times*. Shove the listings to the back, have letters up front, with saucy pictures of Radio 3 announcers, and nude bingo... If that doesn't work wonders for circulation, nothing will."

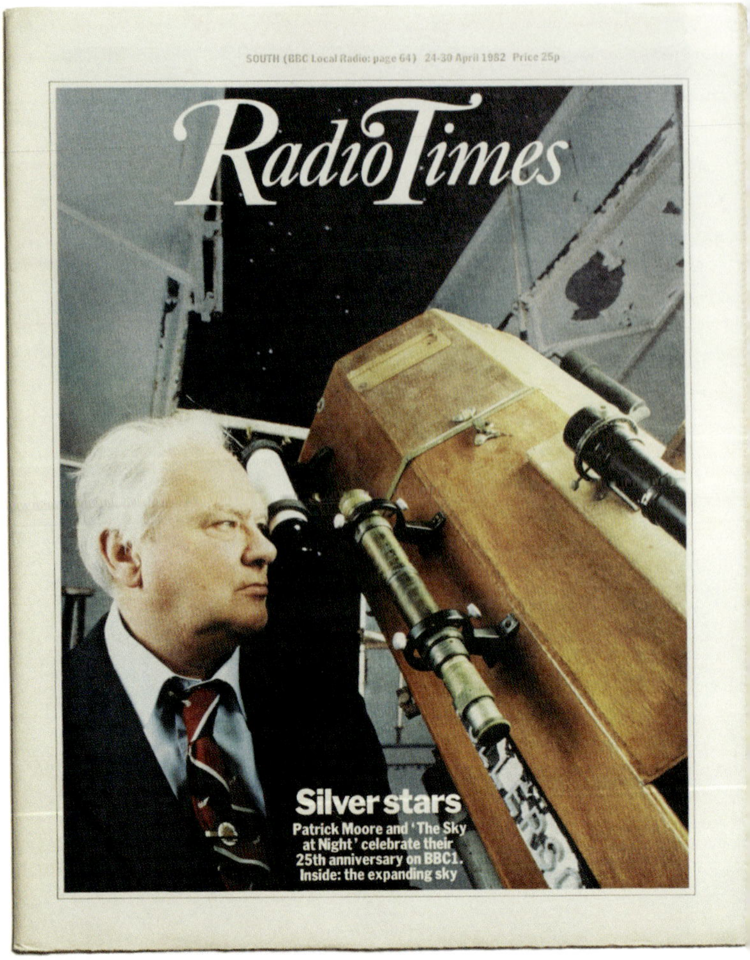

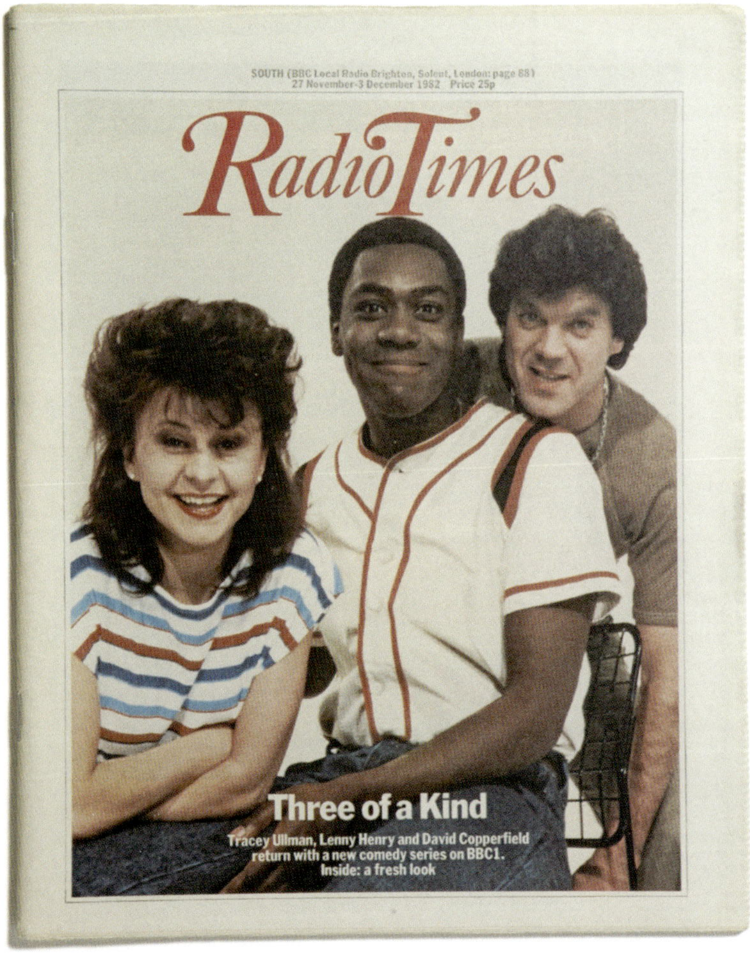

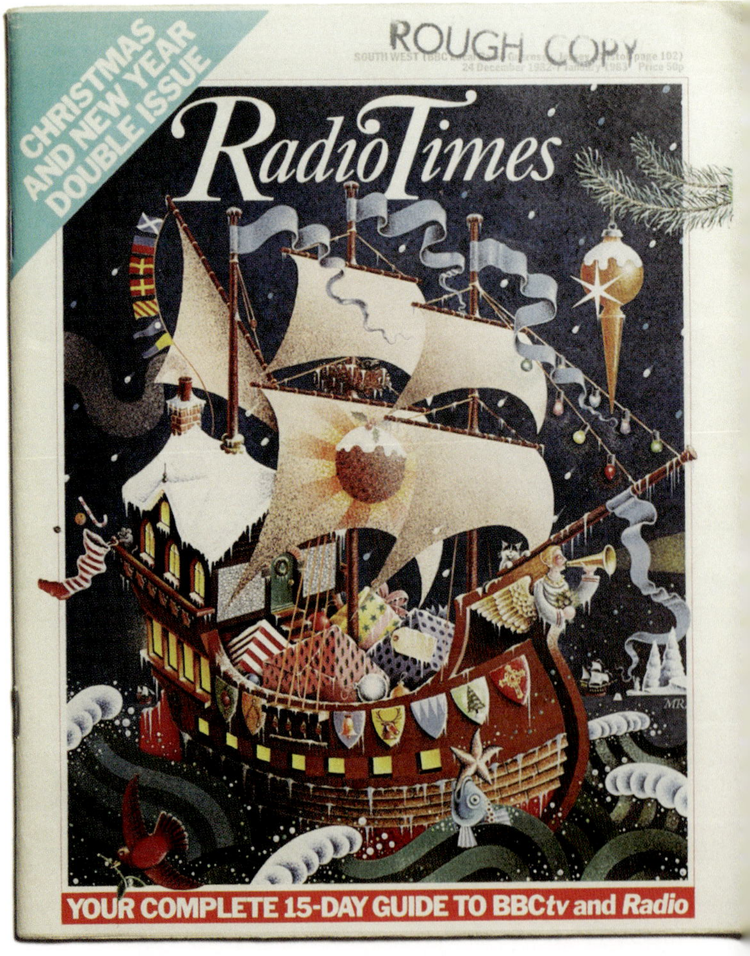

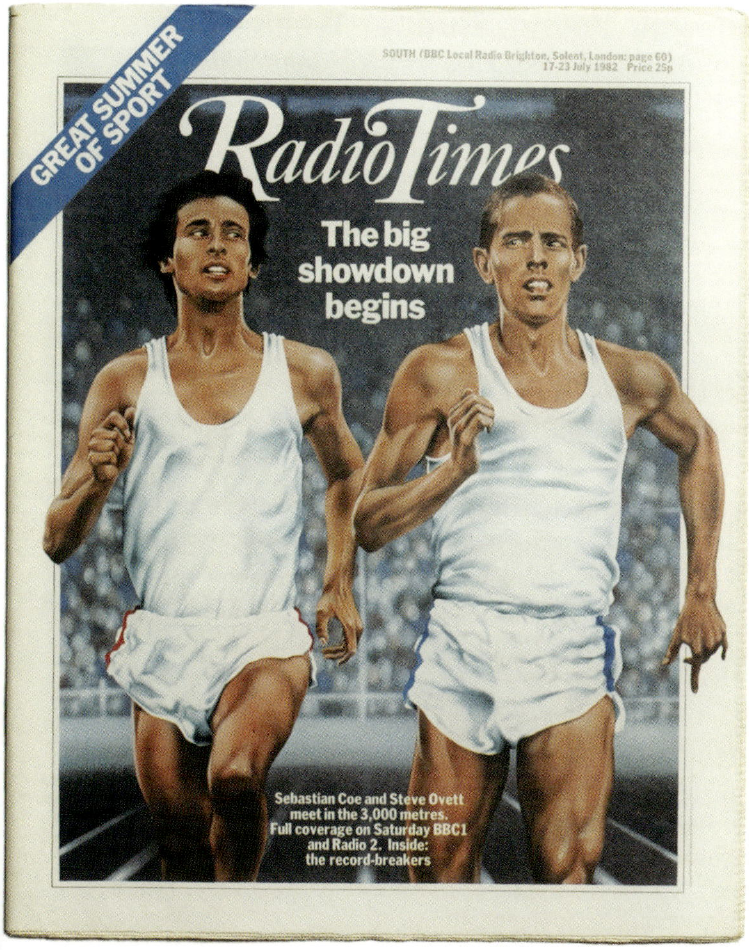

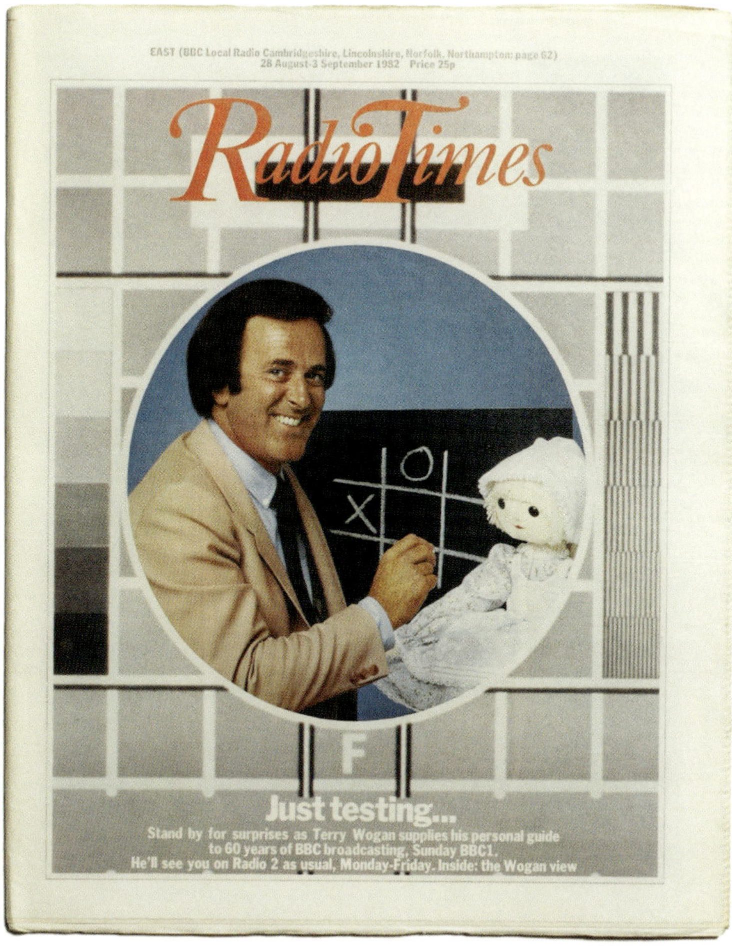

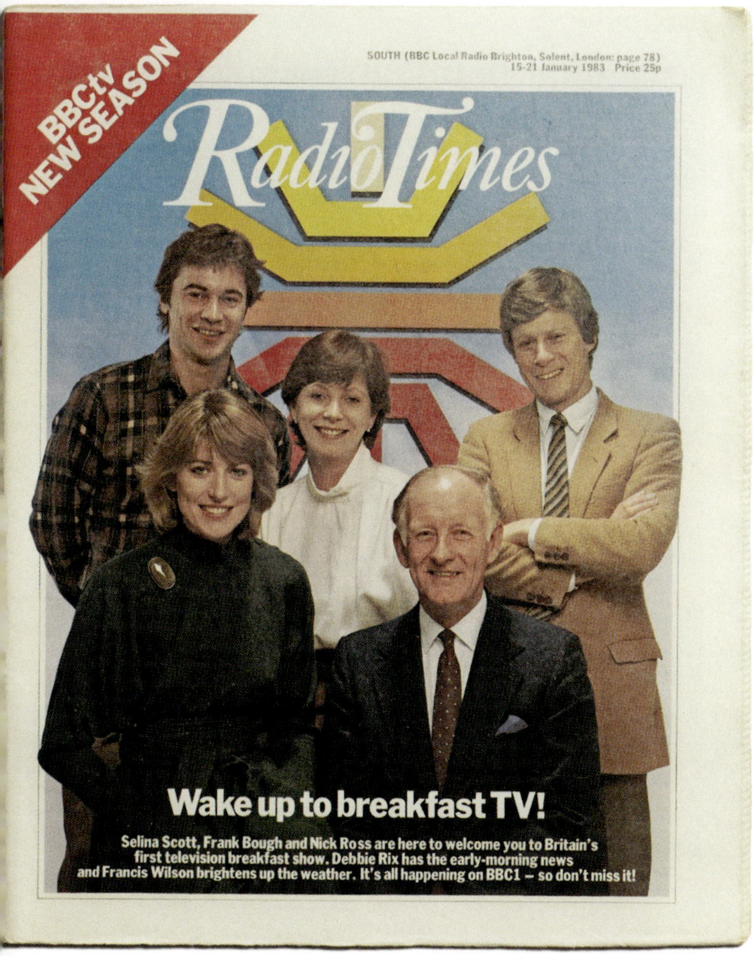

Three of a Kind *(far left)*

Tracey Ullman, Lenny Henry and David Copperfield *(photograph by David Edwards)*

27 November–3 December 1982

Six people had been cast originally but only Copperfield and Henry lasted. They were then teamed with Ullman and a hit sketch show was made. "We're three young kids forging ahead in a fight against mediocre comedy," said Lenny Henry.

Christmas 1982 *(middle left)*

Illustration by Mark Reddy

24 December 1982–7 January 1983

Radio Times asked the stars of the BBC's Christmas comedy specials to tell readers about Christmas presents they'd given and received. Les Dawson's contribution went: "Last year I bought my youngest son an Action Man. When he opened it, he said there was nothing in the box. 'No,' I said. 'It's a deserter.'"

Breakfast Time *(left)*

From left: Francis Wilson, Selina Scott, Debbie Rix, Frank Bough and Nick Ross *(photograph by Ric Gemmell)*

15–21 January 1983

This was the UK's first breakfast television show, making it on to the TV screens of an unsuspecting nation 15 days before the launch of ITV rival *TV-am*.

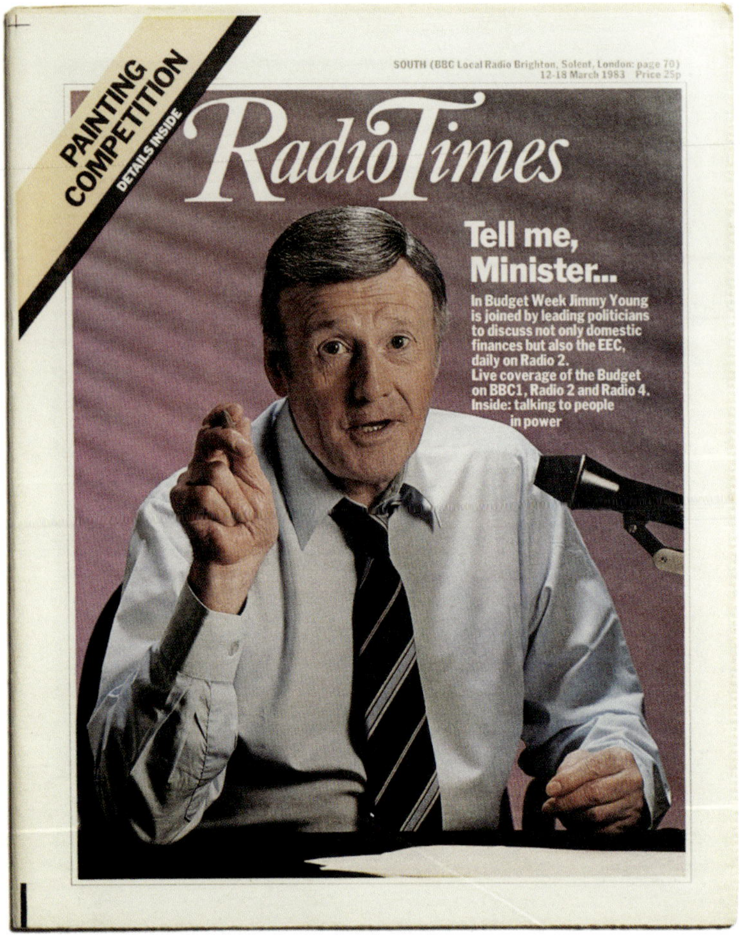

Jimmy Young: Budget Week *(left)*

Jimmy Young *(photograph by Ric Gemmell)*

12–18 March 1983

The Budget fell on the tenth anniversary of Jimmy Young's Radio 2 show, which had grown to mix easy-listening music with politics. Young defended himself against accusations that he was a soft interviewer. "When you don't shout at people, when you're polite – and I always am – but you don't let them go, you'd be surprised at what comes tumbling out."

Britain in the Thirties *(below left)*

Illustration by Ian Beck

23–29 April 1983

A major BBC documentary series looked back to the 1930s – a decade that saw the Depression, the Abdication and the outbreak of war. But there was a bright side, too: great social and technological progress and a golden age of cinema and radio.

Top of the Pops *(below right)*

(photograph by Brian Griffin)

30 April–6 May 1983

The pop show celebrated its 1,000th edition. John Peel wrote about being a *Top of the Pops* presenter and quoted himself saying in a student magazine 16 years earlier that the show "is a national disgrace... all it does is reflect the very worst of popular taste".

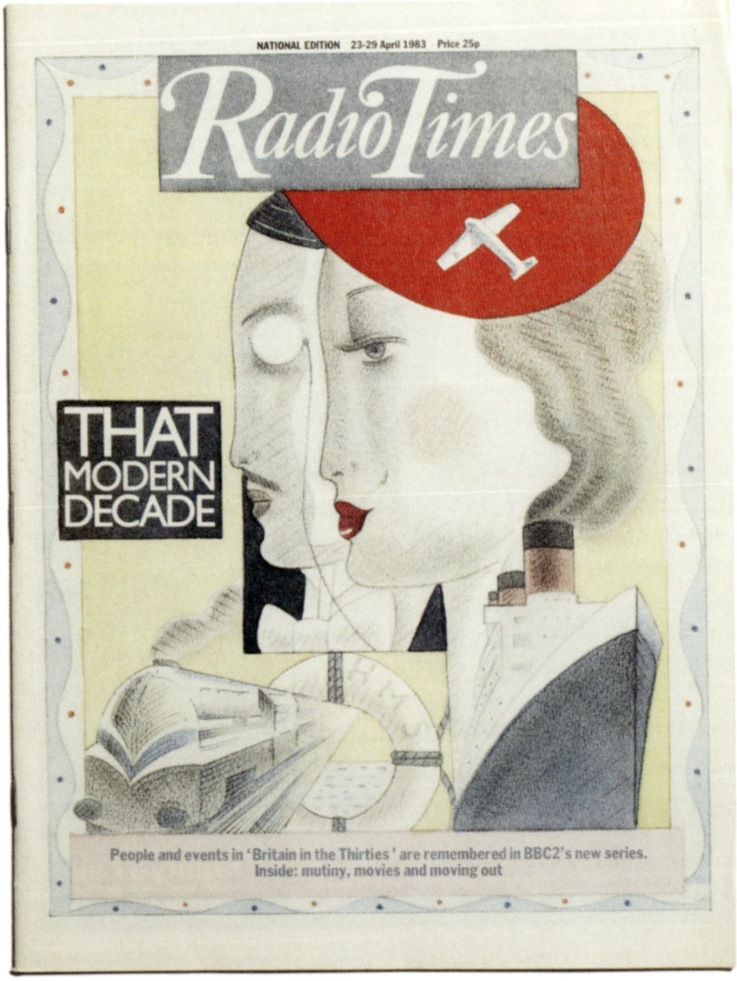

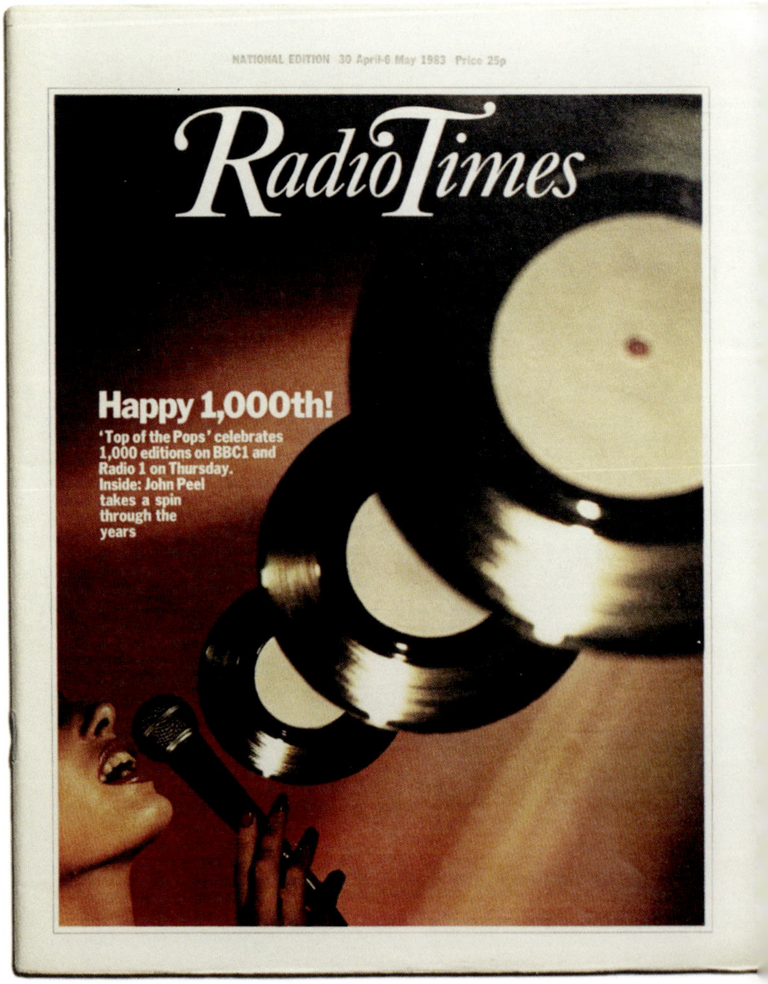

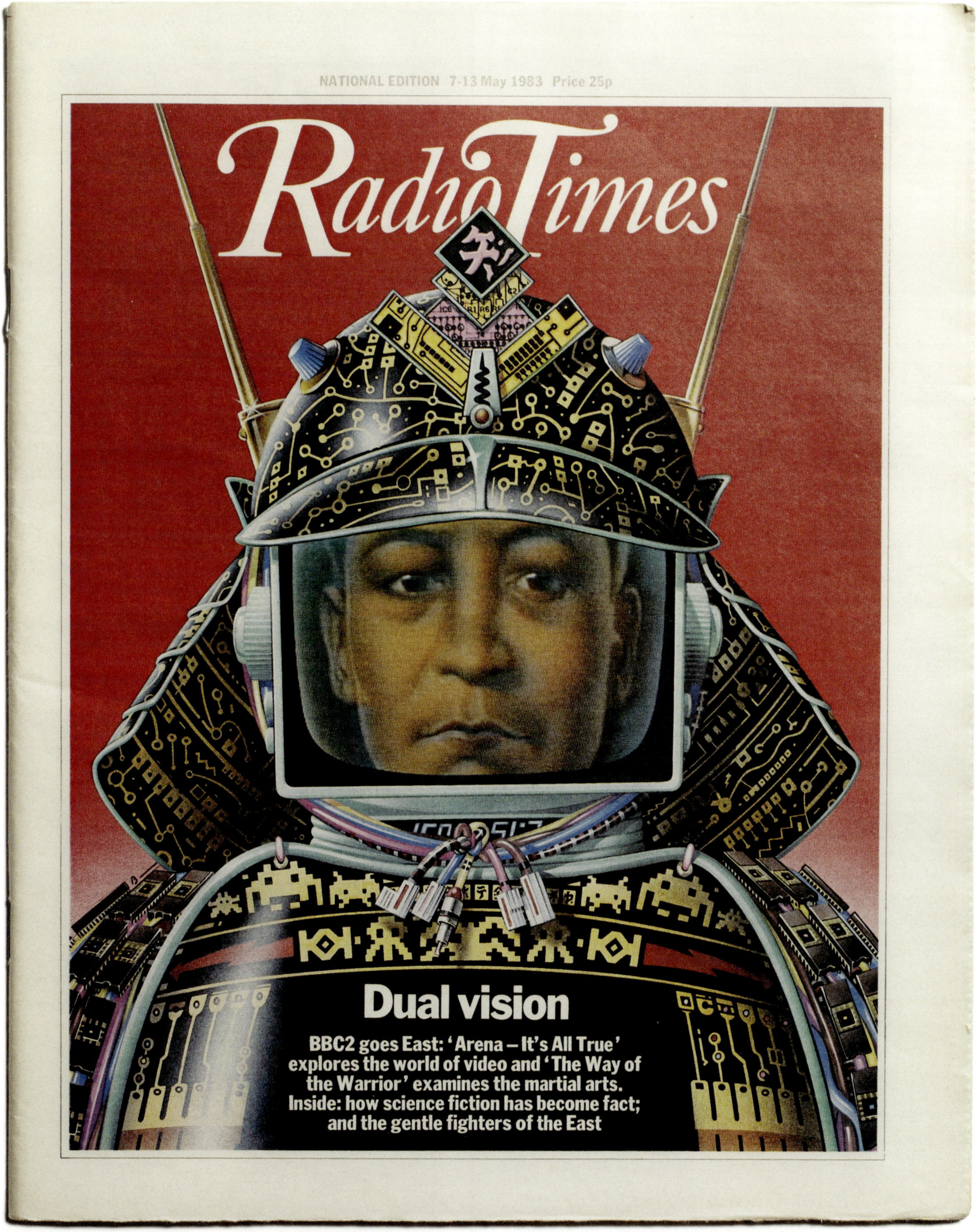

Arena/The Way of the Warrior **Illustration by Mick Brownfield** *7–13 May 1983*

This was a clever way to link two shows on the cover. An edition of *Arena* called *It's All True* looked to the future of television and electronics. It overestimated the impact of video discs and underestimated the number of TV channels (it said we'd have "up to 30 channels of 'pap' entertainment"; we now have a thousand). Meanwhile, the documentary *The Way of the Warrior* looked into the past and present of martial arts.

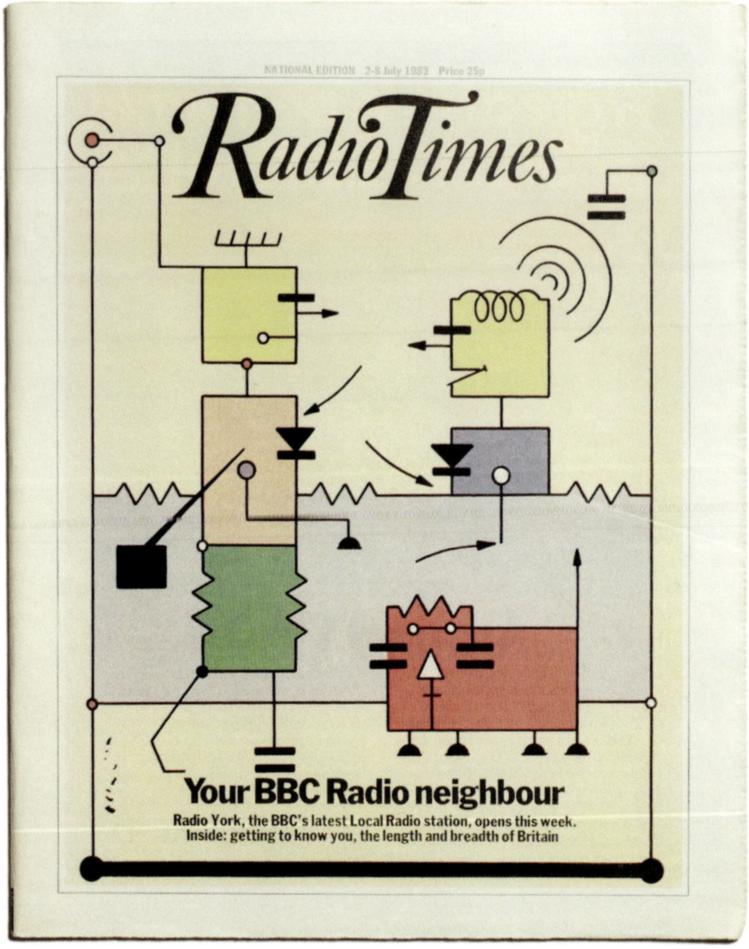

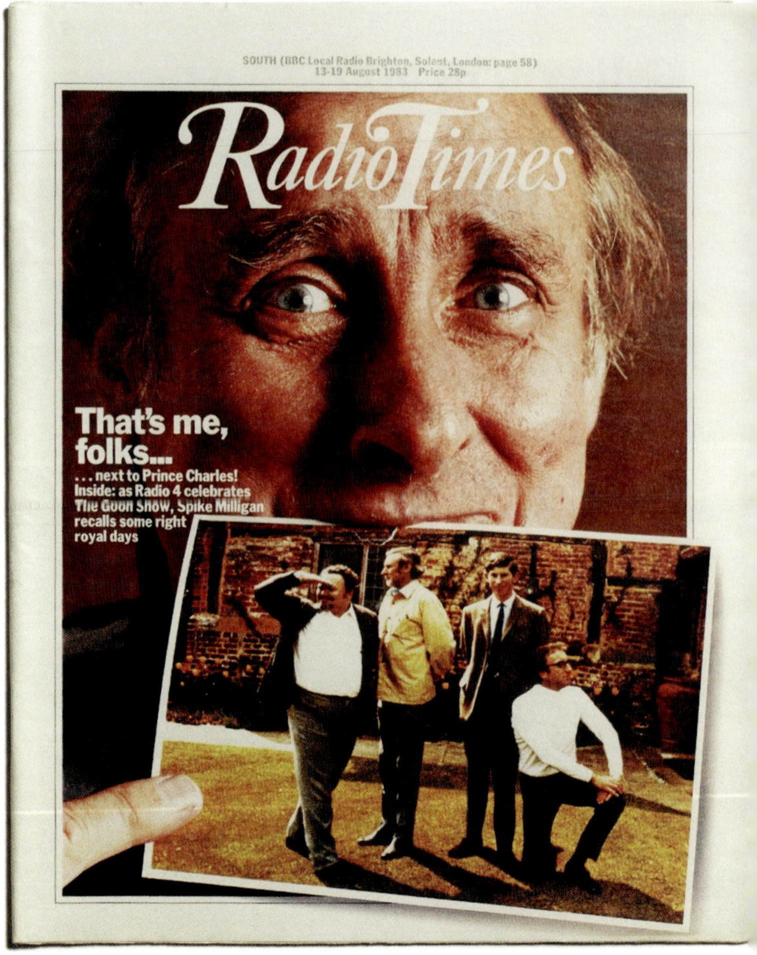

Doctor Who *(right)*

Illustration by Andrew Skilleter

19–25 November 1983

To mark the Time Lord's 20th anniversary, *Radio Times* commissioned an artwork from Andrew Skilleter, who had illustrated many *Doctor Who* novels. A 90-minute BBC1 special, *The Five Doctors,* starred Richard Hurndall (replacing the late William Hartnell), Jon Pertwee, Peter Davison and Patrick Troughton. Tom Baker appeared only briefly, courtesy of old footage from 1979. Anthony Ainley was the villainous Master.

The Thorn Birds *(middle right)*

Ralph de Bricassart (Richard Chamberlain)

7–13 January 1984

Colleen McCullough's novel came to BBC1 as a mini-series made for US TV. It was about an affair between an Australian sheep rancher's daughter played by Rachel Ward and a Catholic priest played by Richard Chamberlain. He said: "I've never come across a character like this before."

Winter Olympics 1984 *(far right)*

Christopher Dean and Jayne Torvill
(photograph by Bob Thomas)

4–10 February 1984

Ice dance duo Torvill and Dean went to the Winter Olympics in Sarajevo carrying the country's gold-medal hopes. Their secret weapon was a dramatic interpretation of Ravel's *Boléro.*

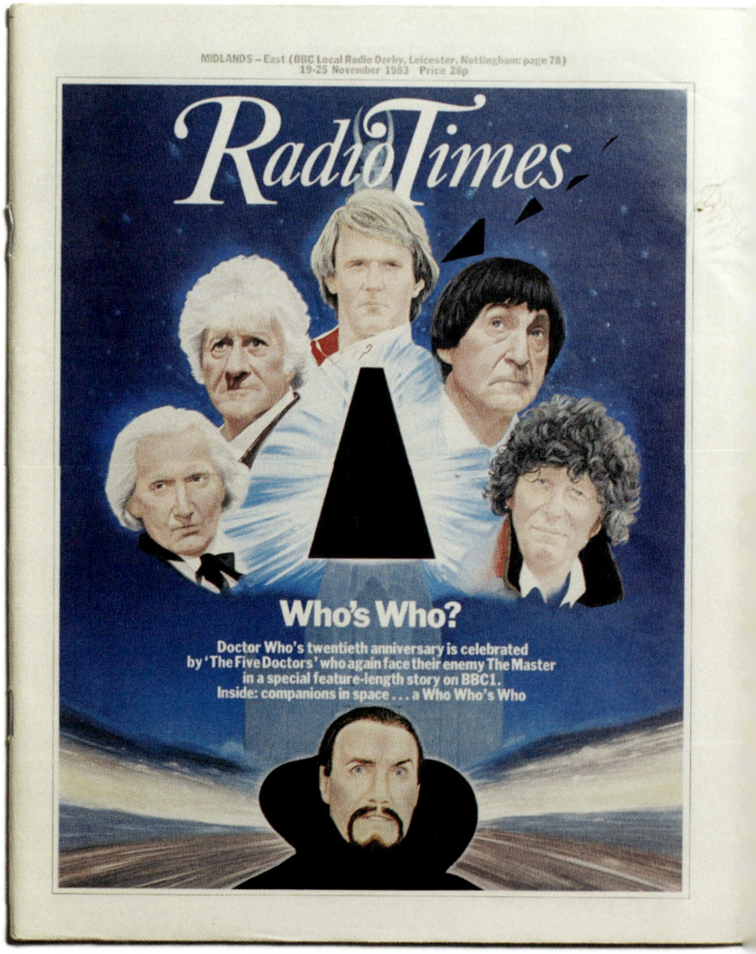

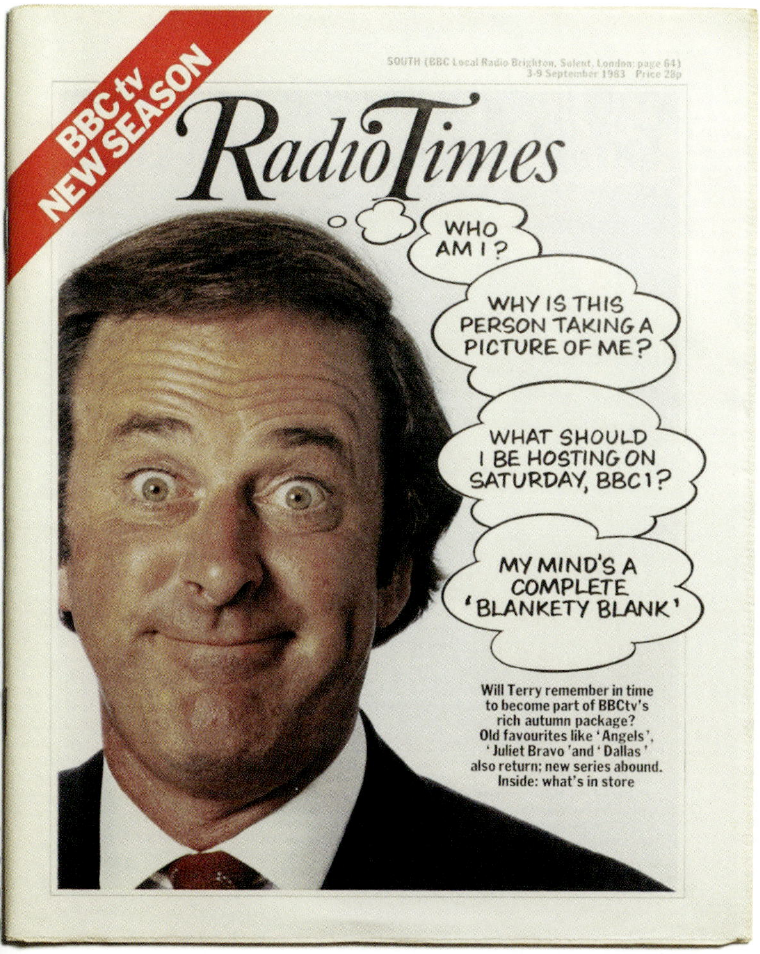

BBC Local Radio *(far left)*

Illustration by Brian Greenwood

2–8 July 1983

A radio circuit diagram marked the opening of Radio York. It was the 30th BBC Local Radio station and manager John Jefferson said: "Being a bright station doesn't mean you have to sacrifice the principles of community radio."

The Goon Show *(middle left)*

Spike Milligan (inset: Harry Secombe, Milligan, Prince Charles, Peter Sellers) ***(main photograph by Brian Moody; inset by Britt Ekland)***

13–19 August 1983

Radio 4 was celebrating the Goons but Spike Milligan wasn't in the mood. "I was paid £25 for writing it and £12 10s for appearing in it. It's on in South Africa and Australia all the time and I get nothing." He also revealed that the inset picture was taken after a lunch at Peter Sellers's house in Surrey, which he organised at the behest of Prince Charles.

Blankety Blank *(left)*

Terry Wogan ***(photograph by Ric Gemmell)***

3–9 September 1983

This was the sixth series of the game show and astrologer Russell Grant was one of three new panellists. He told *Radio Times* that "Terry was charming, in good Leo style".

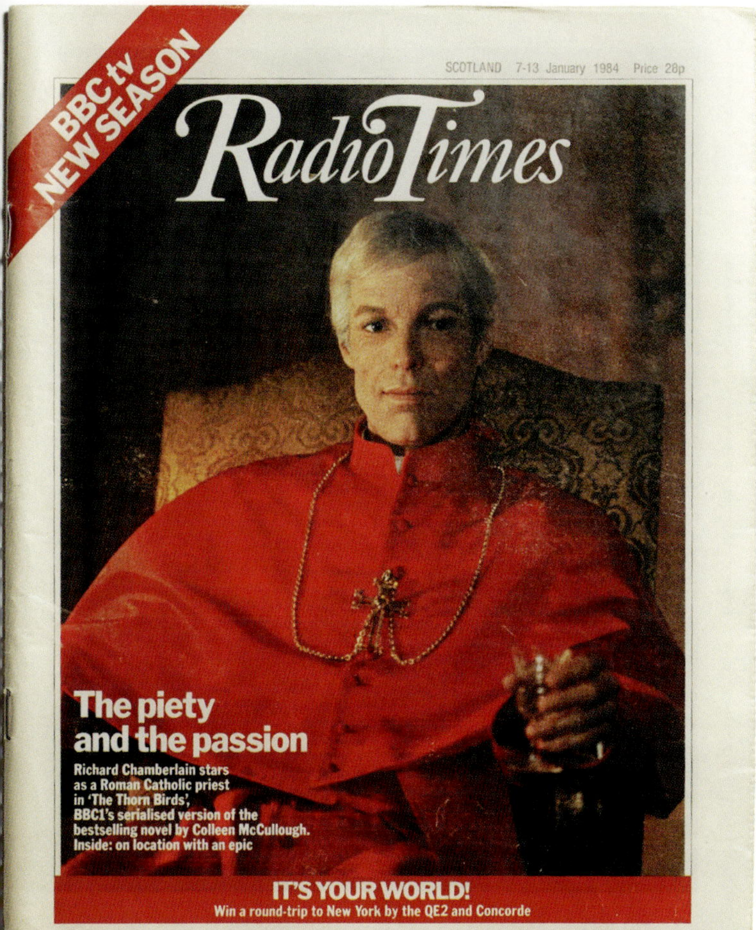

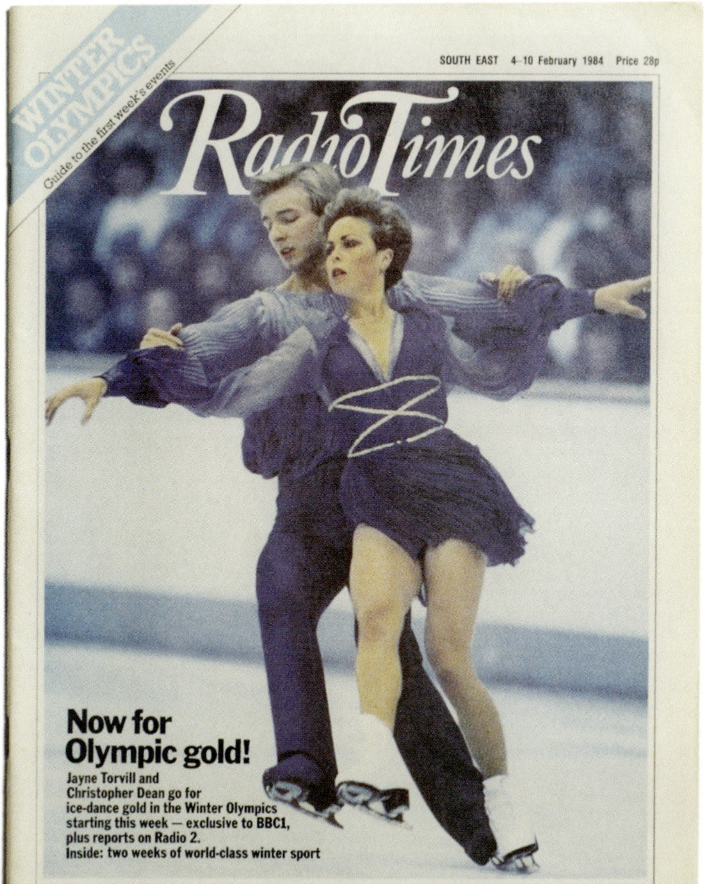

The Young Ones *(right)*

Mike (Christopher Ryan), Rick (Rik Mayall), Vyvyan (Ade Edmondson) and Neil (Nigel Planer)

(photograph by Don Smith) *5–11 May 1984*

Radio Times writer Johnny Black tried – and failed – to interview the cast of *The Young Ones* for their second series. A long tale of woe began in BBC Television Centre when he was told, "They've all gone off to stop Rik bleeding."

Olympics Games 1984 *(middle right)*

(model by Paul Baker; photograph by Chris Ryan)

28 July–3 August 1984

Jonathan Martin, BBC TV's Head of Sport, pondered the problem of broadcasting the Games when the action was happening in Los Angeles while Britain was tucked up in bed. The answer: breakfast-time programmes, a catch-up show at lunchtime and live action and highlights in the early evening.

The Box of Delights *(far right)*

Kay Harker (Devin Stanfield) *(photograph Ric Gemmell)*

17–23 November 1984

Patrick Troughton starred in "the most ambitious BBC children's television series ever". Alan Seymour dramatised it from John Masefield's book and producer Paul Stone said: "Every five or six years, I am seized with a desire to cap the ultimate in children's drama – to better the best there's been."

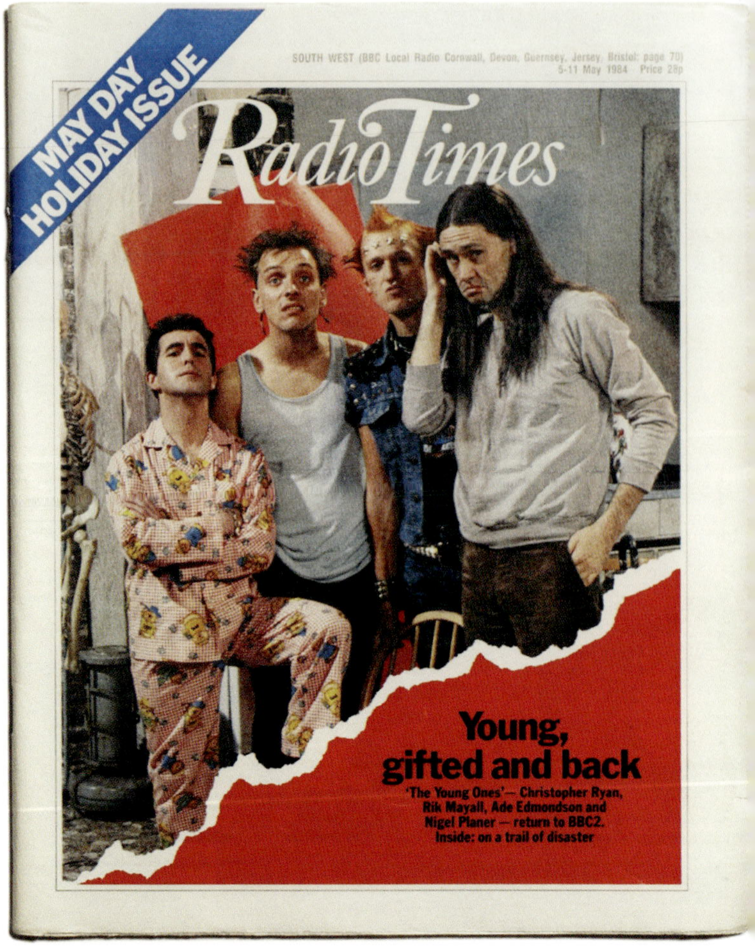

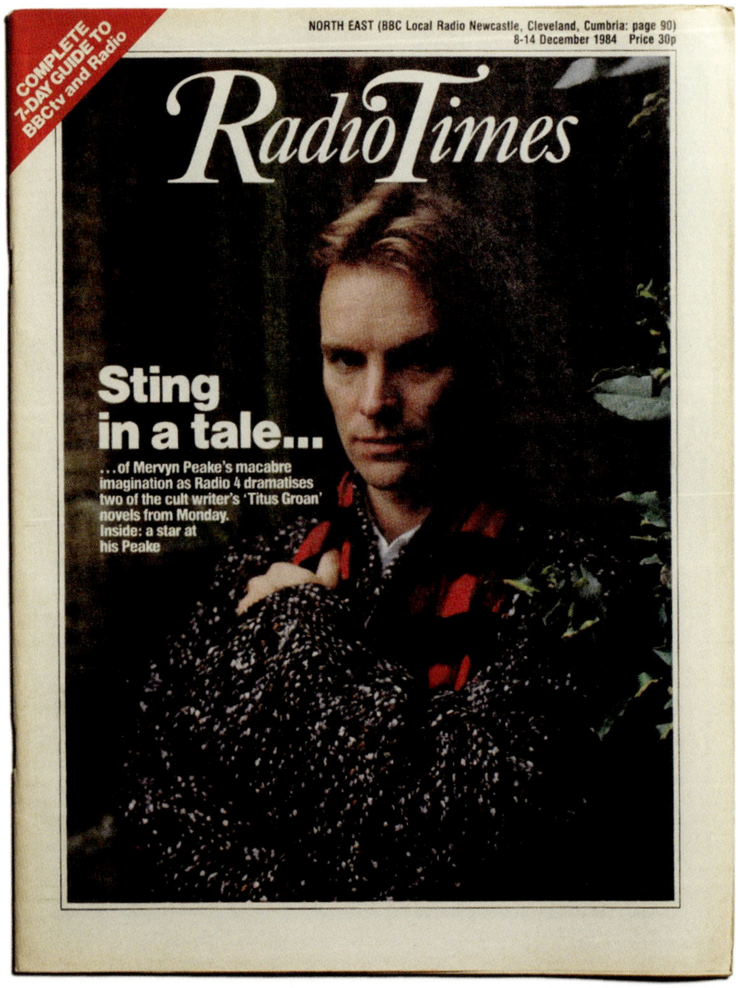

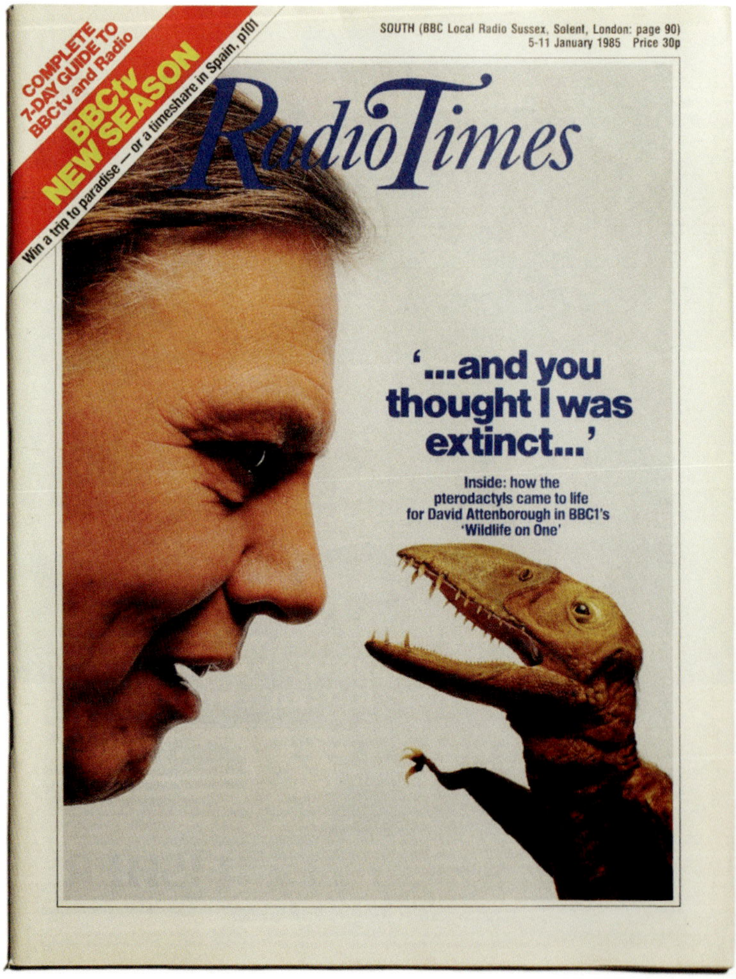

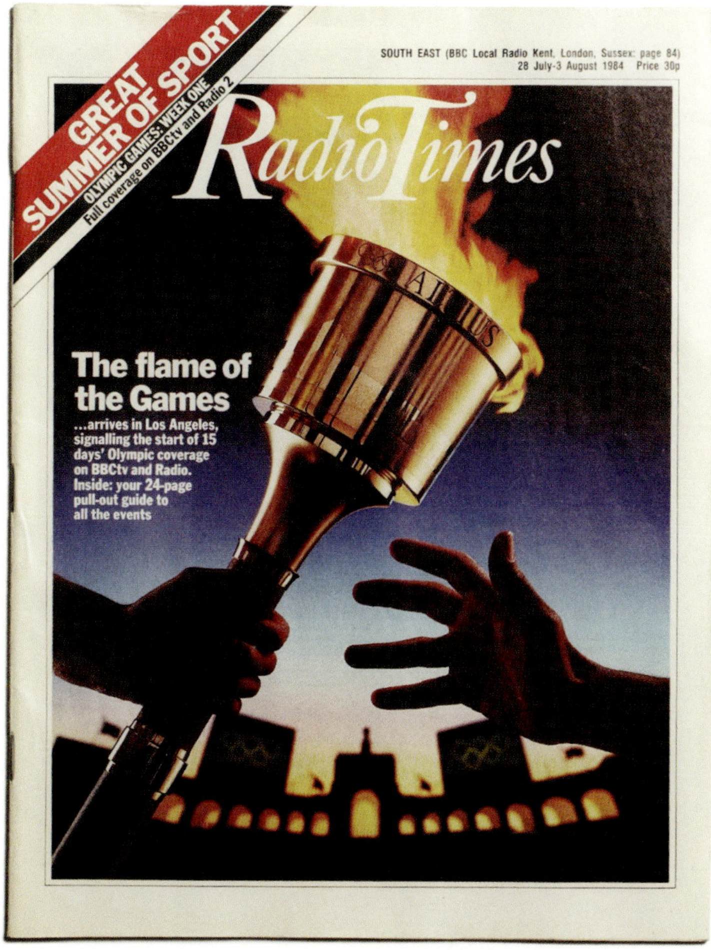

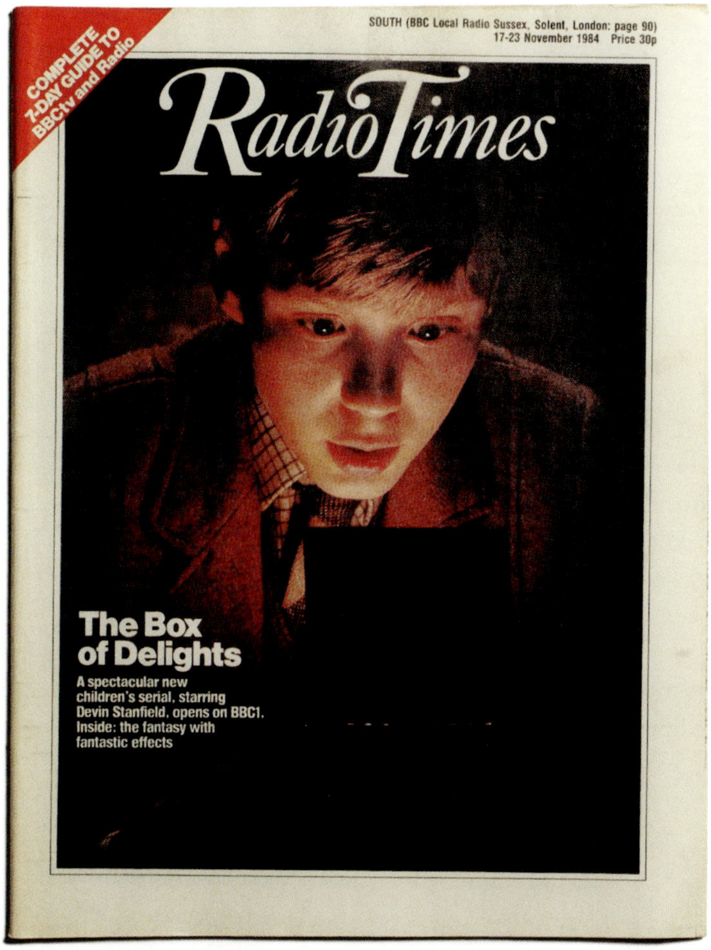

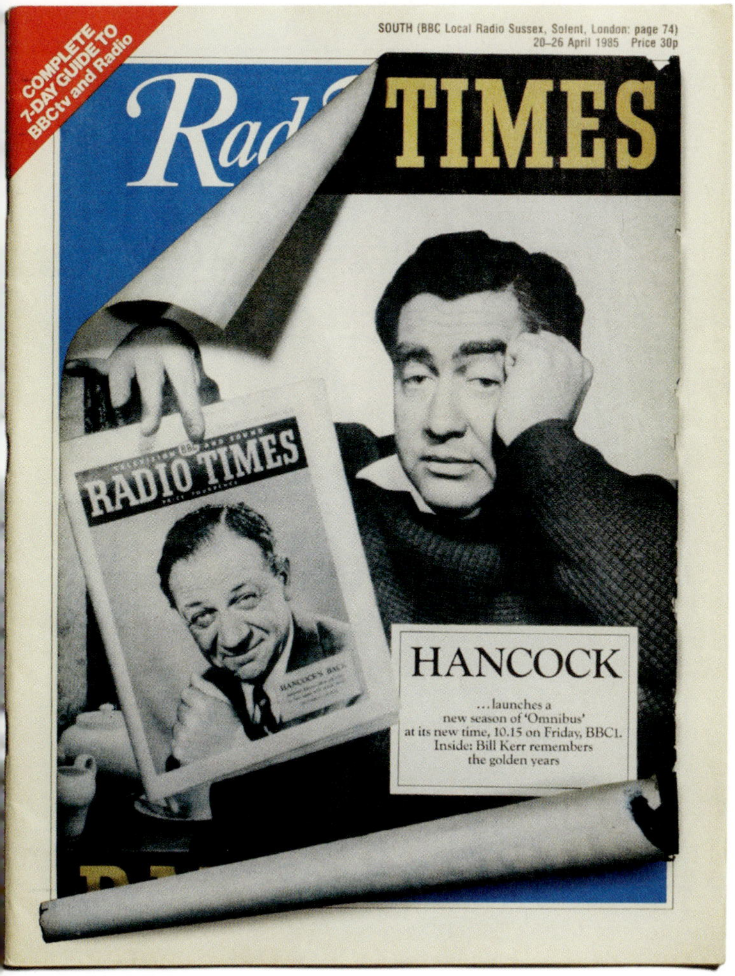

Titus Groan *(far left)*

Steerpike (Sting) *(photograph by Allan Ballard)*

8–14 December 1984

BBC Radio 4 dramatised Mervyn Peake's tale and easily got Sting because he's a fan of the books: "I couldn't put them down. They are so seductive – you start to live inside them. I ended up reading the entire trilogy in a week." He also named "his horse, his dog and his company" Steerpike.

Wildlife on One *(middle left)*

David Attenborough *(photograph by Chris Ridley)*

5–11 January 1985

There were descendants of prehistoric flying reptiles in "bats and birds around the world" and there was also a model with an 11-foot wingspan. "In the air it is altogether magnificent," said Attenborough. "It looks like a living thing. It could even be an albatross... until it gets close."

Omnibus *(left)*

Tony Hancock, inset: Sid James *(photograph by Don Smith)*

20–26 April 1985

That's the cover from 28 February 1960 issue atop this one (see page 114). With Hancock and James now dead, *Radio Times* interviewed the other member of *Hancock's Half-Hour*, Bill Kerr. He said: "It's a mark of his greatness that one can mention Hancock in the same breath as Chaplin and Keaton."

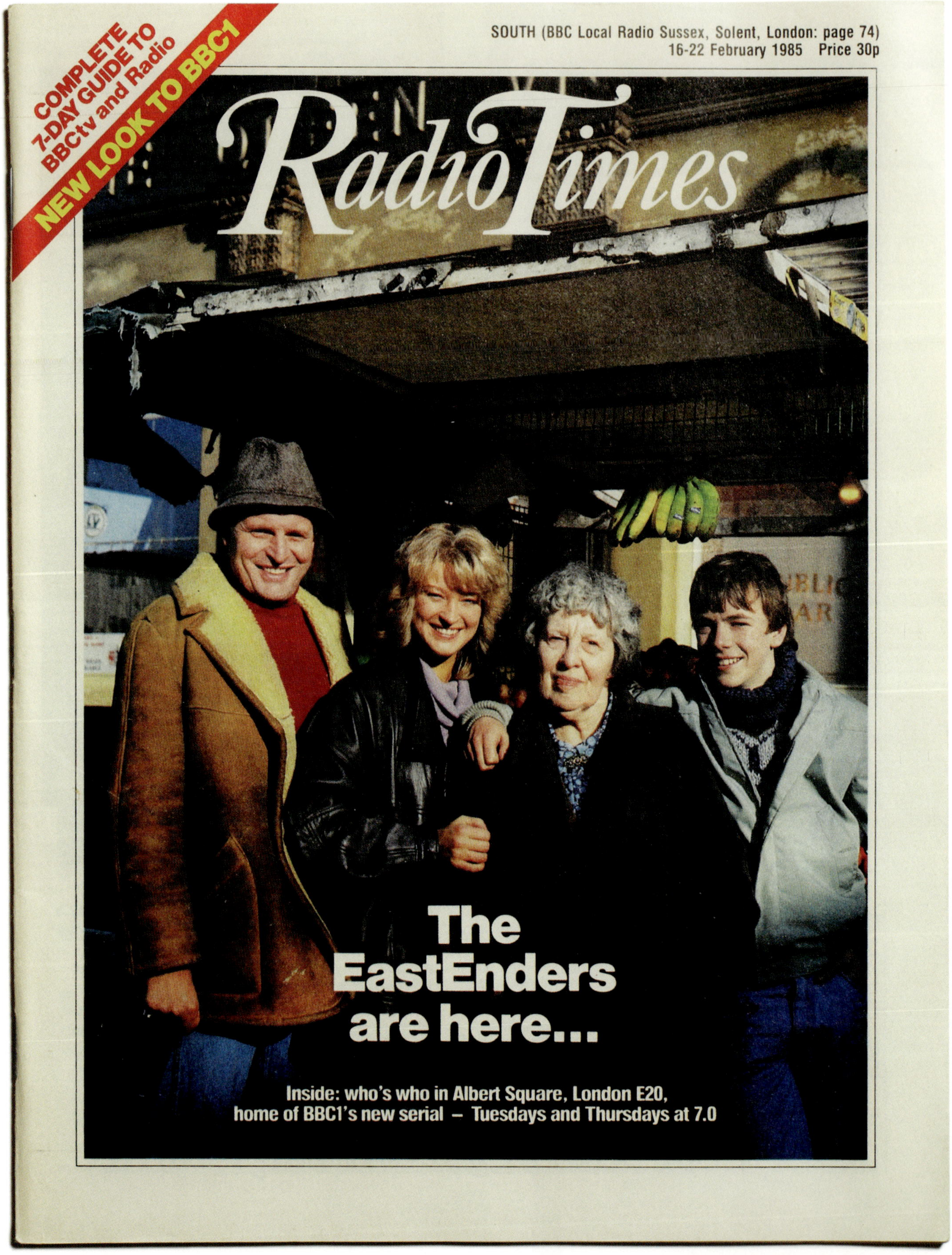

EastEnders **From left: Pete Beale (Peter Dean), Kathy Beale (Gillian Taylforth), Lou Beale (Anna Wing) and Ian Beale (Adam Woodyatt)** *(photograph by Don Smith)* *16–22 February 1985*

Radio Times introduced us to the new soap *EastEnders*, all the characters of Albert Square and their intricate pasts. The show's co-creator Tony Holland wrote: "Families and family life play a large part in everyday happening in the Square."

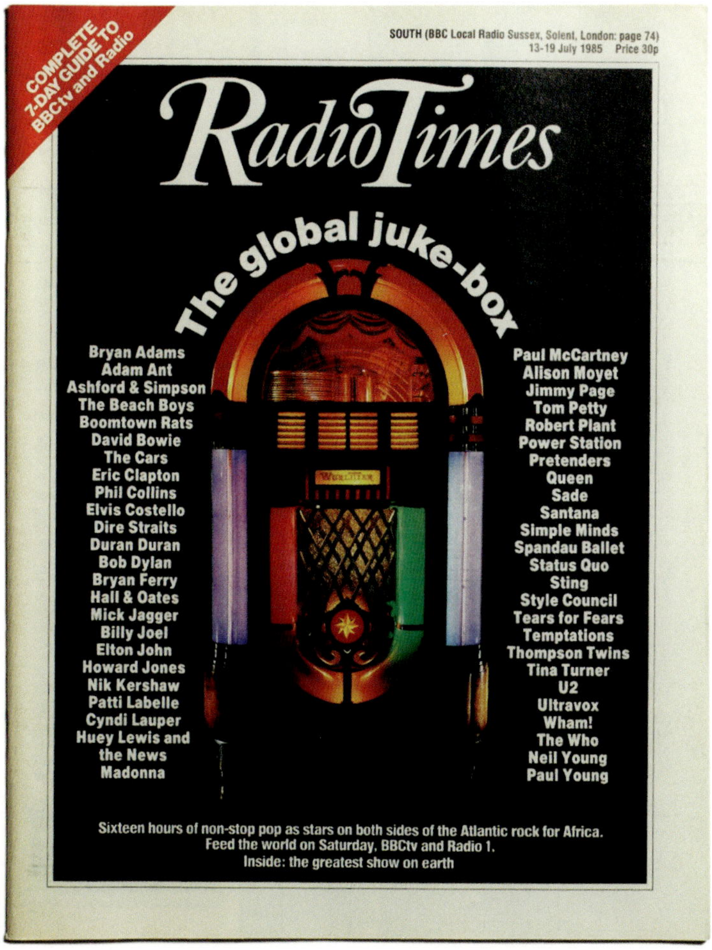

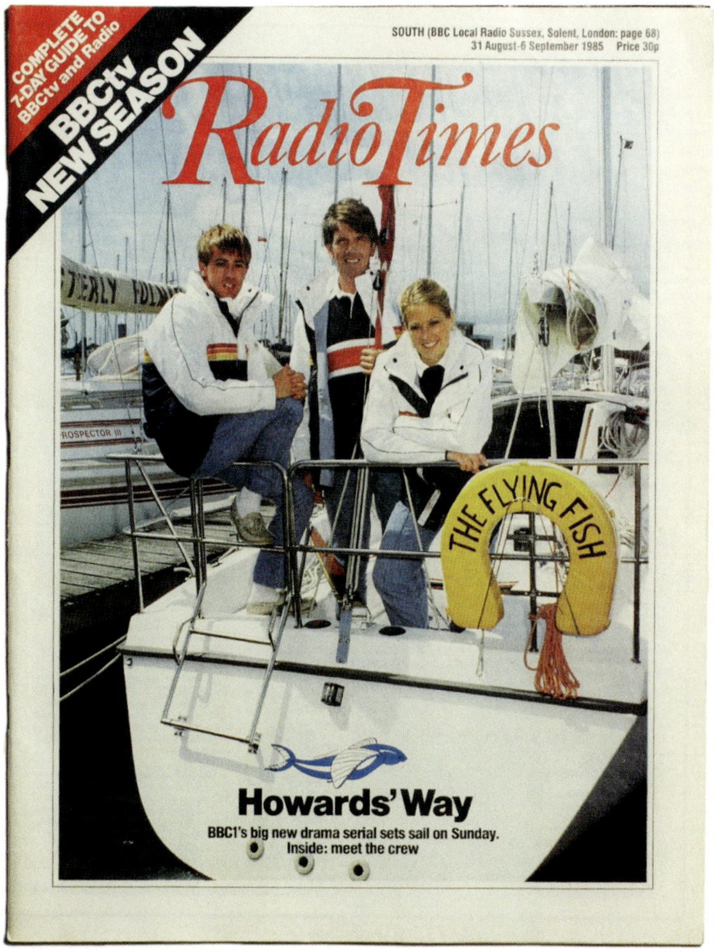

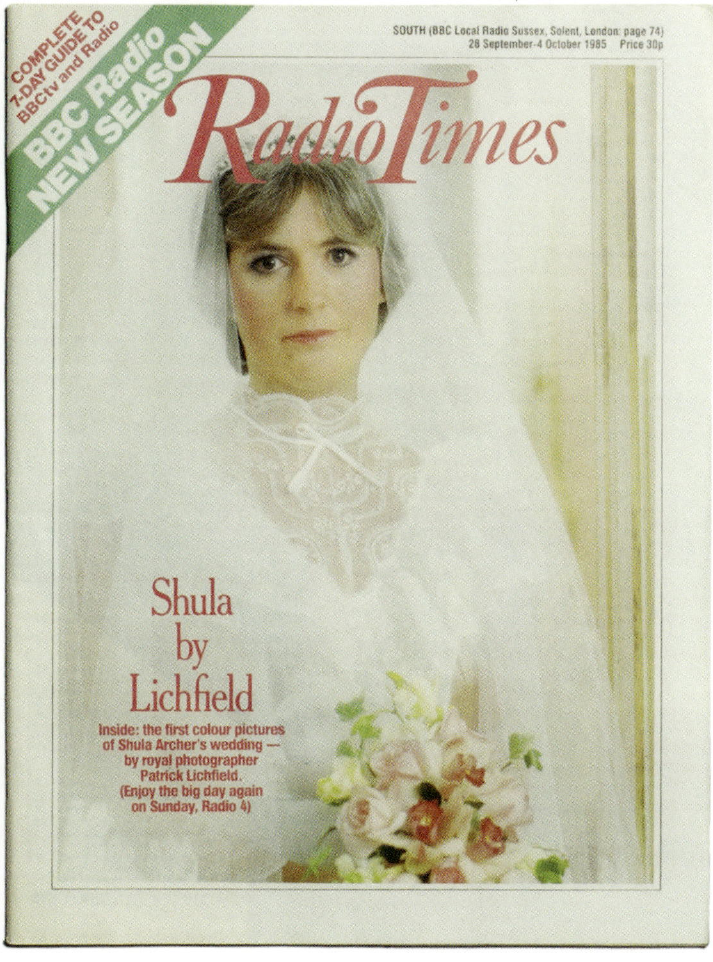

Live Aid *(above left)*

(photograph by Victor Watts, jukebox lent by Graham Hall and Mekkanized Muzik)

13–19 July 1985

Bob Geldof and Midge Ure created the Band Aid single of Christmas 1984 and the Live Aid concerts in response to BBC journalist Michael Buerk's reports from famine-stricken Ethiopia. In an interview in this issue, Geldof told Buerk what his priorities were: "It'll probably be the biggest pop event ever, but that doesn't interest me. It's the amount we can raise. How do you get money to keep people going?"

Howards' Way *(above right)*

Leo (Edward Highmore), Tom (Maurice Colbourne) and Lynne (Tracey Childs) *(photograph by Richard Farley)*

31 August–6 September 1985

The launch of one of BBC1's most popular Sunday-night dramas, telling stories of family, friends, rivalry and a boatbuilding firm. Most of it was filmed around Hampshire and on the river Hamble and the Solent but it was a BBC Birmingham production.

The Archers *(left)*

Shula (Judy Bennett) *(photograph by Patrick Lichfield)*

28 September–4 October 1985

Radio Times made a big fuss over the wedding of Borsetshire beauty Shula Archer and Mark Hebden. Royal photographer Patrick Lichfield took the pictures at "the reception".

'Allo 'Allo *(right)*

Edith (Carmen Silvera) and René (Gorden Kaye)
(photograph by Brian Moody)

19–25 October 1985

The sitcom pastiche of *Secret Army* returned for a second series. Kaye said, "Although it's naughty in places, there is a strong element of taste."

Alas Smith and Jones *(below left)*

Griff Rhys Jones (top) and Mel Smith
(photograph by Iain McKell)

26 October–1 November 1985

Smith and Jones were asked what makes a good comedy sketch. They didn't know. "We had an antiques shop sketch that we could hardly rehearse because we were falling about laughing," said Jones. "But when we tried it in front of an audience, there was an awful silence."

EastEnders *(below right)*

Angie (Anita Dobson) and Den (Leslie Grantham)
(photograph by Don Smith)

22–28 February 1986

By the soap's first anniversary, Walford's Angie Watts and Dirty Den were legends. Paul McCartney told *Radio Times*: "When I get home from a hard day's work in the recording studio, there's nothing better" than *EastEnders*.

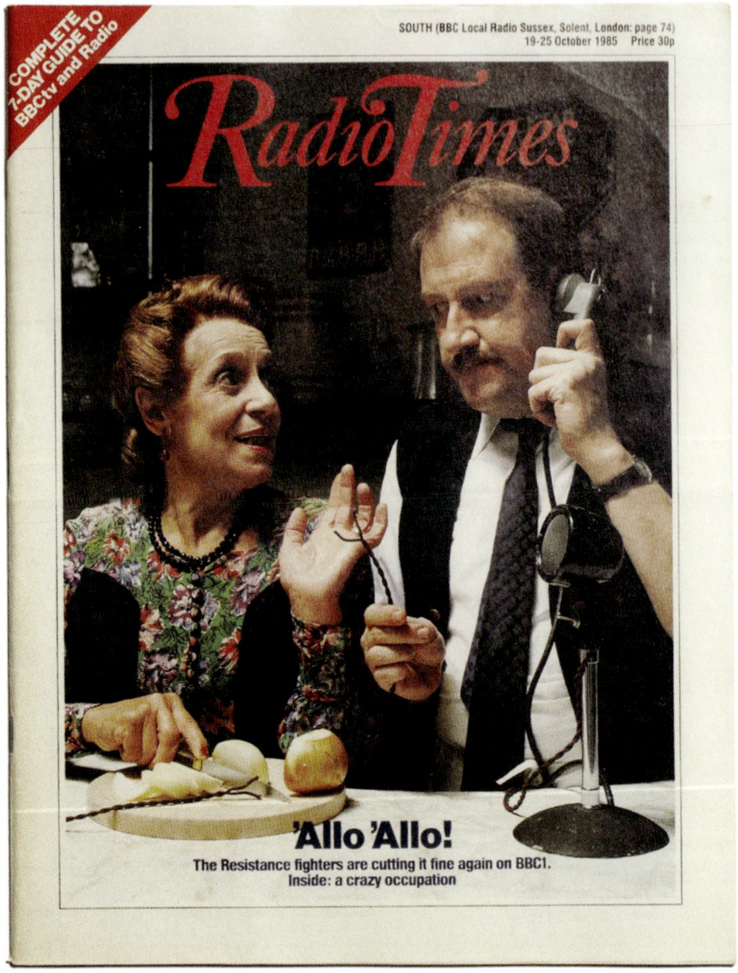

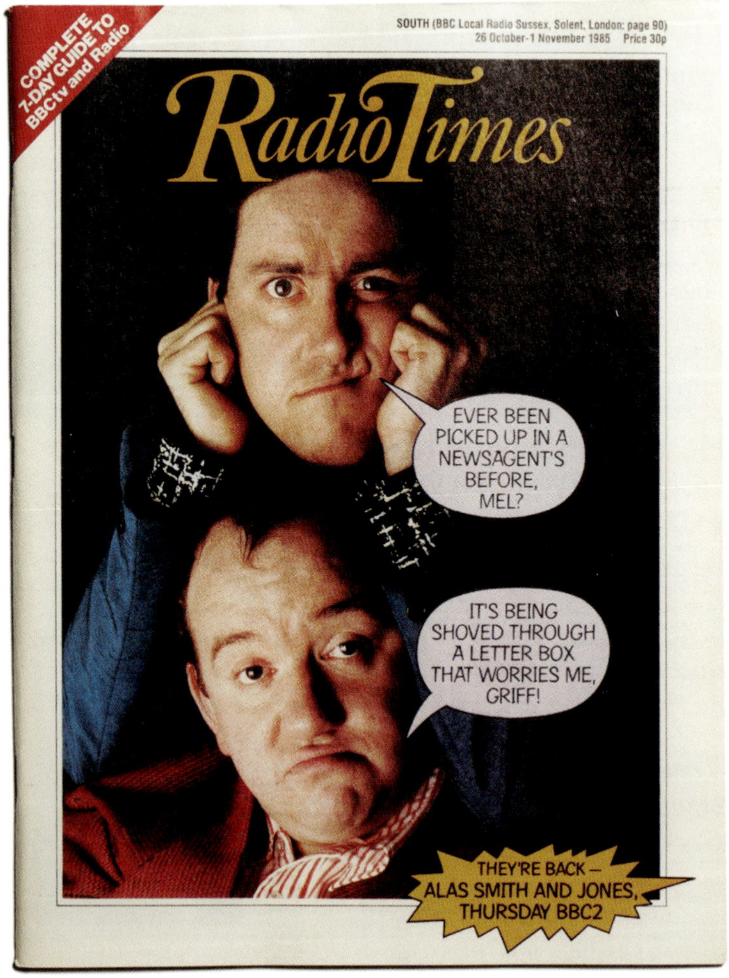

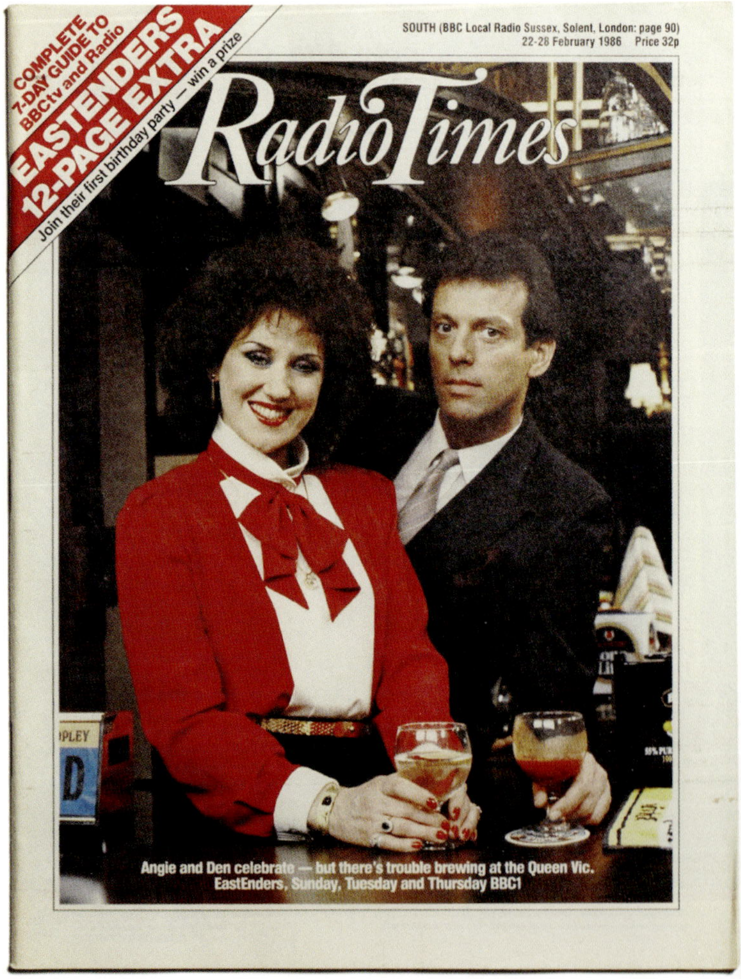

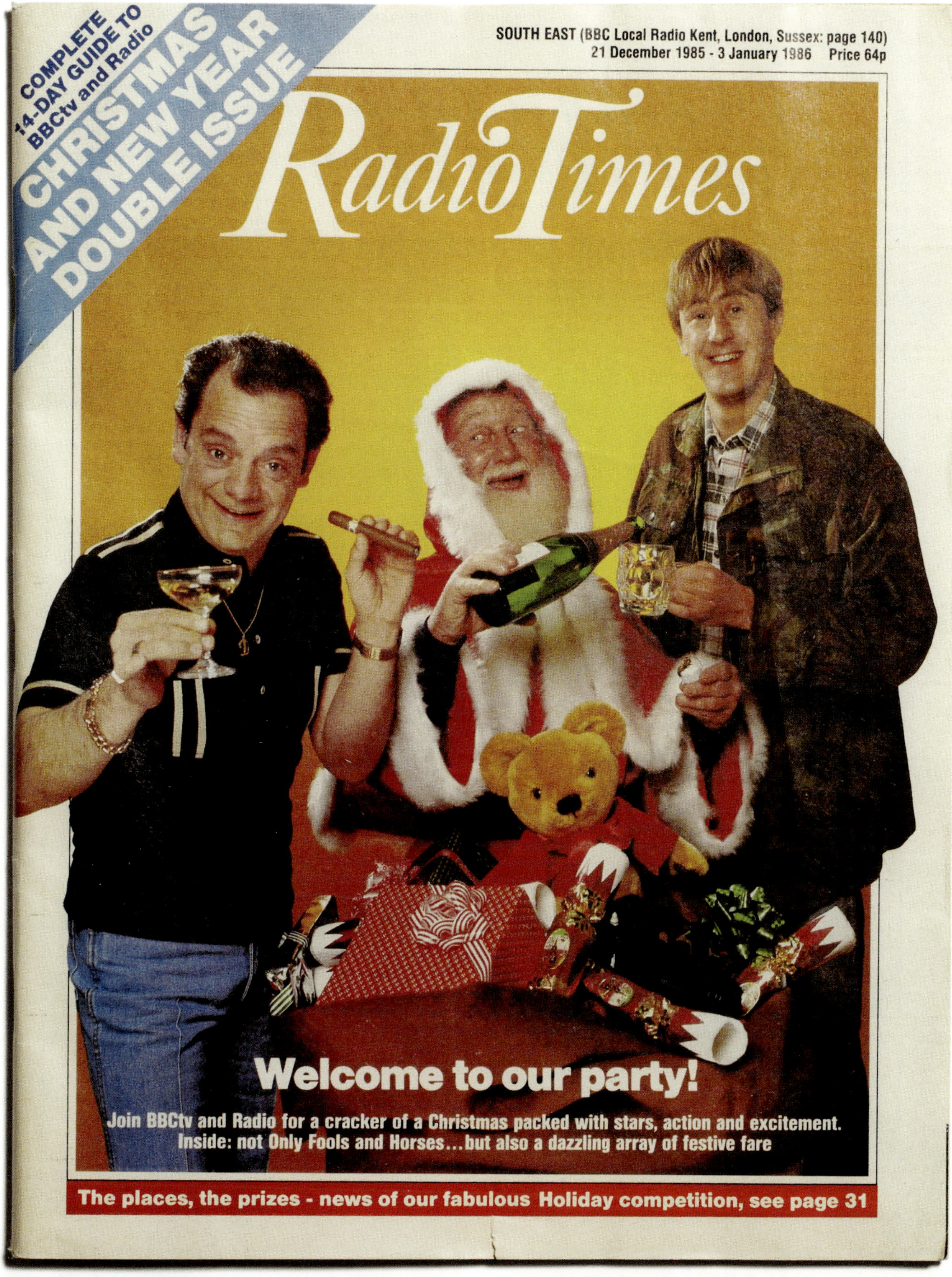

Christmas 1985 ***Only Fools and Horses*** **Del Boy (David Jason), Uncle Albert (Buster Merryfield) and Rodney (Nicholas Lyndhurst)** *(photograph by Allan Ballard)* *21 December 1985–3 January 1986*

Instead of the traditional illustration, *Radio Times* featured the stars of *Only Fools and Horses*, who were appearing in a 90-minute edition of the sitcom that saw Del Boy become a diamond smuggler. That was followed on Christmas Day by *The Two Ronnies* and a *Wogan* special in which Terry Wogan jetted to Denver to meet the Carringtons of *Dynasty* fame.

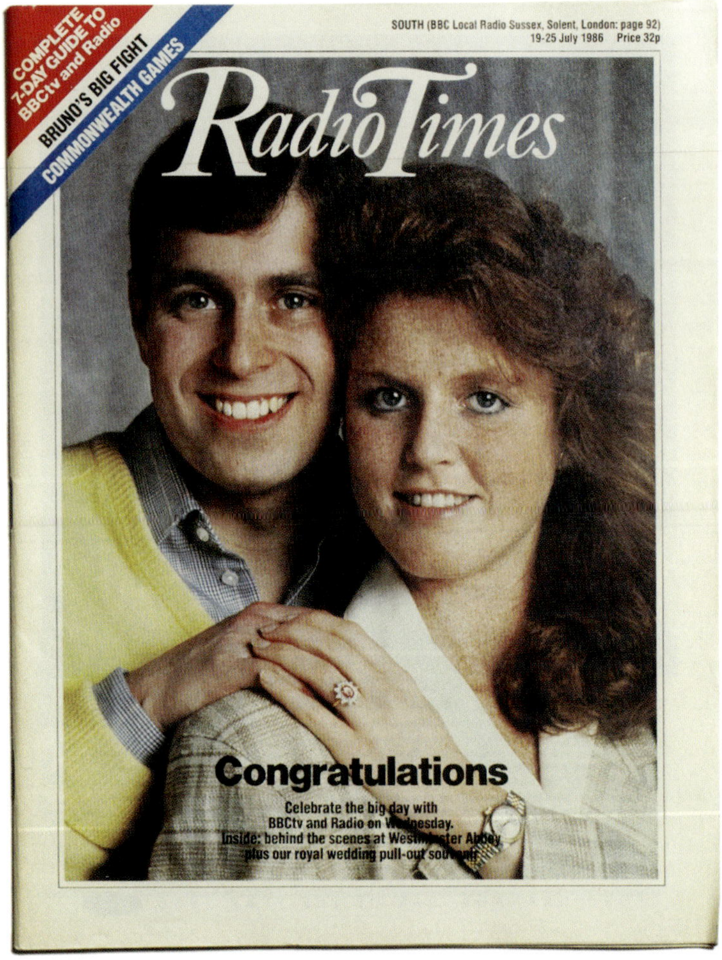

A Royal Wedding *(left)*

Prince Andrew and Sarah Ferguson
(photograph by Gene Nocon)

19–25 July 1986

"It has not, by royal standards, been a long engagement," said *Radio Times* of the marriage of Prince Andrew and Sarah Ferguson. The Wednesday wedding drew a global audience of some 500 million viewers.

The Monocled Mutineer *(below left)*

Percy Toplis (Paul McGann)
(photograph by Clive Landen)

30 August–5 September 1986

"Percy Topis is a modern-day hero performing in days that weren't modern," said writer Alan Bleasdale about a drama that told the story of a British Army deserter in the First World War. Everybody else had plenty to say too: after it was broadcast the *Daily Mail* ran a campaign complaining about the drama's anti-war stance.

Victoria Wood – As Seen on TV *(below right)*

Victoria Wood *(photograph by Brian Moody)*

8–14 November 1986

Victoria Wood didn't just write her series, she wrote the billings for the listings page. A typical example was: " 'Have it your way, Waseem, but if disposable saris don't catch on, count me out!' For cast see Thursday. For fun, try getting out more."

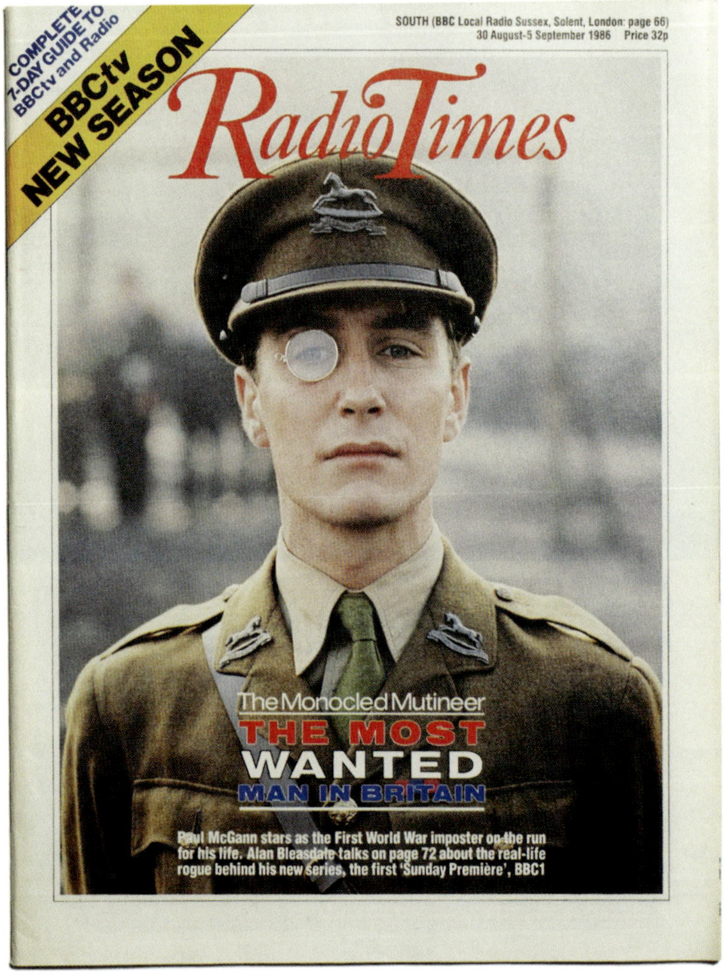

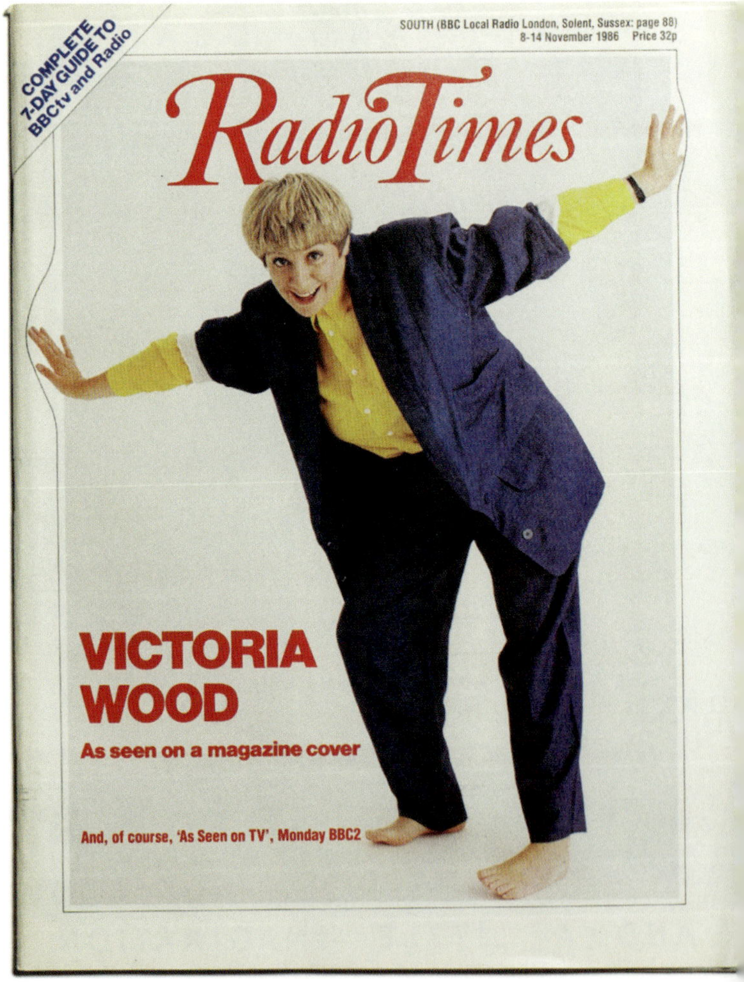

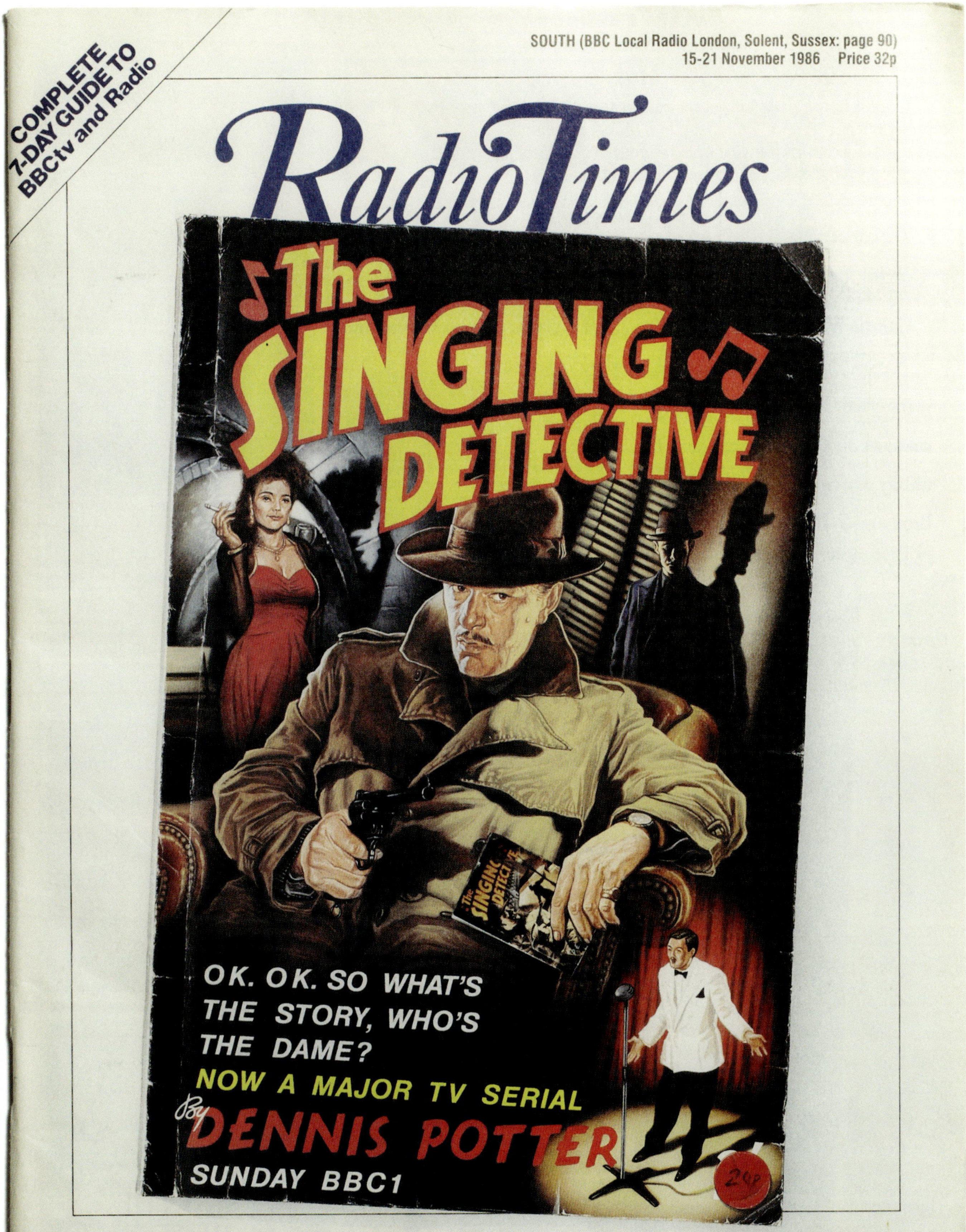

The Singing Detective **Philip E Marlow (Michael Gambon)**

Illustration by Mark Thomas *15–21 November 1986*

"One of the things I wanted to do in *The Singing Detective* is break up the narrative tyranny," writer Dennis Potter told *Radio Times*. Marlow is both the lip-syncing detective and his psoriasis-suffering writer in hospital in Potter's best work.

Tutti Frutti *(right)*

Illustration by John Byrne

28 February–6 March 1987

John Byrne's acclaimed six-part drama starred Robbie Coltrane, Emma Thompson and Richard Wilson and told the story of the silver jubilee tour of Scottish rock band the Majestics. Byrne also drew the cover.

Acting *(middle right)*

Clockwise from top left: Simon Callow, Jonathan Miller and Michael Caine ***(photograph by Brian Aris)***

22–28 August 1987

Maria Aitken gathered Callow, Miller and Caine to present a series about the craft of acting. Miller was directing opera in Italy, Shakespeare at Stratford and launching a season at the Old Vic; Callow was writing a book on Charles Laughton; and Michael Caine "had recently been tangling with that troublesome leviathan in *Jaws 4*."

Today *(far right)*

From left: Sue MacGregor, John Humphrys, Peter Hobday, Brian Redhead ***(photograph by Chris Ryan)***

21–27 November 1987

Radio 4's *Today* celebrated 30 years and about 9,000 editions – but it took years of format changes to make it the hard-hitting news-and-interviews programme it remains today.

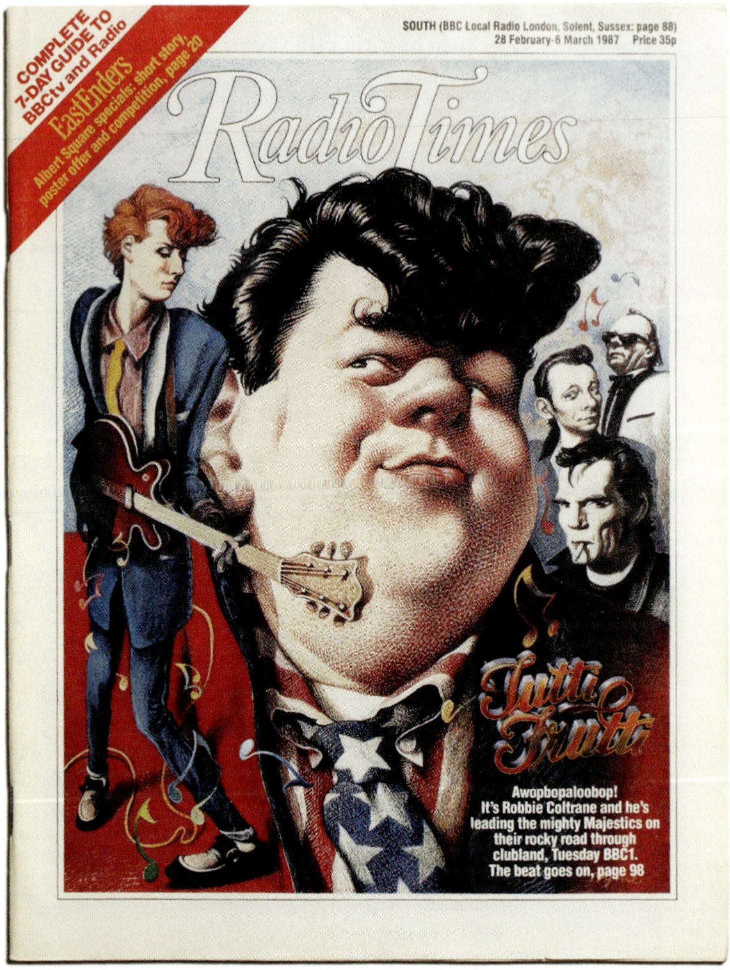

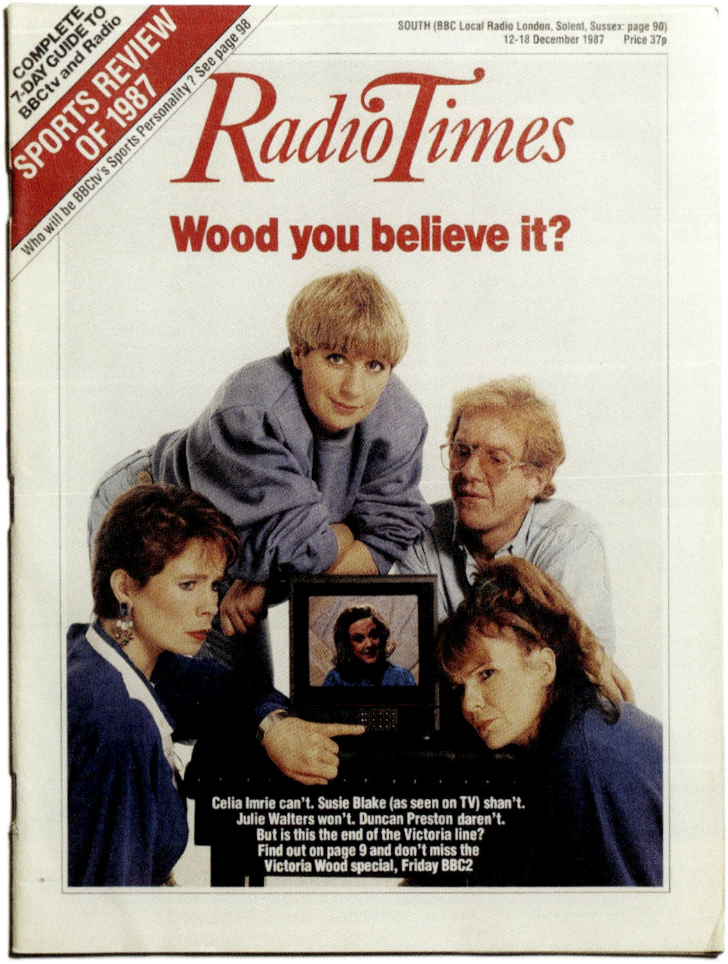

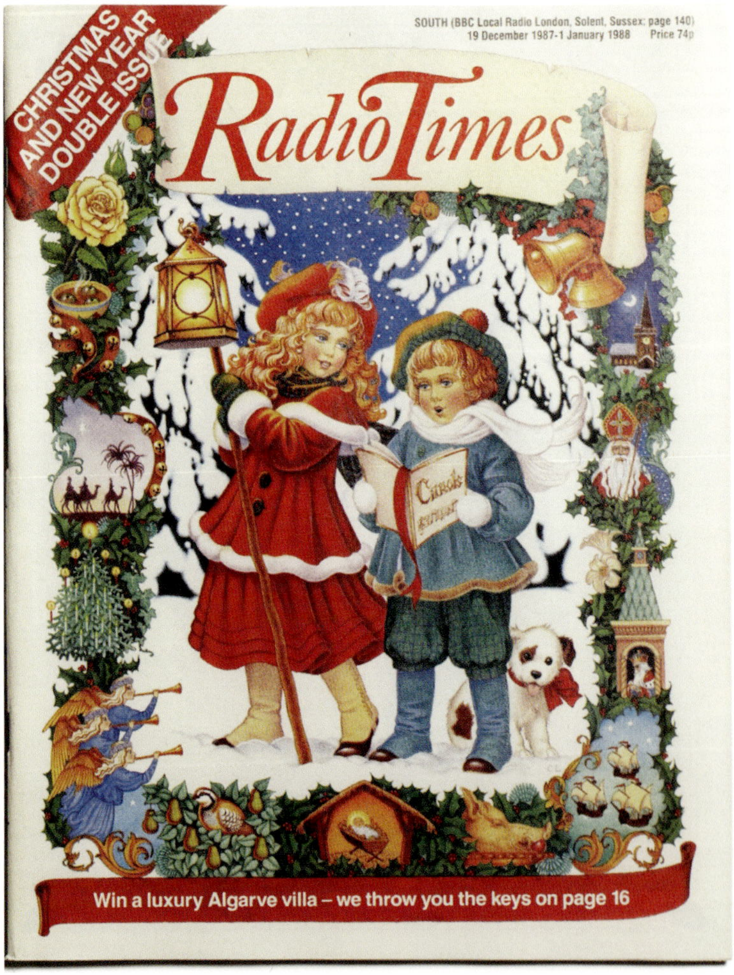

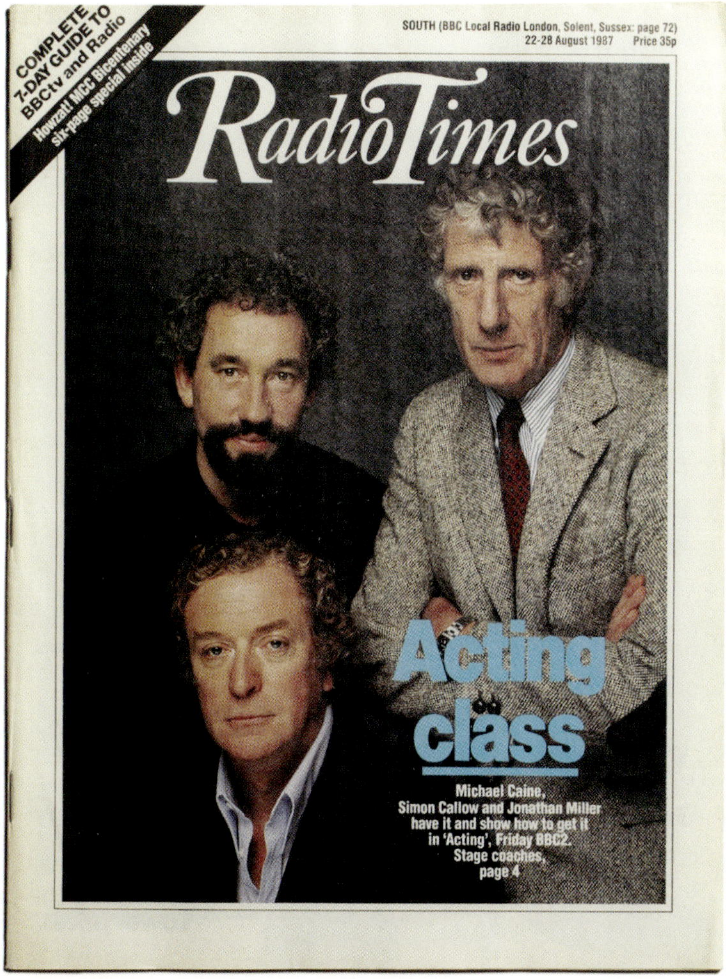

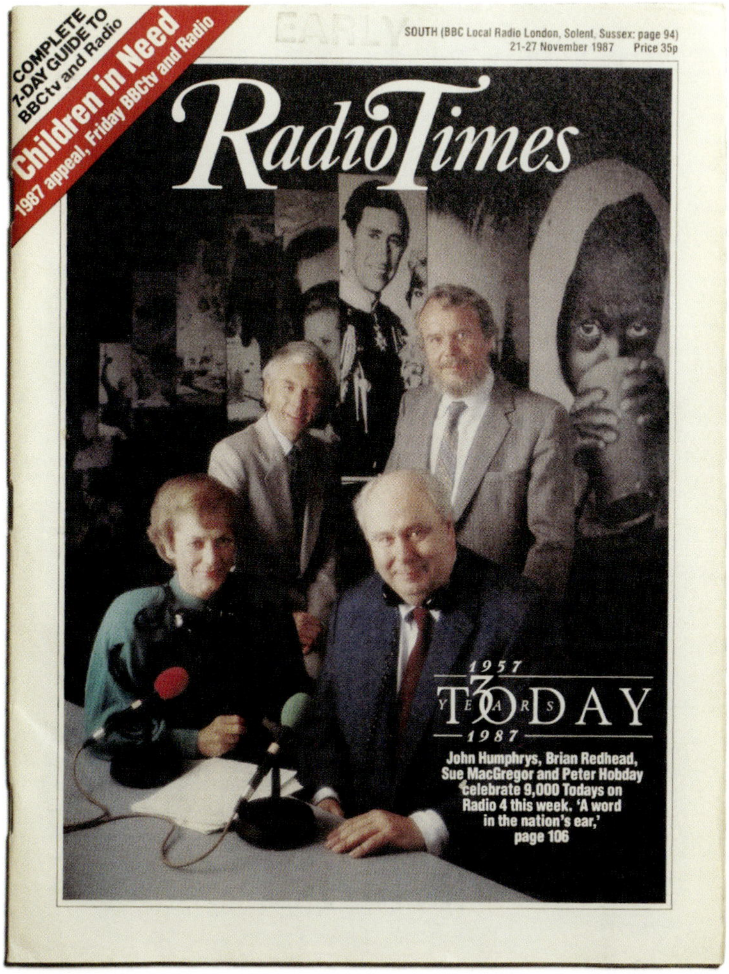

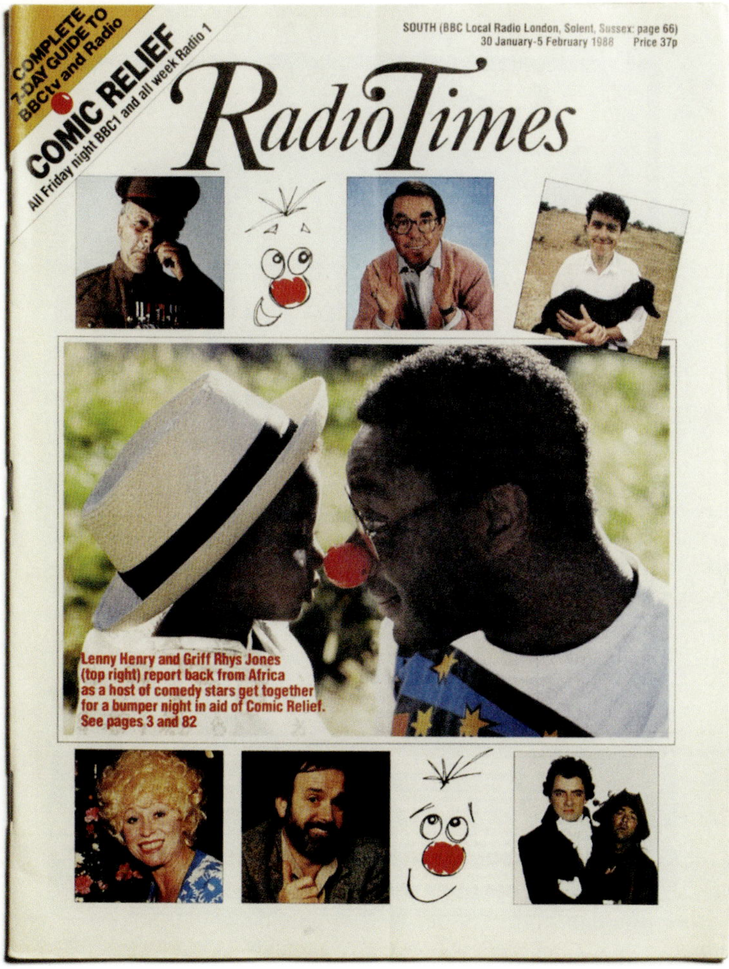

Victoria Wood Special *(far left)*

Clockwise from left: Celia Imrie, Victoria Wood, Duncan Preston, Julie Walters and (on TV) Susie Blake *(photograph by Brian Moody)*

12–18 December 1987

This special marked the last appearance of the *Victoria Wood – As Seen on TV* gang. Imrie said all concerned were sad but: "Vic's quite right to stop now, while it's on an up."

Christmas 1987 *(middle left)*

Illustration by Carol Lawson

19 December 1987–1 January 1988

One highlight of this Christmas was the regular *Two Ronnies* special – and they never made another. Only the cast and crew knew that Ronnie Barker had decided to retire.

Comic Relief *(left)*

Main shot: Lenny Henry *(photograph by Chris Ridley)*

20 January–5 February 1988

Jane Tewson and Richard Curtis formed Comic Relief in 1985, but this was the first Red Nose Day as we know it now, with celebrities gifting their talents in return for public donations to good causes at home and abroad. The first Red Nose Day was watched by 30 million viewers and raised over £15 million (approximately £34 million in today's money).

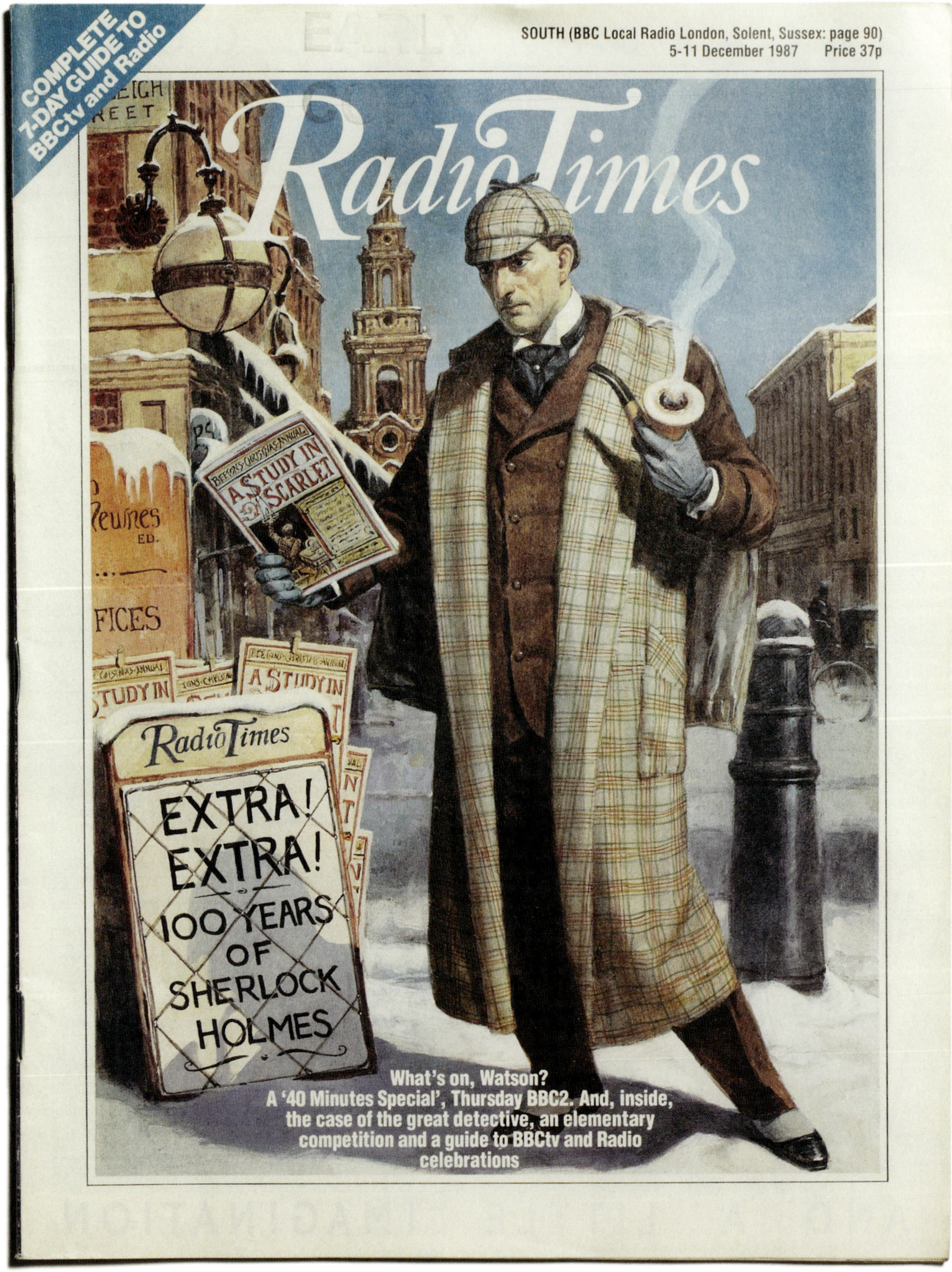

The Case of Sherlock Holmes **Illustration by Paul Slater** *5–11 December 1987*

Sherlock Holmes wasn't the first fictional sleuth but he is certainly the most famous. The Baker Street detective was the subject of the documentary series *40 Minutes* marking his 100th birthday. His creator Arthur Conan Doyle wrote: "It had struck me that a single character running through a series would bind the reader to that particular magazine." Actor Tim Pigott-Smith presented the documentary, having previously played both Holmes and Watson.

French and Saunders *(right)*

Jennifer Saunders and Dawn French
(photograph by Brian Moody)

27 February–4 March 1988

The duo returned for a second run of their comedy. Saunders said: "In some ways a second series is harder to do – and in some ways it's easier. You learn from your mistakes, but it's also harder to think of ideas you haven't touched on before."

Armada *(below left)*

Illustration by Peter Brookes

30 July–5 August 1988

The documentary by Alan Ereira took a fresh look at the story of the Spanish Armada. "Francis Drake was a pirate: Good Queen Bess took a cut of his profits. This stands back from the 400-year-old story of 'victory' and 'defeat'... the Armada must now be seen in a different way."

Floyd on Britain and Ireland *(below right)*

Keith Floyd *(photograph by Red Saunders; food in the photograph was donated to the Salvation Army)*

27 August–2 September 1988

Keith Floyd not only reinvented TV cookery, he was passionate, funny and dedicated. As he set off on a gastronomic tour, his producer David Pritchard said: "He gives it his heart and soul and it's physically draining. There are long moments when he'll gaze at an ashtray and say nothing for hours on end."

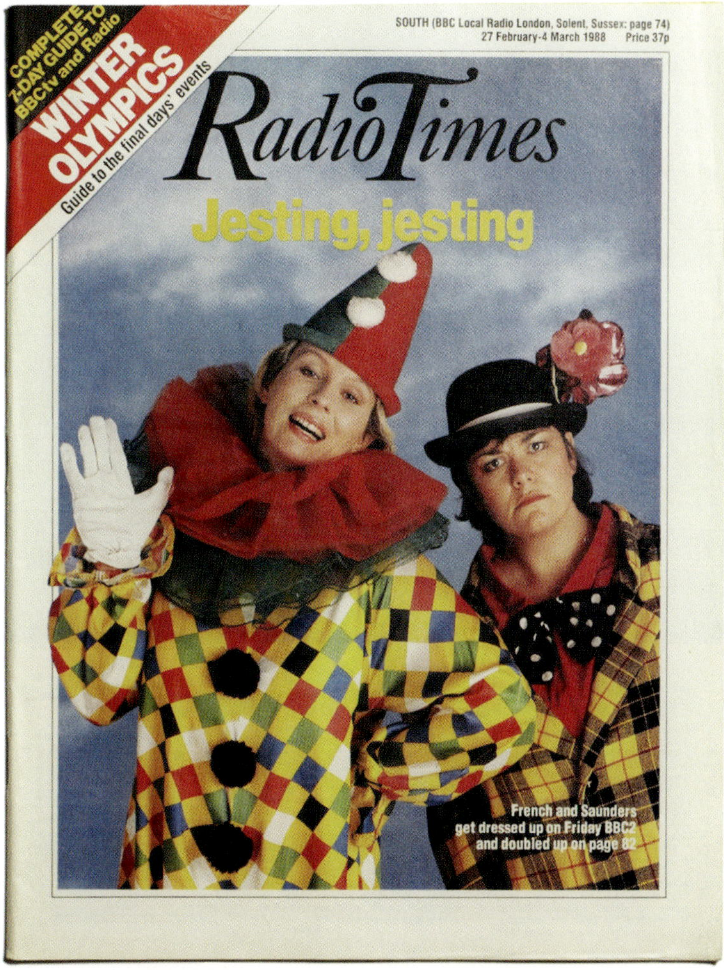

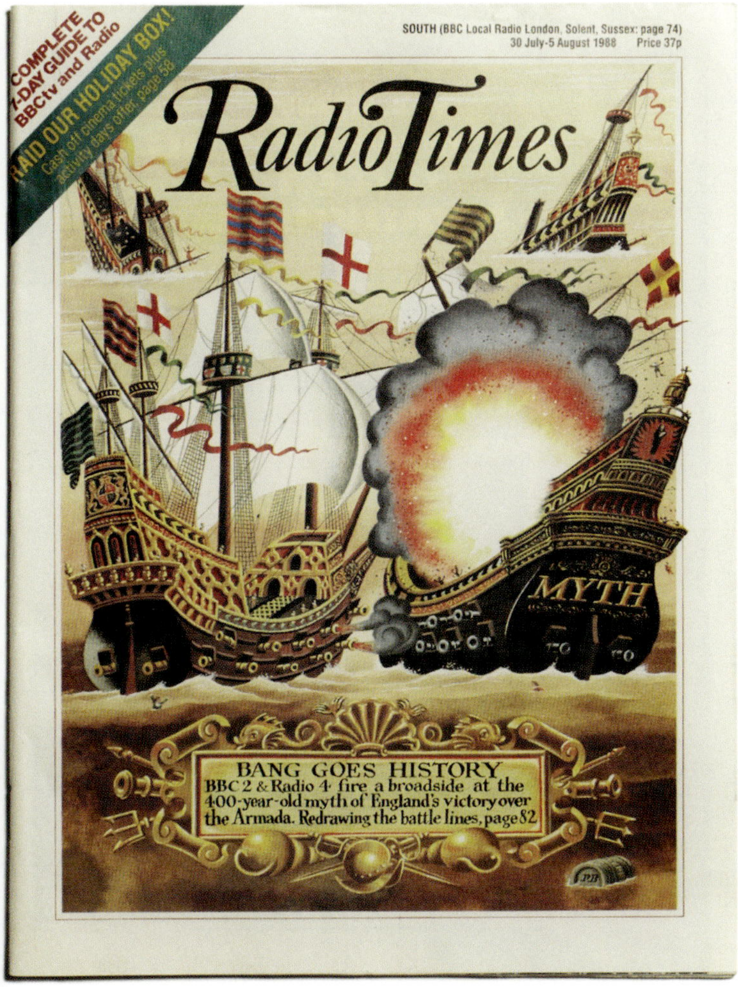

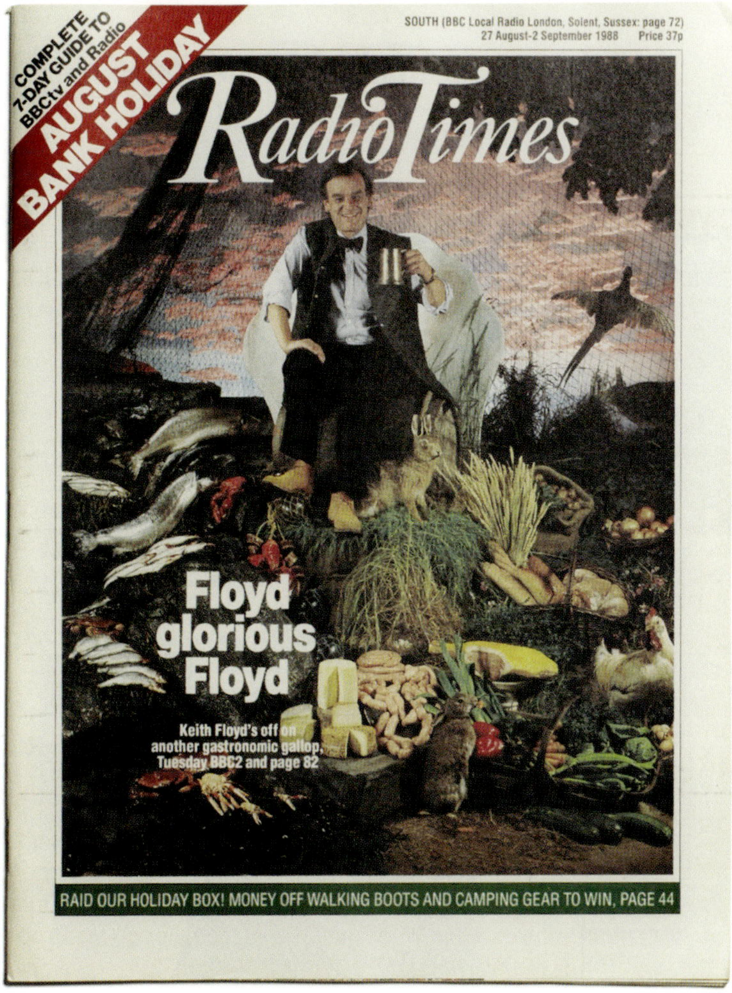

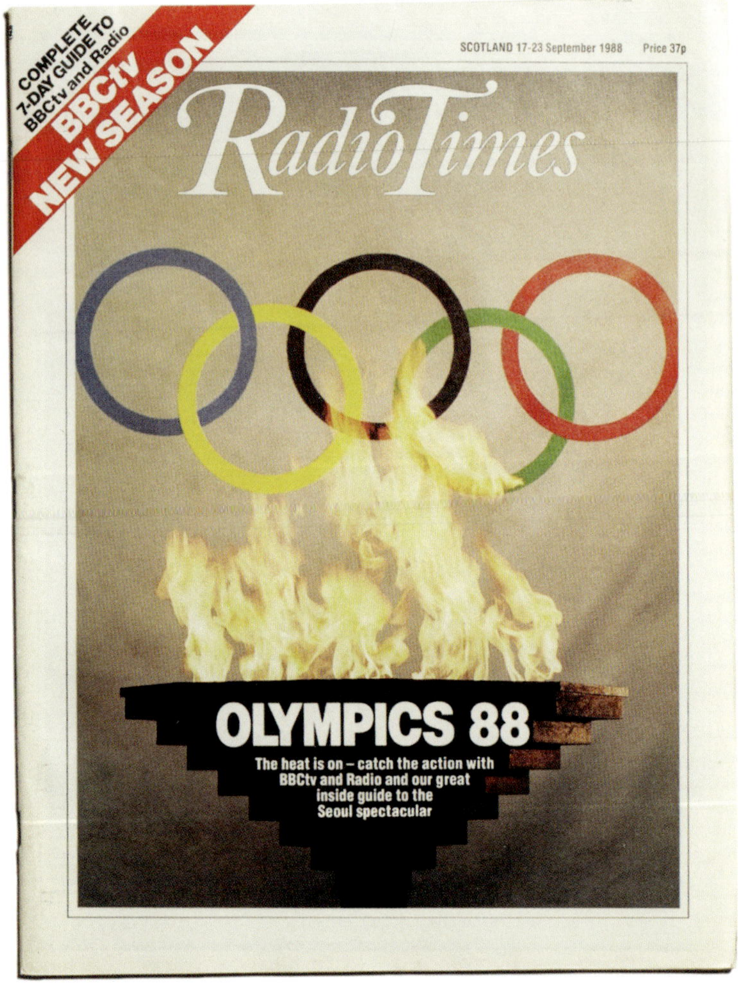

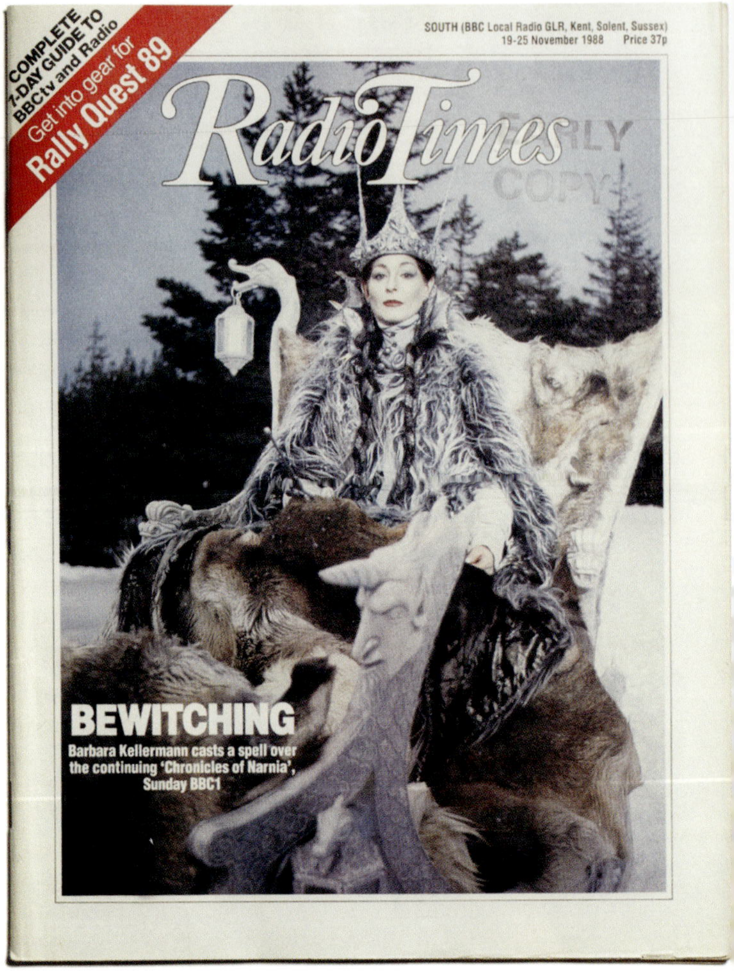

Simon's Triumph *(right)*

Simon Weston *(photograph by Snowdon)*

1–7 April 1989

Weston was aboard the *Sir Galahad* when it was destroyed in the Falklands War and he suffered 46 per cent burns. The BBC series *QED* had featured him in *Simon's War* in 1983 and then followed his recovery in *Simon's Peace* in 1985. Now it was back to see him begin a new charity helping inner-city teenagers.

Lost Worlds, Vanished Lives *(middle right)*

David Attenborough *(photograph by Red Saunders)*

22–28 April 1989

David Attenborough took time out from such series as *The Living Planet* to focus on fossils. He told *Radio Times* that he found them fascinating, but it had been hard to persuade anyone to make the series: "'Fossils don't move about very much.' That was the sort of response I got."

People *(far right)*

Frank Bruno *(photograph by Brian Moody)*

24–30 June 1989

Boxer Frank Bruno took over from Derek Jameson as host of the documentary series, *People*. Bruno said it was about "ordinary people doing extraordinary things" but *Radio Times* was more interested in whether TV was a challenge for Bruno. "Not really," he said. "I'm more nervous talking to you."

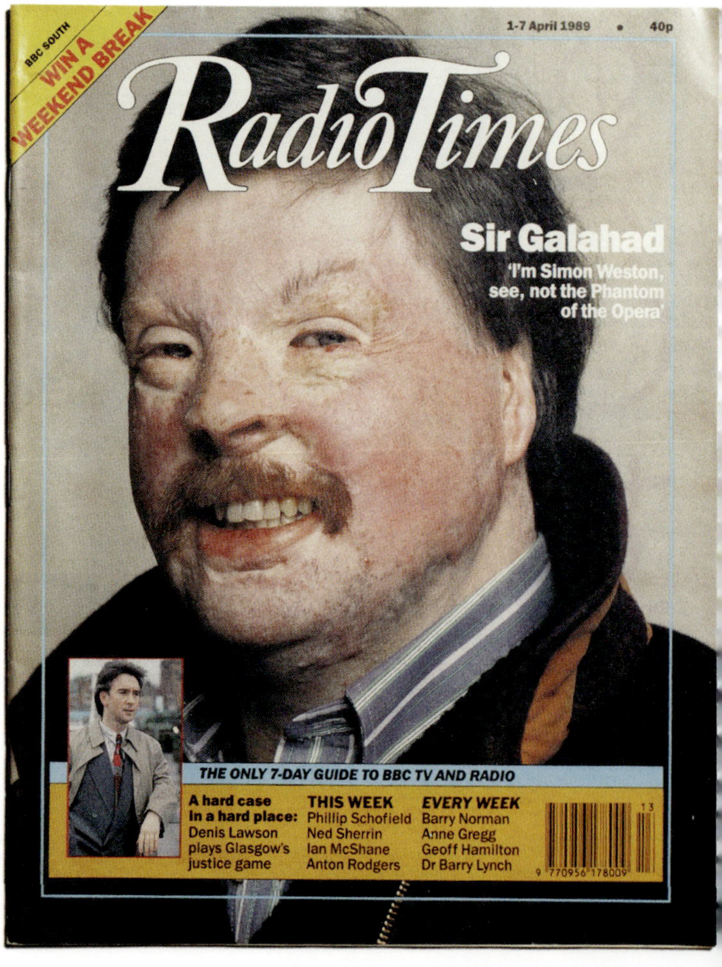

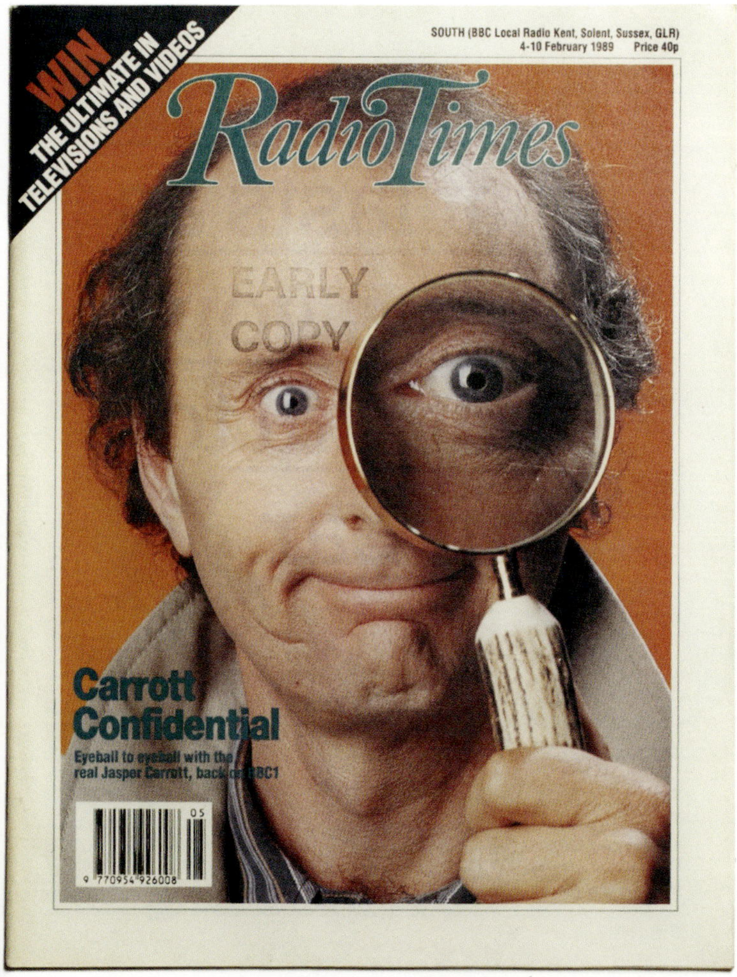

The 1988 Olympic Games *(far left)*

(photograph by Jay Myrdal)

17–23 September 1988

A slightly undernourished cover for the Seoul Games gave way to a thundering 22 pages of preview inside, including a four-page chart for readers to fill in the medal winners in events from archery to yachting.

The Chronicles of Narnia *(middle left)*

The White Queen (Barbara Kellermann)

19–25 November 1988

Barbara Kellermann from *The Glittering Prizes* was unrecognisable under white make-up. She told *Radio Times* that she knew CS Lewis's novels and had "loathed" the horrible White Queen. "But when I actually came to play out her cruellest act, something wonderfully evil took over."

Carrott Confidential *(left)*

Jasper Carrott *(photograph by Allan Ballard)*

4–10 February 1989

Comedian Jasper Carrott said that the success he'd enjoyed meant he'd had to move away from observational comedy: "Things in my life started happening just inside the business and I didn't want to use that," he explained, "but I'd used up all the experiences from the age of six onwards."

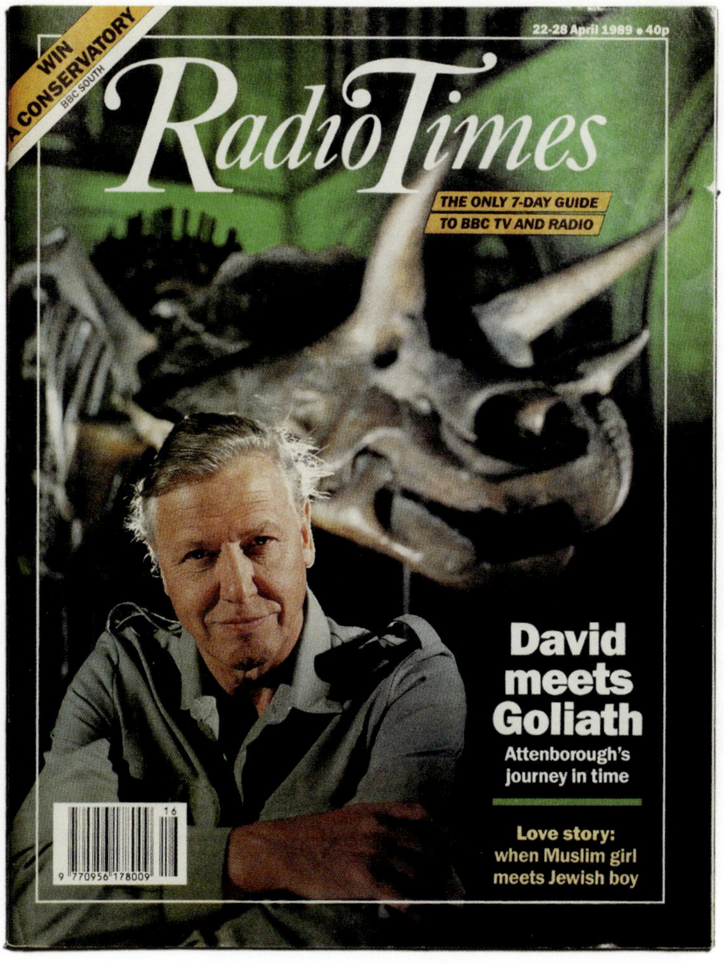

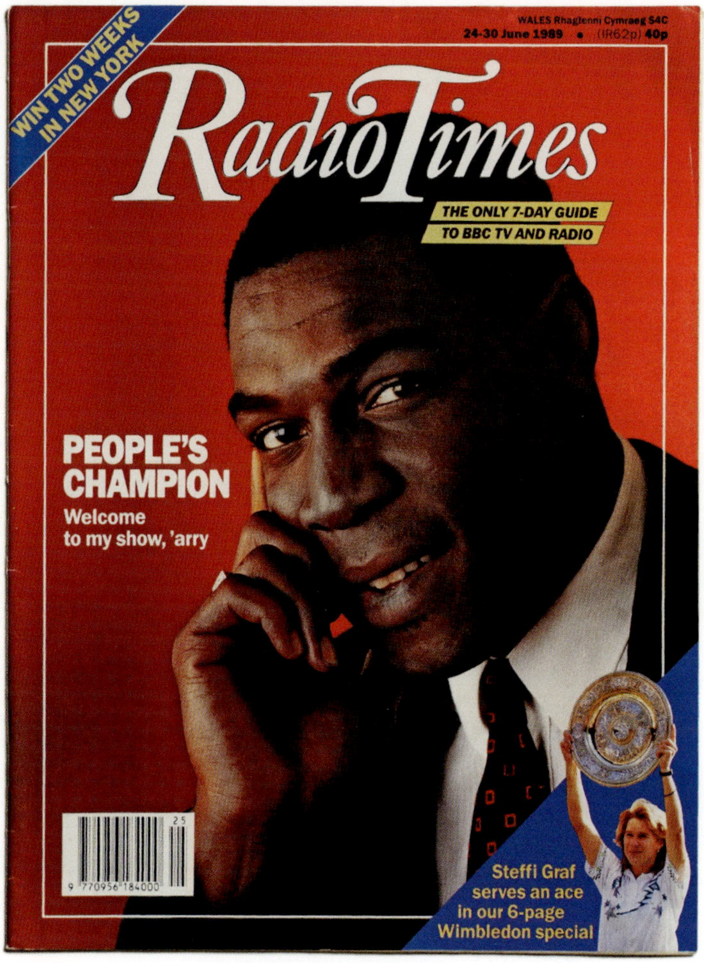

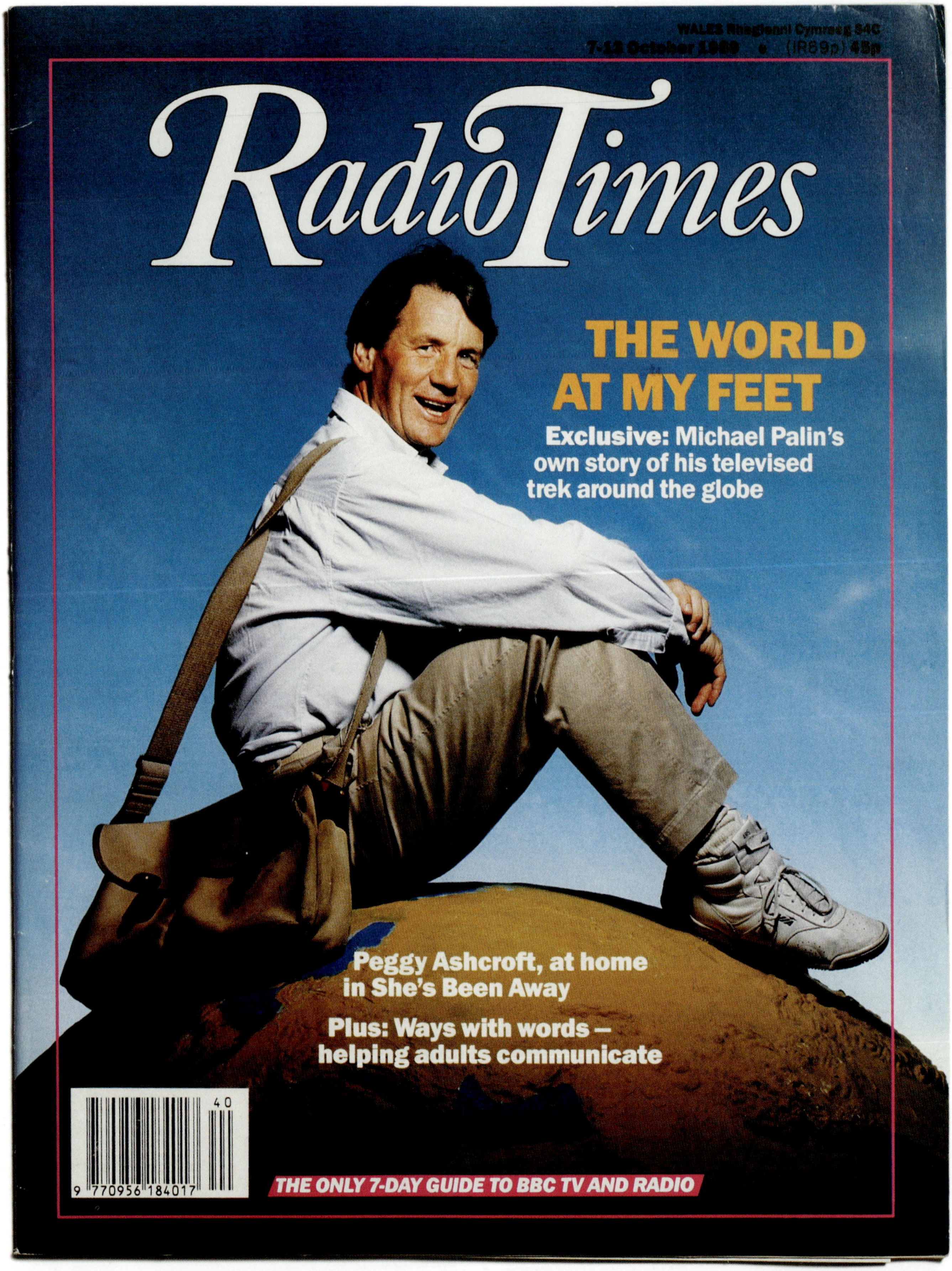

Around the World in Eighty Days Michael Palin *(photograph by Clive Arrowsmith)*

7–13 October 1989

Before this, Michael Palin was a Python: after this, he was a Python – and a world traveller. But he told *Radio Times* that he wasn't the BBC's first choice for the job – "Alan Whicker turned down the idea." Palin was also worried about viewers falling asleep. "How do you make an 11-day trip on a container ship across the Pacific *interesting*?"

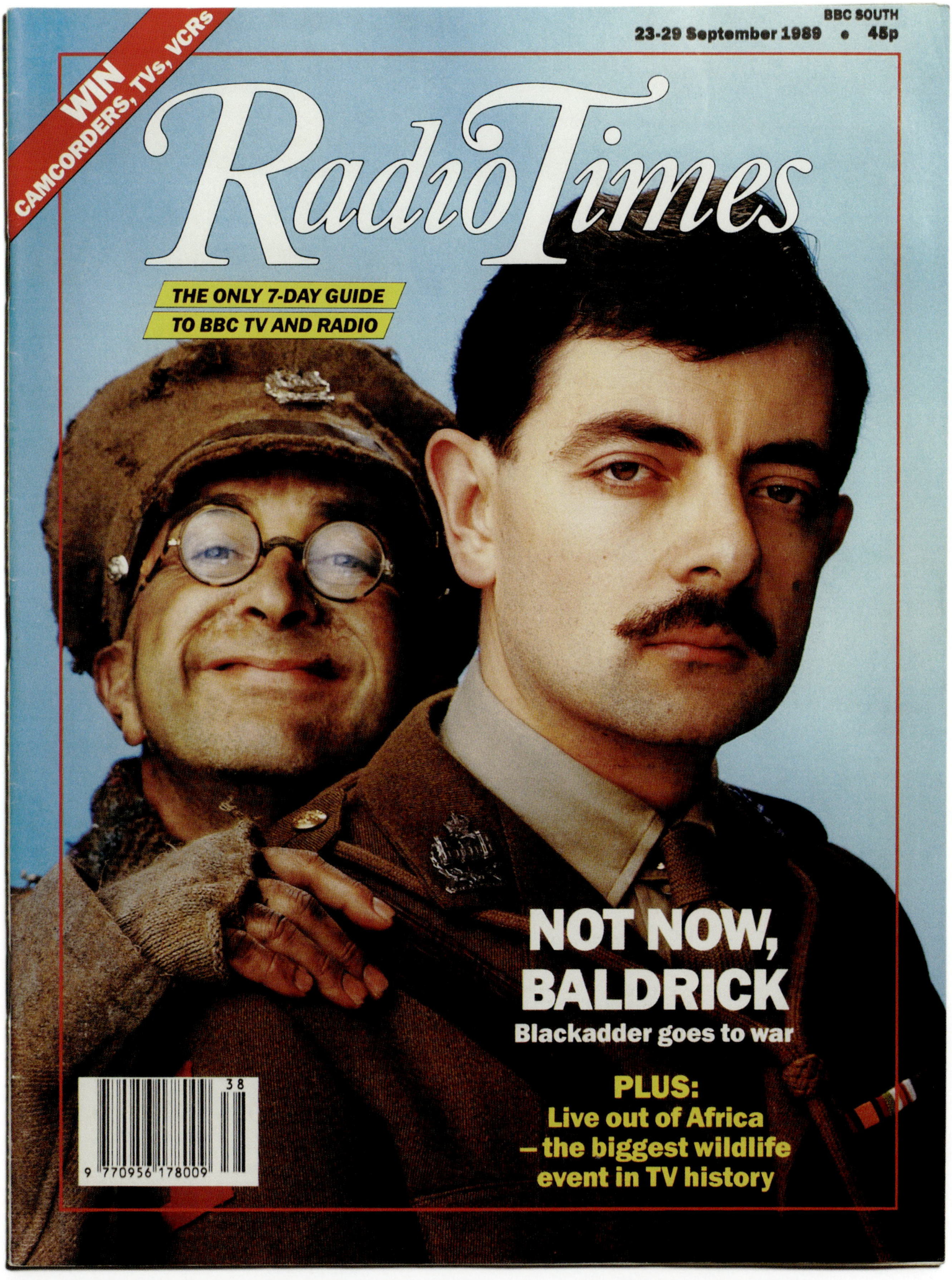

Blackadder Goes Forth Baldrick (Tony Robinson) and Blackadder (Rowan Atkinson) *(photograph by Chris Ridley)* *23–29 September 1989*

The last full series of *Blackadder* saw the action move to the First World War. The only tiny clue that it would include a greater and more serious punch than its predecessors was one comment from Stephen Fry, who said: "The series shows the resilience of the people in those appalling conditions."

1 BBC 1

4.30pm Film premiere
Hook

Fantasy adventure starring **Dustin Hoffman**, **Robin Williams**, **Julia Roberts**, **Bob Hoskins**

Peter Banning – a workaholic lawyer – and his family spend Christmas in London with an old relative, Granny Wendy. The adults arrive home one evening to find that the children have vanished and a note has been left by Captain James Hook. With the help of a fairy named Tinkerbell, Peter sets off for Neverland to reclaim his children.

Captain James Hook.......DUSTIN HOFFMAN
Peter Banning/Peter Pan.......ROBIN WILLIAMS
Tinkerbell.......JULIA ROBERTS
Smee.......BOB HOSKINS
Granny Wendy.......MAGGIE SMITH
Moira Banning.......CAROLINE GOODALL
Jack.......CHARLIE KORSMO
Maggie.......AMBER SCOTT
Liza.......LAUREL CRONIN
Inspector Good.......PHIL COLLINS
Tootles.......ARTHUR MALET
Pockets.......ISAIAH ROBINSON
Ace.......JASEN FISHER
Rufio.......DANTE BASCO
Thud Butt.......RAUSHAN HAMMOND
Don't Ask.......JAMES MADIO
Director Steven Spielberg (1991)
Stereo Subtitled.......83551106 ★★★★

◆ See Films: pages 49–72
◆ Andrew Duncan's interview with Robin Williams: page 16

6.45 Auntie's Brand New Bloomers

The secrets of some of the BBC's most popular and prestigious programmes are revealed when Terry Wogan digs out classic clips from the archives. Those guaranteed to be embarrassed include the stars of *Absolutely Fabulous*, *One Foot in the Grave*, *EastEnders*, *Pride and Prejudice*, *Roughnecks*, *Cardiac Arrest*, *Dangerfield*, *The Brittas Empire*, *Keeping Up Appearances* and *Top Gear*.
Producer Tom Webber Stereo Subtitled 850816

7.30 EastEnders

CHOICE The first of tonight's two offerings from Albert Square. The Vic is full of Christmas cheer while the Fowlers put on a brave face. Pat's plans for a perfect Christmas take an unexpected turn. **See today's choices.**
Part 2 at 8.30pm. For cast see Tuesday 19 December
Stereo Subtitled.......800

8.00 Keeping Up Appearances

CHOICE Plans to hold a pageant don't go quite as Hyacinth anticipated. Could this be remotely connected to the fact that she is organising it? **See today's choices.**

Hyacinth.......PATRICIA ROUTLEDGE
Richard.......CLIVE SWIFT
Elizabeth.......JOSEPHINE TEWSON
Daisy.......JUDY CORNWELL
Onslow.......GEOFFREY HUGHES
Rose.......MARY MILLAR
Emmet.......DAVID GRIFFIN
Vicar.......JEREMY GITTINS
Vicar's wife.......MARION BARRON
Mrs Moody.......UNA STUBBS
Violet.......ANNA DAWSON
Bruce.......JOHN EVITTS
Daddy.......GEORGE WEBB
Mr Crabtree.......TONY STUART
Written by Roy Clarke; Director/Producer Harold Snoad Stereo Subtitled.......6361

8.30 EastEnders

Part 2. Stereo Subtitled.......5496

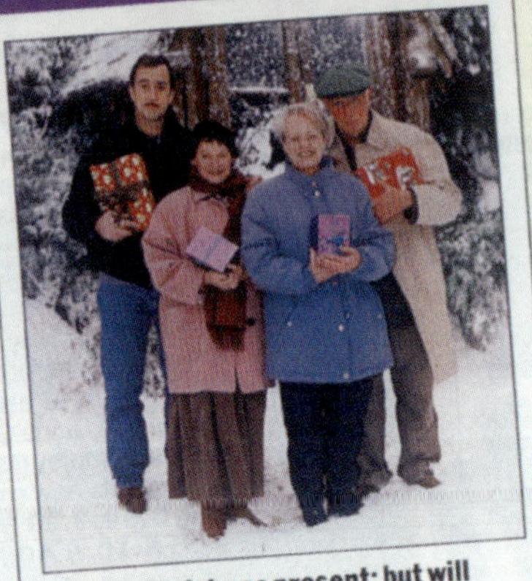

9.00pm Christmas present: but will Victor (Richard Wilson, right) get the chance to enjoy a Christmas future?

9.00 One Foot in the Grave

CHOICE *The Wisdom of the Witch*
A reading of the tarot cards results in a ghastly prediction for Victor and Margaret Meldrew. **See today's choices.**

Victor Meldrew.......RICHARD WILSON
Margaret Meldrew.......ANNETTE CROSBIE
Patrick.......ANGUS DEAYTON
Pippa.......JANINE DUVITSKI
Melvin.......PHIL DANIELS
Lorna.......RACHEL BELL
Christine.......JOANNE ENGELSMAN
Tunstall.......BRUCE BYRON
Gridley.......PETER MCNALLY
Written by David Renwick; Director/Producer Susan Belbin Stereo Subtitled.......7564

◆ See This Week: page 13

10.00 News

With Peter Sissons. Subtitled
Weather Rob McElwee.......513038

10.10 Film premiere
Indecent Proposal

Drama starring **Robert Redford**, **Demi Moore**, **Woody Harrelson**

In danger of losing their dream home, David and Diana Murphy travel to Las Vegas in the hope of gambling their way out of financial trouble. Diana catches the eye of John Gage, an eccentric millionaire, who offers them a million dollars to spend one night with Diana. Are the stakes simply too high for the Murphys?

John Gage.......ROBERT REDFORD
Diana Murphy.......DEMI MOORE
David Murphy.......WOODY HARRELSON
Mr Shackelford.......SEYMOUR CASSEL
Jeremy.......OLIVER PLATT
Day tripper.......BILLY BOB THORNTON
Mr Langford.......RIP TAYLOR
Auction Emcee.......BILLY CONNOLLY
Director Adrian Lyne (1993)
Stereo Subtitled.......864583 ★★★★

◆ See Films: pages 49–72

12.00 I Hate Christmas

A tale of the true spirit of Christmas.
Stereo Subtitled.......5108572

12.05am The Greatest Music Party in the World

The first of two programmes recorded at this month's concert at the NEC in Birmingham. It features an eclectic mix of styles and stars, including David Bowie, Rod Stewart, Diana Ross, Soul II Soul, Lightning Seeds, Des'ree, Echobelly, Alanis Morissette, Alanah Myles, Curtis Stigers and Diana King.
Part 2 on Wednesday 27 December at 1.50pm
Stereo.......5809404

1.35–1.40am Weather

2 BBC 2

5.05pm Today's the Day Christmas Special

Stars from the world of entertainment do battle in this festive edition of the nostalgia quiz using clips and facts from Christmases past. With Martyn Lewis.
Series producer Henry Eagles; Executive producer Mark Rowland Stereo.......2140767

5.35 Some Enchanted Evening

Julie Andrews hosts a centenary celebration from Broadway of legendary lyricist Oscar Hammerstein. Combining interviews, archive clips and performance, the show traces his career in musicals from early work with Romberg and Friml on *Desert Song* and *Rose-Marie*, to *Showboat* with Jerome Kern and his collaborations with Richard Rodgers on *Oklahoma!*, *Carousel*, *South Pacific* and *The Sound of Music*. Among those taking part are Mandy Patinkin, Willie Nelson, Patti LaBelle, Bernadette Peters, Vanessa Williams, Keith Carradine and Dawn Upshaw.
Stereo.......6827632

7.00 Screen Two: Jane Austen's Persuasion

CHOICE A film adaptation of Jane Austen's novel about the enduring power of love. England, 1814: having been "persuaded" several years earlier to reject the proposal of a young naval officer, Anne Elliot suddenly finds him back in her life. **See today's choices.**

Anne Elliot.......AMANDA ROOT
Captain Wentworth.......CIARAN HINDS
Lady Russell.......SUSAN FLEETWOOD
Sir Walter Elliot.......CORIN REDGRAVE
Mrs Croft.......FIONA SHAW
Admiral Croft.......JOHN WOODVINE
Elizabeth Elliot.......PHOEBE NICHOLLS
Mr Elliot.......SAMUEL WEST
Mary Musgrove.......SOPHIE THOMPSON
Mrs Musgrove.......JUDY CORNWELL
Charles Musgrove.......SIMON RUSSELL BEALE
Mrs Clay.......FELICITY DEAN
Mr Musgrove.......ROGER HAMMOND
Louise Musgrove.......EMMA ROBERTS
Henrietta Musgrove.......VICTORIA HAMILTON
Captain Harville.......ROBERT GLENISTER
Captain Benwick.......RICHARD MCCABE
Mrs Smith.......HELEN SCHLESINGER
Nurse Rooke.......JANE WOOD
Mr Shepherd.......DAVID COLLINGS
Lady Dalrymple.......DARLENE JOHNSON
Miss Carteret.......CINNAMON FAYE
Henry Hayter.......ISAAC MAXWELL HUNT
Sir Henry Willoughby.......ROGER LLEWELLYN
Mrs Harville.......SALLY GEORGE
Screenplay by Nick Dear
Producer Fiona Finlay; Director Roger Michell
Rpt Stereo Subtitled.......22658477

◆ Jane Austen books and videos to give away: see page 216

8.40 Close Up

Actor and director Richard Attenborough chooses a scene from Charlie Chaplin's *City Lights*. Rpt Stereo Subtitled..752564
City Lights can be seen tomorrow at 7.00am

8.50 The Queen

Her Majesty the Queen's Christmas message. With signing and subtitles.
Shown at 3.00pm on BBC1 and ITV and 6.20pm on Channel 4 Stereo.......743816

9.00 New series
The Abbey

CHOICE A three-part series, showing on consecutive evenings, in which Alan Bennett goes behind the scenes at Westminster Abbey. *A Royal Peculiar*. Bennett watches the comings and goings in "the Queen's parish church". **See today's choices.**
Director Jonathan Stedall; Producer Andrew Holmes
Part 2 tomorrow 8.00pm Stereo Subtitled..5106

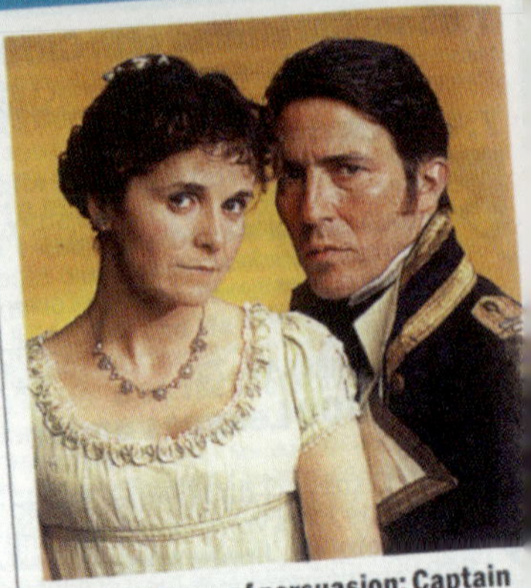

7.00pm Power of persuasion: Captain Wentworth (Ciaran Hinds) closes in on his lost love, Anne Elliot (Amanda Root

THE BBC 100

10.00 Film premiere
Farewell My Concubine

Epic drama, continuing the season of great films celebrating 100 years of cinem Starring **Leslie Cheung**, **Zhang Fen**
Dumped by his mother at an institution where boys are rigorously trained to perform in the opera, Douzi finds protection with the tougher Shitou. Pushed into female roles because o his slight build, Douzi becomes confused about his sexual identity. the years pass, the two become st of the Peking Opera, but they live in turbulent times and sexual and emotional betrayal tear them apar In Mandarin with English subtitles Showing in widescreen format.

Douzi/Cheng Dieyi (young man).... LESLIE C
Shitou/Duan Xiaolou (young man).... ZHANG
Juxian.......
Guan Jifa.......
Na Kun.......
Master Yuan.......MA N
Douzi (child).......
Douzi (teenager).......
Shitou (child).......ZHAO
Shitou (teenager).......
Director Chen Kaige (1993) Stereo ....

◆ See Films: pages 49–72
The next *BBC 100* film is *Man of the West* Thursday 28 December at 11.00pm

12.30am Rowan and Martin's Laugh-in

A compilation of highlights to c the 25th anniversary of the ana comedy show which, during the sixties and early seventies, wo Emmy awards and a cult follow Hosted by Dan Rowan and Dic it launched the careers of Gold and Lily Tomlin and also featu Buzzi, Joanne Worley, Teresa Arte Johnson and British actre Carne. Guests include Samm Johnny Carson, Cher, Peter S Tony Curtis, Michael Caine a Nixon. Rpt Stereo Subtitled....

1.30 A Night at the O

Comedy with the **Marx Brothers**
Stowaways on an ocea false beards and hotel bed-switching lead to the o night of all opening nights.
Otis B Driftwood GROUCHO MARX, F MARX, Tomasso HARPO MARX, Mrs MARGARET DUMONT, Riccardo Bar Director Sam Wood (1935) B/W .

◆ See Films: pages 49–72

3.00–3.10am Weatherv

Radio Times

The Age of Choice

1990–1999

Pride and Prejudice

Fitzwilliam Darcy (Colin Firth)

(photograph by Mark Lawrence)

5–11 July 1997

Two years after Andrew Davies's dramatisation of Jane Austen's *Pride and Prejudice* was first broadcast, Mr Darcy was back on the cover of *Radio Times*. First time round, in September 1995 (see page 257), Darcy had shared the space with Elizabeth Bennet (Jennifer Ehle) but now, in the shape of Colin Firth, he was displayed in splendid isolation, looking the nation firmly in the eye.

In the cover feature, Andrew Davies mused on the reasons why his version had been such a hit – it had been shown in 42 countries. Maybe it was all down to romance – and sexual attraction: Darcy in the bath, Darcy at fencing practice, Darcy locking eyes and hands with Elizabeth Bennet in the ballroom, Darcy emerging from the Pemberley lake in a wet shirt...

1990-1999

A sex symbol in breeches and Helen Mirren at 50. ITV and Channel 4 appear on the listings pages for the first time – and *RT* celebrates its 75th birthday

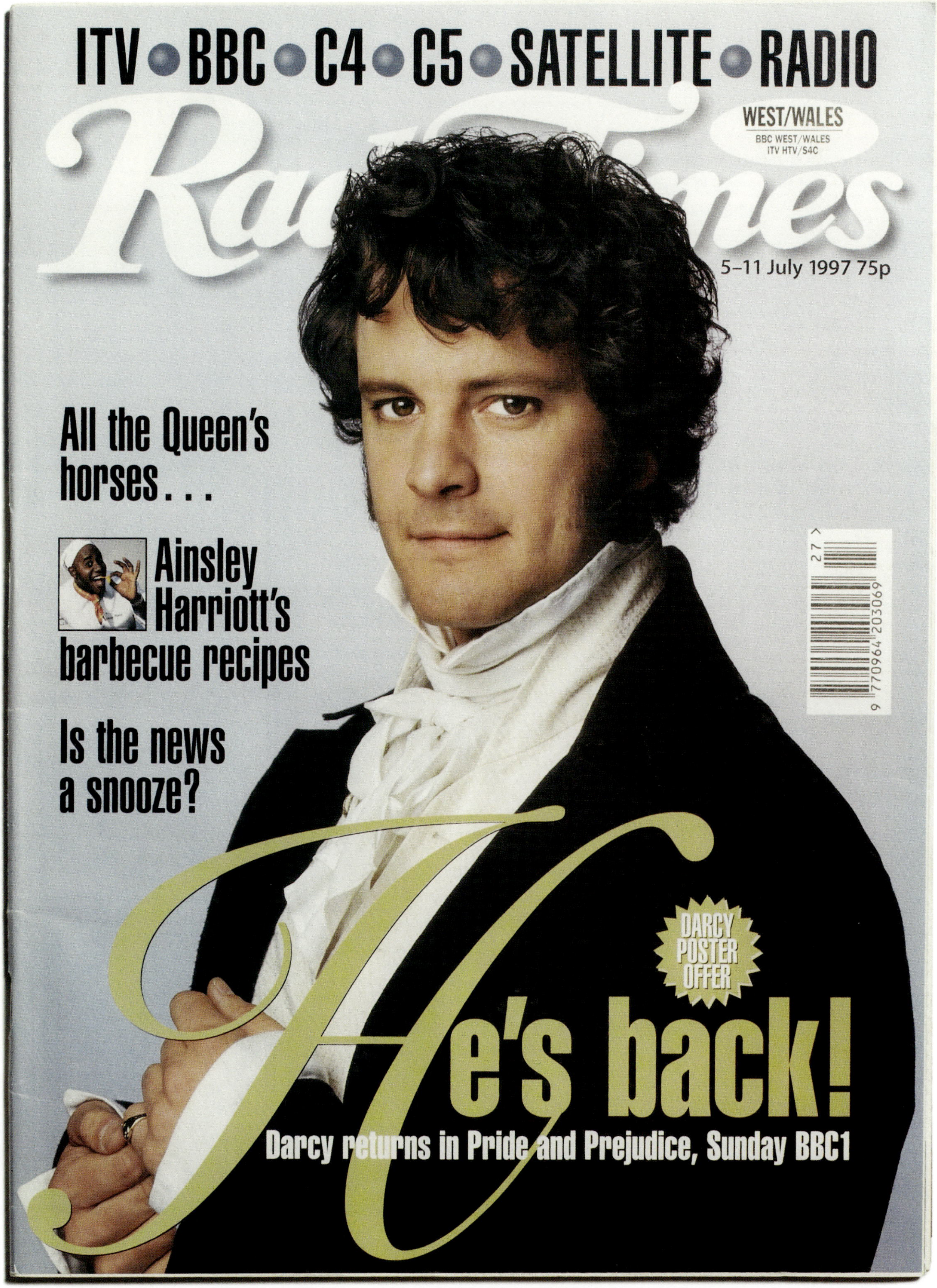
ITV BBC C4 C5 SATELLITE RADIO
Radio Times
WEST/WALES
BBC WEST/WALES
ITV HTV/S4C
5–11 July 1997 75p
All the Queen's horses...
Ainsley Harriott's barbecue recipes
Is the news a snooze?
DARCY POSTER OFFER
He's back!
Darcy returns in Pride and Prejudice, Sunday BBC1

The Trials of Life *(right)*
David Attenborough *(photograph by Steve Shipman)*
29 September–5 October 1990

Three years in the making, the third of David Attenborough's epic natural history series (after *Life on Earth* and *The Living Planet*) looked at animal behaviour through the various stages of life. The footage of chimps hunting monkeys and killer whales attacking sea lions would enter wildlife broadcasting lore.

Comic Relief *(below left)*
Lenny Henry *(photograph by Terry O'Neill)*
9–15 March 1991

"*Radio Times* readers? Better than a barrelful of red-nosed monkeys! Thanks half a million!" So said Lenny Henry in response to *Radio Times* promising to donate half the cover price on the occasion of *Comic Relief III: The Stonker*. It's also the Red Nose Day when Henry's Theophilus P Wildebeeste duetted with Tom Jones in a "Clash of the Codpieces".

Play on One: Out of the Blue *(below right)*
Catherine Zeta-Jones *(photograph by Terry O'Neill)*
17–23 August 1991

Fresh from her eye-catching role in *The Darling Buds of May*, Catherine Zeta-Jones co-starred with Colin Firth in a BBC1 play about a young woman's affair with a film-maker. Some papers labelled it a "Big Sex Romp"; Jones said, "I just take off my top and lie down. I haven't got much to flaunt anyway."

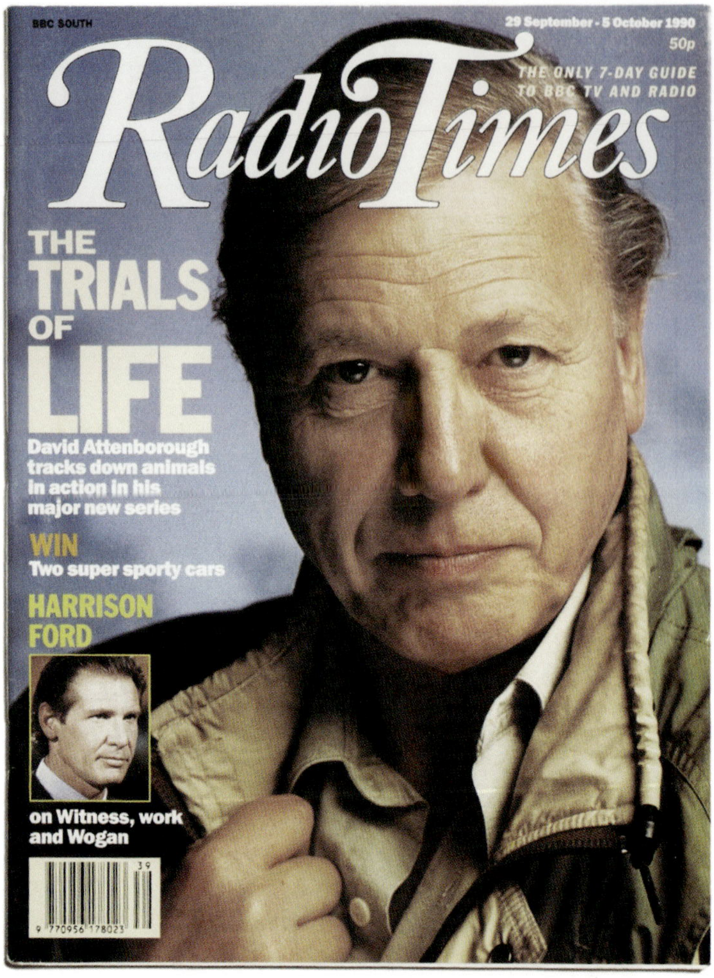

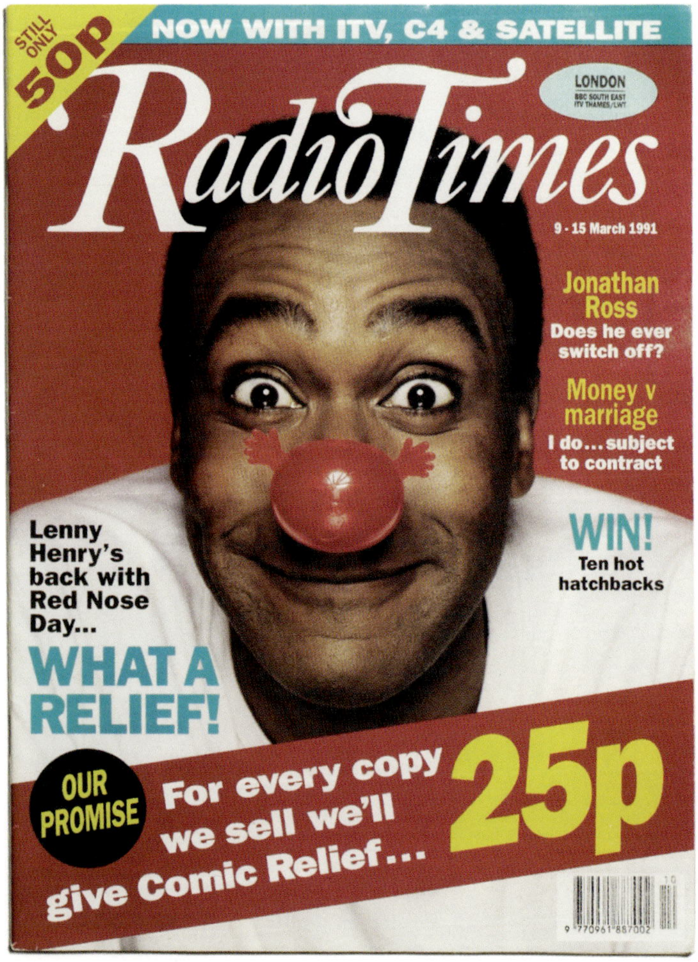

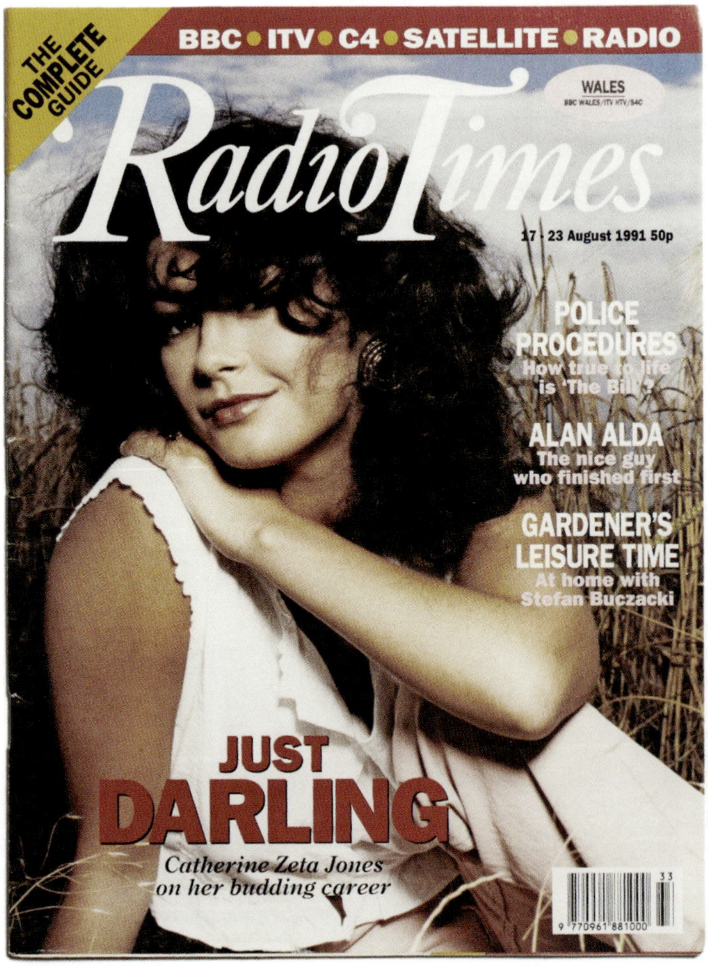

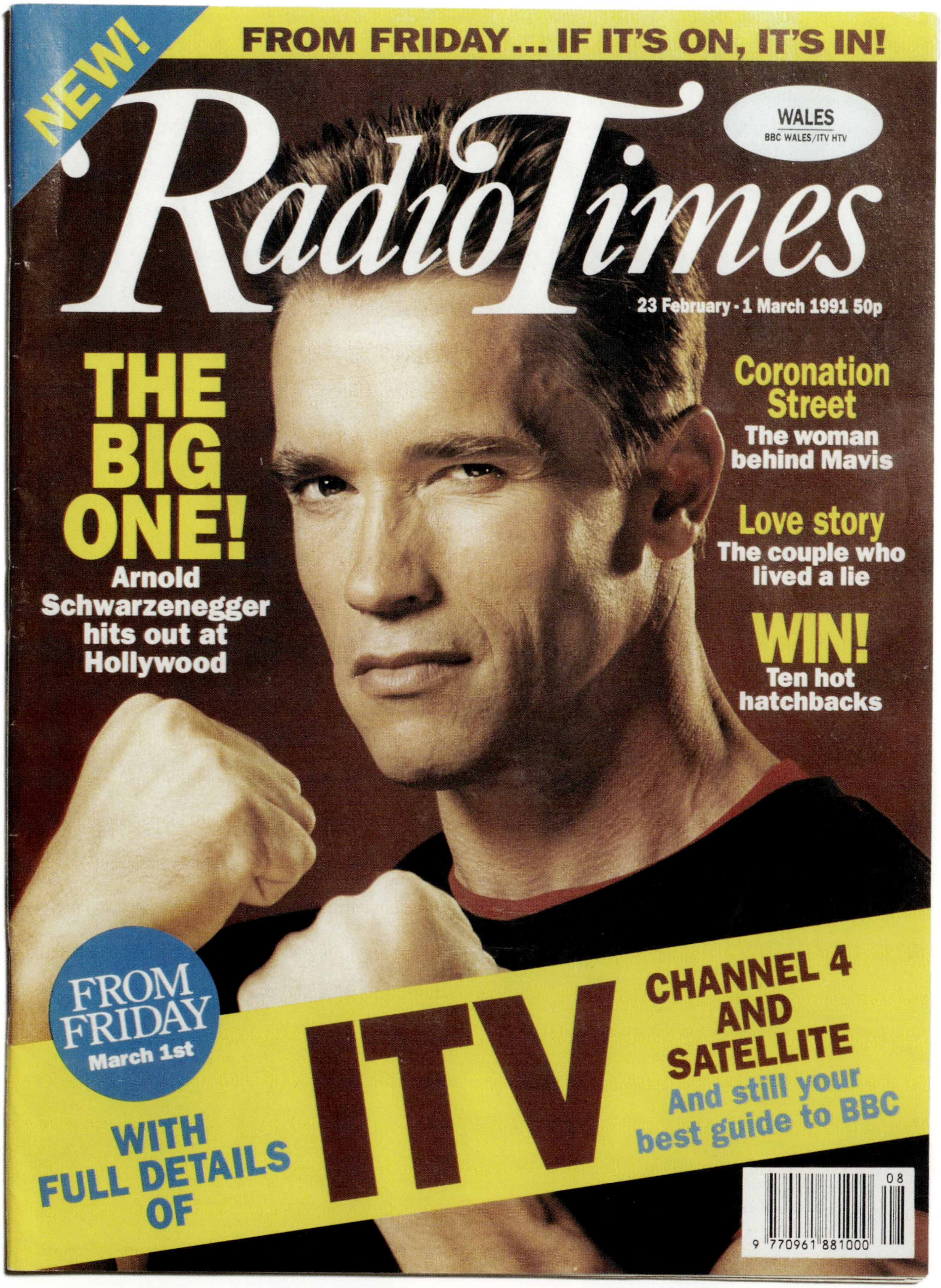

Naked Hollywood **Arnold Schwarzenegger** *(photograph by EJ Camp)* *23 February–1 March 1991*

There may be a big Hollywood star on the cover but the big news for *Radio Times* was the deregulation of television listings, which meant that for the first time, *Radio Times* could print schedules for ITV, Channel 4 and satellite channels, and our competitors could print the BBC's. Things would never be the same again.

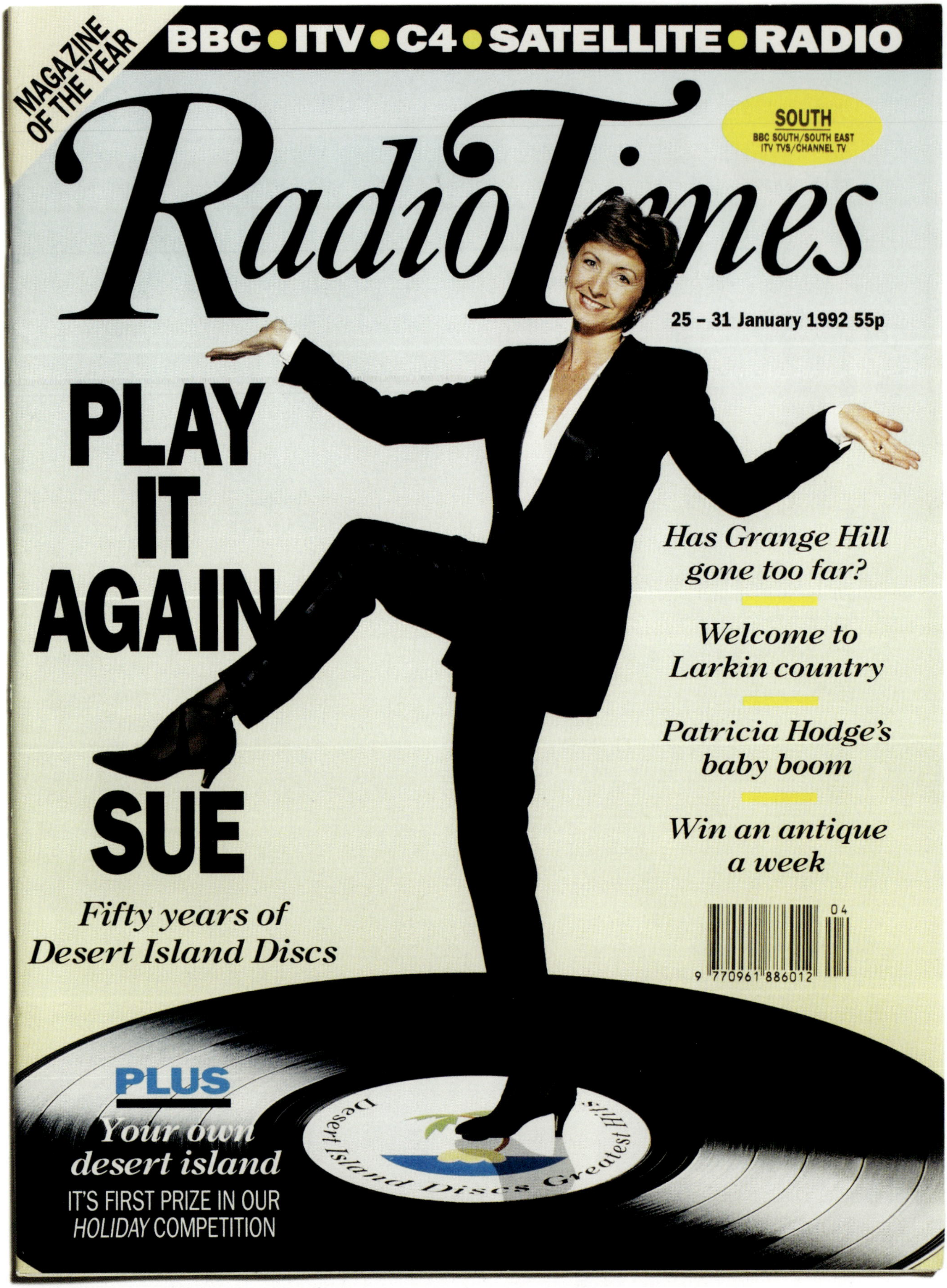

Desert Island Discs **Sue Lawley** *(photograph by Terry O'Neill)* *25–31 January 1992*

The Radio 4 staple celebrated its 50th anniversary with a special edition in which Sue Lawley interviewed then Prime Minister, John Major. His chosen tracks included *The Happening* by Diana Ross and the Supremes and a cricket commentary by John Arlott. His luxury items were a life-sized replica of the Oval cricket ground and a bowling machine.

Galahad of Everest *(right)*

Brian Blessed *(photograph by Chris Craymer)*

7–13 December 1991

Brian Blessed fed his passion for climbing mountains and emulated George Mallory, lost on an ascent of Mount Everest in 1924, when he retraced his boyhood hero's footsteps in a re-creation fraught with danger.

Dame Edna Everage in Person *(below left)*

Dame Edna Everage (Barry Humphries) *(photograph by Terry O'Neill)*

29 August–4 September 1992

As part of Radio 1's 25th birthday party, modest Melbourne housewife and "the best-dressed woman on radio" took to the airwaves with the help of Simon Bates. "I adored him in *Women in Love* – didn't you, darling?"

One Foot in the Grave *(below right)*

Victor Meldrew (Richard Wilson) and Margaret Meldrew (Annette Crosbie) *(photograph by Sven Arnstein)*

30 January–5 February 1993

Television's most irascible man, Victor Meldrew, returned for a fourth series of the BBC1 sitcom (accompanied by long-suffering wife Margaret). Creator David Renwick revealed the caustic thoughts of the curmudgeonly codger, while elsewhere in the magazine, *Casualty* toasted its 100th episode.

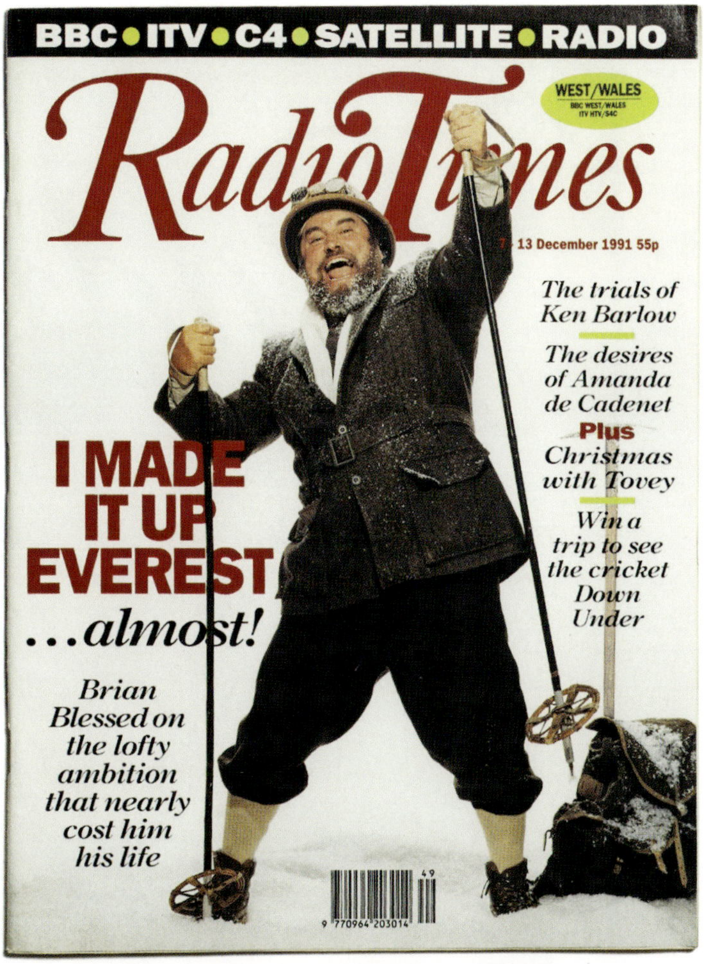

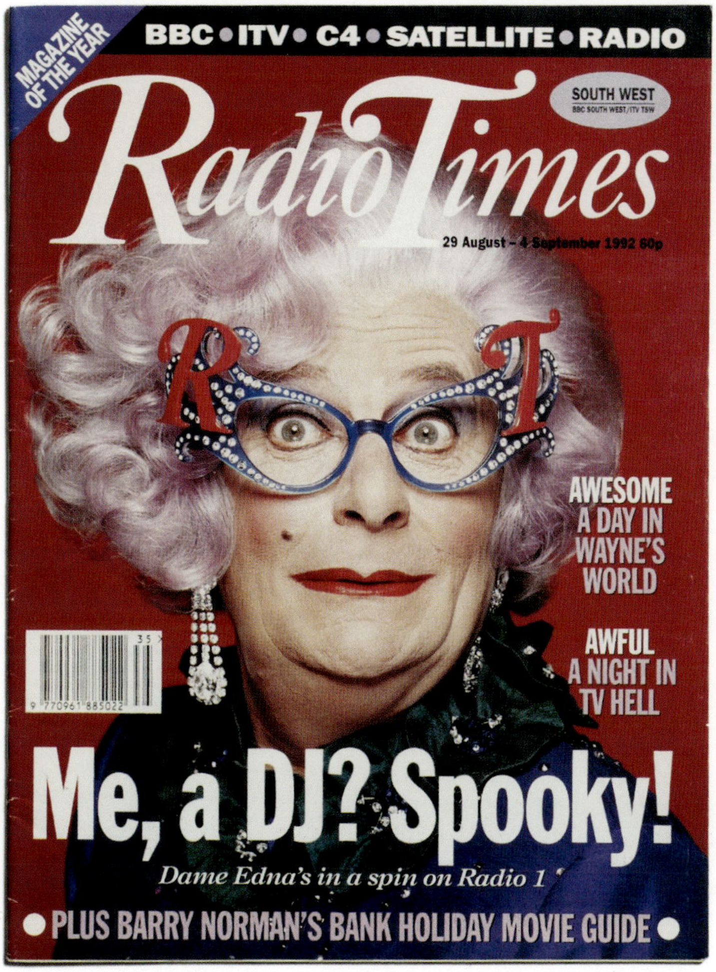

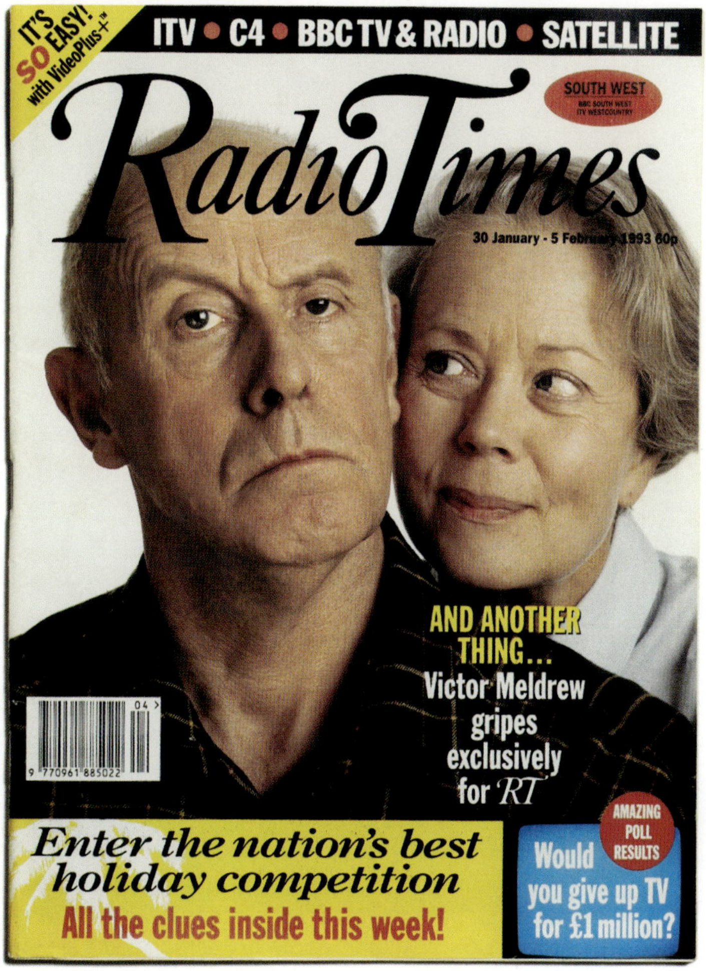

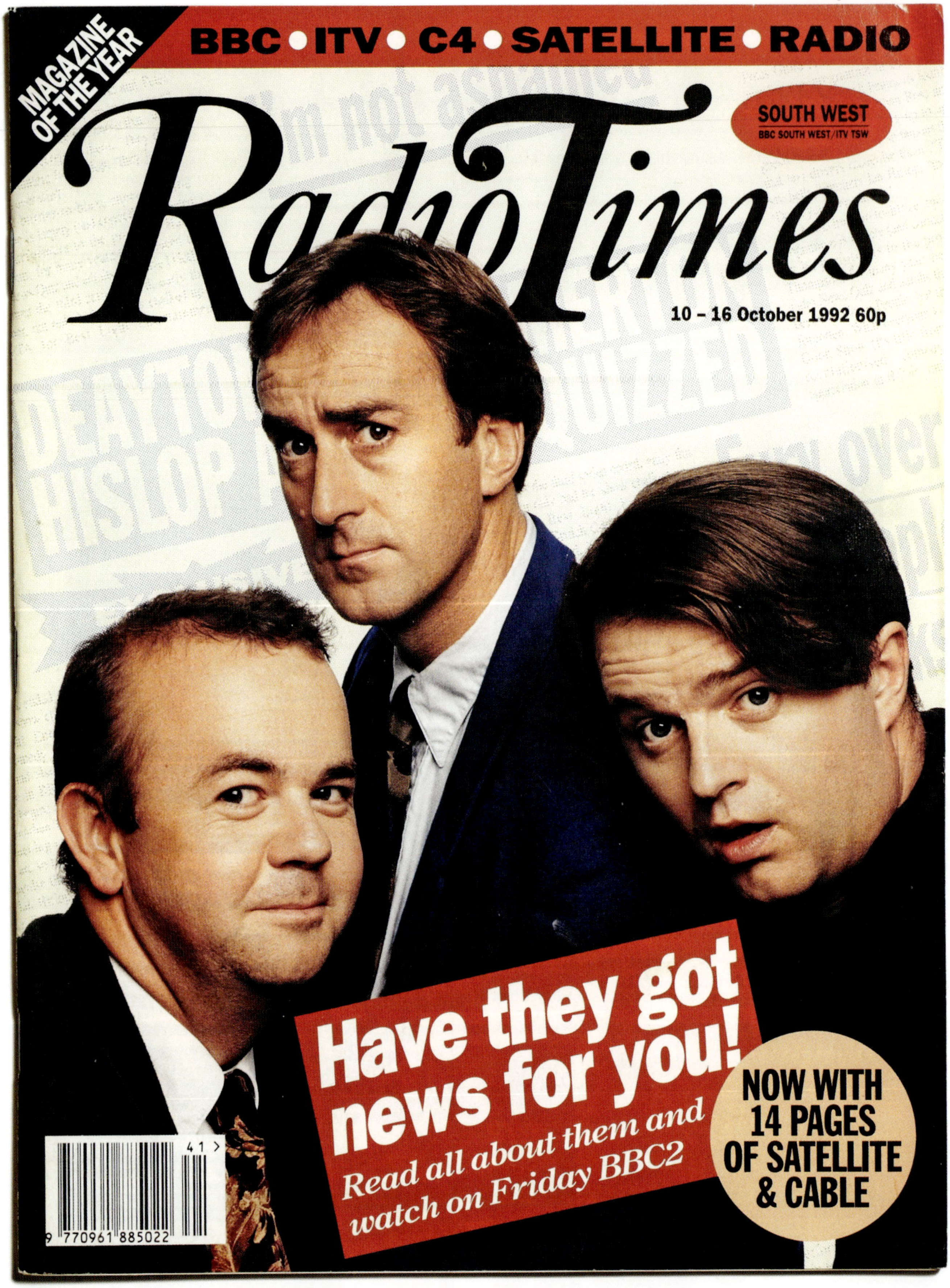

Have I Got News for You **Ian Hislop, Angus Deayton and Paul Merton**
(photograph by Mark Harrison) 10–16 October 1992

"Ian is the conscience, Angus is the brain and I am the spleen," said Paul Merton in a feature to mark the start of the fourth series of the satirical panel show. Deayton was fired as host a decade later after lurid headlines about his personal life. Hislop and Merton remain as captains to this day.

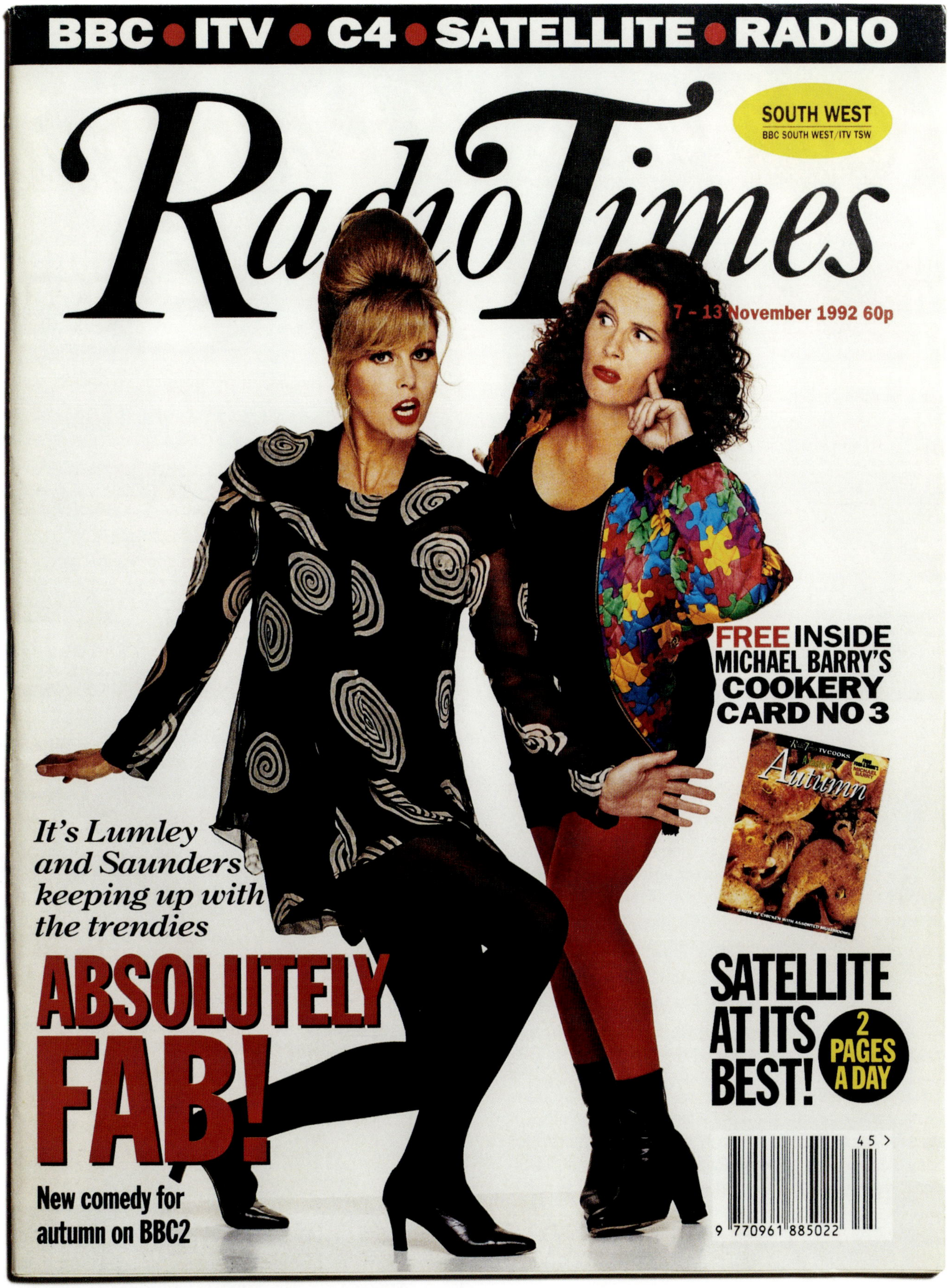

Absolutely Fabulous Patsy Stone (Joanna Lumley) and Edina Monsoon (Jennifer Saunders) *(photograph by Trevor Leighton) 7–13 November 1992*

Jennifer Saunders took a sabbatical from her double act with Dawn French to write and star in this "Women Behaving Badly" comedy series set in the world of media and fashion. It became a huge international success and saw Joanna Lumley jettison her plummy image once and for all to play monstrous best friend, Patsy.

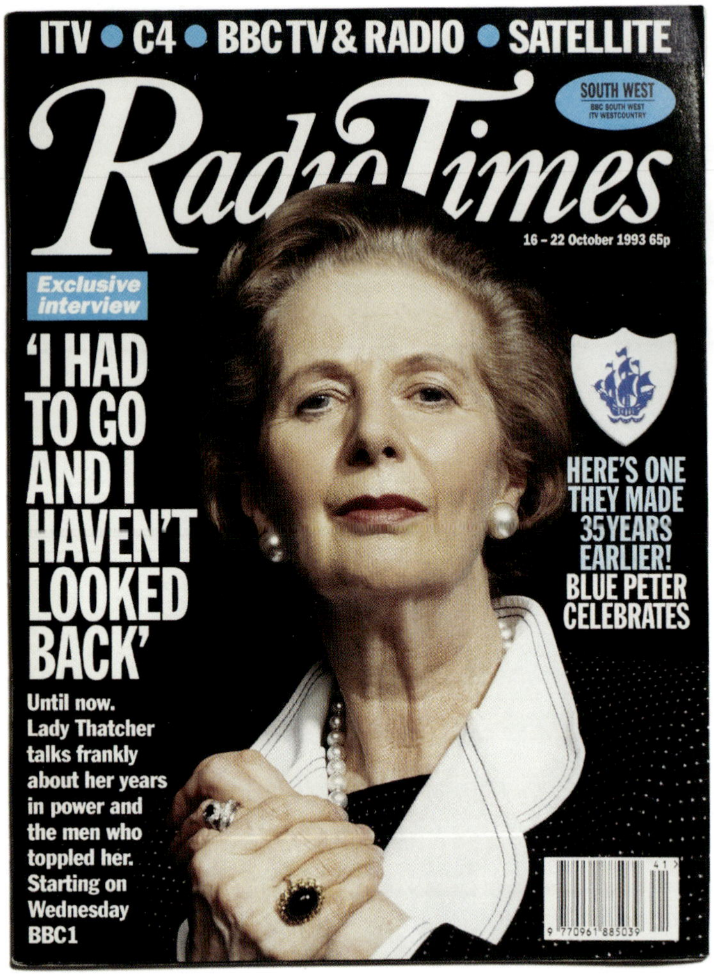

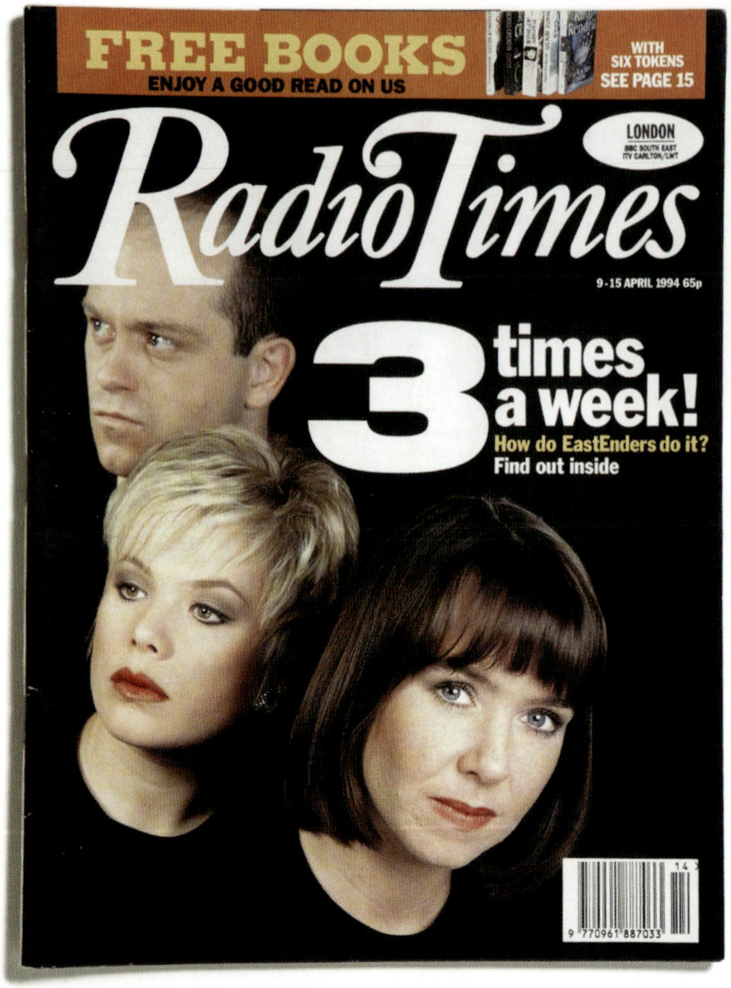

Horror Special *(right)*

Illustration by Ian McKinnell

6–12 August 1994

A BBC1 documentary about Hammer Films inspired *Radio Times* to interview the horror writer Stephen King, screen vamp Kate O'Mara and Hammer stalwarts/programme narrators Christopher Lee and Peter Cushing (who died a few days after the programme was broadcast).

Girl Friday *(middle right)*

Joanna Lumley *(photograph by Brian Ritchie)*

26 November–2 December 1994

In an early example of celebrity-fronted reality TV, Joanna Lumley was marooned on the island of Tsarabanjina off Madagascar for nine days with only a BBC camera crew for company. Lumley built her own shelter, made a pair of "cave-slippers" from a bra and slept alone on the island at night.

Christmas 1994 *(far right)*

Illustration by Bob Venables

17–30 December 1994

This cover is a reworking of the 1924 Christmas edition – see page 27 – by American illustrator Edwin Austin Abbey (but with modern clothes and no cigarettes). It was also a cue for celebrities like Norman Wisdom, Diana Rigg and Cilla Black to reflect on memorable Christmasses past.

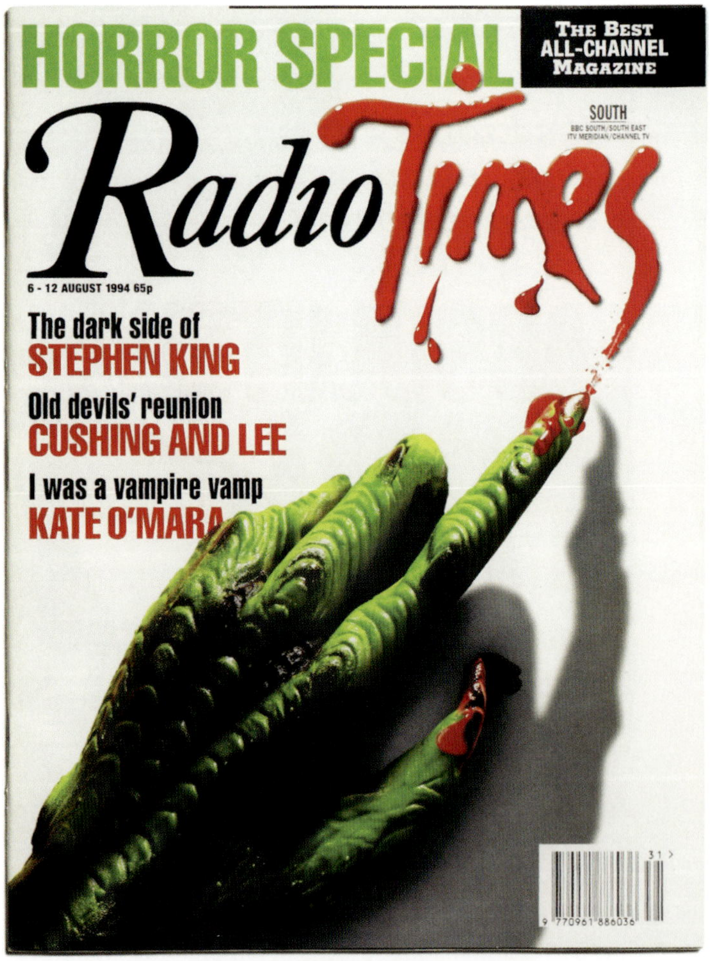

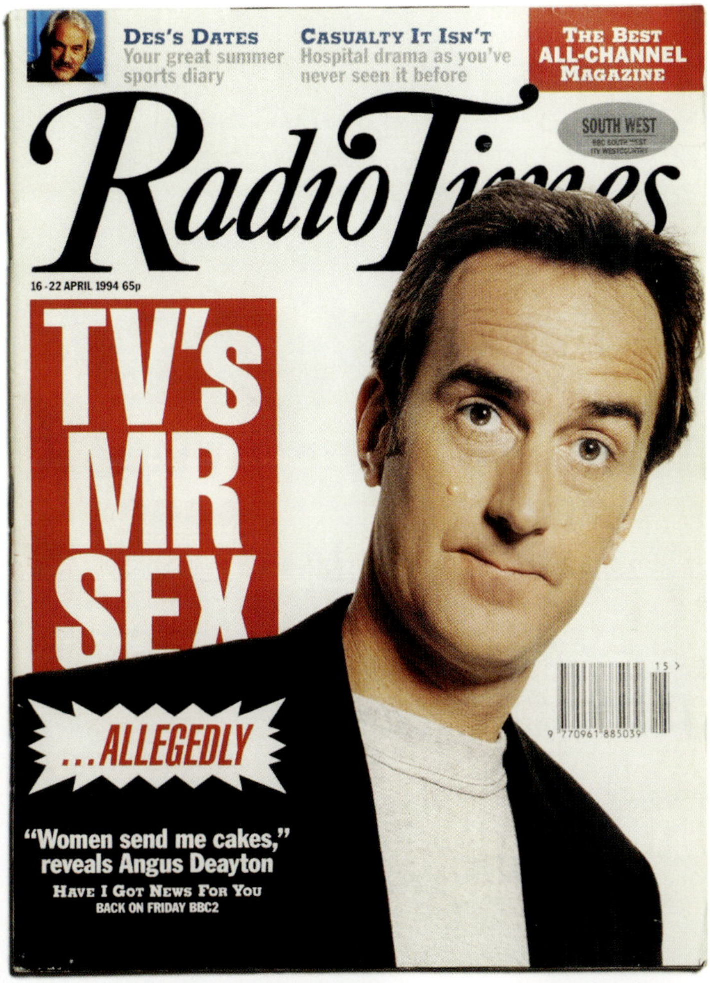

Thatcher: the Downing Street Years *(far left)*

Margaret Thatcher ***(photograph by Nigel Perry)***

16–22 October 1993

Producers Hugh Scully and Denys Blakeway came up with a coup of their own when they persuaded Baroness Thatcher to talk candidly about her 11 years as prime minister and her fall from power in 1990.

EastEnders *(middle left)*

From left: Grant (Ross Kemp), Sharon (Letitia Dean) and Michelle (Susan Tully) ***(photograph by Mark Harrison)***

9–15 April 1994

On the back of a regular audience of 20 million viewers, the BBC soap moved to three times a week. The event was marked with a siege at the Queen Vic pub that put the cover stars at the mercy of a deranged Army buddy of Grant's.

Have I Got News for You *(right)*

Angus Deayton ***(photograph by Terry O'Neill)***

16–22 April 1994

Who would have guessed that an interview with Angus Deayton, in which furore over his private life and his "Mr Sex" nickname were discussed, could now be regarded as prophetic. A spate of tabloid revelations about the host, not to mention ridicule from Ian Hislop and Paul Merton, cost him his job in 2002.

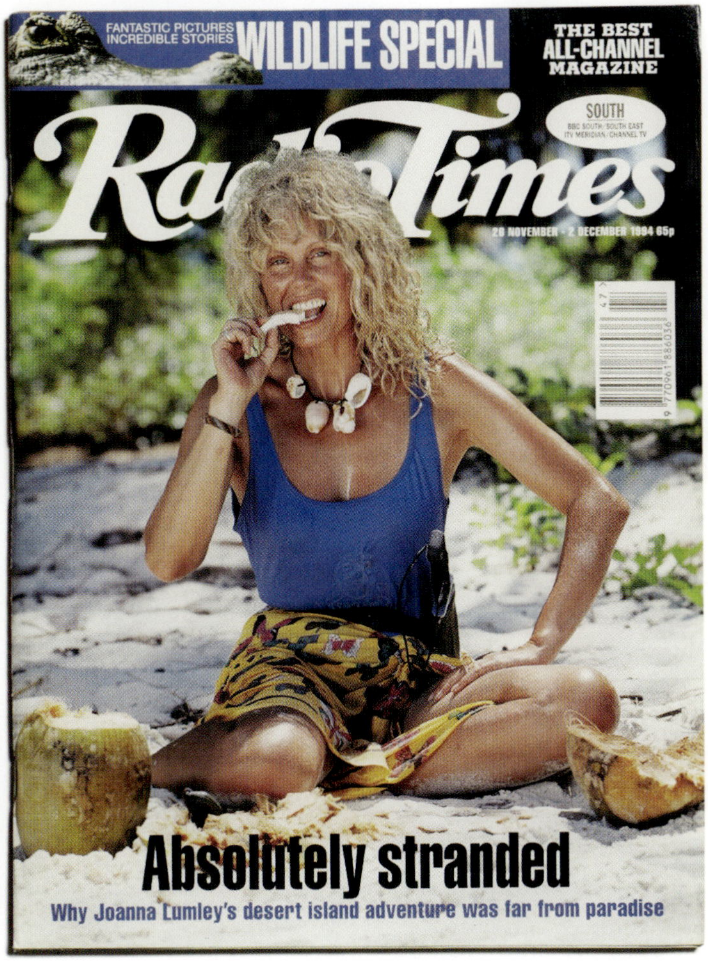

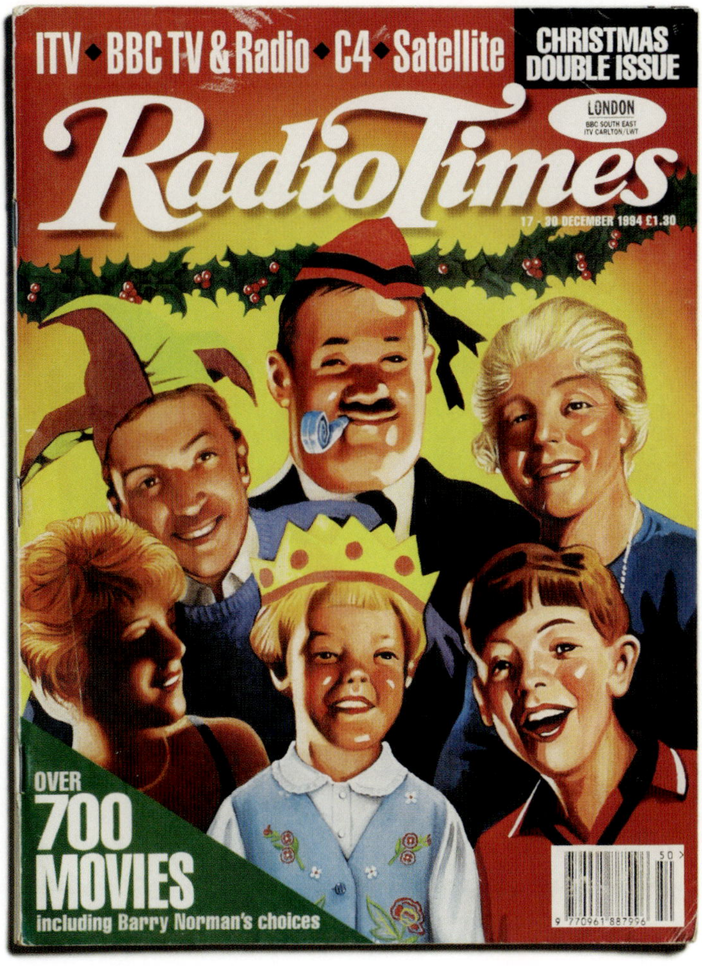

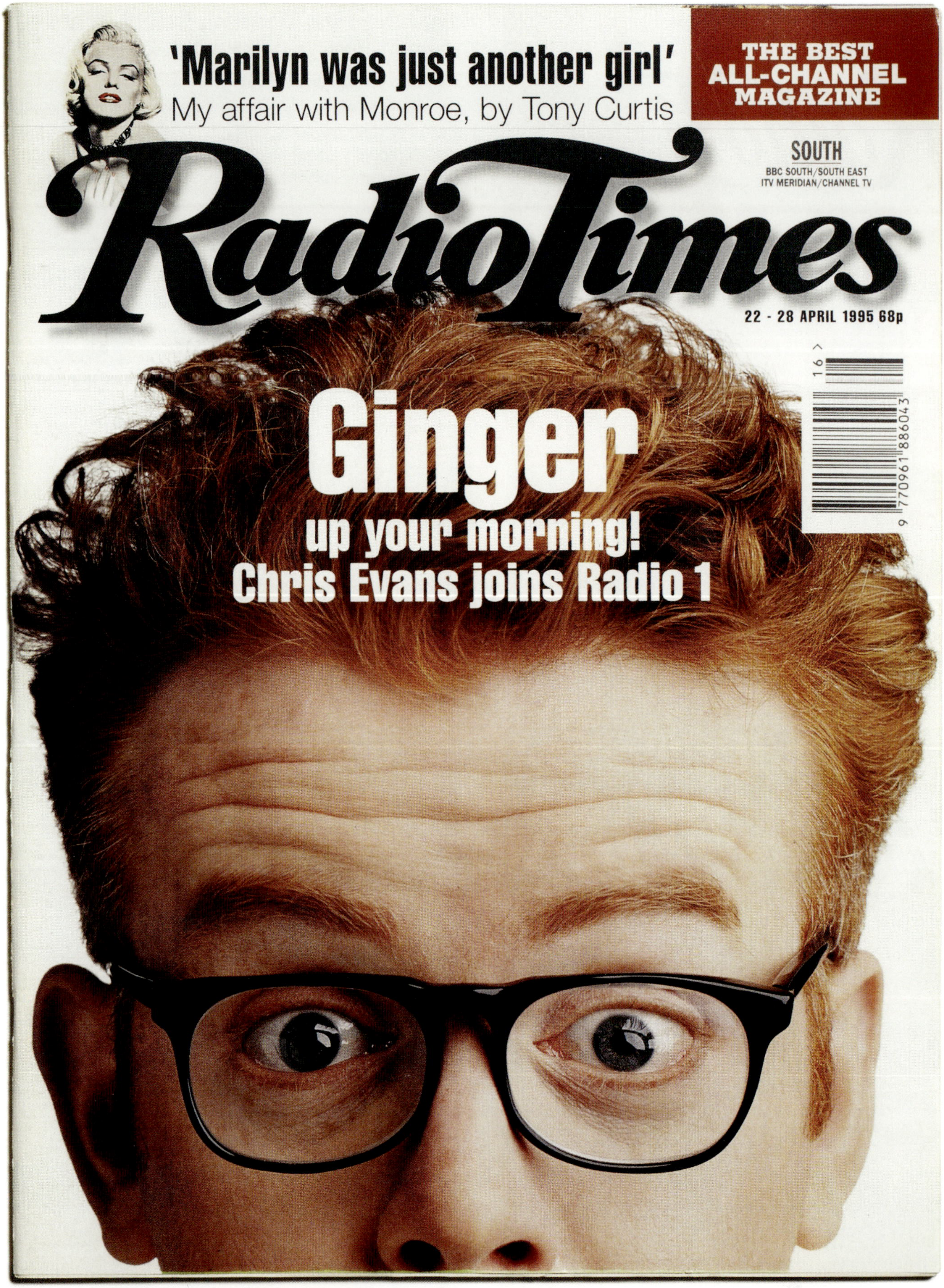

Chris Evans joins Radio 1 Chris Evans *(photograph by Tim O'Sullivan)* *22–28 April 1995*

The arrival of the flame-haired wunderkind, who was hired to boost the fortunes of Radio 1, was the cover story, but the big interview inside was with Hollywood superstar Tony Curtis. The ebullient 70-year-old actor was typically humorous and candid about sex, drugs and Marilyn Monroe.

Censorship Debate *(right)*
(photograph by Ian McKinnell)
27 May–2 June 1995

To coincide with the network premiere of Ken Russell's film *The Devils* (part of BBC2's *Forbidden Weekend*), a five-page feature debated censorship, the censors, the movies that challenged them and the effect on children.

EastEnders *(below left)*
Bianca (Patsy Palmer) *(photograph by Bailey)*
19–25 August 1995

There was a meeting of East End minds as the siren of Albert Square met photographer David Bailey. "She's a flaming redhead with a flaming personality," said Bailey. It's "like being at drama school, improvising. He was brilliant!" gushed Palmer.

Pride and Prejudice *(below right)*
Elizabeth Bennet (Jennifer Ehle) and Fitzwilliam Darcy (Colin Firth) *(photograph by Sven Arnstein)*
23–29 September 1995

Radio Times proclaimed this adaptation an "orgy of Austen" and Colin Firth was already being hailed as the definitive Mr Darcy. All without unbuttoning his shirt. When he did loosen those studs, an international sex symbol was born.

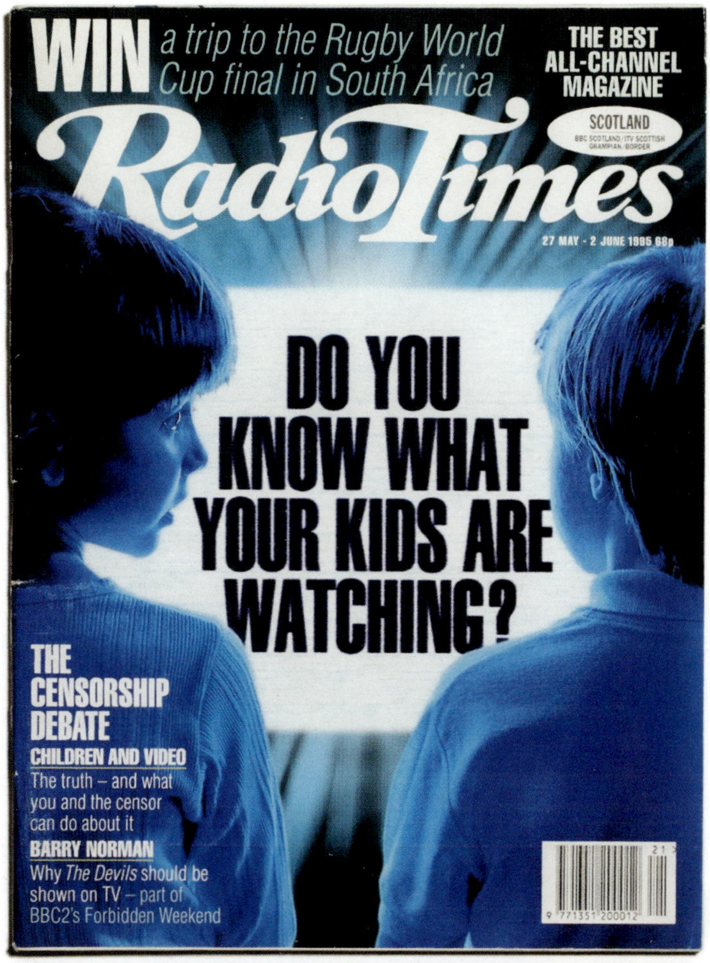

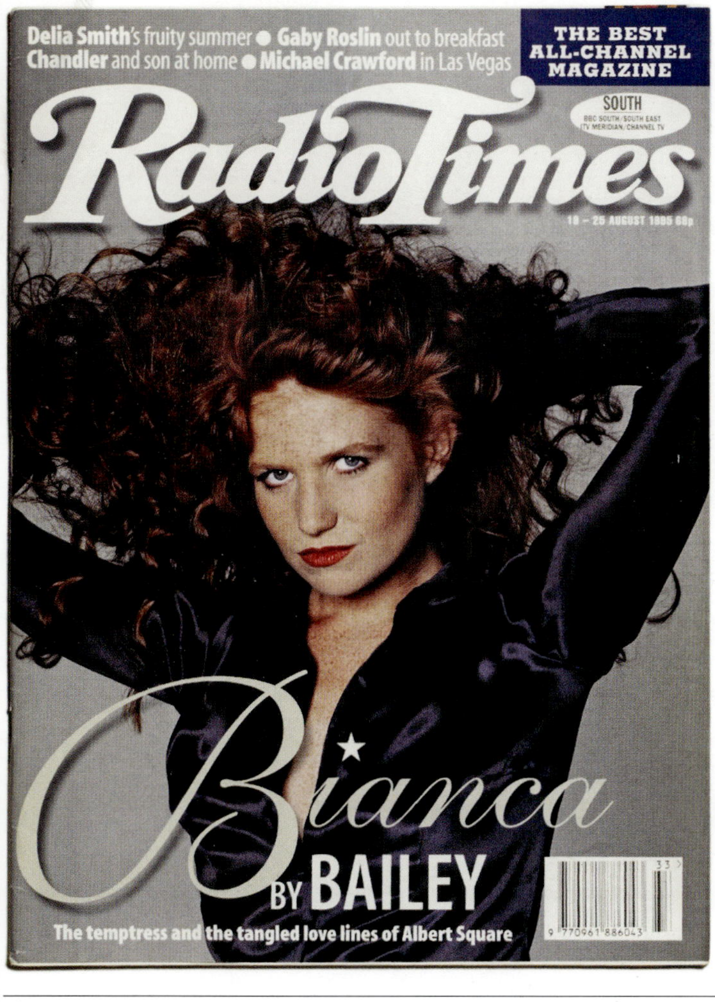

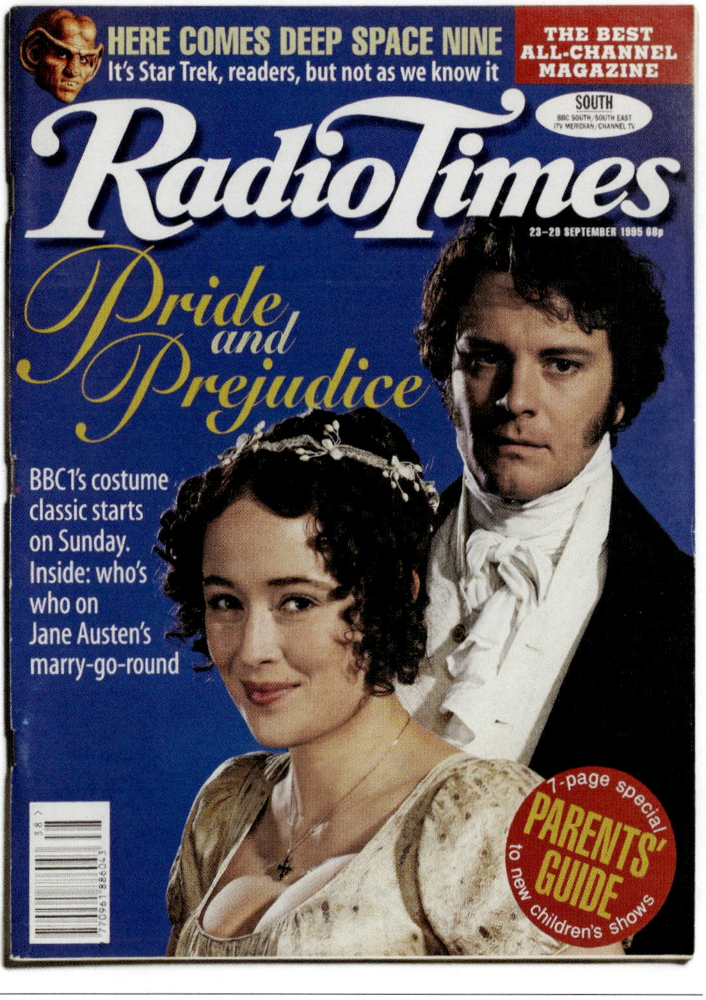

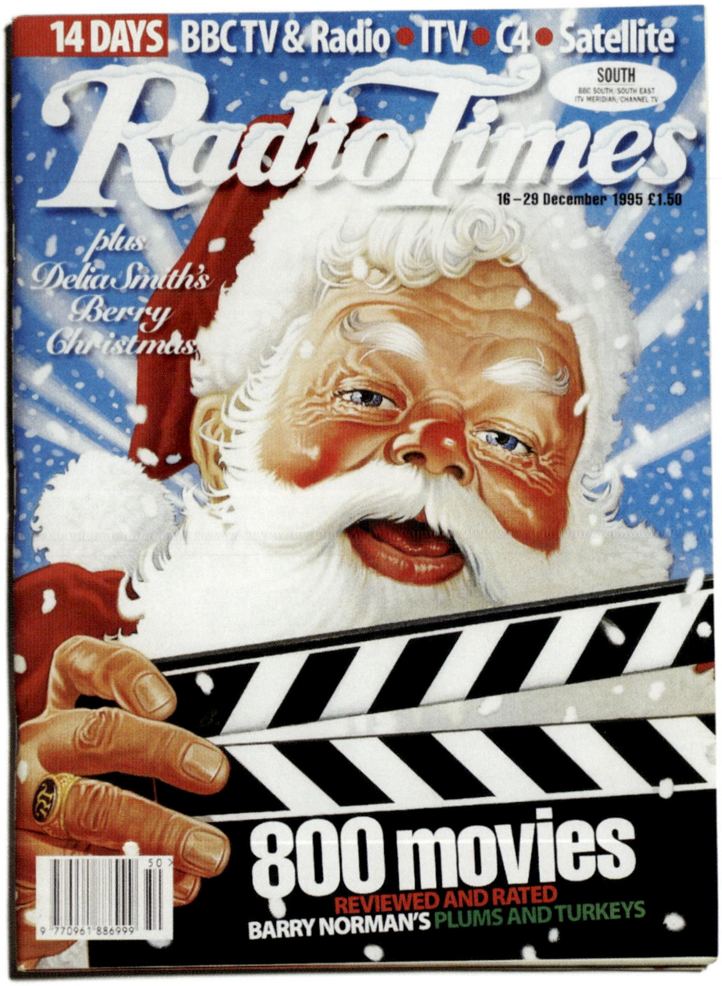

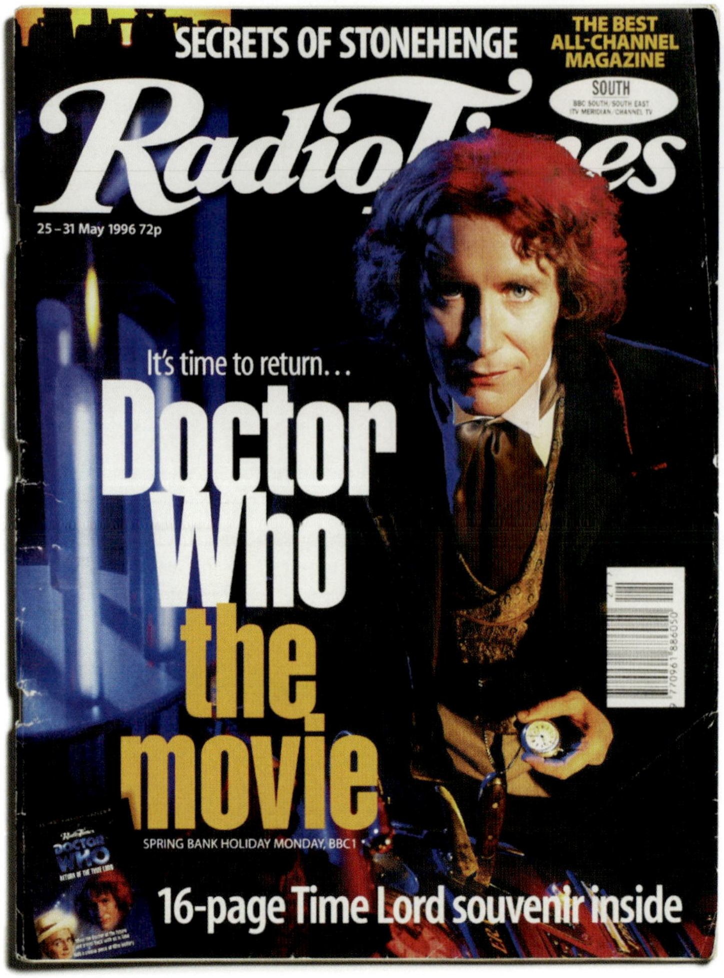

The Day That Changed My Life *(right)*

Christina Hance *(photograph by Patrick Lichfield)*

27 July–2 August 1996

Who's that girl? Not Princess Diana, that's for sure, but single mum Christina Hance, whose life was changed when her photo was entered in a royal lookalike competition. Lord Lichfield provided the cheeky cover.

Woman's Hour *(middle right)*

Helen Mirren *(photograph by Sven Arnstein)*

5–11 October 1996

The 50th birthday of Radio 4's *Woman's Hour* was celebrated by women who had reached (or were on the cusp of) their half-century, including Janet Street-Porter, Clare Short, Maureen Lipman and Dame-to-be Helen Mirren.

Billy Connolly's World Tour of Australia *(far right)*

Billy Connolly *(photograph by Fergus Greer)*

26 October–1 November 1996

Radio Times asked the comedian to keep a diary of his eight-week tour. "Why do they call it 'the bush?'" he mused. "Surely it should be plural – the bushes. Imagine walking across country and suddenly you come across the bush – with four million kangaroos hiding behind it."

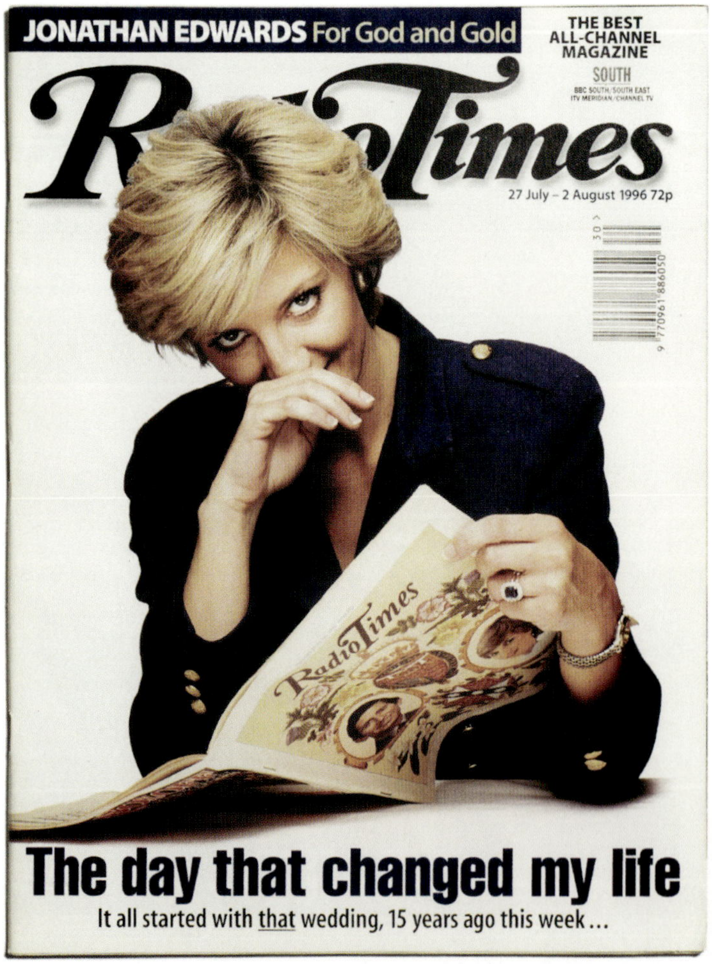

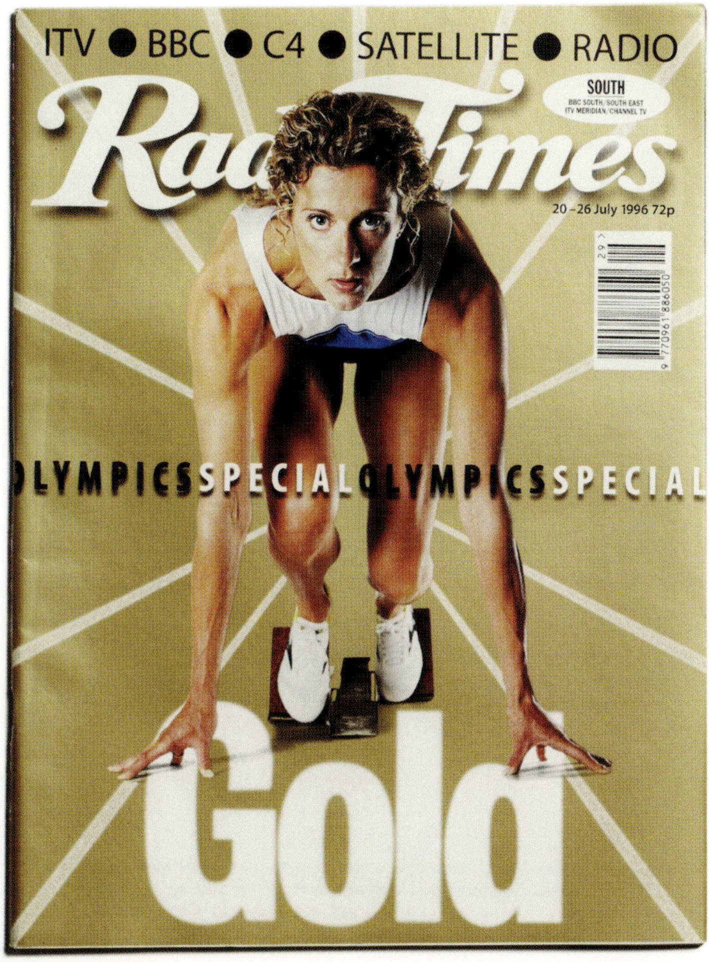

Christmas 1995 *(far left)*

Illustration by Mick Brownfield

16–29 December 1995

Steven Spielberg's *Hook* was the big festive film and its star Robin Williams gave a typically sparky interview. On the turning points in his career: "Being in drag in *Mrs Doubtfire* was one. Better latex than never. The other was stopping drinking. It was great to wake up and discover English was my first language."

Doctor Who *(middle left)*

The Doctor (Paul McGann)
(photograph by Marc Bryan-Brown)

25–31 May 1996

The Time Lord returned after a seven-year gap for a glossy BBC/US co-production with Paul McGann at the Tardis helm. *Radio Times* celebrated with a 16-page souvenir supplement. On set in Vancouver, Alison Graham met McGann, who said: "I can't help thinking of Patrick Troughton, Bill Hartnell and all the others. But I'm doing it my way – that's all I can do."

The 1996 Olympics Games *(left)*

Sally Gunnell *(photograph by Mark Harrison)*

20-26 July 1996

Sally Gunnell was aiming for a gold medal in the 400m hurdles in Atlanta. "I enjoy winning. There is nothing like it. It gives you a high for weeks," she told Andrew Duncan. But there was to be no high: she pulled up injured in the semi-finals.

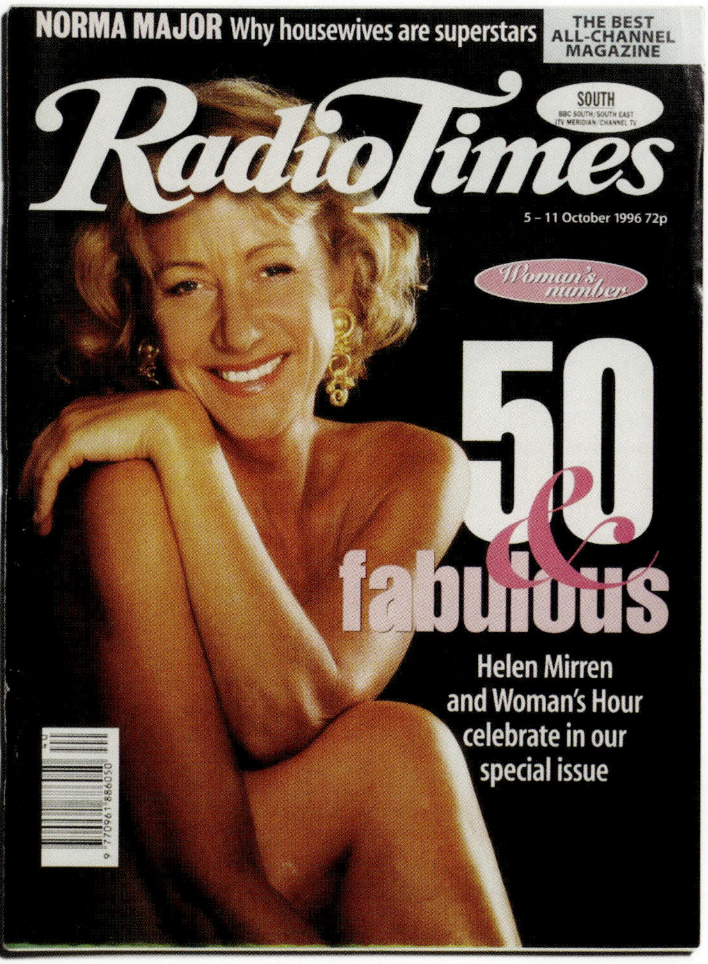

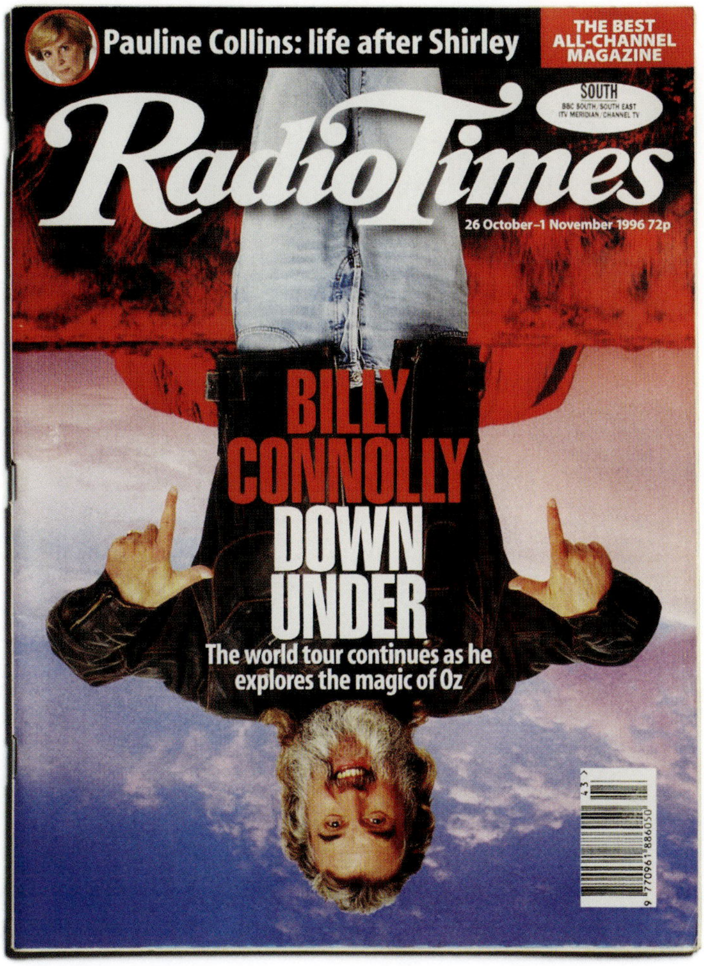

Red Dwarf *(right)*

Clockwise from top left: Kochanski (Chloë Annett), Kryten (Robert Llewellyn), Rimmer (Chris Barrie), Cat (Danny John-Jules) and Lister (Craig Charles)
(photograph by Patrick Demarchelier)

11–17 January 1997

The BBC2 sci-fi sitcom *Red Dwarf* returned after a three-year break. Meanwhile, on Sky 1, there was the start of a new series of *The X Files* with David Duchovny and Gillian Anderson.

They Think It's All Over *(middle right)*

Clockwise from top left: Gary Lineker, Lee Hurst, David Gower, Nick Hancock and Rory McGrath
(photograph by Mark Harrison)

5–11 April 1997

Laughs were more important than correct answers in the sports panel game. As quizmaster Nick Hancock said: "Whatever we say about David Gower, he takes it in good part."

Wimbledon *(far right)*

Cliff Richard and Virginia Wade
(photograph by Nicky Johnston)

28 June–4 July 1997

The cover feature recalled two Wimbledon legends: Cliff Richard's impromptu concert on a rain-soaked Centre Court in 1996, and Virginia Wade's victory in the women's singles in 1977.

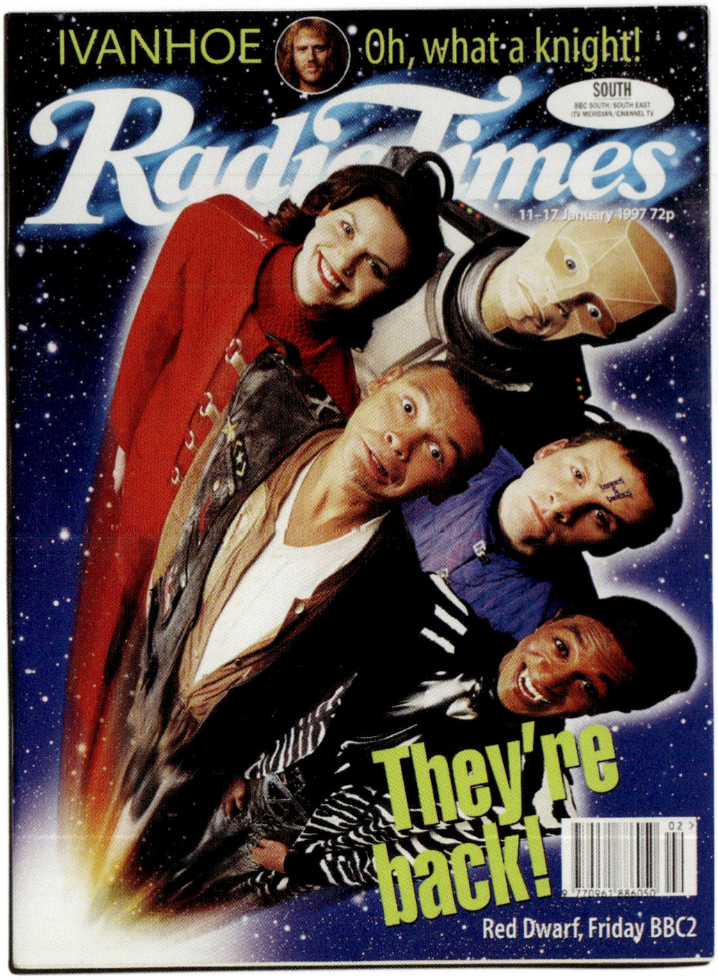

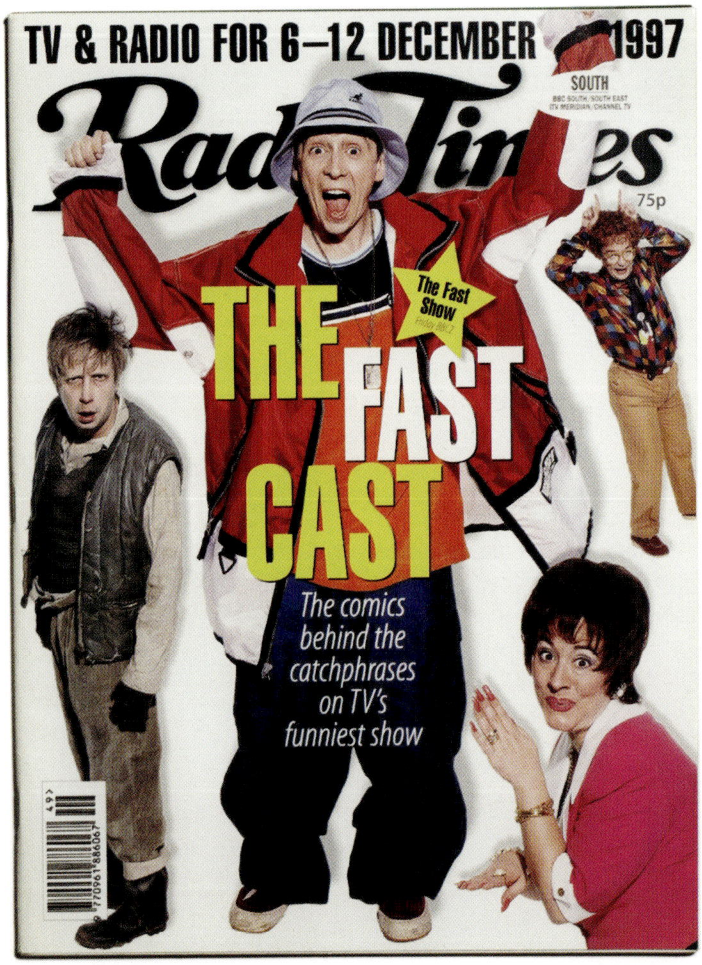

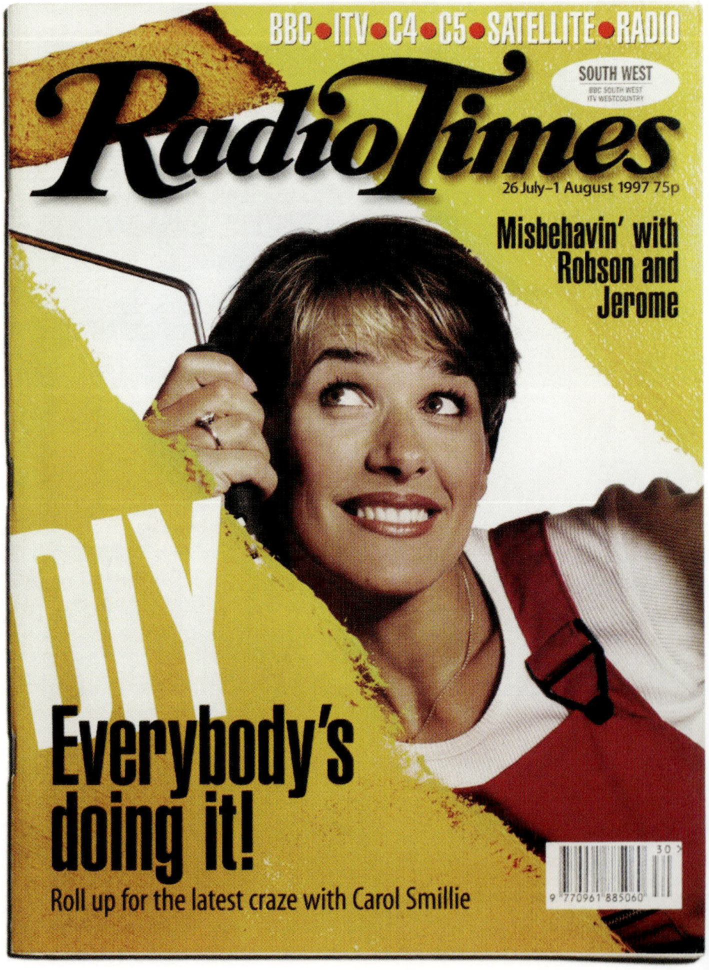

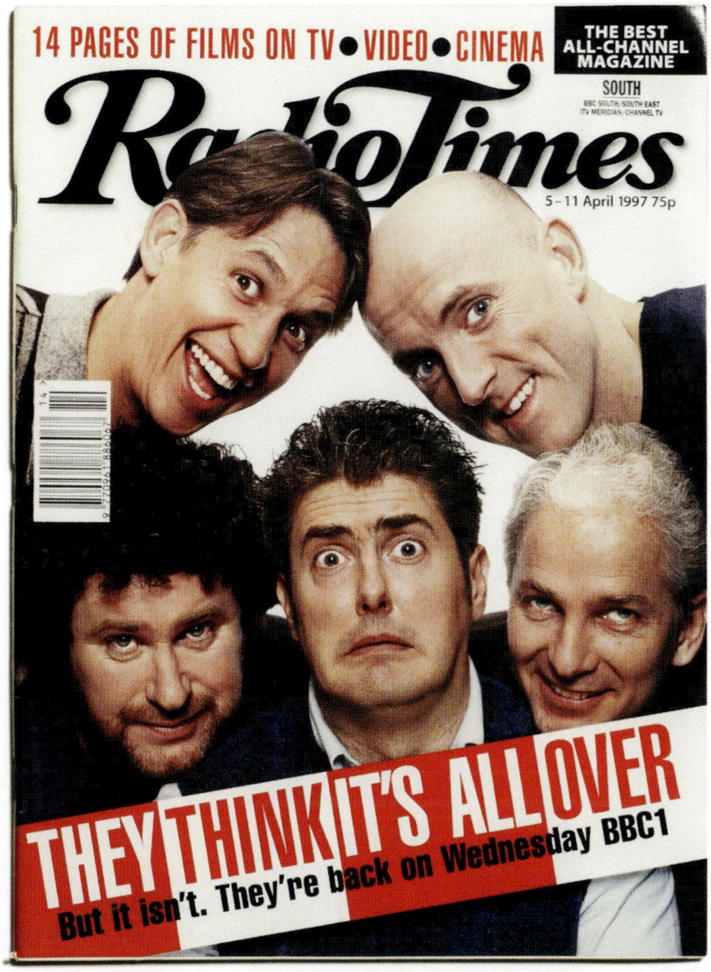

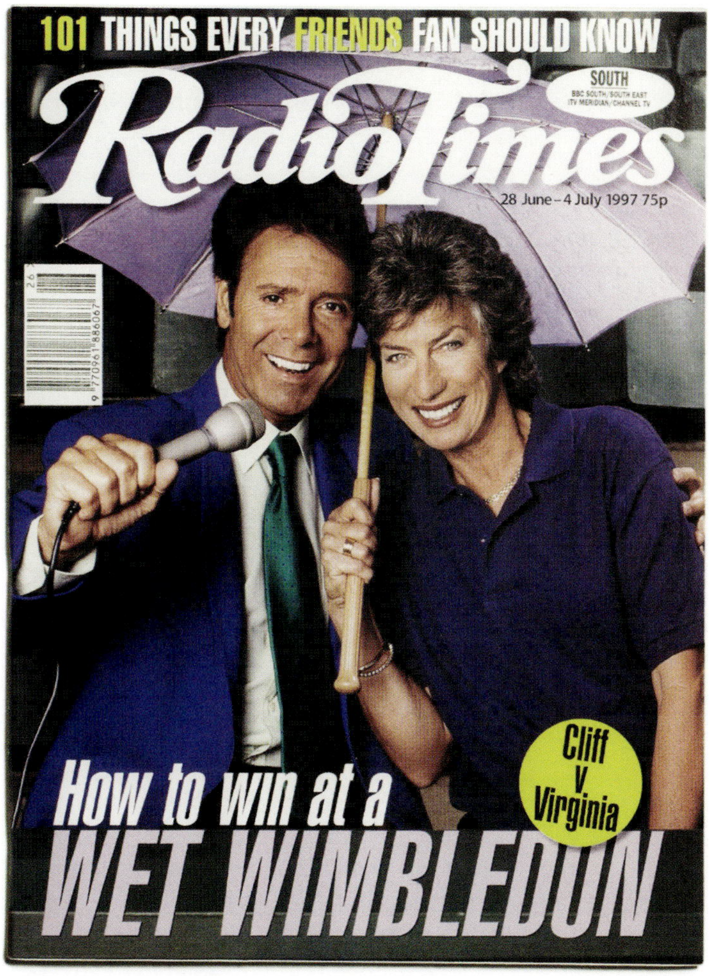

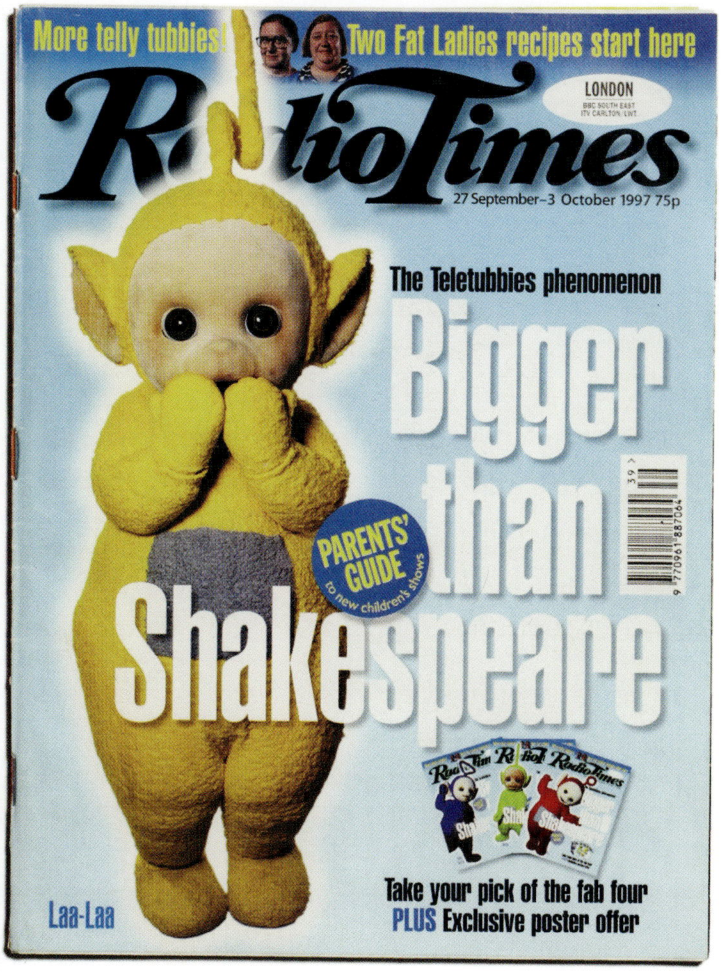

The Fast Show *(far left)*

Clockwise from left: Mark Williams, Paul Whitehouse, Charlie Higson and Arabella Weir
(photograph by Nicky Johnston)

6–12 December 1997

The stars of the sketch show that launched a thousand catchphrases revealed their secrets. Paul Whitehouse said that his mum thought the "Brilliant!" character (the main image on the cover) was him when he was a little boy.

Changing Rooms *(middle left)*

Carol Smillie *(photograph by Mark Harrison)*

26 July–1 August 1997

It was the series that made DIY sexy (and dangerous): couples were let loose on their neighbours' home with £500 and a hammer (while the neighbours returned the favour in their home). But what about the "reveal" when the two couples were shown the transformation? "Just look at their eyes," said presenter Carol Smillie. "They don't lie."

Teletubbies *(left)*

Laa-Laa *(photograph by Mark Harrison)*

27 September–3 October 1997

The children's series had become a huge phenomenon, so *Radio Times* asked the burning question: are Dipsy, Po, Laa-Laa and Tinky Winky bigger than Shakespeare?

Fifty Golden Years *(right)*

The Queen and the Duke of Edinburgh
(photograph by Snowdon)

15–21 November 1997

This week saw a Service of Thanksgiving to mark the 50th wedding anniversary of the Queen and Prince Philip. The cover feature reflected that it was the royals' relationship with the public that had been most challenged over the past half-century, especially in the aftermath of the death of Princess Diana.

Christmas 1997 *(below left)*

Illustration by Kevin Hauff

20 December 1997–2 January 1998

The issue promised "230 pages... and Five Spice Girls..." Posh, Sporty, Baby, Ginger and Scary were the star guests on *Top of the Pops* on Christmas Eve and Christmas Day, and they charmed interviewer Andrew Duncan. "They are easy to mock," he wrote, "but the terrible truth is that I like them instantly."

The Ben Elton Show *(below right)*

Ben Elton ***(photograph by Bill Robinson)***

18–24 April 1998

Comedian Ben Elton was on a roll with his rants. In this issue he despaired over the concept of Cool Britannia. "The truth is you can't buy cool and you can't create it with a label," he wrote. "Cool is in the eye of the beholder."

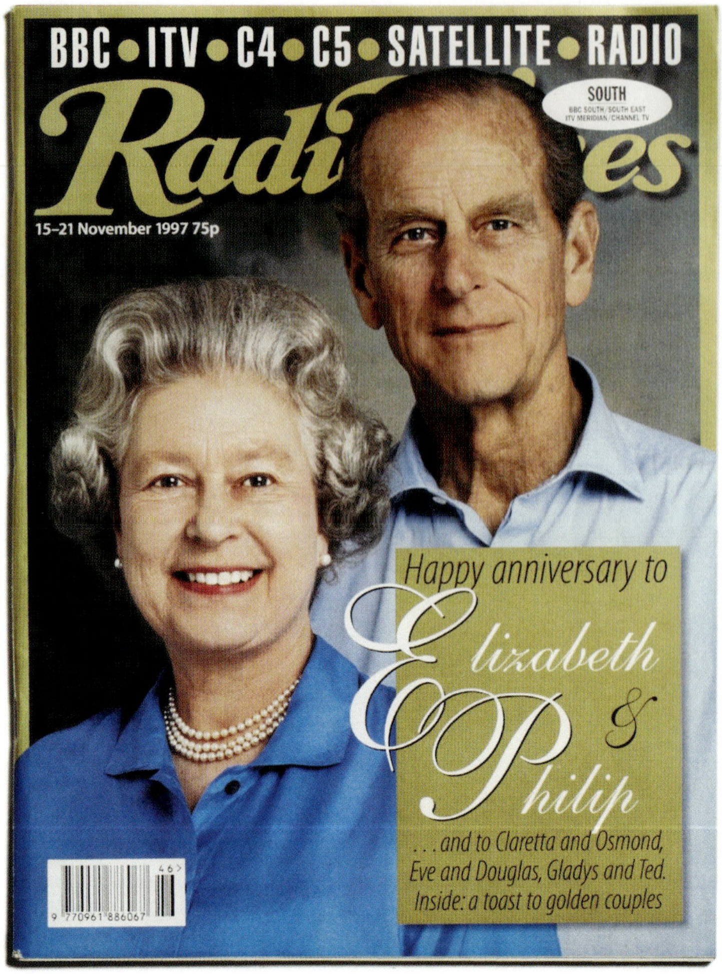

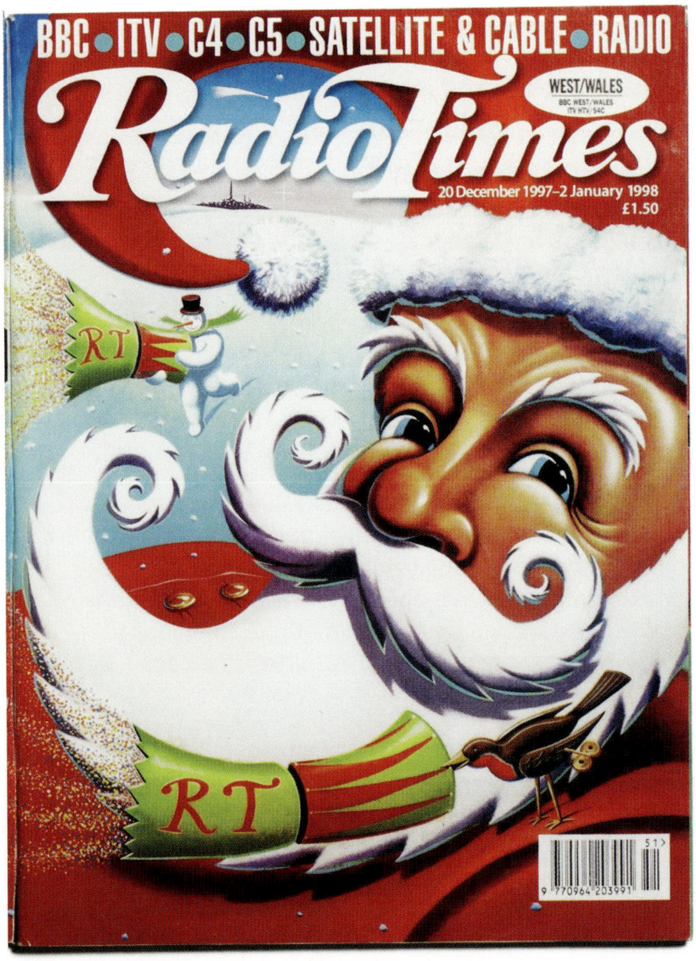

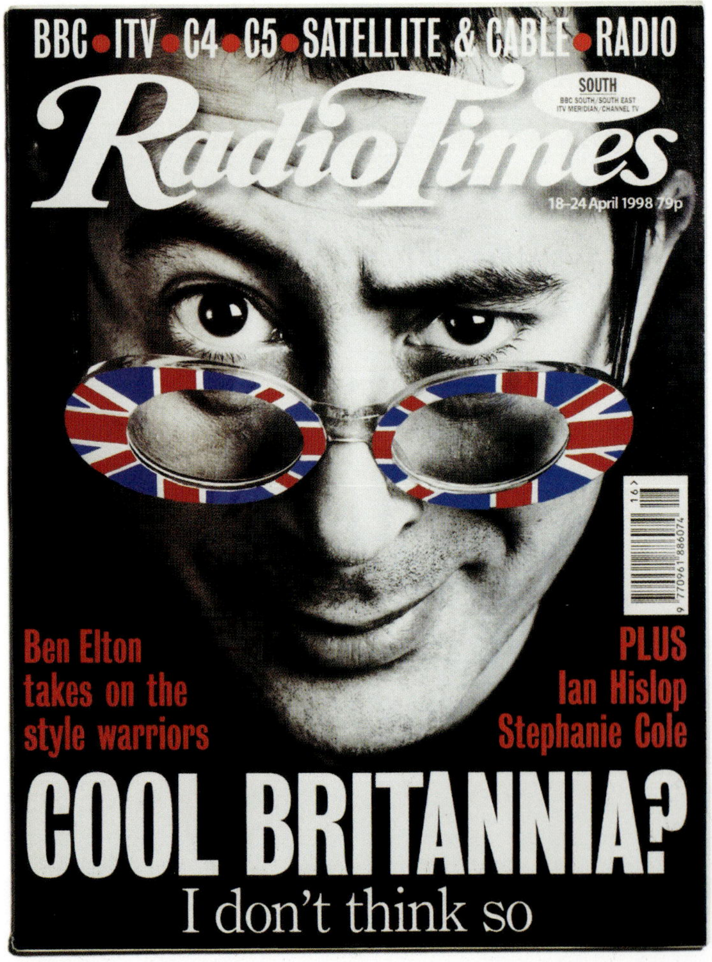

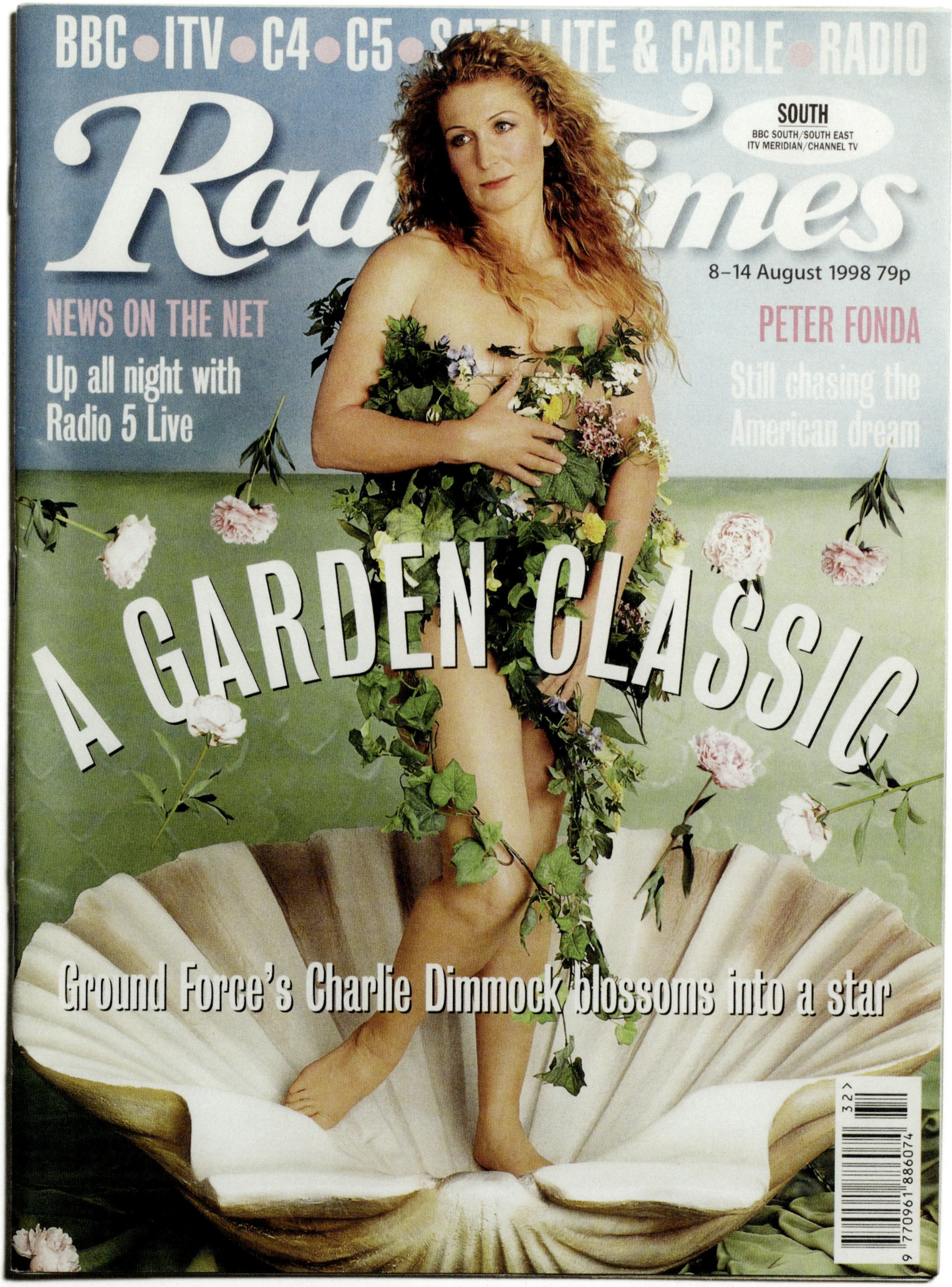

Ground Force **Charlie Dimmock** *(photograph by Sven Arnstein) 8–14 August 1998*

If DIY was the new rock 'n' roll in the late 1990s, gardening was the new soul and Charlie Dimmock ("the pin-up of the strimming classes") was the nation's favourite earth goddess – so *Radio Times* put her on the cover in a pastiche of Botticelli's *Birth of Venus*. Together with Alan Titchmarsh and Tommy Walsh, Dimmock set out to cover the country's gardens in decking (and water features).

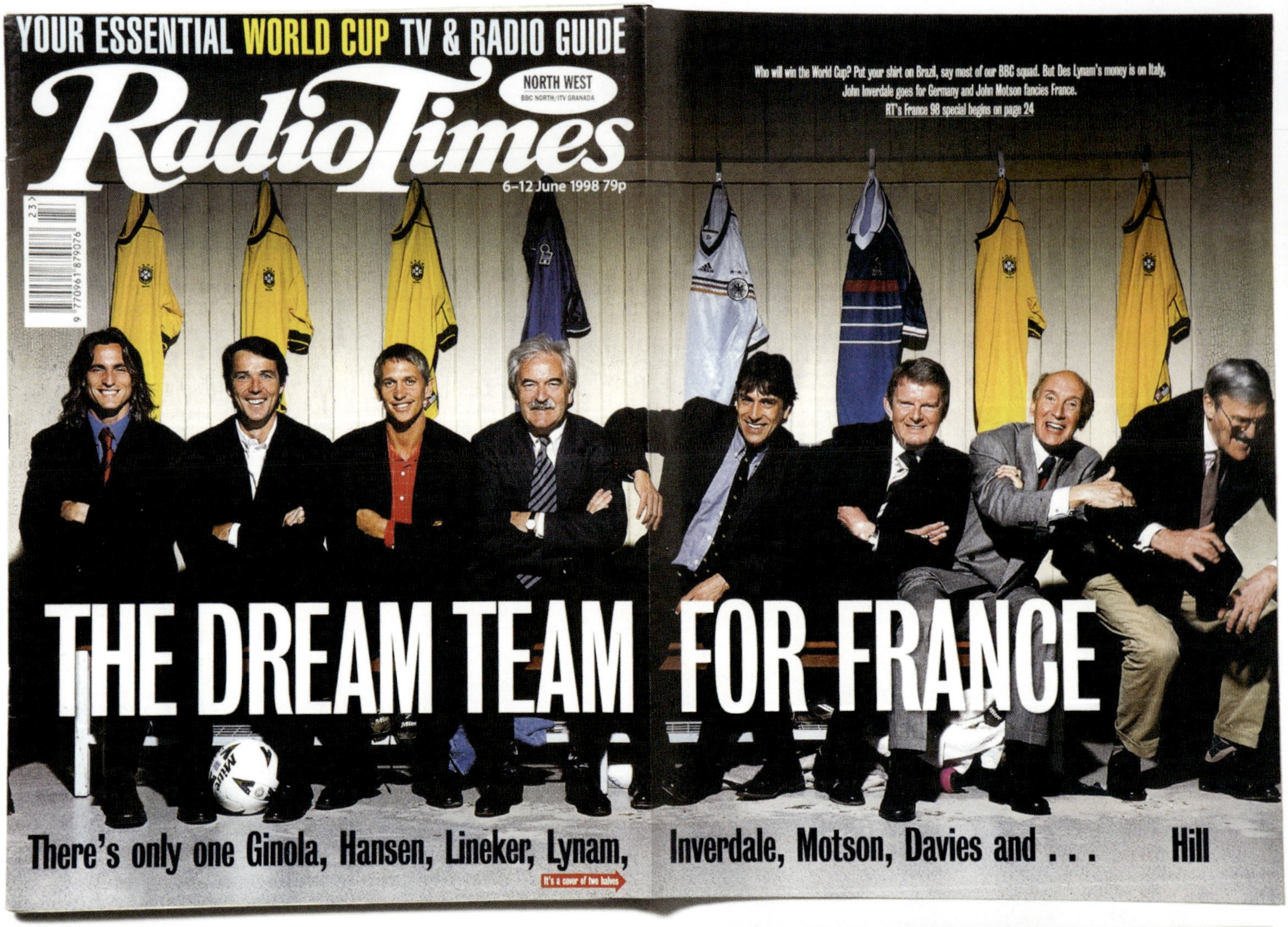

France 98 *(above)*

BBC World Cup broadcasters, from left: David Ginola, Alan Hansen, Gary Lineker, Desmond Lynam, John Inverdale, John Motson, Barry Davies and Jimmy Hill *(photograph by Sven Arnstein)*

6–12 June 1998

As the World Cup opened in France, the BBC sent an eight-strong team of commentators and analysts to cover the action. Each was asked to predict which team would win the tournament, with their choice represented by the team shirt hanging behind them. Most picked Brazil, and only John Motson got it right, opting for France to win. Rumours that the photographer asked the men to line up from the left in decreasing order of handsomeness can't be discounted.

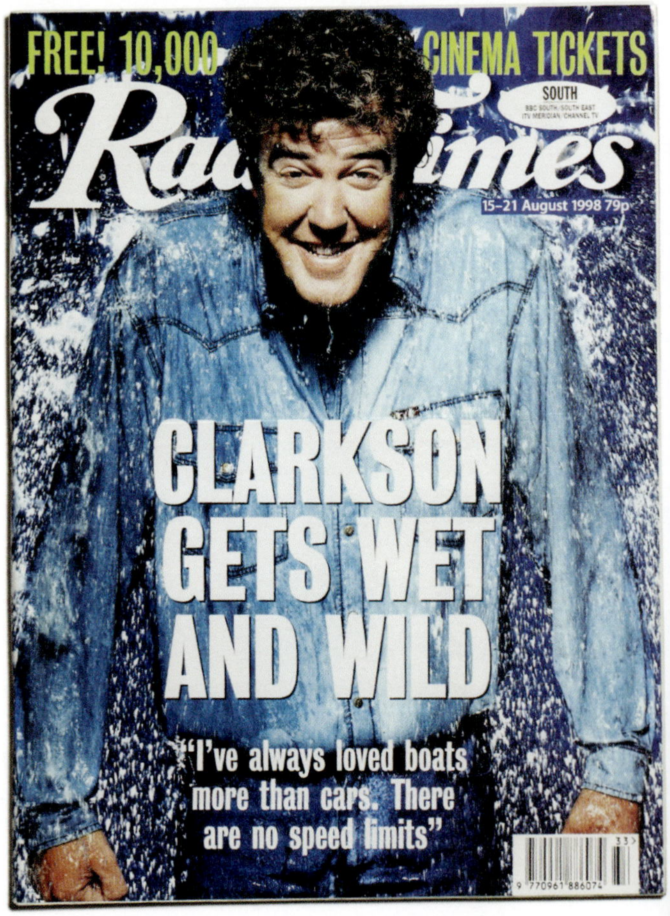

Waterworld *(right)*

Jeremy Clarkson *(photograph by Barry J Holmes)*

15–21 August 1998

"The sea is designed for fish, not boats, so you're not only taking on a machine but also trying to tame the elements," said Jeremy Clarkson on the eve of his new show. The eternally laddish *Top Gear* presenter was now seeking out the marine equivalent of his cars: a Ferrari F355 GTS and a Jaguar XJR.

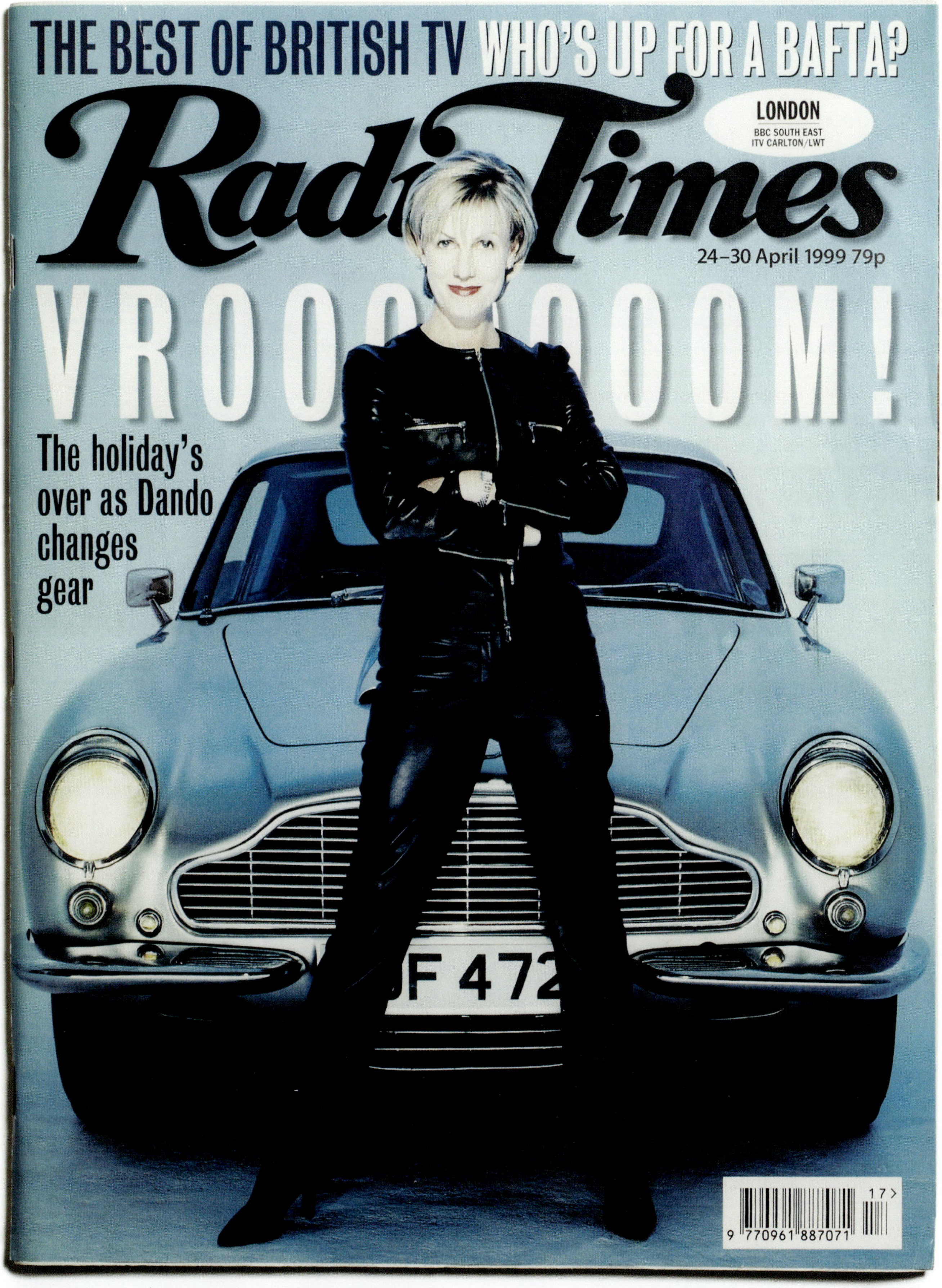

Antiques Inspectors **Jill Dando** *(photograph by Barry J Holmes)* *24–30 April 1999*

Jill Dando had moved on from hosting *Holiday* and the constant travelling it entailed. *Antiques Inspectors*, which saw her behind the wheel of a Mark II Aston Martin DB8, was meant to be her passport to happiness nearer home. But the morning after the first programme was broadcast, Dando was shot dead on the doorstep of her house in London. The back cover of the issue unfortunately carried an advert for books headlined "Couldn't you just murder".

Wallace & Gromit *(right)*

(photograph by Paul Norris)

29 August–4 September 1998

A cheery summer cover launched Wallace and Gromit's TV & Wireless Guide, a new family-friendly section that was edited by the animated inventor and his long-suffering hound.

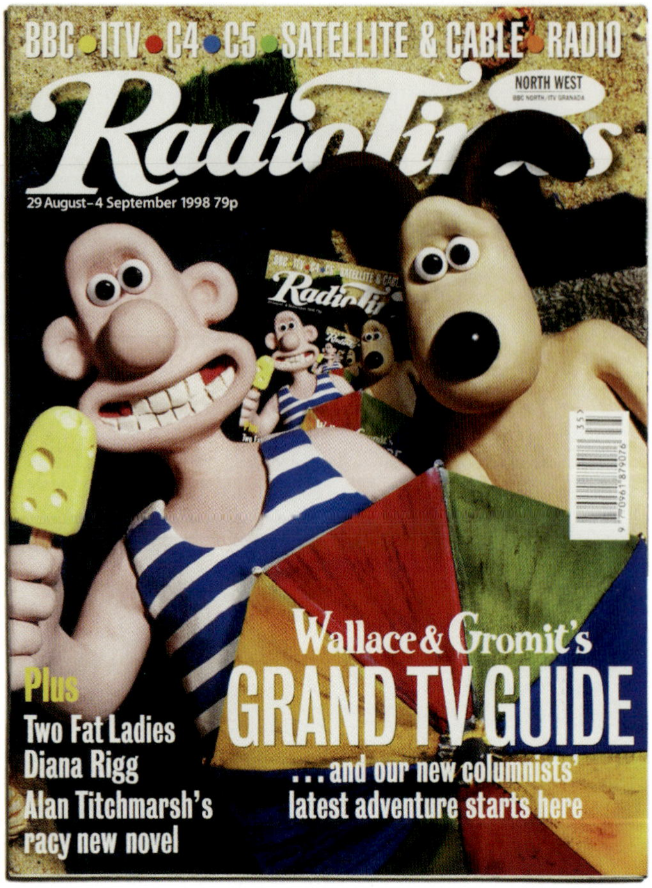

Radio Times's 75th Anniversary *(below)*

From left: John Thaw, Julie Goodyear, Bruce Forsyth, Desmond Lynam, Michael Palin, Amanda Burton, David Jason and Nicholas Lyndhurst, Francesca Annis, Robert Hardy, Christopher Timothy and Peter Davison, Kate Adie, Trevor Harrison, Jemima and Big Ted. On the TV and radio sets: Morecambe and Wise, George Clooney (*ER*), *Cathy Come Home* and *Hancock's Half-Hour*

(photograph by Snowdon)

26 September–2 October 1998

The winners of a 75th anniversary readers' poll on the all-time top radio and TV programmes and people were packed into another fold-out double cover. Celebrity cook and *RT* columnist Delia Smith squeezed in on the strapline.

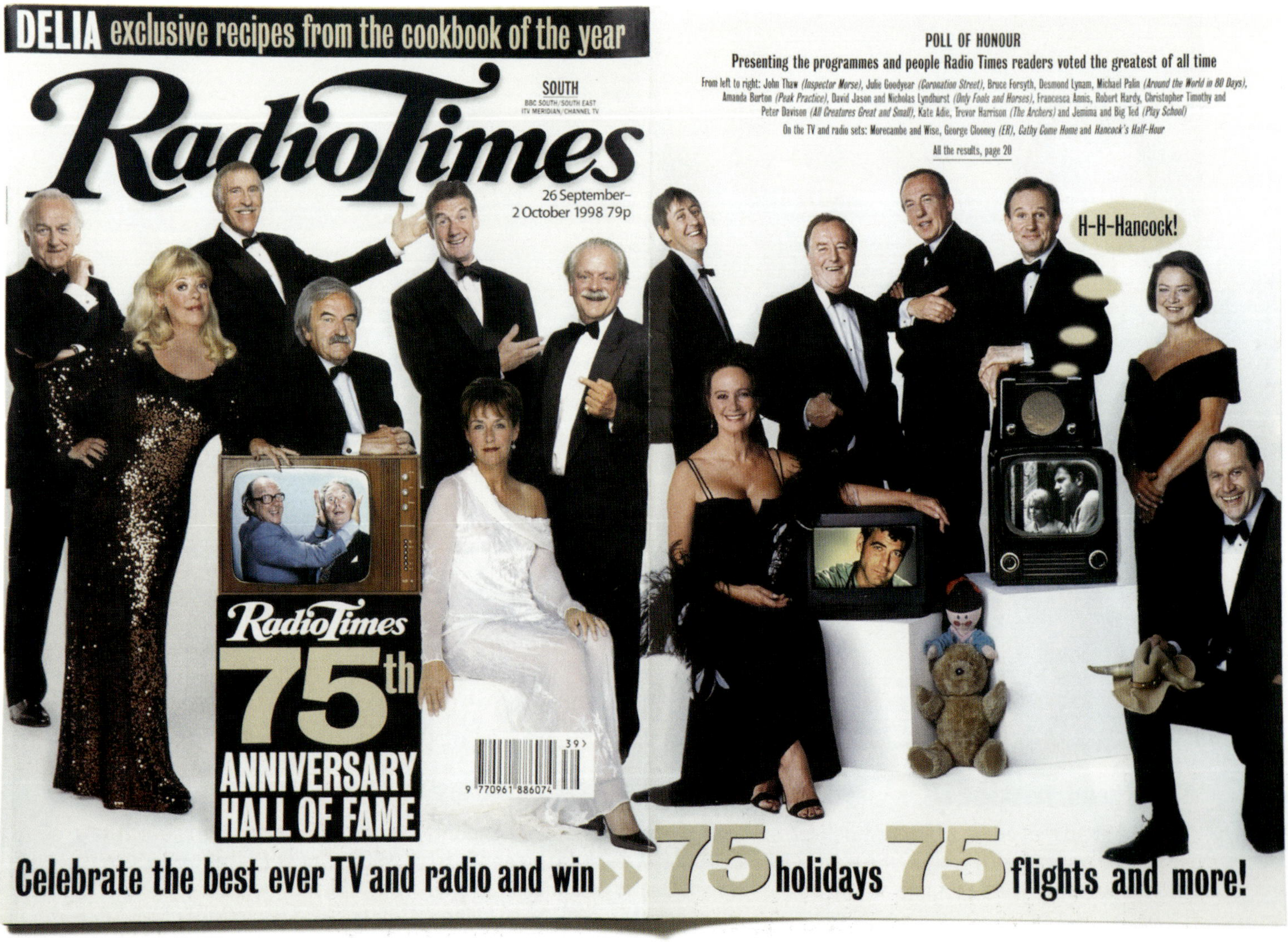

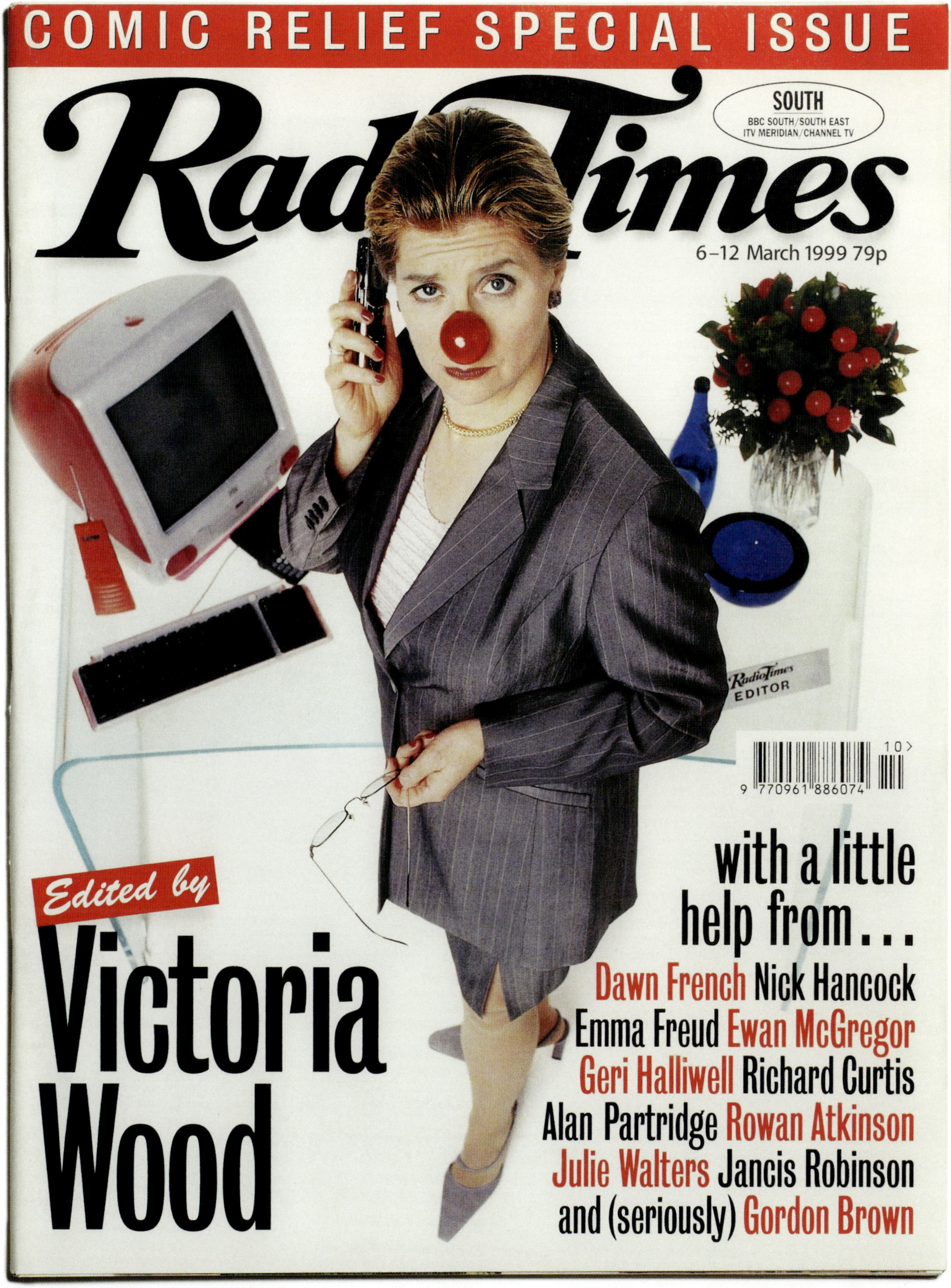

Comic Relief Special Issue **Victoria Wood** *(photograph by Brian Moody) 6–12 March 1999*

Comedian Victoria Wood was appointed guest editor. One of the concepts she wanted to introduce, such as the My Bunion Hell feature, sadly never made it into print. But she did squeeze in Dawn French's column ("Dawn wrote this jolly well. Well done, Dawn!") and a profile of top actress "July Waters" by "Andrea Duncan" (read it and weep).

CHRISTMAS DAY

DAYTIME

BBC1

6.00am Breakfast With Louise Minchin. (S) (HD)
9.00 The Gruffalo Enchanting animation. (R) (AD) (S) (HD)
9.25 Peter Rabbit's Christmas Tale (R) (S) (AD) (HD)
9.50 First Flight A bird transforms a businessman's life. (S)
10.00 LIVE Christmas Day Eucharist Morning service from St Mary Redcliffe, Bristol. (S) (HD) 67564
11.00 Only Fools and Horses The Trotters strike gold. (R) (S) 5624699
12.05pm BBC News Weather (S)
12.15 Shrek the Halls Shrek settles down for a quiet Christmas with Fiona and the babies. (R) (S) (AD) (HD) 8299274
12.40 Madagascar: Escape 2 Africa ★★ Animated comedy sequel featuring the voices of Ben Stiller, David Schwimmer and Chris Rock. **Review p76.** 1098670 (2008, PG) (S) (AD) (W) (HD)
2.00 Top of the Pops Christmas Robbie Williams, RT Girls Aloud, Conor Maynard and Emeli Sandé are among the performers. **See p130.** (S) (HD) 44125
3.00–3.10 The Queen The annual address to the nation and Commonwealth. Rptd 5.15pm BBC2 (S) (HD) 8511361

BBC2

6.00am CBeebies **Baby Jake 6.15 Let's Celebrate Christmas 6.30 The Cow That Almost Missed Christmas**
7.00 CBBC **The Slammer: a Slammer Christmas 7.30 12 Again Christmas Special 8.00 Horrible Histories: Horrible Christmas 8.30 The Story of Tracy Beaker** Double bill.
8.45 Attenborough's Egg Hunt In Madagascar. (R) (S)
9.45 Attenborough's Ark David Attenborough chooses ten animals he would most like to save from extinction. (R) (S)
10.45 Carols from King's The traditional celebration of Christmas from the chapel of King's College, Cambridge. Shown yesterday 6.15pm (S) 6867274
12.00 On the Town ★★★★★ Classic New York-set musical starring Gene Kelly and Frank Sinatra. **Review page 76.** (1949, U) (S) 780800
1.35–3.15pm Singin' in the Rain ★★★★★ Timeless musical set in the 1920s, starring Gene Kelly and Debbie Reynolds. **Review p76.** (1952, U) (S) (AD) 43758212

ITV1

6.00am CITV **6.00 Babar 6.25 The Hive 6.50 Canimals 7.00 Fleabag Monkeyface 7.30 Almost Naked Animals**
7.55 Scooby-Doo and the Alien Invaders ★★★ Animated comedy adventure. The gang get stuck in a town inhabited by aliens. (2000, U) 5281019
9.25 Aladdin ★★★★★ Animated musical adventure featuring the voice of Robin Williams. **Review p76.** 63825403 (1992, U) (S) (AD) (W)
11.10 The Nation's Favourite Christmas Song A countdown of the top 20 tunes guaranteed to get folk in the festive spirit. Shown Saturday 22 December 6.30pm (S) (HD) 2446903
12.40pm Text Santa: One More Time (R) 51923496
1.15 ITV News Weather (S)
1.25 Toy Story ★★★★★ Animated comedy adventure about the secret world of toys. **Review page 76.** 82600800 (1995, PG) (S) (W) (HD)
3.00–3.10 The Queen Annual address. (S) (HD) 8513729

Channel 4

5.40am Children's **The Hoobs 6.05 Little Wolf 6.30 Lost and Found 6.55 Father Christmas**
7.25 The Art of the Snowman and The Snowdog (S)
7.30 The Simpsons Double bill. (R) (S) (AD)
8.20 Dr Seuss' Horton Hears a Who! ★★★★ Animation based on the children's book, with the voice of Jim Carrey. (2008, U) (S) (W) (HD) 15931019
10.00 Gordon's Christmas Cookalong Live The chef's guide to preparing a memorable Christmas dinner. See channel4.com/food for a list of ingredients. (S)
1.55pm The Snowman and The Snowdog Animated sequel to Raymond Briggs's tale. (R) (S) (AD) (HD) 57999903
2.25 Scrooged ★★★ Seasonal comedy starring Bill Murray as a TV executive who can't stand Christmas. (1988, 12) (S) (AD) (W) (HD) 154941
4.20–4.25 The Alternative Christmas Message Presented by comedian Adam Hills. (S) 8164545

Channel 5

6.00am Milkshake! **Thomas & Friends 6.10 Igam Ogam 6.20 Fireman Sam 6.30 Jelly Jamm 6.45 Peppa Pig 6.50 Olive the Ostrich 6.55 Little Princess 7.05 Ben and Holly 7.20 The Mr Men Show 7.35 Thomas & Friends 7.50 Noddy in Toyland 8.05 Fifi 8.15 Peppa Pig 8.35 Roary the Racing Car**
8.55 Inside Hollywood Location reports and showbusiness news.
9.00–1.15pm Gone with the Wind ★★★★★ Oscar-winning romantic drama starring Vivien Leigh and Clark Gable. (1939, PG) (S) (W) (HD) 66653583

BBC1

Doctor Who *5.15pm Christmas Eve 1892 takes a nightmarish turn*

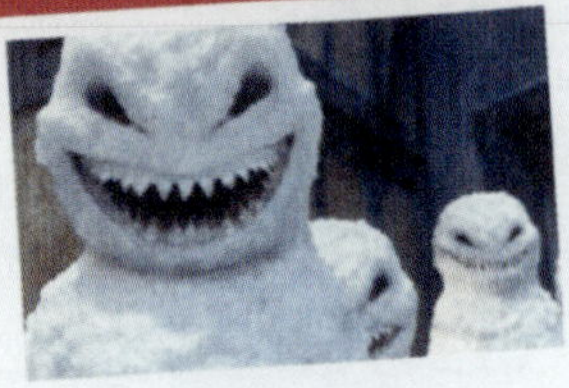

3.10pm Shrek Forever After ★★★
Animated fantasy comedy featuring the voices of Mike Myers, Cameron Diaz and Eddie Murphy. Bored with a life of domesticity, Shrek makes a deal with Rumpelstiltskin that will allow him to return to something like his old life. **Film of the Day: p76.** 5611748
Director Mike Mitchell (2010, U) (S) (AD) (W) (HD)

4.35 Room on the Broom
RT Animated magical tale, based on the children's picture book by Julia Donaldson, about a witch who invites a motley crew of animals to join her on her broom, much to the chagrin of her cat. Featuring the voices of Gillian Anderson and Rob Brydon. **See p130.**
Writers Julia Donaldson and Axel Scheffler; Producers Michael Rose and Martin Pope; Directors Max Lang and Jan Lachauer 5742534
Cast page 234 Repeated tomorrow 9.45am (S) (AD) (HD)

5.00 BBC News Weather (S) 1646075

5.15 Doctor Who
RT **The Snowmen.** 1892: snowfall is making for a picture postcard Christmas Eve, but a chilling menace threatens Earth as an unorthodox young governess, Clara, calls on the Doctor for help. He, however, is in mourning, reclusive and intent on ignoring the problems of the universe. **See p131.**
Writer Steven Moffat; Producer Marcus Wilson; Director Saul Metzstein 482106
Cast pp144/174 Repeated tomorrow 8pm BBC3 (S) (AD) (HD)

6.15 Strictly Come Dancing
RT Taking on the ballroom challenge in this Christmas special are actress Sheila Hancock, comedian Katy Brand, JB from boy band JLS, *Blue Peter's* Helen Skelton, comedian Bobby Ball and retired footballer Fabrice Muamba. Also joining Bruce and Tess is Rod Stewart and a host of familiar faces from *Strictlys* past. **See page 131.** (S) (HD) 3052835

7.30 Call the Midwife
RT As Christmas approaches, a baby is abandoned on the steps of the convent, an event which rallies the Poplar community. **See p130.**

Jenny Lee	**Jessica Raine**	Trixie Franklin	**Helen George**
Sister Julienne	**Jenny Agutter**	Cynthia Miller	**Bryony Hannah**
Sister Evangelina	**Pam Ferris**	Sister Bernadette	**Laura Main**
Chummy Noakes	**Miranda Hart**	PC Peter Noakes	**Ben Caplan**
Sister Monica Joan	**Judy Parfitt**	Dr Turner	**Stephen McGann**

Writer Heidi Thomas; Director Philippa Lowthorpe; Producer Hugh Warren
More cast p182 Rptd Sun 30 December 3.30pm (S) (AD) (HD) 244274

8.45 EastEnders
RT The Brannings pull out all the stops for a wonderful family Christmas. **See page 131.**
Writer Simon Ashdown Cast pages 152/232 774699
Repeated 10.45pm BBC3 (S) (AD) (HD)

9.45 The Royle Family
RT **Barbara's Old Ring.** Barbara goes overboard with presents from a pound shop. **See p130.**

Jim Royle	**Ricky Tomlinson**	Brenda	**Denice Hope**
Barbara Royle	**Sue Johnston**	Ling Su	**Menyee Lai**
Denise Best	**Caroline Aherne**	Betty	**Marie Mitchell**
Dave Best	**Craig Cash**	Petula	**Steve Money**
Joe Carroll	**Peter Martin**	Elsie	**Iris Sharple**
Philomena	**Mary Healey**	Carol	**Lorraine Bruce**
Doreen	**Sheila Vaughan**		

Writers Caroline Aherne, Craig Cash and Phil Mealey
Director Caroline Aherne; Producer Lucy Ansbro (S) (AD) (HD) 763583

10.45 BBC News Weather (S) 690019

11.00 The Vicar of Dibley
Alice miraculously solves the problem of the Nativity play in this episode from 1999. (R) (S) 710922

11.40 On Christmas Night The story of Christmas from Luke's gospel, read by Rachel Morris. (S) (HD) 880090

11.45 Have I Got a Bit More News for You
10/11. An extended edition of last Friday's show with Daniel Radcliffe as the guest host. (Revised rpt) (S) 276081

12.30am Cold Mountain ★★★ Epic wartime romantic drama starring Jude Law and Nicole Kidman. **Review page 77.** 15603626
Director Anthony Minghella (2003, 15) (S) (AD) (W) (HD)
2.55 Weatherview (S) 3888355 **3.00–6.00am BBC News** (S)

HD **BBC1 HD** **Freeview** 101 **Freesat** 108 **Sky** 143 **Virgin** 108

BBC2

Arena: Sister Wendy and the Art of the Gospel *5.25pm*

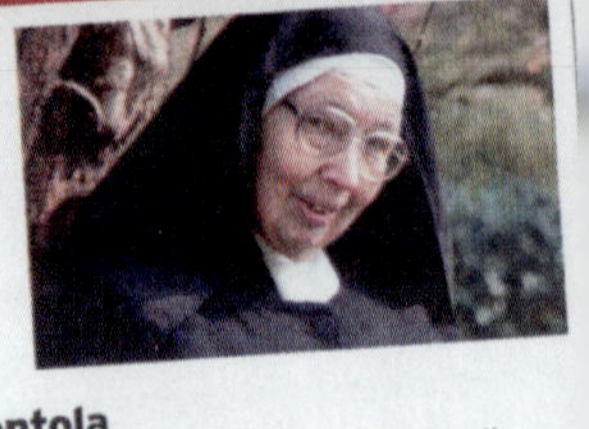

3.15pm Cenerentola
Andrea Andermann continues his series of "live" opera films with a production of Rossini's dramatic work based on the fairy tale *Cinderella*, staged in the rooms and gardens of some of Turin's finest palaces. Introduced by Katie Derham, with Gianluigi Gelmetti conducting the RAI National Symphony Orchestra.

Cenerentola	**Lena Belkina** (mezzo)	Don Magnifico	**Carlo Lepore** (bass)
Don Ramiro	**Edgardo Rocha** (tenor)	Dandini	**Simone Alberghini** (bass-baritone)
Clorinda	**Anna Kasyan** (soprano)	Alidoro	**Lorenzo Regazzo** (bass)
Tisbe	**Annunziata Vestri** (mezzo)		

Producer Andrea Andermann (S) Also on BBC HD 94009

5.15 The Queen
Her Majesty's annual address. Shown 3pm BBC1 (S) (SL) 29574

5.25 Arena: Sister Wendy and the Art of the Gospel
RT The inimitable 82-year-old Carmelite nun and art aficionado burst onto our screens in the 1990s and became an instant star. Here, Sister Wendy Beckett offers an insight into her personal and religious calling while revealing how certain paintings by the greatest old masters can connect the viewer to the emotional insights within the Gospel stories they depict. **See page 130.**
Director/Producer Randall Wright Also BBC HD tomorrow 7pm (S) 6464
Kirsty Wark's arts feast: page 57

6.25 50 Years of Bond Cars: a Top Gear Special
Richard Hammond celebrates 50 years of James Bond films with a look back at 007's cars. 35
Executive producer Andy Wilman (R) (S) (AD)

7.30 Dad's Army
For the Love of Three Oranges. Mainwaring and Pike enter a bidding war for an orange. (R) (S)

8.00 Blackadder's Christmas Carol
Christmas Eve 1850: the kindly Ebenezer Blackadder receives a visit from his loathsome ancestors. R Atkinson stars in this Dickensian parody from 1
Writers Richard Curtis and Ben Elton; Director Richard Boden
Producer John Lloyd (R) (S) (AD)

8.45 The Choir: a Year with the Military Wives
RT Gareth Malone returns to the small chape the military base in Chivenor where, in Fe 2011, he set up a choir for military wives left at while their men are away on duty for months time. Choir members recall the events that fo as their Royal Albert Hall performance paved way for a visit to 10 Downing Street, a numbe Christmas single and a charitable foundation supporting over 60 military wives' choirs in t from Europe to the Falkland Islands. **See pag**
Directors/Producers Steve Jones and Anna Sadowy (S) (AD

9.45 QI XL
Stephen Fry hosts an extended version of ye Christmas episode of the quiz, with Sarah M Phill Jupitus, Danny Baker and Alan Davies.
Repeated Saturday 29 December 11pm (Revised rpt) (S)

10.30 The Sarah Millican Television Programme
Hugh Bonneville and Shane Richie join the as she performs some seasonal stand-up.
Shown Sunday 23 December 10.30pm (S)

11.00 The Christmas No 1 Story
Recalling the battles to top the festive sing
Shown last Wednesday (S)

12.00 Top of the Pops 2: Christmas Festive p from the archives. Shown Saturday 22 December 8pm
1.30–3.20am The Hunchback of Notre Dam Classic Gothic drama starring Charles Lau Maureen O'Hara and Cedric Hardwicke. **Re**
Director William S Dieterle (1939, PG) (BW) (S)

HD **BBC HD** **Freeview** 102 **Freesat** 109 **Sky** 169 **Vi**

RadioTimes

The Digital Age

2000–2013

Doctor Who

The Doctor (Christopher Eccleston) and Rose Tyler (Billie Piper) *(photograph by Mark Harrison)*

26 March–1 April 2005

To relaunch *Doctor Who* for the 21st century – and after a nine-year absence from BBC1 – *Radio Times* produced a special "open-it-up" cover. Peeling back the police-box doors revealed (below) the hot new stars of the programme inside the revamped Tardis.

Radio Times editor Gill Hudson said: "With *Doctor Who* and his Tardis set to invade our Saturday teatimes once more, the big question is: has showrunner Russell T Davies pulled it off? I rather think he has." She was right. The Time Lord gained a new generation of fans and was a ratings and critical hit. Over the next eight years he adorned nearly 30 *Radio Times* covers.

In 2010, Russell T Davies said: "When I was a kid, there was such great currency in a *Radio Times* *Doctor Who* cover." He praised the magazine team for "the joy and imagination with which they approach the show, embracing its optimism, energy and barminess".

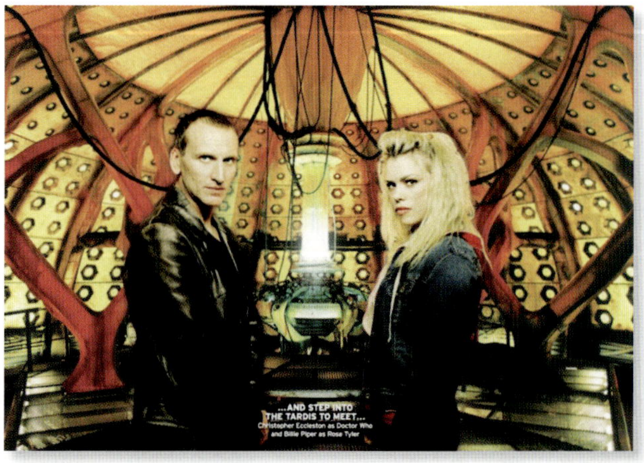

2000-2013

The start of a new millennium and the return of a cult hero; the revival of ballroom dancing, district nurses and baking!

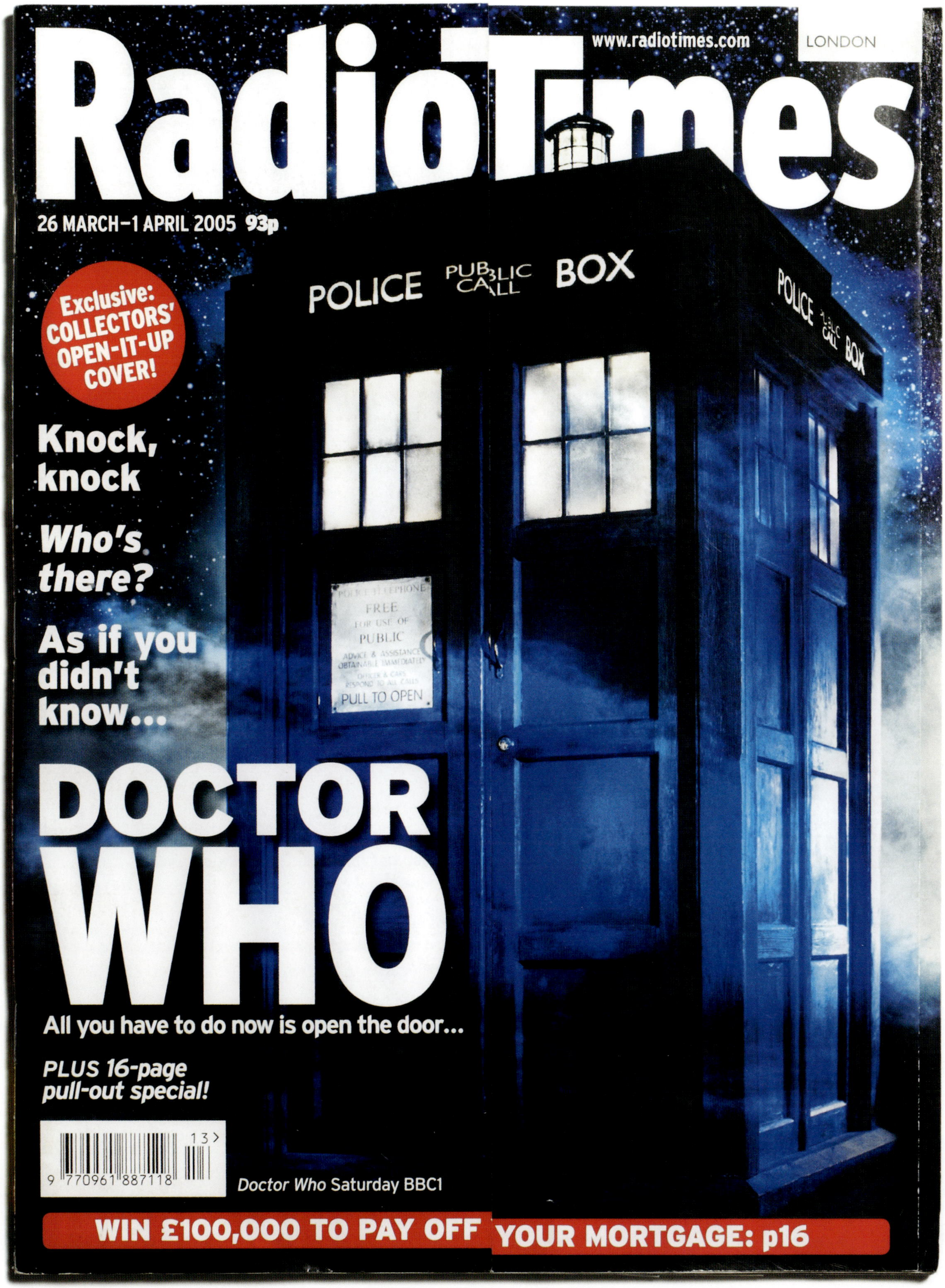
RadioTimes
www.radiotimes.com
LONDON
26 MARCH–1 APRIL 2005 93p
Exclusive: COLLECTORS' OPEN-IT-UP COVER!
Knock, knock
Who's there?
As if you didn't know...
DOCTOR WHO
All you have to do now is open the door...
PLUS 16-page pull-out special!
POLICE PUBLIC CALL BOX
FREE FOR USE OF PUBLIC
PULL TO OPEN
Doctor Who Saturday BBC1
WIN £100,000 TO PAY OFF YOUR MORTGAGE: p16

The Naked Chef *(right)*
Jamie Oliver *(photograph by Barry J Holmes)*
15–21 April 2000

Jamie Oliver was "discovered" in the mid-90s while working as a sous chef at a west-London restaurant. His second TV series proved a big hit, its title referring to his stripped-down, back-to-basics approach to cookery – with added "blokey" banter.

Wimbledon *(below left)*
Sue Barker *(photograph by Alan Strutt)*
1–7 July 2000

Former tennis pro Sue Barker first joined the BBC's Wimbledon team in 1993 and by 2000 had become the familiar face of TV tennis. In an interview with Andrew Duncan, she bemoaned the lack of emotion in the modern game.

Walking with Dinosaurs *(below right)*
(photograph by Ian MacDonald)
5–11 August 2000

The computer-generated dinosaurs were a big hit for the BBC, garnering 216 million viewers across 23 countries. Presented in the style of a nature documentary, the six episodes – originally screened in 1999 and repeated here – took two years to make. *The Ballad of Big Al*, the story of an allosaurus, aired in 2001.

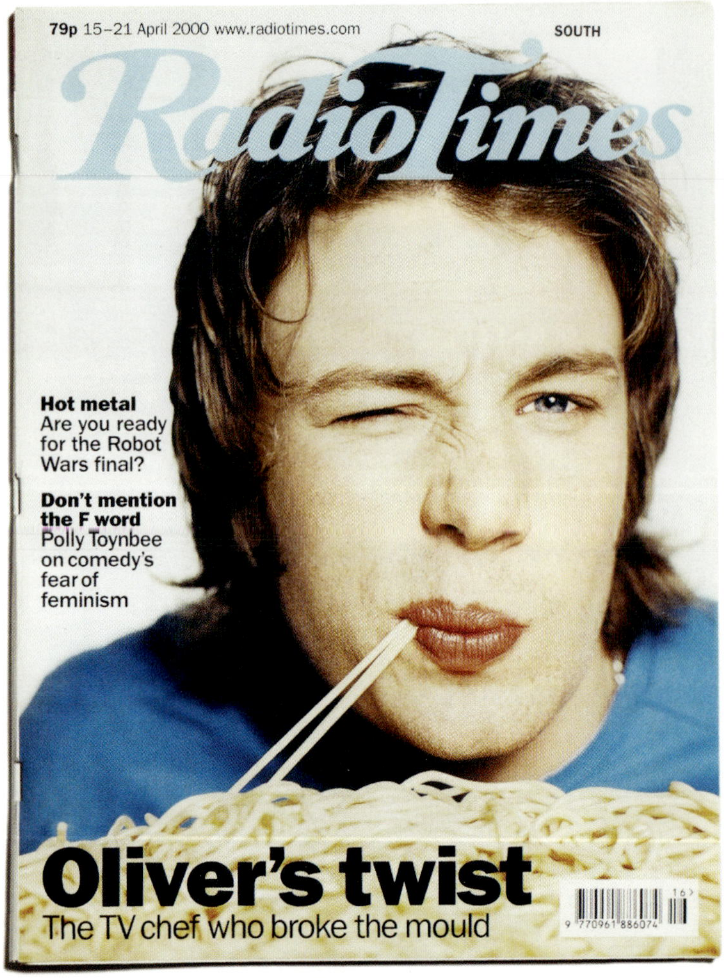

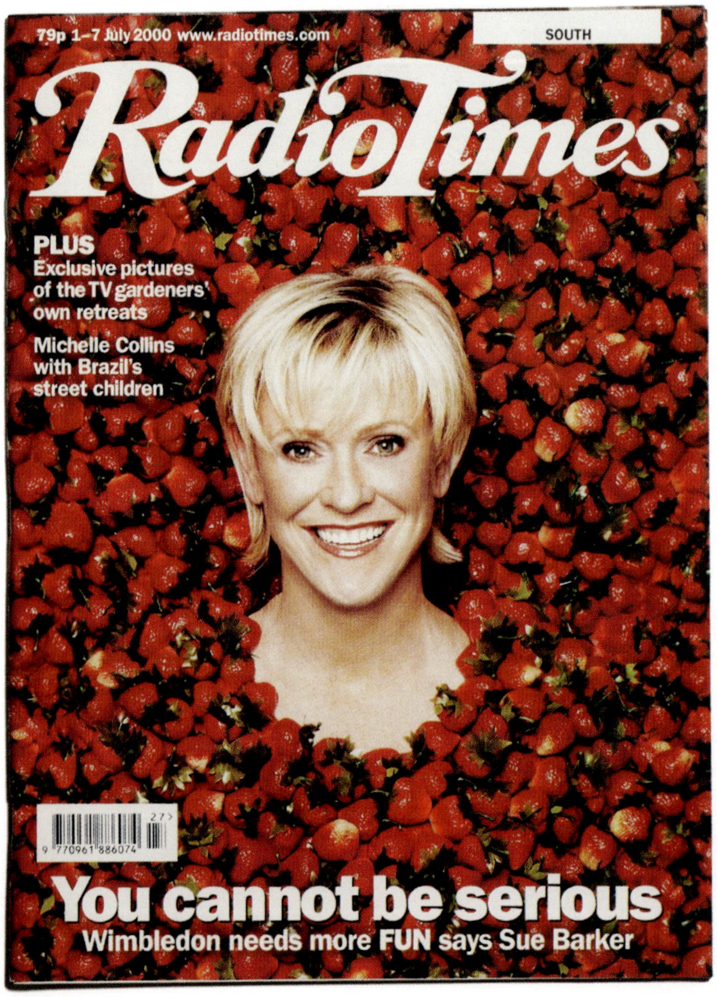

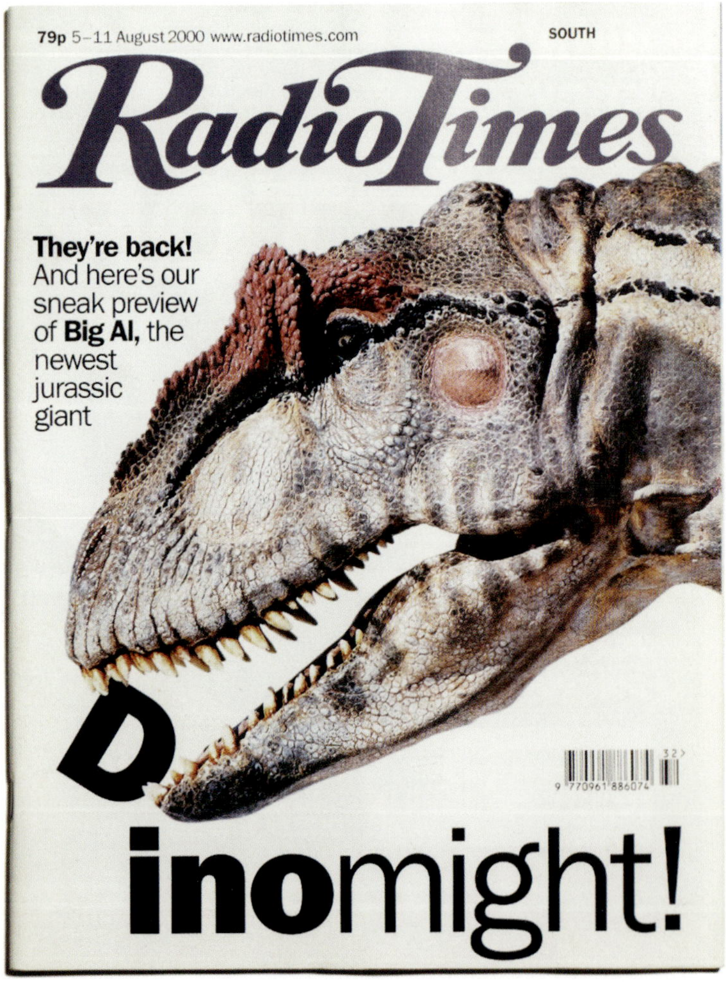

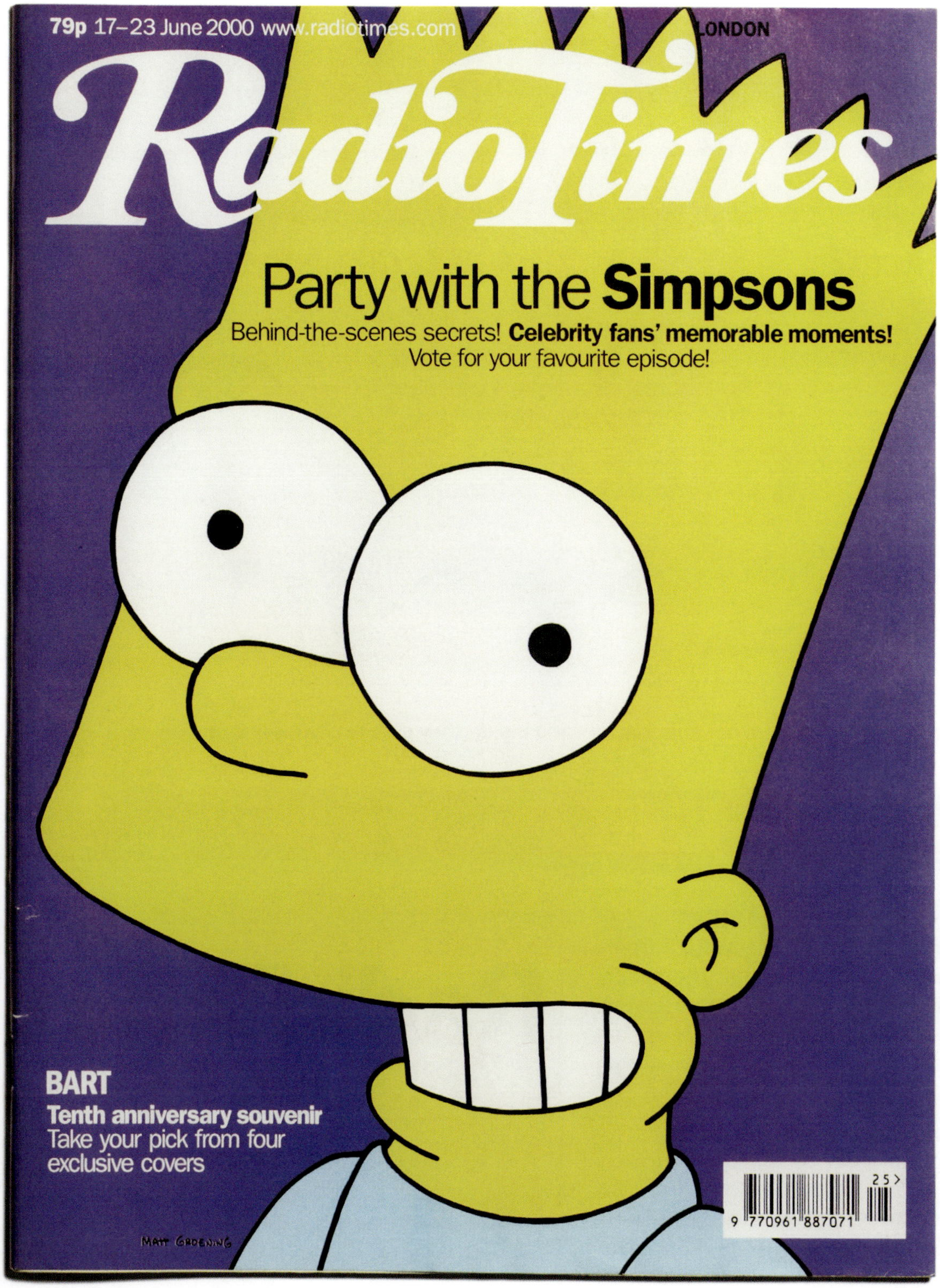

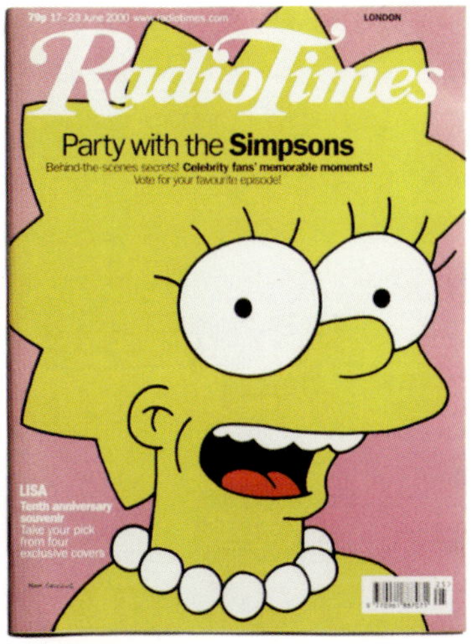

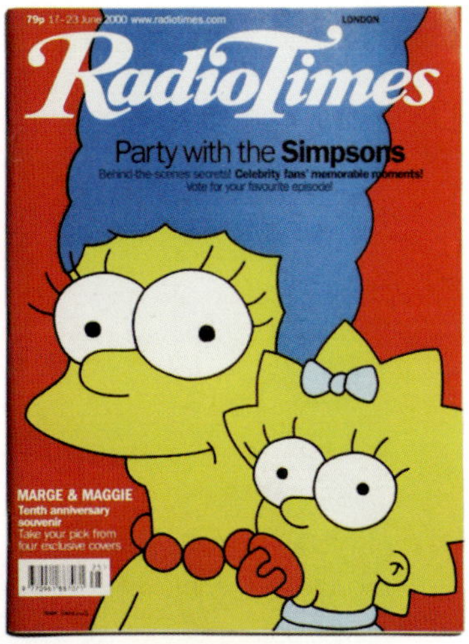

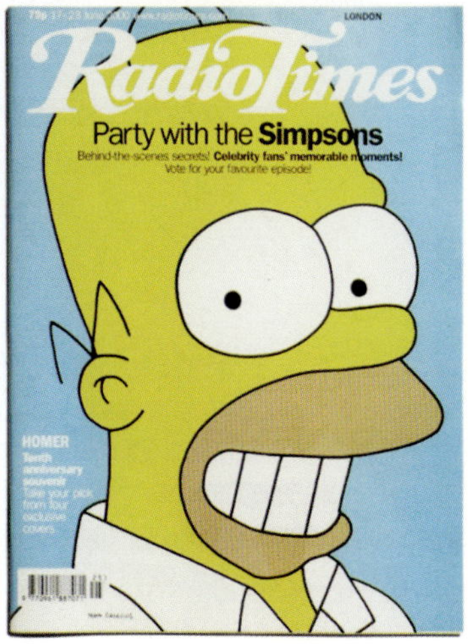

The Simpsons

Illustrations by Matt Groening

17–23 June 2000

"Homer, Marge, Bart, Lisa and Maggie are global superstars, worthy of this week's four covers, specially created for us by the *Simpsons* team," said *Radio Times* editor Sue Robinson. The magazine was marking the tenth anniversary of the world's favourite dysfunctional family. "It's brilliantly written and crosses all age groups," said Paul McCartney, one of several celebrity fans who recounted their favourite moments from *The Simpsons*. There was also a readers' poll to nominate the best episode.

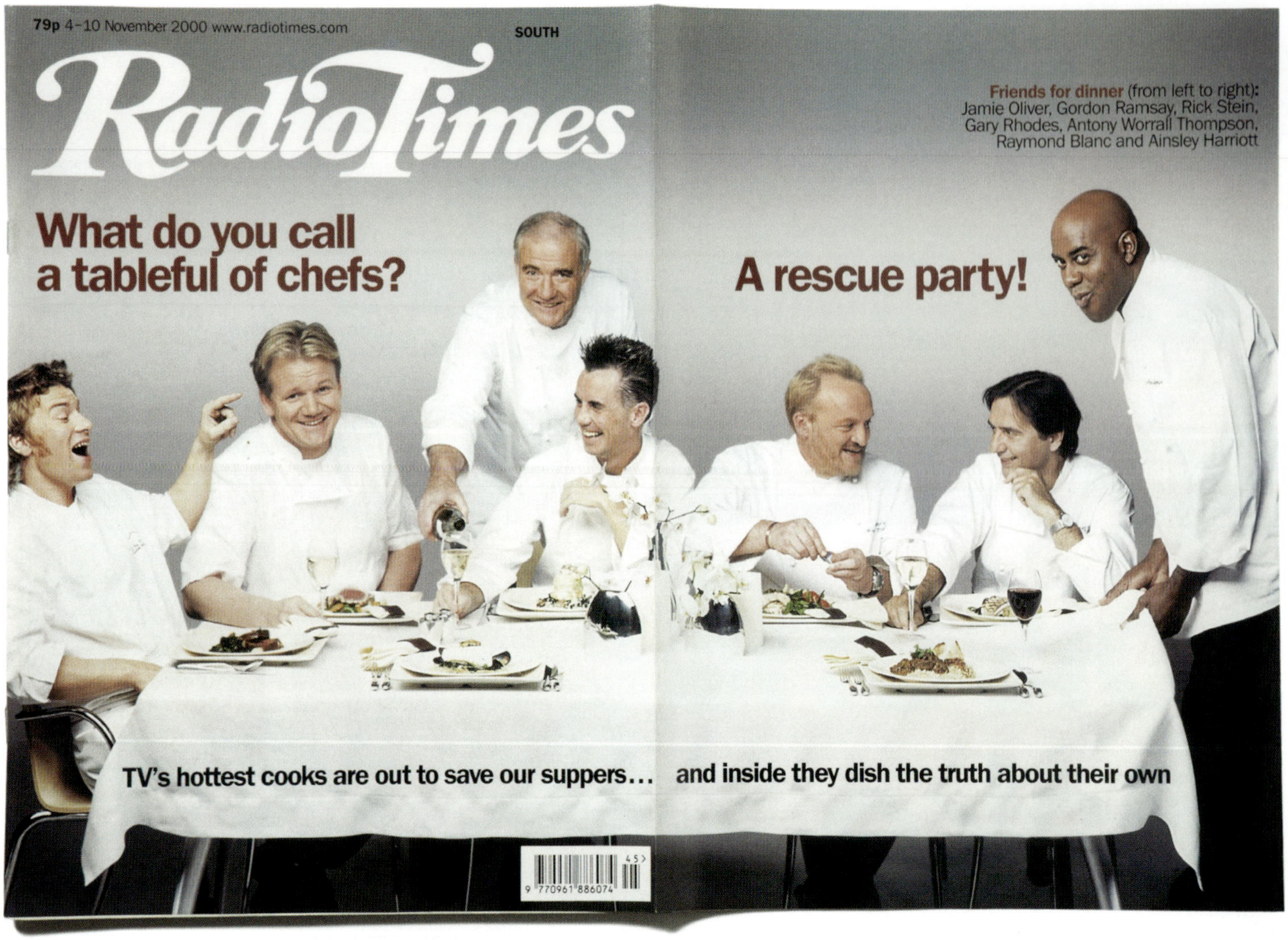

Friends for Dinner *(above)*

From left: Jamie Oliver, Gordon Ramsay, Rick Stein, Gary Rhodes, Antony Worrall Thompson, Raymond Blanc and Ainsley Harriott
(photograph by Mark Harrison)

4–10 November 2000

The top TV chefs were called in to assist unsuspecting members of the public in a new BBC2 series, *Friends for Dinner. Radio Times* featured dinner-party advice from each. Jamie Oliver offered: "Fish pie, big green salad, bottle of wine. Make life easy for yourself. You're there to talk to your mates, not spend the whole night with your head in the oven."

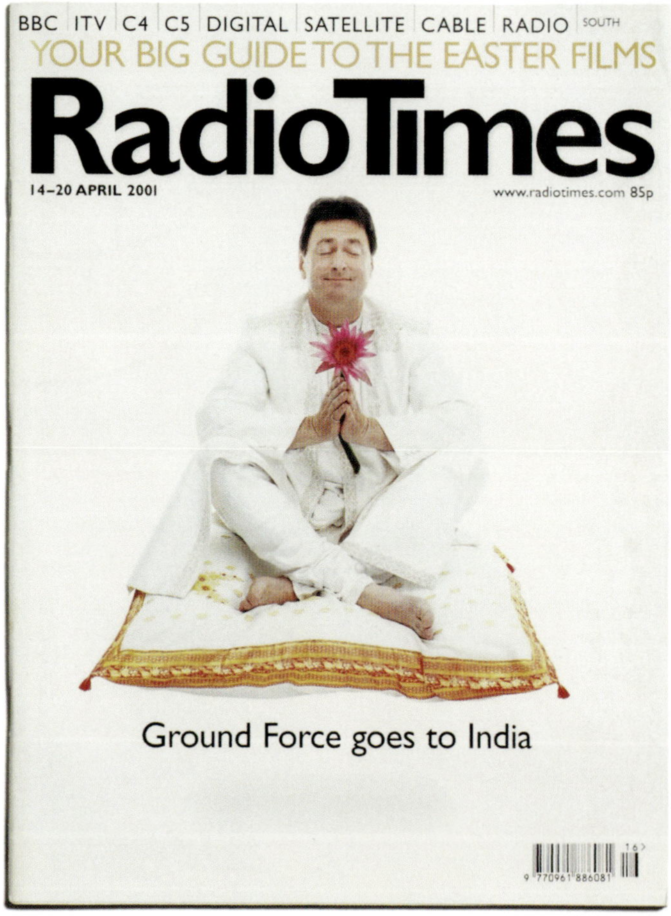

Ground Force in India *(right)*

Alan Titchmarsh *(photograph by Barry J Holmes)*

14–20 April 2001

The cover sported a new-look design, with the familiar curly logo dropped in favour of a clean sans-serif font. Meanwhile, Alan Titchmarsh travelled to India to transform a barren orphanage garden into a blooming oasis, and an Easter special examined the historical evidence of the Crucifixion – to mixed reviews.

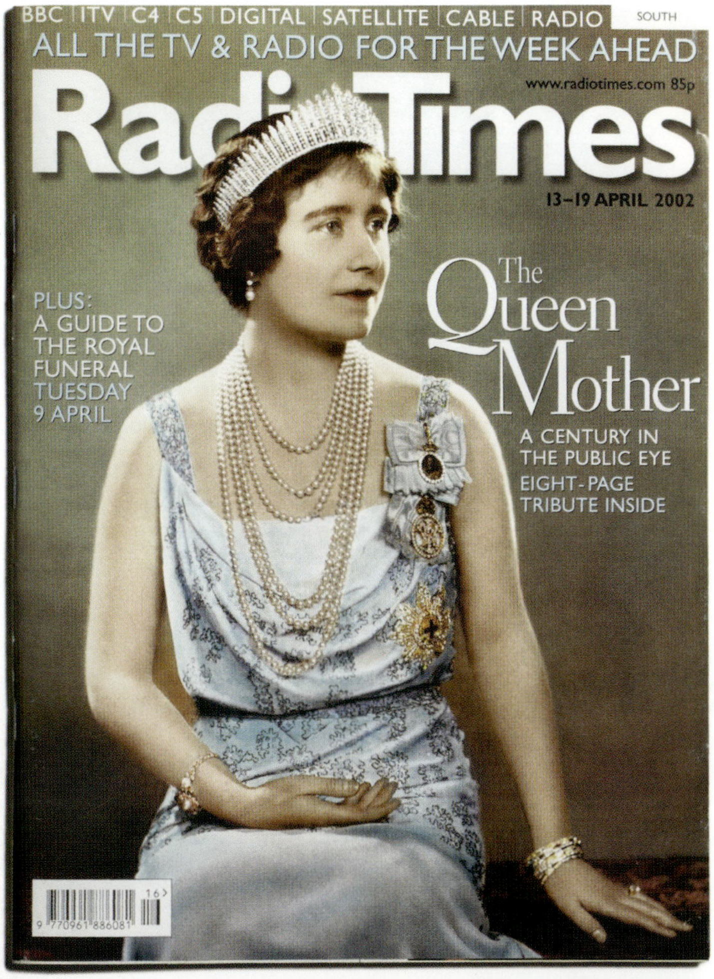

The Queen Mother *(left)*

Photograph by Tom Hustler/hand tinting by Joan Smith

13–19 April 2002

The Queen Mother's funeral was accompanied by an eight-page tribute, and an apology from editor Nigel Horne: "I am sorry that *Radio Times* went to press just before the announcement of the Queen Mother's death, and that the listings pages did not therefore include details for the funeral. Today I hope we will make amends." Veteran newspaper hand tinter Joan Smith admitted that getting a *Radio Times* cover had been a life's ambition.

Radio 2 *(below left)*

Clockwise from left: Terry Wogan, Mark Lamarr, Jonathan Ross and Steve Wright *(photograph by Mark Harrison)*

20–26 July 2002

The cover drew inspiration from the album *With the Beatles* and announced the rebranding of Radio 2 and record listening figures, shedding its fusty image for a cooler, irreverent approach epitomised by the likes of Jonathan Ross and Mark Lamarr – if not Terry Wogan.

Christmas 2002 *(below right)*

Illustration by James Marsh

21 December 2002–3 January 2003

Festive highlights included the *Only Fools and Horses* Christmas special, *The Osbournes* and *Absolutely Fabulous*. *Radio Times* provided a comprehensive 30-page guide to over 2,000 films.

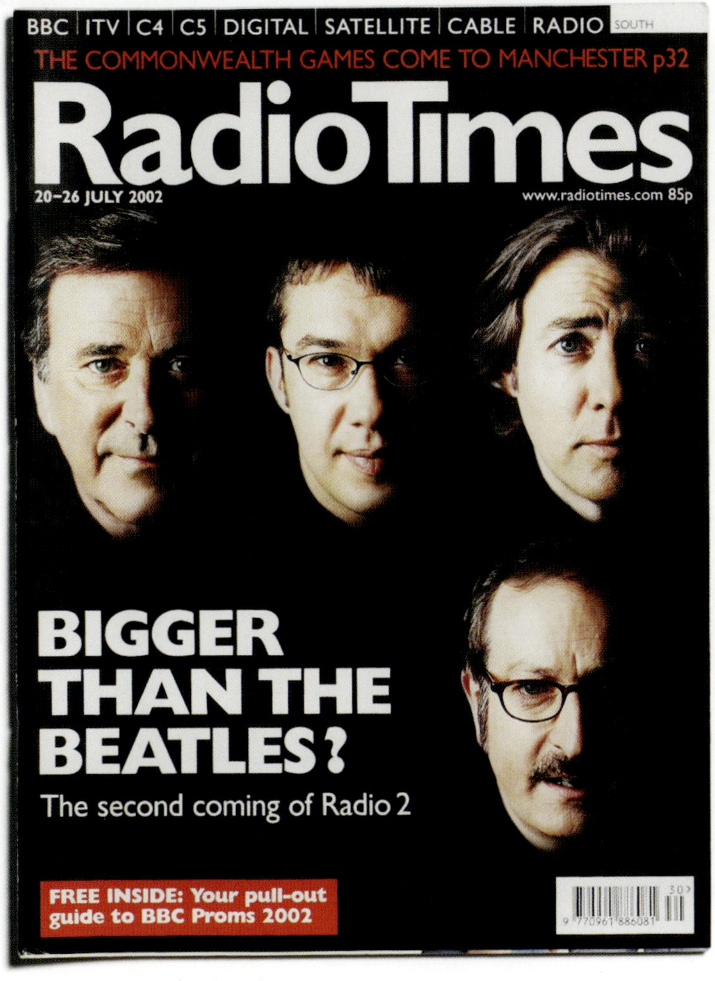

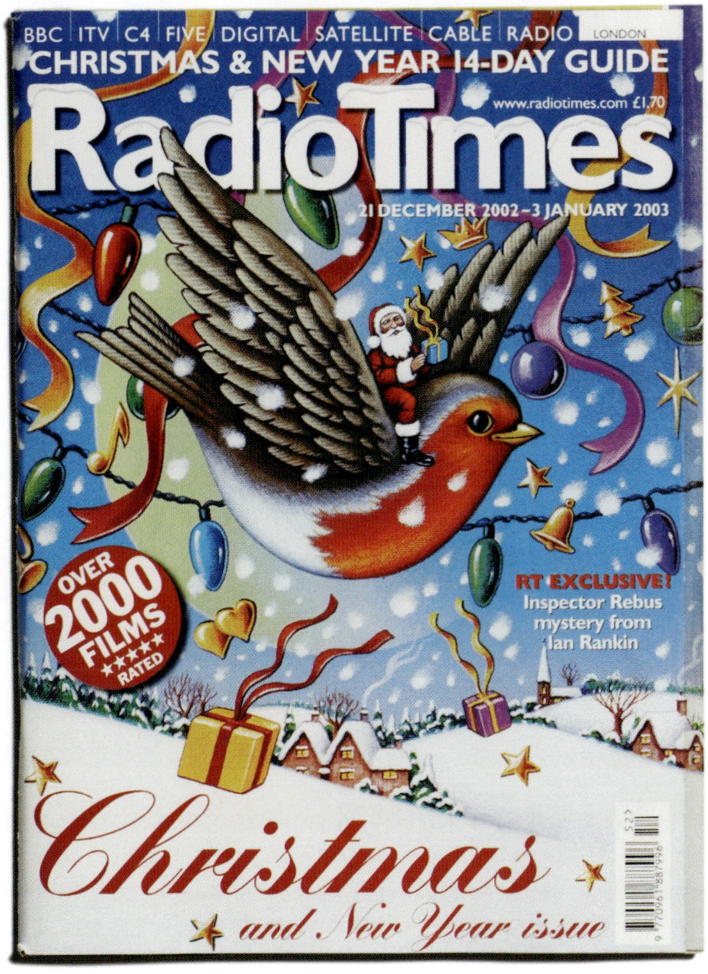

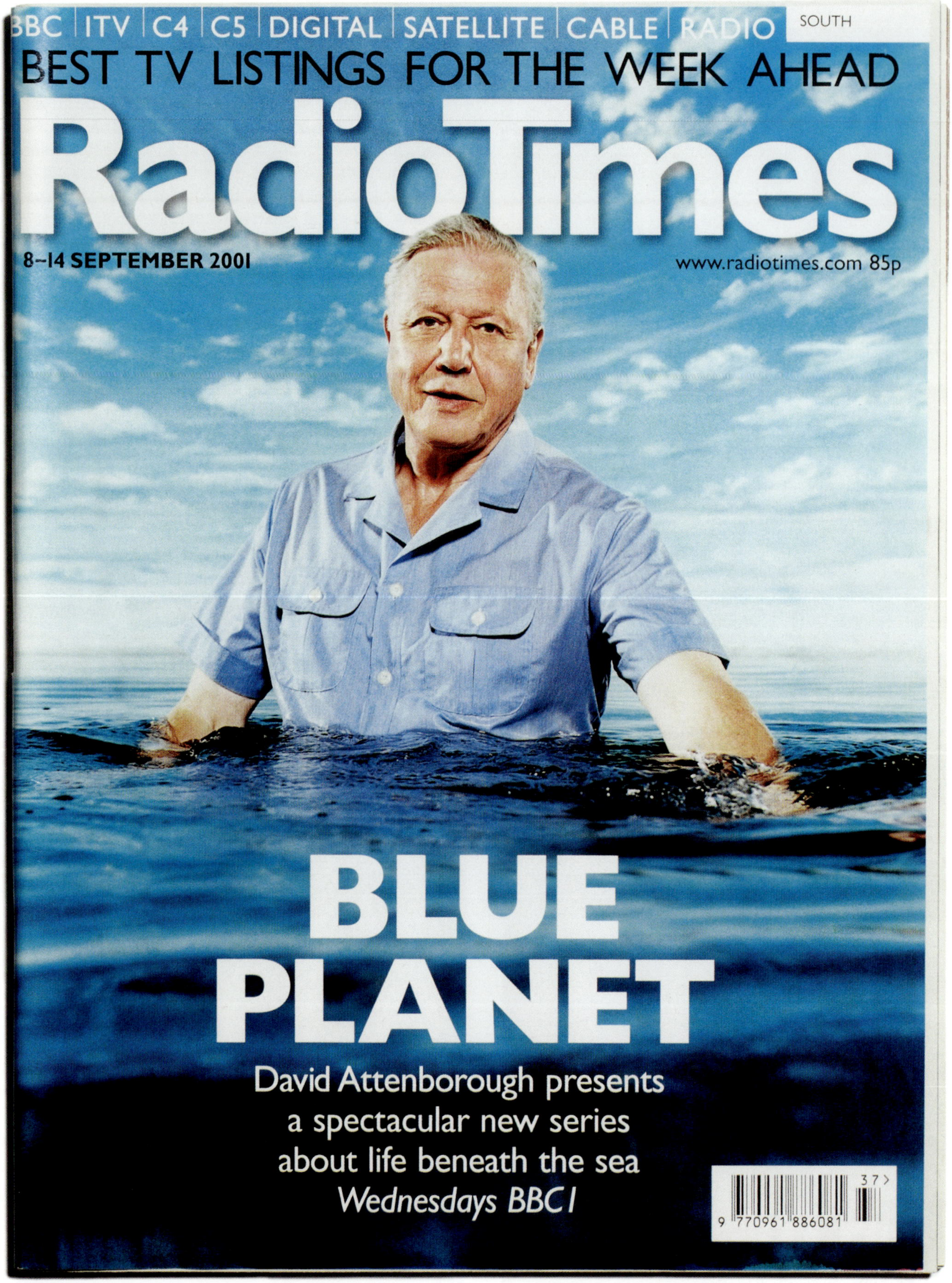

The Blue Planet **David Attenborough** *(photograph by Andy Earl)* *8–14 September 2001*

Any series by David Attenborough is launched by a fanfare of acclaim and *The Blue Planet* was no different. Five years in the making, the eight 50-minute episodes featured amazing underwater photography accompanied by Attenborough's masterful narration. The first episode was broadcast the day after 9/11. The photograph was taken in a water tank in Hertfordshire used to train North Sea oil-rig divers.

Pop Idol *(right)*

Simon Cowell *(photograph by Jason Bell)*

9–15 August 2003

As *Pop Idol* returned to the nation's screens, the *Radio Times* editorial discussed the vast amount of money to be made from successful, simple TV programmes that engage with the viewing public – citing Simon Cowell's moneyspinning show and *Who Wants to Be a Millionaire?* as prime examples.

EastEnders *(below left)*

Den Watts (Leslie Grantham) *(photograph by Colin Bell)*

20–26 September 2003

EastEnders' legend "Dirty" Den Watts emerged from the Walford Canal after a 14-year absence, an event that attracted over 16 million viewers. Meanwhile, Cilla Black commented on the state of broadcasting: "Anyone can be famous now, because anyone can go on television."

Comedy Issue *(below right)*

David Walliams, Ricky Gervais and Matt Lucas *(photograph by Andy Earl)*

15–21 January 2005

Radio Times's third annual review of British TV comedy featured a top 50 rating of the leading comic talent: the success of *Little Britain* put Walliams and Lucas top of the pile, followed by Peter Kay, Jonathan Ross, and Ant and Dec.

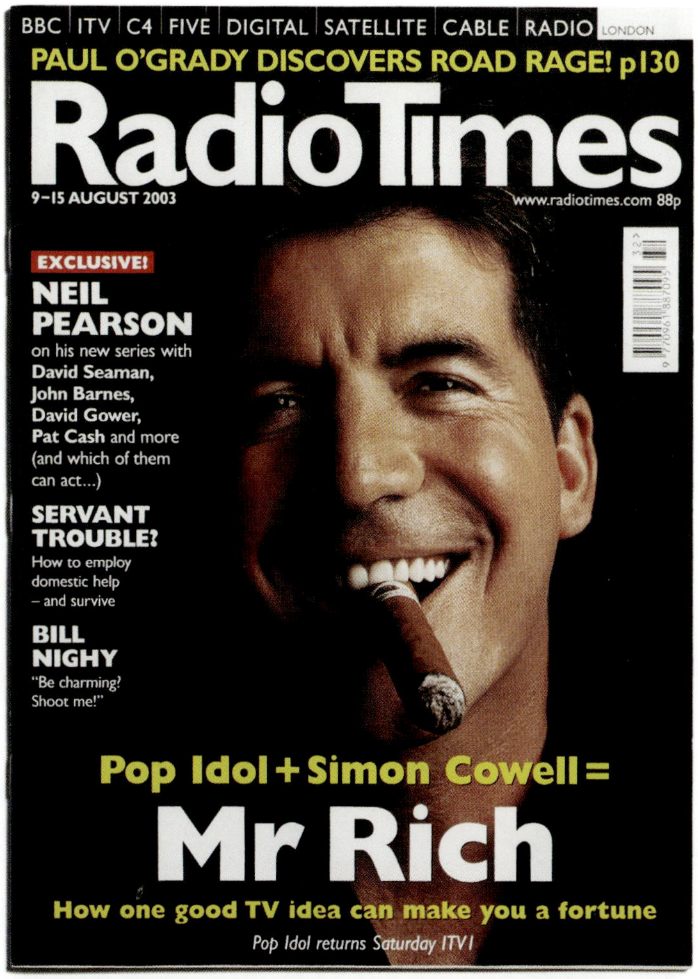

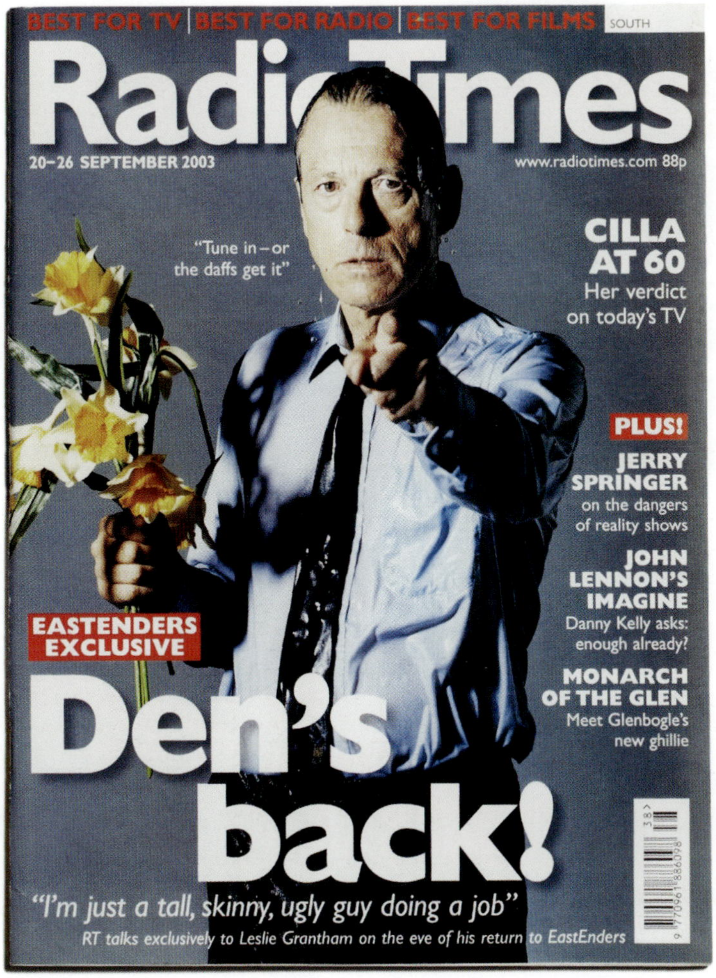

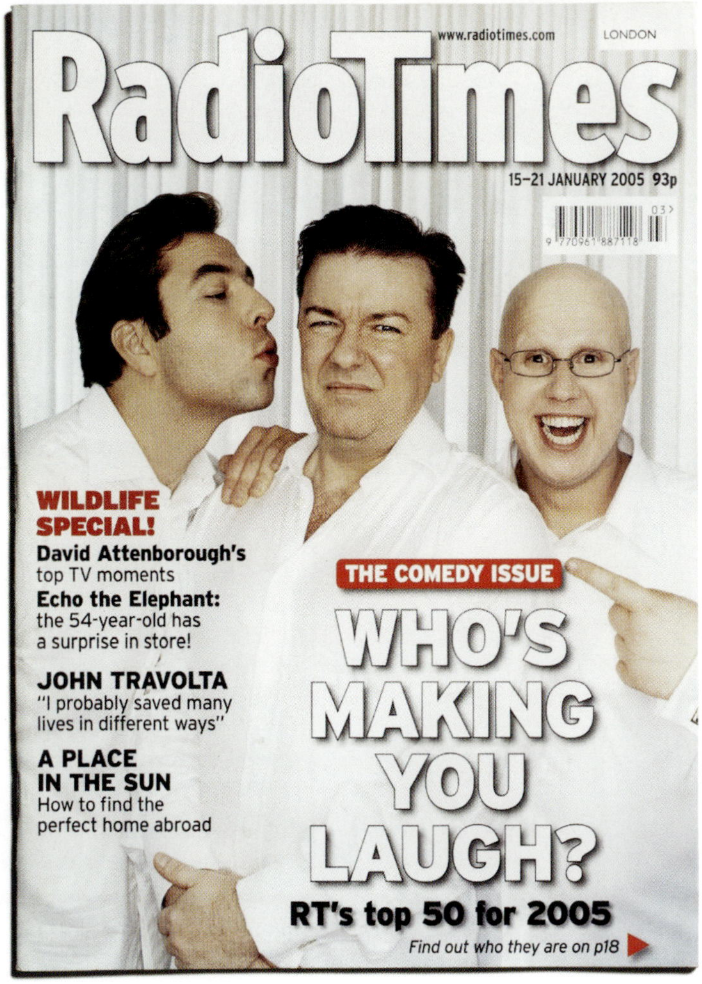

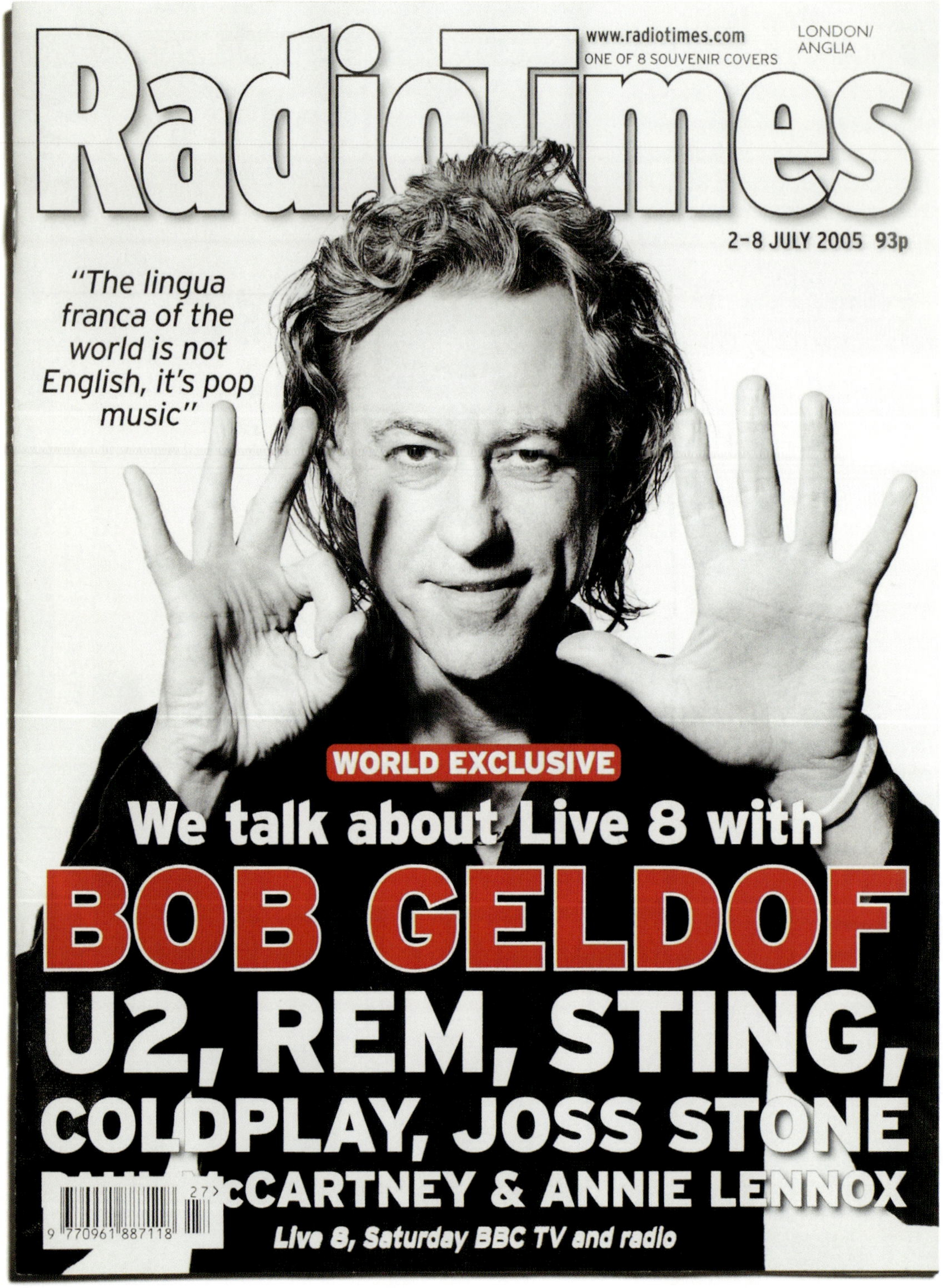
RadioTimes
www.radiotimes.com
ONE OF 8 SOUVENIR COVERS
LONDON/
ANGLIA
2–8 JULY 2005 93p
"The lingua franca of the world is not English, it's pop music"
WORLD EXCLUSIVE
We talk about Live 8 with
BOB GELDOF
U2, REM, STING,
COLDPLAY, JOSS STONE
PAUL McCARTNEY & ANNIE LENNOX
Live 8, Saturday BBC TV and radio
9 770961 887118

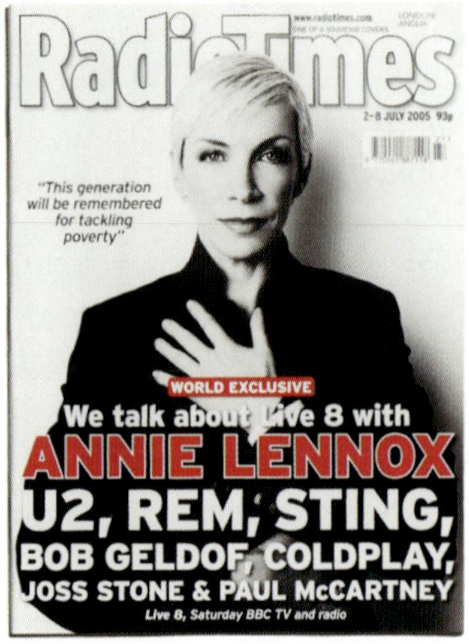
RadioTimes
2–8 JULY 2005
"This generation will be remembered for tackling poverty"
WORLD EXCLUSIVE
We talk about Live 8 with
ANNIE LENNOX
U2, REM, STING,
BOB GELDOF, COLDPLAY,
JOSS STONE & PAUL McCARTNEY
Live 8, Saturday BBC TV and radio

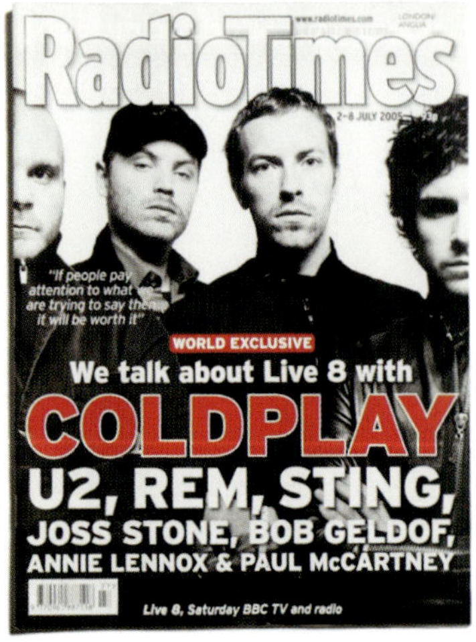
RadioTimes
"If people pay attention to what we are trying to say then it will be worth it"
WORLD EXCLUSIVE
We talk about Live 8 with
COLDPLAY
U2, REM, STING,
JOSS STONE, BOB GELDOF,
ANNIE LENNOX & PAUL McCARTNEY
Live 8, Saturday BBC TV and radio

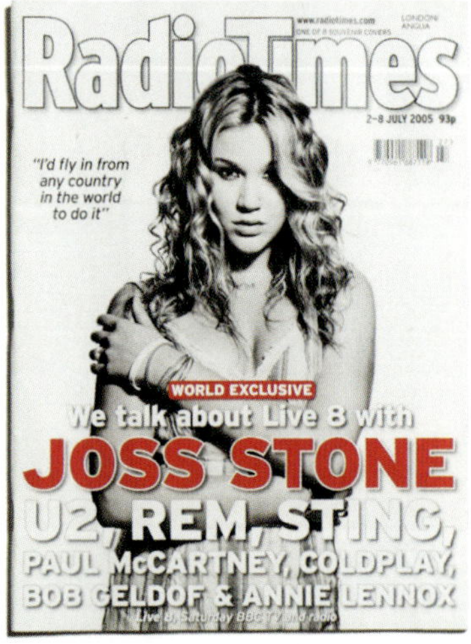
RadioTimes
2–8 JULY 2005 93p
"I'd fly in from any country in the world to do it"
WORLD EXCLUSIVE
We talk about Live 8 with
JOSS STONE
U2, REM, STING,
PAUL McCARTNEY, COLDPLAY,
BOB GELDOF & ANNIE LENNOX

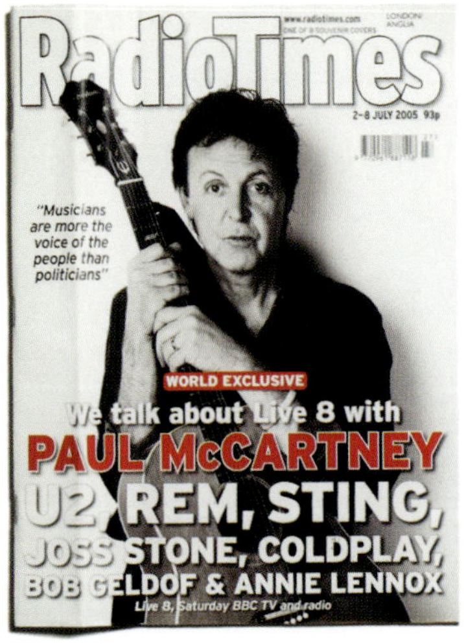
RadioTimes
2–8 JULY 2005 93p
"Musicians are more the voice of the people than politicians"
WORLD EXCLUSIVE
We talk about Live 8 with
PAUL McCARTNEY
U2, REM, STING,
JOSS STONE, COLDPLAY,
BOB GELDOF & ANNIE LENNOX

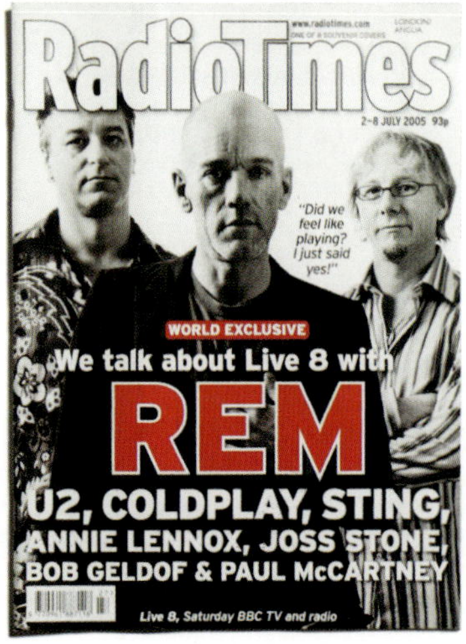
RadioTimes
2–8 JULY 2005 93p
"Did we feel like playing? I just said yes!"
WORLD EXCLUSIVE
We talk about Live 8 with
REM
U2, COLDPLAY, STING,
ANNIE LENNOX, JOSS STONE,
BOB GELDOF & PAUL McCARTNEY
Live 8, Saturday BBC TV and radio

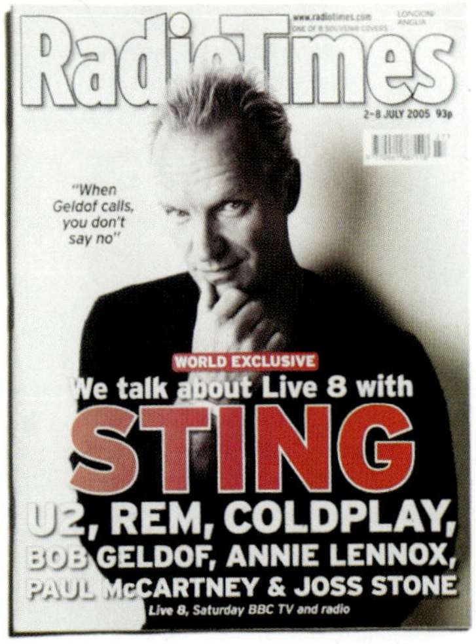
RadioTimes
2–8 JULY 2005 93p
"When Geldof calls, you don't say no"
WORLD EXCLUSIVE
We talk about Live 8 with
STING
U2, REM, COLDPLAY,
BOB GELDOF, ANNIE LENNOX,
PAUL McCARTNEY & JOSS STONE
Live 8, Saturday BBC TV and radio

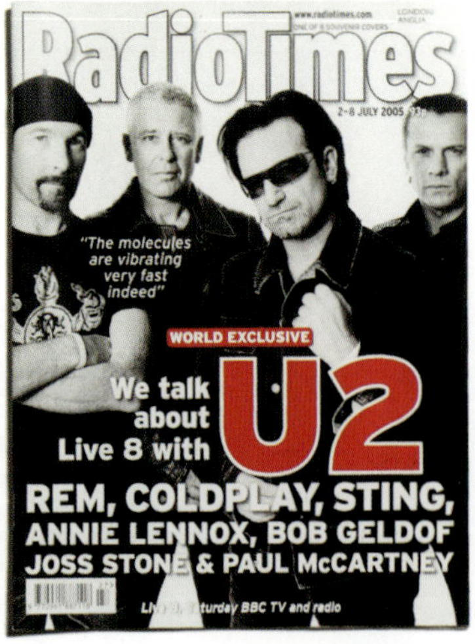
RadioTimes
2–8 JULY 2005
"The molecules are vibrating very fast indeed"
WORLD EXCLUSIVE
We talk about Live 8 with
U2
REM, COLDPLAY, STING,
ANNIE LENNOX, BOB GELDOF
JOSS STONE & PAUL McCARTNEY

Live 8 *(left)*
Clockwise from main image: Bob Geldof, Annie Lennox, Coldplay, Joss Stone, U2, Sting, REM and Paul McCartney
Photographs by Matt Holyoak (Bob Geldof, Joss Stone); Jason Bell (Annie Lennox, Sting, Paul McCartney); Philipp Ebeling (Coldplay, REM); Mark Allan (U2)
2–8 July 2005
Eight different covers were produced to mark the broadcast of the Live 8 charity event. Two decades after Live Aid put global poverty well and truly on the agenda, a total of ten concerts across the world attracted viewing figures of up to three billion.

Prime Suspect *(right)*
Helen Mirren *(photograph by Nicky Johnston)*
14–20 October 2006
One of television's most lauded crime dramas reached its final instalment. Helen Mirren reprised the role of Detective Superintendent Jane Tennison for a seventh time, despite having once told *Radio Times* that "actresses who stick to the same role become an embarrassment".

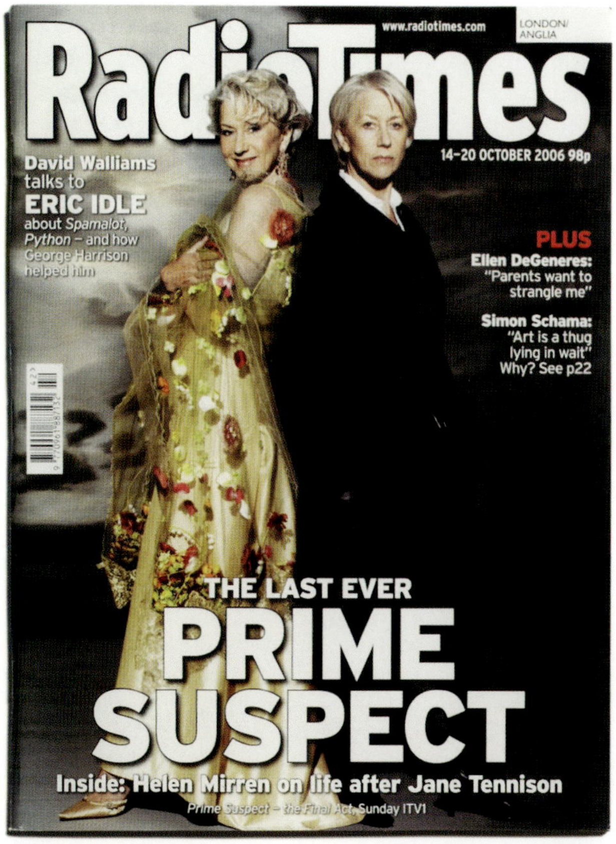

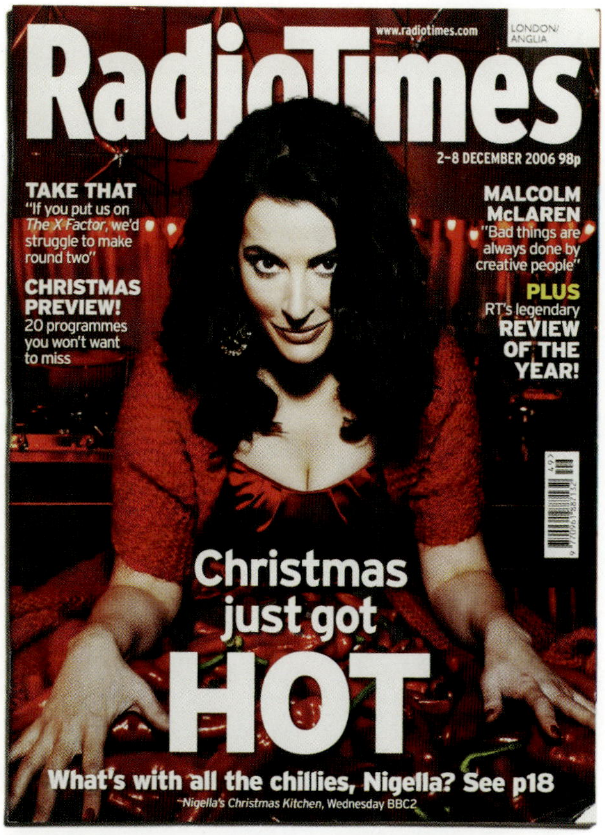

Nigella's Christmas Kitchen
Nigella Lawson *(photograph by Matt Holyoak)*
2–8 December 2006
The successful three-part series *Nigella's Christmas Kitchen* spawned *Nigella Express*, later criticised for "containing scenes of gluttony not seen since the golden age of the Cookie Monster".

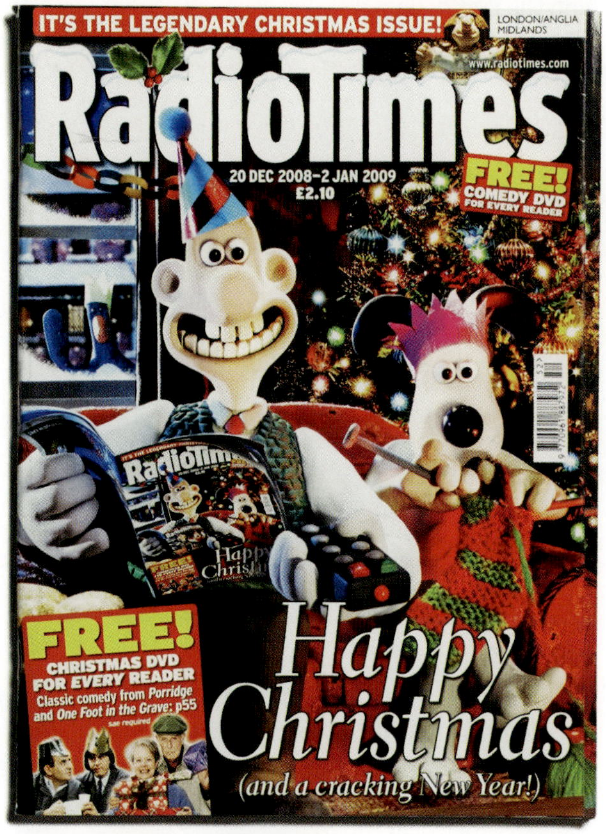

Christmas 2008
Cover tableau by Nick Park
20 December 2008–2 January 2009
On Christmas Day, Wallace & Gromit starred in a new short film, *A Matter of Loaf and Death* – and the duo appeared on the *Radio Times* cover in a tableau specially created by animator Nick Park.

Life on Mars *(right)*
DI Sam Tyler (John Simm) and DCI Gene Hunt (Philip Glenister)
(photograph by Sven Arnstein)

10–16 February 2007

The double-take cover marked the second series of time-warp crime drama *Life on Mars*. The inside cover featured the same photograph but on a *Radio Times* cover with a masthead, fonts and coverlines from 1973 – a neat accompaniment to a series that prided itself on re-creating period details with aplomb.

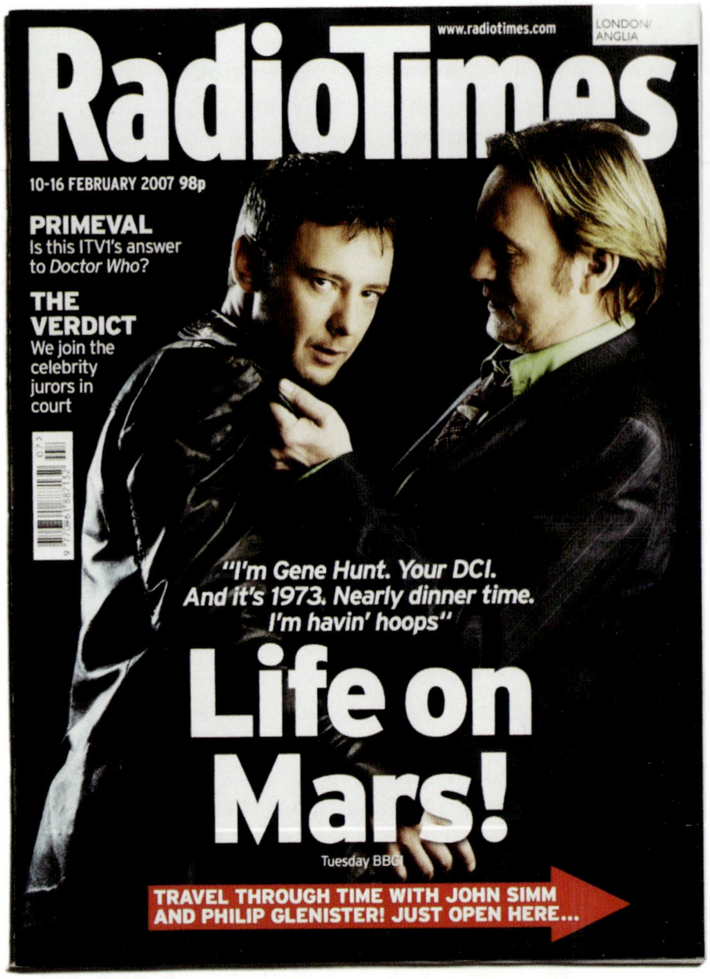

Gordon Ramsay's F Word *(far right)*
Gordon Ramsay *(photograph by Ellis Parrinder)*

10–16 May 2008

Britain's rudest chef returned for a new series on Channel 4. During the photoshoot, Gordon Ramsay caught sight of the cover mock-up with "I must not swear" written out neatly on the blackboard, and commented: "Fat f****** chance, eh, big boy?"

Coronation Street *(right)*
Katherine Kelly *(photograph by Nicky Johnston; background artwork Chris West)*

1–7 August 2009

Katherine Kelly had rapidly become *Coronation Street's* most popular character as barmaid Becky Granger, the latest in a long line of Rovers Return pint-pullers. *Radio Times* saluted the venerable soap with this cover, based on Manet's famous painting, *A Bar at the Folies-Bergère*. "It may not be fine art," said *Radio Times* art director Shem Law, "but the 49-year-old soap is a masterpiece worth toasting. Have this one on us." The issue also went on location with the new star of *Doctor Who*, Matt Smith.

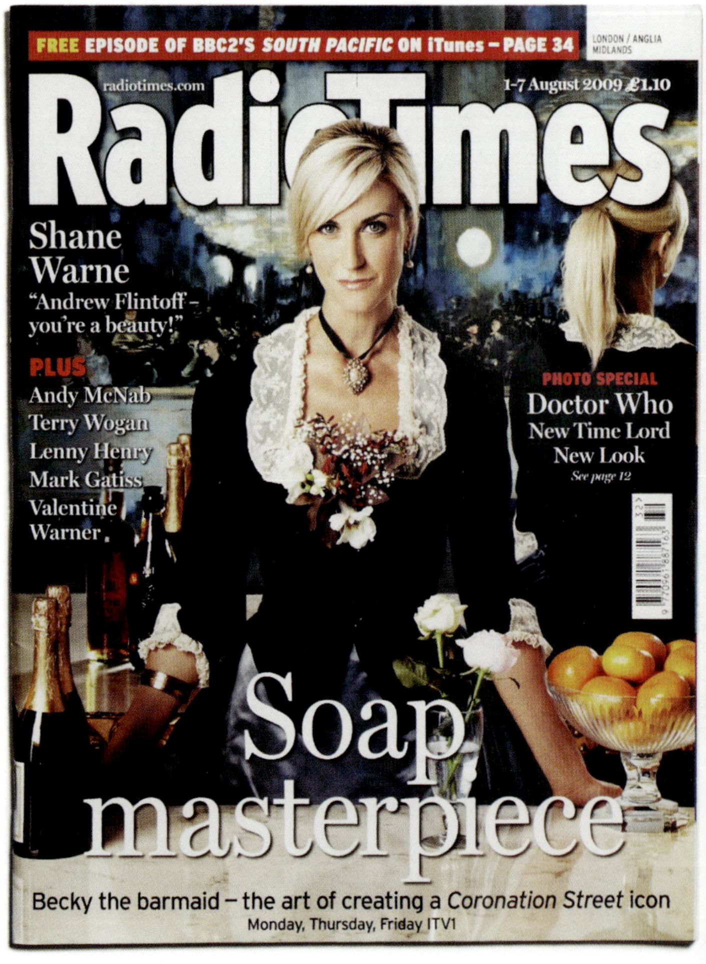

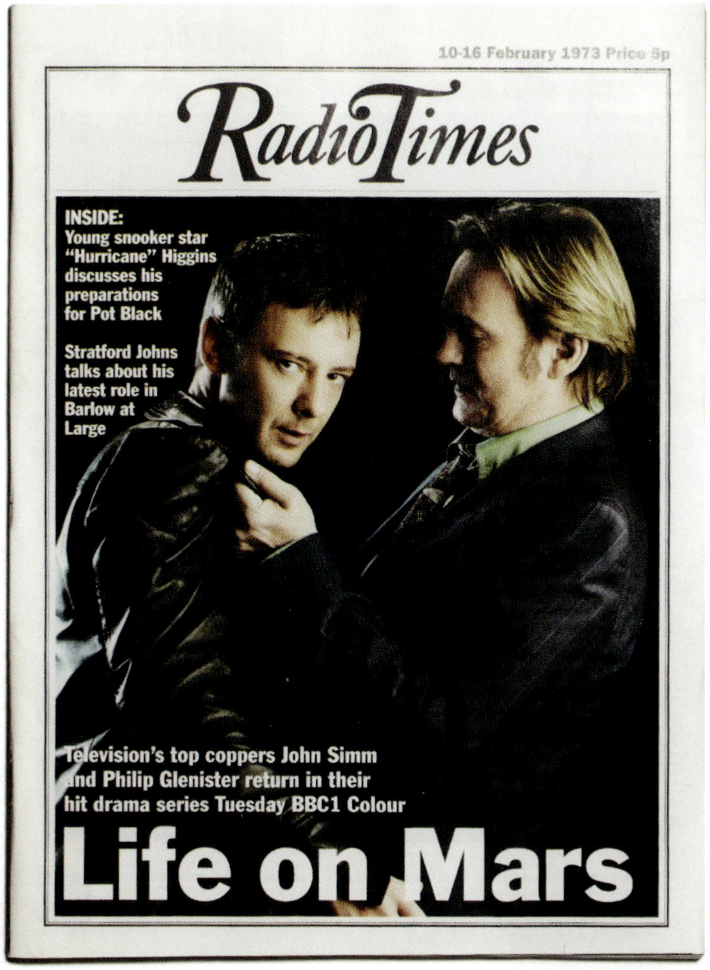

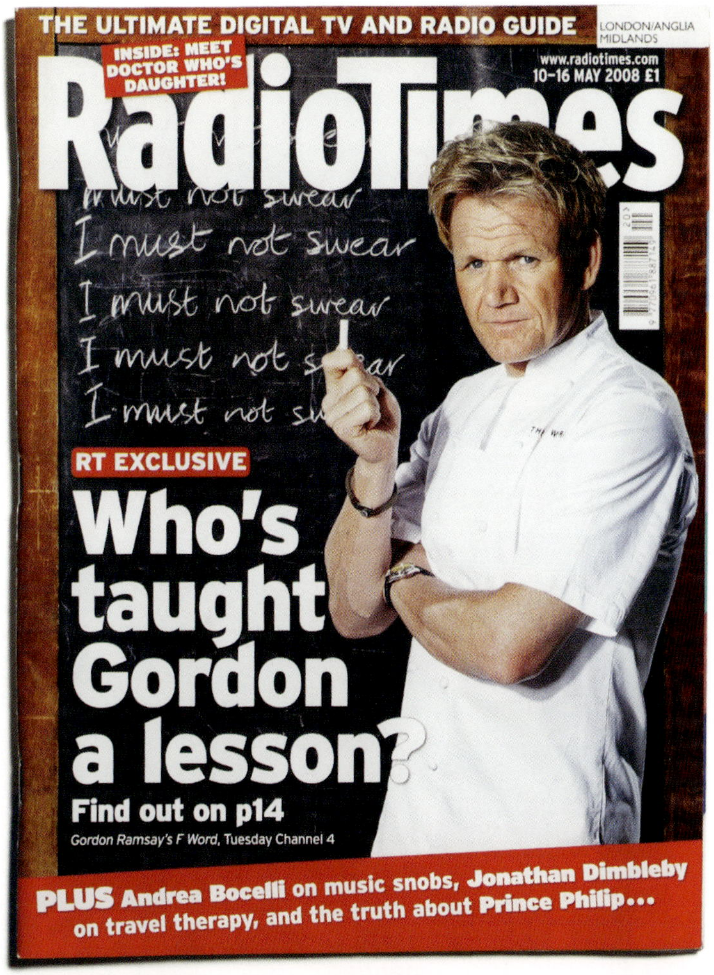

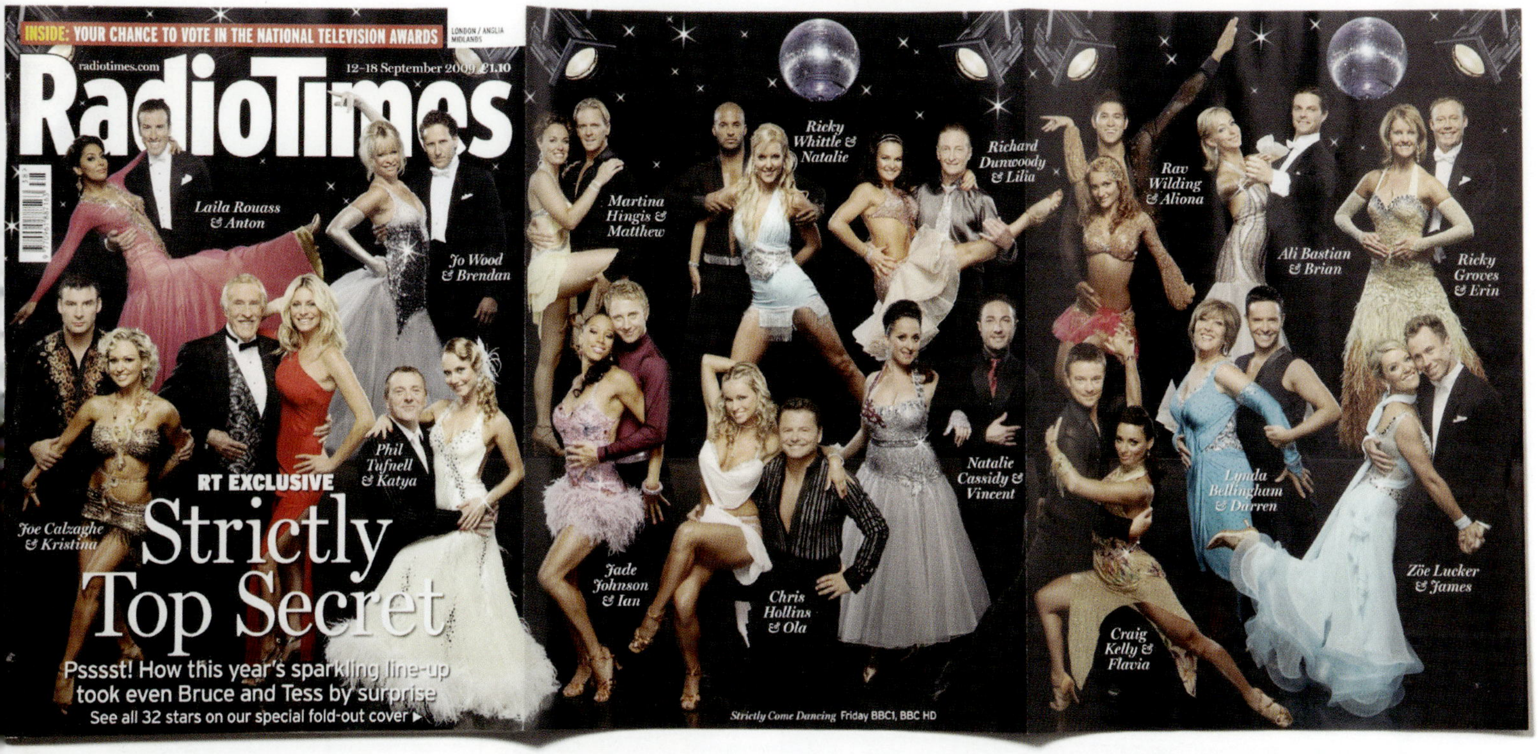

Strictly Come Dancing *(photography by Todd Antony) 12–18 September 2009*

Thirty-two competitors appeared on this fold-out cover to mark the return of the hugely successful dance-fest for its seventh series – eventually won by Chris Hollins and Ola Jordan. Other features included Michael Parkinson bemoaning the state of sports commentary ("Producers must insist commentators think before they speak, shun the cliché and explore the alternatives in what has become a wasteland of babble"), and a profile of the esteemed arts programme, *The South Bank Show*, ending its run on ITV.

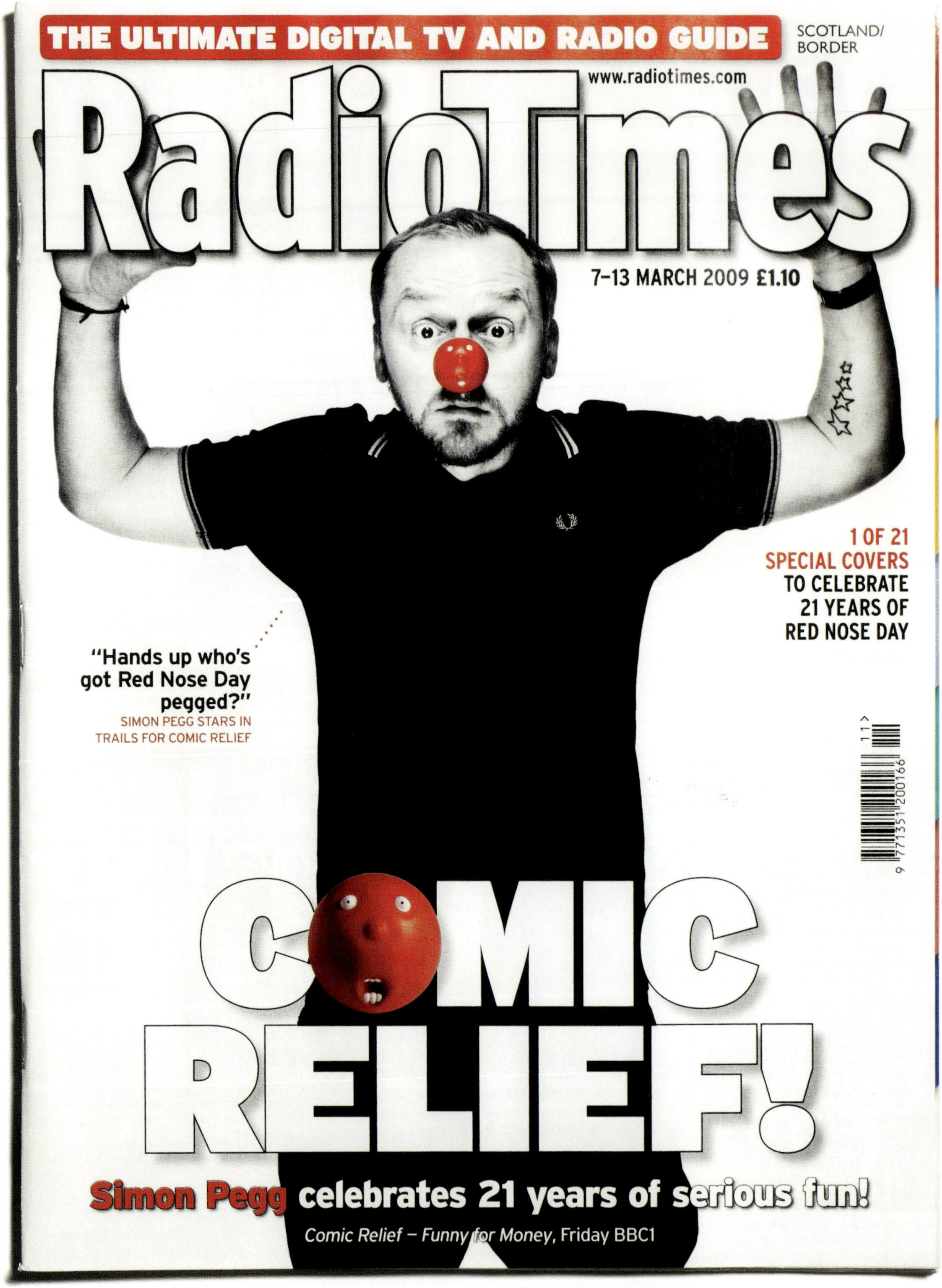

Comic Relief **Simon Pegg** *(photograph by Des Willie) 7–13 March 2009*

Photographs on opposite page by Simon Ridgeway, Mary McCartney, Ray Burmiston, Jon Cottam, Ellis Parrinder, Justin Canning, Gary Moyes and Trevor Leighton

The multiple-cover tradition for special occasions reached new heights on Red Nose Day 2009, with 21 different images featuring the great and the good sporting red noses. £82.3 million was raised by the British public in 2009.

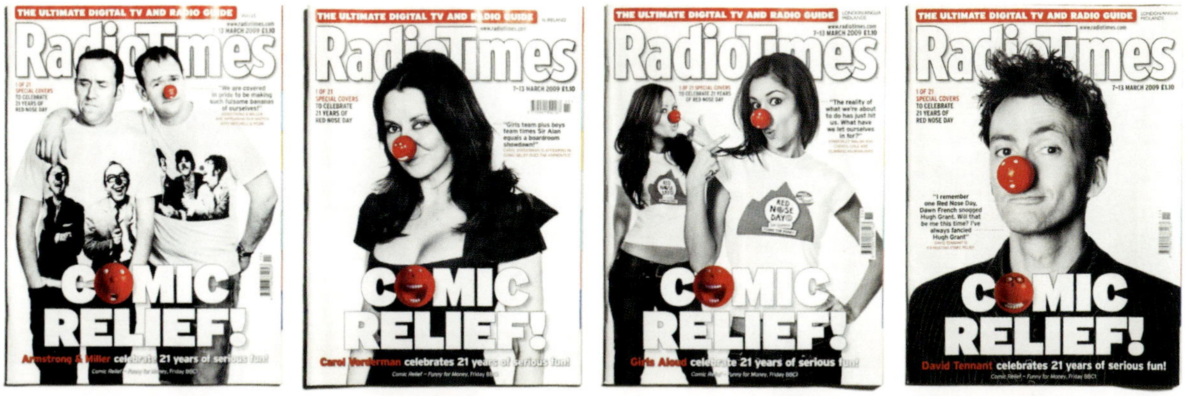

From left: Ben Miller and Alexander Armstrong; Carol Vorderman; Kimberley Walsh and Cheryl Cole; David Tennant

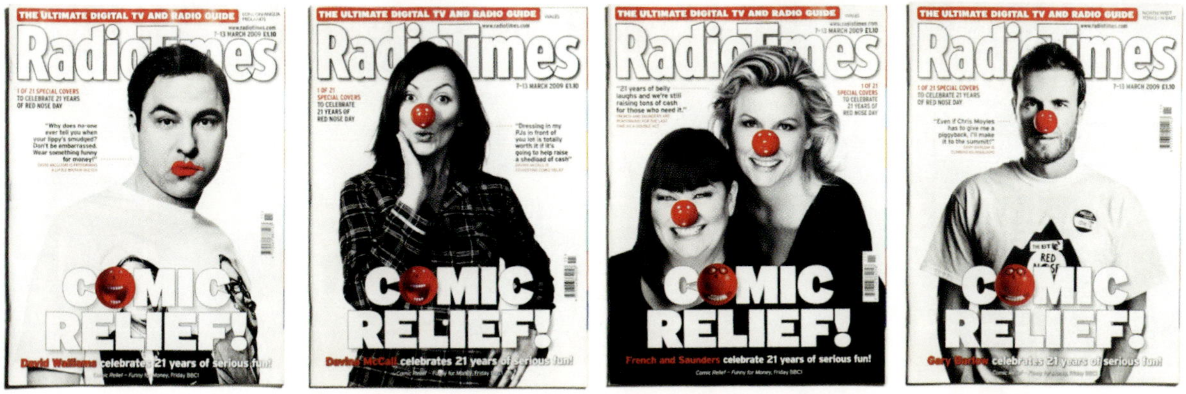

From left: David Walliams; Davina McCall; Dawn French and Jennifer Saunders; Gary Barlow

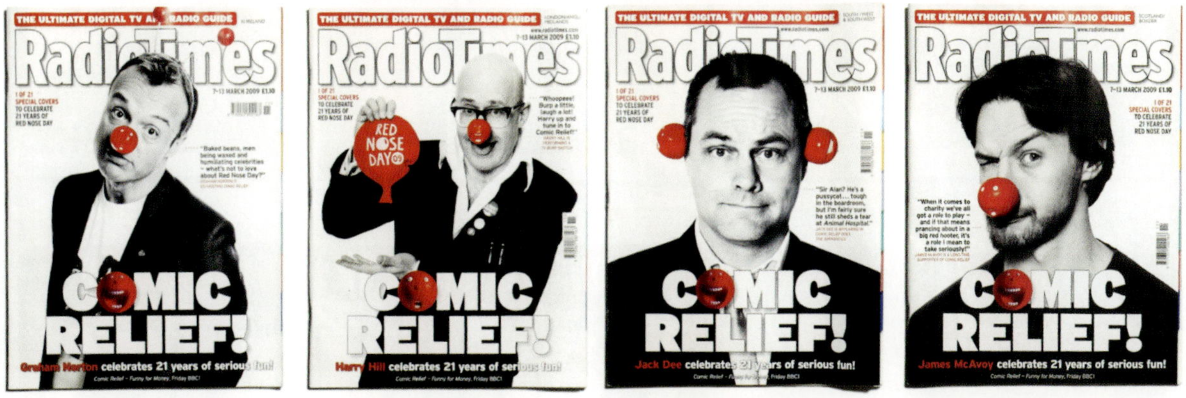

From left: Graham Norton; Harry Hill; Jack Dee; James McAvoy

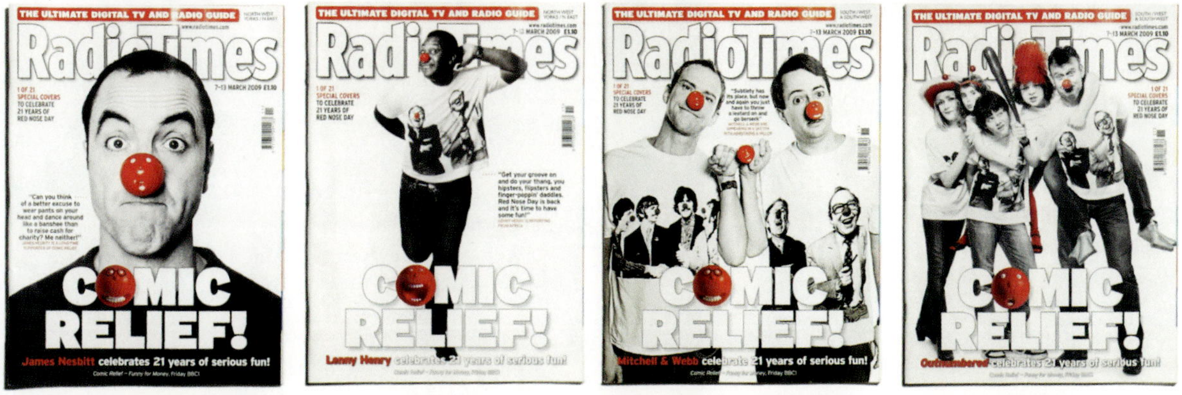

From left: James Nesbitt; Lenny Henry; Robert Webb and David Mitchell; the cast of *Outnumbered*

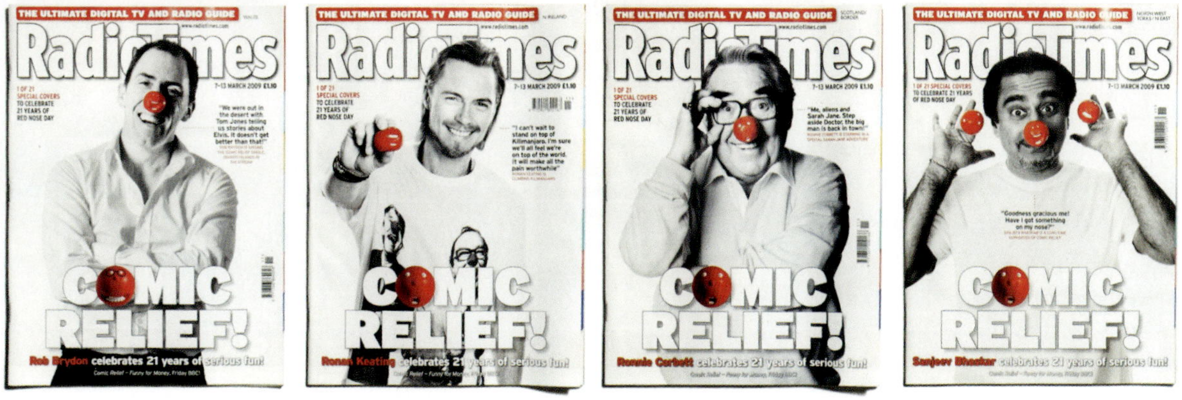

From left: Rob Brydon; Ronan Keating; Ronnie Corbett; Sanjeev Bhaskar

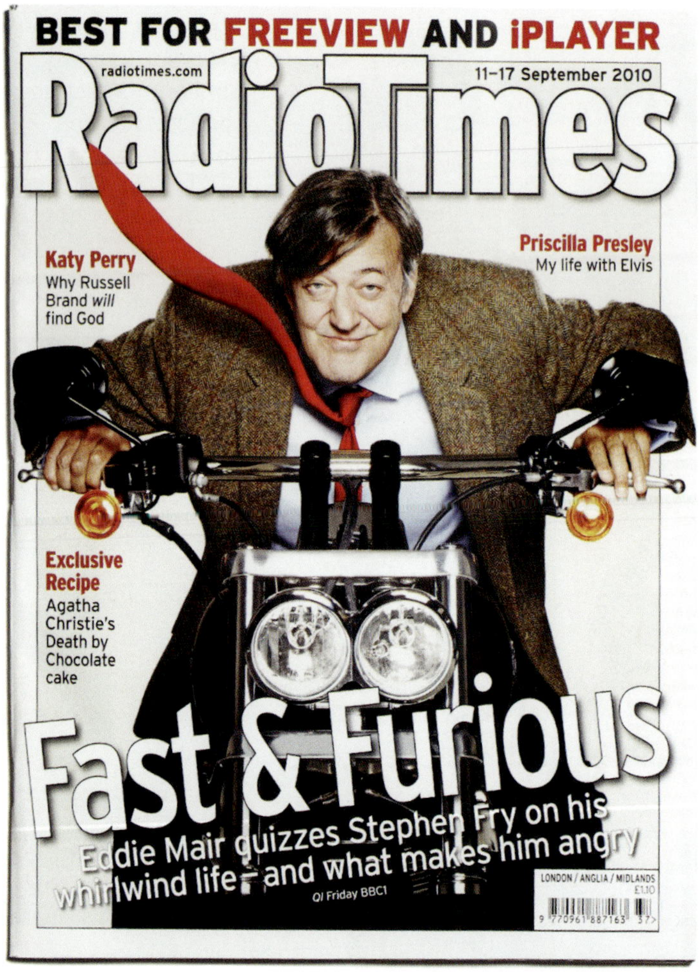

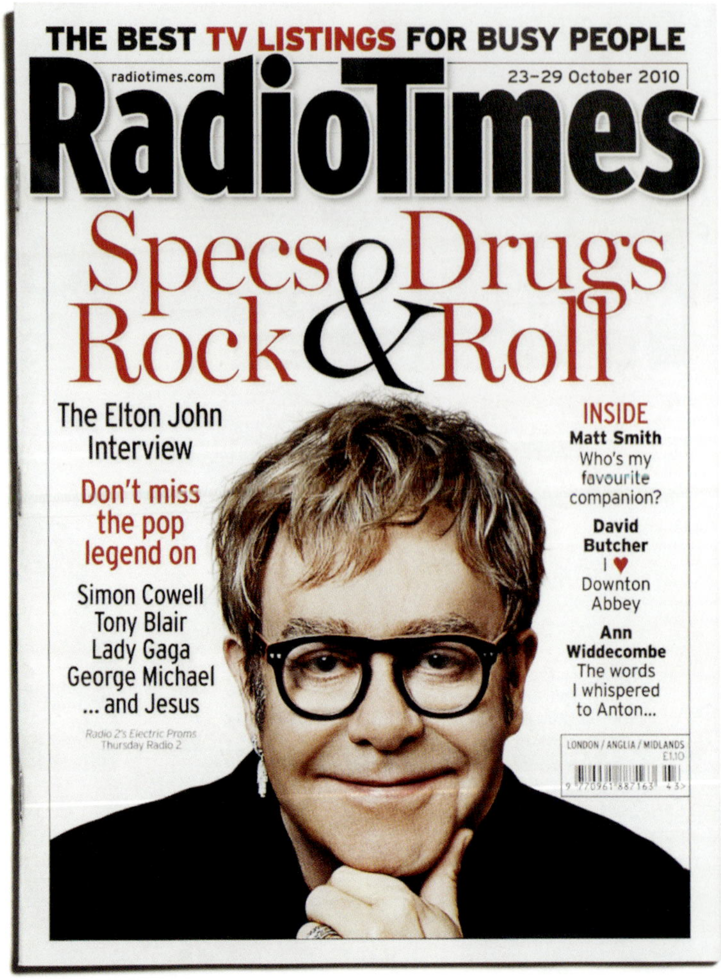

Choosing to Die *(right)*

Terry Pratchett *(photograph by David Levene)*

11–17 June 2011

"The power of television is that it can turn private debates public," said *Radio Times* editor Ben Preston. Author Terry Pratchett, who has Alzheimer's, was making a controversial film about Peter, a man with an incurable disease, who'd chosen to end his life at the Dignitas organisation in Switzerland.

University Challenge *(middle right)*

Jeremy Paxman and Ann Widdecombe *(photograph by Gary Moyes)*

2–8 July 2011

Ex-politician and *Strictly Come Dancing* star Ann Widdecombe tried to grill *University Challenge* host Jeremy Paxman but found it hard not to do the talking. Paxman's response: "You're just making assertions. You're not asking questions."

Life's Too Short *(far right)*

Warwick Davis and Ricky Gervais *(photograph by Mark Harrison)*

5–11 November 2011

"We're standing on the shoulders of giants – comedy giants," said Ricky Gervais during the photoshoot. "I'm handing the baton to Warwick." Never one to stop there, he added: "I like having a dwarf on my shoulders. There, I said it."

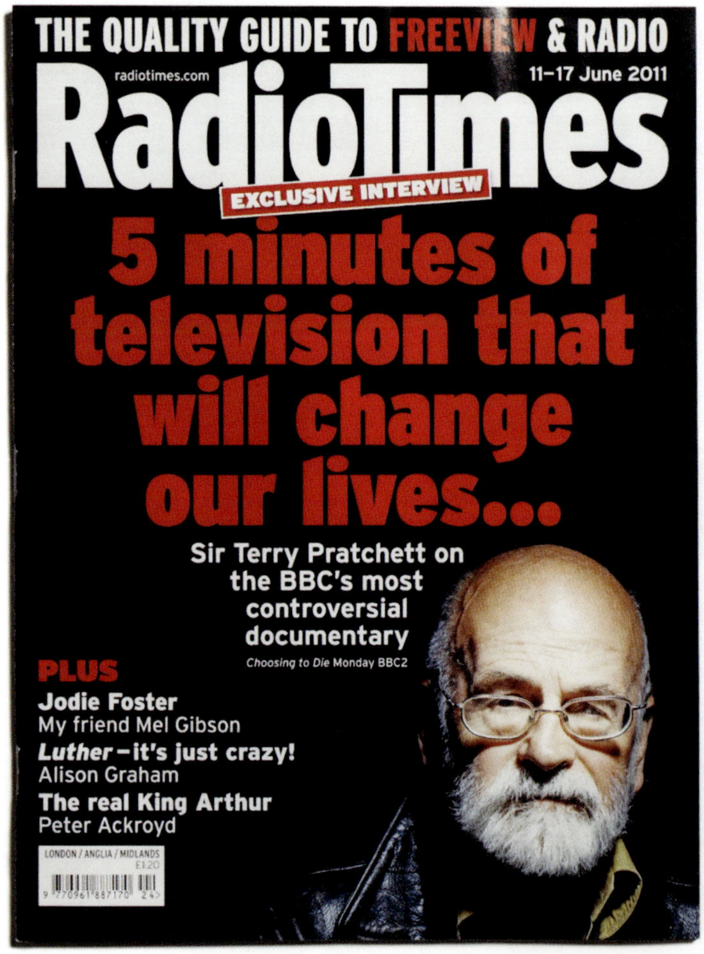

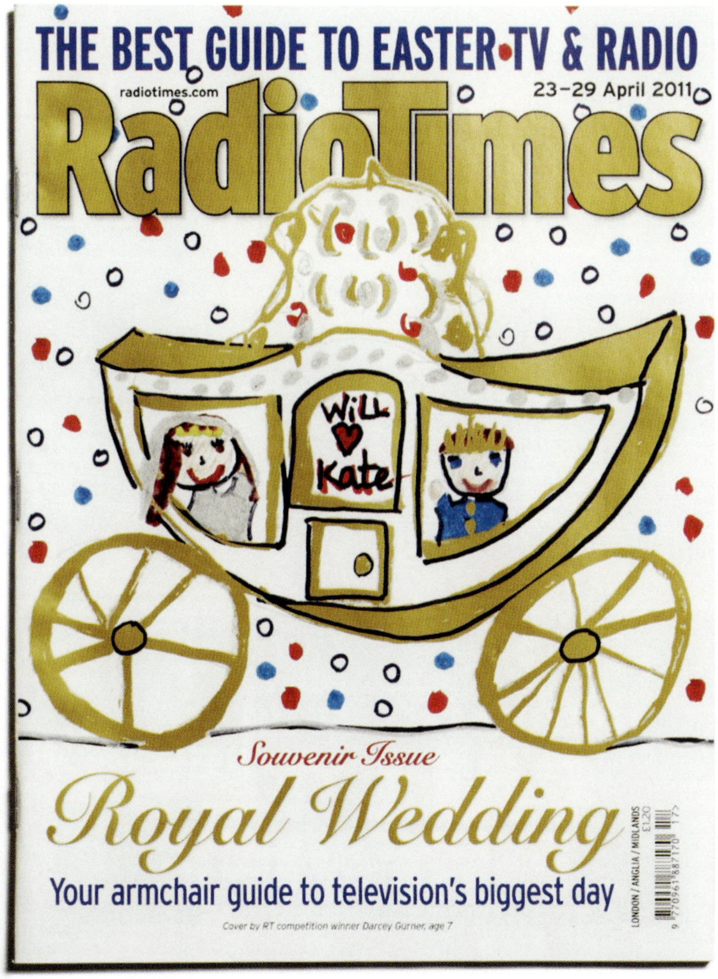

QI *(far left)*

Stephen Fry *(photograph by Mark Harrison)*

11–17 September 2010

Marking Series H of *QI*, that's host Stephen Fry on a Harley-Davidson wearing a Harris tweed jacket. Inside, *Radio Times* had him pose with 55 objects beginning with the letter H. But Fry protested that there were 56: "Haven't you forgotten the big old homosexual in the room?"

Radio 2's Electric Proms *(middle left)*

Elton John

23–29 October 2010

Elton John opened what would prove to be the last of the Electric Proms: after five years, the BBC cancelled the series as part of financial "efficiency savings". He talked openly of politics and drugs but of performing said: "You can't predict the special night, and that makes playing so wonderful."

The Royal Wedding *(left)*

Illustration by Darcey Gurner (age 7)

23–29 April 2011

Art director Shem Law said Darcey's design beat 10,500 others to become the cover for the wedding of Prince William and Kate Middleton. "We had several Doctor Whos and a couple of wrestlers. Some people thought Westminster Abbey wasn't grand enough for the wedding and relocated it to Downton Abbey instead!"

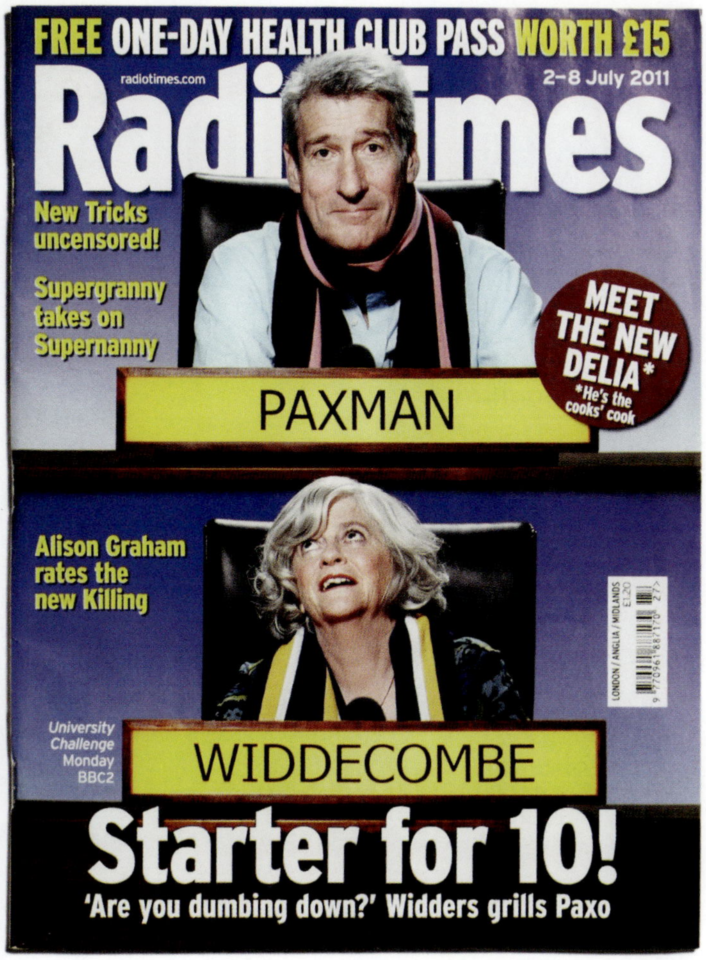

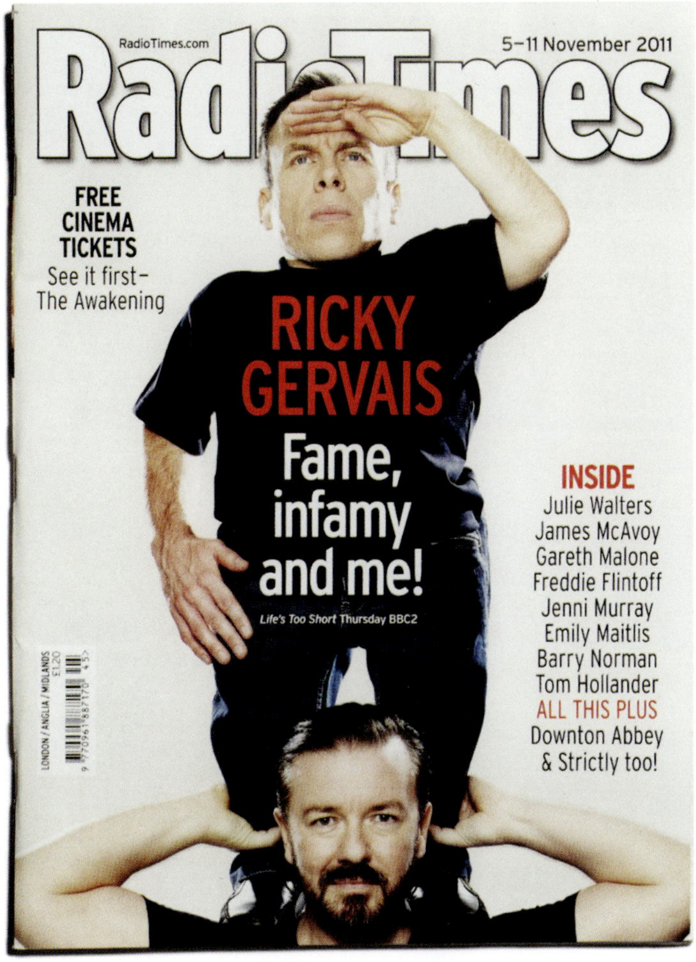

Call the Midwife *(right)*

Illustration by Mark Thomas

11–17 February 2012

Fittingly for the hit drama set in the 1950s, this cover illustration by Mark Thomas was done without computers. He did it at a drawing board on paper, with pencils, brushes and paint.

The Great British Bake Off *(below left)*

Paul Hollywood and Mary Berry
(photograph by Nicky Johnson)

11–17 August 2012

Radio Times asked 2011's *Bake Off* champion Jo Wheatley to "produce a showstopper for the photoshoot with Mary and Paul" and that's her magnificent Victoria sponge right there between Hollywood and Berry.

Attenborough: 60 Years in the Wild

(below right)

David Attenborough *(photograph by Nadav Kander)*

10–16 November 2012

Wildlife presenter Chris Packham got to interview his hero as *Radio Times* celebrated David Attenborough's six decades of natural history films. The cover was shot at Attenborough's home in Richmond, London.

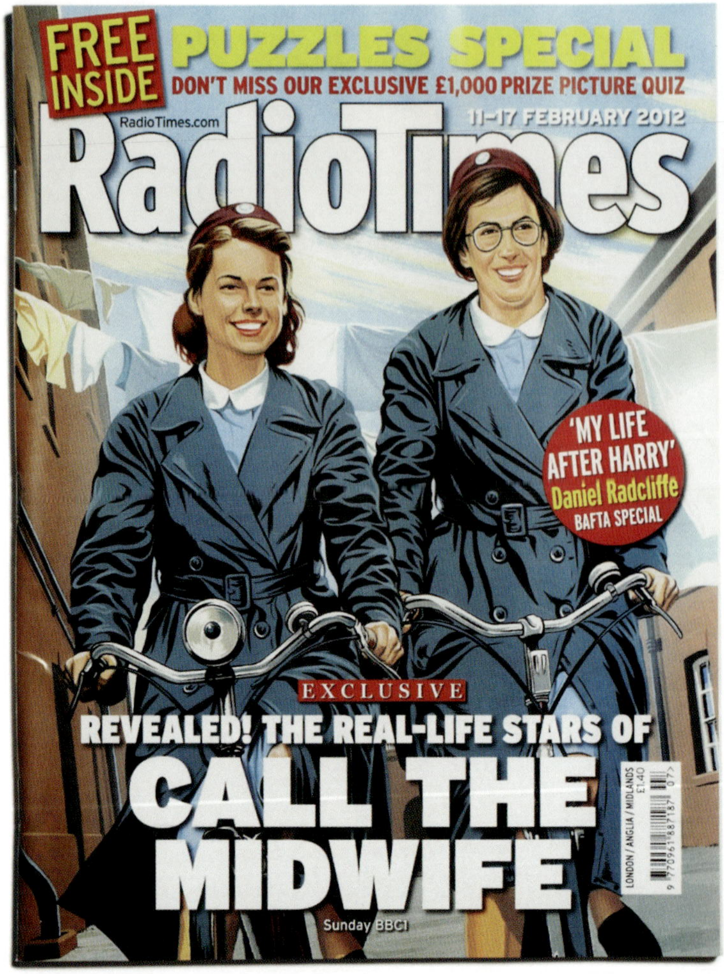

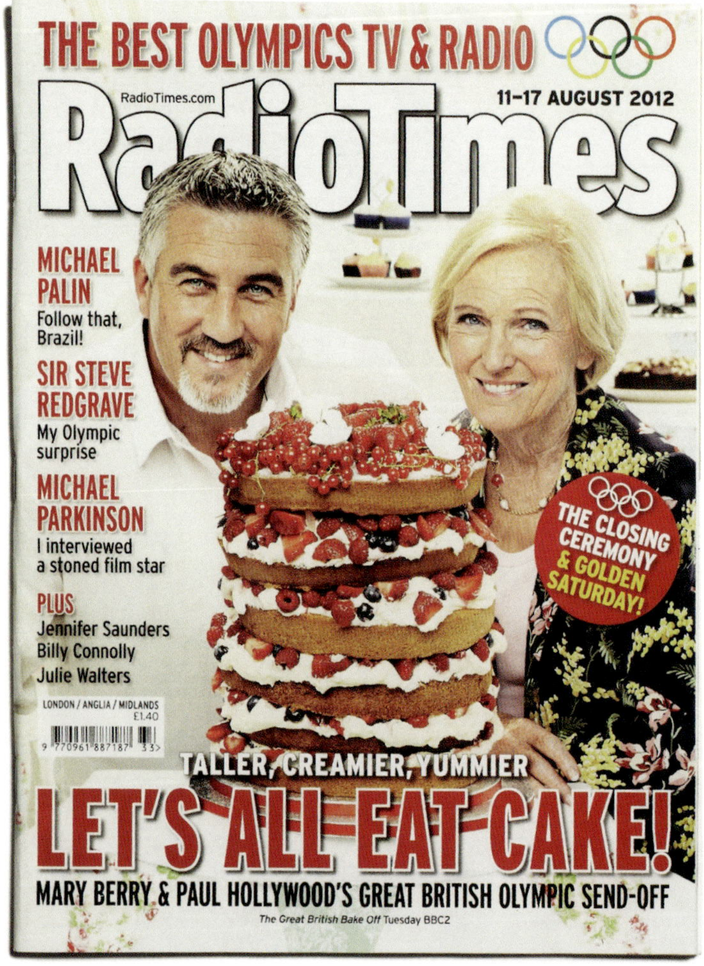

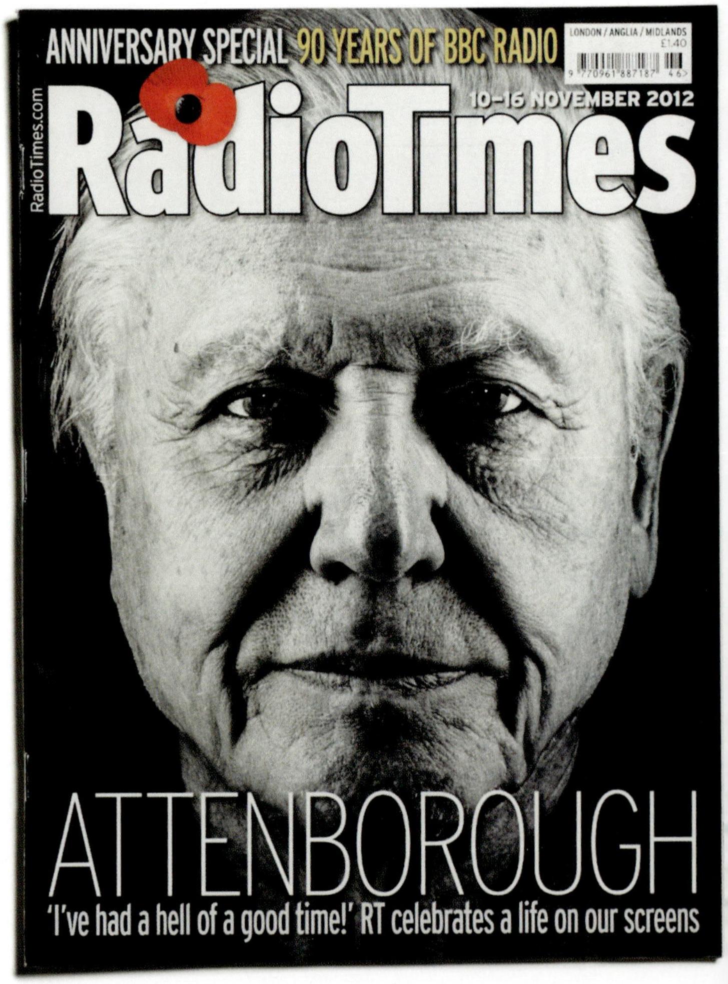

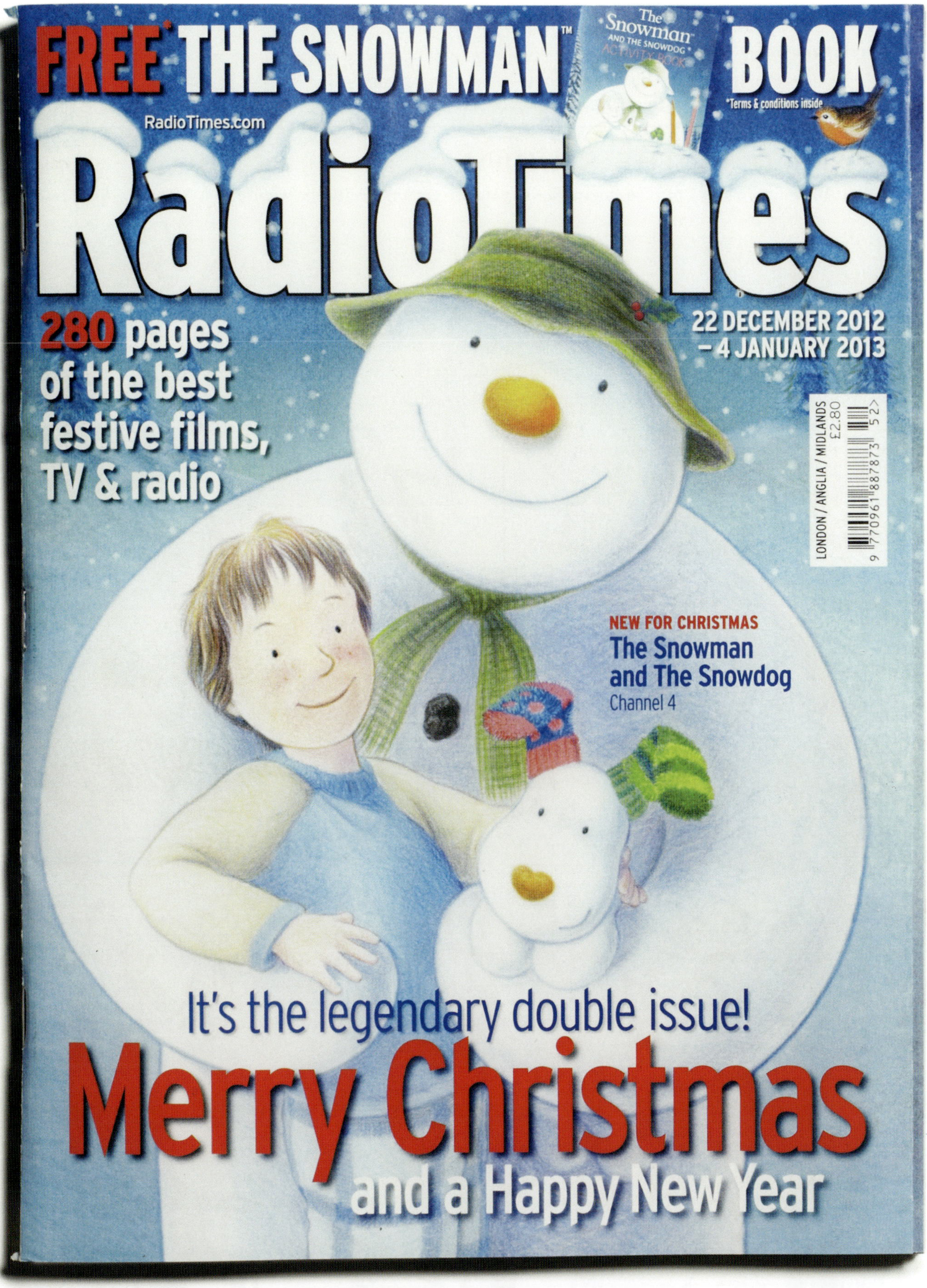

Christmas 2012 **Illustration by Robin Shaw** *22 December 2012–4 January 2013*

The Snowman celebrated its 30th anniversary with a sequel, *The Snowman and The Snowdog* on Channel 4. "I never thought about success," said creator Raymond Briggs. But people who read it as children now read it to their own kids: "It's what every author dreams of." The 24-minute sequel employed 40 artists to create 200,000 drawings using £14,000 worth of Caran d'Ache crayons and cost £2m to make.

A page from the Christmas issue of 1935 Illustration by Mervyn Wilson

20 December 1935

A full-page illustration that made light of the lengths *Radio Times* would go to in order to get the right shot – 78 years later, some things haven't changed...

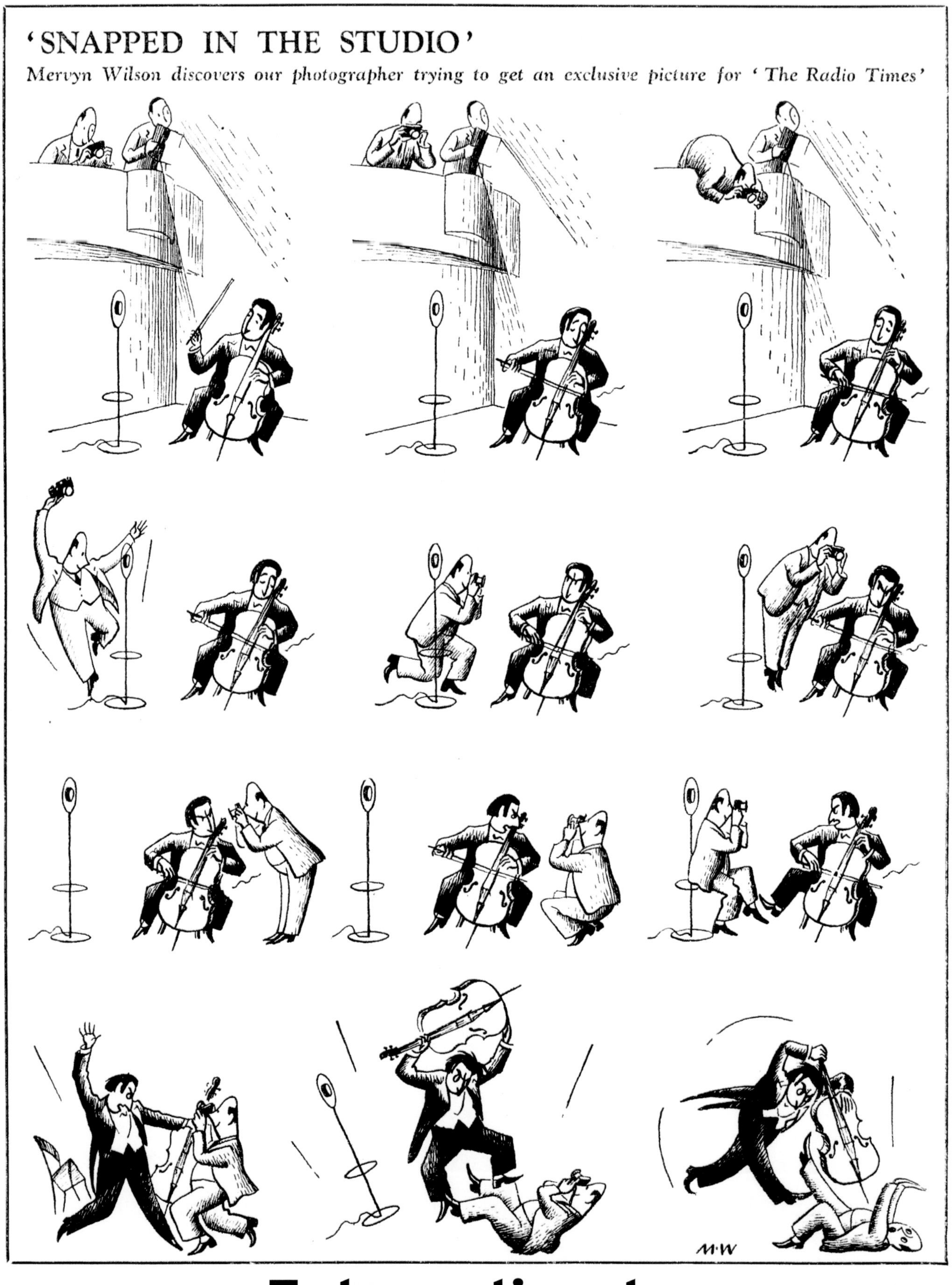

To be continued...